PATHWAYS TO WHOLENESS

Pastoral Care in a Postmodern Age

Pathways to Wholeness

Pastoral Care in a Postmodern Age

Roger Hurding

Hodder & Stoughton

LONDON SYDNEY AUCKLAND

Copyright © 1998 Roger Hurding

First published in Great Britain 1998

The right of Roger Hurding to be indentified as the Author of the Work has been asserted by him in accordance with the Copyright, Designs and Patents Act 1988.

10 9 8 7 6 5 4 3 2 1

British Library Cataloguing in Publication Data
A record for this book is available from the British Library

ISBN 0 340 67129 7

Typeset by Hewer Text Limited, Edinburgh
Printed and bound in Great Britain by
Guernsey Press

Hodder and Stoughton Ltd
A Division of Hodder Headline PLC
338 Euston Road
London NW1 3BH

To students and colleagues
at
Trinity College, Bristol

CONTENTS

PREFACE

This book has been long in gestation and the seeds of its growth were planted in the late 1970s and early 1980s when, before and during a prolonged period of blindness due to diabetes, I worked on my first book, whose title carried the 'double entendre' of *Restoring the Image*. Through two major operations on my right eye, life's visual image *was* mercifully restored, albeit in unilateral form. This harrowing episode and the coincidental experience of picking up the flu-like condition of brucellosis – in my case, in its chronic, long-term form – led to my autobiographical *As Trees Walking*, a work that is slanted toward a practical spirituality of suffering and healing. These combined illnesses led to my retirement from medical practice at the age of forty-five and opened the door toward a wider horizon in theological education.

Throughout my medical career I had maintained a primary interest in psychological medicine and, following the inspiration of the work of Michael and Enid Balint at London's Tavistock Clinic,[1] had committed myself to a psychotherapeutic approach to human illness in both general practice and, for a decade up to my enforced retirement in 1979, in student health. So it was that in 1981 I began, amid the recovery from blindness and the continuing struggle with brucellosis, to lecture part time in pastoral counselling at Trinity theological college, Bristol. In the same year I became one of the 'founding members' of a small gathering of theologians and psychotherapists who met regularly in London and Oxford to discuss the implications of an integrational approach to theology and psychology. One of our cardinal commitments was to initiate, under the auspices of Care and Counsel in London, a series of biennial conferences, beginning at London Bible College in 1983. Following a conference at Trinity College, Bristol in 1985, the venue moved to the more commodious Hayes Conference Centre at Swanwick, Derbyshire in 1987. Thus was born the Swanwick 'consultancy' or 'constituency', which has

been established as the Swanwick Conference for Pastoral Care
and Counselling, an important rallying point for Christian counsellors, psychotherapists and spiritual directors.[2]

A number of Christian counselling centres have grown up since
the early 1980s, at least partly influenced by the example and
impetus of Care and Counsel (under its directors Myra Chave
Jones and Elizabeth Shedden) and the Swanwick conferences.
Network in Bristol, under the successive directorships of David
Mitchell, John Turner and Tim Marks, whose training programme
I pioneered, is one example among many.

My continued writing during the 1980s and 1990s owes a great
deal to this quadruple influence and connection: a medical and
psychotherapeutic background; dialogue with theologians and
psychologists at Care and Counsel and at Swanwick; training
others in counselling at Network; and an expanding involvement
in pastoral studies at Trinity College. Out of these years, with their
attendant first-hand experience of continuing illness, has come a
series of books in the overall area of pastoral care and counselling
– *Roots and Shoots*, *Coping with Illness*, *Understanding Adolescence*
and *The Bible and Counselling*. It is the first and last of these that
have the most relevance to the present volume, the three works
providing sequential and complementary perspectives: *Roots and
Shoots* as a comprehensive overview and critique of counselling
and psychotherapy – in their 'secular' and 'Christian' forms; *The
Bible and Counselling* as a more introductory assessment of the uses
and misuses of Scripture in pastoral care, counselling, healing and
spiritual direction; and *Pathways to Wholeness* as an in-depth study
of the theological and psychological undergirding of pastoral care
in its multiple subcultural contexts.

This most recent book is an attempt to provide a tentative map
of Christian pastoral care within the complex territory of culture's
transition from late modernity to postmodernity. In Part I we
survey the terrain of the contemporary socio-cultural landscape
from the 'twin peaks' of pastoral theology and pastoral psychology. Thus, we explore notions of wholeness as process and goal in
Chapter 1; the concepts of Christian pilgrimage as journey and
story in Chapter 2; the relationship between Church, culture and
selfhood in Chapter 3; and the hermeneutics of text and the
individual's life in today's 'culture of interpretation' in Chapters
4 and 5. Part II begins with the book's pivotal discussion in
Chapter 6, in which ground rules for a pastoral theological method

are laid down and then used in Chapters 7 to 11 to examine five
pathways to wholeness: biblical counselling, the healing ministries, pastoral counselling, spiritual direction and the quest for
social change. Throughout these later chapters an attempt is made
to delineate a 'map' of these five pastoral ministries in terms of
their focus, doctrinal approach, hermeneutics, use of Scripture,
pastoral metaphor, spirituality, theology and conceptual keywords. A summary of these perspectives is given in table form
at the end of Chapter 6 (see p. 175) and this will hopefully provide
a ready reference for the reader.

It is worth saying that, for the general reader, the most accessible
chapters are the first two and Chapters 7 to 11. Even so, Chapters 3
to 6, with their exploration of cultural, hermeneutical and theological considerations, form a theoretical basis to the work. These
foundational areas have been greatly neglected in pastoral studies
and need, I feel, an in-depth appraisal in relation to pastoral theory
and practice. I trust they will be of interest and value to those
readers who have the time and inclination to reflect on the more
contextual and methodological aspects of their Christian praxis.

Throughout *Pathways to Wholeness* I refer to the stories of a
number of people with whom I have had contact through the
years. These stories are deliberately modified and, at times,
blended, so that individual identities and circumstances are obscured and protected; they nonetheless retain the essence of true
encounters with 'living human documents', to use Anton Boisen's
phrase.[3]

The book is dedicated to students and staff at Trinity College
and my prime indebtedness in its writing lies in their direction. I
am especially grateful to my colleagues Robert Forrest, Philip
Jenson and David Runcorn for their supportive and perceptive
comments in the shaping of Chapters 3 and 4, 5 and 6, and 10
respectively. In the writing of such a volume, with its accompanying need to try to master at least the salient texts, I am truly
thankful to the librarians who have aided and abetted me in
tracking down the relevant resources, to those of the British
Library lending service, to Victoria Mier of the University of
Bristol library and, most of all, since I have demanded most of
her, Su Brown of Trinity College. At the same time, my gratitude is
extended to my agent William Neill-Hall and to the editors of
Hodder and Stoughton, particularly to James Catford, Elspeth
Taylor and Judith Longman, for their collective patience and

xiv

PREFACE

encouragement in the book's gestation and delivery. Most especially, my thanks are expressed to my wife Joy who, following her
loving support duing the time of my quadruple bypass and near-
death experience in 1993, has witnessed her husband vanish into
his study, seemingly without coming up for air, over the inter-
vening years. We both look forward to some respite from the pull
of the word processor as we nudge forward on pathways to
wholeness.

ABBREVIATIONS

AV   *Holy Bible, Authorised Version*

CGLE   Ian Ousby (ed.), *Cambridge Guide to Literature in English* (Cambridge: Cambridge University Press, 1993)

CED   *Collins English Dictionary* (Glasgow: HarperCollins, 1991)

DCS   Gordon S. Wakefield (ed.), *Dictionary of Christian Spirituality* (London: SCM Press, 1983)

DCT   Alan Richardson and John Bowden (eds.), *Dictionary of Christian Theology* (London: SCM Press, 1983)

DPCC   Rodney J. Hunter, *Dictionary of Pastoral Care and Counseling* (Nashville: Abingdon Press, 1990)

NDCEPT   David J. Atkinson and David H. Field, *New Dictionary of Christian Ethics and Pastoral Theology* (Leicester: Inter-Varsity Press, 1995)

NDT   Sinclair B. Ferguson and David F. Wright, *New Dictionary of Theology* (Leicester: Inter-Varsity Press, 1988)

NIDNTT   Colin Brown (ed.), *New International Dictionary of New Testament Theology* (Exeter: Paternoster Press: vol. 1, 1975; vol. 2, 1976; vol. 3, 1978)

NRSV   *Holy Bible, New Revised Standard Version, (Anglicised Edition)*

OCEL   Tom McArthur (ed.), *Oxford Companion to the English Language* (Oxford: Oxford University Press, 1992)

SOED   *Shorter Oxford English Dictionary* (London: Oxford University Press, 1967)

INTRODUCTION

A map is not the territory.
Alfred Korzybski[1]

Four years ago, when the idea of this book was taking firmer shape, a small incident with two of our grandchildren sharpened my tentative thoughts on pathways to wholeness and the need we all have for direction-finding. Just a month or so before their visit I had systematically sorted my large collection of Ordnance Survey maps, collected since my teen years with great eagerness as each holiday in some new area of the United Kingdom approached. They had been lovingly set in order from Cape Wrath and the Outer Hebrides to Lands End and the Isles of Scilly, stacked sideways, their spines displayed for easy access, on the bottom shelf of the bookcase in what was to be the children's bedroom for a few nights. That evening, at bedtime, Luke (five and a half) and Verity (four) were soon engaged in a silent, completely absorbed dismantling of the neat row of maps.

Luke seems to have an innate sense of direction and has been fascinated by all things cartographical from an early age. When my wife Joy peered in to evaluate the situation soon after the assault began, Luke, who had just singled out a particular map, opened it and announced, correctly, 'Look! There's Bristol!' He was well orientated for their stay. The next morning Joy chatted with Verity, who was sitting amid the strewn maps, and declared that to leave the maps in such a muddle would make Grandpa sad and suggested that they tidy up the mess together. Verity joined in eagerly, producing a neatly reinstated row of maps whose sequence, so I discovered some days later, appeared to be completely randomised. She agreed readily with Joy that, the next night, she and Luke would not play with Grandpa's maps. It was many weeks before I had the energy to reassemble them.

There seem to be two pointers in this little incident which relate to our exploration of pathways to wholeness. We can say, without stretching our analogy too far, that Luke's triumphant exclamation, 'There's Bristol!' reminds us that, on life's journey, we all need a sense of where we are *now*, a sense of place that is connected with where we have been and holds promise for tomorrow. It is my contention as I write this book, set as it is in the context of Christian pastoral care, that all of us, individually and corporately, can through God's grace and mercy have some appreciation of where we are positioned on our earthly pilgrimage. This may not, of course, be saying very much. We may feel that our sense of direction has gone, that we are, quite simply, lost. It is at such times that we once more need the maps, those reference points from which we can freshly take our bearings.

For some, this may also mean the need for a guide, for a companion who is on the same journey and can offer, for a span of time, exhortation, encouragement, counsel, help with the route-finding. For many, this giving and receiving of direction is hopefully reinforced by a wider and more permanent sense of belonging, of being a valued part of the community, a member in the body of Christ, a pilgrim within a company of fellow-travellers. We may not be able to pinpoint our position on life's maps, to give the precise grid reference of our Christian journeying, but we are a people with a history and a future, and where we are placed in the present needs to be seen in the context of personal and corporate 'story' as well as in an assured destiny. Our span of memory and breadth of anticipation may be limited, but the Christian disciple is assured that he or she is 'in Christ', to use the Pauline term, and that this 'place to be' covers past, present and future. Luke knew all was well, since he was 'connected up' within a loving family that had travelled from Sheffield that day, the map's accuracy confirming the view he had from the grandparental lounge window that Bristol was nearby, and that the next few days held the promise of good things to do and experience – a football to be kicked, treasure to be found with Verity along the coast, good food, drink and hugs from Grannie, stories, board-games, and more hugs, with Grandpa.

The other pointer is linked closely to the first. If we are to have some idea where we are placed on life's pathways, we also need to set our maps in order. Some may feel this is a pointless exercise since life is seen as a terrain of which they cannot make sense, beyond it being a land bound by chains of cause and effect or by chance and accident. Even so, the whole of the history of human-kind is filled with attempts to draw and arrange maps of reality – be it the work of religionists, theologians, philosophers, historians, linguists, aestheticians, scientists, political theorists, economists, psychologists or sociologists.

In this book, the attempt to 'put the maps in order' is made within the overall Judaeo-Christian tradition by setting the para-meters in the theoretical frameworks of pastoral theology and pastoral psychology and, in particular, their bearing on Christian pastoral care and its relation to pathways to wholeness. It is an enterprise that inevitably embraces context as well as text. In other words, the cultural milieu in which our map-making is set – a transition period between modernity and postmodernity – needs to be addressed if we are to take our journeying in and toward God seriously. And, just as in cartography, context and text are closely interwoven (the 'text' of a particular map is read with greater understanding if it is known, for example, that it delineates South-East England just before the motorway system was first introduced) so the links between cultural setting and the inter-pretation of pastoral encounter are comparably interlaced. Con-sequently, questions of the hermeneutics of the relevant 'texts' are tackled, both in terms of seeking to interpret Scripture in relation to pathways to wholeness and to interpet the lives of those who journey toward that wholeness.

At least Verity, with Joy's encouragement, arranged the maps in a neat row. To set them in order afterwards, a system was needed – the simple one of geographical location, from the North of Scotland to the South of England. The 'system' used in *Pathways to Wholeness* is a less straightforward one, as we have just seen, in that it makes use of the complex interplay between postmodernity, a faithful hermeneutics and the frontline of pastoral encounter. However, the resulting ordering of life's maps is, hopefully, made more accessible by an underlying theme – that of story, the story of God's dealings with humankind, the story of God's people set amid community and the story of individual pilgrims who still journey toward the promised land.

Like Luke, I have been a map-maker from an early age. I recall spending many hours in boyhood closely studying maps of that part of Essex, just at the furthest reach of Greater London's north-eastern tentacles, in which we lived. I meticulously copied in blue ink each small meander of our local stream, the River Ingrebourne, followed the confident lines of the main arterial roads in red, etched the mixed woodlands (alternating deciduous and coniferous trees, faithfully rendered) of South Weald and Thorndon Park in green, and delineated the spaced-out, unexciting contours of a relatively flat countryside in brown. Later, in my teen years, my ambition was to be a cartographer, a land surveyor, one who would explore and map remote, uncharted areas in deepest Africa – the romanticised Africa of an earlier era, the land of John Buchan's *Prester John* and Rider Haggard's *King Solomon's Mines*. Although this purpose took me as far as a state scholarship in geography and geology, the map-making urge was carried over into a career in medicine and, latterly, counselling and pyschotherapy, where the contours of human anatomy, physiology and pathology gave way to an exploration of the psyche, of Freud's 'geography of the mind'. Since the end of the 1960s this latter enterprise has been enriched, through the stimulus of colleagues, students, clients, study and reflection, by the progressive development of a map-making exercise in the field of the integration of theology and psychology.

However, in all attempts to depict life's complexities in accessible form we need the reminder of the dictum that heads this Introduction: Alfred Korzybski's, 'A map is *not* the territory.' Just as the intricacies and grandeur of a mountain range are more awesome and spellbinding than maps of the area can portray, so the 'territory' of any aspect of existence is more complicated, rich and wondrous than any of the diagrams, models and 'maps' we might draw to represent it. Luke knew that. He was not deceived by the Ordnance Survey. His 'There's Bristol!' was a small triumph of recognition but he knew, of course, that the excitements of the Clifton Suspension Bridge, the ships in the dock and a pantomime at the Hippodrome were all part of a more engaging reality.

Korzybski's saying, initially given within the discipline of general semantics in the context of words and symbols and their relation to meaning,[2] has a universal appeal to philosophical map-makers. For example, Fritjof Capra uses the phrase to highlight the dilemmas involved in an exploration of the parallels between modern physics and Eastern mysticism, while Jonathan Z. Smith applies the same perspective to the history of religions.[3]

Both these writers emphasise the inadequacy of the 'maps'. Capra contrasts the highly analytical mindset of Western rationalism with the intuitive wisdom of the East. He sees the former's commitment to dividing and distinguishing within the world of reality as a map-making enterprise 'in which things are reduced to their general outlines',[4] whereas the latter insists that 'ultimate reality can never be an object of reasoning or of demonstrable knowledge.'[5] These markedly different approaches to comprehending the universe are highlighted as follows:

> For most of us it is very difficult to be constantly aware of the limitations and of the relativity of conceptual knowledge. Because our representation of reality is so much easier to grasp than reality itself, we tend to confuse the two and to take our concepts and symbols for reality. It is one of the main aims of Eastern mysticism to rid us of this confusion. Zen Buddhists say that a finger is needed to point at the moon, but that we should not trouble ourselves with the finger once the moon is recognized.[6]

The contrast here seems to be between a Western world-view that is always in danger of promoting its maps as substitutes for the wonder and challenge of reality and an Eastern perspective that is willing to lay aside both map and compass once the unknowable is discerned. Let us keep in mind, throughout *Pathways to Wholeness*, the limitations of our map-making and the boundless nature of the God we seek. The pointing finger of any guide on our journeying need not distract us once 'the moon is recognized', once the object of our desire is beheld.

Smith shares Capra's scepticism toward much Western rationalistic map-making. He points out, with Capra, that such analyses oversimplify the complexity of reality but he takes his argument further in raising the question of an imperialistic motive within much categorisation. Broadly, he postulates three mindsets behind attempts to map the cosmos: the view that the universe is chaotic; the belief in a map of the world 'which guarantees meaning and value through structures of congruity and conformity';[7] and a perspective, which he favours, that faces and accepts incongruity and difference. It is with respect to the second of these three stances that he voices his strongest suspicions. Such a unitive view, he argues, is in danger of excluding those who do not fit into our systems. He sees the tendency as ancient and linked to the roots of language. He cites, for example, the attitude within classical Greek culture that 'to be human was to be a Hellene,

to speak in intelligible, non-stuttering speech' and to be, culturally
speaking, 'non-human was to be a barbarian, to speak unintelli-
gible, stuttering animal or childlike speech' – the *bar, bar, bar* of the
so-called barbaric peoples.[8] He sees this excluding perspective in
the nineteenth-century view of the 'savage' as someone who lacks
the mental faculty to differentiate reality beyond the most rudimentary elements and quotes James George Frazer's comment
that such a being is like 'the blind man of Bethsaida, he sees men
like trees and animals walking in a thick intellectual fog'.[9]

Smith carries his argument over into the twentieth century
where it has become fashionable to adopt a more inclusive posture
and 'insist on the holistic character of primitive culture'. Nonetheless, he reasons, both the 'them-and-us' stance of the Victorian
era and the more generous views of today are two sides of the
same coin of an imperialistic style of map-making, for both 'see the
primitive as essentially not-like-us'.[10] His corrective is to follow
the third perspective in mapping reality, that of traditions which
'allow the incongruous elements to stand' and seek 'to play
between the incongruities and to provide an occasion for thought'.
He sums up this stimulating and humanising viewpoint and
enterprise at the conclusion of his essay:

> We may have to become initiated by the other whom we study and
> undergo the ordeal of incongruity. For we have often missed what is
> humane in the other by the very seriousness of our quest. We need to
> reflect on and play with the necessary incongruity of our maps before
> we set out on a voyage of discovery to chart the worlds of other men.
> For the dictum of Alfred Korzybski is inescapable: 'Map is not territory'
> – but maps are all we possess.[11]

In using Korzybski's saying as a framework for this book, and its
exploration of five pathways toward wholeness, I am committed
to seek an openness toward 'the other whom we study' and,
where necessary, 'undergo the ordeal of incongruity' in the attempt to provide a realistic map within the complex terrain of
pastoral psychology, pastoral theology and Christian spirituality.
As we shall be reminded more fully, the wider context is a
postmodern one, which purports to value distinctiveness and
particularity, and the texts for the journey are, ultimately, the
Bible and the human story. Although the two texts interweave and
provide a rich fabric for our map-making, we need to be wary, I

suggest, in ways put forward by Capra and Smith, of the dangers of an oversimplification that reduces, in our case, divine activity and human variety into a monolithic unitary theory that will not allow discrepancy, nonconformity and a measure of uncertainty. By the same token, we should beware any methodology within the pathways that we tread which lays claim to being *the* route that all must take. Such heady confidence is always in danger of reducing the 'God of surprises' to a tamed deity who can only aid the needy within the confines of an accredited rule-book.

Finally, our map-making needs flexibility. All maps need revision and updating from time to time. Even now, I am reminded vividly of the autumn, at the age of fourteen or so, when I cycled into North Essex with my cousin Ken for a few days' camping. We had a map and I, as the 'native guide', was the confident map-reader. All went according to plan until the second full day when, topping a stiff little hill somewhere near the hamlet of Layer de la Haye, we saw before us a large 'inland sea' which filled the landscape where we had expected gently undulating farmland. I, a believer in the inviolability of maps and a reliable interpeter of contours, can still feel something of my utter amazement. We were still a good six miles from the wide mouth of the Blackwater Estuary and this vast expanse of water, barely a mile away, just should not have been there. Still puzzled, we camped that night near the shores of a very present lake, above its very real reedbeds, filled with the very audible chatter of bona fide roosting martins and swallows. It was some time before I established that, within recent years, the shallow valley of the Layer Brook, south of Colchester, had been flooded to form the four-and-a-half-mile long, one-and-a-half-mile wide Abberton Reservoir. My out-of-date map needed drastic revision.

As we seek representations of life's complexities, whether through metaphors, analogies, models or 'maps', we need to keep open to those developments and changes in understanding knowledge that may require us to reappraise our previous attempts to systematise. Let us, then, as we explore five pathways to wholeness, declare a willingness both to accept any apparent incongruities we may meet on the way and, as I needed to do in the case of the all-too-evident reservoir, to adjust our presuppositions accordingly. After all, the object of all map-making is to help us find our way within the real territory of everyday life. Sallie McFague, commenting on the tentative nature of much theologising, uses the comparable analogy of building a house. Here she brings out the essentially practical nature of all worthwhile 'maps', and similar constructs, when she writes:

> As with any construction, the most one can do is to 'live within' it, testing it for its disclosive power, its ability to address and cope with the most pressing issues of one's day, its comprehensiveness and coherence, its potential for dealing with anomalies, and so forth. Theological constructions are 'houses' to live in for a while, with windows partly open and doors ajar; they become prisons when they no longer allow us to come and go, to add a room or take one away – or if necessary, to move out and build a new house.[12]

PART I

THE TERRITORY

1

PATHWAYS TO WHOLENESS:
PROCESS AND GOAL

Walk about before me and be whole.
Genesis 17:1

In using life's maps in whatever territory we find ourselves, we need to ask two questions: What is my destination? and Which route shall I take? The destination may be a minor goal within daily life: some neglected job to complete, an everyday decision to be made, someone to be thanked, or challenged. The route may be simplicity itself: a purchase to be made, a meeting arranged, a fax sent, a letter to be written. At a deeper layer, there are questions of longer-term aims and the weighing up of different routes to achieve those aims: to complete a course of training, to find work after years of unemployment, to pay off a mortgage, to be a better friend or partner. At the profoundest level, issues of ultimate reality raise their head where questions of destination merge with those of destiny, and matters of everyday route-finding mingle with those of a sense of direction in life itself.

It is at this third and deepest level that the perspective of 'wholeness' is raised and the dimension of 'life as journey' can be discussed. Both these themes are subtexts of this book throughout and they will be dealt with more fully and practically in Part II. However, both can be examined in an introductory way at this stage – 'wholeness' in this chapter and 'life as journey' in Chapter 2 – in order to open up a discussion of the theological, psychological and therapeutic aspects of, first, concepts of wholeness and completeness, and, second, journey and story – engaging us with a range of closely linked metaphors of human life.

It is probably true to say that most, if not all, cultures and religions have some concept of *wholeness*, a state of health and completeness that is generally felt to be desirable, if not attainable.

Inevitably, such views depend profoundly on what is believed about human existence. As the presuppositional basis of this book is within the Judaeo-Christian tradition, fuller explorations of different aspects of wholeness will be engaged in in Part II; these include the process of sanctification, issues of healing, growth towards maturity, the mystical union between Christ and the believer, and social and environmental transformation. At this stage, by way of introduction to 'pathways to wholeness', we will examine, albeit briefly, attitudes to wholeness within some of the other major world religions; in a selection of post-Enlightenment ideologies, exemplified by three influential psychotherapies; and, finally, from a Judaeo-Christian perspective.

Wholeness in World Religions

It is instructive to give an overview of beliefs about wholeness in a selection of world religions for at least four reasons:

- such understandings, and a range of closely allied views, are still widespread in those parts of the globe where the religions have their roots;
- their influence has now penetrated innumerable other cultures in our pluralistic societies;
- the so-called New Age increasingly embraces belief-systems from a variety of religions, particularly those from the more mystical traditions;
- postmodernity, as we shall see in Chapter 3, invites us to experiment with and participate in the wares of the philosophical and religious market-place, valuing each product for its own intrinsic worth.

Let us look briefly at an outline of some of the central tenets concerning pathways to wholeness in *Hinduism and Buddhism*; *Confucianism and Taoism*; and *Islam*.

Hinduism and Buddhism

Long before the time of Christ, South-East Asia saw the rise of two distinct belief-systems: Hinduism, with its roots in the religion of the Aryan peoples who migrated into India at about 1500 BC; and

Buddhism, based on the teachings of the *Buddha*, the 'enlightened one', living in the sixth century BC.

Broadly, wholeness is seen, within the multifaceted beliefs of Hinduism, in terms of two principles: *Karma* (action, doing, deed), a route to salvation depending on virtuous thinking and behaviour and necessitating successive reincarnations; and *Brahman*, or the Universal Self, where individual human souls, released from the pains and desires of earthly life, can be seen as the inseparable 'waves' of a blissful 'oceanic state'. One route to achieving reunion with *Brahman* is through the mental discipline of *yoga*. Padmasani Gallup, writing on pastoral counselling in the Hindu cultural context, describes how the four systems of *yoga* may take the individual to an ' "exaltation" beyond all human imaginings', to *santhi*, 'a concept of wholeness, of full integration of mind, body and spirit offered through the yogic systems of hard discipline'.[1]

This blend of asceticism and longed-for release from the cycle of rebirth is modified and, to some extent, ameliorated in Buddhism since Buddha's 'Noble Eightfold Path' offers a 'middle way' of moderation in all things, a pathway to *Nirvana*, a condition of 'nothingness, or self-extinction'. Whereas Hinduism declares continuity of the self, through successive reincarnations, until reunited with the Higher Self, Buddhism postulates the desirability of 'no-self', the final loss of identity and consciousness in the 'no-land' of *Nirvana*.

Confucianism and Taoism

In China, from the sixth century BC onwards, two further contrasting belief-systems emerged. The first, Confucianism, founded by Master K'ung, emphasised the importance of education, ceremonial and social ethics, while Taoism, associated with the supposedly mythical teacher Lao Tzu, pursued a more mystical route 'concerned with a sort of immediate, inner, intuitive enlightenment',[2] the pursuit of the Tao, the Way, or, more comprehensively, the 'Principle which underlies and controls the world'.[3]

As the centuries unfolded, the influence of Buddhism entered China and Korea and, by the twelfth and thirteenth centuries AD, reached Japan where, blending with Taoist ideals, Zen Buddhism was born. This amalgam of beliefs produced a distinctive view of wholeness, for in Zen an emphasis on the art of gracious living, including the studied, socially bonding tea ceremony, was linked with *satori*, a moment of spontaneous awakening and illumination.

It is of perennial interest to observe that, as a generality, these Eastern religions express something of the age-old contrast between two paths towards wholeness: that of *virtuous living* and *scholarly knowledge*, as in much of Hinduism and Confucianism; and that of *the inner life* and *intuitive understanding*, as in Buddhism, especially in its Japanese Zen form, and Taoism. Capra reminds us, in his comparison of scientific reason and mystical intuition, that Eastern religious forms are highly complex and yet certain patterns are discernible:

> The degree to which reason and logic are emphasized [in Eastern mysticism] varies enormously from one school to the other. The Hindu Vedanta, or the Buddhist Madhymika, for example, are highly intellectual schools, whereas Taoists have always had a deep mistrust of reason and logic. Zen . . . prides itself on being 'without words, without explanations, without instructions, without knowledge'. It concentrates almost entirely on the experience of enlightenment and is only marginally interested in interpreting this experience. A well known Zen phrase says, 'The instant you speak about a thing you miss the mark.'[4]

Islam

The three great monotheistic religions – Judaism, Christianity and Islam – see the promise of wholeness in terms of a close interplay between the path of obedience in present reality and an eternal destiny. To a much greater degree than in the Far Eastern religions considered, although their sacred writings are of considerable influence, these Near and Middle Eastern belief-systems are, supremely, religions of the Book – and it is within their Scriptures that we find the clearest teachings on the quest for wholeness.

Islamic belief holds that the faithful keeping of religious, social and ethical duties, as laid down in the Qur'an, are rewarded by paradisical delights in the hereafter, whereas faithlessness, disloyalty and ingratitude result in a 'lostness' wherein the individual 'finally comes face to face with the Real, Allah, his hands empty and his past life meaningless'.[5]

The Qur'an, the transcript of Muhammad's revelations of the early seventh century AD, is undergirded by the *hadith*, an extensive commentary on what the Prophet did and said, and authoritative for much of a traditional Muslim's life. It is here that quite close parallels can be drawn between Islam and the Judaeo-Christian tradition.[6] The faithful Muslim is to follow Muhammad as the 'perfect exemplar', since the Prophet is seen as 'closer to the believers than their [own] selves', to quote the Qur'an.[7] A further Quranic verse reminds the Muslim of the close link between an awareness of God and self-understanding: 'Be not as those who forgot Allah so that He caused them to forget their own selves.'[8] An intregal part of remembering Allah is the ritual ablution, an 'image' of God's forgiveness, opening the way for the worshipper to pray, facing Ka'ba, the sacred mosque in Mecca. This can be seen as a pathway to wholeness, since, to quote Gai Eaton:

> To face in the right direction is to be well on the way to achieve personal integration. It is to be already on the 'straight path' upon which, in his prayer, the Muslim will ask God to lead him, except that in the first case the path is, so to speak, on the horizontal – leading to Mecca – whereas in the second it is vertical and leads to 'the Lord of this House', the Lord of the Ka'ba, God Himself . . . the former is a symbol of the latter and, at the same time, its precursor.[9]

As with the contrasts, already observed, between much of Hinduism and the developing story of Buddhism, and between Confucianism and Taoism, the two differing paths of *reason* and *intuition* can also be seen within Islam's historical development.

Sufism,[10] emerging as early as the eighth century, was in many ways a reaction against the legal formulations of the orthodox Islamic faith, and increasingly embraced a thoroughgoing mysticism that was variously influenced by Eastern Christianity and gnosticism. Its initial asceticism is probably reflected in the term *Sufi*, which may simply indicate one who wears *suf*, undyed wool that implies austere living. In time, the movement shifted its ground from a rigorous self-denial to the more contemplative stance of the 'Sufi way', a 'spiritual itinerary' which fostered the concept of a sainthood where friendship with God was claimed. Orthodoxy, with its adherence to the Qur'an and the *hadith* and its worship of a powerful, transcendent Allah, found a great deal that was threatening in the more intimate path of the 'inner way' with its stress on God's nearness and the disciple's response of trust and love. Following the persecution of Sufis in the tenth century, al-Ghazzali, an expert in Islamic law at the university of Baghdad towards the end of the next century, was a traditionalist who nonetheless explored the Sufi way during his later years and sought a synthesis between the two contrary paths. In seeking to do justice to both the experiential individualism of Sufism and the more structured and communally based nature of orthodoxy, al-Ghazzali brought about a situation where, to quote Ninian Smart, there was no more 'severe friction between the mystic and the theologian'.[11]

Within this brief survey of the world's major religions we have been reminded repeatedly that human religious sensibility gravitates to one of two pathways: either the route of *reason*, marked by faithful obedience to a set of laws and practices, often undergirded by the religion's sacred texts; or the path of *intuition*, featuring a more contemplative and mystical spirituality. Vedanta Hinduism, Confucianism and orthodox Islam largely take the former pathway and Zen Buddhism, Taoism and Sufism the latter. As we shall see throughout this book, the Judaeo-Christian tradition embraces comparable emphases, reflected, not least, within the pathways to wholeness described in Part II.

Wholeness in Post-Enlightenment Ideologies

Drawing on ancient Greek philosophies, particularly those of Plato and Aristotle,[12] and fostering an increasing secularisation of society through the seventeenth and eighteenth centuries, the Age of Enlightenment celebrated three cardinal areas of human endeavour: *reason*, the *natural sciences* and *progress*. In many ways, the first of these was the mainspring for the other two: rationality, and its more resolute companion, rationalism,[13] held centre-stage in the exploration of nature and the pursuit of educational and technological advancement.

Although the Enlightenment was not inevitably irreligious or anti-religious, its metaphysical shift, from acknowledging God as supreme authority in all matters of daily life to a progressive elevation of the primacy of human reasoning, led to a view in which the Deity was seen as superfluous to requirement. There were, of course, notable exceptions to this trend including, for example, Sir Isaac Newton who, in the late seventeenth century, set in train a new, mathematical understanding of the universe, where God was seen as 'the most perfect mechanic of all':[14] unlike the Deists, who saw God as absent initiator, Newtonian physics seemed to allow for a creator who also sustains and provides. Even so, the quintessential voice of the Enlightenment was a bid for autonomy, for a human spirit freed from the perceived restrictions of religious faith. In 1784 Immanuel Kant (1724–1804), the German philosopher, asked the question 'What is Enlightenment?' and summed up the age's credo in the words of the Roman poet Horace: *'Sapere aude!* ''Have courage to use your own reason!'' – that is the motto of enlightenment.'[15]

By the nineteenth century, rationality and empirical enquiry became increasingly established in the realm of the human sciences. Among these, psychology, further influenced by the evolutionary theories of Charles Darwin, carried its investigations into human nature at two levels: that of an examination of what is observable and measurable; and that of an exploration of the inner world of men and women. By the beginning of the twentieth century this attempt to qualify and quantify human psychology could be described in terms of three broad systems – behaviourism, psychoanalysis and personalism, with a fourth system, transpersonalism, emerging from the 1960s onward.[16] By and large, although the history of these four strands overlaps a great deal, there has been a discernible trend within these psychologies, and their attendant therapeutic methodologies, to move increasingly toward more humanising and holistic perspectives: from the extreme reductionism of early behaviourism (human beings as nothing but higher animals or, worse, machines); through the somewhat pessimistic views of classical Freudianism (human beings as the sum of their instincts); the more hope-giving emphases of the neo-Freudians (people as social beings); the optimism of the personalistic psychologies (people endowed with all the inner resources needed for growth); and the transcendental dimensions of transpersonalism (where human need and potential are seen to lie beyond the self).

Nonetheless, every psychotherapeutic approach aims to bring some sort of betterment into the life of the recipient. Early behaviourism, although reducing human interaction to the level of Pavlov's reflex arc and Skinner's operant conditioning, at least sought change toward a more efficient functioning. Behavioural methods, based on unfolding behaviouristic theories,[17] have a well-established place in helping clients overcome anxiety and various phobic states. Further, traditional Freudianism has always aimed to bring relief to conflict-ridden people through a process that seeks to unpeel the layers of the psyche to enable a facing up to what has been repressed, and so, in time, to bring about a measure of reintegration.

However, it is among the modifiers of and rebels against Freud that we find a range of methodologies[18] which begin to fill out the human quest for wholeness: Alfred Adler, with his stress on human choice, purpose and sociability; Melanie Klein, and the British school of psychoanalysis, with their humanising emphasis on the mother–child relationship; Erik Erikson, the post-Freudian, with his step-by-step understanding of the acquisition of identity, intimacy and integrity; the neo-Freudians, such as Karen Horney and Erich Fromm, with their exposition of the importance of social and environmental factors in the search of satisfaction and security. Carl Jung, as we shall see more fully in Chapter 10, stands out from the psychoanalytic stream with his more mystical approach to human nature and his particular goal of 'individuation' as an 'at-one-ment with oneself and at the same time with humanity'.[19]

As we have indicated, the personalistic psychologies, influenced by humanism and existentialism, and transpersonalism, increasingly associated with New Age mysticism, give further impetus to humanity's pursuit of wholeness. This pursuit, within these two systems of psychology, can be traced back, particularly in Germany toward the end of the nineteenth century, to a rebellion against the strictly scientific theories and methods of the earliest behaviourists. Among the philosophers and psychologists who raised their objections, the name of Wilhelm Dilthey (1833–1911) stands out as one of the most consistently outspoken.

Something of a polymath, Dilthey's humanising influence can be seen in the realms of philosophy, sociology and hermeneutics, as well as in the various schools of psychology that emerged in the early years of the twentieth century.[20] Dilthey's 'understanding' psychology challenged the 'explanatory' psychologies of the natural scientists, arguing that human beings are to be seen as living unities capable of individual and social integration, rather than simply as systems of stimulus and response. Broadly, his richer concept of human nature can be seen in the emergence of the holistic psychologies, divided into 'organismic' and 'personalistic' strands, and of Gestalt psychology – all initially taking root in

German soil. The *organismic* strand of holism took a more biological view, seeing wholeness in terms of a total functioning of the human organism, while the *personalistic* strand emphasised the value of personhood and social relatedness in moving toward a unified state. This holism was, in turn, paralleled by Gestalt and, by the second half of the twentieth century, was spawning a vast array of pathways to the fuller life with origins mainly in the systems of personalism and transpersonalism. Among these routes to wholeness, we will briefly consider three representative examples: *self-actualisation*; *Gestalt*; and *psychosynthesis*.

Self-actualisation

While working in New York in the 1940s, it was the German psychologist Kurt Goldstein (1878–1965), one of Dilthey's successors and of the organismic school of holism, who first coined the term 'self-actualisation'. Following his research on wounded German soldiers during and after the First World War, he came to the conclusion that human nature is driven by a single motivational force toward self-actualisation, or self-realisation, the 'tendency to achieve the optimal performance of the total organism'.[21]

Acknowledging the value of Goldstein's work but filling out his biological emphasis with a personalistic approach, Abraham Maslow (1903–70) elaborated his 'holistic-dynamic' point of view from 1935 onward. Over the following years he carried out research on 'relatively healthy college students', as well as contemporary and historical public figures, in order to establish the characteristics of the self-actualising person. These features include: a clear-headed perspective on life's realities; a well-developed acceptance of self, others and the natural order; a 'strongly ethical' stance; spontaneity and creativity; an independent spirit and resistance to the dictates of culture; a capacity for compassion and deeper relationships; and the presence of more frequent 'peak experiences' – mystical events that engage a sense of self-transcendence, such as falling in love, the intense enjoyment of music or art, or gaining inspirational insight.[22] In painting this idealised picture of human completeness, Maslow did not deny the primacy of more basic human needs,[23] such as hunger, thirst, the need for shelter and love, and saw these essential prerequisites of everyday life in continuity with the 'higher' need for an 'ongoing actualization of potentials, capacities and talents', which incorporates 'an unceasing trend toward unity, integration or synergy within the person'.[24]

In his later years, Maslow, as part of a general trend among personalistic psychologists, saw more clearly the limits of a quest for wholeness in purely psychological terms. Although, in 1970, he could still write, 'Psychological health not only feels good subjectively but is also correct, true, real',[25] his main thrust at that time was toward a realisation that human beings need something beyond the self if they are to rise above a sickness of the spirit. Even in this transpersonal vision, though, his humanistic, essentially anti-supernatural, pedigree holds firm:

> I consider Humanistic, Third Force Psychology to be transitional, a preparation for a still 'higher' Fourth Psychology, transpersonal, transhuman, centred in the cosmos rather than in human needs and interest, going beyond humanness, identity, self-actualization, and the like . . . Without the transcendent and the transpersonal, we get sick, violent, and nihilistic, or else hopeless and apathetic. We need something 'bigger than we are' to be awed by and to commit ourselves to in a new, naturalistic, empirical, non-churchly sense.[26]

Gestalt

Among psychologists and psychotherapists, whenever concepts of growth, maturity or wholeness are discussed, it does not take long before the word 'Gestalt' peppers the conversation. The word, and its particular connotations, has taken a circuitous route in the world of psychology over the past hundred years or so – from Germanic philosophical deliberations, through the perennial debate between biological and less reductionist views of human nature and the founding of a therapeutic outlet to the theorising by a charismatic and controversial figure, to an increasingly respected and professionalised body of Gestalt therapists.

The word *Gestalt* was first used within a psychological framework in 1890 by the Austrian psychologist and philosopher, Christian von Ehrenfels (1859–1932), who reasoned that there is a 'gestalt, or form' quality present in the whole of a structure, which is absent from any of the parts that make up that whole.[27] The original discussions centred on questions of the perception of shapes and patterns as distinct from the constituent parts that made up their entirety. In the realm of music, for example, a reasonably attuned ear will pick up and appreciate the overall effect of a sonata or symphony and will not perceive the piece as nothing more than a collection of individual notes arranged in sequence. Further, the very same notes used in, say, Beethoven's *Kreutzer* sonata or Mozart's *Prague* symphony can be rearranged to produce quite different pieces whose musical forms will give their own distinctive impacts on the listener.

Given a general agreement on the reality of such perceptions, the early Gestalt psychologists held differences as to whether sensations, such as seeing and hearing, are structured by some higher mental process or are 'self-organised', so that there is an instinctual immediacy in recognising the simpler patterns in, say, a painting or a piece of music. Von Ehrenfels, and others, of the Austrian Gestalt school held the former view, while Max Wertheimer (1880–1943), Kurt Koffka (1886–1941) and Wolfgang Köhler (1887–1967), forming the Berlin Gestalt school in 1912, maintained the latter. The Berlin school became the trendsetter in Gestalt psychology, many of its adherents, in time, leaving Germany for the United States where, despite their previous resistance to extreme reductionism, they capitulated to the resolutely biological stance of the early behaviourists, giving priority to 'installing quantitative measures and excessive experimental restrictions'.[28]

This criticism of the early Gestaltists was later levelled by Frederick ('Fritz') Perls (1893–1970), who, working as a psychiatrist and psychoanalyst in Germany during the 1920s and 1930s, became disillusioned with orthodox Freudianism and was, in turn, influenced by the post-Freudian Wilhelm Reich (1897–1957). Reichian thinking, with its emphasis that the body is as important as the mind in the development of certain defence mechanisms, was highly formative on Perls's unfolding views. Further influenced by Kurt Goldstein's holism and emphasis on self-actualisation, and by the existential theologians Paul Tillich and Martin Buber, Fritz Perls and his wife Laura, a Gestalt psychologist, worked together – in South Africa from 1933 and in the United States after the Second World War – to develop their distinctive approach. Joining forces with other therapists, as well as writers and political activists, the term 'Gestalt therapy' was agreed upon and, in 1952, the first Institute of Gestalt Therapy was set up in New York.

While Laura Perls has remained a stable, and increasingly acknowledged, figure within Gestalt therapy, Fritz Perls, whose 'flavour' has been described as 'lusty, energetic, colloquial, and charismatic',[29] lived a restless existence during the 1950s and 1960s. Eventually settling at the Esalen Institute in California, Perls spent his latter years as part of the so-called 'human potential movement', a pot-pourri of open-ended approaches to therapy, personal growth and the search for wholeness. Today, much of Fritz Perls's more maverick legacy has been sifted and, where necessary, discarded in a process of increasing professionalisation, where recognised training and standards of supervision and counselling practice are regulated.

Gestalt therapy[30] is a methodology that emphasises that human perception sees the world as made up of coherent, intelligible configurations or 'gestalts'. Following concepts used by the earliest theorists,[31] it is argued that the individual perceives a 'figure', a concentrated, discernible feature, against the 'ground', a less-focused backdrop to the figure. In therapeutic terms, the 'figure' may be a recognised need that the client perceives, such as the pressing necessity of reconciliation with a wronged party. Ideally, effective action is taken – in this case a genuine apology is offered and, hopefully, accepted, and integration is thus achieved within a restored relationship. In this way, the 'gestalt', the overall configuration of figure and ground, is recognised, handled constructively and thus dissolved. Healthy functioning, so the Gestalt therapist reasons, is made up of a series of 'gestalts', each, once perceived, being 'unfinished business' which is subsequently completed.

Inevitably, the path to such psychological wholeness is frequently blocked – by, for example, a lack of self-awareness, an unwillingness to address the perceived need or an inability to integrate the met need. In the face of such maladjustment, Gestalt therapy, through individual counselling or group therapy, seeks to provide a climate in which the client can gain better insight into moment-by-moment experience, the cultivation of a new inner strength and an increased capacity to engage with everyday life. With these aims in mind, the therapist adopts a clear 'here-and-now' style, tailored to the client's specific needs and fostered by the therapist's willingness to share something of his or her own feelings and reactions as counselling progresses. The holistic approach of Gestalt therapy may be further expressed through creative experimentation, in which clients are encouraged to act out what they are feeling, sensing or thinking through art work, a re-enactment of a dream or other dramatisation – such as beating a cushion to discharge (safely!) pent-up anger, or conversing with the imaginary occupant of an empty chair to help objectify tangled feelings or mixed motives.

There is much in this overall methodology, including its openness to present reality, its engagement of the whole person and its quest for integration, that appeals to Christian counsellors and psychotherapists.[32] Let us complete this section with a contemporary view of Gestalt's particular style as a pathway to wholeness:

> A cornerstone of the Gestalt approach is its emphasis on the wholeness of the person in the counselling relationship, not just the intrapsychic or merely the interpersonal dimension. In the counselling process different aspects of a person may be emphasised at different times. These will probably include intrapsychic, behavioural, physiological, affective, cognitive and spiritual aspects of the client's life. The counsellor, however, will always have as a guiding principle the integration of all the many facets of that unique individual. The acceptance and celebration of this multi-dimensional wholeness is also considered a possible goal for the client. This is not 'imposed upon' the client, but is based on a belief that human beings want to experience their wholeness, individual richness and integration of diversity.[33]

Psychosynthesis

In self-actualisation we have seen a process and goal in therapy which is primarily within the humanistic tradition, and in the concept of Gestalt we have a hybrid methodology with roots in organismic holism, existentialism, post-Freudianism and the human potential movement. Psychosynthesis, the brainchild of Roberto Assagioli (1888–1974), is an approach to wholeness that lies among the transpersonal psychologies and avowedly embraces the mystical and spiritual dimensions of life.

Assagioli, born in Venice to a Jewish family, trained in psychiatry with Bleuler and Jung and, in time, entered the world of psychoanalysis. Along with a number of his contemporaries he discarded the mantle of Freud, engaging with a critique of Freudianism in his MD thesis of 1910. In this doctorate he began for the first time to clarify the principles of psychosynthesis as a system which seeks not only to dismember the psyche, as in psychoanalysis, but to reassemble the person's inner life within a process of synthesis.[34] However, the influence of Assagioli's methodology, as with the Perlses' Gestalt therapy, also lies beyond the individual and has applications in organisational development, team management, education and the creative arts. As well as in Italy, centres for training in psychosynthesis are established in many other European countries, including the United Kingdom, and in North America.

Assagioli's concept of personhood has certain parallels with those put forward by Freud and Jung, although his underlying anthropology is less naturalistic than Freud's and more akin to Jung's transcendental perspective. Psychosynthesis postulates that the human personality comprises three levels of the unconscious: the *lower*, consisting of primitive urges, drives and phobias (similar to Freud's notion of the id); the *middle*, made up of those psychological elements that are readily available to consciousness (as in Freud's preconscious, the source of our 'Freudian slips'); and the *higher*, whence come our intuitions, inspirations and creativity. These three unconscious levels are enveloped by the boundless *collective unconscious*, the Jungian idea of a vast repository of human experience built up through history and across the cultures and expressed through fairy tales, folklore and symbol. Consciousness in Assagioli's model comprises the *conscious self*, observing those other parts of the personality within its 'field of consciousness', and the *higher Self*, a permanent centre beyond or 'above' the conscious self which can be 'thought of as existing both within and outside time'. The concepts of the 'conscious self' and the 'higher Self' are linked by the 'Will', a psychic function that, when developed, enables us to make choices. Assagioli's notion of 'self' and 'Self' are part and parcel of many of the transpersonal psychologies, with their conceptual links with Eastern mysticism and the ethos of much New Age thinking.

Psychosynthesis is a full-orbed methodology that sees human functioning as comprising six basic elements – thought, desire, sensation, feeling, imagination and intuition – which are expressed *bodily*, *emotionally* and *mentally*. This holistic perspective nonetheless acknowledges that there is imbalance within individual human lives and a tendency to identify with just one of these three modes of expression, to the neglect of the other two. For example, the keen footballer's life may revolve around athleticism and prowess on the pitch; the singer's very existence may be caught up almost entirely with feelings and emotions; the academic's *raison d'être* may be completely absorbed in the world of the intellect. Within such preoccupations there may, further, be the development of 'subpersonalities', role-like states which, unless the person recognises that they are simply aspects of the overall personality, may act subversively. The footballer's marriage may be jeopardised by unconscious conflict between the subpersonalities of 'rebel teenager' and 'dutiful husband'; the singer's career may be threatened by unexamined tension between 'tragic heroine' and 'strict mother'; the academic's research capabilities may be undermined by unacknowledged polarisation between 'recluse' and 'responsible colleague'. Where such identifications are proving problematic, psychosynthesis aims to redress the balance, seeking to help the client disidentify from the warring subpersonalities, to engage the conscious self, exercise the Will and thus move towards a greater harmony in his or her day-by-day functioning.

Assagioli advocates a range of techniques to aid the process of change and reconstruction. In the early, more analytic stages of therapy, methods may include the invitation for the client to write out his or her autobiography, thus uncovering forgotten memories and buried conflicts. Through disidentifying with newly recognised subpersonalities, the client gets in touch more fully with the 'I' of the conscious self, learning to relax into states of 'being' rather than frenetic 'doing'. As a sense of self-awareness increases, the therapist seeks to encourage the client in the deliberating and purposeful engagement of the Will, 'as connection between I and Self', giving 'access to the transpersonal'.[35] This movement is facilitated by a range of reflective and meditative techniques including dream analysis, the use of music as a relaxation exercise for individuals or groups, and inner dialogue, where the client sees his or her higher Self as personified as an 'Inner Teacher', reached and engaged with via an imagined 'Inner Journey'.

It is here that we are at the heart of psychosynthesis, since the ultimate goal of this approach concerns the union between the 'I' of the conscious self and the higher Self. Assagioli saw this in terms of 'the discovery or creation of a unifying centre' and 'the formation or reconstruction of the personality around the new centre'.[36] Although this lofty ambition is acknowledged to be a difficult task that can never be fully achieved, psychosynthesis seems to leave the door open to the variety of understandings of 'a unifying centre' furnished by a range of belief-systems. Douglas

Mathers, for instance, cites the examples of those who, 'with no spiritual orientation', maintain 'profound respect for the uniqueness of an Other' or, more specifically, those Buddhists who see in the transpersonal 'the Buddha nature',[37] while Assagioli points to a Christian mystical tradition which sees 'the Self as the Inner Christ'.[38]

In this section we have examined three pathways to wholeness which, although firmly within the psychological tradition, offer holistic approaches which allow for and, in some cases, address directly the spiritual dimension: self-actualisation, with its acknowledgment of peak-experiences; Gestalt therapy, with its multidimensional bid for the completions of life's 'unfinished business'; and psychosynthesis, with its goal of integration 'into the conscious personality of higher psychospiritual elements of which it is not consciously aware'.[39] Further, the holism of these methodologies leads, in the case of self-actualisation and psychosynthesis at least, to an expanded vision of human wholeness, to Maslow's awareness that we need something 'bigger than we are' and Assagioli's desire for ultimate completeness:

> We seem to sense that – whether we conceive it as a divine Being or as cosmic energy – the Spirit working upon and within all creation is shaping it into order, harmony, and beauty, uniting all beings (some willing but the majority as yet blind and rebellious) with each other through links of love, achieving – slowly and silently, but powerfully and irresistibly – the Supreme Synthesis.[40]

It is within the Judaeo-Christian tradition that we see a pathway to wholeness that unashamedly celebrates a divine Being who not only engages by his Holy Spirit with the world order to bring it, in the fullness of time, to 'order, harmony, and beauty' but invites all humankind – even where 'blind and rebellious' – to walk in interdependent relationship with the One who declares 'I am the Way'.

Wholeness in the Judaeo-Christian Tradition

So far we have considered, in outline, a range of traditional world religions and a selection of post-Enlightenment psychologies to illustrate something of the rich diversity of routes toward wholeness that humankind pursues. Broadly, we have noted the tendency of a twin emphasis among such pathways – sometimes held in combination, sometimes the source of division: an emphasis on 'here-and-now' engagement with the life-changing ground rules of religious faith or psychotherapeutic practice; and a stress on a 'one-day-all-will-be-well' belief which embraces a more inward and mystical journey. Vedanta Hinduism and Gestalt therapy may be seen as examples of the former, Taoism and 'Supreme' psychosynthesis as instances of the latter.

More succinctly, these two ways may be seen as essentially a question of *process* and *goal*. In other words, wholeness is to be regarded as both a dimension of life that we can engage with on a day-by-day basis by the choices we make, the actions we take, the words we say, and an ultimate destiny that we can aim for and, hopefully, eagerly anticipate. In the more integrated religions and psychotherapeutic methodologies process and goal are all of a piece: the way we live today interweaves with what we may become. The Judaeo-Christian tradition is no different with respect to the general principle of process and goal, of 'becoming' and, ultimately, 'fulness of being'. Nonetheless, it makes its own unique claims, not least with respect to both the daily, life-changing engagement with God and neighbour and the promise of eventual fulfilment as a new people in a 'new heaven and a new earth'.[41]

The biblical account of wholeness is an exceedingly rich and complex one. Process and goal are addressed, to varying extents, for the individual, the extended family, the tribe, the nation, the land, the people of God and for creation itself. The stories, poetry, symbols, metaphors and analogies used weave an intricate tapestry of concepts of wholeness: forgiveness, healing, liberation, restoration, redemption, salvation, sanctification, holiness, fruitfulness, maturity, completeness, Christlikeness, glorification. A number of these aspects of the process and goal of wholeness will be addressed under the five pathways of pastoral care in Part II. For the moment, let us consider two foundational elements in the biblical picture of wholeness: 'shalom', transliterated from the Hebrew *salôm*; and 'completeness', linked with the Greek word *teleiotes* and its cognomens.

Shalom

Shalom is one of the 'big words' of the Hebrew Bible. Although readily translated as 'peace' it means a great deal more than

simply the absence of war. Occuring more than two hundred and
fifty times in the Old Testament, shalom 'covers well-being in the
widest sense of the word',[42] incorporating notions of contentment,
health, prosperity, justice, unity and salvation – at individual,
communal, national, international and creational levels. This far-
reaching view of wholeness can be represented by three examples.
The first, at a *personal and intimate level*, implies physical safety and
a reassured mind: 'I will lie down and sleep in peace, for you
alone, O LORD, make me dwell in safety' (Ps. 4:8). The second, at
the *political level*, relates to economic goodwill and trade between
the kingdoms of Tyre and Israel: 'There were peaceful relations
between Hiram and Solomon, and the two of them made a treaty'
(1 Kings 5:12). And the third, at the *universal level*, brings the
prophetic voice to proclaim the promise of wholeness to the
created order:

> The wolf will live with the lamb, the leopard will lie down with the
> goat, the calf and the lion and the yearling together; and a little child
> will lead them . . . They will neither harm nor destroy on all my holy
> mountain, for the earth will be full of the knowledge of the LORD as the
> waters cover the sea. (Isa. 11: 6–9)

As indicated in Psalm 4:8, this personal and relational sense of
well-being is not self-manufactured. It is a gift of God. Multi-
faceted, it is like some rare and priceless gem, which, miraculously, given humankind's inherent bias toward conflict, turmoil
and discord, is offered to the people of God, if they will but allow
it. Gideon, fearful at an angelic visitation, exclaims 'Ah, Sovereign
LORD! I have seen the angel of the LORD face to face!' In response to
his servant's acute sense of mortality, Yahweh insists on shalom:
'Peace! Do not be afraid. You are not going to die.' As a memorial
to his encounter with the divine, Gideon builds and dedicates an
altar to 'Yahweh Shalom': 'The LORD is Peace' (Judg. 6:22–4). At
the communal level, this gift of shalom, experienced by the
psalmist and Gideon, is expressed in perpetuity by the priestly
blessing of Numbers 6:24–6: 'The LORD bless you and keep you;
the LORD make his face shine upon you and be gracious to you; the
LORD turn his face towards you and give you peace.'

The rabbinic tradition of later Judaism cultivated the seed of
shalom to bear fruit in everyday human interchange. The Hebrew
phrase for 'to greet', meaning to ask after a person's peace and,

thereby, to wish that peace on the recipient, 'turns the act of greeting into something approaching an act of blessing'.[43] The declaration of 'shalom' in the market-place or on the high road becomes a form of benediction caught up with 'the very essence of that salvation expected by the Jews'. In this way, the symbolism of greeting, reinforced by rabbinic teaching on the value of the peacemaker, resonated with Jesus's fuller declaration of a 'new commandment': 'Love one another. As I have loved you, so you must love one another' (John 13:34) – an exhortation that, radically, offered shalom to everyone, even enemies.[44]

This shalomic pathway to wholeness is reinforced, as we have just suggested, in the New Testament's teaching on love and peace, where the God-originating nature of 'shalom' at personal, communal and cosmic levels,[45] seen in the Hebrew Bible, is echoed in the life and teaching of Jesus Christ and the early Church. Jesus declares himself to be the spring of this refreshing sense of well-being: 'Peace I leave with you; my peace I give you' (John 14:27) – and the element of 'greeting as blessing' is carried over into the apostolic letters, implying that peace, and the accompanying riches of grace, mercy and love, is to be seen as the gift of God through Christ.[46] The more fully trinitarian context and resourcing of shalom is implied in, for example, Romans 15, where, in relation to following 'Christ Jesus' (15:5), Paul declares this benediction: 'May the God of hope fill you with all joy and peace as you trust in him, so that you may overflow with hope by the power of the Holy Spirit' (15:13).

As in the Old Testament, we find that this peace is to be relational: both within the 'household of faith' – 'Make every effort to keep the unity of the Spirit through the bond of peace' (Eph. 4:3), and amid the wider community – 'If it is possible, as far as it depends on you, live at peace with everyone' (Rom. 12:18). The realism – 'make every effort' and 'if it is possible, as far as it depends on you' – of these Pauline injunctions is exemplified by the story of Annemarie, as told by Joann Wolski Conn.[47]

Annemarie, in her mid-30s and described as 'sad, confused, and tired', is a theology teacher 'devoted to high school students' and has been a member of a religious community for fifteen years. Experiencing a protracted period of darkness in her Christian faith, and torn between her feminist leanings and the seemingly unyielding sexism of church structures and officials, she approaches Janice, a highly regarded spiritual director.

Annemarie says, 'My religious life seems to be falling apart . . . I can't seem to pray' and 'I can't relate to Christ anymore . . .' and declares that she feels closer to a female fellow-teacher than to most of the sisters in the community. After responding in a cautious and general way, Janice, through addressing more specific issues, comes to her most important question: 'What do you most want to do, Annemarie?' Annemarie, her voice 'choking with emotion', replies, 'I want to know how, or if, I can still relate to Christ.' This heartfelt declaration enables Janice to see Annemarie's 'willingness to stay with this darkness' and desire 'to search for Christ in this "desert"'. Through prayer, reflection and further discussion over the following year of spiritual direction, Annemarie comes to a new level of peace and wholeness:

This was not an absence of conflict within her nor an elimination of struggles to live her feminist spirituality within a patriarchal church. For her, the peace centered on a new experience of the meaning of 'charity.' She was discovering, from experience, that what she used to think meant 'being nice to everyone, silently tolerating community dissension,' now meant 'giving the time to develop the level of sharing that intimacy demands.' This experience gave her a deep, 'dry' satisfaction, not an emotional 'high.' She believed that she was now beginning to experience the true 'shalom' of the gospel.[48]

Completeness

The New Testament words teleios (complete, perfect), telos (end, conclusion, goal) and teleiotes (completeness, perfection) have their roots in classical Greek usage, where telos, for example, developed from such meanings as 'turning point' or 'culminating point', begins to have the inference of 'goal' or 'completion' in terms of human physical and intellectual development.[49] Under pre-Socratic philosophy, this 'goal of life' was seen as 'delight in the beautiful', while Plato and Aristotle shifted life's ultimate objective from the realm of aesthetics to that of ethics, where 'happiness and bliss' were the outcomes of virtuous lives.[50]

Within the polytheistic world of Greek thought God was viewed as arche kai telos, the beginning and the end of all things,[51] a perspective held dear in the Judaeo-Christian tradition and, in many ways, the key to unlocking the door of meaning supplied by telos and teleios, and their derivatives. For God is, by definition, a

God whose very nature speaks 'wholeness' and 'completeness' and who both calls out a people to be whole and complete and supplies the wherewithal for the goal to be achieved. Let us look at two examples, one in the Old Testament, furnished by the Hebrew root *tamim* and translated by *teleios* in the Greek Septuagint, and one in the New Testament.

In Genesis 17, *El-Shaddai*, God Almighty or, even, God the Mountain One,[52] reaffirms his covenant with Abram, broadening the baseline of simple, responsive trust described in Genesis 15:6 ('Abram believed the LORD, and he credited it to him as righteousness') to embrace new names – Abraham and Sarah, father and mother of many (Gen. 17:5, 15), a new people (17:9–14), and a new calling to personal wholeness (17:1–3): 'When Abram was ninety-nine years old, the LORD appeared to him and said, "I am God Almighty; walk before me and be blameless. I will confirm my covenant between me and you and will greatly incease your numbers." Abram fell face down . . .'

Here, Yahweh declares to his servant that it is in the name, and therefore the nature, of God Almighty, the One who is a veritable mountain of rock-like reliability, that the call to 'be blameless' can make sense – both as *process* and *goal*. Abram, now Abraham, is to live out blamelessness and completeness in faithful obedience to the covenanting God who is both dependable companion and ultimate destination. Frederick W. Bush, writing on this passage, offers his own translation for Yahweh's invitation: 'walk about before me and be whole', and points out that 'the Hebrew syntax clearly makes the covenantal promise of verse 2 a consequence of that command: "walk . . . so that I may confirm my covenant" '.[53] Abraham and, by inference, the people of God, are to journey before the Almighty One, living out an observed lifestyle that is to be marked by wholeness and completeness. That the enterprise was not fully successful on the human side is writ large in the unfolding story. And yet, the 'covenant of promise' stands, for the fulfilment of the command 'be blameless, be complete, be whole' depends, mercifully, not on human nature's ability to storm the heights but on the nature of the God who steps down from those very heights. As Bush puts it, covenant, as 'a divine dispensation of grace and blessing confirmed by oath', ultimately depends only 'on the character of the gracious God who makes it'.[54]

In the New Testament, we meet a comparable injunction, to that declared to Abraham, in the words of Jesus to the gathered disciples: 'Be perfect (*teleioi*), therefore, as your heavenly Father is perfect (*teleios*)' (Matt. 5:48). The context is the catechetical one of instruction by question and answer, where the listeners are challenged to a loving generosity of spirit that supersedes the more restricted perspectives of some of the Old Testament texts. In contrast to the partial love that has its favourites and excludes others, followers of Christ are to model on the all-inclusive largesse of 'your Father in heaven' who 'causes his sun to rise on the evil and the good, and sends rain on the righteous and unrighteous' (5:45). Once more the challenge that is both process and goal is given: 'Be whole, be complete, be perfect.' As with Abraham's encounter with Yahweh, the promise lies in the nature, example and enabling of the heavenly Father. As Wiord Popkes puts it, commenting on this passage in the context of God's transforming love: 'Jesus's instruction is both encouragement and exhortation, setting a goal, showing a way, and promising fulfilment.'[55] Completeness, hallmarked by 'Father-love', lies in the travelling and in the journey's end.

More broadly, the use of *telos* and *teleios* in the New Testament is divisible into two main sections, each emphasising goal and process: the eschatological and the anthropological.[56] The Greek *eschatos* (extreme, last, least) and *eschaton* (end) have, in the New Testament, a dual connotation with reference to both the 'new age' ushered in by the incarnation, death and resurrection of Jesus Christ and the 'last days' of God's 'final, consummative action' of judgment and salvation.[57] The 'now' and 'not yet' dimensions of *telos* and its derivatives are brought out by Reinier Schippers when he writes, 'The end . . . is the consummating conclusion of a dynamic process, the goal of which manifests the realization of its meaning and its intentions.'[58] Completeness and wholeness are here caught up on a cosmic scale where the process and goal of post-incarnational history are fulfilled and achieved in the risen Christ, the one who declares, 'I am the First and the Last. I am the Living One; I was dead, and behold I am alive for ever and ever! And I hold the keys of death and Hades' (Rev. 1:17–18).

Anthropologically, *teleios* engages notions of growth and completeness. Here, there is both a step-by-step process of transformation of Christian character and an ultimate goal of Christlikeness. A frequently used analogy in the New Testament is the developmental one of progression from childhood to adulthood: from the transient sustenance provided by the milk of 'the elementary truths of God's word' to the 'solid food' that nourishes the 'mature', the *teleion* (Heb. 5:12–14); from the fragility and suggestibility of 'infants . . . blown here and there by every wind of teaching' to those who, 'speaking the truth in love', are 'becoming mature', *teleion* (Eph. 4:12–15).[59]

And yet we can say that Christian disciples are both 'mature' and are, at the same time, 'becoming mature' – are both 'given fulness in Christ' (Col. 2:10) and are being changed 'into his likeness with ever-increasing glory' (2 Cor. 3:18). There is a given *status*, as well as process and goal, in the concepts surrounding *teleios*. Schippers puts it this way: '*Teleios* denotes not the qualitative end-point of human endeavour, but the anticipation in time of eschatological wholeness in actual present-day living. Christian life in the NT is not projected idealistically as a struggle for perfection, but eschatologically as the wholeness which a person is given and promised.'[60]

I still vividly recall a strongly felt interchange with a close schoolfriend when we were aged sixteen or so. We were visiting a mutual friend's house, along with one or two other fellow-schoolboys, and were also in the company of the mutual friend's mother. I was holding forth on the subject of maturity, declaring, and not anticipating any dissenting voices on the matter, that we, teenagers that we were, were 'growing in maturity'. My close friend's riposte was a strong one, along the lines of: 'What are you saying? Speak for yourself. I'm mature already!' Indeed, this particular friend was a tall, well-built, strapping young man, whose physical and sexual maturity were beyond dispute. My muttered response, trying to explain that I was referring to more of an inner growth toward becoming more and more adult, fell on deaf ears. After all, he was bigger than me!

And so, we can say that the 'completeness' that we are called to as Christians is, as in the contrary emphases that my teenage friend and I gave, a threefold matter: status – 'we are mature in Christ'; journeying – 'we are growing in maturity in Christ'; and arrival – 'when he [the Christ] appears, we shall be like him, for we shall see him as he is' (1 John 3:2). Popkes brings all these strands together, eschatological and anthropological, when he writes:

Wholeness is thus nothing exceptional for Christian existence, no idea of perfection never attained. Rather, it is the direction of God's work with us, becoming real even now. The concept of wholeness shares both of the two aspects: 'already now' and 'not yet'. God in his wholeness, with the fulness of his revelation, will and love, draws us into his wholeness, leading us along the way towards the final completion in the eschaton.[61]

Summary

Humankind at heart seeks for wholeness. That is not to deny that there is much in human nature that, perversely, pulls the other way and invites fragmentation – leading to loss of individual peace of mind, to broken relationships, to divided communities, to racial hatred, to betrayal of one nation by another, to rebellion, terrorism and war. And yet, as we have seen in this chapter, there is a foundational thirst for connectedness, for unity, for completeness, for a sense of arrival and fulfilment that inspires and sustains countless human beings in their quest for the promised land. The quest may be one of more limited horizons rather than for any ultimate goal, yet it is nonetheless a search for better things, however modestly defined: for employment, job satisfaction, an enriching friendship, a successful deal, a game well played, an exam passed, a poem written, a mountain climbed. Jim Crumley, the Scottish climber, points to the strong urges that drive him 'among mountains': 'There are a handful of mountains and mountain landscapes to which I return addictively like an un-requited lover craving favours, secrets, intimacies.'[62] Here, the sexual imagery reminds us of how intrinsic to our human nature is the desire for union, completion and ecstasy – whether in braving the elements to conquer a favoured peak, in the consummation of a love-match or in the pursuit of and abandonment to the Holy.

In this chapter we have outlined a selection of the vast range of pathways to wholeness sought out by men and women. In some of the main world religions we have witnessed the human quest for completion taking either a primarily reasoning and practical path of obedience to the faith's particular ground rules or an essentially intuitive and contemplative path that stresses the mystery and mysticism of the 'inner journey'. Inevitably, the religious way, whatever its intrinsic belief-patterns, has to address both the nature of humanity and the existence, or otherwise, of God or gods. It is with respect to the former that we see a variety of understandings of personhood and its desired destiny, ranging from the state of 'no-self', as in classical Buddhism, to a sense of union between the self and the higher Self.

Selfhood, of course, is one of the central preoccupations of personalistic psychology and its hybridisation with psychoanalytic and transpersonal influences. As we have seen, the psychological quest for wholeness for the self takes many forms, including self-actualisation – the realisation of personal and relational fulfilment, the holism of Gestalt whereby subpersonalities are unmasked and dissolved, and the panoramic vistas of psychosynthesis where individual, social and cosmic integration are sought. In some ways we come back to our starting-point here, since there is an increasing acknowledgment in psychotherapeutic circles that the person needs to reach out beyond the self to the numinous, the supernatural, cosmic consciousness, the higher Self, to God. In other words, the psychological quest becomes the religious, or spiritual, quest.

We have seen, further, that the Judaeo-Christian tradition broadly parallels the twin pursuit of other world religions and of the major psychotherapies – for a wholeness that engages both the 'now' and the 'not yet', that is both process and goal. And yet, as we have also noted, the Hebrew Bible and New Testament engage us with a God who is not only sought as the source of all wholeness but who, in the first place, initiates the seeking. Abraham is called to 'walk about before me and be whole', and Jesus points to the same God, the God of Abraham, Isaac and Jacob, and declares 'be complete and whole as your heavenly Father is complete and whole'. The Christian call not only carries us beyond the personal to the relational, the communal, the environmental and the universal, as do other religious and psychological quests, but, uniquely, is made, resourced and fulfilled by our trinitarian God.

Walter Brueggemann, writing in the context of Christian preaching, and drawing an analogy with psychotherapy and its slow, often step-by-step road to constructive change,[63] declares that the 'purpose of preaching and of worship is transformation' and asks, in the postmodern situation of the 1990s and beyond, 'How do people change?' He argues that people 'do not change, or change much, because of doctrinal argument or . . . moral appeal' but, rather, 'by the offer of new models, images, and pictures of how the pieces of life fit together', all having 'the particularity of narrative to carry them'.[64] This creative and enriching storyline of the journey toward wholeness is summed up by Brueggemann as follows:

> What is yearned for among us is not new doctrine or new morality, but new world, new self, new future. The new world is not given whole, any more than the new self is given abruptly in psychotherapy. It is given only a little at a time, one text at a time, one miracle at a time, one poem, one healing, one pronouncement, one promise, one commandment. Over time, these pieces are stitched together into a sensible collage, stitched together, all of us in concert, but each of us idiosyncratically, stitched together in a new whole – all things new![65]

Here, the goal of wholeness, of 'all things new', needs the process of day-by-day, piecemeal faithfulness, where the 'new world . . . is given only a little at a time'. Thus the journey is engaged upon and the storyline unfolds. In the next chapter we shall explore the notion of pathways to wholeness in terms of the going, the remembering and the storytelling, recalling throughout the anticipation of journey's end and the promised land beyond.

2

PATHWAYS TO WHOLENESS: JOURNEY AND STORY

Look at every path closely and deliberately. Try it as many times as you think necessary. Then ask yourself, and yourself alone, one question . . . Does this path have a heart? If it does, the path is good; if it doesn't it is of no use.

Carlos Castaneda[1]

At the beginning of Chapter 1 we posed two fundamental questions that we can ask of life: What is my destination? and Which route shall I take? In response to the first we considered the goal of 'wholeness' as proposed in some of the world's major religions, in three psychotherapeutic approaches and within the Judaeo-Christian tradition. In this chapter we shall use the second question as a springboard to explore the idea of 'life as journey'. We will keep in mind the destination of wholeness, at the same time acknowledging that human weakness, vagary and downright sinfulness can rob any one of us of a sense of direction. The notion of a journey does not necessitate that we will take a route that is wholesome and life-giving, let alone simply in our best interest. If our aim is to reach the summit of a mountain that we have heard offers an exhilarating climb and spectacular views, we will not make that particular journey if we are waylaid by inertia, laziness or, for that matter, the legitimate counterclaims of everyday affairs. The simple but daunting fact is that in the 'journey of life' there are decisions to be made and circumstances to be acknowledged. I may want to climb the mountain but the summit-route may be closed by quarrying, the travel to the area too expensive for my pocket, or I may have become bed-bound by long-term illness. Whether through decision or circumstance, our route-finding can feel a precarious affair. John Dunne expresses the uncertainties well when he writes:

There is a dilemma that arises whenever one chooses a road in life. It is
that of 'the road not taken.' If I give my life to something, then I have
not given it to something else; if I share my life with someone, then I
have not shared it with someone else. No matter what road I take, there
will be a loss: there will be a road – in fact, many roads – I have not
taken.[2]

In considering 'life as journey' we must, inevitably, also address
'life as story' for as we journey our stories unfold. Without
journey, without some movement outwards and forwards in life,
there is no story. And stories need to be told. Without remembering and sharing our stories, we cannot make sense of our journeying – whether for ourselves or for our fellow-travellers. Let us then
consider both 'journey' and 'story', endeavouring in these interweaving concepts to engage with their essentially experiential
nature and some of their theological, psychological and pastoral
implications.

Journey

The idea of life as journey is as old as humankind: it is written into
the order of things. Ancient texts and archaeological discovery
reveal individuals, families and communities who, from time to
time, set out from hearth and homestead into the unknown,
whether in response to military threat, natural disaster, economic
necessity, the desire to conquer, wanderlust or the call of the gods.
Other peoples, of course, have always been nomadic. Freed from
the ties of land tenure and responsive to changes of weather and
season, they have travelled desert and tundra in search of better
pasture or to follow the migrations of animals whose hides and
flesh provide livelihood. The sedentary, too, have their journeys.
The innumerable small journeyings of daily life – to sow, tend,
hunt, gather, buy and sell – provide local paths of necessity which
serve to shape the overall direction of personal and communal life-
journeys, in matters of birth, growth, marriage, sex, ageing and
death.

The dimension of journey in human existence is not simply a
question of geographical travel or, indeed, of life's rites of passage
– however important these realities are in moulding character and
circumstance. The perspective to 'life as journey' which is the

prime concern of this book is that relating to questions of beginnings, purpose, route-finding and destination – all with respect to
pathways to a higher goal. Such considerations have been part and
parcel of myth and legend in many cultures from ancient times:
the Mesopotamian *Epic of Gilgamesh*, in which a perilous journey is
undertaken to seek out the secret of immortality; the courageous
voyage of Jason and the Argonauts in search of the Golden Fleece;
Rama's brave endurance of many trials to rescue his wife Sita from
Ravana, the demon king of Ceylon; the Arthurian quest for the
Holy Grail; the voyages of Sinbad the Sailor; and, among more
recent creations, Tolkien's epic tale of the Hobbit journeying into
the very fiefdom of Mordor, and Steven Spielberg's bravura film
of Indiana Jones's intrepid adventures in *Raiders of the Lost Ark*.

Such fabulous tales, coupled with the sagas of historical figures
like Alexander the Great, Eric the Red, Hannibal, Jeanne d'Arc and
Napoleon, can fire the imagination and stir the spirit in life's more
mundane journeys. As a child, my hero-figure was the intrepid
Ulysses, pitted against every conceivable adversity and somehow
surviving both palpable terror and subtle allurement: neither the
rampaging excesses of a Cyclops nor the seductive chanting of the
Sirens could finally thwart my Greek sailor's destiny.

In my teen years my intrigue with the seemingly impossible
mission turned to an absorbed interest in polar exploration,
particularly that of Scott's ill-fated last expedition. Once more a
formative hero-figure stood out – this time in the shape of Edward
Wilson. He was a perfectly matched model for me at a stage when
my interest in mapping unknown terrain, my enjoyment of bird-
watching and painting, my newly found Christian commitment
and prospect of studying medicine, responded eagerly to what I
was reading of him and his relating to his colleagues. Medically
qualified, appointed as Chief of the Scientific Staff and Zoologist, a
keen naturalist, a competent artist, a Christian of great moral
integrity, 'Uncle Bill' Wilson was described by Scott in glowing
terms:

> Words must always fail me when I talk of Bill Wilson. I believe he really
> is the finest character I ever met – the closer one gets to him the more
> there is to admire. Every quality is so solid and dependable; cannot you
> imagine how that counts down here? Whatever the matter one knows
> that Bill will be sound, shrewdly practical, intensely loyal and quite
> unselfish. Add to this a wider knowledge of persons and things than it

is at first guessable, a quiet vein of humour and really consummate tact, and you have some idea of his values. I think he is the most popular member of the party, and that is saying much.[3]

Although the personality of Edward Wilson appealed to my adolescent idealism, it was the concept of journey as both test and revealer of character that gripped my attention more fundamentally. Described by Scott as 'the hardest journey that has ever been made' and by Wilson as 'the wierdest bird-nesting expedition that has been or ever will be', the 'Winter Journey' of 1911 was the one that most engaged my dreams and waking hours. Three men – Wilson, as leader, 'Birdie' Bowers, 'the incomparable, the indomitable', to use Scott's phrase, and Apsley Cherry-Garrard, 'another of the open-air, self-effacing, quiet workers' – braved the darkness, extremely low temperatures and blizzards of an Antarctic winter to pull heavily laden sledges for sixty-seven miles, and back again, over crevasse-riven ice-fields in order to collect eggs from a colony of the rare, and barely investigated, Emperor penguin.[4] Enduring frost-bite, sleeping-bags and clothes rendered stiff and unfoldable by ice, an all-encompassing darkness and temperatures in the region of −70°F, the resolute three reached the penguin rookery at Cape Crozier after five weeks. Five precious eggs were taken, two bursting in Cherry-Garrard's fur mitts, which were fastened round his neck, as they climbed the ridges out of the nesting area. Their hardship had been extreme enough in reaching their goal, but now, as they returned to an igloo they had constructed as a temporary base-camp, the weather worsened dramatically. In the ensuing storm, logged at force 11, they lost first their tent, pitched to protect provisions, and then, as the hurricane raged on, the roof of the igloo. Cherry-Garrard later wrote of this 'worst journey in the world':

> I expect the temperature was pretty high during this great blizzard, and anything near zero was very high to us. That and the snow which drifted over us made a pleasant wet kind of snipe marsh inside our sleeping-bags, and I am sure we all dozed a good bit. There was so much to worry about that there was not the least use in worrying; and we were so *very* tired. We were hungry, for the last meal we had had was in the morning of the day before, but hunger was not very pressing.
>
> And so we lay, wet and quite fairly warm, hour after hour while the wind roared round us, blowing storm force continually and rising in the gusts to something indescribable.[5]

Why had this epic story of human endeavour, and, some would say, foolhardiness, gripped this particular schoolboy so compellingly? Even with hindsight, and a fair amount of self-awareness, it is hard to know. Given that each generation of adolescents needs its ideals and idols in order to shape and mould emerging early adulthood, it is not surprising that some, at least, of my generation should have been stirred by the heroic acts of our recent forebears. Be that as it may, my own particular models continued in the same vein: Ulysses; Edward Wilson; 'Titus' Oates – who walked out to his death to save his last three companions on Scott's fateful return journey from the South Pole; a range of mountaineers, especially the solo climbers who first assailed the formidable North face of the Eiger in winter. Without pressing interpretation too far, such journeyings point to the personal appeal of 'going it alone', of 'battling against the odds', of an independent, self-sufficient streak in me which has been both a bane and a blessing. On the positive side, such idealism has been a valuable preparation for a life of recurring illness and debility, of struggling with symptoms in the 'lonely places', of learning to come to terms with solitude. On the negative side, it has led to a slow, slow response to the need for others – not least for my basic human need to depend on the Lord who declares, 'apart from me you can do nothing'.[6]

I have spelt out some aspects of early influences autobiographically to illustrate something of the way in which 'pathways to wholeness', whether of the individual or the community, can be seen in terms of 'life as journey'. We have noted, briefly, that this journeying can be seen in terms of a people's travelling and in relation to the successive stages of life – from the cradle to the grave, and, more fully, with regard to those models that shape our destinies. Given the formative dimension of life's journeys, let us now consider 'journey' with respect, first, to the God who calls out a journeying people and, second, to ourselves in our struggle to respond to the God of journey.

Journey and God

In Cormac McCarthy's *The Crossing*, volume two of his Border Trilogy, two teenage brothers, Billy and Boyd Parham, cross the border from New Mexico, in the United States, into Mexico to recover six horses stolen from their murdered parents' ranch. Having retrieved one of the horses, Keno, and established that the town of Cassas Grandes might hold the key to their quest, they asked the way of a thin old man in the dusty square of a roadside hamlet.[7] Watched by four men, 'dressed in ancient and sunfaded suits' and seated on a bench nearby, the old man uses a whittled stick to sketch in the dust a panoramic map of the country ahead. Paid a peso for his pains by the boys, the old man walks away but, once he has disappeared, is laughed at for his efforts by the spectators. One of the men says that what they beheld 'was but a decoration' and asks 'when had that old man last journeyed to those mountains?' Another of the men counters this scepticism, saying 'it was a mistake to discount the good will inherent in the old man's desire to guide them for it too must be taken into account and would in itself lend strength and resolution to them on their journey'. But a third man rose and gestured to the two boys to follow him out of the square into the street beyond. Telling them of certain landmarks in the country to the east and pointing to the track they must take, he gives his blessing to Billy and Boyd. We read:

> He asked if they were brothers and they said that they were and he told them to care for one another in the world. He nodded again toward the mountains and he said that the serranos had good hearts but that elsewhere was another matter. Then he wished them luck again and called upon God to be with them and stepped back and raised his hand in farewell.[8]

Here are three responses to our desire for direction on life's journey. The first discounts the fumbled attempt of another to point out the way. The second acknowledges the value of well-meant intention where another's good will can sustain the traveller, even in territory with no reliable maps. The third adds the dimensions of caring companionship, the reality that not all those met on the way will be good-hearted, and the inestimable worth of God's abiding presence as we travel. It is this third stance that resonates most faithfully with the journeying God set forth in the Bible.

The Journeying God

The Hebrew Bible and the New Testament abound in reference to the God who journeys and calls his people to journey with him.

There is a sense in which the whole span of the Scriptures is a journey for humankind – from the agrarian existence of Eden to the city of new beginnings, 'the Holy City, the new Jerusalem' (Rev. 2:2), and this is a journeying in which the God of journeys is profoundly implicated. Noah is called to embark on unknown waters with his precious zoological cargo and 'God remembered Noah and all the wild animals and the livestock that were with him in the ark' (Gen. 8:1). Abram and his extended family uprooted themselves from his father's settlement in Haran and trekked for five or six hundred miles in response to Yahweh's covenant-backed command: 'Go to the land I will show you' and 'I will make you into a great nation and I will bless you' (Gen. 12:1–2a). And supremely, in Old Testament terms, the Israelites set out from the bondage of Egypt for the promised land with the journeying God, who, by day, 'went ahead of them in a pillar of cloud to guide them on their way and by night in a pillar of fire to give them light' (Exod. 13:21).

The companionate presence of Yahweh was no guarentee of the faithfulness and obedience of his fellow-travellers, and so a purposive journey was waylaid into forty years of going round in circles. And yet the God of journeys was more than equal to the Israelites' recalcitrance, for the process of wilderness wandering was to achieve not only the inheritance of land but a nudging toward the goal of wholeness: 'to humble you and to test you in order to know what was in your heart, whether or not you would keep his commands' (Deut. 8:2). But God's journeys are not always pathways to the land of delights, since a rebellious people may, in repeatedly spurning 'the good way' of the tried and trusted 'ancient paths' (Jer. 6:16), be obliged to journey into a strange and unwelcoming land. And yet there is still hope and promise, even in exile, from the God who is always on the move: 'Forget the former things; do not dwell on the past. See, I am doing a new thing! Now it springs up; do you not perceive it? I am making a way in the desert and streams in the wasteland' (Isa. 43:18–19).

This 'new thing' that the God of journeys declares, this 'way in the desert', is of course the promise given by a 'voice of one calling: "In the desert prepare the way for the LORD; make straight in the wilderness a highway for our god" ' (isa. 40:3). here the way is to be paved for the greatest journey of all: the mysterious coming of a god who 'made himself nothing, taking the very nature of a servant, being made in human likeness' (phil. 2:7).

It is in Jesus Christ, the Promised One, that the God of journeys is most fully revealed. All those elements given in the Mexican's blessing of Billy and Boyd Parham – a caring fellowship of the road, discernment of the realities of human nature and the promise of a companionate God who provides, protects and guides – are writ large in the life and teaching of Jesus as he journeys from cradle to carpenter's bench, from Nazareth to Galilee and the dark road to Jerusalem.

This sense of movement on the road to the cross and resurrection is caught up by the use of the Greek word *hodos*, way, road, highway, way of life.[9] Stephen Barton brings out this journeying element in the account of Jesus's life given in Mark's Gospel. He points out that one of the characteristics of Marcan spirituality is the 'all-pervasive' theme of discipleship as 'following' Jesus, denoting a 'path or journey metaphor' which is 'associated specifically with Jesus as the one who is "on the way" (*en te hodo*) and who "goes before" (*proagein)'.[10] The structure of this metaphor is particularly clear in the central section of Mark where the journey of Jesus from Caesarea Philippi to the ascent to Jerusalem is described. Strikingly, each of the three passion predictions that are the hallmark of the journey coincide with the phrase 'on the way' (Mark 8:27, 9:33–4, 10:32). The third and most haunting of these is commented on by Barton in terms of the figurative use of *hodos*:

> So the journey is not just a progression of the topographic kind. It is even more, and at the same time, a journey of revelation and spiritual encounter. Only thus can we explain the language of epiphany, the 'fear' and 'amazement', which characterizes the response of the disciples as they follow: 'And they were *on the way* (*en te hodo*) going up to Jerusalem, and Jesus was *going before* (*proagon*) them; and *they were amazed* (*ethambounto*), and *those who followed* (*hoi akolothountes*) *were afraid* (*ephobounto*).'[11]

In John's Gospel the metaphor of journey, of being 'on the way', is extended and personalised so that Jesus can say of himself, 'I am the way (*ego eimi he hodos*) and the truth and the life. No-one comes to the Father except through me' (John 14:6). Here we see that Jesus is not only our fellow-traveller but is the journey itself, the journey to wholeness, to an intimate relationship with God. This sense of journeying is carried over, following Jesus's journey's end

with his cry from the cross, 'It is finished' and his new beginnings
in resurrection, ascension and pentecost, so that God's new people
are seen as a journeying community, 'followers of the Way'.[12]

And so a journeying God raises up a journeying people. If we
take the whole biblical record, from the stories of Noah and
Abraham through to the missionary dispersal of the early Church,
we see a pilgrim community that, on the one hand, is vulnerable
and prone to wander from the Way and, on the other hand, is held,
chastened and encouraged by the ever-present God of journeys.
And here there is challenge for today's Church as it seeks pathways to wholeness. For example, Brueggemann writes of Western
Christianity's present danger of being held back by 'commoditi-
zation' – 'the outcome of greed, acquisitiveness, and idolatry, the
reduction of everything and everyone . . . to a commodity, a
means, an object of control'.[13] He sees this elevation of 'commodity' as a product of self-sufficiency and in opposition to 'covenant',
where life is received 'from the other, from God and neighbor,
rather than from self'.[14] Using 'Israel' as a model, he sums up the
need for the 'Western church' to rediscover its call to respond to
the journeying God:

> Israel must leave the garden, leave Ur, leave Egypt, leave Sinai, leave
> Babylon. Israel is always led, always on the way to newness. The
> Western church now faces a like departure from old 'flesh pots.' The
> text suggests that this traveling, departing people does not travel in
> safety, but always in vulnerability. But it also does not travel alone. The
> text invites a memory of 'traveling with,' a hope of 'fellowship with,'
> and a present practice of 'communion with.' This 'being with' liberates,
> subverts, and finally may overcome the terrible power of numbing
> commoditization.[15]

Journey and Self

Brueggemann's opposition of 'covenant' by 'commodity' reminds
us that the greatest obstacle to journeying toward wholeness is the
demotion of God and neighbour and the promotion of self. And
yet the thrust of a biblical anthropology is that the self does have
its place – in harmony with God, neighbour and its own self-
awareness and self-respect. Ideally this threefold relating is seamless, each part of the fabric of life being distinctive and yet subtly
interwoven with the other two. Put succinctly, we are to respond

to 'Love the Lord your God' and 'Love your neighbour as yourself' (Matt. 22:37–9) with our whole being.

How then are we to find the key to our pathways to wholeness where the right balance can be struck between God, neighbour and self? The story, and theology, of John S. Dunne is most instructive at this point.

As an afterword of his fifth book, *The Reasons of the Heart*, Dunne traces the closest of links between his life's pathway, his stage-by-stage self-understanding and the writing of his books. Declaring 'My method is my journey',[16] he records three main phases of his pilgrimage, each summed up in a confessional statement: 'I will die', 'I am' and 'I shall live'. We can take these three self-declarations as a structure for our consideration of 'journey and self'.

'I will die'

Dunne's first book was to be part of an ambitious project – a work that traced political theology from ancient times to the present day. While compiling material for this first volume, on the Greek city-states, he developed the feeling that he was 'piling up lumber' and that his heart 'was elsewhere, and that it was drawing [his] mind along after it'.[17] Aged thirty at the time and acutely aware of his passing youth, he found in the great Babylonian poem, the *Epic of Gilgamesh*, a resonance that exactly fitted his inner turmoil. Following their adventures together, Gilgamesh is profoundly grief-stricken when his close friend dies, and sets out on a quest to the ends of the earth to discover the secret of unending life. The hero fails in his search for immortality, achieving instead a measure of wisdom. Dunne saw himself 'in a position very like that of Gilgamesh' and resolved to change the subject of his first book, *The City of the Gods*, to that of 'man's quest of life through the ages'. In the end he formulated the question, 'If I die someday, what can I do to fulfill my desire to live?'[18]

Jon Nilson, in his paper on the theology of John Dunne,[19] sees Dunne's step of literary relinquishment as a radical dying to self. Quoting from an interview with Dunne carried out by Kenneth Woodward, Nilson writes:

To abandon a project that could have brought him security and esteem in favour of a personal quest that had no certain direction and result was daunting. It was a kind of death, since it entailed something of the

'letting go of everyone and everything that is called for in death' . . .
He had to be willing to let go of everything, the benefits and securities
of his career, community, and faith, for he had come to experience the
'tremendous chasm between the answers you have already from a
religious tradition and the real questions that come up in your life.' He
had no guarantee that the journey which lay ahead of him could ever
bridge it. Nonetheless, he set out on a way.[20]

'I am'

Whereas Dunne saw his first work as a book 'about times', his
second, *A Search for God in Time and Memory*, he described as a
book 'about lives', where ' "I am" is an answer to "I will die" '. In
preparation, he sketched out his autobiography 'not for inclusion
in the book but to prepare [himself] to understand the stories of
others'. And so he reflected on the lives and very different
philosophical contexts of Paul the apostle, Augustine and Kierkegaard, picking up the common thread of a quest that led each of
them to Christianity.[21] In this enterprise Dunne came to believe
that, to find God, 'we must give over the quest for certainty for a
quest of understanding' and this understanding is to be achieved
by 'passing over to the standpoint of other lives and times and
coming back to that of our own lives and times'. He cites his
personal experience in which, 'passing over' to Augustine's 'I am'
declaration in the *Confessions*, his 'coming back' gave him his own
authentic 'I am' voice.[22]

Dunne continues to explore this process of identification with
others, and subsequent enrichment of his own life, in his next two
books – *The Way of All the Earth*, in which he 'passes over' to world
religions 'to see how God comes among us and how we walk with
God' and *Time and Myth*, in which he 'comes back' to the 'standpoint of self', seeking wholeness on this 'home ground'.[23] And yet,
as with Dunne's experience of 'I will die', his continuing quest is
not without its cost: 'When my life opened up before me all the
way to death, I became very lonely . . . "I am" had raised a
question too . . . that of the loneliness of the individual.'[24]

'I shall live'

Dunne sees the chief role of his fifth book, *The Reasons of the Heart*,
as 'the changing standpoint of a person who says "I am and I will

die, yet shall I live"'. As he began to write the book, his 'sense of
the spiritual adventure' was tempered by 'an unresolved loneliness', a loneliness which, during the three years of writing,
dissolved into 'a sense of being heart-free and heart-whole in
the journey with God'. His pathway to wholeness involved an
imaginative journey, in which he 'envisioned a person going out to
meet his loneliness in solitude and then returning to meet it again
in the human circle'. Within this outward and homeward journey
both the 'I am' of solitude and the 'I will die' of the return to
vulnerable human community were 'caught up in the "I and
thou"' of 'a journey with God'.[25]

Nilson further traces this continuity of method and journey in
Dunne's sixth and seventh books, The Church of the Poor Devil[26]
and The House of Wisdom[27] where, respectively, a 'passing over' to
the poor, 'to let them change our minds and hearts', and the
struggle to find a unity of perspective where God says, 'my eyes
and my heart will be there for all time' are addressed.[28] In the
latter book, Dunne sees the figure of Wisdom as 'the reality' of
God's knowledge and love, a reality which can be variously
described as the 'eyes and heart' of God, of Christ and, indeed,
of the individual pilgrim. The encounter with Wisdom leads to 'a
subtle change . . . in seeing and feeling, in knowing and loving'.[29]

Step by step within his pilgrimage, Dunne sees that the human
journey can only find fulfilment with the journeying God. Nilson,
defining theology as 'reasoned speech about God', commends
Dunne for resisting the temptation to define his theological calling
exclusively in terms of 'intepreting sacred, doctrinal, and classical
texts'. Dunne, rather, has 'discovered a method by which experiences of the heart yield their light to the mind' and 'has become a
genuine theologian, one who dares to speak of God'.[30] And the
God of whom he speaks is the God revealed by Jesus Christ:

> And when it appears that Jesus is the way, the truth, and the life, as is
> said in the Gospel of John, 'I am the way, the truth, and the life,' this will
> be because in the person of Jesus one somehow finds a light on the
> mystery of oneself and others, which one can find in no other person.[31]

We can see, with Dunne, that the self, restored through Jesus
Christ, can only find its true destiny through a companionate
journeying with God and neighbour.

Story

It was in the early hours of Friday morning on 4 March 1993 that the ambulance came. After barely a month of realising the gravity of my newly experienced dizzy spells and low-grade chest pain, we had needed to call out the duty doctor soon after midnight. As I was swung bodily into the vehicle I noticed the darkness in the surrounding houses and said, 'All this drama and no one to see it!' 'Don't you believe it!' replied one of the ambulance men.

With such minimal symptoms it had been hard to accept that, within a space of a few weeks, my perspective on life had shifted from a sense of day-by-day coping with the manageable condition of diabetes to one of imminently threatening death. Lying back on the stretcher, feeling every bump of the road's irregularities, chatted to by the friendly, competent crew and followed by Joy in the family car, I knew I was on a journey, not simply the one of a dozen miles or so to the hospital but an unknown journey set in motion by the GP's visit – the wheels of fortune moving inexorably toward unpleasant investigations, major cardiac surgery and an unknown future.

Admitted to the coronary care unit for rest, observation and medical tests, it was a week later that the consultant shared the results of the recent angiography with Joy and me. The three of us sat close together as he explained the gravity of the situation wherein all main coronary arteries, and a major branch of one of them, were blocked to a potentially fatal degree. His message was ominously simple: 'We must operate soon – preferably within the week.'

Although I had experienced recurring illness since my teen years and a number of very invasive procedures and operations, especially from the late 1970s onwards, this was the first time I faced what felt to be a decision about two alternative routes that each offered the strong possibility of imminent death. Aged fifty-nine and with a track record of moderate but significant physical restriction for over forty years, I nonetheless greatly valued life, the love of friends and family and my limited opportunities in the fields of counselling, lecturing and writing. Added to this basic human longing for continuity was the mixed blessing of my medical knowledge! The logic for surgery was strong and yet I wrestled with a series of inner questions: Given the mildness and very recent onset of my symptoms, was I really in extreme danger of a massive and final heart attack? Having endured so many stretches of illness and major operations in recent years, did I really have the resolve and reserve to face 'the big one'? Knowing the potential complications of heart surgery – including a stroke or, indeed, death on the table – and being aware of the particular dangers of a fatal outcome as a longstanding diabetic with a very low blood pressure, was I taking the better route in agreeing to an operation? Suddenly, the alternative, medical course of taking a large dose of aspirin daily looked more enticing than bypass surgery within the week!

Over the next few days, supported by Elaine the ward sister, Dawn the staff nurse, appointed to help me with practical details, Paul the cardiologist, Judith the hospital chaplain, and, of course, friends and family, my emotions began to catch up with my thoughts. On the Wednesday night five days after my admission, Paul came and sat on my bed to see how my thinking was shaping. He was completely unpressurising and assured me that God would show me the way forward. Later, as I lay on my bed before sleep, the simple words written by our son Simon on a card depicting a very cheerful family of sperm whales joyfully riding the waves, came to mind: 'Choose Life.' As I nudged toward my dreams, 'Choose Life' came, quite simply, to mean, 'Choose the bypass.'

Throughout this week or so of anticipation and trepidation Joy and I kept coming back to the image of a tunnel. At first the tunnel seemed dark and foreboding for both of us, but Joy came to see light at its further end, while, for me, there was a bend in its course which hid the unknown. In time, I too sensed the light beyond the tunnel's end but was unsure whether it signified the cheering eventuality of post-operative recovery or the light of eternity.

Transferred to another hospital at the weekend for surgery on the Tuesday, the theme of the tunnel continued to haunt us. As I lay on the bed following premedication, I shared with Joy my reflections on the design of the curtains that had been discreetly pulled around us. I had lived with these for a few days and had seen in each whorled and scalloped repeat-pattern a semblance of a tunnel. As I wrote in my journal a week later, recalling my pre-operative feelings:

A tunnel, yes, but not a tunnel of sombre gloom and darkness and, further, *not* a long tunnel . . . For me two further dimensions had been evoked as I lay . . . and prayed . . . and relinquished: the short and decorative qualities of the tunnel resonated beautifully with Rache's painting [which she, our younger daughter, had given me a few days before] where the tunnel was a rainbow tunnel and the light and wonder not far away, just beyond the blood red gleam of resurrection; and, further, that the tunnel itself (on the curtain fabric) was, in profile (in *cross*-section) a crown of thorns. What rich imagery, and with Joy's sweet smile so close, it felt more like a babe slipping towards a safe slumber than a grown man with a problem or two! Praise be!

Later that day a quadruple bypass was performed, confirming the urgent nature of my condition, in that the cardiac surgeon found that one of the main coronary arteries was so blocked that he could not penetrate it with a probe. Returned to the intensive care unit, I slipped in and out of consciousness at, for me, undefined hours. When I first woke, prostrate, intubated, a respirator breathing for me, my first, fleeting thought was 'This can't be glory. I'm sure heaven isn't cluttered with all this medical machinery!'; and my second thought was 'I can't move and yet I'm pretty sure I haven't had a stroke'. Some time later I had an out-of-body experience where my conscious self floated several yards away to the right of the recovery bed. I could see my sleeping form and the bleeping and flashing monitors beyond. As I looked, my consciousness was aware of an overwhelming sense of peace: I *knew* all was well.

What I did not know was of what Joy, on the end of the phone at home, was painfully aware: that I was still bleeding from within the chest wall and that the surgical team were talking of operating a second time. In due course, the haemorrhage stopped, the tracheal tube was removed, Joy was at my bedside, and several exhausting days unfolded in which I dipped in and out of a series of life-threatening medical complications.

This is the bare bones of the story from my point of view. Joy and other members of our family, and indeed each of our friends, would tell a different tale – making up a kaleidoscope of memories, viewpoints and interpretations. This patchwork of impression and detail was undergirded by three broad, connected themes that weave their way in and out of the collective stories. First, God was clearly abroad in the providential series of events which brought us to and through a major crisis; second, a sense of community was writ large in the network of paramedics, doctors, nurses and other hospital staff and the chain of prayer and practical support that we, as a family, received from fellow church members; and, third, a more pastoral dimension interwove with the other two themes, expressed through the ministrations of our vicar, other church leaders, the hospital chaplain and the patient and supportive listening and explaining of the ward sister and her appointed staff. We can take these three themes as a structure for our consideration of the wider theological, communal and pastoral aspects of 'story'.

Story and God

The entire Scriptures are charged with story from beginning to end. We might talk of the 'micro-stories' of everyday events in the lives of individuals, families and small communities and the 'macro-stories', or 'metanarratives',[32] of creation- and salvation-events engaging whole peoples and historic interventions on a grand scale. And yet the Bible seems to assume and argue that the 'foreground' elements in the lives of, say, Hagar, Miriam, Caleb, Jonathan, Naomi, Baruch, Cornelius and Lydia are as integral, in their way, as the more 'high profile' perspectives that surround the lives of, say, Abraham, Moses, Joshua, David, Ruth, Jeremiah, Peter and Paul. In turn, such lives – God's 'little people' as well as the 'key' figures – are caught up with the broad canvas of the giving of covenant and commandment, with exodus, the occupation of the land, with exile and the return – all anticipating and foreshadowing a new covenant, a new people and a new creation, brought through the fulfilment of messianic promise in Jesus Christ and the sending of the Holy Spirit.

What are the links, if any, between the notion of the journeying God we examined earlier and that of the story-giving God? Fundamentally, we can say that it is as we journey that we build up memories of that journey, and, as we remember and declare that remembering, stories are born. Further, it is in the telling of our stories that we can find strength and inspiration for tomorrow, and the continuance of our journey. For example, as I looked back at my journal for the spring of 1993, recalling the events, thoughts and emotions surrounding my bypass operation, and struggled to find words to share something of its story for this chapter, I have been freshly challenged to face the need to trust the Lord of life and death in all things. Memory of the past, awareness of the present and anticipation of the future give content to the time-span of our journeying. And the journeying God portrayed in the Judaeo-Christian tradition is also the God who calls a people to remember, to tell their stories and thus to gain confidence for the road ahead:

> Be careful to follow every command I am giving you today, so that you may live and increase and may enter and possess the land that the LORD promised on oath to your forefathers. Remember how the LORD your God led you all the way in the desert these forty years, to humble you and to test you in order to know what was in your heart, whether or not you would keep his commands . . . Observe the commands of the LORD your God, walking in his ways and revering him. For the LORD your God is bringing you into a good land. (Deut. 8:1–2, 6–7)

The linkage between the God who calls forth a story-telling people in both Old and New Testaments and the stories that engage us in our everyday lives is part of the province of *narrative theology*,[33] where 'narrative', in this limited sense, can be defined as 'The general or inclusive term for a story or account of any events or experiences, fact or fiction, long or short, detailed or plain'.[34] Stanley Hauerwas is fully aware that the emphasis on narrative can trap the unsuspecting into a relativism where 'every community – and worse, every individual – has their own story and there is no means for deciding that one story can be preferred to another'.[35] If my bypass story was allowed to become too central in my life, regardless of any testing out in relation to God's story in Christ Jesus or, for that matter, the stories of others whose lives interweave with mine, then the danger of narrative's potential autonomy is clear. Hauerwas urges upon us a primarily 'constructive theological task': 'Our concern must be to understand better how to live appropriate to the God whom we find in the narratives of Israel and Jesus, and how these stories help provide the means for recognizing and critically appropriating other stories that claim our lives.'[36]

However, amid the debate on what issues are the legitimate focus of narrative theology, Hauerwas and L. Gregory Jones argue that the concept of narrative is not only central in our understanding of God through story and the biblical text, but that it provides the key to *how* we reason, debate and come to know about God and ourselves. They write:

We are concerned with suggesting that narrative is neither just an account of genre criticism nor a faddish appeal to the importance of telling stories; rather it is a crucial conceptual category for such matters as understanding issues of epistemology and methods of argument, depicting personal identity, and displaying the content of Christian convictions.[37]

The process of how we come to know some truth or other or arrive at reasonable conclusions can be seen to link closely with this more developed notion of 'narrative' where, to quote Mark Hargreaves, 'what defines narrative is the presence of a beginning, a middle and an end'.[38] If I am to grow in understanding of God and his ways, I at least need to see where insight about or experience of him fits into the bigger picture, into the narrative of, say, salvation – with its own distinctive unfolding of a beginning, middle and end.

Story and Community

The story of my cardiac illness, hospital admission and subsequent operation was set within several overlapping narrative contexts, including those of our family, the worlds of individual friends, the institutional life of two hospitals and the corporate story of the local church that Joy and I attend. It is this context of the Church that Hauerwas describes as having the 'primary social task . . . to be itself – that is, a people who have been formed by a story that provides them with the skills for negotiating the danger of this existence, trusting in God's promise of redemption'.[39] He goes on to reflect skilfully on the notion of a 'story-formed community' within Richard Adams's *Watership Down*[40] to shed light on the Christian Church – 'a community formed by the story of Christ'.[41]

Hauerwas examines the four main rabbit communities of the novel, judging their significance primarily 'by their ability to sustain the narratives that define the very nature of man, or in this case rabbits'.[42] Seeing *Watership Down* as 'fundamentally a political novel', he sees Sandleford, the warren that is about to be bulldozed out of existence, as a 'traditional class society' hall-marked by loyalty to a 'strong and competent leader', in this instance the Threarah. Leaving Sandleford of necessity, the rabbits reach the second community in the story, a warren of no name, having no Chief Rabbit and adopting a permissive, heedless *laissez-faire* attitude of tolerance to all and sundry. Efrafa, under the brutal tyranny of General Woundwort, is a 'highly organized and regimented totalitarian society' stamped by servile, unquestioning obedience. Watership Down, the fourth community, is the ultimate goal of the rabbits' journey, 'an ideal society for which there is no ready analogue'.[43]

Rabbithood is dominated by narrative for, as Adams writes, 'There is a rabbit saying, "In the warren, more stories than passages"'[44] and its tradition is founded on and pervaded by one supreme story: 'The Blessing of El-ahrairah'. Beginning with 'Long ago, Frith made the world', the story tells how one of his creatures, El-ahrairah, who had many, many wives, sired so many young 'that even Frith could not count them'. In the face of the voracious appetite of rabbitkind and the ravaging of all green things, Frith sternly warns El-ahrairah that if he, Prince Rabbit, cannot control his people then he, Lord Frith, would have to control them. But El-ahrairah would not listen and Frith sets out to trick him and his kind into a measure of subjection, by gifting all the animals and birds with distinctive gifts. El-ahrairah is oblivious, as he joyously anticipates his own gift, that 'the fox and the stoat and the weasel' have been given an insatiable hunger-lust for rabbit meat. Warned of the fate of his kind by a swift, the Prince Rabbit flees over the hills only to hear the voice of the approaching Frith. In panic, El-ahrairah begins to dig his first burrow and Frith, breasting the rise, sees the rabbit's bottom sticking out of the hole. Frith insists on blessing El-ahrairah but, since the rabbit would not stop his feverish attempt to escape, he declares, 'Very well, I will bless your bottom as it sticks out of the hole. Bottom, be strength and warning and speed for ever and save the life of your master. Be it so!' And so Prince Rabbit, newly endowed with a white bobtail and powerful hind legs for burrowing and fleeing his enemies, knows Frith to be his friend.[45]

Hauerwas thus takes the political implications of *Watership Down*, with its fourfold model of society – *traditional*, *permissive*, *totalitarian* and *ideal* – and reminds us of the integrative power of our foundational story. We, too, have a 'story of a prince' and, as with El-ahrairah, our prince was 'defenceless' before the forces of darkness and yet the harbinger of a 'hidden power' expressed through 'truth and love'.[46] Linking the themes of society and story, we can proclaim the centrality of the Prince of Peace in terms of the founding of the Church as a 'community of character', to use

Hauerwas's phrase, and the unfolding of a narrative by which we are to live. Hauerwas brings us this challenge:

> By recovering the narrative dimension of christology we will be able to see that Jesus did not have a social ethic, but that his story is a social ethic. For the social and political validity of a community results from its being formed by a truthful story, a story that gives us the means to live without fear of one another. Therefore there can be no separation of christology from ecclesiology, that is, Jesus from the church. The truthfulness of Jesus creates and is known by the kind of community his story should form.[47]

Story and Pastoral Care

Although the pastoral care I received at the time of my cardiac crisis from hospital staff, church members, friends and family was of the highest order, not everyone, inevitably, seemed to allow the reality of my particular story to be heard. Joy and I found that a frequent rejoinder to our declaring something of our situation was a speedy response that was well meant, but had the effect of dampening any attempt to share just how we were feeling amid our particular story. A common pattern was: 'Bypass surgery? Nothing to it! My Jack had one, three years back. Right as rain now!' We became unduly sensitised, since everyone seemed to have a bypass story, and the dark tunnel that we faced seemed to have no place in the clean, bright world of breezy, anecdotal reassurance. What is the place of 'story' in pastoral care? Is it a self-indulgence to expect to be heard? Is it simply a commonplace to be tolerated or dismissed by others? Or is its effective telling an essential part of a pathway to wholeness?

In recent years a number of writers, many influenced in particular by the works of Charles V. Gerkin and Donald Capps,[48] have sought to address such questions as these in the contexts of pastoral care and counselling. We will look more fully at the influence of Gerkin and Capps at a number of points in the coming chapters, not least in examining the links between hermeneutics and life-story. Fundamental to our argument at this stage is the acknowledgment that, to use Gerkin's words, 'the self maintains its sense of being a self primarily by means of the interpretation of life as a story'.[49] Let us consider story and pastoral care in terms of *self-identity*, *narrative-worlds* and the *pastoral encounter*.

Self-identity

There is no doubt that a sense of self is tied closely to an awareness of story. The five-year-old child, say, can be confident as to who she is because memory and the building up of day-by-day experience serve to assure her that her name is Louise, after Auntie Lou whom everyone likes and who gives lovely presents, that she can now ride a bike without stabilisers, that she was chosen to be Mary at the school nativity play and that she can go higher than Mark, her older brother, on the swing. Erik Erikson, although not expressly using the language of 'story' and 'narrative', nonetheless is implicitly aware of these dimensions in his use of the 'epigenetic principle' in his theories of the development of human identity. Within this principle, derived from the study of foetal growth, 'anything that grows has a ground plan, and . . . out of this ground plan the parts arise, each part having its time of special ascendancy, until all parts have arisen to form a functioning whole'.[50] Erikson applies these concepts to his notion of the step-by-step progress of personality, the transition of each of its eight stages marked by a 'crisis' – a time of special vulnerability where the person begins to realise his or her potential at a new level of maturation.

If we take the example of Louise, she is now just within the fourth of Erikson's stages, that of 'industry vs. inferiority'. Her confidence clearly shows that she has assimilated the 'basic trust' in others, a sense of 'autonomy' and the ability to show 'initiative', hallmarks of the first, second and third stages respectively, and is now applying herself, as her story unfolds, to achievements at school and at home. There will be times when a sense of inferiority threatens her equilibrium as when, playing Mary at Christmas in front of the school, she drops the baby Jesus and nearly everyone laughs. Crucially, though, she sees that her much-loved form teacher does not join in with the mirth and, following the play, receives warm affirmation from her for the way she picks Jesus up, ticks him off and proceeds with her part.

Hopefully, Louise will continue on the pathway to maturity through the successive stages of an identity established in adolescence, of learning about intimacy in adult relationships, of demonstrating responsible membership of society and establishing her values and commitments as her years advance. Throughout, she will ideally keep in touch with her story and the stories of

those around her – avoiding the temptation to ostracise her older
brother Mark, because she does not approve of the woman he
marries, or fall out with Aunt Lou over her will. As Gerkin puts it,
'To lose the sense of story line in one's life is to lose the sense of
being a self.'[51]

Narrative-worlds

As a backdrop to her life, Louise's 'narrative' will have its own
beginning, middle and end. Its content or 'world' may, for example, prove to be any of the following: pleasing others at all
costs; seeking to make as much money as possible; aiming to bring
justice and mercy into a troubled society; marrying and having
many children; or following a particular belief-system wherever it
may lead. What is implied in this brief selection of alternative
'narrative-worlds' for Louise's life is that our stories inevitably
have their moral and ethical aspects. Choice as well as circumstance plays its part in fashioning narrative. Put another way, we
may opt for 'false' stories where we live a lie by denying our
humanity, uniqueness, need for others or responsibility to play
our part in personal and societal relationships, or we may opt for
'true' stories where we 'learn to regard others and their difference
from [us] as a gift'.[52]

To take examples of the respective routes of a *false* story and of a
true story, with their accompanying *narrative-worlds*, we can follow
George Stroup in considering the phenomena of 'alienation' and
'conversion'. He argues that there are 'at least two different
dimensions or levels to personal identity narratives': *chronicle*,
which is 'simply the sum of those events, and experiences which
constitute an individual's personal history';[53] and *interpretation*, an
autobiographical venture, where a 'form or shape or pattern is
culled from the chronicle and projected over the whole'.[54] We
could, for instance, have a 'chronicle' of Louise's story in which the
dates and episodes of her life are listed in a matter-of-fact and
even-handed way. Or, we could present an 'interpretation' of her
narrative, a slanted biography where, for example, we might
concentrate on her developing athletic prowess and its significance in the community in which she lives. It is the interplay
between chronicle and interpretation, so Stroup reasons, that can
give the clue to an understanding of 'alienation' and 'conversion'
in a person's life-story.[55]

If we continue with Louise's developing 'narrative-world', we might see her undergoing a major period of alienation from the individuals and communities that make up her life. Let us say that her dislike of Mark's wife, Judith, has led to an estrangement from her brother and the issue over Aunt Lou's will, in which Louise has been demoted in favour of Mark, has aggravated her growing antipathy toward members of her own family. Landing a managerial job in a leading sports shop in a city the other side of the country, she is able to escape the community of her roots and cut her ties with those who have been nearest and dearest. Earning good money, she decides to 'live it up' in her new environment, moving into a range of settings where she mixes with well-known personalities in the worlds of media and the arts and falls in and out of a series of sexual relationships with attractive men. Within her newly acquired narrative-world, we can say, to follow Stroup,[56] that her identity is increasingly caught up with an 'alienation' that involves 'the repression or negation of chronicle' in the 'conscious act' of an interpretation that denies her rural, family-orientated and sports-filled background.

In time, though, Louise, through her working connections, falls desperately in love with Steve, a keen athlete who also happens to be a Christian. Although he is prepared to meet and appreciate her friends among the glitterati, she soon begins to see that Steve's faith and values, and those of his Christian community, present a potential 'collision of narratives' if their friendship is to continue at any depth. Torn between the disowned 'narrative-world' of her childhood and adolescence, that of the city's all-absorbing social scene and the disturbingly far-reaching world-view of her new man-friend, Louise faces a crisis of identity and direction. Her danger is either to absorb this new world unreflectingly out of her devotion to Steve or to flee back to a life of continuing denial and hedonism. She may, though, with the loving encouragement of others, experience 'conversion' in which she finds her way to Christ, to 'the lengthy, difficult process of reinterpreting . . . her personal history in [the] light of the narratives and symbols that give the Christian community its identity'.[57]

The Pastoral Encounter

If Louise, amid the turmoil engendered by the clash of her contrary narrative-worlds, were to seek pastoral help, how might our consideration of 'story' help in that encounter? We can aim to answer this question by focusing on *narrative identity*, *hearing the story* and *changing the story*.

Narrative Identity

Following Paul Ricoeur's term *'l'identité narrative'*,[58] Ruard Ganzevoort writes that every individual develops a 'narrative identity' through 'telling the stories of his or her life', creating 'a central character in the story' which is 'the image of the individual's identity one strives to construct and maintain'.[59]

As we have seen, Louise has lost the continuity of her story in the successive narrative-worlds that she has been inhabiting: Is she Louise, lover of family and popular athlete? Is she Louise, go-getting, good-time girl without a past? Or is she Louise, Steve's faithful friend and potential Christian disciple? In order to find fresh answers to the question 'Who am I?', Louise needs to find a valid way of rediscovering her *narrative identity*, hopefully through the pastoral encounter. That encounter may be through any one of the models considered in Part II, including pastoral counselling and spiritual direction. Here, we will take the model of pastoral counselling with its strong emphasis on the therapeutic relationship and its awareness of psychodynamic, as well as spiritual, factors.

Hearing the Story

Ganzevoort cites four main characteristics of narrative that need to be kept in mind in hearing the story: 'plot', 'setting', 'character' and 'tone'.[60] The *plot* is a 'recognizable pattern of events' which, in turn, contains the 'subplot' of the 'underlying personal narrative'. In Louise's case, both plot and subplot have become complicated through the experience of alienation from her past and yet, within the pastoral encounter, crucial elements in her personal narrative may be revealed through 'emotionally charged memories and expectations'. Although, in the early stages of pastoral counselling, Louise may resist reference to her hidden past, clues may be given to the counsellor by largely non-verbal means, such as a clenched fist or a flushed face every time her brother Mark is mentioned. In time, the story of her antagonism toward Mark, Judith and the wider family may explode into the counselling relationship through the recall of angrily expressed memories and the anticipation of bitter encounters ahead.

Setting refers to 'the constellation of social, cultural and other context factors' and attention paid to these contexts may further reveal aspects of the personal narrative. For Louise, a series of social environments await exploration and clarification: the domestic and rural settings of her early years; the world of amateur athletics; the linked everyday realities of the sports shop; night-life in the city with her glamorous friends; and the enjoyable but newly challenging set of relationships with Steve and within his Christian communal context.

Within the cumulative setting of Louise's narrative the question of *character* needs to be raised. Here the term refers to 'personal context: persons and relationships that are perceived as primary in importance'; and the accent is on the word 'perceived', since it is Louise's way of seeing who are the significant people in her life that offers another key to unlock the door of understanding her narrative-world and narrative identity. In hearing her story, it is likely that the centrality of Steve in her current situation will present readily. In time, the emergence of a residual longing for Josh, one of her former man-friends, who appealed greatly to her more hidden artistic and creative side, reveals another dimension to her narrative that Louise needs to acknowledge and, if possible, integrate into her self-understanding and future choices. As the counselling proceeds, other *dramatis personae* of her life-story are declared, although their importance to her may be initially denied or grudgingly admitted. Gradually, her brother, parents, Auntie Lou, her favourite primary school teacher and others enter the counselling dialogue and begin to recover, hopefully, something of their primacy in Louise's recounted narrative.

The *tone* of her story is the 'overall atmosphere' in which her account is given. We have already indicated the emotional charge of sections of Louise's storytelling, and the 'messages' given by anger, resentment, anxiety, fear, guilt, calmness, generosity of spirit, courage, hopefulness and loving attitudes need to be observed, for they can give the profoundest meaning to the plot, setting and character of her narrative.

Changing the Story
Carolyn Bohler, writing on the use of storytelling in pastoral counselling,[61] points out that there is more to hearing the stories presented by people seeking help than simply allowing the narrative to spill over, unchecked and unchallenged. She cites three main responses on the part of the counsellor:

1. *Hearing well*, where every effort is made to listen actively, engaging in careful observation of each nuance of the narrative and its presentation. Bohler, writing in a Christian context, urges us to 'espouse a theology in which God hears more than God speaks' and adds that we, as pastoral counsellors, 'are required to be with, not over; to hear insight, not just to give it; to trust God in the process, not to be "gods" ourselves'.[62]

2. *Hearing, then giving a twist of meaning*, assisting the counsellee to 'reintegrate her or his past events with a new feeling tone, as she or he gains a fresh perspective about the self, relationships and the future'. One technique which can aid this transformation is that of offering metaphors that can 'embrace a truth without demanding it'.[63] In Louise's situation, an awareness of the priority of athleticism in her life, on the dance floor and in the bedroom as well as on the sports field, may prompt the counsellor to say, 'It seems to me, Louise, that your life is about being the first to reach the winning post.' Floating such a metaphor within the counselling relationship can only be hazarded where time has been spent and a measure of understanding and trust built up. This 'twist of meaning' may throw a shaft of light on Louise's narrative, enabling her to face her competitive spirit and reflect upon the possibility of a less driven future.

3. *Prohibiting stories*, in which the person seeking help is interrupted in his or her storytelling since continuance would be counterproductive, or even destructive. Bohler gives three examples of relevant situations:[64] where the client seeks to dwell in the past through recounting historic story, thus avoiding facing present reality; in behavioural therapy, where the pressing need is for a breakthrough in, say, the fear of crowded streets rather than an endless recounting of the earlier narrative; and in the treatment of chemical addiction, where there may be a strong temptation to escape into storytelling as a defence against having the much-loved habit challenged and eradicated. For Louise, the first of these contexts is the most likely one for intervention. If, for example, she insisted, even within the late stages of the pastoral encounter, on repeatedly rehearsing her early antipathies toward her sister-in-law, the counsellor may feel obliged to interrupt the flow with, 'You seem to be going over the same ground endlessly. I would like to suggest that we shift the focus from your resentments toward Judith when Mark first married her and bring our discussion up to date by asking, How do you *now* feel about her?'

As we follow Bohler's and Ganzevoort's alternative approaches to story in pastoral counselling, we can begin to see that, step by step, Louise's story may begin to change in a way that is constructive and integrating for her and her significant relationships and social contexts. It is here that the question of significant others may be crucial in her transition from alienation to a more constructive narrative identity. In the context of Christian counselling, Ganzevoort points to the research of the Dutch writer, W. A. H. Kox,[65] who investigated the conversion of 'non-religious youth' to membership of 'charismatic churches' and found that it is 'social attraction' that precedes the acceptance of the group's Christian doctrine. As Ganzevoort puts it: 'In pastoral work and in the life of a community of faith it is not meaningful doctrines that count most, but meaningful relationships.' For Louise, struggling with her various narrative-worlds and trying to make cohesive sense of her past, present and future, it may well be her relationship with Steve and her new friendships with other members of his Christian community that may grant her 'a meaningful interpretation of the life events encountered'.[66]

It is within this unsettling but hope-giving process of 'changing the story' that Louise in effect discovers, to use Ganzevoort's term, new 'referential figures', defined as 'the persons, groups, or belief systems that provide the primary orientation for interpretations'.[67] Inevitably, these figures may be 'either supportive or detracting' and Louise will need discernment and courage in choosing between, for example, the community of faith and the hedonistic milieu of some of her acquaintances. It is within this transition that the pastoral counsellor may prove to be a 'referential figure' of far-reaching influence:

> The pastoral aim is to establish a relationship that offers openness and acceptance, so that the two stories of divine and human revelation may come to merge and a new understanding and interpretation may emerge. Pastoral counselors and others may function as a referential figure, through which an orientation on the transcendent God may lead to meaningful interpretations . . . Although the counselee has to interpret in his or her own way, the counselor will try to maintain the central elements of the Christian tradition and biblical revelation.[68]

Summary

As we have considered pathways to wholeness in terms of journey
and story and explored these themes through a range of personal
pilgrimages and narratives, we have been continually reminded of
the three interrelated perspectives of *God, self* and *community*.
There is no stasis in the picture for we have a journeying and
story-giving God who calls us to travel forward on life's adventure
but to do so reflectively, as we recall and retell our stories. And this
is a path of transformation while we follow in the Way, a path
where personal and communal narrative identity and narrative-
worlds may be changed radically through constructive referential
figures, including, for some at certain stages in life, those of
pastoral carers and counsellors. The central 'referential figure',
though, is Christ himself whose journey and narrative took him
through the darkness to the light beyond, 'who for the joy set
before him endured the cross' (Heb. 12:2). It is through him that
our narrative-world and narrative identity are changed, since 'We
are "storied people" because the God that sustains us is a "storied
God," whom we come to know only by having our character
formed appropriate to God's character.'[69]

In the next chapter we need to address what it means to be a
'storied people', on the road to wholeness and sustained by a
'storied God', within our present culture – a culture peopled by
those of many faiths and no faith, caught within the melting pot of
modernity's world of intellectual certainty and the safety of
scepticism and postmodernity's world of conceptual uncertainty
and the risk-taking of the unfettered imagination.

3

PATHWAYS TODAY: TAKING OUR BEARINGS

All that is solid melts into air.
Karl Marx[1]

In seeking to map pastoral reality and its pathways to wholeness we need to take our bearings in the context of contemporary culture. This is a task fraught with presuppositional uncertainty, since Christians have always struggled over culture. From the earliest times there have been issues and tensions surrounding the Church's relationship with the prevailing societal structures of the day. At times, the people of God have stood out against the wider community's cultural trappings, as when believers in the early years of the Roman Empire refused to eat meat offered to idols and campaigners against the slave trade challenged the status quo in late-eighteenth-century England. In other periods, the Church has shown a remarkable conformity to cultural trends, and indeed has been the main shaper of those trends, as in the establishment of Christianity as state religion following the emperor Constantine's conversion (AD 312) and throughout much of european history since, up to the modern era. from time to time, where the main-stream church has become compromised or grown complacent, minority groups of christian believers have rocked the culturally sanctioned boat by agitating for a renewed faith or a reformed society.

But where are we today? How are we to understand contemporary culture? What stance are we to take toward it? How are the journeying, storied people of God to respond to the journeys and stories that motivate the lives of countless others within society? What is the relationship between present-day pastoral care and the counter-claims of the prevailing culture on concepts of God and the self? An attempt will be made to answer these and similar questions by a consideration of, first, the meaning of culture; second, its handling by the Church and its broad relevance in today's world; third, an examination of the rise and influence of modernity; fourth, an appraisal of postmodernity; fifth, an exploration of selfhood in the light of these discussions; and, finally, an appraisal of the challenge contemporary culture presents to Christian understandings of pathways to wholeness.

Culture

The word 'culture' has its roots in the Latin verb *colere*, to till, as do two other, seemingly unrelated words: 'cult' and 'cultivation'. The bridges between the three English words lie, on the one side, with the sense of a cult, or *cultus*, as 'a specific system of religious worship'[2] and, on the other, with the emphasis on cultivation as a refining process that is toiled over. It is a heartening thought that the first human engagement with the environment is pictured as Adam's call to work and take care of Eden[3] – a commitment to cultivate the earth that, by definition, sees the birth of culture and, in the fullness of time, the development of the cultus of a worshipping community.

The concept of culture is notoriously difficult to define, the third edition of *Collins English Dictionary* (1991), for example, giving eleven distinct definitions and uses of the word. In the world of literary scholarship, Raymond Williams sees the potential confusion as resting in the variety of disciplines that lay claim to an understanding of culture, and Roger Lundin, following Williams, points to the gradual movement from the early uses of the word, in 'tending crops or animals', to its application, 'early in the modern period, to human development in a general sense'. Acknowledging the 'exceedingly complicated history of the modern usage of the word', Lundin writes that culture 'designates that complex, interlocking network of symbols, practices, and beliefs at the heart of a society's life'.[4]

Such a general definition clearly embraces every aspect of a people's world, be it one of close bonding to the land and agrarian or pastoral simplicity, or one of urban sophistication and high technology. The Masai's commitment to ancestor worship, tribal and familial loyalty and a currency in cattle, and the Western city-dweller's commitment to individualism, business loyalty and the world money market, are examples, equally, of culture, of a 'cultivating' of life's environmental possibilities. And these possibilities include the so-called 'low' culture of folk, popular and 'streetwise' lifestyles of dress, music and the visual arts, as well as the 'high' culture of revered tradition. All this is simply to express varieties of uniqueness in the peoples of the earth, varieties that are both historically rooted and open to developmental change in the future. David Augsburger sums up the human faces of culture when he writes: 'The Westerner, since Descartes, defines the self as saying, "I think, therefore I am." The African says, "I participate, therefore I am"; the Oriental, "I belong, therefore I am"; the Palestinian villager, "I reside in this village, therefore I am." '[5]

Culture and the Church

If we are going to take our bearings as pastoral carers within contemporary Western culture, it is important to address more fully the question of the relationship between the Church and the prevailing culture of the day. There have been a number of attempts to analyse the range of positions taken by Christians in relation to society's cultural beliefs and practices. Among these, the schema produced by H. Richard Niebuhr (1894–1962) is still perhaps the most influential. Based on a series of lectures given in 1949, his *Christ and Culture* postulates five stances taken by the Church in its attitude to culture. These comprise three overall positions: Christ *against* culture, Christ *of* culture and Christ *above* culture, the third being further subdivided into 'synthesis', 'dualism' and 'conversionism' (see below).[6] 'Christ-against-culture' and 'Christ-of-culture' are seen as the polarised stances of Church history, 'Christ-above-culture', with its three variations, as the middle-ground viewpoint of the 'Church of the centre'. Charles Kraft acknowledges both the foundational value of Niebuhr's structure and its limitations in the light of more recent cultural studies.[7] He proposes the following eight categories,[8] in effect including Niebuhr's five:

1. God-*against*-culture
2. God-*in*-culture
   a) God as cultural hero
   b) God as endorsing my culture
3. God-*above*-culture

a. God-above-culture-and-unconcerned (deism)
b. God-and-culture affirmed (Niebuhr's 'synthesis')
c. God-and-culture in tension (Niebuhr's 'dualism')
d. God as transformer of culture (Niebuhr's 'conversionism')
e. God-above-but-through-culture (Kraft's preferred position).

This is not the place to fill out the detail of this complex schema, except to comment briefly on some of the pastoral implications of the three main categories. There will be further reference to elements in these positions in Part II.

First, the 'God-against-culture' stance is, I suggest, one that has arisen largely from a misreading of Scripture. The vehemence of some of the excluding attitudes we shall meet in our consideration of 'biblical counselling' can be traced, for example, to a rendering of *kosmos* in 1 John 2:15–17 as the 'whole world order' rather than those elements within human society that militate against God, as suggested by the telling litany, 'the desire of the flesh, the desire of the eyes' and 'the pride in riches' in verse 16 (NRSV).[9] Second, the 'God-in-culture' positions can lead to a dangerous rationalisation that God is inevitably 'on our side' in every attitude and decision fostered by the favoured culture. Such mindsets can be seen in the extremes of Zionism and Islamic fundamentalism within the Middle East conflict. In the pastoral context, 'God-in-culture' viewpoints may trap a Christian individual or community into a 'Jesus will sanction all we do' attitude, where, to follow Kraft, the forms of a culture may take precedence over 'the *functions* to which these forms are put and the *motivations* of those who employ them'.[10] And so Christians who live and witness in, say, an inner city's street culture, or in, for instance, a suburban, middle-class milieu, may come to believe that God identifies wholeheartedly with all the trappings of, on the one hand, the unpredictability and 'differentness' of a clubland lifestyle, or, on the other hand, the respectability and 'niceness' of the status quo.

Whereas the 'God-against-culture' and 'God-in-culture' positions both have the danger of engendering a sense of moral superiority – either 'God is on my side *against* culture' or 'God is on my side *in* culture', the 'God-above-culture' viewpoints at least have the advantage of allowing God to be God. Pastorally, though, the 'deistic', 'synthetic' and 'dualistic' stances each offer pitfalls for the unwary. *Deism* proposes an absentee God who has washed his hands of the human endeavour, allowing cultural experimentation a completely free rein and leaving men and women to pursue autonomous destinies without let or hindrance. Niebuhr's *synthesis* seeks the seamless blending of Christ and culture in society's structures and institutions. Its idealistic stance can, for example, lead to turning a blind eye to institutional injustice and oppression and, pastorally, to simplistic, over-trusting attitudes that see no evil in the social environment, only in the life of the individual. This attempt to 'bring Christ and culture . . . into one system of thought and practice tends, perhaps inevitably,' so Niebuhr states, 'to the absolutizing of what is relative, the reduction of the infinite to a finite form, and the materialization of the dynamic'.[11] The *dualism* of Niebuhr's analysis holds Christ and culture in paradox, a paradox in which God is full of grace and humanity full of sin – a sin so pervasive that, in this view, 'All human action, all culture, is infected with godlessness.'[12] Pastorally, we can see how this perspective, with its neglect of creation theology and humanity's call to bear the image of God, can undermine an individual's self-esteem and sap a community's will to change society.

It is in Niebuhr's 'conversionism' and Kraft's 'God-above-but-through-culture' position that we have the greatest potential for a pastoral theology and pastoral psychology which are open to a fully orbed, trinitarian, biblically sensitive understanding of the God who is both Lord of all and abroad in and through human culture. Niebuhr here sees Christ as the transformer of culture, where 'culture is under God's sovereign rule, and [where] the Christian must carry on cultural work in obedience to the Lord'.[13] If culture is transformable, then it must be in need of transformation, and Niebuhr freely acknowledges the corrupting effects of human sinfulness on society and its structures: '[Human culture] is perverted good, not evil; or it is evil as perversion, and not as badness of being.'[14] Kraft takes a similarly redemptive line to Niebuhr, although he sees the 'forms and functions' of culture in a more neutral light as essentially vehicles which God chooses to use in order to communicate with humankind. The transformable elements, for Kraft, lie more in the *uses* to which cultural forms and functions are put, although, in time, transformed individuals and groups of people may also engage with the restructuring of society.[15]

We can take the emphasis given in these two views as offering a useful model for the Church's relationship with culture. Their value lies in the dynamic quality of the perspective, that is to say, that cultural forms and usage can be changed for the better where the people of God respond to and co-operate with divine initiatives in Christ and through the Holy Spirit. Theologically, the godward side of the equation points to the sovereignty of the Trinity ('God-above-culture') and the divine engagement with humanity ('God-through-culture'). Anthropologically, the human side of the equation points to humankind's ontological calling, 'created . . . in the image of God' (Gen. 1:27), and God's mandate to men and women to 'fill the earth and subdue it' (1.28). Brian J. Walsh and J. Richard Middleton bring these two latter elements together, when they write:

> The primal command to subdue the earth . . . is a cultural mandate. In all our cultural activities and affairs – that is, in all human actions, artifacts, relationships and institutions by which we interact with and develop creation – human beings provide evidence of their God-given rule of the earth. The image of God, in its central reference to the idea of subduing the earth, designates humans as cultural-historical beings.[16]

Culture Today

Any overview of culture needs to take note of influences from past traditions, from more recently established trends and from elements that seem to be shaping the future. In terms of today's societies this requires some assessment of three principal cultural strands: the *premodern*, the *modern*, and the *postmodern*. Although these strands, with their use of the word 'modern', can be seen as integral to the history of *Western* civilisation, the concepts behind them have global application. The planet has contracted dramatically in terms of time and space throughout the twentieth century and so now we can be sharply aware, either through personal travel or through images on the screen, of the premodern in, say, rural Greece or upland Kenya, and of the modern and postmodern in any of the world's capitals. Even more tellingly, in many parts of the world all three strands can be witnessed by a stroll through the nearest large town or city. A walk in downtown Bristol, just ten miles from where I live, soon reveals, amid the shining shopping malls, the high-tech and 'pick and mix' fashions of the modern and postmodern, huddles of unkempt young people whose struggle for existence mirrors all too readily the dispossessed poor of premodernity.

In addressing these three cultural strands we shall focus mainly on modernity and postmodernity since these are the prime contexts of today's pastoral care. At the same time, the interpenetration of the premodern into contemporary society will be kept in mind throughout. Essentially, we will view the modern in the light of the premodern and the postmodern in the light of the modern.

Here, and throughout the book, I shall primarily use the term 'modern*ity*', with prefixes when appropriate, rather than 'modern*ism*'. Although the distinctions between them are far from rigid, I shall follow the tendency to see the former group of words as emphasising the social and attitudinal aspects of the culture and the latter as signifying the more systematic and philosophical elements. As a result, modernity and postmodernity can be talked of in terms of 'condition', 'project', a 'body of experience' or a 'state of mind' and modernism and postmodernism as a 'style', 'school of thought' or 'cultural movement'. There is clearly a great deal of overlap between these concepts. David Harvey brings the two broad categories together: 'Modernism is a troubled and fluctuating response to the condition of modernity produced by a particular process of modernization.'[17]

To help us take our bearings in the territory of modernity and postmodernity, let us first examine the three cultural strands mentioned above by way of brief thumbnail sketches of life in Britain in the 1750s, 1950s and 1990s.

The 1750s

My own ancestors were poor farm-labouring families in the mid-eighteenth century. Following a marriage to a Roman Catholic woman in west Dorset in the 1720s, they fell victim to the anti-Catholic sentiment of the time, seeking and receiving relative safety by settling in Stourton, Wiltshire, a parish where the protective influence of the Catholic Lords Stourton meant they could continue to keep the rites of the Roman Church over the following century. As far as can be gleaned from county records, their lives were typical of the labouring poor of premodernity – lives that, although often harsh and hard in the extreme (with, for example, the constant threat of removal to a former parish for the handouts that might keep them on the breadline), at least had a certain structure that gave a measure of stability within a highly localised world. The key word for the premodern could be said to be 'Providence': there was a sense of order that arose from a hierarchy of provisional help. However low in the pecking order of God, Church, Parliament, aristocracy, local squirearchy, farmers, craftsmen and 'inarticulate poor', there was a belief that thrift and keeping on the right side of the law were rewarded, if not in this life, in the hereafter. Along with a trust in the givenness of the way things were, there was a sense of kinship and generational continuity that, however hard the struggle, saw the seasons and the cycle of birth and death as offering some hope that each generation might relive the 'modes of life of its forerunners'.[18]

The 1950s

The two-hundred-year leap from the premodern mid-eighteenth century to the Britain of the 1950s is a leap of astronomical proportions, socially and culturally speaking. The rise and rise of modernity from its seedbed in the Enlightenment was signalled by one salient watchword: 'Progress'. The certainties of 'Providence' in the premodern world had given way to the blandishments of an industrial and technological advance that nurtured human autonomy and breathed hope into postwar Britain. Where life in the 1750s was governed by a fixity ordained by class, gender and lineage, the 1950s saw many in a situation of increasing choice and new possibilities: 'being' was giving way to 'becoming'. Perhaps the ikon of this call into the future was the television set, and its staged premiere the coronation of Elizabeth II. In 1953 the nation gathered on lines of chairs – 'just like the pictures' – to view the royal spectacular. Within twelve months the number of sets in private use had doubled and over the next few years audiences declined dramatically at the cinema, while the number of books borrowed from the lending libraries also plummeted. Television continued to be the window through which the modern world was seen – a world that both lifted the human spirit with the promise of better things over the horizon and dashed those very hopes with the fear of dark forces, unleashed in an age without Providence.

The 1990s

By the 1990s it can be argued that another major cultural shift was well under way. Many see the 1960s as a gateway through which a whole range of new understandings about humankind and its place within the cosmos advanced, so that the following decades would experience a social and conceptual climate which may be described as *post*modern. There is a continuing debate as to whether postmodernity is a clearly definable cultural milieu which is quite separate from modernity or whether it is, rather, an expression of 'late' or 'high' modernity.[19] We will pick up this issue again as we examine these concepts in greater depth in the following sections. However we envisage the postmodern, though, there is no doubt that the 1990s can be viewed as a decade of distinctive sensibilities, some in clear continuity with the modern, some declaring new ways of perceiving the world. Among the latter, we might single out the idea of 'Pluralism' as something of a byword – a byword under which 'all groups have a right to speak for themselves, in their own voice, and have the voice accepted as authentic and legitimate'.[20] Even so, under-girding this central tenet of postmodernity, as we shall see, is the deliberate eschewing of the certainties of premodernity and modernity: faith in religion, in science, or in any of life's '-isms' is to be resolutely left behind. Thus, life in the 1990s, amid all the wonderment of the conquest of cyberspace and the bewilderment of life in the market-place, hangs in the balance between a pluralism that celebrates 'difference' and 'otherness' and a jettisoning of old values that can, ultimately, lead to the void. David Lyon asks a searching question of modernity's role in this potential decline: 'Did modernity, by secularizing providence into progress, initiate the unravelling of the social-cultural fabric now associated with nihilism?'[21] We will seek to address some of the issues that cluster around this question, especially in relation to Christian pastoral care, in the coming sections.

Modernity

The rationality and scientific enquiry of the seventeenth and eighteenth centuries offered a carefully defined and ordered route toward the ever new horizons of 'Progress'. The prime mover of this journey of objectification was the French philosopher, René Descartes who, during the winter of 1619–20, immured himself before a fire in a room in Germany and resolved to reason his way to the barest essentials for human reflective activity. Seeking to discard all certainties, including those provided by his five senses and by his formerly held mathematical proofs, he proceeded to his famous declaration: '*Cogito, ergo sum*: I think, therefore I am', adding, in his recall of the event, that this insight 'was so certain and so evident that all the most extravagant suppositions of the skeptics were not capable of shaking it'.[22]

This 'unshakeable' path of Cartesian logic, though undergirding the scientific endeavour and industrial expansion of the post-Enlightenment era, was to run on to less stable terrain as the nineteenth century unfolded. Two main developments contributed to this unsettlement – romanticism and revolution – and each, together with the continuing pursuit of cognitive knowledge, combined powerfully to give birth to modernity.

By way of reaction to the impeccably precise reasoning of the Enlightenment, the late eighteenth and early nineteenth centuries saw the rise of a new way of celebrating human individuality, that of exploring the intuitive and imaginary, the world of the subjective. The so-called Romantic movement embraced a range of ideologies, including the quest for beauty in the poetry of William Wordsworth and Samuel Taylor Coleridge, the emphasis on an individual's intuitive spiritual experience in the works of the American essayist Ralph Waldo Emerson and the commitment to 'immediacy' and 'relationality', as against 'conceptual distance',[23] in the hermeneutics of the German theologian Friedrich Schleiermacher. This strand in the creation of modernity served to foster a powerful emphasis on the understanding of selfhood in experiential and liberating terms.

The rise of romanticism, with its bid for self-expression and creativity, was bound up with another surge of the human spirit – that of the revolutions in America, in the 1770s, and France, in the 1790s, against perceived socio-political injustice. Once more the 'order of things' was under threat, and the radical fervour of the late eighteenth century was carried over as a source of inspiration for the democratic and socialist movements of the first half of the nineteenth century. The year 1848 stands out in revolutionary history as a year in which 'government in every major European capital except London and St Petersburg . . . appeared to be in retreat'.[24] This was the year, too, of the publication of Karl Marx's *The Communist Manifesto*, in which the threat of the shaking of a premodern trust in 'Providence' and the Enlightenment belief in the sure-footedness of rationality was clearly expressed: 'All that is solid melts into air, all that is holy is profane, and men at last are forced to face with sober senses the real conditions of their lives and their relations with their fellow men.'[25]

These three influences – residual Cartesian logic, romanticism and 'creative destruction' – are each constituent of the complex social and cultural phenomena of modernity and modernism. By definition, the modern project is a mix of stability and uncertainty. It rejects, or at least discounts, the premodern past with its confident claims in a providential God. Replacing faith with rationality and religion with science, it commits itself to autonomous human endeavour. The future is eagerly anticipated in the name of 'Progress', but it is also feared, since revolution, iconoclasm and the relentless pursuit of knowledge can unearth darker forces. Marshall Berman expresses the duality of the modern in these terms: 'To be modern is to find ourselves in an environment that promises adventure, power, joy, growth, transformation of ourselves and the world – and, at the same time, that threatens to destroy everything we have, everything we know, everything we are.'[26]

Already unsure of itself, modernity was to find its confident, unitive voice increasingly drowned out by the babel-voices of a 'postmodernity' which sought to discount not only a providential past but a progressive future – voices that spoke in many subcultural tongues and represented many diverse worlds, celebrating a kaleidoscopic and splintered, ever-present 'here and now'.

Postmodernity

As we have noted earlier, the concept of postmodernity is controversial. Some, like Anthony Giddens, see so-called 'postmodernity' as essentially descriptive of 'late' or 'high' modernity. Others, like Keith Tester, stress that postmodernity is simply *post*-modernity – 'a point of critique of modernity which is nevertheless dependent on modernity'.[27] Yet others, including many philosophers, social scientists and theologians, fully acknowledge the usefulness of the term in relation to profound cultural and societal changes which have taken place in Western civilisation since the late 1960s and early 1970s. Most accept that, in today's world, the presuppositions of modernity and postmodernity coexist, albeit and by definition, as we shall see, at variance with each other. David Lyon sums up much of contemporary thinking on the matter when he writes: 'The idea of postmodernity may yet turn out to be a figment of overheated academic imagination, popular hype, or disappointed radical hopes' and yet 'it is worth pursuing' since 'it raises our sensitivity and helps us see certain issues as problems to be explained'.[28]

Whereas the roots of modernity can be traced back to the soil of the Enlightenment and the forward thrust of a Cartesian logic which honoured the individual subject in the quest for progressive knowledge, many have attributed the rise of postmodernity to the seminal works of the German philosopher Friedrich Wilhelm Nietzsche in the second half of the nineteenth century. Nietzsche (1844–1900) challenged the citadels of Enligtenment rationality and objectivity in a profoundly persistent and consistent way, condemning the pursuit of reason as a perverted form of the 'will to power', wherein the 'knowing ones' assumed mastery over the ignorant. Prophetically, it can be argued, he anticipated a 'new age' in which the rational is so demoted that concepts of 'truth', 'history', 'religion', and any universal explanatory process concerning God and humanity, are deemed null and void. In the moral realm, Alasdair MacIntyre points to a Nietzschean logic which argues that 'if there is nothing to morality but expressions of will, my morality can only be what my will creates'.[29] Thus Nietzsche celebrates the ascendancy of will over reason: 'We . . . *want to become those we are* – human beings who are new, unique, incomparable, who give themselves laws, who create themselves.'[30]

This self-determining notion that dispenses with the foundational thinking of the past, seeks to dismantle the 'givens' of the structures that make up human life and yet invites the 'differentness' of innumerable human autonomies, is the harbinger of the postmodern self. The three resulting characteristics of postmodernity – antifoundationalism, deconstructionism and pluralism – will be examined in due course: the first and last in this section and the third, deconstructionism, in the next chapter. Let us illustrate the flavour of this profound undermining of modern rationalism in the imagined world of Ridley Scott's film *Blade Runner*.[31]

Set in Los Angeles in November 2019, the editor's cut edition (1991)[32] presents a particularly bleak picture of a world where the 'will to power', and the attendant unstitching of what is 'true' and 'real', reign supreme. The scene opens in a gaunt cityscape lit intermittently by great balls of fire and surveyed from above by the ceaseless patrol of spacecraft. Genetic engineers have produced an army of robotic slaves, known as replicants, who are used 'off-world' in 'the hazardous exploration and colonisation of other planets'. Among the replicants, who are virtually identical to human beings, an élite corps, the NEXUS 6, is superior in strength and agility and has members at least equal in intelligence to their creators. Even so, all these simulacra are restricted by a life-span of four years. Following a bloody mutiny by a NEXUS 6 combat team, replicants have been declared illegal on earth and special police squads – blade-runner units – have been requisitioned to kill any trespassing replicants on sight, an event described in policespeak as 'retirement'.

Four of these 'skin jobs' have been identified walking the streets of the city and Deckard, played by Harrison Ford, is assigned to 'retire' them. Inevitably – even in the soulless world of the postmodern metropolis – love interest stirs and 'Deck' falls for Rachel, a fifth, recently created replicant, whose 'humanness' is particularly beguiling, including, as it does, an 'implant of memories' to fill out a constructed past. The film throughout plays on questions of 'what is real?': Rachel seeks to convince Deck of her earlier existence by showing him a photograph of herself, supposedly, as a child with her 'mother'; Zhora, another replicant, dressed up to look like a store-front display model, is hurled through a series of arcade windows full of tailors' dummies when shot by the blade runner; Roy, the leader and the most violent of the skin jobs, echoes Descartes when he says to a genetic designer, 'I think, Sebastian, therefore I am.' Over against this world of blurred boundaries and deep uncertainty, the ghettoisation of the Los Angeles of the twenty-first century continues in the crowded squalor of Chinatown and the littered streets of urban decay.

Let us look, now, at the Nietzschean themes mentioned above in the light of some of the postmodernist elements found in *Blade Runner*.

Antifoundationalism

For Deckard and Rachel, human and replicant respectively, both the past and the future are drained of meaning. All we know of Deckard's personal history, as with Rachel's supposed earlier existence, is in his possession of some family photographs: 'truth' is tied to 'image'. And the film ends with, at best, ambiguity, as the couple make off (together, or not; we are not quite sure) with the words of the police chief hanging in the air: 'It's too bad she won't live. But then again, who does?' As Nicholas Wolterstorff puts it, 'On all fronts foundationalism is in bad shape.'[33] *Blade Runner* paints a picture in which the old certainties have been replaced by pandemic fear: the foundations of Western civilisation, laid firmly within a Romano-Christian history and held together by the tenets of religion, law and science, have been undermined by human anti-rationalism and wilfulness and by a Nietzschean exultation in the 'death of God'.[34]

This antifoundationalism has been charted, and, in many cases, celebrated by a cluster of French philosophers writing from the 1960s onwards: among these, the names of Jacques Derrida, Michel Foucault, Jean Baudrillard and Jean-François Lyotard stand out as cardinal contributors to the debate on postmodernity. Lyotard sums up the Nietzsche-inspired erosion of historical continuity and the 'grand explanations' of life's meaning when he writes, 'Simplifying to the extreme, I define *postmodern* as incredulity toward metanarratives.'[35] The metanarrative of the Judaeo-Christian tradition we considered in Chapter 2, and all other unitive accounts of the world order – such as Marxism and, indeed, the universalising claims of science, on which Lyotard concentrates – are not only scrutinised but are denied as worthy of belief.

The loss of the grand narrative inevitably means that the significance of life's *lesser* stories begins to evaporate. Personal history becomes inconsequential in human relating since, according to Lyotard, 'language games are the minimum relation required for society to exist'[36] and this 'social bond [though] linguistic . . . is not woven with a single thread'.[37] Like a game of chess whose rules are crossed with those of, say, draughts and dominoes, the daily intercourse of life can only make sense at the level of doing one's best with a variety of linguistic ground rules. Deckard and Rachel could only survive in their tentative relating if each can get the words right and, hopefully, find a stir of responsiveness in the other.

In the Introduction we considered Korzybski's dictum 'A map is not the territory' in terms of the map-making enterprise of this book. Jean Baudrillard kicks the ground of territory, as it were, from under our feet by declaring, 'Henceforth, it is the map that precedes the territory.'[38] Just as the surface texture of language has ousted narrative, so the maps we make take precedence over the territory we seek to depict. In other words, representation has superseded reality. It is the world of the television and computer screens that entices us most down this route of 'hyperreality' (where reality itself is both 'more and less real').[39] Here the 'maps', images and representations of reality engage us through video games, electronic personal organisers, the Internet, virtual reality, broadcast films and soap operas.

An innocent example of this shift in reality was seen at a party thrown by a woman prison governor for members of her staff and other guests. The occasion was held at the time, in BBC's television series *EastEnders*, when the much loved Arthur Fowler was held in prison unjustly. A placard at the party, 'Free Arthur Fowler!', was scrutinised by a very puzzled visiting barrister, Oxbridge-trained and erudite, whose television-watching was restricted to *Newsnight*. His thoughtfully enquiring question, 'Who's Arthur Fowler?' was met by howls of disbelief: Arthur Fowler *is*; the imagined is more real than reality.

At a much profounder level, Baudrillard 'envisages a postmodern landscape in which there is no reality underlying the virtual map'. He cites the Gulf War of 1991 as an 'unreal war, war without the symptoms of war, a form of war which means never needing to face up to war, which enables war to be perceived from deep within a darkroom'.[40] There is no doubt that the language games of the coalition's warlords, reminiscent of *Blade Runner*'s talk of 'retirement' as a euphemism for execution, served to cushion harsh reality for the passive viewer: to 'pick off' instead of 'kill'; to 'soften up' for 'bombard enough to destroy morale'; to 'take out' for 'destroy'; 'interdiction' for 'destruction'; and 'collateral damage' for the 'killing of civilians and non-military targets'.

The influence of Nietzsche, and 'new luminaries'[41] such as Lyotard and Baudrillard, has been a relentless unpicking of the ancient garment of a world dominated by divine providence and human reason, not least in its more modernistic guise where God is demoted and the progress of science and technology elevated. The destructive path of antifoundationalism moves inexorably toward nihilism, through the troubled, steadily vanishing country of no past, no future, no meaning, no reason, no reality and, ultimately, no territory. Jonathan Culler comments on the sheer folly of this downward route to oblivion:

If 'sawing off the branch on which one is sitting' seems foolhardy to men of common sense, it is not so for Nietzsche, Freud, Heidegger, and Derrida; for they suspect that if they fall there is no 'ground' to hit and that the most clearsighted act may be a certain reckless sawing, a calculated dismemberment or deconstruction of the great cathedral-like trees in which Man has taken shelter for millennia.[42]

Pluralism

Although we have painted a dark, monochrome and, in the last analysis, indecipherable picture of postmodernity's headlong dive into nihilism, it is worth repeating that contemporary society is still a complex organism where 'late' modernity and the post-modern interpenetrate. Further, there is a brighter, more hopeful strand in the painting of postmodernity, that of a pluralism which celebrates difference and otherness. This strand, to pursue our analogy, is not wholly light but is, perhaps inevitably, a mixed picture of hopefulness and potential meaninglessness.

It was Nietzsche's successor in the relay race toward post-modernity, Martin Heidegger (1889–1976), who brought into the philosophical debate an emphasis on 'Being' and 'beings' which opened up the way to an affirmation of distinctiveness. He resisted the Nietzschean track toward nihilism, exploring, rather, the beingness of our humanity through the use of the German word *Dasein*, variously translated as 'being-there' or 'being-here', or, as Anthony Thiselton puts it, meaning 'almost "human being," since it characterizes human existence in contrast to that of objects . . . such as tables and chairs, or stones and mountains'. Thiselton takes the concept further when he writes that *Dasein* 'is to be understood in terms of possibility rather than actuality, and also in terms of that individuality whereby "my" existence is always mine'.[43] Heidegger, then, counters the nega-tivism of Nietzsche and his followers with a more affirmative perspective on humanity, a perspective that has carried over into contemporary culture and has thus helped foster an individualism which values both human uniqueness and human otherness.

There are, of course, many other strands within postmodernity's pluralism. Heidegger provides an important philosophical influ-ence on, for example, Michel Foucault's studies of the 'otherness' of mental illness, madness and life in prison and on the works of Emmanuel Levinas, which explore the realms of ethics and morality and reveal the 'real face of postmodernity . . . the face of the other',[44] where the 'Other is, for example, the weak, the poor . . . whereas I am the rich or the powerful'.[45] More broadly, the range of liberation movements – in areas of gender, race, class and the environment – which rose up from the 1960s onwards in the face of the monoliths of State, technology and the war machine, wove their distinctive ethos into the rainbow cloth of contemporary culture. This crossing of social and ecological boundaries has been aided and abetted by the giddying rate of the compression of time and space since the advent of electronic telecommunications. An evening's viewing or surfing in cyberspace can bring the back-streets of Calcutta, the culinary delights of the West Indies, the Brazilian rain forest, an e-mail from Japan or a browse through a library in Sydney, all collapsing into the living-room or study. A visit to the supermarket or the city centre reveals a degree of the same interpenetration of different worlds made up of different customs, languages, beliefs, ways of eating and dressing. 'Hetero-pia', to use Foucault's word, 'where apparently incongruous worlds coexist is our situation.'[46]

As we have already stated, there are two sides to the pluralism of postmodernity: the bright one of a rich diversity and celebration of human otherness; and the dark one of a self-centredness that pulls up the drawbridge against all that is perceived as strange, different, alien. David Harvey sums up the duality of the post-modern when he writes that, on the one hand, 'in its concern for difference, for the difficulties of communication, for the complex-ity and nuances of interests, cultures, places, and the like, it exercises a positive influence'. On the other hand, 'while it opens up a radical prospect by acknowledging the authenticity of other voices, postmodernist thinking immediately shuts off those other voices from access to more universal sources of power by ghet-toizing them within an opaque otherness, the specificity of this or that language game'.[47]

In the face of our overview of modernity and postmodernity, and their often contrary contributions within the complexity of today's societies, let us now consider questions of selfhood within contemporary culture before, finally, examining a Christian pas-toral response to our discussion.

The Contemporary Self

We have already visited certain contemporary notions of the self: in Chapter 1, we examined three psychological pathways to wholeness: self-actualisation, Gestalt and psychosynthesis; in Chapter 2, we looked briefly at self-identity, in the context of narrative and in relation to Louise's story. Keeping in mind the pastoral implications, we now need to assess more closely the nature of the self in relation to the social and cultural influences of 'late' modernity and postmodernity. As we do so, it is important to remember that today's society is a mishmash of modern and postmodern influences, and human selfhood lives amid the ensuing confusion. Just to take one aspect of the self's uncertainties: the modern self is essentially an autonomous being which lives centre-stage; the postmodern self is in a much less self-assured place, since it is de-centred and in danger of fragmentation. Many today are caught in their struggle to live out their lives between holding on to some semblance of premodernity in seeking to maintain elements of traditional morality, securing the rationalism and scientific basis of the modern life, and trying to find a way amid the loss of societal landmarks in the strange and unknown country of postmodernity. Keeping in mind the often contrary psychodynamics of contemporary culture, we can consider the self of today under two main headings: the *consumer self* and the *relating self*.[48]

The Consumer Self

One of the hallmarks of postwar culture in the West, at least for the more privileged in society, has been the increasing opportunity of choice. The range of that choice has varied from one decade to another, depending on the socio-economic climate. In the boom years of the 1960s, for example, school-leaving was commensurate with job-finding and, for many, that shift from the one engagement to the other was the result of at least two or three optional ways forward. In the Thatcherite 1980s, by contrast, the rise in unemployment for the many was accompanied by the rise in remuneration for the few: the 'yuppie' generation had choice at every level – not only in the pickings of privileged work, but whether to wear Armani or Yves St Laurent, whether to buy

Porsche or BMW, or both. And yet, regardless of circumstances, to be human as a 'contemporary self' is to choose; and, although comparatively few have all of life's major options, choice can still be made by most of us in the everyday: which football team to support, which brand of beer to drink, which breakfast cereal to eat, which TV programme to watch, which book to read. The 'consumer self' of today can be considered under two headings: *lifestyle* and *narcissism*.

Lifestyle

Over the twenty-five years that Joy and I have attended Christ Church in Clifton, it has been intriguing to observe the evolution of choice in men's wear at the Sunday services: from Guernseys, through a sequence of striped Breton tops, rather more daring Next for Men jerseys, Norwegian pullovers, Fair Isle designs, plain cotton T-shirts and sweaters, Mid-West check shirts to a recent flush of zipped fleeces. At a superficial level, such gentle gradations of middle-class fashion are an expression of a consumer society which gives attractive choices for those who can afford to respond. At a profounder level, they are part and parcel of an aspect of our humanity, since how we choose to appear in terms of clothes, hairstyle, adornments, accent and inflexion of speech, gestures and general demeanour are a fair approximation of the sort of persons we see ourselves to be, or want to be seen as. Anthony Giddens undergirds this point with reference to the contemporary notion of 'lifestyle':[49]

> We all not only follow lifestyles, but in an important sense are forced to do so – we have no choice but to choose. A lifestyle can be defined as a more or less integrated set of practices which an individual embraces, not only because such practices fulfill utilitarian needs, but because they give material form to a particular narrative of self-identity . . . All such choices . . . are decisions not only about how to act but who to be. The more post-traditional the settings in which an individual moves, the more lifestyle concerns the very core of self-identity, its making and remaking.[50]

As has already been indicated, the 'making and remaking' of self-identity through lifestyle may be an unachievable luxury for the marginalised and dispossessed. Even so, Giddens argues, the habits of lifestyle are also 'constructed through the resistances of ghetto life' and may be 'as strongly affected by globalising influences' in such contexts as in 'more affluent strata'. He cites the example of a black woman who is a single parent and who, in spite of the rigours and restrictions of her life, is still able to be aware of women's struggles generally and who is forced, circumstantially, to make the best of her relationships and friendships. However, the uphill struggle may be too great and the tasks required of her given 'lifestyle' may be 'a source of despair rather than self-enrichment'.[51] As Zygmunt Bauman puts it, in relation to post-modernity's preoccupation with the TV screen, 'To many, reality remains what it always used to be: tough, solid, resistant and harsh. They need to sink their teeth into some quite real bread before they abandon themselves to munching images.'[52]

Narcissism

At the opposite end of such deprivation there is a quite different pastoral dilemma for a number in contemporary society. As we have seen, postmodernity encourages the break from modernist certainty and thus ceases to offer a trustworthy basis for life's choices. For many, a new security is sought in consumerism – a 'society dominated by appearances' – in which people live 'as though surrounded by mirrors', searching 'for the appearance of an unblemished, socially valued self'.[53] Among those preoccupied by image, some will be trapped by a narcissism which lacks 'full engagement with others' and 'depends on continual infusion of admiration and approval to bolster an uncertain sense of self-worth'.[54]

Although the psychoanalytic tradition sees the narcissistic personality as encumbered with a childhood difficulty in acquiring basic trust,[55] certain recent writers suggest a close linkage between the social realities of contemporary culture and the condition. For example, Richard Sennett views the rise in 'narcissist character disorders' as relating to the 'demise of public life', where modern cities are riven by thoroughfares that isolate rather than being the providers of open meeting places; and Christopher Lasch points to the threat of cataclysmic global risks as a key factor in encouraging privatised 'survival strategies' that include a narcissistic consumerism.[56] Giddens concedes that 'modern social life tends in some part to promote' narcissism but, rightly I believe, also stresses the psychological origins of the trait, where the child has been unable to 'separate out its own psychic boundaries'.[57]

For one London-based young woman the journey to a liberation from a restricting maternal voice to carve out her own identity as independent professional, wife and mother has been an uphill struggle against the odds. Even after years of therapy there is a stong gravitational pull back to the low self-esteem, guilt feelings and separation anxieties of childhood and adolescence. The movement from a dependency, dominated by a deeply ingrained attitude that 'mother knows best' and a narcissistic lifestyle which seeks identity through the message, 'Look at my clothes, my beauty; value me', to an interdependence that can say, 'We make our choices and I play my part in those choices, for better or worse' is, perhaps, typical of many who seek to establish 'who they are' in a postmodern, consumerist society.

The Relating Self

The word 'relationship' is a quintessentially post-Enlightenment word. First coined in the mid-eighteenth century as an abstract noun to denote 'The state of being related',[58] it has become, in modern times, one of the most widely used words in personal communication, often indicating a more concrete use of the term, as in 'Do you have a relationship?' The multiplicity of choices presented by high modernity and postmodernity inevitably invades the world of human relating as well as that of lifestyle or, in other words, to use Giddens' phrase, 'the project of the self' faces a host of options in life-planning, including not only what to wear and what to eat but who to be with. With regard to the relational dilemmas of the contemporary self we can consider two perspectives: the *pure relationship* and the *privatisation of passion*.

The Pure Relationship

During the mid-1970s, while preparing for a range of talks I had been asked to give on sexuality, marriage and family life, I came across Nena and George O'Neill's *Open Marriage*, already proving to be a bestseller in the United States. This book advocated a style of married relationship which I was already meeting in the young adults that I counselled in the student health service of the University of Bristol, where I had been working since 1969. The

O'Neills challenged the traditional, premodern 'closed' marriage, with its exclusivity and sexual faithfulness, and put forward the model of 'open' marriage, marked by companionship, honest communication and an openness to develop further relationships, 'with or without sex'.[59] This book, of course, was perfectly in accord with modernity's opening up of choice, and concurrent undermining of traditional morality. At the same time it did a great deal to discard the sexism and inequalities of many conventional marriages. Inevitably, its 'openendedness' loosened the marital ties for some: the 'separate persons' of the 'one flesh: separate persons'[60] of marriage became as enticing in its inclusivity as the 'one flesh' of many past marriages had become bound, rejoicingly or otherwise, to their exclusivity. One female postgraduate of the early 1970s had, in this sense, become thoroughly modern when she came to my consulting room on a medical matter and declared, 'We are getting so close in our marriage that we have decided to separate, as our individuality is being threatened.' She came to see me next a year later, sad and depressed in her loneliness and the knowledge that her husband was living with another woman.

Anthony Giddens's notion of the 'pure relationship' arises within his carefully analysed critique of the contemporary condition. The moorings of the traditional social context have been slipped and so the pure relationship is, 'as it were, free-floating', its 'purity' resting in its single-minded quest 'for what the relationship can bring to the partners involved'. Since the relationship – which may be that of friendship, marriage or a sexual liaison outside wedlock – is not held by society's conventions, and is thus more readily threatened by adversity, it is not easy for those involved to 'coast along'.[61] True to high modernity's reflexive style, and nudged continually by magazine articles and programmes on the television and radio, there is a tendency for a running self-questioning: 'How am I doing?', 'Am I meeting his/her needs?' 'Is he/she meeting mine?' 'Will it all work out?' Within the agonisings and uncertainties, the pure relationship can only be mutually satisfying and fulfilling, Giddens argues, where there is 'the development of trust based on voluntary commitments and an intensified intimacy', a trust that is 'psychologically stabilising' since it reinforces the 'basic trust' of childhood and the reliability of 'caretaking figures'.[62] The fragility of this untethered relating is acknowledged by Giddens:

The pure relationship contains internal tensions and even contradictions. By definition, it is a social relation which can be terminated at will, and is only sustained in so far as it generates sufficient psychic returns for each individual . . . The possibility of dissolution . . . forms part of the very horizon of commitment. It is not surprising that rage, anger and depressive feelings swirl through the contexts of pure relationships and . . . intimacy may be psychically more troubling than it is rewarding.[63]

The Privatisation of Passion

Another aspect of the relating self of modernity is that of the 'privatisation of passion'.[64] The word 'passion' (from the Latin *passio*, suffering), linked anciently with the sufferings of Christ and Christian martyrs, has changed radically in its meaning through the centuries. In the medieval period its connotations were essentially in the expression of religious fervour, from Tudor times its use spread to that of any overpowering emotion and, since the seventeenth century, its meanings include that of 'sexual desire or impulse'.[65] As Giddens puts it, the notion of passion has become 'secularised and confined mainly to the sexual sphere', leading to the separation of 'sexuality' from 'the more general and diffuse eroticism' of the past.[66] Passion is for the privacy of the bedroom rather than the place of public worship.

This privatisation of passion and sexuality is seen by Giddens, along with the search for 'pure relationship', as part of 'the reflexive project of the self'. Once sexuality, in the modern sense of the word, 'went behind the scenes', it 'became a property of the individual, and more specifically, the body'. Here, Giddens argues, the eroticism of premodernity, with its attendant gravitation toward guilt, is replaced by 'an association of sexuality and self-identity and the propensity to shame'.[67] In other words, the modern self has, not least in the area of sex, been cut off from guilt, deriving from 'feelings of wrongdoing', and is more prone to shame, which 'depends on feelings of personal insufficiency'.[68] An awareness of culpability before a holy God, a court of law or an offended fellow-citizen is replaced by a sense of inner disgrace before the reflexive self. And this sense of shame works against the pure relationship, since it 'eats at the roots of trust more corrosively than guilt, because shame is involved in a fundamental way with the fear of abandonmemt in infancy'.[69]

We can see something of the powerful psychological and social forces at work in the quest for the 'pure relationship' and the attendant 'privatisation of passion' in the agonised words of this woman who sought emotional closeness:

> I have a constant feeling of never being satisfied for some reason. Either he's not calling, or when he's calling, it's not romantic, and so on . . . I've been so scared all the way, thinking to myself, no matter what happened, giving him the benefit of the doubt, 'Let me trust, let me trust,' . . . I've always been so afraid, wondering, 'Will somebody stay?'[70]

The deep longing expressed by this woman for a relationship that not only feels right but offers continuity and security is typical of the dilemmas of the contemporary self. As we have seen, the self may be self-regarding, eaten up by naricissism or shame, or it may be reaching out, celebrating its latest lifestyle, searching perhaps for private passion in a 'pure relationship'. Either way, whether the drama of life is seen in tragic, melodramatic, comic or farcical terms, the modern self is centre-stage. Men and women who are truly modern can thus be depicted as standing in the spotlight of their own self-reflection, independent spirits who, whether they struggle with low self-esteem and frustration or celebrate a sense of well-being and achievement, at least anticipate a future: whether tragedy or comedy, the play must go on. As we have seen, the ground is kicked from under the feet of this stance of optimism or wishful thinking by the inroads of postmodernity.

God and Contemporary Culture

In the face of a culture where the 'solidities' of modernist self-confidence are continually melting into the thin air of post-modernity's dalliance with 'hyperreality', and where consumer-ism and the restless search for the 'pure relationship' are the hallmarks of the contemporary self, what hope, if any, can be offered to and through the storied, journeying people of God? We have seen, in the writings of H. Richard Niebuhr and Charles Kraft, viewpoints toward culture which encourage the possibility of a godly transformation of its structures and attitudes. At the same time, of course, we may need reminding that the Church is inevitably part of culture. Christianity, in all its forms, cannot function in a vacuum – whether in the Graeco-Roman world of the first century or in the globalised postmodernity of the twenty-first century. And the reality of enculturation[71] applies, not least, to the calling of Christian pastoral care. As William Clebsch and Charles Jaekle state, 'Pastoral care has always utilized current psychologies'[72] and the psychological insights of each culture are part of the 'given' of the societal environment which needs to be weighed in the balance of Christian appraisal and used, or not used, accordingly.[73] Examples of this process can be seen in the influence of Greek Stoicism on John Chrysostom in Constantinople in the fourth century, of Aristotle's understanding of humanity on Thomas Aquinas in the thirteenth, and the powerful emphasis on reason and will on post-Enlightenment pastors like John Keble in the nineteenth. But how might pathways to wholeness fare in the cultural milieu of the world of high modernity and postmodernity at the dawning of a new millennium? Let us seek to address this question under two headings: 'back to the future?' and a 'theology of hope'.

Back to the Future?

One of postmodernity's ubiquitous features is a 'pick-and-mix' attitude to the past, shown, for example, in the pastiche of much contemporary architecture and in the arbitrary selectiveness of many a theme park and museum, where history is plundered and paraded as 'heritage'. In the face of postmodernity's tokenism toward its roots it is no surprise that solutions to contemporary cultural blind alleys are sought in the past. Among those who advocate such a 'back to the future' approach, the social scientist Jürgen Habermas and the moral philosopher Alasdair MacIntyre offer distinctive agendas.[74]

For Habermas the key to society's needs lies in the recovery of modernity as an 'unfinished project'.[75] He traces the seeds of ruin in Western civilisation back to the crossroads in post-Enlightenment thinking at the time of Georg Wilhelm Friedrich Hegel (1770–1831), the first philosopher 'for whom modernity became a problem'.[76] Habermas seeks to recover the elements of 'an undamaged intersubjectivity that the young Hegel first projected as an ethical totality'[77] as a corrective to modernist individualism's tendency to pick and choose its way through life.[78] Thus, Habermas aims to re-establish a communal spirit and socio-political responsibility for contemporary living.

MacIntyre takes the search for lost foundations even further back in time. Whereas Habermas wants to rescue postmodernity through a return to early modernity, MacIntyre delves deep into premodernity to rediscover a moral tradition that predates Christianity. Taking the long-neglected concept of the 'virtues' from the writings of Aristotle and Homeric poetry,[79] he reminds today's society of a world where courage and friendship were valued and commitment to kith and kin was woven into the fabric of civilisation. As he puts it, 'morality and social factors are in fact one and the same in heroic society'.[80] At the conclusion of his seminal work *After Virtue*, MacIntyre reminds his readers that, just as the Dark Ages which followed the collapse of the Roman Empire were in some measure redeemed by the call to community in the early monastic movement, so there is a modicum of hope in contemporary culture, in which 'the barbarians are not waiting beyond the frontiers; they have already been governing us for quite some time'. That hope, he concludes, is not in 'waiting for Godot', a symbol of postmodern passivity in a meaningless universe, but in an expectancy for 'another – doubtless very different – St Benedict',[81] one who can bring communal responsibility into the quest for 'the human good'.

A Theology of Hope

Can we, though, rescue the culture of today by a journey 'back to the future'? Can we 'recover the lost innocence which characterized the self of modernity, let alone that of the pre-modern'?[82] More fully, are the optimism of modernity and the moralism of premodernity sufficient to gainsay the pessimism and amorality of postmodernity? Many would argue that neither the heady wine of modernist 'Progress' nor the darker brew of postmodernist 'Nihilism' can be remedied by simply putting the clock back. A new potion is needed, one that will revive contemporary culture by a new realism which engages both a remembered past and a promised future.

As we saw in the last chapter, the Christian Church has just such a calling in its need to recover both 'story' and 'journey' for its people and for the wider community. In the context of postmodernity, Brueggemann writes:

The task of reframing, which addresses the extremities of our life, works at two awesome tasks. On the one hand, by *supplanting amnesia with memory*, it gives back to the congregation the forgotten past. On the other hand, by *supplanting despair with hope*, it gives back to the congregation its future.[83]

In the face of postmodernity's obsession with 'the wager on the immortality of the present',[84] in which any notions of historical continuity and life beyond the grave are denied, the need for such a *theology of hope* is all the more pressing.

If we pursue Keith Tester's analogies between the more purposeful journeying of modernity and the ancient concept of pilgrimage, and the loss of a sense of linear time in postmodernity and the restless condition of nomads, we have a useful picture for the recovery of hope and promise in today's society. On closer scrutiny, both the modern and the postmodern are found wanting. As Tester puts it, 'the tragedy . . . of the modern was . . . the impossibility of the achievement of the future', since modernity was 'too busy carrying out projects of constuction and deconstruction'.[85] Conversely, with the rejection of metanarratives and their propensity to make sense of history, the postmodern 'nomads' are 'stuck in an inescapable present'.[86] Modernist pilgrims are too busy with their map-making to engage the territory of the future: postmodern nomads are lost in a featureless desert without map or compass. A Christian theology of hope seeks to address both groups: offering a sense of a redeemed past and an assured future to the nomadic condition of postmodernity; and inviting the modern into a truer pilgrimage where the arrogance of human autonomy gives way to a celebration of life 'in the image of God'.

Jürgen Moltmann,[87] long recognised as one of the main contributors to a theology of hope, argues that 'the sin of unbelief is manifestly grounded in hopelessness' and that hopelessness can be expressed in two forms: a 'presumption' which is 'a premature, selfwilled anticipation of the fulfilment of what we hope for from God'; and a 'despair' which is 'the premature, arbitrary anticipation of the non-fulfilment of what we hope for from God'. It can be said that these two manifestations of contemporary hopelessness echo, respectively, the wilfulness of the autonomous modern and the rootlessness of the nihilistic postmodern. Cancelling the 'wayfaring character of hope', these presumptive and despairing attitudes 'demand impatiently either fulfilment "now already" or "absolutely no" hope'.[88] Moltmann concludes that in neither attitude lies 'the power to renew life, but only in the hope that is enduring and sure'.[89]

This 'enduring and sure' hope is caught up with the concept of eschatology, traditionally summed up as the 'doctrine of the last things', including the second coming of Christ in glory, the resurrection of the dead, the final judgment and the renewal of the created order. Moltmann, however, points out the danger of relegating eschatology to an apparently distant future, 'like a loosely attached appendix that wandered off into obscure irrelevancies.' He rightly emphasises that a healthful understanding of the 'last things' must include their engagement with the 'here and now': 'From first to last . . . Christianity is eschatology, is hope, forward looking and forward moving, and therefore also revolutionizing and transforming the present.'[90] And this living today in the light of tomorrow is, in Moltmann's theology, profoundly christocentric and all-embracing. The once-incarnated, crucified, risen Lord has made, and continues to make, his journey into the future, and this demonstration and realisation of the 'way' demands a theology of hope that is grounded in life's everyday socio-political and environmental realities:

> To believe means to cross in hope and anticipation the bounds that have been penetrated by the raising of the crucified. If we bear that in mind, then this faith can have nothing to do with fleeing the world, with resignation and with escapism . . . It sees in the resurrection of Christ not the eternity of heaven, but the future of the very humanity for which he died. That is why it finds the cross the hope of the earth. This hope . . . espouses in all meekness the cause of the devastated earth and harrassed humanity, because it is permitted possession of the earth.[91]

Moltmann's theology of hope is, moreover, ideally suited to the needs of the contemporary self. The self of high modernity and postmodernity is, as we have seen, caught up in a state of flux somewhere between an individualism and subjectivism that still anticipates progress in life – whether as part of the 'big picture' of the technological revolution or in the daily search for 'privatised passion' within the 'pure relationship' – and a Nietzschean fragmentation of meaning and significance. Within the transition between these two states of hopelessness – presumptive and despairing respectively – Anthony Thiselton argues that the post-modern self 'has greater realism than the illusory optimism of the self of modernity about human nature and society' and yet it 'can find hope only in the context of a theology of promise'.[92] Even so, without the new realism of Christian hope, the postmodern self readily slides from its 'greater realism' about 'human nature and society' into a decline toward paranoia, cynicism and nihilism. Thiselton contrasts the residual hopefulness of modernity with the blame-giving stance of the postmodern, a 'contrast between a courageous or accepting "That's Life"' in the former and 'an accusatory "It's Them"' in the latter.[93]

Christian hope includes both 'the act of hoping' and 'the idea of the object hoped for'.[94] It is profoundly linked with the trinitarian nature of God: he is described as 'the God of hope' (Rom. 15:13); Jesus Christ is declared to be 'our hope' (1 Tim. 1:1); and the power of the Holy Spirit is the means whereby the believer 'may overflow with hope' (Rom. 15:13). The expectations of hope – including salvation, resurrection and eternal life – are summed up in the Pauline phrase, 'Christ in you, the hope of glory' (Col. 1:27). As we have seen in Moltmann, Christ is both guarantee of an assured future and ever present in his people to engage with his much-loved and needy world in the 'here and now'.

And yet the genius of a Christian theology of hope is not in an over-confident certainty that borders on an arrogance toward contemporary culture. The shoulder-shrugging 'That's Life' of the autonomous modern self or the finger-pointing 'It's Them' of the rootless postmodern self can only be drawn to the Christ who is 'the hope of glory' by an approach that listens as well as speaks, suffers with as well as celebrates, receives as well as gives. Moltmann urges on us theological concepts that 'do not give a fixed form to reality' but are, rather, 'expanded by hope and anticipate future being'. This attitude of a hopefulness which is confident without being inflexible is 'grounded not in the will to dominate, but in love to the future of things'.[95] Perhaps the key to commending the God of hope in the contexts of modernity's belief in its own maps and postmodernity's unmappable world of the 'hyperreal' is to remember that Christian hope is classically inseparable from faith and love, where faith 'hopes in order to know what it believes' and where 'the believing hope will itself provide inexhaustible resources for the creative, inventive imagination of love'.[96]

In conclusion, as we take our bearings in a culture whose landscape is both inviting and bewildering, let us take heart as a pilgrim people who follow the 'God of hope'. There is promise of a 'new heaven and a new earth', the territory is to be redeemed as succeeding cultures come and go, each to be challenged and transformed by the Lord of all. And there is ample provision for the journey. Isaiah 40 uses two metaphors which cut human society down to size: our existence is likened to the transience of wild grass and the mindlessness of domestic sheep! And yet the metaphors are not to demote our humanity but to remind us of our vulnerability and our need to trust. Two declarations assure us for the pathways ahead: "Here is your God!" and 'the word of our God will stand for ever' (Isa. 40:8–9). These confident claims provide the backdrop of our next chapter as we consider the question of our understanding and interpretation of the guiding texts and principles of our pastoral journey.

4

PATHWAYS INTERPRETED: HERMENEUTICS OF THE TEXT

Every child arrives at the meaning of a word only through hermeneutics.
Friedrich Schleiermacher[1]

Contemporary society is in many ways a 'Culture of Interpretation'.[2] Much of life today is spent in trying to understand the world we live in, offering this or that way of seeing things, challenging the views and conclusions of others, both trusting and doubting the so-called 'experts'. We are so bombarded by messages and images which vie to inform, educate and influence that we are spoilt for choice. And this freedom to choose is both a blessing and a bane: it both liberates and paralyses – not only can many of us enjoy the luxury of deliberating over what to wear for a wedding, which car to buy and where to go on holiday, we may also be gripped by uncertainty through conflicting advice about where to send our children to school, which insurance policies to take out and what treatment or therapy to adopt when we are ill or need counsel. How are we to make right choices – not only in everyday matters but in life's big decisions? In other words, how are we to read the signs in a world of transition between the self-assured claims of the modernist *cognoscenti* and the multiple voices of postmodernity, where every pathway can beguile with its own unique brand of reality? To be more specific, in the context of the pastoral calling in a 'high' modern and postmodern age, how are we to engage with the task of interpreting both the Judaeo-Christian texts and the lives of those who seek help? Before examining these questions more fully, I would like to illustrate some of the features of contemporary interpretation, or hermeneutics, in the light of a quintessentially postmodern novel, Julian Barnes's *A History of the World in 10½ Chapters*.[3]

It has been said that the postmodern novel moves away from

the 'complex but nevertheless singular reality' of modernist imaginative writing to a consideration 'as to how radically different
realities may coexist, collide, and interpenetrate'.⁴ We see this
'pluralism' of 'radically different realities' in Barnes's book where
a series of seemingly unconnected cameos of human history is laid
out in apparently haphazard fashion. I say 'seemingly unconnected' since the common thread of traditional and modernist
literature – the human condition – is cleverly de-centred by
bringing in the unlikeliest of creatures – the lowly woodworm
– as a recurring, at times consequential, at times inconsequential,
motif. The triumph of this humblest of God's creatures over the
pride and vanity of humankind is told with consummate ironic
skill in Chapter 3, 'The Wars of Religion'. Here the might of the
sixteenth-century Church in rural France is brought down by the
unseen woody mastications of an army of these 'diabolic bestioles'
who had the audacity to make the much revered throne of the
Bishop of Besançon into their dwelling-place. The throne was
hoisted into the church rafters 'lest any child or stranger might
by chance sit on it and thereby profane it' and only lowered into
the sanctuary on the occasion of the Bishop's annual pilgrimage. In
the year 1520 the customs of that pilgrimage were carried out, as
ever, to the letter. Having blessed the local villagers from the step
of the church, duly processed up the nave, followed 'at subservient distance by his flock', and prostrated himself before the altar,
the richly apparelled Hugo, the current Bishop, 'lowered himself
upon his throne'. It was then that tragedy struck, for the throne
collapsed and the Bishop fell, 'striking his head upon the altar step
and being hurled against his will into a state of imbecility'. Later,
to their horror, the 'terrified petitioners' examined the Bishop's
throne and found in the collapsed leg 'a vile and unnatural
infestation of woodworm'. The roof was duly examined and
discovered to be riddled by the workings of these miscreants.

It is in the subsequent court case concerning the activities of the
bestioles, and yet carried out in the absence of the malefactors, that
the learned doctors of the Church engage with the hermeneutics of
the Scriptures. Bartholomé Chassenée, the procurator for the
defence, looks to the first chapter of Genesis to demonstrate the
innocence of the tiny creatures in relation to a God who not only
saw that his creation was good but who beneficently provided for
'every creeping thing' food, including 'every tree upon the face of
the earth', and who summoned those same creeping things to be

'fruitful and multiply and replenish the earth'. He asks, 'What have these humble *bestioles* done since the day of Creation but exercise the inalienable rights conferred on them at that time, rights which Man has no power to curtail or abrogate?' Cleverly, he turns the tables on the petitioners who have brought the case against these humblest of animals, which are simply living out their creation ordinance, by challenging their sinful judgmentalism: 'Cast out the beam from your own eye before you seek to extract the mote from the eye of another.'

The lawyer representing the aggrieved inhabitants of the village also implicates Scripture, but this time it is to question Chassenée's demotion of humanity's juridical rights in the face of invertebrate innocence. He asks, 'Is it not clear from the holy book of Genesis that the animals which were created before man, were so created in order to be subservient to his use?' Referring to Exodus, the Psalmist and the apostle Paul to support his view of human superiority, he seeks to clinch his argument by returning to the first chapter of Genesis, aiming to show the lack of hermeneutical scruple in the reasoning of the defence lawyer. Although he concedes that God 'gave the trees unto those creatures which have the instinct to devour trees', he triumphantly declares that the Lord did not give those selfsame creatures 'the cut wood'. His concluding rhetorical questions seem irrefutable:

Did the Lord intend when He permitted a creature to burrow within the oak tree that the same creature had the right to burrow within the House of the Lord? . . . And does the Lord instruct His servants to pass by on the other side while His temples are devoured and His Bishops reduced to a state of imbecility?[5]

If this deliciously ironic court scene can serve to remind us of the subjectivism and special pleading we often bring to the 'hermeneutic of the text', elsewhere in Barnes' novel we see the linked challenge of the 'hermeneutic of the life'. The novel abounds in the interpretative ambiguities of human lives, frequently staged in maritime settings where they are 'all at sea', ranging from the uncertainties surrounding the fates of the shipwrecked men in Géricault's painting *The Raft of the Medusa* to the day-dreams and nightmares of Kathleen Ferris, deserted by a sexist partner and adrift with her two cats on a poisoned ocean. It is in the retelling of the story of Noah's ark, with which the book opens, that we can see a particularly clear link between the hermeneutics of text and life. That link is, of course, inevitable in such a life as Noah's since we have no more direct access to him than through text, aided and abetted by an oral tradition. Even so, Barnes's whimsical revisionism offers us a potential example for a pastoral hermeneutic.

An articulate woodworm, one of seven such stowaways on board the Ark, provides an alternative account of Noah's voyage and, indeed, his character. This account can be trusted, unlike the 'much repeated version' of the human species, and is reinforced by the animals, which, unlike the lowly woodworms, were *chosen* and can thus confidently trace their ancestry back to the Ark. In the woodworm's reality the 'Ark' was a whole flotilla of ships, since a much greater capacity was needed for the entire animal kingdom than could be provided by 'something a mere three hundred cubits long'; the duration of the Deluge was 'about a year and a half', rather than the forty days and forty nights of the Genesis narrative; and the Flood lasted for 'about four years' and not the hundred and fifty days of the traditional account.[6] The most hard-hitting of the woodworm's deconstruction of the familiar story, though, is in the description of Noah himself. Instead of the picture of this patriarch as 'a righteous man, blameless among the people', the invertebrate view is that 'Noah was not a nice man'; he was given to bullying his living cargo with his gopher-wood stave and, along with his family, treated the animals as a 'floating cafeteria', thus depriving posterity of many strange and beautiful creatures.[7] The woodworm's account of reality concludes by drawing the reader's attention to the apparent inconsistency in the traditional story between the godly, blameless Noah of Genesis 6–8 and the inebriated, son-cursing Noah of Genesis 9:18–25. Rather than allowing Noah a very human lapse, not rare after imbibing new wine, the woodworm points out that 'Old Noah had always enjoyed a few horns of fermented liquor in the days before Embarkation' and that his many mishandlings of his fleet of ships 'turned him into a soak'. And even though biblical scholars might try to explain away 'the drunkenness, the indecency, the capricious punishment of a dutiful son' as the behaviour of a different Noah from the perceived hero of the voyage, the woodworm knows that the two Noahs are one and the same – a 'depressing yet predictable case of alcoholic degeneration'.[8]

Although not wanting to draw profound conclusions about the handling of the biblical text from Barnes's postmodern excursion into the Old Testament, it seems to me that the woodworm's version of narrative and character serves to illustrate both the seductiveness and challenge of the hermeneutical enterprise. In seeking to interpret the words of Scripture or the life-stories of those who receive pastoral care, we need to avoid both the traditional temptation to read into the text and life only what is seen to be acceptable (Noah as the godly man who could do no wrong) and the postmodern woodworm's temptation to read into the text and life such alternative views that elevate the neglected parts to the point of universalisation (Noah has always been a sad case).

Let us now look more fully at the contemporary challenge to a faithful reading of both the text and the life, keeping in mind the context of responsible pastoral care and heeding the warnings of Barnes's *bestioles*. We will consider the 'hermenetics of the text' in this chapter and the 'hermeneutics of the life' in Chapter 5.

Interpreting the Text

Although today we live in a 'culture of interpretation' and the study of 'hermeneutics' as a discipline dates primarily from the seventeenth and eighteenth centuries, human beings have always been interpretive creatures, trying to make sense of the world around them. In ancient Greek civilisation it was the messenger Hermes who plied to and fro between the gods and mortals, bringing divine judgments on the ways of humankind, and in early Judaism the term *midrash*, meaning 'interpretation and narrative', paralleled the Greek useage of *hermeneia* for 'communication', 'translation' and 'interpretation'.[9] Jesus himself, on the road to Emmaus with the unnamed two disciples, exercised an interpretive 'hermeneutics' when, 'beginning with Moses and all the Prophets, he explained (*diermeneusen*) to them what was said in all the Scriptures concerning himself' (Luke 24:27). For Paul the apostle, according to Ulrich Luz, 'the Old Testament is not in the first place something to understand; but *it itself creates understanding*'.[10] In his use of a hundred or so references to the Jewish Scriptures, mainly in Romans, 1 and 2 Corinthians and Galatians, Paul taps into a tradition 'which is the basis for understanding what God has now done in Christ "when the time had fully come" (Gal. 4:4)'.[11]

In order to gain an appreciation of today's hermeneutical context for pastoral care, I propose we examine an outline of the history of biblical interpretation, following the broad subdivisions of premodernity, modernity and postmodernity which we used in the previous chapter.

Premodern Biblical Interpretation

As we have seen, premodernity is characterised by a widespread belief in an ordered universe where life's patterns and hierarchies are laid down and human conduct for the perceived good of family, village, town or country is ruled over by divine providence. Not least within the Christian tradition of the West, providential justice and mercy are declared and mediated by the Church in its handling of the holy Scriptures. The people, whether directly or through the ministrations of monk or priest, are the people of the Book. Let us consider the span of premodern interpretation of that Book in two main sections: the *early and medieval Church*; and the *Reformation*.

The Early and Medieval Church

Although Roger Lundin sees the hermeneutics of the classical and Christian worlds as a practice which involves 'the effort to translate what was taken to be a divine, authoritative word into language that would have power and relevance for a particular community',[12] it would be a mistake to see premodern bibical interpretation as 'all of a piece'. Both the early and medieval Church, as well as the New Testament, adopt a range of hermeneutical methods to translate the 'divine, authoritative word' into language which speaks clearly into communal life. Broadly, the tradition divides into two main streams: the contemplative *lectio divina*, or 'spiritual reading'; and the more rigorous approach of 'exegesis', which seeks to 'come to an accurate historical understanding of the point that the scriptural text in its own right makes'.[13] Gillian Evans illustrates these very different trends in the approaches of Rupert of Deutz (1070–c.1129) and Anselm of Canterbury (1033–1109) respectively, where Rupert pursues an 'aesthetic satisfaction in Scripture which is inseparable from spiritual understanding'[14] and Anselm is committed to an exegetical study in order to establish doctrinal clarity, a style summed up in the Augustinian phrase 'faith seeking understanding'. And yet, as Anthony Thiselton points out, these two 'levels' of a biblical hermeneutic are closely allied in that Anselm is one of those who help shape the conceptual framework within which the alternative contemplative tradition can function.[15] In other words, 'spiritual reading' can be likened to the enjoyment of a delectable view whose boundaries are clearly defined by the well-constructed window frame of Christan orthodoxy. We shall find both these aspects of interpretation clearly represented in the pastoral methodologies described in Part II of this book.

More comprehensively, the broad traditions of the 'spiritual' and 'doctrinal' readings of the Bible can be summed up within the fourfold schema used by Augustine of Hippo (354–430), formulated by Gregory the Great (c.540–604) and dominating medieval hermeneutics up to the time of Luther: (i) *the literal meaning* which 'arises from the historical situation and context of the text'; (ii) *the allegorical interpretation*; (iii) *the moral meaning* which 'embodies a practical application for present conduct'; and (iv) *the anagogical meaning* which 'embraces the horizon of the future consummation'.[16] This interpretive grid is, for the premodern Christian, enlivened by the illuminating work of the Holy Spirit. Origen (c.186–254), for example, continues the biblical tradition that the Spirit both inspires the text and renders it effective in the lives of believers: without that Spirit, 'the words remain only "earthen vessels"'.[17]

Augustine's handling of Scripture can be taken as representative of this pre-Reformation style of hermeneutics. Whichever of the four strands he pursues he sees the use of the Bible in terms of 'the enjoyment of God' – Father, Son and Holy Spirit.[18] Within this relational, God-centred approach he follows the established Patristic tradition of the figural understanding of the text, in which 'allegory' and 'typology' are seen as legitimate ways of interpretation.[19] The precise definition of these terms is disputed, but, broadly, according to Thiselton, typology 'represents a parallel, analogy, or correspondence between two or more *historical events*; whereas allegory represents an extension of meaning in terms of parallels, analogies or correspondences between two or more *ideas*'.[20]

We can see examples of typological approaches in some Pauline statements as when, for instance, in Galatians 4:24–6, he refers to Genesis 16:15 and 21:2 to show a correspondence between, on the one hand, the inheritance of the bond-woman Hagar and the enslaved 'present city of Jerusalem', and, on the other, that of the free woman Sarah and 'the Jerusalem that is above' which is also free.[21] Here Paul does not lose sight of the historical dimension in both Old and New Testaments. In contrast, Augustine produces, in, for example the story of the Good Samaritan, analogies which are fully allegorical in that there is an 'extension of meaning' between a range of ideas. Here, the 'certain man' is seen as Adam; Jerusalem is the 'heavenly city of peace'; Jericho represents our mortality; the thieves are the devil 'and his angels'; and the 'half-dead' condition of the man indicates that he is 'subject to life in knowing God' and 'subject to death through sin'.[22] In his use of allegory Augustine seeks to follow a hermeneutical rule whose priority is the love of God and neighbour: 'To carefully turn over in our minds and meditate upon what we read till an interpretation be found that tends to establish the reign of love.'[23]

The Reformation

Hans Frei argues that the 'literal and historical reading' of Scripture found in premodernity has never been wholly lost in Western Christendom and, indeed, that it discovered a new impetus during the Reformation, when it was established as 'the regnant mode of biblical reading'.[24] Martin Luther (1483–1546) and John Calvin (1509–64) stand out as cardinal representives of a reforming mode of interpretation which, although following the broad principles of the earlier understandings of the Bible, nonetheless laid down distinctive ground rules for a simplified hermeneutics. Differences between them are matters of emphasis rather than essence.

It is perhaps the doctrine of 'perspicuity of Scripture' (claritas scripturae) that most distinguishes the interpretive style of the Reformers. In the context of Erasmus's claim that the biblical text is insufficiently clear to warrant human certainty, Luther exclaims that it is 'a shameless blasphemy that the Scriptures are obscure . . . Those who deny the perfect clarity and plainness of the Scriptures leave us nothing but darkness . . . I would say in the whole of Scripture that I do not allow any part of it to be called obscure.'[25]

Within this debate, it can be said that Erasmus (c.1469–1536), in playing down 'the literal, contextual, or historical meaning of the text', leans more to 'the spiritual or allegorical', appealing to the Bible's ' "hidden" wisdom':[26] where Erasmus follows the strand of interpretation typified by Rupert of Deutz, Luther stands squarely within the tradition of Anselm of Canterbury. Further, although Luther kept to the fourfold scheme of medieval interpretation in his earlier years as a monk and allegorised 'everything',[27] he later, pursuing the 'plain' or 'natural' meaning of Scripture, declares of analogies and allegories: 'I know they are nothing but rubbish.'[28] Even so, the mature Luther did allow the allegorical to have a place in biblical interpretation, but only to serve as illustration for what can be established elsewhere in the text.[29]

As well as a commitment to the perspicuity of the Scriptures and an aversion to the too-ready usage of allegory, Luther and Calvin also hold to a view that Christ is the central subject of the entire Bible. For Luther the presence of Christ is pervasive throughout the text: 'Take Christ from the Scriptures, and what more will you find in them?';[30] whereas for Calvin, as Frei points out, 'not all texts referred either directly or indirectly to Christ, but by and large the Old Testament either predicted or else prefigured Christ and the salvation . . . he was to institute'.[31] Either way, both Reformers declare an interpretive approach wherein the reader, guided by the Holy Spirit, engages with the living God. As Luther sees it, 'the word of God always comes as *adversarius noster*, our adversary'[32] and such an encounter cannot leave the faithful reader unmoved or unchanged. Similarly, for Calvin the Bible 'communicates and informs' so that scriptural interpretation involves a two-way traffic between the words of Scripture and the lives of those exposed to their challenge. As Frei writes of Calvin's hermeneutical stance:

> The reader, not the text, is to be illumined by the internal or inspiring testimony of the Spirit so that he may discern the written biblical word to be God's own Word, intended for his own and the Church's edification. The text is God's Word in its own right and communicates the truth quite clearly.[33]

We will return to this Christ-centred, Spirit-inspired and exegetical tradition when we consider 'biblical counselling' in Chapter 7.

Modern Biblical Interpretation

Although we have used the term 'hermeneutics' interchangeably with 'interpretation' in our discussion of the premodern Bible, it was not till the eighteenth century that hermeneutics as a discipline of study was fully established. There were earlier explicit uses of the term[34] but the 'hermeneutics of enquiry', to use Thiselton's phrase to describe Lutheran and Calvinistic interpretation, gradually gave way to the broader concept of 'general' biblical hermeneutics. This process, egged on by Enlightenment rationalism and autonomous individualism, witnessed the steady erosion of the Reformers' approach to Scripture, where historic event, literal meaning, coherent narrative and practical application as a unified whole began to crumble.

One of the prime movers in this incipient collapse is seen to be the radical Dutch thinker Benedict de Spinoza (1634–77) whose *Tractatus Theologico-Politicus* (1670) represents the Cartesian shift toward elevating human reasoning over notions of reliable divine revelation. He writes that Scripture 'speaks inaccurately of God and of events, seeing that its object is not to convince the reason, but to attract and lay hold on the imagination'. Here, the historical veracity and God-given trustworthiness of the Bible give way before a functionalism which seeks simply 'to move men and', Spinoza adds, 'especially uneducated men, to devotion'. The word of God as 'our adversary', to use Luther's phrase, is disengaged from historic reality and offered as a mere aid for, in today's terms, 'mentally challenged' piety.[35] Thus we see the beginnings of an expansion of the study of hermeneutics to embrace the viewpoint of the *interpreter* – whether sceptical or orthodox – as well as the text's original historical setting. As Thiselton puts it, 'hermeneutics in the more recent sense of the term begins with the recognition that historical conditioning is two-sided: *the modern interpreter, no less than the text, stands in a given historical context and tradition*'.[36]

We can trace the consequences of this wider emphasis in the unfolding story of the hermeneutics of modernity under two headings: the *historical-critical method*; and the *hermeneutics of understanding*.

The Historical-Critical Method

Even though, as we have already said, the 'literal and historical' reading of Scripture has never been wholly lost in Western Christianity, certain elements in post-Reformation Protestantism developed the residual strand of a more subjective approach to the interpretation of the text, which we saw, for example, in the medieval hermeneutics of Rupert of Deutz. Counted among these are some of the later German pietists who, although in the Lutheran tradition and affirmative toward a literal and grammatical understanding of the Bible, nevertheless sought 'higher' layers of meaning within the text. Jacob Rambach (1693–1735), a follower of the pioneering pietist August Hermann Francke (1663–1727),[37] was a hermeneutician who pursued such an approach, arguing for both a scholarly commitment to God's Word and an openness to the Holy Spirit's enabling in order to discern a 'spiritual sense' over and above the text's more self-evident meaning. The influence of Rambach and others led to a handling of Scripture wherein an 'expanded force' or 'emphasis' pertained to the text's individual words, 'so that they have as much meaning and resonance attributed to them as they can possibly bear'.[38] This twin post-Reformation route of a continuing tendency to a literalistic use of the Scriptures, on the one hand, and an attitude which sought supercharged layers of special 'emphasis' in the text, on the other, is a trend still visible today in the more fundamentalist branches of, say, 'biblical counselling' and in the more untethered examples of some 'inner healing' approaches.

According to Frei, modern theology can be seen to have its roots in English Deism at the turn from the seventeenth to the eighteenth century.[39] Although the earlier Deists clung to a 'two-storey' view of Christianity,[40] where the 'ground floor' was occupied by an everyday rationalism and the 'upper floor' by the domain of a faith that held on to such 'unprovable' concepts as the Trinity and salvation in Christ, later proponents moved toward a greater scepticism where the ground floor threatened to take over the whole building. Imbued with a commitment to Cartesian rationality, the Deists essentially challenged the notion of divine revelation, asking whether such an idea is 'conceivable or intelligible' and, if so, whether, in the face of biblical miracles and the links between Old Testament prophecy and their fulfilment in the New, such a conclusive view is sustainable.[41] Deist influences spread to the continent and, in such figures as Johann Salomo Semler (1725–91), the 'historical-critical' method of hermeneutics was born.

Semler, moving away from the historic influence of German pietism at the University of Halle where he taught, argued that the application of scriptural interpretation should take place primarily 'in accordance with universal moral [spiritual] and religious principles' with the result that 'one can no longer believe in the equal inspiredness of all the books of the Bible'.[42] His interpretive method included a careful evaluation of Scripture's use of language, an attentive assessment of the 'historical circumstances of a biblical discourse' and a painstaking attempt to match these appraisals with the current needs of one's fellow human beings.[43] The point of departure here from earlier hermeneutical approaches lay essentially in the historical-critical method's commitment to putting aside the idea of God's revelation in favour of *the primacy of human reason* in weighing up the pros and cons of historical and cultural context. The Bible was, in effect, treated by 'general hermeneutics' as any other written document would be treated.

Rationalistic interpretation reacted against both traditional streams – against what were seen to be the plodding literalism of Reformist orthodoxy and the flights of fancy among the pietists – to offer a unitive system toward the 'plain' text, so that, by the end of the century, 'belief in layers of meaning in a single text – literal, typological, and spiritual or mystical had virtually disappeared as a major force'.[44]

Liberal theology has been described as a theology where 'a God without wrath brought men without sin into a Kingdom without judgment through the ministrations of Christ without a cross',[45] and, although, as we shall see in later chapters, Christian liberalism can be viewed in much more constructive lights, H. Richard Niebuhr's jibe can be levelled with some truth on the trends within the historical-critical method as the eighteenth century gave way to the nineteenth. The progressive split between historical authenticity and the perceived meaning of the text, initiated by the Deists and continued under the rationalist scrutiny of a radical biblical criticism, came to its widest point under the influence of the German liberal theologian D. F. Strauss (1808–74). Many liberals in the late eighteenth and throughout the nineteenth century, who had discarded any belief in the deity of Jesus Christ, nonetheless pursued 'the quest for the historical Jesus'.[46] Among the numerous 'lives of Jesus' written at this time, it was Strauss's *Life of Jesus*, published in 1835, that set the sceptical cat among the traditionalist pigeons. He concentrated on the 'historical conditioning' of the authors of the Gospels and viewed the biblical narratives as 'myths' – stories which tell 'in history-like fashion either absolutely inexperienceable matters, such as facts of the supernatural world, or relatively inexperienceable ones, where due to the circumstances no one could have been a witness'.[47] His uncompromising rationalism led him to conclude 'that the "historical Jesus" has neither historically nor theologically . . . any connection with the "Christ of faith" '.[48] In our 'two-storey' universe there are no stairs nor lifts between the ground floor of human reason and an upper floor which may not even exist.

The Hermeneutics of Understanding

In the last chapter we considered two contributive strands in modernity: post-Enlightenment rationalism from the seventeenth century onward; and the rise of romanticism in the late eighteenth and early nineteenth centuries. And just as Cartesian reason in the realm of biblical interpretation unfolded inexorably toward an increasingly sceptical historical-critical methodology, so the equally individualistic Romantic movement fed a hunger for a 'hermeneutics of understanding'. While Strauss persisted with his prime focus on the text, a new emphasis gained momentum in which the interpreter also became the centre of attention. Instead of only asking 'What does this text mean?', the hermeneutician began to add, 'How do I, the interpreter, understand what I read?' It was this movement between the words as detached subject-matter and the reader or hearer as involved subject that led the way toward a psychologising hermeneutics by the end of the nineteenth century and throughout the twentieth. The prime mover in initiating this self-reflective journey was the German philosopher and preacher Schleiermacher.

Echoing Schleiermacher's own words on Frederick the Great, Karl Barth said of Friedrich Schleiermacher (1768–1834): 'He did not found a school, but an era',[49] and, increasingly, not least in the English-speaking world, the contribution of this great German Protestant to 'new horizons' in philosophy, theology and hermeneutics is undisputed.[50] The influences on his creative thinking were many and various, including the Christian pietism of his upbringing, the romanticism of his contemporaries, the historical-critical emphasis of J. S. Semler at the University of Halle, and, perhaps most profoundly, Immanuel Kant's (1724–1804) challenge toward the limits of 'pure reason' and questioning of the very basis of human understanding.[51]

It is impossible to do full justice to Schleiermacher's complex and innovative thinking in the limited space within our discussion but it is worth taking note of some of the cardinal aspects of his *hermeneutics of understanding*. First, it is important to realise that his view of interpretation was panoramic. He once wrote, 'Every child comes to understand the meanings of words only through hermeneutics',[52] and it is the universal effort of children to comprehend their environment with little or no pre-understanding that can be seen to exemplify Schleiermacher's hermeneutical approach. Unlike the 'knowingness' demonstrated by his predecessors, who mapped out a widely understood and systematic route to appraising the text, he asked 'What were the conditions under which human understanding could take place at all'.[53]

Schleiermacher's response to his own question was a creative one and a new departure in the fiercely rationalistic world of the historical-critical method. As we have seen, his approach to the mystery of human knowledge was on a broad front and within its range he embraced a duality of understanding which he sought to hold in fine balance. He declared that the process of knowing involves two complementary principles: a 'divinatory', 'psychological' or 'feminine' one, to use his terms, which emphasises relatedness; and a 'comparative', 'technical' or 'masculine' one, which stresses the critical and objectifying. In handling the written text, these two principles operate in harmony:

> By leading the interpreter to transform himself, so to speak, into the author, the divinatory method seeks to gain an immediate comprehension of the author as an individual. The comparative method proceeds by subsuming the author under a general type . . . Divinatory knowledge is the feminine strength in knowing people; comparative knowledge, the masculine. Each method refers back to the other . . . The two methods should never be separated.[54]

Thiselton points out that the issue here is that of *'immediacy and relationality* as against *conceptual distance'* and that Scheiermacher's stance, whether in the matter of the interpreter seeking 'immediate comprehension of the author as an individual' or in the wider contexts of 'life and selfhood', is one that more closely resembles 'empathy between two friends, than the solitary exercise on whch Descartes embarked'.[55]

It is this acute awareness of the 'otherness' of the text and person that distinguishes Schleiermacher's hermeneutical endeavour and marks out his relational commitment to God as 'Other' in his theology. Frei says of Schleiermacher's theological system that its 'every doctrine was formative only to the extent that it was . . . a direct expression of faith or the living religious relation with God'.[56] This view is born out in Schleiermacher's presentation of a Christian apologetic to the sceptical intellectuals of his day and in his declaration that the 'common element' in all true piety is 'the consciousness of being absolutely dependent or, which is the same thing, of being in relation with God'.[57]

Inevitably, not least linked with the pietistic and romanticist tendencies in his approach, Schleiermacher has been criticised by orthodox theology. H. R. Mackintosh, for example, accuses him of a theology that 'is less concerned with God than with man's consciousness of God'[58] and Schleiermacher has been variously indicted with 'subjectivism', 'individualism' and 'psychologism'. And yet, as Hans Frei and Anthony Thiselton point out,[59] such condemnations do not do justice to, respectively, the balance he held between his 'divinatory' and 'comparative' methods, his emphasis on the relational and 'otherness', and his commitment to the full interpretive process. His place in the history of hermeneutics is incontrovertible and the thoroughness of his exploration of human understanding anticipates a number of twentieth-century developments. Thiselton sums up the breadth of Schleiermacher's hermeneutical contribution in these words:

> Schleiermacher's conception of the hermeneutical task . . . involves the author's thought, experience, and situation; the content, context, language, and effects of the text; the first readers of the text, including their linguistic and other capacities and competences; and the consciousness and experience of later interpretation.[60]

As we shall see in the next chapter and in several of the pathways considered in Part II, Scheiermacher's comprehensive 'hermeneutics of understanding' have quietly leavened the dough of the developing psychological comprehensions of human selfhood through the nineteenth and twentieth centuries.

Postmodern Biblical Interpretation

A number of the hermeneutical strands we have so far considered have continued to play their part in the unfolding story of biblical interpretation. The more literal and grammatical methods, as we have already indicated, thread their way through various restatements within Reformed, evangelical and fundamentalist traditions; figural approaches feed into the rise of so-called 'biblical theology',[61] following the Reformation; the historical-critical method persists in a range of emphases, including 'source', 'form' and 'redaction' criticism;[62] and the influence of Schleiermacher can be traced, for example, in the work of Wilhelm Dilthey (1831–1911), Hans-Georg Gadamer (b. 1900) and the existential hermeneutics of Rudolf Bultmann (1884–1976).[63]

Dilthey, whose 'understanding' psychology we considered in Chapter 1, carries over Schleiermacher's duality of critical judgment and relational evaluation into a developed emphasis on 'interconnectedness', where an understanding of history is found through the common bond of what it means to be human. As Dilthey puts it, 'Understanding is a rediscovery of the I in the Thou . . . This identity of mind in the I, in the Thou, in every subject within a community, in every system of culture . . . and of world history, makes possible the joint result of the various operations performed in the human studies. The subject is here one with its object.'[64] This holistic vision includes the interpretive enterprise, taking the Schleiermacherian bridge from the historicity of the text to an understanding of the author even further, so that, as we shall discuss in Chapter 5, he opens the way toward a hermeneutics of selfhood.

Although Dilthey's methodology can be seen as falling within the paradigm of modernity, in that he sought to achieve a comprehensive system of 'human understanding',[65] Gadamer, who criticises Dilthey's attempts to systematise,[66] is increasingly regarded as a transition figure between modernity's commitment to the unified view and postmodernity's antifoundationalism and pluralism.[67]

Perhaps best known of Gadamer's more 'modern' contributions to our understanding of hermeneutics is his notion of the 'two horizons', where the word 'horizon' is 'used metaphorically to denote the limits of thought dictated by a given viewpoint or perspective'.[68] We live on a hillside not far from the city of Bristol. Even though the site is exposed, our back garden is hemmed in by a screen of trees and shrubs, giving, especially in the summer, a very limited horizon. In the winter, when the sycamores and ash have shed their leaves, our horizon is greatly expanded to include a line of distant limestone hills and the sweep of Bristol, ten miles to the east. If we were instead surrounded by a dense coniferous wood, rather than by deciduous trees, and were too infirm to climb higher up the hill behind us, our perspective would remain restricted, although valuable in its own right: our understanding of wider horizons could only be by hearsay. And so, we can say, in the context of hermeneutics, that we need to engage with both the limits of our own immediate viewpoints as interpreters and with the perspectives of the interpreted within the 'landscape' of the text or of another self.

However, Gadamer takes his metaphor further. To return to the picture of where we live, our 'horizon' obviously changes as we move about, whether within the restrictions of our back garden or during a car trip or walk within the wider view of our winter landscape. At the same time, wherever we go we take our previous experiences and understandings with us. As Gadamer puts it, within the context of hermeneutics, 'The horizon is . . . something into which we move and that moves with us. Horizons change for a person who is moving. Thus the horizon of the past . . . which exists in the form of tradition, is always in motion' and the 'pre-judgments that we bring with us' make up 'the horizon of a particular present'.[69] Genuine understanding, Thiselton adds, 'takes place when there occurs a fusion of horizons . . . between the past and the present, or between the text and the interpreter'.[70] And yet, at the same time, in order to move toward Gadamer's 'fusion of horizons', there is a need for both the 'distancing' of critical study and an 'openness' toward the written word.[71] By analogy, we might add, a comparable fusion of perspectives is sought in the pastoral encounter, where the distancing of objective appraisal and an openness to another's reality are both required.

The more postmodern elements in Gadamer's philosophy are brought out by Anthony Thiselton and Susan Hekman. For example, Thiselton writes that Gadamer sees life as a 'game' in which we, the 'players', setting aside our own wishes and preoccupations, lose ourselves as we respond to the game's purpose, ground rules and developments. Here the emphasis is on overall 'performance', the uniqueness of each and every game and, at the same time, the irrelevance of the individual's consciousness.[72] Behind this metaphor, we can see once more postmodernity's preoccupation with 'image' and plurality, at the expense of the de-centred self. Hekman makes a comparable, but more generalising

point, when she refers to Gadamer's attack on the Enlightenment's
self-assured certainties and its dismissal of 'tradition' and 'prejudice', the latter term used by Gadamer for 'the pre-understandings that make all human communication possible'.[73] She sees
Gadamer's thesis that 'all human understanding is contextual,
perspectival, prejudiced, that is hermeneutic' as fundamentally
opposed to modernity's conception of science and its unitive
viewpoints.[74]

Beyond Gadamer's hermeneutics of transition, we find a range
of more fully fledged postmodern approaches to interpretation.
The scene is a complex one and is probably best summarised for
our purposes under two headings: *deconstructionism* and *reader-
response theory*.

Deconstructionism

When we discussed postmodernity in the last chapter we examined two of its main features – *antifoundationalism* and *pluralism* –
and left the third, *deconstructionism*, for consideration in the context of contemporary hermeneutics. Historically, the philosophy of
deconstructionism arises from a blend of Nietzschean influence, as
we shall shortly see, and the theorising of 'semiotics', defined as
'the study of signs and symbols, especially the relations between
written or spoken signs and their referents in the physical world or
the world of ideas'.[75]

The notion of 'signs' in human and animal behaviour is very
ancient. Hippocrates, for example, initiated the importance of
signs in physical illness and today's doctor is carefully trained
to distinguish between 'symptoms', bodily or psychological sensations of which the patient complains, and 'signs', clinically
discernible features which point to underlying illness: chest pain
made worse by deep breathing is a symptom; the rasping sound of
a pleural rub, detected by stethoscope, is a sign. Comparably, we
have grown used to the idea of signs or 'signals' in, for example,
the ethologist Desmond Morris's book *Manwatching*[76] and in
counselling, where trainees are taught to look out for the 'messages' given by non-verbal communication, such as the evasion of
eye contact, the clenching of a fist whenever a certain relative is
mentioned, or a frown when the question of a fee is raised!

We can consider the rise of deconstructionism under the names
of two linguistic philosophers: de Saussure and Derrida.

De Saussure

The best-known figure in the development of modern semiotics is generally thought to be the Swiss linguist Ferdinand de Saussure (1857–1913).[77] He compares the use of language to a game of chess in which the operational value of each individual piece rests solely in its relationship with all the other pieces, set within the total structure of play. Here, meaning is understood in terms of 'difference': each piece is defined in terms of its functional differentness to all other pieces. Similarly, in the field of linguistics, de Saussure declares, 'In language there are only differences.'[78]

A further principle that de Saussure stresses is that of 'arbitrariness'. He states that the link between the 'signifier' (a word) and the 'signified' (the object indicated by the word) is always an arbitrary one, whose ground rules are purely linguistic and thus divorced from their historical and social contexts. For example, it is arbitrary that in English we have just the one word 'brown', whereas French speakers have the choice of *brun* and *marron*, and that in Latin and Greek the terms *amo*, *philo* and *ero* are in one-word form, where in English and German we have two-word forms: 'I love' and *ich liebe*.[79]

De Saussure's work in linguistics, including his emphases on 'structure', 'difference' and 'arbitrariness', lived on and was formative in the rise of 'structuralism'[80] from the late 1920s through to the 1950s, when the term began to be used more widely to embrace, for example, social and cultural issues in the writings of Claude Lévi-Strauss. However, it was in the late 1960s, when the stream of modern semiotics was infused by a revival of Nietzschean philosophy, that deconstructionism began to take hold. In fact one writer, Terry Eagleton, has committed himself to declaring 1968 as the year that a post-structuralist and deconstructing philosophy began to take hold. In relation to the extraordinary number of international cataclysms that occurred that year, including the assassinations of Martin Luther King Jr and Robert Kennedy, the rash of student riots and labour strikes that erupted in European cities, the invasion of a liberalising Czechoslovakia by Russia, and the Tet offensive in Vietnam, he writes, 'Unable to break the structures of state power, post-structuralism found it possible instead to subvert the structures of language.'[81] As Roger Lundin adds, with regard to deconstructionism's targeting of linguistics rather than politics, for many of its adherents 'it has become a means of waging the intellectual equivalent of risk-free guerilla warfare'.

Derrida

At the end of the section on antifoundationalism (p. 80), we left Nietzsche, saw in hand, on a branch and poised above the void with three companions: Freud, Heidegger and Derrida. And it is Derrida's acknowledged indebtedness to the other three, it can be argued, that has carried on their collective work, in Jonathan Culler's picture, of 'a certain reckless sawing' which deconstructs 'the great cathedral-like trees in which Man has taken shelter for millennia'.[82]

Born in 1930, the French philosopher Jacques Derrida is seen as a central figure within the project of deconstructionism.[83] Taking the Saussurean notions of 'arbitrariness' and 'difference', but demoting that of 'structure', Derrida engages with the 'science of writing' or 'grammatology', shifting the modernist hermeneutical emphasis on the author and declaring that the text has its own life force in which there are multiple interpretations of possible meanings. In fact, we 'can never reach any "final" point of the interpretation of meaning. One semiotic process leads on to another, and none is grounded in "reality" or in the external world.'[84] Or, as Lundin puts it, for Derrida 'language begins to *deconstruct* itself even before a critic trains his or her gaze upon it'.[85]

Even so, Derrida uses the term 'writing' on a wide base to cover all modes of communication that are not vocal: he declares, 'We say "writing" for all that gives rise to inscription . . . cinematography, choreography . . . pictorial, musical, sculptural "writing".'[86] It is here that we see a movement from modernity's *logocentrism*, where meaning is located in words, to postmodernity's *iconocentrism*, where a shifting ground of possible meanings is caught up in image, collage and montage.

At one level, this may seem an innocent enough eventuality, not least since the contemporary Western world is brimful of surface style and 'meaning'. Here every 'text' we are invited to read – whether on television or video, at the cinema or through the Internet, in the art gallery or listening to synthesised 'world' music – offers a seemingly endless plethora of interpretations. The more sinister underbelly of this post-structuralist state of affairs, as we have already indicated, is the resurrection of a Nietzschean worldview: a culture of interpretation in which 'truths are illusions about which one has forgotten that this is what they are'.[87] As with Nietzsche, so with Derrida, for in the face of a destructured universe with meaninglessness and emptiness at its centre, he picks up with the Nietzschean 'joyous affirmation' of 'a world of signs without fault, without truth, and without origin'.[88] Lundin sees this semiological world 'without fault' as Derrida's 'utopian ideal, a world in which intellectual history becomes a great video arcade, and every character or idea in that history is but one more game meant to heighten the pleasure of the postmodern player at the controls'.[89]

This retreat from historical context and meaningful text to the one goal of free-floating 'pleasure' is in stark contrast to the richness of the Bible's hermeneutical treasure-house, where the 'arbitrary' gives way to significance, where humanity is defined by intrinsic value as well as Saussurean 'difference', and where 'structure' is undergirded by a 'sure foundation'.

Reader-Response Theory

Where 'deconstructionism', with its close links with antifoundationalism, is undoubtedly the bleaker face of postmodern hermeneutics, 'reader-response theory' can be seen as a re-humanising endeavour within contemporary biblical interpretation. Whereas Derridean post-structuralism dismisses the historical and social context of author, text and interpreter, leaving only the surface 'writing', reader-response theory at least recovers and enlarges the role of the *reader* and the more *literary* aspects of Scripture. As Edgar McKnight, tracing the reaffirmation of the Bible's historicity during the 1970s[90] and fully aware of concurrent deconstructive approaches to interpretation[91] declares, in postmodernism 'the reader and the text are interdependent' in such a way that 'the text is actualized by the reader in a fashion that the text may be said to actualize the reader'.[92] Here is a dynamic engagement between a creative process as to how the living Scriptures can be seen and the life-changing responsiveness of the reader and the 'reading community'. We can examine this particular brand of postmodern hermeneutics under two headings: the *Bible as literature*; and the *reader's response*.

The Bible as Literature
First, we need to acknowledge with Stanley Fish that what we recognise as literature 'is a function of a *communal decision* as to what will count as literature'.[93] This emphasis is backed by *The Oxford Companion to the English Language* which acknowledges the

impossibility of defining the primary sense of literature exactly, since its unfolding is marked by at least three factors: a fluidity made up of its nature as 'an imitation of life'; its 'effect on the reader'; and its susceptibility to different fashions with regard to its forms of poetry or prose.[94] Even so, as McKnight states, the literary side of this fluid interchange between text and the reader-community does not need to mean any loss of the Bible's distinctiveness. He concedes that the 'process of reading biblical literature' is comparable to the reading of all literature in terms of 'intellectual and emotional pleasure', but adds that 'biblical literature is different from other literature as it reveals a transcendent world and . . . "traps" readers to become a part of that world'.[95] This experience of entrapment by a unique text evokes Luther's dictum: 'The Bible is alive, it speaks to me; it has feet, it runs after me; it has hands, it lays hold on me.'[96]

As well as employing this dynamic metaphor of the Scriptures in terms of ensnaring the reader into its 'transcendent world', MacKnight uses the picture of a nut and its protective shell to illustrate the special contribution of the 'reader-oriented literary approach' which he advocates. He argues that all previous styles of hermeneutics, including the 'dogmatic' tradition of the ancient and medieval Church and the 'historical' method of the Enlightenment, gave readers 'information', whereby the 'nut was extracted and the shell discarded'. In contrast, McKnight's approach seeks to appreciate both 'nut' and 'shell': 'To see the Bible as literature . . . is to value the texture and the content.'[97] This valuing of literary texture *and* transcendent content 'does not mean that the text is minimized'. It means, rather, that 'the text is taken just as seriously as before' and in such a way that 'it is able to speak to the reader in his or her contemporary idiom'.[98]

The Reader's Response

The balance between text and reader can, however, be lost, and certain reader-response approaches tend so to elevate the readers' role that the text is moulded into the image of the reading-community.[99] Even so, as we have seen, McKnight seeks to hold the 'interdependence' between the written word and the particular needs and hopes of the reader or group of readers. Here, the emphasis is not only on the uniqueness and sacredness of the Scriptures but on the need for readers to 'retrieve' the Bible 'from the museum' and 'relate it' to contemporary life.[100] If Scripture is truly from God then engaged reading will rescue it from all approaches that see its pages as exhibits of a disengaged past and rediscover its ever-fresh life force for the present.

This process is seen as a creative one, which involves both the mind and the heart, and can be likened to engagement with the 'artistic text in general', which is 'so filled with meaning' that, to quote Jurij Lotman, it 'transmits different information to different readers in proportion to each one's comprehension'.[101] For anyone who has engaged with the 'artistic text' in, say, a novel or poetry appreciation group, the experience of the rich variety of ways that the text is received, understood and enjoyed is well known. Similarly, where the Scriptures are studied together a range of meanings and pertinent applications can be discovered, even within the simplest story or briefest passage of teaching. For example, individuals discussing an account as well known as the Parable of the Prodigal Son may variously identify with: a sense of waste or of fresh hopes in the life of the younger son; feelings of being taken for granted or resentment in the elder son's response to the party's perceived excesses; or a fresh glimpse of the largesse of God's forgiveness and restoration in the father's eager, heartfelt embrace of his wayward son. For others again the active reading of the same account may be responded to at a communal level where the thrust of the story is seen, for example, to relate to questions of societal responsiveness in celebrating the return of those who 'come to their senses' and seek to disentangle themselves from life's degradations. McKnight sums up this creative enterprise as relating to a biblical text which appeals to 'the reader's capacity for imagination and need for meaning that coheres with the reader's own situation in the world'.[102]

In this way there is both a 'reimaging of the sacred'[103] and a 'redefining of the self':[104] both God and the reader can be revisited and seen in new, challenging and transforming ways, where biblical texts 'provide resources for the creation of a comprehensive universe, which . . . sees the human in the light of the divine and the divine in the light of the human'.[105]

Summary

This overview of the story of the interpretation of the Scriptures reminds us that, as with Julian Barnes's stowaway woodworm and the learned doctors in sixteenth-century France who debated the fate of the humble creature's miscreant descendants, there have been many different ways of understanding the Bible down through the centuries. Variously, we have seen a great range of emphases from the traditional views that uphold the 'plain text' or find layers of allegorical meaning within it, through progressive questionings which wrestle with the authenticity of original authorship and historical setting, the emergence of more intuitive understandings to counterbalance post-Enlightenment rationalism and an increasing focus on the interpretive process, to the postmodern shift toward the dismemberment of the text, plurality of meaning and the creative response of the reader.

Within Part II we will explore something of the way these variant 'hermeneutics of the text', and the attendant 'hermeneutics of the life' which we look at in the next chapter, influence and are used by pastoral care's 'pathways to wholeness'. For the moment, I would like to close with two metaphors used by contemporary interpreters of the Scriptures: the 'compost heap', emphasising the part played by the *text*; and 'reading against the grain', stressing the role of the *reader*.

Although Joy and I are keen gardeners, we have never quite conquered the seemingly simple process of really effective composting. Today the emphasis is on closed womb-like containers and an alliance with an army of purchased worms which achieve the right mix of decomposing vegetable waste at great speed. Even so, our more traditional open-mesh system gradually gives us a passable compost which, in spite of seemingly immortal peach-stones, tea-bags and squeezy-bottle tops, is most productive for mulching and improving our heavy soil. On the whole the compost heap greatly enriches the garden, although it also generates surprises, such as a crop of potato plants or spring onions.

Walter Brueggemann, following Stuart Hampshire, sees the Bible as 'the compost pile that provides material for new life'. It comprises 'deposits of old growth that have been discarded, but that continue to ferment' to provide 'resources' for renewal. As with most garden compost, Scripture 'contains seeds of its own' and 'sprouts and grows more than and other than we had in mind'.[106] Here is a view of the text which, in some ways, echoes the adversarial nature of Luther's Bible and, at the same time, meshes with the balanced interchange of the 'reader-response' approaches where both the reader reads the text and the text reads the reader.

Not only am I a merely average compost-maker, I am especially incompetent in the field of carpentry. Even so, one of the few things I learned in school woodwork lessons is that you should never plane 'against the grain'. David Clines takes this term and applies it to the reading of the Scriptures. Writing in the context of interpreting the Pentateuch, he says that 'most readers . . . have subscribed to the ideology of the text; they have read with the grain of the text', that is, they have concurred with the broad themes of the creation, the flood and the choice of one family, one people and one land. Like Barnes's woodworm, though, he proposes alternative readings, pointing out 'how differently the narrative would sound if one read against the grain', if, for example, one engaged with the viewpoint of an Egyptian or Canaanite, rather than an Israelite. In such conceived settings, what a contrast of perspective might be found over the Red Sea Crossing or the entry into the Promised Land! And, Clines shrewdly declares, 'We need not suppose that reading against the grain of the text is a sign of disrespect for the text.' Instead, what is 'disrespectful to the text is to assume that it will say what it is we would like it to say'.[107]

In both Brueggemann's picture of the compost heap as a metaphor for the text and Clines's bid for the reader to read against the grain, we find two of postmodernity's more constructive reminders in the plurality of *possible meanings* and the value of the *imagination*[108] in biblical hermeneutics. Such fresh awareness of the mystery of God and the surprises contained in his Word need not tip us from our contemporary contexts toward the downward slopes of postmodern antifoundationalism and deconstructionism. Bernhard Anderson holds the balance well when he writes:

> The sober realization of our 'location' does not, in my estimation, mire us in interpretive relativism, as though the Scriptures and other literary works are 'like a picnic to which the author brings the words and the reader the meaning,' to invoke the celebrated words of Northrop Frye. To be sure, we come to the Scriptures in our social location and hopefully, with some creative imagination; but the words of Scripture, spoken or written in their own context, may criticize where we stand, limit our use of them, and challenge us with their strange social setting and theological horizon.[109]

Chapter 5

PATHWAYS INTERPRETED: HERMENEUTICS OF THE LIFE

In short, the self of self-understanding is a gift of understanding itself and of the invitation from the meaning inscribed in the text.

Paul Ricoeur[1]

We have seen that in a culture of interpretation everything is subject to the quest for understanding and, within the context of Christian journeying, we have singled out the hermeneutics of the text and of the life for consideration. For these two, as we have noted, are inextricably bound together. The text of Scripture is interpreted by the reader and that selfsame text interprets the life of the reader. And as we explored the story of the hermeneutics of the text we observed that that close interpenetration between the Bible and human selfhood gained momentum from the time of Schleiermacher and the Romantic movement onward. Figures such as Dilthey and Gadamer have carried the torch of a 'hermeneutics of understanding' well into the twentieth century, within which progressive waves of continuing historical-critical and existential approaches have largely given way to the inroads of structuralism, deconstructionism and reader-response theory. In our contemporary culture, as we have observed in the musings of Barnes's 'postmodern' woodworm, the interplay between text and reader leads to multiple meanings for both parties.

The 'hermeneutics of understanding' established a clear corrective to the relentlessly objectifying trend of the post-Enlightenment 'historical-critical' method. This fresh engagement with the human factor in interpretation, launched in Schleiermacher's emphasis on the more 'intuitive' or 'divinatory', as well as on the more 'technical' or 'comparative', was continued in Dilthey's commitment to 'interconnectedness' and Gadamer's proclamation of a 'fusion of horizons', in which a critical 'distancing' accompanies an 'openness' to the given text. In each of these methodologies there emerges the possibility of *relationship*: in Schleiermacher's bid for 'otherness', likened by Thiselton to 'empathy between two friends';[2] in Dilthey's 'rediscovery of the I in the Thou'; and in our extrapolation of Gadamer's 'horizons' into the need for both 'distance' and 'openness' in the pastoral encounter.

A crucial fourth figure has emerged within the metamorphosis of hermeneutics from a sometimes arid encounter with just the objectified text to a hopefully more heart-warming exploration that includes both written documents and human selfhood as legitimate territories for interpretation. Paul Ricoeur (b. 1913), the French philosopher,[3] challenges both the Cartesian confidence in the power of the reasoning self and the Nietzschean antifoundational shattering of that confidence[4] – in effect, Nietzsche declares, 'I doubt better than Descartes'.[5] Ricoeur, rather, sees beyond 'the alternative of the cogito and of the anticogito' to an unfolding 'hermeneutics of the self' which, in the Schleiermacherian tradition, culminates in 'the dialectic of selfhood and otherness', where 'The *autonomy* of the self will appear . . . to be tightly bound up with *solicitude* for one's neighbor and with *justice* for each individual.'[6]

This historic shift in hermeneutical enquiry is being taken up increasingly in the field of pastoral studies. A significant initiator of this trend is seen in the 1920s and 1930s in the pioneering studies of Anton T. Boisen, who introduced theological reflection into the interpretation of mental illness. To some extent building on Boisen's ground-breaking work, two outstanding contributions of the 1980s are those of Charles V. Gerkin, a pastoral psychologist looking primarily to the influence of Schleiermacher, Dilthey and Gadamer, and Donald Capps, a pastoral theologian who draws comparable conclusions from the thinking of Ricoeur. Where Gerkin writes within the more circumscribed field of pastoral counselling, Capps sets his discussion in the wider context of pastoral care. Taking this range of theological and psychological perspectives in order, we will consider the overall 'hermeneutics of life' under four main headings: *living human documents*; *soft-focus hermeneutics*; a *translation model* and *interpreting the postmodern self*.

Living Human Documents

One of the concepts that I have baulked at during my career as a medical practitioner lies behind the traditional use of the word 'case' to describe a patient's clinical condition. In medical student days in London, and during subsequent hospital work, I objected to the reductive implications of a ward deemed full of medical or surgical 'cases'. The use of this term often seemed to be accompanied by an attitude that was in danger of losing the rich fabric of a human story in a summary listing of a patient's 'signs and symptoms'. At its worst, a ward sister or senior doctor might say to a student, 'There's a couple of heart cases on Ward 11 for you to examine' or 'Mrs Jones is an interesting case; make sure you have a look at her before the ward round'.

And yet, of course, the term does not need to be misused and the notion of 'case studies' and 'case histories' is integral to important elements in the accurate appraisal of human needs and situations in a variety of professional contexts. For example, Harvard Law School began to substitute traditional lectures with the study of individual cases in 1871 and, in the realm of psychiatry, Freud established the value of case studies from the 1880s onward. However, it was the work of Anton T. Boisen (1876–1966) and his notion of 'living human documents' that were integral to making early links historically between the study of case histories, pastoral education and theological reflection.

Boisen, training consecutively in linguistics and theology, had a lifelong interest in psychological matters – not least, it seems, because of his own episodic collapse into mental illness. In his autobiographical *Out of the Depths* he traces the strands in his own story which may have contributed to a shattering series of psychotic breakdowns that began in 1920. In his earlier years he had been haunted by the influence of his powerful father who died, after a scholarly career in modern languages, when Boisen was seven years old and whom the son idealised as a great academic teacher. Although his family background was a liberal Christian one, it was his loyalty to the memory of his father that, so he wrote of his early adult life, 'had become one with my religion'.[7] Hemmed in by the 'potent force' of his dead father's omnipresence and tormented by inner conflict over his sexual desires, he nonetheless found his training for ordination at Union Theological Seminary supplied three of his happiest years. Meeting the case study method for the first time through the tutelage of the religious educationalist George Albert Coe in his second year at the seminary, and, following his first breakdown, studying social ethics and case presentation at Harvard Divinity School under the physician Richard C. Cabot, Boisen became increasingly committed to the exploration of the relationship between mental disorder and religious experience in the lives of 'living human documents'.[8]

Starting in 1924 at Worcester State Hospital as one of the first full-time chaplains to mental hospitals in the United States, he developed his distinctive, case-centred approach for the training of theological students until his retirement in 1942. Here was a 'pioneer of pastoral assessment',[9] to use Glenn Asquith's phrase, who not only focused on the primacy of accurately recorded personal story in the understanding of human need but also allowed his own journey 'out of the depths' to shape his theological and psychological reflection. Clearly by his later life he had left behind the ghost of his father's pervasive presence and could write that 'parents are merely representatives of a higher loyalty' – a 'higher loyalty . . . represented by [the] idea of God', an idea that 'stands for something which is operative in the lives of all men whether they recognize it or not'.[10]

Although one of the co-founders of Clinical Pastoral Education (CPE),[11] Boisen both warned the movement of the dangers of an uncritical assimilation of the currently favoured views of Freud[12] and stressed that theological training needs to emphasise the social as well as the individual, a balanced approach neglected by the individualistic bias of many of Boisen's successors in CPE.[13] His methodology not only sought to free seminarians from the incursion of a psychoanalytical mindset and engage them with the 'actual social conditions'[14] of hospital patients, but it also adopted a highly inductive approach toward theological understanding, reasoning from careful observation of the particular to form general conclusions. Students were instructed to begin 'not with traditions and not with systems formulated in books, but with the open-minded exploration of living human experience' in order 'to build up a body of generalizations'.[15]

Asquith summarises the assumption behind Boisen's objectives as one in which 'the individual experiences of mentally ill persons will have general application to the student's understanding of the religious lives of "normal" persons, thus enhancing the student's ability to function as a minister'.[16] Here, in pioneering form, we have a pastoral method which is committed to active listening, painstaking recording of the story of each 'living human document' and an awareness of the closely interwoven nature of the psychological and the theological. Mental illness, in this way of thinking, may be seen as a fall into the dark places. And yet, in spite of the sense of anguish and lostness experienced, it may also prove to be a potential gateway to spiritual awakening – not least when the times of darkness and recovery are accompanied by supportive fellow-travellers, be they friends, family members or trained psychiatric or pastoral carers.

The crucial component of Boisen's notion of 'living human documents' is that of the need to 'get the story right'. The patient's narrative furnishes a text ripe for understanding and so the case history, mediated through exhaustive questionnaires, careful note-taking and duplication for group discussion, is of the essence. This method, adapted to the conditions of psychiatric evaluation, is too exhaustive for general medical practice and most pastoral contexts. Although largely replaced by audio and video recording in, for example, psychotherapeutic training programmes, and by the selectively remembered 'verbatim report'[17] in many contemporary clinical and pastoral settings, the centrality of the personal account is integral to the pastoral encounter.

Here is a hermeneutics of the self whose open-minded respect for the 'document' of a human life is as committed to cautious and reflective interpretation as the most diligent and circumspect scholar is to the hermeneutics of the biblical text. And this is not a straightforward path for the pastor, counsellor or psychotherapist. As I know from my own experience in the practice of medicine it is all too easy to project one's diagnosis and conclusions on to the patient's account. Once the trained mind fastens on to a stray comment or phrase used by the person in need it can readily fall into the trap of 'reading' the living human document in a way that fits neatly with one's untested hunches and firmly held presuppositions. In discussing this issue the other evening with a group of colleagues who work in the psychiatric and social services, one man, a consultant psychiatrist, warmed to the point and said that once a set piece of diagnostic jargon took hold – such as the notion of a 'flight of ideas' held to be symptomatic of schizophrenia – then any open-mindedness toward the patient's story flew out of the window. A flight of ideas in the patient leads to a flight of ideas in the psychiatrist!

The value of Boisen's concept of the 'living human document', as we have seen, has penetrated much clinical and pastoral practice. For myself, the legacy of medical and psychotherapeutic training has been paramount in establishing a comparable discipline of careful note-taking and record-keeping. Within the counselling and spiritual direction that I do, coupled with the supervision of the same, the importance of 'getting the story right' and, where appropriate, producing a 'verbatim report' on remembered interchange with the client or directee, are integral to the interpretation of the relevant life's narrative. Boisen's commitment to the patient's account, although too meticulous in its most developed form for many contemporary contexts, including my own therapeutic endeavours, carries some powerful points into current pastoral practice. Asquith raises two of these: a reminder that the 'busy pastor' needs, nonetheless, to find the time to learn 'the details and the background of the parishioner's situation' in order to be 'more prescriptive' and thus 'more effective'; and, second, a calling 'to think theologically about human experience'.[18]

Stephanie, a young postgraduate in history, came to see me as a Christian who was struggling with her sexual identity and fearful of her lesbian tendencies. Overwhelmed by a dominant and controlling mother who seemed to rob her of a sense of 'being her own person' whenever she visited the parental home, she was drawn to a series of passionate relationships with contemporary and slightly older women – women whose selflessness, social skills and humour she especially admired and coveted. Some chapters of the 'living human document' of her story were opened over the limited time I was able to see her and, because of her clear history of religious commitment, our discussions included a focus on some elements of her thoughts and feelings about the links, if any, between her inner turmoil and her Christian faith. She declared a slippage from the happier former times of her discipleship and concluded that, although her mind could still see the relevance of Christianity, her emotional life did not match that conviction. As in so many clinical, counselling and pastoral encounters, here was an unresolved fragment of someone's 'living document' that was shared over limited time and yet, hopefully, contained within its exposure to active listening and tentative interpretation the potential for transformative growth within a particular unfolding story of human experience and theological reflection.

Soft-Focus Hermeneutics

Boisen's work with 'living human documents' has been both built on and extended to give an interpretation of the text of a life which is based on a 'soft-focus' approach to pastoral counselling and its relationship to the underlying disciplines of pastoral theology and pastoral psychology.[19] In photography and the visual arts generally the technique of soft focus, in blurring boundaries and obscuring definition, can lend a picture an element of mystification which invites enquiry and reflection. Where the mystery of a portrayal is at its most intriguing the viewer may need to resort to the less hard-edged language of metaphor in order to make some tentative sense of what is seen. Wendy Beckett, for example, in seeking to interpret Mali Morris's painting *A Vision of the Mermaids* (1983), is forced toward language that is abstract and symbolic:

> We get the impression that the painter does not 'understand' the picture any more than we do. Mermaids are another species, creatures of the imagination, born to an atmosphere different to our smoke-polluted air. We could almost equate mermaids with angels in their essential unlikeness to fallen man. What, then, do the Mermaids see in vision? Horizons and verticals of colour, strange seaweed-like whirls and squiggles, all afloat in an almost transparent matrix. All we can or are asked to do is to *receive* this vision, let its beauty move us, be stilled by its motionless peace. We can take from it no concrete word or message.[20]

Since human experience is also rarely clear-cut or self-evident, the pastoral engagement can be similarly viewed in soft focus, in which the interpretation of the stories, lives and encounters of those involved allows for the understanding of the partially obscured or enigmatic through the use of symbol, parable and analogy. John Patton, bringing this approach into the limelight in his seminal paper of 1981, lays down an emphasis on form and language in the counselling process, where 'theological truth, when closely related to the concrete richness of human experiencing, is most effectively interpreted with a soft focus of symbolic and sometimes multiple meanings'.[21] We can explore this interplay between 'theological truth' and the softly focused language of the pastoral encounter under two main headings: *pre-understandings in pastoral counselling*; and *parable and the cross*.

Pre-understandings in Pastoral Counselling

In his *The Living Human Document* Charles Gerkin addresses the most fundamental presuppositional basis of the therapeutic encounter: the relationship between the theological and psychological understanding of a human life. He offers a 'hermeneutical theory' of pastoral counselling[22] in which he seeks an 'even-handed usage of both psychological and theological paradigms'.[23] His aim is to reflect on counselling practice in such a way that, on the one hand, theology is not subordinated to 'psychotherapeutic theory' and, on the other hand, 'psychotherapeutic language' is not subsumed 'into a heavy-handed insistence on the authority of theological word usage and God talk'.[24] Here there is an attempt to find a balance between the sort of eager assimilation of Freudianism that Boisen warned against and a reactionary Christian stance that is unbudging in its use of the 'language of Zion' in the face of psychological understanding. The particular value of Gerkin's contribution to a hermeneutical theory of pastoral counselling lies in the primacy he gives to 'the Christian mode of interpretation' in dialogue with 'contemporary psychological modes of interpretation'.[25] In the pastoral encounter Freud and Rogers have their say but, where necessary, they give way to Christ and Paul.

It is worth saying at this stage that, in my work at Trinity College in the late 1990s, I am still meeting the need for theological students to hear Gerkin's voice. It is by no means rare to find, especially among certain male students, a clearly held prejudice against things psychological. This attitude is perhaps commoner among men who have been brought up with the stereotyping imprint that to be male is to be physically and mentally strong and to leave things emotional and reflective to the opposite sex. Such an unexamined mindset can be reinforced in students who have been nurtured in an overly doctrinaire form of belief. Often, it seems, their previous understanding of the Bible and Christian theology stands like an unyielding bulwark against any perspective about human nature that cannot be upheld by precise chapter and verse in the pages of Scripture. Conversely, other theological students who have worked as, say, doctors, social workers or clinical psychologists, have genuine difficulty in meshing their psychological understanding with the theology that is presented to them day in, day out.

However, we need to see that the pastoral counsellor must bring more than reasonably integrated theological and psychological reflectiveness to the encounter with men and women in need if a fair interpretation of their lives is to be found. Here the 'pre-understandings' held by both parties should be kept in mind. Generally speaking, we can say that we all bring to every human encounter our own presuppositions – whether they are the impressions gleaned from others of a company's record which we bring as applicants to a job interview; the prejudices fostered toward a particular colleague who has sought us out for a 'frank discussion'; or the unrealistic expectations we may hold of someone with whom we have fallen in love. In counselling and spiritual direction it is clear that both parties bring to the early stages of the developing relationship a whole range of expectations shaped by previous experience, set ways of thinking and established patterns of emotional response. A counsellor, for example, may know she has difficulty in helping older women since her relationship with her mother still has certain unresolved elements. This pre-understanding may make her reluctant to take on such clients or, where she goes ahead circumspectly, her foreknowledge may prove an ally within the therapeutic relationship. Similarly, someone seeking spiritual direction for the first time may feel daunted by his preconception that spiritual directors are aloof, austere figures who dispense restrictive advice straight from the mouth of the Almighty. Having taken the plunge, it may take some time for such a directee to accept that he is simply on a journey with a soul-friend who has his best interests at heart.

Gerkin develops his commitment to pre-understandings in pastoral counselling by looking to Gadamer's notion of the two horizons and the Schleiermacherian emphasis on the hermeneutical circle. We can further clarify the application of these insights by the consideration of a brief case history.

Horizons of Understanding

We saw in the previous chapter (see p. 111) the use Gadamer makes of the need to work toward a 'fusion of horizons' in the interpretation of the text and we hinted at the possible transference of this concept to the pastoral encounter. Gerkin clarifies the connection in the 'beginning phase' of counselling by noting the counsellor's awareness of the two horizons: that of the 'narrative story line' in the client's life and that of the accompanying 'preunderstanding shaped by the previous hermeneutical process' of the counsellor's own life. Thus the counsellor brings to the therapeutic relationship both a measure of self-understanding, gleaned, for example, from earlier counselling experiences and supervision, and an openness to 'the truly new and unique, once-as-never-before qualities of the other's story'. Here the wise counsellor seeks to avoid using the interpretive process 'as templates or molds into which to force all new disclosures' but rather 'as soft, tentative images of who the other may indeed be'. This softly focused search carries pastoral counselling toward 'a fusion of horizons of understanding' in which the understanding of both parties 'may be enlarged and illuminated'. Lest this quest seem idealised, Gerkin correctly acknowledges the asymmetry of the counselling relationship: '[In] a fusion of horizons of understanding . . . lies the hope that both life stories, that of the help seeker and of the helper, may undergo transformation, though by its nature pastoral counseling will focus primarily on altering the hermeneutics of the self of the one seeking help.'[26] Here is a bringing together of two personal narratives that is hopefully transformative for the pastoral counsellor and the person in need, although, inevitably and by definition, it is the latter's 'horizon of understanding' that is the central interpretive agenda for both parties.

Hermeneutical Circle

The notion of the hermeneutical circle has become an *idée fixe* in the study of interpretation. Systematised by Schleiermacher,[27] its usage runs through Heidegger, Bultmann, Gadamer and Ricoeur and is now common currency among hermeneuticians. From the beginning the term has generated multiple shades of meaning: the simple circularity between the interpreter's investigative questions of the text and the reshaping of those questions by what is read; the interplay between the comprehension of the whole text through its individual parts and of the parts by an understanding of the whole; and the interchange between the interpreter's preunderstandings and what is examined. It is in this last emphasis, likened by Thiselton to a spiral rather than a circle,[28] that we can see the clearest implications for the dynamic of the pastoral encounter: 'Here the initial preliminary understanding . . . with which we approach the text or person to be understood becomes modified, corrected, and refined as that which we seek to understand "speaks back", in turn, to the interpreter.'[29]

Gerkin takes this Schleiermacherian 'hermeneutics of under-standing' and applies it to pastoral counselling. Citing Bauman's dictum that 'Understanding means going in circles' through 'an endless recapitulation and reassessment of collective memories',[30] he sees the therapeutic encounter in terms of 'a circular pattern that moves from the immediate counseling relationship to the arena of current life relationships to the history of significant relationships, back to the counseling relationship itself'. Within this circularity, the 'flow of conversation' is loosely structured by the twofold process of the counsellor's enquiry and the 'construc-tion of interpretive possibilities'.[31]

Here is a softly focused format that nudges the continuing pastoral encounter from its initial pre-understandings through the altered perceptions of a developing therapeutic relationship toward a fusion of the participants' horizons. And just as, in traditional hermeneutics, the committed reading of the text can release the text's life-changing effectiveness, so the creative use of a pastoral hermeneutical circle can release the God-given human potential in the lives of those therein engaged. This overall process of constructive change can be viewed as subject to the 'trinity' of 'understanding, interpretation, and application'.[32]

A Hermeneutical Case Study

Following a year's struggle in his new job as a solicitor in a nearby town, Grant phoned me to query the possibility of counselling. Married with two children and in his late thirties, he had had a strong sense of God's calling into his present situation. Even so, he was full of self-doubt as to whether he had misjudged that call, a state of mind that was already leading to something of a crisis in the marriage – not least since his wife Jane had forfeited a fulfilling teaching post to make the move.

It is interesting, in terms of Gerkin's analysis, to reflect on the pre-understandings that he and I brought to the early stages of the counselling relationship. Grant had shared a little of his story with the psychiatric friend of one of his colleagues and had been urged to visit his GP for antidepressants. He was not only reluctant to take that step, as he wanted to 'understand' why he was so troubled, but he also declared his desire that I should address the 'spiritual' as well as the 'psychological' aspects of his crisis of direction. For myself, I was aware that I had mixed feelings about taking on this particular counsellee. On the one hand, my experience and long-held views responded sympathetically to Grant's wish to avoid medication, as long as any elements of depression did not work against his responsiveness to the therapeutic process. On the other hand, I felt ambivalent about his request that we include the 'spiritual', not because I would want to exclude automatically such a fundamental dimension so much as I would hope that such a declared agenda would not trap us into compartmentalising this or that aspect of his life.

The 'pre-understandings' were duly noted and what proved to be a lengthy period of counselling ensued. Within the developing relationship Grant's 'horizon of understanding', concerning his perceived call from God, his way of handling decisions that inadequately engaged Jane's plans and wishes, and the patterns built up in his story since childhood, was explored and, where appropriate, cautiously interpreted. Although this softly focused approach centred on Grant's 'horizon', my own 'world' was also illuminated and expanded by the pastoral encounter – not least in a fresh reminder how, in my own life, certain questionable decisions can too readily be rationalised as 'God's will'.

Throughout this process the hermeneutical circle between us meant a constant re-evaluation of how best to interpret Grant's life. At the end of many sessions, especially in the early months of counselling, I knew that my tentative conclusions about him might need reassessing and modifying as further encounters unravelled his story. For example, one of my initial impressions of him was of a selfish preoccupation with his own destiny, at the expense of Jane, the children and a range of other important people in his life. In time, though, in seeking to 'read' his story, that story 'spoke back' in ways that revealed a deep desire for the best in the lives of those around him, albeit a desire that needed freeing from its blind spots. Eventually, a measure of fusion of our two horizons developed which, hopefully, has encouraged Grant forward into a widened and more accountable 'horizon of understanding'.

Parable and the Cross

So far, we have seen the way Charles Gerkin unravels a soft-focus hermeneutics for pastoral counselling, demonstrating an approach which acknowledges the prime importance of both the counsellor's and the counsellee's pre-understandings, and a process which seeks the fusion of the parties' 'two horizons' and engages a hermeneutical circle of 'understanding, interpretation, and application'. Within this brief he continues to hold a balance, as we have seen, between his psychological and theological pre-understandings – between, in particular, his acknowledgment of the value of object relations theory[33] in 'the formation of the integrated self'[34] and his commitment to an expansion of self psychology's[35] remit to include 'all aspects of the self's interpretive life, including the ultimate aspect of its life in God'. Thus, Gerkin's therapeutic goal is that of 'integration and wholeness', conditions which, in keeping with this book's approach, 'retain a certain ambiguous . . . quality' where 'wholeness remains proleptic, a fragmentary anticipation of that final wholeness for which we hope'.[36]

Gerkin's 'pathway to wholeness' provides a rich methodology that sees his theological perspective as offering 'both a normative direction for evaluating changes taking place in the lives of persons as a result of pastoral counseling' and 'a normative check on our own and our counselees' desires concerning change'.[37] This perspective is true to the calling of pastoral counselling, as we shall see in Chapter 9, in that it is *incarnational* in its emphasis.

Further, it offers an incarnational christology with 'a theology of the cross' at its centre.[38] He sees here, in accordance with Romans 8:22–4, that 'creative transformation' involves 'both suffering and waiting for the work of the Spirit', where both counsellor and counsellee 'must suffer the agonies of change as they await the fruits of change'.[39] For the person seeking help this may mean the realisation that progress is often painstakingly slow; for the helper it may refer to the demands of entering another's agonies and frustrations, becoming freshly aware of one's own vulnerabilities and unresolved memories. Within the hermeneutical process that nudges toward transformation, Gerkin sees that, in 'a limited human sense', 'the vicarious suffering of the pastor embodies the suffering of Christ on behalf of as well as in the place of another'.

This may seem to be an extravagant claim on first reading but it is essential to emphasise the 'limited human sense' of Gerkin's analogy and to add his awareness that 'the pastor is therefore not left entirely on his or her own' within the demands of pastoral counselling. He holds the balance when he writes: 'The counselor's identity as a follower of Christ . . . provides both a model and an authorisation for the suffering work of counseling ministry.'[40]

Amid the unfolding of his incarnational approach, Gerkin looks to the writings of John Dominic Crossan and Sallie McFague for further help in the interpretive task of pursuing the 'fusion of horizons of understanding' in pastoral counselling. He takes Crossan's schema of five ways of using language to construct the 'world' that a person's story 'creates and defines' and applies these insights to his soft-focus hermeneutics.[41] Myth, apologue, action, satire and parable[42] are considered, but, for the purpose of our emphasis on Gerkin's 'theology of the cross', I propose taking the use of the *parabolic form*, together with its attendant linkage with *myth*.

Myth

In everyday speech the word 'myth' is often synonymous with 'lie' or 'falsehood': 'How dare you accuse me of theft! It's a complete myth that I stole your purse', or 'To me the idea of a loving God has to be a myth in the face of the world's suffering'. Although the term derives from the Latin and Greek *mythos*, simply denoting a 'story', its more pejorative and popular sense may have its roots in pre-Socratic writings where the rational truthfulness of *logos* was contrasted with the deceitful storytelling of *mythos*.[43] We meet this dismissive connotation in the Pastoral Epistles and 2 Peter, where, for example, Timothy is commended as a 'good minister of Christ Jesus' and urged: 'Have nothing to do with godless myths and old wives' tales' (1 Tim. 4:6–7).

However, there is an alternative meaning to 'myth', widely used in philosophy, theology and linguistics, where the term refers to a story or narrative that is valued for its validity rather than as to whether it is historically accurate or not. The account of Adam and Eve in Genesis 2 and 3 can legitimately be regarded as myth in this sense. Christians are divided on the historical and geographical veracity of the record's details but many will accept its mythic quality in terms of giving a valid understanding of humanity's creation and fall from grace. It is this second sense of the word that Crossan uses to develop his 'theology of story' and that Gerkin carries over into his hermeneutical theory of pastoral counselling.

Crossan declares that 'Myth establishes world' and Gerkin writes that the pastoral counsellor, from early in the therapeutic relationship, 'focuses on evoking the underlying mythic narrative

of the help seeker's life'. This narrative may, of course, whether it
is historically correct or not, have a validity that is questionable.
For example, a young man who seeks counselling may hold
resolutely to a mythic understanding that, since he is the apple
of his mother's eye, he is attractive to all women and will have no
trouble in picking a mate. This degree of self-assurance may have
led the counsellee into a number of relationships that are marked,
on the one hand, by his arrogant and unrealistic expectations of
the woman concerned and, on the other, by her rapid disenchant-
ment. The pastoral counsellor, following Gerkin's interpretive
approach, will aim 'to enter the world the story has constructed
in order to seek to change it *from the inside*'.[44] And so the young
man's 'mythic story of the self' is carefully evoked so that, step by
step, he is enabled to see the flaws in his mythic narrative and,
with the counsellor's help, come to a truer and humbler self-
assessment and, in time, to relationships of loving mutuality.

Parable

According to Crossan, where myth establishes world, parable
subverts world. Although myth, in its establishing of a people's
or individual's 'world' of ideas, priorities and understanding of
life, can exist without ever being undermined by parable, parable
cannot exist without a mythic 'world' to subvert. As Crossan puts
it: '[A parable] is a story deliberately calculated to show the
limitations of myth, to shatter world so that its relativity becomes
apparent.'[45] And so the 'story' or myth that I have set up to
establish my 'world' rests secure and unassailed unless countered
by another 'story', in parabolic form, that might shed a new,
transformative light on my mythic narrative. The revelatory
experience that the encounter with parable entails is often unner-
ving and in sharp contrast to the comforting voice of myth. Put
graphically, 'You have built a lovely home, myth assures us; but,
whispers parable, you are right above an earthquake fault.'[46]

This 'way of subversion' is writ large in the parables of Jesus.[47]
Here, what is familiar and 'safe' (the established 'world' of the
hearers) is presented initially and the story is unravelled with
grunts and nods of agreement and assent until the parabolic 'twist'
is reached. At this point the audience is arrested by the unexpected. There may be a *reversal*, so that, for example, the normally
commended is suddenly condemned – as in the Parable of the

Pharisee and the Tax Collector (Luke 18:9–14), or the usually despised is dramatically honoured – as in the Parable of the Good Samaritan (Luke 10: 29–37). There may be a *revelation*, an entering of the extraordinary into the ordinary, as in the Parables of the Lost Sheep, the Lost Coin and the Lost Son (Luke 15), where the surprise is that the largesse and joy of everyday recovery is matched among the angels of God. There may be the shock of a *contrary priority*, as in the Parable of the Rich Fool (Luke 12:16–21), where an egocentric business acumen is suddenly faced with eternity. For those who listen, to quote Sallie McFague, 'The secure, familiar everydayness of the story of their own lives has been torn apart; they have seen another story . . . another context or frame for their lives [that] might be a possibility for *them*.'[48]

In the setting of pastoral counselling, the challenging of the counsellee's 'world' by parable is probably at its most effective when, as in the parables of Jesus, its impact is least expected. Rather than through the insertion of 'illustrative or suggestive stories' by the counsellor, Gerkin argues that the 'best parables' may 'simply happen at the "right time" in the counselling process' and may on occasions 'carry the impact of a revelatory experience disclosing ultimately significant truth'.[49]

While on retreat at a Welsh convent in November 1994, I was on the receiving end of such a parabolic 'revelatory experience' which served to subvert in a fresh way the myth of Christian activism which still lurked half-hidden in my 'world'. The sister who was guiding me through an eight-day Ignatian retreat, left with me a clipping which included these words of Bernard of Clairvaux:

> If you are wise, you will show yourself rather as a reservoir than as a canal. For a canal spreads abroad water as it receives it, but a reservoir waits until it is filled before overflowing, and thus communicates, without loss to itself, its superabundant water. In the Church at the present day, we have many canals, few reservoirs.

Through the preceding years recurring illness had taught me much about the need to relinquish a number of activities and the striving, competitive spirit which often accompanied them. It was, though, during retreat, that the choice between the metaphor of the 'reservoir' or 'pool' and the 'canal' or 'channel', as a guiding principle for the next stage of my unfolding 'story', became a freshly subversive moment of truth. In response, I found myself echoing Richard Foster's resolution, 'We have determined to be reservoirs.'[50]

The Supreme Parable

Most understandings of Christianity see the cross of Christ as central to the plan of God's salvation. Its very centrality has invited theologising on a grand scale – not least at the coal face of pastoral theology, where the Gethsemanes and Golgothas of men, women and children echo the all-encompassing suffering of the Son of God. Crossan presents us with just one of the many creative reflections on Christ's passion which may shed light on the anguish and ambiguities of pastoral situations. He argues that, in the early Church, there was a transition from an understanding of Jesus as the teller of parables to a perception of him as 'the Parable of God',[51] as the ultimate subverter of our comfortably self-centred lives. Crossan sees the work of the parabolic Christ as essentially cruciform: 'The Cross replaced the parables and became in their place the supreme Parable.'[52] It is the self-sacrificing death of the Suffering Servant which, supremely, pulls us up short by its declaration of extravagant redemptive love and brings our preoccupied lives to crisis-points of choice.

Gerkin takes Crossan's metaphor and applies it within his own incarnational approach to pastoral counselling. He puts forward the role of the pastoral counsellor as potentially representational of the Christ of the cross as 'the Supreme Parable of God', where, within this 'parabolic imagery, our ministry becomes one of subversion, of seeking to change the mythic narratives of others' lives from the inside by the quality of our presence with them'. In this way, Gerkin declares that the pastoral relationship itself can become parabolic, 'giving to the narrative of the other person a new twist that opens the story to a fresh and lively possibility'. There is no presumption in Gerkin's analogy, no demotion of Christ's supremacy, since 'the good pastoral relationship remains in the lower case; in its ordinariness, its human everydayness, it represents and, on occasion, discloses the extraordinary – the gift of God'.[53]

My encounter with the sister at the Welsh convent remained 'in the lower case'. Although, through the metaphorical language of 'reservoir' and 'canal', a parabolic element in the pastoral relationship gently subverted my own 'mythic narrative', God's servant saw herself as essentially an observer of heaven's engagement with 'ordinariness'. To quote her, she regarded herself as not only a privileged 'fly on the wall' but a 'very shy fly' at that!

A Translation Model

Whereas Gerkin looks primarily to the interpretive tradition from Schleiermacher through Dilthey to Gadamer for his softly focused hermeneutical approach to pastoral counselling, Donald Capps takes the closely analytical tenets of the theologian and philosopher Paul Ricoeur as the centre-piece in his 'translation model' for pastoral care. Since Ricoeur can be seen within the continuing trends of a 'hermeneutics of understanding', there is necessarily some overlap between Capps's and Gerkin's methodologies – not least with respect to the notion of 'pre-understanding', the concept of the hermeneutical circle and the importance of parable in the pastoral encounter. Given this strong measure of common ground we will concentrate more on the distinctiveness that Ricoeur brings to Capps's concern for a hermeneutic that provides 'a very promising method . . . for understanding and evaluating pastoral actions'.[54]

Paul Ricoeur, as we saw at the beginning of this chapter, questions both Descartes's autonomous knowingness and Nietzsche's rejection of even the possibility of objective knowledge. By the same token, aware of the Cartesian shortcomings of the historical-critical method, he seeks, rather, to move forward to a ' "post-critical moment" of openness to the biblical summons',[55] while at the same time remaining 'faithful to the original intention of Schleiermacher's hermeneutics'.[56] His approach is an integrational one, since he aims to bring together both the objectivity of the natural sciences' commitment to 'facts' and the subjectivity of the social sciences' reliance on 'signs'. He sees the key to the dialogue between these often factious potential partners in the discipline of semiology (see pp. 112–15), where the 'explanatory' note of the former meets the 'understanding' focus of the latter: 'It is within the . . . sphere of signs that the process of objectification takes place and gives rise to explanatory procedures. And it is within the same sphere of signs that explanation and comprehension are confronted.'[57]

Using the 'model of the text', he demonstrates a range of

parallels between a hermeneutic of the written word and a hermeneutic of the self. Within this correlation, he argues that the heart of interpretation engages both a more subjective 'guessing' and a more objective process of 'validating', analogous to Schleiermacher's 'divinatory' and 'comparative' methods respectively. Once more, a hermeneutical circle operates – in this case between the intuitive 'guess' and the reflective 'validation', but 'this circle is not a vicious circularity' in which the interpreter is locked into a 'cage' of unverifiable subjectivism.[58] The key to freedom from such imprisonment, Ricoeur argues, lies in the 'personal commitment' of the interpeter within the overall enterprise of balancing objective explanation and subjective understanding.[59] Here, there is a need for a critical 'distancing' whereby the meaning of an action, whether that of an author in his or her writing or another individual engaged in everyday life, is seen to be less in the original intentions of either party and more in the multiple constructions that are possible to the relatively detached observer. In this way, with reference to the text and, by implication, a person's actions, what 'has to be understood is not the initial situation of discourse' but their 'power of disclosing a world'. [60]

This debate will seem an obscure one to many pastoral carers but it is worth saying here that Ricoeur's analysis taps a rich seam of material for everyday use in understanding the lives of people in need. Capps takes a number of these hermeneutical insights and applies them to his pastoral methodology, asking 'What are the major factors involved in understanding a text, and what are their counterparts in pastoral action?'[61] We can examine the essence of his 'translation model' under four headings: the *pastor's intentionality*; *world-disclosure*; *personal appropriation*; and *hermeneutics of suspicion*.

The Pastor's Intentionality

At this stage it is worth noting that the use of the terms pastoral care and pastoral counselling has some variation between the United States and the United Kingdom. Quite commonly in North American usage, and especially within Episcopalian and Catholic contexts, the word 'pastoral' refers exclusively to the ordained pastor, and so pastoral care and counselling are activities carried out by the priest or minister. Although this way of handling the words is part of the British tradition too, there is also a widespread use of the terms to denote caring and counselling which is simply carried out by Christians, especially in the contexts of the local church or specifically Christian counselling organisations. Such Christian carers and counsellors may be lay or ordained. My own use of 'pastoral' is in the latter sense, a calling which may come to any member of the 'priesthood of all believers'. Keeping in mind Capps's North American emphasis, but allowing a wider context for the British reader, let us consider his understanding of the pastor's intentionality within the vocation of pastoral care.

One of my relaxations is to attend a small book group which attempts to read and then discuss a novel a month. Any member of such a gathering will know something of the range of diverse opinions expressed on a particular work: 'It's quite brilliant! I've never read anything so compelling', 'I found it quite disturbing. The central plot led me on, but I felt betrayed by the ending' or 'The whole thing's a sham. There's no decent storyline and as for the characters – they're non-existent!' Sometimes a book is read where an author's note declares something of the circumstances and thinking behind the writing. But this rarely helps the group, since, somehow, the work takes on its own variety of meaning and significance, regardless of the author's original intentions. As Ricoeur puts it, 'The text's career escapes the finite horizon lived by its author.'[62]

Capps, following Ricoeur's analogy between the text and human action, shows how, in the setting of pastoral care, the pastoral action's career, in effect, 'escapes the finite horizon' lived by the Christian minister. Just as my book group spends its time interpreting 'serious' literature, rather than the latest 'pot-boiler', so Capps focuses on 'meaningful' pastoral actions, rather than on a pastor's every encounter with others, however trivial or inconsequential. And so, in the context of, say, visiting a sick parishioner in hospital, supporting a grieving family, organising a soup run for the homeless or engaging with a project to counter local racism, it is argued that 'the intentionality of the pastor is . . . better revealed through the action itself than the pastor's conscious intentions'.[63] This is not to say that his or her intentions are irrelevant, so much as to emphasise that just as authors are known by their texts so pastoral carers are known by their actions. The maxim, 'Actions speak louder than words' and Jesus's warning about the false prophets, 'By their fruit you will recognise them'

(Matt. 7:16) resonate well with Capps's conclusion.

And here some important distinctions emerge between pastoral counselling and its wider context in pastoral care. For in the former, with its more contractual setting, the intentionality of the counsellor rightly comes to the fore. The very essence of counselling presupposes, through training and growing experience, the need for acute self-awareness in the counsellor and a commitment to motives that seek the best for the counsellee within the boundaries of the therapeutic relationship. The more action-based nature of much pastoral care, although it will still require its listening skills and an openness to a person's possible need for counselling, shifts the emphasis away from the pastor's intentionality to an interpretation of his or her activity. As Capps puts it, 'pastors are held responsible for their actions and not for what they thought they were doing'.[64]

And so, with the focus on 'intentionality revealed' in the action itself, the pastoral encounter, to use Ricoeur's term, is 'depsychologized'.[65] Unlike the counselling model, the emphasis moves from the need to unpick motive and examine intent to an honest appraisal of the action and its consequences. As one friend expressed to me during our car journey to a church leaders' meeting and in response to my comment on the complexities of motivation, 'I've given up looking at my motives. I just get on with what needs doing!'

World-Disclosure

Just as we have seen, in Ricoeur, that the meaning of a text relates both to the original, and limited, purposes of the author and, of far greater significance, to the 'world' engendered by the text, so, in pastoral actions, there are, according to Capps, two kinds of meaning: those linked with the 'immediate situation' and those which have a 'world-disclosive potential'.[66] It is the latter that is to be the focus of the hermeneutical theory of pastoral care. And so, where a Christian carer engages with individual or corporate needs within the Church or wider community, he or she should seek to be open to the revelatory nature of the encounter: 'What is there to be learned from this person's or group's experience?' 'How can the local church or community adjust and change in relation to what has happened?' 'What fresh understanding is there for me as I seek to interpret the other's story?'

Let me take a simple example. Some years ago, when I was blind, I visited a dying friend a couple of times, following the simple intention of comforting her amid the pains and nausea of her final weeks. Due to my own disability I was taken to her bedside by another friend, a member of staff at the church we attended. Left together, I attempted to bring some solace to this emaciated young mother of three. However, the pastoral encounter possessed a greater significance than the simple notion of my visit. I found, as I listened to her struggles over pending death and, in time, made my way home, that *I* had been on the receiving end of *her* comfort and that a world was being disclosed in which people in the tightest corners give the greatest blessing to others. The sometimes hidden resource that empowers such 'missionaries of comfort' is proclaimed by Paul in 2 Corinthians 1:3–4: 'Praise be to the God and Father of our Lord Jesus Christ, the Father of compassion and the God of all comfort, who comforts us in all our troubles, so that we can comfort those in any trouble with the comfort we ourselves have received from God.'

Further, Capps, following Ricoeur, argues that 'world-disclosure' takes place essentially through the 'genre' or 'form' of the text and, by implication, of the human action. We have already seen the interpretive value of the parabolic form in Gerkin's softly focused approach to pastoral counselling, where, on occasions, the 'best parables . . . carry the impact of a revelatory experience disclosing ultimately significant truth'.[67] This valid insight into one clear route for 'world-disclosure' is included in Ricoeur's wider analysis of biblical genre and their revelatory potential. In his essay 'Toward a Hermeneutic of the Idea of Revelation', first presented in 1976, he discusses five generic discourses found in the Scriptures: the *prophetic*, where revelation is presented 'in the name of another, in the name of Yahweh';[68] *narrative*, in which 'the author often disappears and it is as though the events recounted themselves';[69] *prescriptive*, revelation's 'practical dimension' which instructs the reader in 'the will of God';[70] *wisdom*, a 'reflection on existence'[71] that binds together the spheres of 'human action' and the 'world';[72] and *hymnic*, a sense of God expressed through the 'three figures of praise, supplication, and thanksgiving'.[73] In all this, Ricoeur argues against a notion of revelation which is 'formulated in a uniform and monotonous fashion'; he declares, rather, a 'polysemic and polyphonic concept of revelation' that is awash with multiple meanings and voices.[74]

And so Capps takes Ricoeur's fertile understanding of the
biblical text and his 'analogy between texts and human actions'[75]
and applies these to the pastoral encounter. He urges the Christian
to pay attention to 'genre' or 'form' within the encounter, since
once we 'know the form of the pastoral action' we can 'begin to
understand what kinds of world-disclosure are possible and what
kinds are not'.[76] We shall look more fully at Capps's 'formative'
approach in Chapter 9 but, for the moment, it is worth noting that,
in his *Biblical Approaches to Pastoral Counseling*, he explores three
particular 'forms' of pastoral care – grief, premarital and marital
counselling – and links each of these with insights from, respectively, three biblical 'forms' – the psalm, proverb and parable.
Within these structures he anticipates world-disclosures which, in
order, address 'the limits of our endurance (and need of comfort)',
'the limits of our moral insight (and need for instruction)' and 'the
limits of human comprehension (and need for reinterpretation)'.[77]
Lest this emphasis on 'form' seem too contrived in the face of
disparate human need, Capps also urges on the carer an openness
to the 'metaphorical content' of the pastoral action, 'because it
concerns the meanings of a specific action and thus its own unique
possibilities for world-disclosure'.

When, for example, I seek to support someone through the
experience of loss – be it a situation of bereavement, a broken
relationship or redundancy – I need to be aware of the form or
'shape' of grief, in terms of initial disbelief at the loss's reality,
ensuing anger and then the struggle of adjustment and re-engage-
ment. Here I can anticipate world-disclosures that point to the
'limits of endurance', to the pain and anguish of separation from a
loved person or situation. But I need, too, if I am to be open to the
'unique possibilities for world-disclosure' in this particular encounter, to listen to its 'metaphorical content'. For Hugh, struggling with
a friendship that had threatened his own marriage, it was his sense
that he and his friend had stumbled into a ravine, while his wife and
children remained on the plateau above, that disclosed his world of
ambivalence in the face of a choice between two losses – that of the
'forbidden' relationship which had come to mean so much to him,
or that of a loving family unit. From the depths of the ravine rose
two difficult paths, the one climbing back to a life of marital
commitment, the other, his friend's path, ascending steeply out
of his reach. It was the disclosive power of this metaphor that faced
Hugh with the need for decision and action.

Personal Appropriation

While writing this section I am also rereading a novel for the book group I belong to: Barbara Kingsolver's *Animal Dreams*,[78] set in the 1980s in the imaginary town of Grace, Arizona. The central figure, Codi Noline, in her early thirties, returns to Grace, the setting of her childhood, aware that her father, Homer, the local doctor, believes himself to be suffering from a fatal brain disease. Early in the book it is clear that the relationship between Codi and her much-loved sister, Hallie, and their father is a strained and ambivalent one. The piecing together of Codi's story – the death of her mother soon after Hallie's birth, the girls' strict upbringing at the hands of Doc Homer and the various loves of her life during her teen and early adult years – takes place through a series of skilfully recounted revelations. And yet, as in any good book, the questions nag through much of the telling: 'Why can't Codi remember the dramatic flood that nearly swept the two sisters away during their childhood?' 'Is Doc Homer really as ill as he believes?' 'What is the significance of Viola Domingos and "the grave of a great grandmother who is no part of this family"?';[79] 'Why "Animal Dreams"?' I look forward to the book group's discussion and to a greater clarification within the disclosure of Codi's 'world'.

Comparably, in the realm of pastoral care, Capps argues that a pastoral action is completed only when it has been understood and that understanding 'entails personal appropriation of the action's world-disclosures'.[80] And just as I am needing to reread Codi's narrative to find a fuller appreciation of her world, so, in the context of pastoral care, it may take repeated returns to the 'story' before the lessons of what has happened can be appropriated by all concerned. Within this process there may be a recasting of attitude and self-awareness which will, hopefully, influence future pastoral ministry. Let me illustrate 'understanding as personal appropriation' in Lucy's story.

Lucy was seeing me on a regular basis for spiritual direction during a time of transition in her developing career. With a background in teaching modern languages, she had been considering for several years the possibility of entering full-time Christian work. It was not that she had denied the God-given nature of her time as a teacher, so much as she had a growing conviction that her communicative skills should be used in a different sphere of service.

During this period of negotiating a change of direction, she was caught up with a small group of fellow church members in caring for Margaret, a young woman who had become progressively ill with what was thought to be a particularly virulent form of multiple sclerosis. Lucy, having left her teaching post, was the most available of the group and spent a great deal of time responding to Margaret's physical and emotional needs. The situation had been one of containment but, increasingly, it became one of inordinate demand on Lucy's time and energy. Margaret, although bound to a wheelchair, seemed unduly secretive about her illness. Living alone and out of contact with her parents, she insisted on keeping the diagnosis from anyone but her doctor, the community nurse who visited her regularly and the small circle of carers from the local church. For a few weeks Lucy received daily phone calls from Margaret, and during that time, supported by the curate, she sought to clarify the chain of clinical and pastoral responsibility. Then one day, Clive, one of Lucy's friends, happened to be passing Margaret's flat and saw the supposedly terminally ill patient running up the path to her door! Clive promptly informed the vicar – who took the opportunity to pay a pastoral visit to challenge the unsuspecting Margaret – and Lucy, who came to see me within a day or two when the full force of the deception was being painfully experienced. Margaret had so elaborated the web of entanglement around her that she had even produced a different voice to simulate that of her 'community nurse', who, from time to time, had 'phoned' Lucy with an update of the situation.

The personal appropriations needed in such a dramatic disclosure of a manipulative 'world' of fantasy and falsehood are, of course, both profound and varied. It was not just Lucy and her friends who had been deceived. In different measures the whole local congregation had been fooled and the vicar, curate and myself, as Lucy's spiritual director, had all been caught up with Margaret's 'story' at various degrees of removal. Certainly, all of us who were most centrally involved needed to take time to face the range of emotions that the situation aroused, including disbelief, anger, outrage, guilt and a sense of betrayal. In all this it was important that we attended, following Capps, 'not just to what literally took place, but to those possibilities the action projects'.[81] If Lucy and the other carers – and, of course, Margaret herself – were to learn from this grim experience, then we had to weigh up the 'possibilities' around the pastoral encounter: 'Could the deception have been exposed sooner?' 'How well supported was Lucy in her often lonely vigil?' 'What balance of "grass-roots" care and pastoral oversight is needed for the future?' In all this we needed to grow in wisdom – a wisdom granted through mature reflection and the pain of reorientation for the future. Here, the hermeneutic of our personal lives could be at its most productive for Christian discipleship. As Capps concludes:

> In approaching a text or action, one is interpreted by it. To be 'interpreted by' a pastoral action is, in effect, to become more self-aware. The basic religious rationale for this view is that self-awareness is the basic quality we share with God; it is what justifies our claim to be created in the image of God.[82]

Hermeneutics of Suspicion

Some years ago, in Margaret Thatcher's heyday as prime minister, I cheekily sent a card to a good friend who is staunchly Conservative in his political convictions. The card, posted in London and using a House of Commons franked envelope, purported to come from Margaret herself, commending my friend for his loyal support and diligent service in the cause of the party. If my friend was taken in at all it was for the briefest fraction of a second. Inevitably, though, he then engaged over the next week or so in seeking to narrow the field as to who the imposter behind the card might be. The issue did not concern the substance of the text, which, in different circumstances, could have been genuine, so much as the nature, motives and mindset of the author. In interpretive terms, my friend was engaging in the 'hermeneutics of suspicion'.

Paul Ricoeur points to the three great influencers of nineteenth-century world-views in the arenas of philosophy, politics and psychology – Nietzsche, Marx and Freud[83] – as heralding a 'new era of hermeneutical work, the era of hermeneutical suspicion'. These three heavyweights were concerned to show that the 'texts' they wrestled with were imbued with an illusory sense of reality, or 'false consciousness'. They moved beyond Cartesian doubt in 'things' to doubt the very consciousness of the doubter.[84] As Capps notes, Ricoeur sees all three 'demystifiers' as regarding culture itself as the overall 'text' to be examined and, from their respective views, found wanting. 'For Marx it was the false consciousness of domination and submission, for Nietzsche of will, and for Freud of desire.'[85]

Ricoeur seeks to learn from these 'masters of suspicion' by acknowledging the need for caution and circumspection in approaching life's texts, but at the same time, he offers a 'hermeneutics of retrieval' to counterbalance a 'hermeneutics of suspicion'. In holding both these interpretive processes, he aims to avoid unthinking gullibility on the one hand and destructive scepticism on the other. Put more positively, for Ricoeur, to quote Anthony Thiselton, hermeneutics 'may be summed up in the two principles: "willingness to suspect", which destroys idols, and "willingness to listen" which retrieves the power of symbols and communicative texts'.[86]

In pursuit of this goal Ricoeur, as we have just seen, acknowledges the importance of 'symbol'[87] as the key to unlocking a great deal of the 'true consciousness' of the text. Here, symbol is seen as that which represents and makes immediate something of the seemingly inaccessible and mysterious, as when Maya, our two-year-old granddaughter, clutches her 'doo-doo', her sodden linen 'transitional object', as an acceptable and ever-present 'symbol' of a parent's comfort. For Ricoeur, the hermeneutical balance is achieved by moving beyond the 'first naïveté' of 'an unquestioned dwelling in a world of symbol', as seen in, to quote Lewis Mudge, 'one-possibility cultures', to a 'second naïveté', where the reader engages with a discerning hermeneutical exploration of 'symbolic and metaphorical texts'.[88] Maya will, of course, in time move beyond the 'first naïveté' of her 'unquestioned dwelling' in the world of her 'doo-doo' to a 'second naïveté' where the complexities of later childhood, adolescence and adult life are explored with, hopefully, a healthy balance between a constructive 'retrieval' of what is of value and an appropriate suspicion of what is doubtful.

Capps takes these insights and applies them creatively to the pastoral encounter, following Ricoeur in giving priority to the influence of two of the 'masters of suspicion': to Marx, with his emphasis that false consciousness ends 'when what man says is equal to what he does, and when his work is truly equal to his being'; and to Freud, with his focus on human desires as the root of any discrepancy between what a person says and means. Thus, in the pastoral situation a 'critical distance' is achieved through a combined interpretive approach of 'suspicion' and 'retrieval' which takes note of human susceptibility to deceive or be deceived in the complex interrelationships between what is wished, what is said and what is done. And, most crucially, Capps offers his 'translation model' to aid the *pastor's* self-reflection as a test of his or her pastoral integrity. Here he poses three questions, the first two using Marxian insight to probe the minister's actions and calling, and the third looking to the Freudian link between desire and world-disclosure to evaluate pastoral effectiveness:

1. 'Is there an essential congruence between the pastor's intentionality in the action itself and the action's appropriation by others?'
2. 'Is the pastor's praxis, as reflected in this action, a true reflection of his/her pastoral self-understanding?'
3. 'Do the world-disclosive possibilities of the action address the fundamental human desires of individuals for whom they are intended?'[89]

Let me give a simple example in which these three questions are addressed. In 1976, at a time when we knew that I was going progressively blind as a complication of diabetes, Joy and I requested of our vicar at Christ Church, Clifton, the Reverend Paul Berg, a service of commitment to the will of God in our situation. It was decided that Paul would lay hands on us both during a specially arranged time of prayer and worship, to be held in the main body of the church after the regular evening service. We had talked the situation through very carefully with Paul and all three of us consequently knew that, statistically, the likelihood of blindness in both eyes was a strong one. The gathering came at the end of a tiring weekend in which I had given five ill-prepared talks at a residential conference of mostly single twenty- and thirty-year-olds. In spite of the quality of the talks (!) there was strong and loving support for Joy and me from the conferees and a considerable number of them swelled the ranks of the hundred or so at the 'laying-on-of-hands' service.

Here, the pastoral intentionality was clear in relation to the pastoral action, since it was understood that the service was one of commital to the unknown will of God – whether the coming years be ones of unimpaired vision, partial-sightedness or blindness. There was an openness to the possibility of healing but also a

willingness to accompany St Paul in his conviction of trust in a
Lord who declared 'My grace is sufficient for you, for my power is
made perfect in weakness' (2 Cor. 12:9). Second, having discussed
with our vicar the implications of prayers for healing and the
pastoral dilemmas around issues of degrees of faith and 'unan-
swered' prayer, it was clear that his customary practice (or
'praxis') and his 'self-understanding' were all of a piece as a
man who held in balance a realistic 'down-to-earthness' in his
dealings with people and a confident trust in God's power to
change lives. And, third, as far as we could judge from the sense of
corporate prayerfulness and loving support, underscored by the
hopes and longings of fellow-Christians whom we knew and who
attended the service, the 'world-disclosive' possibilities of the
occasion fitted well with the people's desires – for divine intervention and enabling in the face of illness, troubled relationships
and life's other struggles. Here was a pastoral hermeneutic which
was suspicious of any false claims for instant and 'magic' cures
and yet embraced the hope of a retrieval of God's true lovingkind-
ness.

Interpreting the Postmodern Self

We saw in Chapters 3 and 4 that postmodernity can be summed
up in its three cardinal dimensions – antifoundationalism, deconstruction and pluralism. And, by definition, we can further conclude that the manifestations of the postmodern in human
cultural, societal and personal life will vary within a spectrum
which runs from a destructive nihilism, where the reality and
value of metanarrative and virtue are denied, to a range of more
constructive stances where the richness and variety of human
experience, story and possible destiny are celebrated, largely
through the exploration of myth, symbol, metaphor and parable.
Consequently, understandings of what it means to be a postmodern self have a comparable spread. We can briefly consider
two contrasting pictures of contemporary selfhood – each providing a viewpoint for 'interpreting the postmodern self': the *liberal
ironist* and the *postmodern Christian.*

The Liberal Ironist

The first viewpoint is that of Richard Rorty and his notion of the 'liberal ironist'. In his *Contingency, Irony, and Solidarity*, Rorty puts forward a philosophy which, following Nietzsche, discards any claim to 'knowing the truth' and sees human life as 'contingent', depending for its existence and understanding on historical circumstance rather than on the 'givenness' of any blueprint for human nature or divine creative action. In this Nietzschean view, 'self-knowledge' is 'self-creation',[90] a continuous reinventing of selfhood paralleled by ever-new experimentation with language, for, as Rorty puts it, 'Truth . . . cannot exist independently of the human mind' and 'where there are no sentences there is no truth'.[91]

The central figures in this deconstructed scene are the 'ironists', people who are 'never quite able to take themselves seriously' because they realise that 'the terms in which they describe themselves are subject to change':[92] as contingent beings, they are subject to the chances of history and the vagaries of new language games. Among such, Rorty favours the 'liberal' ironist where, ideally, the individual is part of a culture that is 'enlightened, secular, through and through' and in which 'no trace of divinity' remains, 'either in the form of a divinized world or a divinized self'.[93] This is a society that, freed from its foundations, seeks to redefine itself around the metaphorical language of the poet, rather than the theologising of the priest or the rationality of the scientist.[94]

The third strand in Rorty's postmodern world, 'human solidarity', arises, not from any notion of a common, shared humanity – since, as we have seen, the idea of such 'givenness' is rejected – so much as in the acknowledgment of 'similarities with respect to pain and humiliation', where 'people wildly different from ourselves' are 'included in the range of "us" '.[95] Here, the ironist, the private individual who seeks to live with the ambiguities of self-definition, may be stirred by liberalism, the public face of a society that will not tolerate cruelty and oppression. Thus, the liberal ironist – through 'imaginative identification' with the sufferer and not, Rorty insists, through 'the love of God, or the love of truth' – is able to 'envisage' and 'desire to prevent' the 'humiliation of others'.[96]

The Postmodern Christian

Roger Lundin, in his *The Culture of Interpretation* (1993), offers a critique of the deconstructed postmodern self, as typified in the writings of Rorty, and argues for a recovery of the Christian faith in the context of postmodernity. Lundin picks up on Rorty's use of the word 'therapeutic' as descriptive of those elements in contemporary culture in which 'we lose faith in the power of language to mirror the truth' and acquire instead a 'newfound appreciation' of 'its capacity to help us get what we desire'.[97] Here, according to Lundin, is manifest a 'secular eschatology of desire' in which 'the kingdom to come' offers an 'expansive and flexible freedom', put into 'the service of the self's quest for expression, acquisition, and satisfaction'.[98]

This self-regarding world of the 'therapeutic self' is contrasted with the Christian's search for 'something greater than the stunning reflection of his or her own desiring countenance', a listening to 'the proclamation of the Word of God' which is 'more than the echo of his or her own voice'.[99] In this 'search for something greater', Lundin warns that the Christian can easily be 'beguiled by the blandishments of deconstruction', in that the poststructuralist's commitment to dismantling the edifice of scientism's certainties and exposing the power games of contemporary culture may appear to be allied to the Church's prophetic voice against modern idolatries and injustice. The Christian, rather, is to distinguish between 'poststructural indeterminacy' and 'the idea of mystery', between 'the vertiginous play of interpretation that has given up on truth' and 'a biblical sense of mystery' which addresses 'a truth that encompasses men and women even as they fail to comprehend it fully'.[100]

In postmodernity's 'vertiginous play of interpretation', Lundin does not deny the need to re-examine traditional language creatively in order to understand and communicate with the contemporary self. In contrast to Rorty's longing for a 'half-formed new vocabulary which vaguely promises great things',[101] Dietrich Bonhoeffer's attempt to find a way to mediate the 'profound this-worldliness of Christianity' to a secular culture is expressed, just months before his death, in a letter to his friend Eberhard Bethge: 'I don't mean the shallow and banal this-worldliness of the enlightened, the busy, the comfortable, or the lascivious, but the profound this-worldliness, characterized by discipline and the constant knowledge of death and resurrection.'[102] Lundin sees this courageous effort to produce a 'new vocabulary', which *more certainly* promises 'great things', as a premonitory 'rejoinder to the cultured weariness of Rortyan postmodernism'.

We can see in Lundin's affirmation of Bonhoeffer that Christian belief and practice do not have to bow to the more subversive elements of postmodernity. In the contexts of clinical and pastoral care, the unfolding work of Boisen, Gerkin and Capps has shown that the contemporary self can be interpreted with compassion and understanding – where people are viewed as 'living human documents', human story is taken seriously and a softly focused hermeneutic prevails in the light of the Judaeo-Christian meta-narrative. Such pastoral carers and counsellors, in effect, challenge the apparently inexorable outworkings of postmodern antifoun-dationalism and deconstructionism toward the de-centred self, who is closed to truth-claims and at the mercy of society's power-interests. The Christian postmodern, rather, seeks to ac-knowledge the potential riches of the third limb of postmodernity – pluralism – without allowing its more excessive elements to submerge the distinctive 'givens' of the Christian tradition. Thi-selton puts the need for such discernment well when, assenting, on the one hand, to the inevitability of 'hermeneutical pluralism', he writes:

> On the other hand, *Christian theology would move into self-contradiction if it ceased to evaluate the prohibition of idolatry, the message of the cross, and the universality of eschatological promise as merely context-relative*; as the *product* or *construction* of a particular social culture with no claim to offer a *universal critique* of life and thought, and even a *metacritique* of other criteria of thought, understanding, and action.[103]

In summary, we can suggest, the key to a constructive herme-neutics of the life in a postmodern age lies in the Schleiermachean tradition through Dilthey, Gadamer and Ricoeur rather than the Nietzschean one through Derrida, Lyotard and Rorty. In the former's expression through, particularly, Gerkin and Capps, we see a pastoral methodology which is polysemic and polypho-nic, to use Ricoeur's terms, breathing life into the understanding of the postmodern self through the well-oxygenated air of the Bible's multiple forms and metaphors.

Having ventured in Part I to explore the 'territory' of our

contemporary pathways to wholeness, through an appraisal of
process and goal, journey and story, modern and postmodern
culture and the hermeneutics of text and life, Part II of this book
will be taken up with one of the many possible 'maps' that can be
used to find our pastoral bearings. This map will be delineated
with an openness to the many-voiced nature of the Scriptures, the
multiple meanings found within the rich inheritance of Christian
spirituality and an awareness of postmodernity's invitation to
value each individual pathway to wholeness in its own right – an
awareness which seeks the undergirding of a trinitarian theology
of hope throughout.

PART II

THE MAP

6

PATHWAYS CHARTED: MAP-MAKING FOR THE JOURNEY

The need to create reliable cognitive maps of the world has been carried to the point where the person prefers the map to the territory, the menu to the meal, the model to the reality.

David W. Augsburger[1]

So far we have studied the terrain through which our journey toward wholeness is taking place. We have explored a landscape which, at times, looks complex, puzzling and dangerous and, at other times, seems exhilarating, inviting adventure and unknown possibilities over the horizon. This is a territory that can be unlocked through story – the need to remember, retell and anticipate – and the recovery of metanarrative, the big story that makes sense of the domain. It is also a territory that is both known, made familiar and tamed by modern map-makers and appraised as liable to slippage, subsidence and the loss of landmarks by postmodern commentators. The comprehension of the guide to this much-loved and much-feared landscape is found in the interweaving interpretation of both text (see Chapter 4) and human life (Chapter 5).

As we now turn to the task of producing a map of the territory, we need to heed the warning that modernity's propensity to analyse and systematise can seduce the cultural cartographer into believing that the definitive map *can* be drawn, that every topographical rise, fall and delineament of every human context can be accurately depicted. David Augsburger, quoted at the head of this chapter and writing in the context of cross-cultural counselling, points to the contemporary danger of 'cultural encapsulation', in which the would-be map-maker has such a strong 'desire to reduce the complexity of the world' that he or she slips into preferring 'the map to the territory, the menu to the meal, the model to the reality'.[2] As we saw in the Introduction, 'a map is *not* the territory' and throughout Part II of this book we should sit loose to the map-making enterprise, remembering that the territory of the enculturation of God's world is always richer, more intriguing and mysterious than our attempts to capture and confine its essence.

At the same time, as we noted in Chapter 3 (see p. 75), postmodernity offers us an equally powerful seduction in the opposite direction. Whereas the modern invites us to celebrate the effectiveness and accuracy of our maps in representing reality, the postmodern entices us to believe that our maps are all the reality there is. The corrective to both blandishments is, once more, in Korzybski's dictum, 'A map is not the territory': in the case of modernity, we need to be reminded that the territory is more wondrous than our maps and, with respect to postmodernity, we need to resist the temptation to say that territory and map are one and the same.

In seeking a balance between these opposing dangers, it is worth noting that, however many different types of map are drawn of a landscape, there will be certain salient features that are discernible on all of them: a mountain or a lake cannot be hidden, unless there is a deliberate choice to remove all foundational topography! Comparably, in the cartography of pathways to wholeness, there are certain monolithic elements that are non-negotiable in any attempt to be true to the Judaeo-Christian tradition.[3] The immovable 'mountain' of both map and territory is the Lord God himself, revealed supremely, so orthodox Christian belief declares, in the life, death and resurrection of Jesus Christ and through the mediation of his Spirit.

And so, keeping in mind the twin pitfalls of modernity and postmodernity, let us delineate our map of pathways to wholeness under three main headings: *pastoral care*, which is, as it were, the very landscape that we seek to map; *a pastoral theological method*, giving us the tools for both our map-making and engagement with the terrain; and *mapping the pathways*, in which we will focus on the key to the ensuing map in terms of doctrine, Scripture, metaphor and spirituality.

Pastoral Care

The notion of pastoral care, it can be argued, is as old as human need and the calling to respond to that need. Within the Judaeo-Christian tradition the impetus to care for others lies in the revealed nature of Yahweh – who 'defends the cause of the fatherless and the widow, and loves the alien' (Deut. 10:18) – and the unfolding perception of God as Trinity, three persons within the one godhead, interrelating in perfect love and calling the emerging Church to respond to the summary of the 'entire law': 'Love your neighbour as yourself' (Gal. 5:14). This neighbourly love is to be all-inclusive, boundary-crossing and tailored to precise human predicament: Jesus urges his followers to love their enemies;[4] exemplifies a love that breaks Judaistic taboos toward Samaritans, women, children and work, even healing work, on the Sabbath;[5] and challenges God's people to respond to the communal needs of hunger, thirst, homelessness, lack of clothing, sickness and imprisonment.[6] It goes without saying that such wide-sweeping compassion includes within its compass love toward family, friends and fellow-believers – the last, at times, the most difficult love, since there may be little or no 'natural' affection involved. Leanne Payne is realistic about the high calling of Christian love when she writes, 'We love confusedly, we fallen ones; the journey of life is for setting love in order.'[7]

It would be incorrect, though, to equate Christian love with pastoral care, as the latter is simply one manifestation of that love. Perhaps one of the most helpful ways of visualising the essence of pastoral care in biblical terms is to see its close links with the Greek word *paraklesis*, exhortation, encouragement, comfort, consolation. Jacob Firet takes this term as part of a threefold picture of 'pastoral role-fulfilment', comprising proclamation (*kerygma*), teaching (*didache*) and pastoral care (*paraklesis*). These three pastoral 'modes' are clearly interrelated, so Firet argues, and yet there is in the parakletic ministry something 'which lies in a different sphere from that of the authoritative proclamation of salvation and the didactic unfolding of it'.[8] He sums up this pastoral calling in these words: '*Paraklesis* is the mode in which God comes to people in their situations of dread, suffering, sin, despair, error, and insufficiency', bringing them into 'the joy of new obedience' and a readiness 'to fulfil special tasks within the body of Christ'.[9]

We can look more closely at this transformative work by posing two questions: What is pastoral care? Does it need an underlying theology? In Chapter 9, we will ask 'Why *pastoral* care?' as we examine the links between the metaphor of the shepherd and pastoral care and counselling.

What is Pastoral Care?

From ancient times pastoral care has been simply what Christians do as part of their neighbourly love toward needy fellow human beings. Although great stretches of the history of pastoral care have invested the shepherding role[10] in that of the ordained minister, the thread of the 'priesthood of all believers', however tenuous at times, has also run throughout the centuries – to free women as well as men, laity as well as clergy, to respond to the call to care for others in the name of Christ. Since it is modernity's bid to analyse, define and systematise, it is only in comparatively recent times that attempts have been made to clarify a precise understanding of pastoral care. We will consider two contemporary definitions.

The first, that by William A. Clebsch and Charles R. Jaekle and published in 1964, has become interwoven with a number of appraisals of pastoral care[11] and still serves as a useful baseline:

> The ministry of the cure of souls, or pastoral care, consists of helping acts, done by representative Christian persons, directed toward the healing, sustaining, guiding, and reconciling of troubled persons whose troubles arise in the context of ultimate meanings and concerns.[12]

Although this definition has been criticised by Stephen Pattison for its apparent clericalism ('representative Christian persons'), individualism ('troubled persons') and problem-centredness (focus on 'troubles'),[13] it is worth drawing out two of its clauses for constructive comment.

First, the overall division of historic pastoral care into 'healing, sustaining, guiding, and reconciling'[14] has a pragmatic usefulness in terms of an understanding of the rich inheritance of *cura animarum*, the cure of souls, to use an established alternative term. I have been using this analysis in discussions with theological students for nearly fifteen years now and still find that the four *functions* of care resonate well with contemporary debates on pastoral issues: for example, the relationship between a theology of healing and a theology of suffering (these two subsumed in Clebsch and Jaekle's *healing* and *sustaining* functions respectively); between pastoral counselling and spiritual direction (under *guiding*); and around notions of forgiveness and church discipline (under *reconciling*). This fourfold structure is a valuable contribution toward the map-making enterprise of Part II of this book.

Second, Clebsch and Jaekle's notion of 'representative Christian persons' is more open to misunderstanding in the light of the current debate on pastoral care. As we saw in the last chapter (see p. 138), there is a tendency in the North American scene to equate the 'pastoral' with the 'clerical', whereas, in a British context, although that view is still represented, pastoral care and counselling are generally regarded as the potential province for *all* Christian carers. In fact, Clebsch and Jaekle adopt an 'in-between' position, seeing their 'representative persons' as people 'who, either *de jure* or *de facto*, bring to bear upon human troubles the resources, the wisdom, and the authority of Christian faith and life'. Although such 'commonly' hold 'the office of authorized pastors', they may possess 'no churchly office whatever'. Either way, Clebsch and Jaekle seem to argue, the local church is safeguarded from the well-intentioned but wayward ministrations of the inept and self-authorised by, among other things, the possession and exercise of 'the authority of a company of Christian believers'.[15] Whereas Pattison is right to criticise them for their individualism, Clebsch and Jaekle clearly also see pastoral care in a communal and corporate Christian context.

The second major definition of pastoral care for our consideration is one offered in the magisterial *Dictionary of Pastoral Care and Counseling*, published in 1990 and edited by Rodney J. Hunter. This book provides an invaluable resource for the documentation of the development of the pastoral calling throughout the twentieth century, especially in its North American context. Hunter writes:

Pastoral care is considered to be any form of personal ministry to individuals and to family and community relationships by representative religious persons (ordained or lay) and by their communities of faith, who understand and guide their caring efforts out of a theological perspective rooted in a tradition of faith.[16]

This definition holds up well in the light of contemporary understandings of pastoral care. First, it is worth saying that this is not a specifically Christian declaration in that it implicitly acknowledges, in the general phrases 'representative religious persons' and 'their communities of faith', the reality of post-modern pluralistic societies. The dictionary discusses, for example, personal care in native American traditional religion as well as, clearly within the history of the Old Testament's shepherding metaphor, Jewish caring and counselling. Second, the definition avoids the individualistic tendencies of earlier writers and proclaims the twofold element of interdependence: with respect to the recipients of pastoral care in their 'community relationships'; and as the supportive context of the 'communities of faith'. Third, there is no equivocation around such doctrines as 'the priesthood of all believers', since the 'personal ministry' is carried out by 'representative religious persons (ordained or lay)'.[17] The fourth point – the reality of an underlying 'theological perspective rooted in a tradition of faith' – will be considered in the next subsection.

An Underlying Theology?

Historically, pastoral care has often been diffident, and even coy, about claiming a need for an underlying theology. Its emphasis has been intensely practical and the idea of theologising in the face of an anguished request for guidance, the last words of a dying parishioner or the weeping of a grieving relative has often been far from the intentions of the sensitive pastor. Perhaps something of Brueggemann's thought hovers at the back of the mind: 'The serpent is the first in the Bible to seem knowing and critical about God and to practice *theology* in the place of *obedience*.'[18]

But all this side-stepping of theology can be seen to be a failure of nerve, since, to quote David Tracy, 'all our experience, indeed all praxis, is theory-laden'[19] and pastoral care, a ministry of front-line experience, is as 'theory-laden' as any other human enterprise. Elsewhere, Tracy declares that '*praxis* is correctly understood as the critical relationship between theory and practice whereby each is dialectically influenced and transformed by the other'.[20] And this, surely, is the heart of the matter for pastoral care, since its theology, as with all theology, needs to demonstrate the critical interface between theory and practice: a *praxis* in which theory is shown forth in enlightened practice and practice informs theory with the cutting-edge of everyday life. To reflect on the anguish and distress of a young woman dying of cancer, to be angry with God and face unanswerable questions, and then to return to the bedside to make some feeble attempt at companionship in suffering, is about *doing* theology – a pastoral theology that is praxis.

Theology itself has many shades of meaning. Most definitions emphasise its essentially mediatoral and communicative style, seeking to translate the mysteries of God into accessible language. Luther opted for simplicity and profundity: 'Theology is nothing but grammar, applied to the words of the Holy Spirit.'[21] G. Ernest Wright stresses its scriptural basis: 'Theology may . . . be defined as the discipline by which the Church, carefully and with full knowledge of the risk, translates Biblical faith into the non-Biblical language of another age.'[22] David Tracy expresses a comparable, though broader, declaration when he writes, 'Theology is the discipline that articulates mutually critical correlations between the meaning and truth of an interpretation of the Christian fact and the meaning and truth of an interpretation of the contemporary situation.'[23] This last definition fits well with the hermeneutical climate of today's postmodern culture and is a stance that we later adopt in considering a pastoral theological method.

Traditionally, theology can be subdivided into *fundamental theology*, addressing such foundations of the faith as the existence of God and the nature of revelation; *systematic theology*, the attempt to give shape and pattern to the detailed content of Christian belief; and *practical theology*, comprising such 'ministerial activities' as preaching (homiletics), teaching (catechetics) and pastoral care.[24]

In the Europe of the mid eighteenth century,[25] *pastoral theology* began to emerge as a potential subdiscipline within the concurrent development of practical theology. Throughout the next two centuries practical theology was caught up in an essentially pragmatic approach to human need, in which its offspring, pastoral theology, was seen as simply the province of a theological reflection that undergirds the 'activities' of pastoral care.

This love affair with functionalism was fanned into further ardour by the advances of the new disciplines of dynamic psychology[26] and the psychology of religion[27] during the early years of the twentieth century. It is here that Edward Farley's criticism of much practical theology bears on the nature of pastoral theology too – a theology without the backbone of a substantial base of theory, 'a combination of a functionalist temper', focused on ministerial action,[28] and 'one or two extratheological disciplines that provide the scholarly aspect'.[29] This indictment has proved true both sides of the Atlantic, for many theological colleges and seminaries still allow pastoral theology to be the Cinderella within the faculty, seeing its role as beyond the pale of academic theology and concerned solely with the messy business of human life, aided and abetted by theoretical input from such disciplines as psychology and sociology.

And yet there is hope for a pastoral theology which is true praxis, where, as we have seen, there is a mutually transformative interplay between theory and practice. A wind of change blew into the clergy-dominated, pragmatic world of a psychologised pastoral care through the influence of Anton Boisen, whom we met in the last chapter. His emphasis on a reflective theology that took seriously the loves and trials of 'living human documents' was later revived in Hiltner's shepherding perspective, which, in turn, sought a pastoral theology that 'draws conclusions of a theological order from reflection' on 'the operations and functions of the church and the minister'.[30] Such approaches have been further developed, modified or challenged by a range of contemporary theologians that include Paul Ballard,[31] Stephen Pattison,[32] Elaine Graham[33] and David Deeks,[34] in the United Kingdom, and James Lapsley,[35] Don Browning,[36] Edward Farley and David Tracy, in the United States. Here there is a sharp awareness that, to quote Ballard, pastoral theology is a 'primary theological activity' that pays attention 'to the particular and concrete', to the realities of the immediate situation in the lives of individuals, people in relationship, groups and institutions.[37]

As we explore the five pathways to wholeness in the coming chapters, we will pick up with the particular emphases brought by a number of these pastoral theologians and by other writers in the areas of theology and spirituality. Throughout, we will be aware that each pathway tends to favour its own theological and spiritual stance. Although a great range of methodological positions can be taken up, broadly we will find two main polarities are returned to again and again: an emphasis on law, ethics, ground rules and foundational 'givens', on the one hand; and a stress on experience, story, imagination and personal and communal encounter on the other. Where too much weight is given to the first, there is a danger of steamrollering human need and differentness;

where the second is overplayed, there may be a slippage into untethered, uncontainable individualism and widespread relativism.

Rabbinic Judaism has the wisdom to observe these polarities sharply and, at its best, to argue that the two perspectives be held in balance. Abraham Joshua Heschel sees their contrast as a 'contest' between *halacha* and *agada*. Of these two Hebrew concepts, he writes:

> Halacha represents the strength to shape one's life according to a fixed pattern; it is a form-giving force. Agada is the expression of man's ceaseless striving which often defies all limitations. Halacha is the rationalization and schematization of living; it defines, specifies, sets measure and limit, placing life into an exact system. Agada deals with man's ineffable relations to God, to other men, and to the world . . . Halacha deals with law; agada with the meaning of the law.[38]

Among the pastoral theologians whose methods we shall consider there is, inevitably, a pull toward one extreme or another, toward law or story, ethics or experience, *halacha* or *agada*. And, we can add in terms of our contemporary debate, this polarity is also displayed in the parallel pull between modernity's commitment to foundational knowledge and system, on the one hand, and postmodernity's celebration of narrative and antifoundationalism, on the other. For example, in Don Browning's *fundamental practical theology*, we see a systematic approach that shows elements of both modernity and *halacha* in its bid to rediscover the importance of an ethical and obligational framework for all pastoral and communal care.[39] By way of contrast, we can say that Elaine Graham's *transformative Christian practice* demonstrates a more fully worked postmodern stance, in which *agada* features strongly in her commitment to a practical wisdom that openly values human 'otherness' and pursues a liberational pastoral theology toward the oppressed and disadvantaged.[40] In establishing our methodological approach we will seek to hold a balance between these approaches, open to the ethical groundbase required by *halacha* and, at the same time, responsive to the experiential and narrative qualities of *agada*. The search is for a method that is both mindful of God-given universals and open to a liberative, gender-sensitive approach that values particularity and differentness.

A Pastoral Theological Method

In many ways, the differences between Browning's 'practical reasoning' and Graham's constructively feminist 'Christian practice' highlight the dilemmas of forging a satisfactory pastoral theology in the melting-pot of contemporary society's mishmash of premodernity, modernity and postmodernity. How far are we to return to premodern understandings of God and humanity? And if we are to recover the traditions, do we do so by switching off from today's cultural mêlée? Or do we, following Richard Niebuhr's 'Christ-above-culture' rather than 'Christ-against-culture' (see pp. 67–70), engage with the contemporary scene? And if we do that, is it to be the one-way traffic of a proclamation that does not listen, or a commitment to a dialogue that takes seriously modern certainties and postmodern uncertainties? Either way, is our emphasis to opt for clear ground rules, as in the Jewish understanding of *halacha*, or to give priority to narrative and experience, as in *agada*? Or, in cultural and philosophical terms, does our Christian praxis shift ground and, if so, how far does it move into modernity's elevation of reason or, to be really brave, or foolish, into the exciting, confusing world of postmodernity's antifoundationalism, deconstructionism and pluralism?

In our pastoral context, such questions address the matter of *a pastoral theological method*, where, to quote Bernard Lonergan, *method* is 'a normative pattern of recurrent and related operations [which] yields cumulative and progressive results'.[41] However, it has long been recognised that the methodical is not necessarily equated with insight, as is shown in Polonius's oft-quoted aside concerning Hamlet: 'Though this be madness, yet there is method in't.'[42] Method, in Lonergan's words, 'is not a set of rules to be followed meticulously by a dolt. It is a framework for collaborative creativity.'[43] At its best, it is a joint enterprise that is freed from inflexible formulae and engages creatively with the task in hand. At its least cluttered, it is essentially autobiographical, since it concerns the creative process of life's pilgrimage. As John S. Dunne puts it, 'My method is my journey.'[44]

The method proposed in surveying the five pathways to wholeness seeks to be *transcendental, cautiously foundational, correlational* and *liberational*. Under the banner of practical theology and its offspring, pastoral theology, it is essentially a method of praxis, in which theory and practice interrelate in mutual transformation – a front-line form of *doing theology*.

A Transcendental Method

Transcendence is one of those big theological words, like immanence and immutability, that can silence a discussion in a house group or Bible study by its mystifying lack of precision. It is, by definition, one of those 'beyond' words that will not be pinned down.

Generally speaking, transcendence is used in two main, related senses. The first is its broad useage to denote those perspectives and understandings that are above and beyond the everyday and material. Here there is a sense of mystery and incomprehensibility before the seemingly unknowable. It was the experience of being overwhelmed by transcendence that led Job to cry, 'Surely I spoke of things I did not understand, things too wonderful for me to know' (Job 42:3). Second, transcendence is used more specifically and theologically to denote the distinctiveness of God as above and beyond the creation. This too, of course, was intrinsic to Job's experience, for his humbling took place before the awesome power and wonder of a creator who was over and against Job as his creature: 'Then the LORD answered Job out of the storm [and] said: "Who is this that darkens my counsel with words without knowledge?"' (Job 38:1–2).

Colin Gunton shows how modern theology, following the inheritance of Kant, Schleiermacher and Hegel, has encouraged 'a move from seeing God as "outside" to locating him "within" the world', thus shifting from a historic theology of transcendence to the various fashionable theologies of immanence of today. He goes on to argue that modernity's rejection of the 'otherness' of God is a tragically mistaken one, since the modern fear of a deity who is over and against humanity is the misplaced fear of a loss of human autonomy. Rather, he writes, 'Theologies of transcendence allow for human independence and freedom by leaving a space between the divine and the human.'[45] Thus, modernity has made 'the cure worse than the disease': by rebelling against a misconceived 'alienating otherness', it threatens 'the true otherness of the world'. The desire for independence leads to the loss of interdependence, of 'otherness-in-relation, both personal and cosmic'.[46]

More specifically, and in accordance with the 'theology of hope' we outlined in Chapter 3, the transcendental method of this book is essentially *trinitarian*. The concept of the Trinity – of one God, three persons – has always been difficult for human minds. The story is told of a guide who, pointing out the various features on the gatehouse of Trinity College, Cambridge, announced grandly, 'And here, ladies and gentlemen, are the four persons of the Trinity: the Father, the Son, the Holy Ghost, and the Blessed Trinity Himself.' And yet, whatever understanding of trinitarian mystery we may grope toward, it is the *relational* aspect that can give us greatest heart and insight for our pastoral calling. As Jürgen Moltmann puts it, writing of the Spirit's relation to the Father and the Son, 'personhood is always being-in-relationship'.[47] And so, a pastoral theological method, with its commitment to *otherness* and *relatedness* in the lives it seeks to help, will, if it is to be truly Christian, be open to the otherness and 'being-in-relationship' of the triune God – in other words, to a trinitarian transcendence.

A Cautiously Foundational Method

In Chapter 3 we charted postmodernity's unpicking of the foundations that had been laid by successive waves of religious and, increasingly since the Enlightenment, scientific and technological certainty. Although preceded by the 'givens' of earlier Judaeo-Christian tradition, it was the wedding of Western notions of truth with that heritage that has formed the bedrock of *foundationalism* so vigorously attacked by the postmodern imagination. Nicholas Wolterstorff sees that bedrock as the establishment of 'a body of theories from which all prejudice, bias, and unjustified conjecture have been eliminated'. And, 'on all fronts', in the face of postmodernity, 'foundationalism is in bad shape'.[48]

Many, if not most, Christians react to the loss of what is foundational with anxiety. In fact, such people need to take heart, for the central thrust of postmodernity's antifoundationalism is an attack on the orderly, systematised edifice of modernity's certainties. If, in Wolstertorff's words, 'foundationalism is in bad shape', we should see that it is the modern self-confidence in the authority of 'reason', 'experience' and 'ideology' that is in 'bad shape', rather than, necessarily, the fundamental tenets that underpin the Judaeo-Christian faith.

In the context of a pastoral theological method, both Browning and Graham, to different degrees, carry the torch of antifoundationalism within their methodologies.[49] In doing so, they both, however, seek to hold back from the dizzying drop into the black hole of postmodern nihilism. It is one thing to question the ground we stand on, it is another to bulldoze it out of existence! At the same time, though, they demonstrate the difficulties of antifoundationalism's path, for it is a natural human wish to re-establish something 'foundational', whether it is Browning's particular brand of ethical reasoning[50] or Graham's communal practical wisdom.[51] It is here that Christian pastoral carers should rejoice, since the momentum of antifoundationalism, in its dismantling of modern knowingness, opens up the way for a pastoral theological method that is brimful with Lonergan's 'collaborative creativity', where ancient verities are rediscovered and deconstructed truths are reconstructed.

We noted at the beginning of this chapter that the enterprise of contemporary conceptual and methodological map-making needs to choose a route between modernity's overdefinition and a postmodern deconstruction that leaves no map. The way forward for the Christian map-maker, it was suggested, is to see that there are certain elements of 'foundational topography' that cannot be gainsaid. The 'mountain', we argued, is God himself. And so, we can say, there is a tentative middle path between the extremes of a foundationalism that universalises 'reason', 'experience' or 'ideology' as *the* mainstay of life and an antifoundationalism that dismisses all grand understandings, including an understanding of God, in the name of differentness and particularity.

Colin Gunton, I believe, offers the right pointer to the direction needed in this quest for 'non-foundationalist foundations': it lies in our *attitude of mind*. Having outlined the need to 'find the moments of truth' in both universality and particularity, he asks, 'If we are finite and fallible human beings, should we not rather seek for a concept of truth that is appropriate to our limits, both in capacity and in time and space?' Here is a step down from the lofty heights of Enlightenment reason to a humbler, more tentative place, where an awareness of our creatureliness as divine image-bearers helps us realise that our map-making is always searching for greater clarity. 'It is a rationality appropriate to created knowers in a world with which they are continuous.'[52]

And so, in terms of re-establishing appropriate 'non-foundationalist foundations', we can say that our pastoral theological method is to be not only transcendent but also cautiously foundational, undergirded, in Gunton's words, with a *created* rationality.

A Correlational Method

Having laid out a method that is cautiously foundational in declaring the otherness and relatedness of God, we need to turn our gaze from the heavenlies to the many contexts of pastoral practice, be they street corner, family kitchen, local church, counselling room or hospital bed. What can we add to our pastoral theological method in the face of the human condition at the frontline of Christian praxis? It is, I suggest, a *correlational* method that is best suited to the often uncomfortable realities of 'doing theology'.

As both Browning and Graham point out, current pastoral theology owes a great deal to a correlational approach. Paul Tillich (1895–1965), seeking to reconcile Freudian insight and traditional Christian understanding, established the trend with his *method of correlation*, in which systematic theology 'makes an analysis of the human situation out of which the existential questions arise' before demonstrating 'that the symbols used in the Christian message are the answers to these questions'.[53] The one-way explanatory style of this approach is challenged and revised by David Tracy, and, in turn, further modified by Browning.[54]

In *Blessed Rage for Order* (1975) and *The Analogical Imagination* (1981) Tracy addresses contemporary pluralism in theology and the wider culture respectively, presenting a 'revisionist' correlational approach for today's Church. In the earlier book he puts forward his distinctive method against the backdrop of a critique in which 'classical liberalism, classical orthodoxies, various kinds of neo-orthodoxy, and various radical alternatives' are found wanting as adequate models for 'the present theological task'.[55] In turn, he offers a 'post-liberal' theology which challenges 'both secularity and traditional Christianity . . . in accordance with publicly available criteria for meaning, meaningfulness, and truth'.[56] In the later book, he carries over the debate into the relevance of such a theological method in the public worlds of society and academia, as well as the Church.[57]

In his 'revisionist model for contemporary theology', Tracy declares that the two principal sources for that theology are

'Christian texts' and 'common human experience and language'. In contrast to Tillich's one-way street of correlation, Tracy's method seeks the two-way traffic 'of correlating the principal questions and answers of each source'.[58] Inevitably, this is a hermeneutical task, which 'articulates mutually critical correlations between the meaning and truth of an interpretation of the Christian fact and the meaning and truth of an interpretation of the contemporary situation'.[59] All in all, Tracy's method acknowledges clear Christian declaration within the pluralities of postmodernity:

> A theological pluralism which could rest content in the merely aesthetic pleasure of a pluralist world is unworthy of the commitment of the Christian theological traditions to the Word as bearer of meaning and truth for all humanity, or to the seriousness of the present crisis of meaning in our increasingly global community of inquiry.[60]

Although the postliberalism that Tracy adheres to will be addressed more fully in Chapter 9, it is worth saying now that his revised correlational method is one well suited, as demonstrated by Browning,[61] to the pastoral encounter. It takes seriously the harsh and complex realities of people's lives, offering a listening ear to what seems to be *actually* happening, rather than a reflex response which reacts to the situation because the 'rules have been broken' and 'something must be *done*'. Such pastoral engagement may, of course, take place at the personal or communal level. The latter may concern, for example, laws relating to the status of incoming refugees, issues around abortion on demand or situations of suspected sexism in the workplace, and is to be undertaken correlationally correlationally by the Church – a body that needs to see itself as, to quote Browning, 'a community of moral discourse', desirous of creating 'a truly human society, even if that society is not always explicitly Christian in all respects'.[62]

And so we seek a pastoral theological method which is not only *transcendental* and *cautiously foundational*, but is also *correlational*, engaging with pastoral need at personal, familial, communal and socio-political levels by a process of two-way listening, speaking and acting that takes seriously the human condition.

A Liberational Method

The fourth and final dimension of our pastoral theological method is *liberational*. Here, a cautiously foundational awareness of a transcendental God of otherness and relatedness, carried through into a correlational method that engages personal and communal pastoral need, must face, I suggest, the requirement to seek 'liberation' in the light of private and public inequities. The God of Israel and of Jesus is a liberative God. As Moltmann puts it: 'Exodus theology is not yet resurrection theology, but resurrection theology must always include exodus theology and must again and again be embodied in acts that liberate the oppressed.'[63]

Elaine Graham's 'transformative Christian practice' offers a profoundly liberational method that is also open to feminist and narrative theologies. True to postmodernity's celebration of particularity and differentness, she puts forward a *practical wisdom* that is the very 'medium by which truth-claims and value-commitments come into existence'.[64] This formative wisdom serves to mould attitudes where human otherness, or *alterity*, is valued and where 'the irreducible difference and mystery of the other' demonstrates 'a moral community [that] is heterogeneous and pluralistic', rather than hidebound by 'a universal set of needs and qualities'.[65] Here, once more, we see that Graham's approach to human reality is one of *agada*, in contrast to Browning's tendency toward *halacha*. Thus Graham, through the exploration of 'difference and alterity' in the stories of women's experiences and the accounts of other marginalised groups, engages with 'the disclosive function' of practical wisdom.[66]

To illustrate such *disclosure*, she cites a range of examples from the work of Nancy Fraser, in which a number of 'runaway' needs, starting as issues dealt with in the private domain and breaking loose into public consciousness, serve to reveal the mismatch between women's perceived needs and the established norms and meanings of a patriarchal society. Thus, self-help groups, tenants' associations and women's health groups have helped redraw the boundaries between the 'public' and 'political', on the one hand, and the 'private' and 'domestic', on the other, on such issues as the valuing of housework, the need of child-care, accusations of 'date rape' and the realities of sexual harrassment in the workplace.[67]

And so, Graham argues, the 'practical wisdom' of Christian

practice needs to be guided by the question, 'What does it disclose/foreclose?' In other words, what values and preconceived ideas lie behind the pastoral encounter – both those that reveal what is just and liberating and those that expose what is unjust and restrictive? Here, Graham acknowledges the tension between the traditions of history and contemporary experience, arguing that the latter, in, for example, the feminist movement, 'may reveal the foreclosures and fault-lines of historic practices'. Once more, we are reminded that we are set in a culture of interpretation, in which the past is not seen as 'a fixed and concrete event' so much as a source for disclosure, wherein 'the enduring availability of possible meanings' are 'available for reinterpretation'.[68]

In Graham's liberational method we see a pastoral theology which permeates a Christian practice that is gender-sensitive, charged with practical wisdom, respectful of otherness and disclosive of 'new horizons' within a postmodern context. Here, the very *difference* of each pastoral engagement is allowed to speak forth its own reflectiveness and wise resolutions.

Thus, all in all, we have a pastoral theological method that seeks a balance between *halacha* and *agada* within its transcendental, cautiously foundational, correlational, liberational style, providing, at its best, a God-centred praxis which can be described, simply, as *doing theology*.

Doing Theology: Praxis Revisited

Laurie Green, with his hands-on approach of *doing theology*, demonstrates, I suggest, the essence of the pastoral theological method we have explored. Based for ten years as vicar of the parish of Erdington, beneath Birmingham's Spaghetti Junction, and, subsequently, as principal of the Aston Training Scheme, which offered theological education to men and women prior to ordination training, Green has a great deal of first-hand experience of theological praxis in urban settings. In *Let's Do Theology* he puts forward a 'new model' of theology which has arisen from the needs and situations of the people among whom he has worked, and pays particular attention to issues of 'liberation, context, action, power, oppression and spirituality'.[69] Here is an approach, containing transcendental, foundational, correlational and liberational elements, which may be used by individuals or groups and 'moves around continually from action to reflection and from reflection to action'.[70]

Green's earlier book, *Power to the Powerless*, provides rich illustration of this active and reflective theology. Soon after the founding of the ecumenical project of St Chad's, Erdington in 1974, the combined Anglican and Methodist congregation carried out a major analysis of the locality and its needs, putting strong political pressure on local government to finance a community centre for the area.[71] This awareness was carried over in 1979 into the Parables in Action Group, a regular gathering of socially and racially mixed church members who, together with Laurie Green as their vicar, sought a 'democratised' theology, 'reclaimed as an essential component of every Christian's kitbag'.[72]

As the group looked at gospel parables its members began to appreciate two dynamic elements: Jesus's clear understanding of his contemporary reality; and his appreciation of the continuity between the Jewish people's history and the 'present and imminent reality of the Kingdom of Heaven'. Armed with these insights, they decided that, in order to find out how the parables really worked, they needed to be subject to a parabolic process themselves. And so, for the coming months, they resolved to use the identified twofold ingredients of the parable to re-examine carefully the present realities in their part of Birmingham, research the history of its people and the structures within which they lived and, 'simultaneously and imaginatively', reflect on what God might want of them in the situation.[73] Thus, the group used what was, in effect, a *revised correlational method*, as they searched the library archives, poured over maps and tape-recorded the memories of ageing residents to recover Erdington's past and, in turn, assessed 'present realities' through collecting demographic material, drawing up a checklist they could all use and sharing subjective impressions to balance objective data.

Newly aware that their locality was viewed as 'that area with lots of problems!', the group raised a number of critical questions: 'What can be affirmed from our past? What from our past do we denounce? Which developments were good and which bad? Who made the decisions and who did they affect?'[74] As they studied the contemporary scene they began to uncover a range of uncomfortable facts to which they had perhaps turned a blind eye, including: the degree of anxiety among residents concerning deteriorating properties, increasing street violence and high unemployment; the repeated reference in government reports to 'low moral and intellectual standards' and to 'problem families'; and the high level of air pollution recorded within their motorway-dominated skyscape.[75]

Having identified the experience of powerlessness and frustration in the local community, the Parables in Action Group moved on to further reflection, realising that their church had allowed itself to become distant to the people, most decisions on policy were made by outsiders, the present helping organisations were struggling and often ineffective, relevant skills and information were in short supply and the residents' low self-esteem was 'fed by popular myth and biased media'.[76] Turning from one of Tracy's two principal sources for theology – 'common human experience and language', back to the other – 'Christian texts', the group once more exposed themselves to the parables by acting out a few of them, to experience them 'from the inside'.[77]

It was the story of the Good Samaritan in particular that revealed a range of stark correlations between the well-known parable and their situation. Amid the ensuing discussion, Madeleine, one of the group members, said, 'Just like the Samaritan, we are actually where the parishioners are, we're right on the spot. Even if we could only act as an information centre for people, that would be something.'[78] The group, seeking to keep its horizons wide as it reflected further, repeatedly came back to the notion of some sort of advice bureau, a need that had been pinpointed by a previous government survey, which stated that 87.6 per cent of the local residents had asked for just such a provision.[79] After fourteen months of deliberation and careful planning, supported by diocesan and other local money, the Community Advice Centre was opened in 1981, hopefully 'a small parabolic light in the present urban darkness'.

Looking back at the project, Sue, another of the group's members, expressed the spirit of Green's democratised process of 'doing theology' well when she declared:

> We've been helped to discover that theology . . . can be done today. It's a practical exercise that involves action, like the setting up of an Advice Centre or whatever, and reflection upon that action. We have experienced a feeling of growing self-confidence in ourselves as theologians. Theology is too important to be left to the ministers of the Church.[80]

And so we have established the value of a pastoral theological method which is *transcendental, cautiously foundational, correlational* and *liberational*, demonstrating its loving Christian *praxis* through *doing theology* within a repeating interchange between *action* and *reflection*. This will be our methodological basis as we unfold the mapping of the pathways to wholeness.

Mapping the Pathways

A map-making enterprise, if it is to make sense to others, has to decide in advance what aspects of the terrain are to be surveyed and thus depicted. Is it to be a map that shows land use, sites of special scientific or conservational interest, the historical geography of an area, lines of communication, the morphology of the landscape or its underlying geology? Whatever the overall objective, there also have to be decisions about what is to be included and what excluded. So far, having taken our bearings within the territory of contemporary culture, we have begun to establish that our mapping of pathways to wholeness, in the context of Christian pastoral care, needs to include a portrayal of a pastoral theological method. And just as every cartographer – even a flat-earther! – has a view on the nature of what is being mapped, so we have worked toward a theology that is ably demonstrated in the praxis of Laurie Green's 'doing theology'.

Before delineating in detail in the coming chapters each of the pathways – biblical counselling, the healing ministries, pastoral counselling, spiritual direction and social transformation – in terms of their theological style and quest for wholeness, it remains to outline four other parameters of the proposed map, not so far considered: *doctrine, Scripture, metaphor* and *spirituality*. For clarification throughout the remainder of the book the reader might like to refer to Figure 1 below. This gives an overview of the developing schema to include the four parameters just mentioned, as well as four others culled from our exploration of pathways to wholeness.

Doctrine

Within contemporary society 'doctrine' is often seen as a particularly formidable word, out of touch with postmodernity's emphasis on plurality and the discarding of metanarrative. It has a hard-edged, joyless sound and is guaranteed to dampen

	BIBLICAL COUNSELLING	HEALING MINISTRIES	PASTORAL COUNSELLING	SPIRITUAL DIRECTION	SOCIAL CHANGE
FOCUS	Cognition Behaviour	Journey Back	Relationality Psychological maturity	Inner journey Spiritual maturity	Community Environment
DOCTRINAL APPROACH	Propositional	Experiential-expressive	Experiential-expressive Cultural-linguistic	Two-dimensional (Propositional & Experiential-expressive)	Cultural-linguistic
HERMENEUTICS	Exegetical	This-is-that	Soft-focus Intratextual	Spiritual reading (*lectio divina*)	Hermeneutics of suspicion
USE OF SCRIPTURE	Prescriptive	Therapeutic	Formative	Imaginative	Socio-political
METAPHOR	Teacher Evangelist	Healer Deliverer	Shepherd	Priest (desert-dweller, soul-friend, midwife)	Prophet Wise one
SPIRITUALITY	Evangelical Postevangelical	Charismatic Pentecostal	Liberal Post liberal	Catholic Eastern Orthodox Celtic	Liberation Feminist Third-eye
THEOLOGY	Foundational	Experiential	Correlational	Transcendental	Liberational
KEY WORDS	Word Cross	Spirit Power	Trinity Covenant	Presence Mystery	Exodus Freedom

Figure 1: A Map of Pathways to Wholeness

debate and stop conversation in today's experience-loving society.

Even so, George Lindbeck argues that doctrine is the lifeblood of all religions. In the context of Christianity, for example, he writes that the doctrines of the Church are 'communally authoritative teachings regarding beliefs and practices', which are seen to be 'essential to the identity or welfare of the group in question'. Declaring 'the inescapability of doctrine', he reasons that even those faiths that see themselves as free of doctrinal encumbrance, such as Quakerism, become 'by definition operationally creedal', in that their so-called 'creedlessness' is claimed 'as a mark of group identity'.[81] Here, as it were, members of the relevant body, in declaring that they do not hold to specific teaching, demonstrate a certain solidarity in a doctrine of 'no doctrine'.

Either way, Lindbeck does not expect too much of doctrine. Inspiration is preferable, he argues, but, unfortunately, 'saints and prophets are rare' and so doctrinal decisions, although 'poor substitutes' for the inspirational, 'are preferable to uninspired and unreflective prejudice'. He divides approaches to today's doctrines, which can be 'both firm and flexible, both abiding and adaptable',[82] into three main groupings: *propositional*; *experiential-expressive*; and *cultural-linguistic*. We will look at these in detail at appropriate points in the coming chapters, but, for the moment, it is worth sketching an outline of each of them.

Most theologically orthodox streams in Christianity hold *propositional* approaches. Here there is an emphasis, given the commitment of faith, on what is knowable through *cognition*: appeal is made to the Christian believer on the basis of the reasonableness of doctrines which function 'as informative propositions or truth claims about objective realities'.[83] And such 'truth claims' are indissoluble; although they can be denied or watered down, they cannot be eradicated. Conversely, what is once false will always be false. As we explore doctrinal styles within the pathways to wholeness, we shall see the essence of propositonalism expressed, for example, in the cognitive-behavioural style of biblical counselling, in the evangelical wing of the healing ministries and in the more traditional Catholic and Eastern Orthodox proponents of spiritual direction.

Contemporary attitudes to doctrine are widely characterised, Lindbeck observes, by what he calls *experiential-expressive* approaches. Contrasting with propositionalism in almost every respect, these replace the cognitive resolve to adopt a 'discursive' style, in which conclusions are reached through reason and argument, with an emphasis on the *expression of experience* that is 'nondiscursive', or intuitive.[84] Whereas propositional doctrine appeals primarily to the mind and issues in declarations of credal belief, the experiential-expressive stance – demonstrated, for example, in pastoral counselling's 'liberal tendency' – lays its weight on the *inner life* and is shown forth through the world of symbols.[85] In this split between clear doctrinal statement and an emphasis on intuition, experience and symbol we see, once more, something of the polarity between *halacha* and *agada* respectively. A number of contemporary theologians aim to combine the best of these two strands in what Lindbeck calls a 'two-dimensional' approach.[86] Although we will meet elements of this combined style in the charismatic approaches of the healing ministries, its clearest expression is seen in the pathway to wholeness of spiritual direction.

The third main section of doctrinal styles, the *cultural-linguistic* approaches, sums up Lindbeck's preferred viewpoint. Here, the emphasis is on 'those respects in which religions resemble *languages* together with their correlative forms of life and are thus similar to *cultures*', where the latter are understood 'as idioms for the constructing of reality and the living of life'.[87] Whereas propositionalism focuses on a cognitive mindset, based on a foundational faith, and experiential-expressivism on the 'inner life' and its intuitive links with symbolism, cultural-linguistic approaches look to the *outer life* of culture and language and to a *regulative* or *rule* theory of doctrine.

The novelty of such 'rule theory', Lindbeck argues, is that it does not place 'the abiding and doctrinally significant aspect of religion' in 'propositionally formulated truths', much less in 'inner experiences', but in 'the story it tells and in the grammar that informs the way the story is told and used'.[88] Here, in contrast to the premodern roots of much propositionalism and the lineage of experiential-expressivism in the romantic and autonomous strands of modernity, we can say that the cultural-linguistic approaches, in their narrative and interpretive styles, are quintessentially postmodern. Lindbeck argues that this last approach is the domain of the 'post-liberal' and we shall continue to see a strong emphasis on culture and language amid the postliberal elements in the pathways of pastoral counselling and social transformation.

All in all, Lindbeck's sentiments, echoed in the variety of the five pathways to be considered, are summed up well when he writes:

It seems that from the very beginning [Christianity] has been committed to the possibility of expressing the same faith, the same teachings and the same doctrine in diverse ways. This is illustrated by the
multiplicity of Christological titles in the New Testament. No particular
words or specific interpretive notions are uniquely sacrosanct.[89]

Scripture

Fellow-travellers on pathways to wholeness see Scripture in
diverse ways – as lifeline or quicksand, authority or literature,
as guidebook or puzzle, as currently relevant or hopelessly ar-
chaic. And just as we have noted a variety of approaches to
doctrine among contemporary Christians, so we will find a diversity of viewpoints and practices relating to the place and
usefulness, or otherwise, of the Bible on the pastoral routes
examined. We have already discussed, in Chapter 4, the vexed
question of how to interpret the text of Scripture and, in Walter
Brueggemann's simile of the 'compost heap' and David Clines's
injunction to 'read against the grain' (p. 119), observed examples
of ways that readers today are seeking fresh and refreshing ways
of approaching the Bible. It remains now to outline briefly some of
the main groupings found in handling the Scriptures on the
Christian journey.

David Kelsey addresses 'a situation that is theologically open
and characterized by rich theological pluralism', in which a
number of 'theological positions' are examined, each claiming
to be 'in accord with scripture'.[90] In this appraisal he provides
a helpful overview of the uses of Scripture through an evaluation
of major stances adopted in the work of seven theologians: B. B.
Warfield, Hans-Werner Bartsch, G. Ernest Wright, Karl Barth, L. S.
Thornton, Paul Tillich and Rudolf Bultmann. First, there is a broad
subdivision between the first two and the remaining five, in that
the former see Scripture as holding its authority through its
'content', while the latter view that authority as resting primarily
in Scripture's 'function'. And so, in summary, Warfield and
Bartsch look to the 'authoritative element in scripture' as 'its
doctrinal and conceptual *content*'[91] respectively, while the action-based functionalism of the Bible is expressed by Wright
and Barth through 'narrative', Thornton in 'literary image', Tillich
in 'religious symbol' and Bultmann in 'kerygmatic myth'. Kelsey
concludes his assessment of this rich vein of understandings of the

Scriptures by emphasising their commitment to Christian community and a praxis that reaches out beyond the walls of the local church:

> For such theologies the concrete contexts in which biblical texts function precisely as 'Christian scripture' are a set of activities that are constituent of the church's life: preaching the gospel, celebrating the sacraments, doing the liturgy, teaching the doctrine and lore of the faith, giving pastoral care, offering service to the world's needy, making prophetic judgment on immorality both in the lives of members of the community and in society generally.[92]

We shall keep in mind Kelsey's analysis of different uses of the Bible, and the hermeneutical emphases behind them, during our survey of the five pathways to wholeness.

Metaphor

Everyday language is full of metaphor. When we use phrases like 'time is money', 'I could eat you', 'Let's sift the evidence', 'Stop fishing for compliments', we are speaking metaphorically. There is no literal intention in the words – the second example, for instance, does not usually imply imminent cannibalism! The use of metaphor, rather, is seen where two things are compared concisely 'by saying that one is the other',[93] but, at the same time their meanings are kept distinct. Or, to quote G. Lakoff and M. Johnson, 'The essence of metaphor is understanding and experiencing one kind of thing in terms of another.'[94] To say, 'The kingdom of heaven is like a mustard seed' (Matt. 13:31) engages two domains – God's kingdom and the hedgerow, and the mystery of the former is at least partly fathomed by the familiarity of the latter.

Many metaphors are so much part of the language that they cease to arrest and stimulate. In contrast, a fresh metaphor can open up new horizons, or, as we noted in the last chapter, in Ricoeur's phraseology, be 'world-disclosive'. Sallie McFague cites the example of 'war is a chess game' as a metaphor that stirs the imagination to see military engagement in terms of strategy, feints and endgame. As in most, if not all, metaphors, the picture given is a partial one: there is more to war than manoeuvres, and the account given by a game of chess necessarily leaves out the elements of human destructiveness and brutality.[95]

The partial nature of metaphor is perhaps at its clearest in trying to express the mystery of God. As McFague says, metaphor 'always has the character of "is" and "is not"'. To say, for example, 'God is mother' is not to define God *as* mother, so much as to 'invite us to consider some qualities associated with mothering as one partial but perhaps illuminating way of speaking of certain aspects of God's relationship to us'.[96] It is inevitable that the Bible's God-talk is brimful of such suggestive metaphorical language: 'the Shepherd, the Rock of Israel' (Gen. 49:24); 'the LORD God is a sun and shield' (Ps. 84:11); '[God] will cover you with his feathers, and under his wings you will find refuge' (Ps. 91:4); 'the Word was God' (John 1:1); 'Jesus said again, "I tell you the truth, I am the gate for the sheep"' (John 10:7); 'our "God is a consuming fire"' (Deut. 4:24; Heb. 12:29).

Further, in terms of our postmodern context, there is the need, according to McFague, for theologians to 'think experimentally', risking 'novel constructions in order to be theologians *for our time*'.[97] Thus the overt metaphors of the Scriptures, and those that lay more hidden in the text, are extended, amplified, and even added to, by the metaphorical theologian, who tries out 'new pictures that will bring the reality of God's love into the imaginations of the women and men of today'.[98] This seems to me to be a wholly worthwhile enterprise, as long as 'extrascriptural' images are assessed by the yardstick of Scripture, bearing in mind the need to read the text both 'between the lines' and 'against the grain'.[99]

There are, in effect, two opposing poles around this stance. The metaphorical is a dimension of life that is shunned by the rigid propositionalist, who may side-step biblical metaphor, with its invitation to the creative and imaginative, in the relentless pursuit of uncompromising instruction and clear-cut statement. At the other extreme, the postmodern world of virtual reality may see the metaphorical as its very life-blood. As McFague has it: 'Fundamentalism fails to appreciate that the language of theology is metaphorical, and deconstruction refuses to acknowledge that there is anything but metaphor.'[100]

Metaphors are the building blocks that make up *models*. Donald Capps argues that, although a single metaphor may not have the power to do so, a 'loose collection' of metaphors, as in the Book of Proverbs, may combine to form 'a model of human life' that comprehensively embraces its 'social, natural, and personal' perspectives. Put differently, McFague declares that 'a model is a metaphor with "staying power" . . . a metaphor [that] has gained sufficient stability and scope so as to present a pattern for relatively comprehensive and coherent explanation'.[101] Either way, our map-making enterprise seeks a model made up by a metaphor, or metaphors, with 'staying power'.

We have already discussed various bids to provide pastoral care and its underlying theology with suitable metaphors and models. We noted, for example, Seward Hiltner's commitment to the 'shepherding perspective' (see note 14) and Ricoeur's declaration (p. 141) of a 'polysemic and polyphonic concept of revelation' made up of five genres of discourse: the prophetic, narrative, prescriptive, wisdom and hymnic.[102] Alastair Campbell puts forward the images of shepherd, wounded healer and wise fool as depictions of the pastor's character.[103] Capps takes these three metaphors further, as reflecting 'three distinctive pastoral self-understandings that are capable of integrating one's praxis'.[104]

From my own reflections, teaching and writing over the last decade or so, and, taking due note of the work of Ricoeur, Campbell, Capps and others, the metaphors of pastoral self-understanding that I propose to explore in the coming pages are those of *teacher* in the prescriptive and propositionalist world of biblical counselling; *healer* and *deliverer* within the more 'experiential-expressive' style of the healing ministries; *shepherd* in the contextual and relational sphere of pastoral counselling; *priest* (in the forms of 'desert-dweller', 'soul-friend' and 'midwife') in the mediatorial domain of spiritual direction; and *prophet* and *wise one* within the praxis of social transformation.

Spirituality

The final parameter that both links and distinguishes the various pathways to wholeness is that of 'spirituality', a term that has become more widely used and misused in the realms of religion and theology, and, indeed, life itself, than words like 'empathy' and 'congruence' have in the fields of counselling and psychotherapy. Tom Lubbock, reviewing the Radio 4 programme *Only Connect*, wrote that 'the magic word was "spirituality": infinitely preferable to either faith (sounds gullible) or religion (sounds strict), being founded on the unshakeable rock of self-expression'.[105] And, with the rise of the transpersonal psychologies and the merging of New Age experimentation with the fundamental human longing for significance, meaning and connectedness, spirituality has spread through the verbal landscape like fire in a Dorset heath.

Starting life within French mysticism in the seventeenth century, and used in its early years dismissively for a piety that was out of touch with the sweat and toil of everyday life,[106] the word 'spirituality' covers an ancient concept that has been freshly taken on board by many religious beliefs in our pluralistic society, not least by a range of perspectives within the Christian Church – extending from the realms of Celtic, Catholic and Eastern Orthodox practice to a cautious welcome in more evangelical and charismatic circles. Spirituality is a wide term used by a wide range of people. David Benner points up its universalism when he writes that *natural spirituality* is 'the response to a deep and mysterious human yearning for self-transcendence and surrender'. This yearning can be further expressed through *religious spirituality*, 'a relationship with the power or being who serves as the focus of self-transcendence and as the meaning of life' – 'a movement toward the true God or . . . some other god'. From this frame of reference, we can clearly then talk of, for example, Hindu, Muslim, Jewish or Christian spiritualities.[107]

As we have noted, religious spirituality implies relationship – with God, a god, or gods – and definitions of Christian spirituality rightly emphasise the relating aspect of discipleship. Central to Christianity, of course, is the person of Jesus Christ and so the simplest declarations of a spirituality that is truly Christian are christocentric. Paul Edvokimov, the Orthodox theologian, for example, sees the maturing process within Christian spirituality as 'Christification',[108] a work of grace begun through Christ, continued in Christ and completed by Christ. Joann Wolski Conn, declaring that the term spirituality 'refers to both a lived experience and [increasingly] an academic discipline', widens the focus of the former to that of a 'trinitarian, christological, ecclesial religious experience'.[109] This experience, further, needs to embrace issues of justice and mercy in society, if it is to avoid a retreat into a privatised faith that, to quote Kenneth Leech, loses its humanity and becomes 'nothing more than religiosity'.[110]

Taking these relational, trinitarian, christocentric and liberational perspectives, we can define Christian spirituality as *that dimension of human existence which emphasises the living out of a commitment to God in every area of life (personal, social, political, ecological), in relationship with Christ, sustained by the Holy Spirit, and within the contexts of the believing community and the wider world.*

Backed by this definition, we will explore the relevance to pathways to wholeness of a range of Christian spiritualities, from evangelical, charismatic, liberal, Catholic and radical traditions. Throughout, we will be mindful that each mode of pastoral care – biblical counselling, inner healing, pastoral counselling, spiritual direction and social transformation – needs something of the adventurous and forward-looking spirit of the Texan priest who claimed that Christian spirituality should be 'a spirituality for pioneers rather than settlers'.[111]

Summary

In Chapters 3 and 4, we established that the three salient features of postmodernity are antifoundationalism, pluralism and deconstructionism and showed that these perspectives, when taken to their extremes, slide inexorably toward relativism and nihilism: toward, in Jonathan Culler's words, a 'certain reckless sawing, a calculated dismemberment or deconstruction of the great cathedral-like trees in which Man has taken shelter for millenia'.[112] In this chapter, we have tried to clarify a pastoral theological method which seeks to discern what is of value in the postmodern project: to rescue 'non-foundationalist foundations', to use Gunton's phrase, from what is antifoundational; to celebrate particularity and otherness within pluralism; and to seek a circumspect reconstruction of the 'ancient pathways' in the face of deconstruction.

And so, to this end, we have laid out the plans for our mapping of pathways to wholeness. We have surveyed the terrain of Christian pastoral care, noting its long history in the functions of healing, sustaining, guiding and reconciling, and observing its more contemporary voice in addressing the personal and communal needs of a pluralist society. We have explored the theology that undergirds today's pastoral care and have demonstrated, in Browning's 'fundamental practical theology' and Graham's 'transformative Christian practice', two notable commitments to clarify the calling of pastoral theology in the present climate of high modernity and postmodernity, commitments that serve to illustrate the polarity between *halacha*, law, and *agada*, story. In turn, we have elaborated a pastoral theological method as the necessary tool for both delineating the map and for engaging with the territory. This method is to be transcendental, cautiously foundational, correlational and liberational, a trinitarian and christocentric approach that takes seriously the questions and answers of those in need and celebrates the otherness and relatedness of both God and fellow human beings within its Christian praxis. Finally, we have established a key to the map of pathways to wholeness, pinpointing doctrine, Scripture, metaphor and spirituality as signposts to indicate the particularities and differentnesses of the routes to be explored: biblical counselling, inner healing, pastoral counselling, spiritual direction and social transformation.

At last we can engage with the five individual paths. As we do so, let us recall that the landscape is much more wondrous and complex than our attempts to map the possible ways through it. Maps are fun, but they are, inevitably, simplifications of the territory. Let the words of David Kelsey, writing of his own piece of descriptive cartography on the uses of Scripture, be an apt cautionary note at this stage of our journey:

> The work of God the Holy Spirit . . . is not patient to systematic mapping . . . Theological proposals are concerned with what God is now using scripture to do, and no degree of sophistication in theological methodology can hope to anticipate that![113]

BIBLICAL COUNSELLING: THE TRANSFORMED MIND

Scripture . . . is not an encyclopedia, but a tool for making encyclopedias.
Richard Lovelace[1]

In the general mêlée at the 1980 Christian Booksellers' Convention in London, where my first book, *Restoring the Image*, was being launched, I was accosted by an earnest young man who, knowing I was putting forward a church-based approach to counselling, asked me, 'Do you follow Jay Adams or Narramore?' Taken aback by the presumption that there could only be two possible pathways in the Christian counselling scene, I replied, with some relish I have to admit, 'Neither!'

In many ways, though, the young man's urgent question sums up much of the story of a range of Christian approaches to counselling which sought to respond to the incoming tide of secular counselling, comprising successive waves of behaviourism, Freudianism and humanistic psychology, with an attempt to recover the power and relevance of Scripture in meeting human need. Many Christians, for example, had responded to Freud and his successors through the 1930s and beyond, as we saw in the context of Anton Boisen in Chapter 5 (see pp. 122–5), with *assimilation*, eagerly and uncritically absorbing such fetching new notions as that human malaise is, fundamentally, a question of neurosis rather than sin. In the 1940s and postwar years, the humanistic basis of Carl Rogers's psychology proffered a non-directive, client-centred counselling style that became the central credo of the rapidly rising counselling movement. In many ways, this more optimistic and more relationally based method (human being as personhood) proved more readily enticing to Christian pastoral carers than the earlier blandishments of behaviouristic reductionism (human being as machine or simply higher animal) and of Freudian psychoanalysis (human being as the sum of instincts). In the face of such widespread assimilation of secular methodologies, a second response among Christians, that of *reaction*, began to find a voice, especially in the ranks of evangelicals from the 1960s onward, many claiming to be even more 'biblical' than their Bible-loving predecessors. A third response by Christians, that of *dialogue*, has moved more and more into centre-stage among those who were formerly assimilative or reactive, among liberals and conservatives alike.[2] It is here that we come back to the young man's comments, since we can see in today's so-called 'biblical' counselling an evangelical spectrum, ranging from Jay Adams's more excluding and reactive style to Clyde Narramore's more integrational and potentially dialogical one.[3]

We will consider the strengths and weaknesses of biblical counselling, our first pathway to wholeness, under two main headings: *exclusion or integration?* and *the way forward*.

Exclusion or Integration?

Since the 1950s, when Clyde Narramore first put forward an approach that heralded the possibility of integration between faith and psychology, and the late 1960s, when Jay Adams launched a brand of Christian counselling that, in essence, excluded psychology, a battle has raged to and fro between these two broad stances as to which can be more truly dubbed 'biblical' counselling. Some practitioners, notably Lawrence J. Crabb, have adopted something of an in-between position, a viewpoint that might be described as 'cautiously integrational'. Whatever the precise vantage point, the whole debate lies within the realm of the more fundamentalist, evangelical and Reformed sections of the Christian Church and hinges, ultimately, on just how the Scriptures are seen in relation to perceived human need.

The evangelical tradition holds to a view of the Bible as *the* inestimable resource through which God declares himself and his dealings with humankind: in other words, a *revelational* view. Even so, there is a split between perspectives that keep solely to the text of Scripture as *special* revelation, wherein God's Word is seen as all-sufficient *in itself* for all that is needed in terms of understanding and transforming human nature, and those that allow that the Bible *also* points beyond itself to a God who speaks through creation, history and human experience, in *general* revelation.[4] In terms of our notion of pathways to wholeness, do we have a purely special revelational route-finder, where the words of Scripture are our sole guide within a dark and alien landscape, or is the Bible not only the clear revealer of the way to God but a generous companionate resource which points out to a wondrous, sometimes obscure, sometimes illuminating, terrain?

Let us look more closely at the story and essence of the two stances within biblical counselling: the more excluding, special revelational style, typified by Jay Adams and his 'nouthetic' counselling; and the more integrational styles, often holding an openness to both special and general revelation, of Clyde Narramore and his successors. Third, we will examine the continuing debate between and within these two broad standpoints.

Excluding Biblical Counselling

It is not my purpose here to repeat my critique of Jay Adams's methodology, as described in *Roots and Shoots*,[5] so much as to spotlight some of its continuing emphases in order to clarify the contemporary debate on what it means to be 'biblical' in Christian counselling. It is my contention that the phenomenon of biblical counselling, whether in its excluding or integrational forms, does not have the sole rights to Scripture and that each of the five pathways under consideration in this book can be true to the Bible in some aspect or other of its rich revelation. Even so, it is in the issues that surround the rival positions of 'exclusion' and 'integration' that we find, because of their evangelical, Scripture-loving pedigree, the most overtly focused discussion.

Jay Adams, a Presbyterian pastor in Pennsylvania and New Jersey and lecturer in homiletics at the Westminster Seminary, Philadelphia, experienced a great deal of frustration during the early 1960s as he tried to counsel needy Christians with the Freudian and Rogerian insights of the day. He declares that his distinctive *nouthetic counselling* was launched in 1969 on the back of two cardinal influences: the neo-behaviourism of O. Hobart Mowrer and the presuppositionalism of Cornelius Van Til, professor of apologetics at Westminster. Working under the tutelage of Mowrer in the summer of 1965, Adams readily responded to his mentor's open challenge to the widely accepted 'medical' model of mental illness and strong avowal of the 'moral' model, in which such terms as 'neurosis' and 'psychosis' are discarded in favour of an acknowledgment of real guilt and personal responsibility.[6] This re-evaluation of human 'mental' dysfunction in terms of sin rather than sickness was reinforced by Van Til's strong commitment to a 'two kingdoms' view of humanity, in which no one is neutral and all live out their lives in accordance with 'conceptions of reality' – either Christian or non-Christian. His presuppositional view is uncompromising: 'All men are either in covenant with Satan or in covenant with God.'[7]

Following these leads, nouthetic counselling incorporates the centrality of personal culpability, the universal dividing line of presuppositionalism and, by inference, a strong suspicion toward 'secular' helping professionals such as clinical psychologists and psychiatrists.[8] In line with these emphases, Adams looks to the usage of *nouthesia* and *noutheteo* in the Greek New Testament as giving the context and flavour of Christian counselling methodology. The words, with their connotations of warning, instruction and admonition, are used in situations of relating within the Christian fellowship[9] and, in the Van Tilian sense, are words of 'a world run by the counsel of God'.[10] Adams is consistent in his approach in that nouthetic counselling is committed to helping the *believer*, because, he writes, 'you can't *counsel* unbelievers in the biblical sense of the word (changing them, sanctifying them through the work of the Holy Spirit . . .)':[11] conversion to Christ, he argues, is the prerequisite for authentic 'biblical change' through Christian counselling.

The biblical change that Adams writes of is, in essence, a change of mind and action[12] that is effected through the open use of scriptural texts during counselling. This *cognitive-behavioural* enterprise, in fact, sees the Bible's text as *the* resource for personal transformation: 'All that is needed to form values, beliefs, attitudes, and behavioral styles is in the Scriptures. Indeed, no other book can do so.'[13] Further, Adams's methodology is largely *propositional* and *prescriptive* in its handling of the Bible;[14] that is to say, biblical statements and propositions (the Book of Proverbs and Pauline Epistles are happy hunting-grounds)[15] are explicitly used within the counselling encounter and are often prescribed for the counsellee to learn and apply as 'homework' between sessions. The touchstone of Adams's approach is seen to lie in Paul's declaration to Timothy that 'All Scripture is God-breathed and is useful for teaching, rebuking, correcting and training in righteousness' (2 Tim. 3:16), since, Adams states, this verse indicates that 'the Scriptures themselves are nouthetically oriented'.[16]

Although Adams's methods have been much criticised for their strongly directive and excluding style,[17] there is evidence that certain of his colleagues and followers, as is often the case where the legacy of a powerful leader is taken up by others, have adopted a less confrontational and more inclusive stance. In 1968 Adams was joined by John Bettler, a fellow-pastor, in the founding of the Christian Counseling and Educational Foundation (CCEF) at Laverock in Pennsylvania. In 1977 the National Association of Nouthetic Counselors was launched and its views began to be promoted through the *Journal of Pastoral Practice*. This organ, in turn, became the *Journal of Biblical Counseling* in 1993. Significantly, in an interview conducted by David Powlison with Adams and Bettler that year, the narrower term 'nouthetic' counselling[18] had clearly given way to the more comprehensive one of 'biblical' counselling.[19] Further, Bettler's gentler and more inclusive approach is evident in the discussion between the three men. Where Adams's personal style is described as 'tough' and, at times, 'overwhelming', Bettler says of himself, 'If you aren't an exuberant person, counseling won't work if you start shouting'; where Adams focuses on training the ordained as counsellors, Bettler widens the remit to include lay people; and where Adams follows Van Til closely in emphasising 'the antithesis between belief and unbelief', Bettler seeks, less confrontationally, to 'recycle' error 'in the light of truth'.[20]

And yet, given the commitment of a nouthetic counselling that has claimed the high ground of *biblical* counselling, there remains the need to clarify a stance that is, given its pedigree as a reaction to a psychologised culture, essentially *excluding*. John Bettler, arguing from a Presbyterian tradition that looks back to the Westminster Confession of 1646, seeks to begin the process of establishing a 'confession of faith for those who claim to be biblical counselors'. Acknowledging the differences among such, he goes on to say that 'we have stronger commonalities', including a trinitarian creed, which also, in accord with evangelical orthodoxy, declares a belief in 'the authority of the Word of God' and that the Bible is 'the infallible rule of faith and life inspired of God'. In the context of applying such a standpoint to the counsellor's view on the place of the past in the counsellee's life, he declares the need 'to do the dangerous job of drawing circles, drawing lines', where anyone 'within the circle is biblical', anyone 'outside the circle is not'.[21]

Integrational Biblical Counselling

Christian counsellors who seek an integration of insights from theology and psychology are seen by many in the more excluding biblical counselling movement as definitely 'outside the circle'. Even so, there is a strong corpus of evangelical opinion which has grown up around what is seen as a Bible-based calling to integration. With its earliest North American roots in the 1950s and 1960s in the partially integrational approach[22] of Clyde Narramore, the founding of the Christian Association for Psychological Studies (CAPS) in 1952 and the Graduate School of Psychology at Fuller Seminary in 1965, it became an increasingly sophisticated and professionalised body through the 1970s and 1980s.[23] The launching of the *Journal of Psychology and Theology* by the Rosemead School of Psychology in 1973, as 'an evangelical forum' for the integration of these two disciplines, and the *Journal of Psychology and Christianity* by CAPS in 1982, to 'provide scholarly interchange among Christian professionals in the psychological and pastoral professions', were landmarks on the continuing road toward an integrational biblical approach[24] in the world of pastoral care and counselling.

Parallel movements can be seen in broadly evangelical circles in the United Kingdom: the founding of the Clinical Theology Association, under the aegis of Frank Lake, in 1962;[25] the formation of the Institute of Christian Counselling, directed by Selwyn Hughes, in 1975;[26] the development of a number of integrational-style Christian counselling centres over the next decade or so, including Care and Counsel in London, Network Counselling in Bristol[27] and the Oxford Christian Institute for Counselling in Oxford; and the setting up of the Network of Christians in Psychology (NeCIP) in 1989, as a forum for the integration of faith with psychological training and experience. The launch of the Association for Christian Counsellors (ACC) in 1992 has seen the more excluding stream of the British Association of Biblical Counsellors (ABC), set up in 1984,[28] join with a number of more integrational counselling organisations to form a monitoring and accrediting body for Christian counsellors, supervisors and training courses.

Since the early 1970s the debate between psychologists and theologians, each bringing to the other the distinctiveness of presupposition, goal and method intrinsic to their respective discipline, has proceeded with a series of checks and balances in the quest for a measure of theoretical and practical integration. The foundational stone laid in this edifice of dovetailed building materials has been named so often that its nature, essential to the construction's coherence, is easily dismissed as a truism. This is the simple but profound statement: *all truth is God's truth*. The philosopher Arthur Holmes puts this declaration into perspective. Arguing on the basis of a Christ-centred biblical theology, he writes:

> The early church claimed that all truth is God's truth wherever it be found. The *focus* here is on truth. But the ultimate *locus* of truth is God. If he is the eternal and all-wise creator of all things, as Christians affirm, then his creative wisdom is the source and norm of all truth about everything. And if God and his wisdom are unchangingly the same, then truth is likewise unchanging and thus *universal*. If all truth is his, and he understands fully its interrelatedness, then truth is *unified* in his perfect understanding.[29]

It is important, in terms of our discussion, to note two things here. First, we need to see that the statement 'all truth is God's truth' emphasises *God's* truth: it concerns the knowingness of the creator and redeemer and his willingness to reveal that truth, rather than the frailty and fallibility of human reason. Second, if *all* truth is God's truth, then the door is open toward the possibility of integrating partial human understandings of the innumerable facets of God's world, be they in the realms of art or science, law or politics, psychology or theology.[30]

One of the first major explorations of the task of integrating psychological and theological insight from an evangelical view-point is presented by John D. Carter and Bruce Narramore.[31] On the basis 'that God is the source of all truth', Carter and Narramore argue that 'there is no inherent conflict between the *facts* of psychology and the *data* of Scripture'.[32] Any apparent discrepancy between the two is therefore laid at the door of either misguided psychological theorising or mishandled biblical interpretation. Since psychology and theology are, in a sense, 'both anthropologies',[33] integration can be seen in terms of psychology's commitment to 'raising questions and providing data' that, in turn, 'bear on our theological understanding of the human being' and theology's expression of 'divinely revealed truths that speak to psychology's developing view of humanity'.[34]

Following, in broad outline, H. Richard Niebuhr's analysis of the different positions taken up by Christians with reference to Christ and culture (see pp. 67–70), Carter and Narramore present four main stances held with respect to the relationship between psychology and theology; each of these has its 'secular' and 'sacred' version. We can summarise these as follows: the *Against* model, closest to our 'excluding' position, in which either psychology discards theology, especially in its special revelational form, as irrelevant or destructive, or vice versa; the *Of* model, an assimilative stance in which 'good' psychology and 'good' theology are mutually, and at times uncritically, absorbed; the *Parallels* model, in which psychology and theology provide distinctive and essentially unconnected perspectives on human nature; and the *Integrates* model, wherein 'secular' and 'sacred' versions collapse before a viewpoint that 'requires a full commitment to both the learned facts of psychology and the revealed truths of Scripture'.[35]

These four models can be likened to the interchange between two lovers: the Against model depicts a permanent lovers' tiff in which there is no common ground and each is convinced that he or she is right; the Of model shows a cosy relationship of living in each other's pockets to such an extent that individual identity is blurred; the Parallels model demonstrates a 'bed and breakfast' mentality in which each goes their separate way having experienced brief snatches of contact over sex, toast and coffee; and the Integrates model indicates a 'one flesh, separate persons' match in which both common ground and difference are understood and celebrated.

But, of course, even faithful lovers have their difficulties; and integrationists, as well as having much in common, have been prone to fall out, and make up, over a range of issues. Just as one of the prime matters for a couple to settle is that of the balance of power in their relationship (does one take precedence over the other, or are they committed to equality?), so among the more central issues discussed by integrationists is the foundational one of what priority to give, if any, between special and general revelation and, by inference, between theology and psychology. For example, Lawrence Crabb, writing in 1981, in adopting what I call a 'cautiously integrational' view,[36] acts as a potential bridge-head between the more excluding position of biblical counsellors like Jay Adams and John Bettler and the more fully integrational stance of John Carter and Bruce Narramore. Even so, his position is taken to task by James D. Guy, who criticises Crabb's rating of 'special over general revelation, or theology over psychology' and expresses, instead, a desire for 'open dialogue' between these perspectives in a spirit of 'epistemological humility'.[37]

In a pivotal paper published a year later,[38] Kirk E. Farnsworth seeks to take the debate beyond these earlier deliberations by raising the question of *method*: he asks, *How* is the integration between the two disciplines to be effected? He addresses his enquiry through an understanding of integration as a 'process of discovering, verifying, relating, and applying God's truths through theology and psychology'[39] and commits himself to an essentially *interpretive approach* which resonates well with the hermeneutic of the text and of the self that we considered in Chapters 4 and 5:

> The primary data-base for theology is the Bible and for psychology, the human person. That is, the Bible is a data-base whose texts must be read, or interpreted . . . The same holds for psychology: The human person is a data-base whose experience and behavior must be ana-lyzed.[40]

From such data, Farnsworth allows three routes for the com-prehension of God's revelatory truth: a *propositional* one, through the interpretation of the Scriptures; a *natural* one, in the realm of observable human (and non-human) behaviours; and an *existential* one, involving the analysis of human experience. In other words, he widens the remit of the discussion to encompass not only special revelation but a general revelation that embraces 'subjec-tive phenomena such as feelings and religious experiences such as prayer', as well as the observable and objective.[41]

Here, in Farnsworth's emphasis on 'nonrational' as well as rational knowledge, including the Pauline notion of a 'knowing that passes understanding (Ephesians 3:19, Philippians 4:7)',[42] we are reminded of Schleiermacher's 'hermeneutics of understanding' (see pp. 107–9), comprising both relationality and objectivity, closely resembling, to quote Thiselton once more, 'empathy be-tween two friends, [rather] than the solitary exercise on which

Descartes embarked'.[43] In all this, Farnsworth's integrational method moves toward a notion of *embodied integration*, a commitment to right living (orthopraxy) as well as right thinking (orthodoxy), seeking 'to fully know God's truths in His multi-faceted creation, in other words, to know God'.[44]

The Continuing Debate

Following the papers by Crabb, Guy, Farnsworth, and the last's respondents, in 1981 and 1982, the academic debate on 'model development' for the integration of theology and psychology, apart from a trickle of papers,[45] went to ground. Everett L. Worthington, writing in 1994,[46] sees this relative silence as indicative of a third phase in the field (subsequent to the early years, prior to 1975, when the writings were 'unsystematic and rudimentary' and the productive second phase from 1975 to 1982 when a range of models for integration were put forward). He regards this most recent period as preoccupied with both the empirical study of *inter*disciplinary integration and a commitment 'actually to do the task' of *intra*disciplinary integration, asking 'How do I integrate my faith with my theory and practice of psychology (or psychotherapy)?'[47] Worthington responds to this question himself with a carefully reasoned construction 'to help trainees and other interested professionals articulate their own Christian theory of counseling'.[48]

Even so, as John A. Ingram puts it, writing of Worthington's emphasis on the 'how-to' of intradisciplinary integration, 'more than "nuts and bolts" methodological information regarding Christian integrative model-building is needed'.[49] Ingram, rightly I believe, seeks to face the comparative silence over integrational theory since 1982 by raising a fresh challenge for a theoretical basis that takes seriously its present context in a 'modern/postmodern age'. In fact, we can say more broadly that there is an often hidden dimension that lurks behind the agendas of the integrationists, and, for that matter, the excluding biblical counsellors too, and that is the relationship, if any, between such endeavours to carve out scriptural models of theory and practice and the influences of contemporary culture. In a sentence, we can argue that much of the dispute between excluding and integrational biblical counsellors, and among the various emphases debated by the integrationists, lies in the degree of impingement on biblical counselling from modernity and postmodernity.

Modernity and the Biblical Counsellor

We saw in Chapter 3 that the hallmarks of the modern mind, with its roots in the Enlightenment, include the residual Cartesian strand of *individual knowingness*, a bid for a cast-iron certainty that elevates human rationality before a world that is eminently knowable. There is strong historical evidence that evangelicalism has inherited this bid for the primacy of reason and has thus incorporated its dictates into the handling of Scripture and attempts to communicate a Christian apologetic. Alister McGrath, for example, locates the roots of this trend within the expansion of the evangelical faith through the revivals and renewals of the eighteenth century.[50] One clear strand, he argues, can be seen in the influence of the Scottish 'philosophy of common sense', with its commitment to the value of empirical scientific enquiry and its opposition to the scepticism of David Hume (1711–76).[51] This anti-sceptical streak and avowal of Enlightenment rationality permeated the conservative Calvinistic theology of the Presbyterian seminary in Princeton, New Jersey through the thinking and teaching of, among others, Princeton College's former, Scottish-born president, John Witherspoon (1723–94). Among those so influenced, Charles Hodge (1797–1878) and Benjamin Breckinridge Warfield (1851–1921)[52] stand out as two of the most influential theologians of the nineteenth century in terms of setting the tone and agenda for an evangelical understanding of Scripture as inspired, inerrant and fundamentally appealing in propositional form to the rational mind. McGrath sums up the insidious way that the 'common sense' school infiltrated Hodge's understanding of how to handle biblical words: for Hodge, 'Words can be known directly and immediately by the human mind, without the need for any intermediaries. To know the words of Scripture is thus to know immediately the realities to which they relate.'[53]

It can be argued, as McGrath does, that the mixed inheritance of conservative Christianity and Enlightenment rationality from the Old Princeton School lives on in branches of modern American evangelicalism. He cites the example of Carl F. H. Henry who affirms a belief in a 'logically consistent divine revelation' and thus runs the danger, McGrath argues, of making 'an implicit appeal to a more fundamental epistemological foundation' than that of Scripture itself – a foundation in which 'without non-contradiction and logical consistency, no knowledge whatever is possible'.[54]

And it is here, I suggest, that we can discern the influence of modern knowingness on the biblical counselling movement, both in its excluding and integrational forms. It is salutary to note, for example, that the New Testament scholar, John Gresham Machen (1881–1937), who had studied under Warfield, and Cornelius Van Til, a former pupil of Machen's, left Princeton Theological Seminary in 1929 in the face of its 'inclusive' Presbyterianism and founded Westminster Theological Seminary in Philadelphia, where both Jay Adams and John Bettler later studied. Although the subsequent formation of the Orthodox Presbyterian Church, in response to the perceived liberalism of the Northern Presbyterian Church, sought to safeguard the essence of Reformed Calvinism, there seems little doubt that the deep commitment to Hodge and Warfield's particular cognitive and propositional style persisted.

And so, in the case of excluding biblical counselling, we see an inheritance which, not surprisingly, in opting for a high view of reason and the self-evident nature of words, puts undue weight on cognition, proposition and textual self-containment in its interpretation of Scripture. Thus special revelation, albeit profound and essential for salvation, is stressed to the neglect of general revelation, even though the Bible itself also proclaims the latter. A truncated agenda is the result, in which Scripture may be reduced to 'a code book of theological ordinances'[55] and where God's rich and wondrous world is perceived, in essence, as 'enemy territory'. So, for example, the discipline of psychology is firmly put in its place. It is allowed to be 'illustrative' and 'provocative'[56] but is not permitted to enter into face-to-face dialogue with theology, let alone contemplate an integration of its insights and perspectives with the latter discipline. David Powlison, one of the leading apologists for the more excluding form of biblical counselling, refers to the spirit of Machen's classic work *Christianity and Liberalism* (1923), and its wholesale rejection of the liberal stance, as echoing over the years into the contemporary debate between psychology and theology. With a strongly excluding polemic, he writes:

> The logic and drift of the integrationist movement has not been a biblical logic and drift. The church is reaping the consequences. Integration or inundation? The deluge is upon us. If Machen wrote his book today, he would entitle it Christianity and Psychologism. The modern psychological evangelicalism, the intellectual flood in which we float or against which we swim, is not Christianity.[57]

Postmodernity and the Bible Counsellor

As we have mentioned, the legacy of Enlightenment rationality in modern knowingness has also left its mark on the integrationists' agenda. In its maxim 'all truth is God's truth', there is a tendency, as in the excluding forms of biblical counselling, to elevate the cognitive and propositional at the expense of other levels of human knowledge and scriptural genre. For example, Stephen M. Clinton, in his critique of integrational models,[58] takes James Guy to task and says that he 'widened the base for theology and historicized it' through his openness, for example, to the Church's historic creeds.[59] 'As an evangelical theologian', Clinton protests against this perceived shift, declaring that Guy 'moves the base of the discussion from the propositions of Scripture (and their individual and systematic implications as the Word of God) to the propositions of noninspired people'. We see, perhaps, something of Charles Hodge's view of the immediacy and complete accessibility of the Bible's words when Clinton adds, '[Scriptural] meaning is discoverable through a grammatical, historical hermeneutic, and is intelligible to all people.'[60]

However, integrationists have found an increasing need to address the realities of the paradigm shift from high modernity to postmodernity. An awareness of the reductionist tendency of modernity's love affair with human reason has led a number of writers in recent years to widen the integrational debate to embrace issues surrounding *otherness* and *difference*. Guy's paper (1982), in response to Crabb's more propositionalist stance, appears as one of the first critiques to acknowledge the need for integrationists to receive 'diversity, controversy, and plurality . . . with respectful tolerance, even affirmation', as opening the door to a fuller and richer dialogue that leads to an 'increased understanding of revealed truth'.[61] Here, true to the tradition of evangelical integration, there is a continuing commitment to a revelational theology. Further, Guy widens the horizon beyond that of a strictly cognitive approach to Scripture that cannot lift its eyes beyond the foreground of proposition. He reminds his readers of the Bible's diverse genre – 'commands, prayers, proverbs, parables, poetry, stories, and history', and the variety of its language – 'symbolic and metaphorical, as well as literal'.[62]

Other voices of the early 1980s that tentatively address postmodern perspectives include Farnsworth's *embodied integration*, which we considered earlier, with its holistic openness to divine revelation through the non-rational, as well as the rational, and through experience, as well as the textual, and Randie L. Timpe's acknowledgment of the 'epistemological and metaphysical limits' to integrating psychology and theology.[63] Steve Bouma-Prediger, in his paper on the typology of integration (1990), owns that the Enlightenment ideal of 'objective, neutral scholarship . . . can no longer be sustained' and that we now live in a more intensely *interpretive* climate where 'all knowledge is guided by human interests and grounded in commitments of various kinds'. In such an atmosphere, each would-be integrator of faith and professional calling needs to face his or her personal presuppositions and prejudices.[64]

It is John Ingram, though, who addresses most fully and openly the question of a Christian model of integration in a 'modern/ postmodern age'. Looking to and extending J. F. Rychlak's 'complementarity' model for psychology,[65] Ingram offers a Christian integrative approach that takes 'from both modern and postmodern perspectives'. In this he seeks to move away from modernist reductionism, while retaining the value of modern research's 'limited scope', and, at the same time, he pursues, in the name of postmodernity, 'more holistic, integrative models' which are able to 'accommodate more than one mode of thought and practice'.[66]

Rychlak puts forward four distinctive, complementary 'groundings' on which psychological theories have been generally based: *Physikos*, using physical science for such concepts as energy, force and constancy; *Bios*, with its emphasis on organic process and genetics; *Socius*, which includes social and historical constructs; and *Logos*, drawing on 'the patterned order of experience' to give personal and mental constructs. Ingram develops Rychlak's theory in two respects: he moves beyond the relatively static notion of 'groundings' to the more dynamic concept of 'dimensions', wherein one conceptual level can influence another; and, in a 'postmodern spirit of a plurality of perspectives', he adds a fifth dimension to the schema, *Theos*, in which explanatory models for psychology can be drawn from religious belief systems, authoritative texts and metanarratives.[67] In effect, Ingram offers a 'theologosociobiophysical' model:[68] a somewhat unwieldy term compared to the more familiar 'biopsychosocial' model of psychological literature, but, nonetheless, aiming to do justice to the rich complexity of what it means to be human.

Although Ingram concedes that each of his fivefold dimensions can interact with any other (for example, *Bios* with *Theos*, as when a gastric upset tends to work against a time of reflective prayer), he also acknowledges that the model can make sense hierarchically – either from the more reductionist 'bottom up' viewpoint or from the more expansive 'top down' direction.[69] The 'bottom up' perspective is by far the commoner in most psychological debates. Here, the analogy is a constructional one in which each 'grounding' or dimension builds in increasing complexity on the previous level: from the *physical* and *biological* through the *social* and *logical* to the *theological*. Freud, for example, argued for much of his psychodynamic theory at the level of physical science, in terms of cathexis and the principle of constancy,[70] while conceding the legitimacy of an evolutionary 'biology of the mind'. By and large it was his successors, and detractors, who 'ascended' to the social (as with Karen Horney and the neo-Freudians),[71] logos-centred (Viktor Frankl and his logotherapy)[72] and theological (in Jung's, albeit largely unstructured, supernaturalism)[73] levels.

Seeing most Christian integrational endeavours as tied primarily to *Logos* and *Theos*, as implied, for example, in the title of the influential *Journal of Psychology and Theology*, Ingram argues that such 'fall short of a comprehensive integrative product'.[74] Besides opening the discussion toward a more comprehensive 'bottom up' perspective, he also explores the further possibilities of a 'top down' viewpoint. In this alternative understanding the structure is imposed from above: from the *theological* and *logical* through the *social* and *biological* to the *physical*. Here, radically and in keeping with postmodern holism (and, indeed, Judaeo-Christian revealed theology), Ingram can say: 'from a top down perspective, all things could be experienced at all times by God's omniscient and omnipresent consciousness, and therefore need not in any final sense be dependent on the experiencing aspect of finite sentient beings for existence.'[75] Thus, Ingram puts the more conventional, modernist 'bottom up' and the more holistic, partially postmodernist 'top down' perspectives together into a single format, in which both directions 'could potentially yield different types of questions, data and explanations' and where both viewpoints, though not necessarily reconcilable, are needed.

Ingram illustrates the potential of his multidimensional, 'two way' model in the case of alcoholism, an area of addiction that is usually handled by a 'bottom up' approach. Adopting the 'top down' direction, but acknowledging the interplay between all five dimensions, we can recall the widespread awareness of spiritual and moral aspects (*Theos*) of alcohol use and abuse, not least in the 12-Step treatment of Alcoholics Anonymous; the well-reasoned guidelines hammered out for the handling of alcohol (*Logos*); the social and legal aspects of drinking which clarify acceptable and unacceptable behaviour (*Socius*); appropriate care and use of the body in relation to alcohol (*Bios*); and issues surrounding the production and marketing of intoxicating beverages (*Physikos*).[76]

All in all, Ingram puts forward a model of integration which, in effect, owns a God who speaks from the 'top down', and seeks human responsiveness from the 'bottom up', through special and general revelation. Further, this modern/postmodern enterprise aims to embrace an anthropology which celebrates a more fully conceived humanity than either the reductionism of scientism (with its truncated form of 'bottom up' approach, neglectful of 'groundings' above the *Physikos* and *Bios* levels) or the reductionism of biblicism (with its top-heavy form of 'top down' viewpoint, tending to ignore levels 'beneath' *Theos* and *Logos*).

Biblical counselling, whether excluding or integrational, needs to take heed of the commitment of such as Guy, Farnsworth and Ingram with their courage to ask questions of evangelicalism's dalliance with modernity and to explore the possibilities of an engagement with postmodernity that does not compromise 'the faith that was once for all entrusted to the saints' (Jude 3).

The Way Ahead

We have given an overview of the story of biblical counselling so far: the first stirrings of a cautious evangelical *affirmation* of much of value in the new realm of secular counselling psychology in the 1950s; a strong reaction toward the dangers of pyschologising pastoral care, expressed by the *excluding* stance of nouthetic counselling's birth in the 1960s; and the increasingly sophisticated journey of *integration* between a biblical theology and valid insights from the discipline of psychology, from the 1970s onward. It remains necessary to open up a more constructive debate for the way forward.

We can consider the future of this particular pathway to wholeness under three main headings: *in search of a metaphor; law needs story*; and *theology needs spirituality*. In doing so, we will keep in mind the four parameters for such a pathway, looked at in outline in the last chapter – doctrine, Scripture, metaphor and spirituality.

In Search of a Metaphor

I have found that one of the hardest dilemmas to crack in assessing the five pathways to wholeness is the matter of their individual relationship with the rich repository of biblical metaphor. Seeking to avoid the modernist trap of too neatly categorising and tying too close a knot between each pathway and a particular role and calling, I have nonetheless pursued the possibility of a salient functional metaphor or two from the Scriptures as summing up the essence of this or that route toward wholeness. My premise has been that the God who has called men and women to pastoral responsibility, as recorded in the pages of the Old and New Testaments and within the annals of church history, still makes that call today – even within the contexts of the post-Enlightenment rise of the secular psychologies, the counselling movement of modernity and the pluralistic therapies of postmodernity.

The potential metaphor, or metaphors, for biblical counselling has proved especially difficult to discern, since, if this pathway is to be true to the full impact of the Bible, it seems to me that it will incorporate the entire range of callings: priest, prophet, wise man or woman, pastor, teacher, preacher, evangelist and, most paradigmatically and, ideally, underlying all, suffering servant.

Even so, as I have juggled the possibilities in the face of biblical counselling's literature, and reflected on Jacob Firet's summary of the Church's calling (see p. 157) in *kerygma* (preaching), *didache* (teaching) and *paraklesis* (pastoral care), it seems to me that much biblical counselling, particularly the more 'excluding' brand, has centred on the first two functions rather than the third. This is not to say that the parakletic ministry is completely absent from this pathway, for many biblical counsellors, among both excluding and integrational approaches, clearly have a pastoral heart. It is to point out, rather, that a great deal within the cognitive and propositionalist styles of much biblical counselling is inevitably and primarily linked with the metaphors of preacher, teacher, and, by inference in a 'pre-counselling'[77] sense, evangelist.

In this context, it is especially pertinent to note that Jay Adams, the founder of nouthetic counselling, trained initially in homiletics and has always held his biblical counselling ministry in close association with his calling as a preacher and teacher. Further, there is a clear acknowledgment by many biblical counsellors, completely in tune with their evangelicalism, of the centrality of the call of the evangelist – often as a vocation that is complementary to and distinct from the call of counsellor and, at times, as in the case of Adams's methodology, as a necessary precursor to effective counsel.[78]

However, although the metaphors of preacher and evangelist are common adjuncts to the work of biblical counselling, it is the metaphor of *teacher*, I believe, which is the cardinal paradigm[79] for this pathway to wholeness. Jay Adams, for example, in discussion with John Bettler and David Powlison in 1993, looks back to the foundational years of nouthetic counselling and declares: 'The decision was made that we're fundamentally going to use counseling as a means of teaching.'[80] The broadly didactic is implied when Lawrence Crabb, in searching for an acceptable model of counselling, writes that our priority must concern itself with 'which ideas are true and which ones move people in directions that ultimately are good'.[81] Gary Collins points to the need that counsellees have, not only for direct instruction but for 'observing mentors (including the counselor) and thus developing practical skills for more constructive living.'[82]

Biblical counsellors, such as Adams, Crabb and Collins, are indeed true to the Scriptures when they stress the importance of the educative. Moses, for instance, in addressing the Israelites, declared his pedagogical calling from Yahweh – who 'directed me . . . to teach you the decrees and law you are to follow' (Deut. 4:14); the fruit of David's restoration, following Nathan's indictment of his adultery and murder, was to 'teach transgressors [God's] ways' (Ps. 51:13); and the Book of Proverbs offers a treasure-house of instructional wisdom. Jesus himself stands in the line of the rabbinic tradition as one who, for example, stood to read from the prophetic writings and sat to expound their meaning (Luke 4:16–21) and yet bore the stamp of supreme teacher,[83] 'because he taught as one who had authority, and not as [the] teachers of the law' (Matt. 7:29).

Even so, Christ did not come to abolish the God-given law of the Old Testament but, rather, to fulfil it.[84] As N. T. Wright puts it: 'The whole Torah is vindicated in Christ, even as God is vindicated in Christ.'[85] It is in the scriptural concept of Torah (instruction from Yahweh),[86] and the continuing place of law within the life of the believer and the community, that we can most fruitfully view the links between biblical counselling and the metaphor of teacher.

Law needs Story

In Chapter 6 we saw how most, if not all, of the pathways to wholeness are subject to the danger of a bid for either the pole of a strong rationality and deep commitment to rules, guidelines and clearly marked boundaries, all reinforced, as we have seen, by modernity's elevation of reason and knowingness, or for the pole of the experiential, narrational, intuitive and mystical, encouraged today by postmodernity's celebration of otherness and difference. We have argued throughout that our humanity and our Christian journeying requires *both* these strands, albeit redeemed from the more baleful influences of the modern and the postmodern. We illustrated the need for a balanced polarity between these two emphases by looking to A. J. Heschel's analysis of the Torah (see p. 163) as comprising *agada* as well as *halacha*, experience as well as ethics, story as well as law.

Christians have been very neglectful of the concept of Torah (*tôrâ*) within the biblical canon. Held by Jewish tradition as the first five books of the Bible – the Pentateuch or 'the book of the law' – and said to comprise 'five-fifths of the law', Torah, in terms of its continuing signifance and relevance, has often been discarded by Christianity, not least in its evangelical form, in the mistaken beliefs that the gospel 'does away with' law and that to embrace law inevitably equates with a slide into legalism. And yet a closer reading of the Pentateuchal text, and a fuller awareness of its intrinsic balance of *halacha* and *agada*, law and story, helps to clarify the essential oneness of Old and New Testament as an unfolding narrative of God's creative, redemptive and law-giving acts. Indeed, the account in the Pentateuch, with Israel's experience of Yahweh as law-giver on Sinai as its central motif, can be viewed, in New Testament language, as a story of *justification*, of how God saves the people, and a continuing story of *sanctification*, as life begins to be lived out on the land and under the law.[87] Such perspectives accord well with Jesus's words, 'Do not think that I have come to abolish the Law or the Prophets; I have not come to abolish them but to fulfil them' (Matt. 5:17) and the Pauline rebuttal of the notion that faith and law are at loggerheads: 'Do we, then, nullify the law by this faith? Not at all! Rather, we uphold the law' (Rom. 3:31).

The corrective to all this is that *halacha* needs *agada*, law needs story, ground rules need freedom, head needs heart. Heschel likens the 'code of conduct' of *halacha* to a musician's score and adds, 'Rules, principles, forms may be taught; insight, feeling, the sense of rhythm must come from within.'[88] And just as the act of making good music needs a balance between musical theory and a creative impulse that usually comes from long practice and an evolving story of musical experience, so a commitment to pastoral care needs to find a level of equilibrium between its Christian ground rules and its attention to human narrative.

But, as we have seen, post-Enlightenment rationality can push Christian ministries, particularly the more cognitive forms of biblical counselling, toward the elevation of proposition and principle, to the neglect of story and experience. Often this trend arises through a propensity to handle scriptural statements as discrete entities, prescribed for a counsellee's troubled spirit or besetting sin, where little attention may be paid to the person's narrative and inner life. As Waldemar Janzen observes, in the context of Old Testament ethics, the acceptance of 'ethically relevant' texts 'in isolation' can combine with 'the affinity of Western mentality for abstract thinking' to foster within the Church 'a tendency to detach law from story'.[89]

There is a measure of encouragement, though, in that, in the wider remit of latter-day 'excluding' biblical counsellors like John Bettler and David Powlison, as well as in the comprehensive approaches of many integrationists, a more fully orbed hermeneutic is emerging in which the *kerygmatic* and *didactic* elements of classical biblical counselling are allowing the development of *parakletic* perspectives that are more open to the stories of God's people. Walter C. Kaiser comments that '*tôrâ* probably comes from the Hebrew verb meaning "to point [out the direction one should go]"'. He notes that in the Book of Proverbs, Torah's teaching is often linked with the picture of a 'path', and adds, 'God's law was meant to be a light on one's path: it was intended to point out which direction a person should go.'[90] May biblical counselling, as it continues its Christian journeying in a postmodern age, be increasingly committed in its theory and practice to the direction-finding *halacha* and *agada* of 'the perfect law that gives

freedom . . . the royal law found in Scripture, "Love your neighbour as yourself"' (Jas. 1:25; 2:8). It is in the reclamation of
paraklesis and the filling out of *didache* to include story as well
as law that biblical counsellors can more fully engage, in both their
counselling theory and practice, with this 'royal law' that expresses neighbourly love by taking human narrative seriously.

Theology needs Spirituality

Just as biblical counselling, if it is to be true to the Bible and the
best in its evangelical tradition, needs an awareness of story as
well as law, by the same token it needs a theology which is
embodied through an appropriate spirituality.[91] Put differently,
just as psychology needs theology if its understanding of human
nature is to engage with the divine perspective, so theology needs
spirituality if its attempts to grasp God's ways are to be earthed in
Christian discipleship. Anciently, there was no rift between the
two: to study God was to wonder at God, to seek to understand
God was to respond to God in faith and obedience. We see this
seamlessness between theology and spirituality implied when
Paul writes that 'no-one knows the thoughts of God except the
Spirit of God' and that any understanding and declaration of
God's ways is likewise Spirit-given, so that we may speak, 'expressing spiritual truths in spiritual words' (1 Cor. 2:11–13).
Historically, though, there has often been a separation of the
paths between theologising and the spiritual endeavour,[92] a split
that a number of leading evangelicals are seeking to heal.[93] James
Packer, for example, wants 'to arrange a marriage', between a
systematic theology that is 'practised as an element in our spirituality' and a spirituality that is seen as 'an implicate and expression of our systematic theology'.[94]

Behind the desire to reunite theology and spirituality is an
awareness that all is not well in the state of evangelicalism. It is
seen to be both weak in its theology and singularly lacking in a
coherent sense of spirituality. Mark Noll and others, writing in the
context of American Christianity, see evangelicalism as largely
deficient in knowledge of the theological tradition, seriously
lacking an intellectual cutting-edge and bedazzled by 'TV culture,
entertainment culture, the cult of self-absorption, and various
other anti-intellectualist forces'.[95] Alister McGrath, in his assessment of British evangelicalism, is less condemning, but acknowl-

edges that a great deal of slippage theologically has come about where evangelicals, in the face of biblical criticism, have either capitulated to a more liberal stance or retreated into a 'dogmatic and simplistic fundamentalism'.[96] On the matter of evangelical spirituality, David Parker[97] and McGrath[98] both express a concern at the clearly palpable fact that many erstwhile evangelicals, given the perceived spiritual desert of their own tradition, crave for the refreshing springs of Catholic, Eastern Orthodox and Quaker spiritualities.

Of comparable concern, in the eyes of evangelicals who seek to hold to what is best within mainstream evangelicalism, is the related stir caused by the publication in 1995 of Dave Tomlinson's *The Post-Evangelical* and the tide of identification that swept around the book and through the subsequent debate.[99] The central thrust of Tomlinson's concern is to tap into a deep well of longing, once more for a rediscovered spirituality and theology – perspectives that shake off the mantle of an evangelicalism seen to be embedded in modernity and step out into a Christian faith that is *post*modern and *post*-evangelical, where, for example, a 'consciousness of truth is . . . found less in propositional statements and moral certitudes and more in symbols, ambiguities and situational judgements'.[100] Others, like Nigel Wright[101] and Alistair Ross,[102] have stopped short of Tomlinson's step *beyond* evangelicalism's 'perceived limitations' and yet, like Tomlinson, ask the hard questions of those same limitations in order to set forth, respectively, as 'radical evangelical' or as an evangelical 'in exile' within his own native faith tradition. The debate around the positions taken up by post-evangelicals, radical evangelicals and evangelicals in exile is less important in terms of their precise distinctions than with respect to their shared longing for a more rigorous and robust theology and a richer and more wonder-filled spirituality.

Following David Bebbington's classic summary of evangelicalism's cardinal characteristics as *conversionism, activism, biblicism* and *cruciformism*,[103] we can take the last two as essential indicators of the health of the evangelical faith (and, thereby, of today's biblical counselling) with respect to its theology and potential spirituality. The other two – conversionism and activism – and their need to be balanced by concepts of process and maturation, in the case of the former, and by reflection and contemplation, in the latter, will be intrinsic to the assessments of pathways to wholeness in Chapters 9 and 10 respectively. We will look at evangelicalism's 'biblicism' and 'cruciformism', and at a theology that needs spirituality, under the headings of *Word-centredness* and *Cross-centredness*.

Word-centredness

Since childhood I have been a typical product of modernity in that words for me have been something of a life force. As a boy of eight or nine countless hours were spent with my best friend, Chris, pouring over dictionaries to see how many words we could make from such megaliths as 'antidestablishmentarianism' and, our favourite, 'floccinaucinihilipilification'. I created two volumes of my very own 'Roger's Book of Knowledge' and delighted in the magic of words from faraway places – Popocatepetl, Aconcagua, Limpopo, Kanchenjunga . . . This logocentrism, as we have seen, is the quintessence of the modernist project, for words are not only the gateway to understanding and knowledge, as in my childhood exploration of the lexicon, they can also be the vehicle for arrogant knowingness, control and power. And evangelical theology, and its derivative spirituality, is both legitimately Word-centred and, by that very token, especially susceptible to modernist idolatry of the word.

We have already noted that biblical counselling has, perhaps inevitably, inherited something of a post-Cartesian mindset in its tendency to look to propositionalism and cognitive-behaviourism in the handling of Scripture. Such a stance has been strongly criticised by George Lindbeck as 'intellectualist' and 'literalist,'[104] and for some of the more fundamentalist elements in biblical counselling this criticism needs to stick. However, there is a more subtle point to be made. It is one thing to be rigidly held by head knowledge, the power of logic and a commitment to the objective 'facts' of the Bible; it is quite another to own that scriptural doctrine includes much that *is* propositional, cognitive and beha-vioural: 'The law of the LORD is perfect' (Ps. 19:7); 'be transformed by the renewing of your mind' (Rom. 12:2); 'I will show you my faith by what I do' (Jas. 2:18). As McGrath rightly points out, 'It remains axiomatic for evangelicals that both revelation and doc-trine have cognitive or informative aspects.'[105]

And yet evangelicalism, and thereby biblical counselling, is in continual danger of truncating its theology by putting all its

PATHWAYS TO WHOLENESS

doctrinal eggs in the one basket of propositionalism. Thus evangelical theology and its potential spirituality are impoverished. How might this imbalance be addressed?

First, it seems essential that evangelical Word-centredness is allowed to be just that – not a logocentrism that opts only for the biblical proposition but one that dares to permit the full impact of Scripture's rich and varied genres and figures of speech, including narrative, metaphor, symbol, vision, dream, wise sayings, poetry and parable. Biblical counsellors, in seeking to be true to God's revelation in Christ, need to listen afresh to those theologians who both take every part of the Bible's text seriously and seek to discern its singular voice amid the Babel sounds of postmodernity. Walter Brueggemann, for example, declares a major shift in interpretive practice in which 'knowing consists not in settled certitude but in the actual work of imagination' – a work that engages 'the human capacity to picture, portray, receive, and practice the world in ways other than it appears to be at first glance when seen through a dominant, habitual, unexamined lens'.[106] In this enterprise he takes the analogy of *drama* and, in true postmodern fashion, focuses on the 'little stories' of the text, committing himself to side-step modernist systematisation in favour of a reading that is true to the Bible's Jewish roots, honouring texts that are 'disjointed, "irrational", contradictory, paradoxical, ironic, and scandalous'.[107] He declares of this bold step away from former knowingness and the 'large, compelling, reductionist summaries' of the past:

> [It] is done one item at a time, one memory, one vision, one image, one narrative at a time, which partly flow together, but not completely . . . The outcome will not be doctrinal or moral coherence. It will be, rather, an energizing, liberating process of imagination that permits us to process the feared, cherished parts of our own life, to process them in the context of this Other who with us traverses the stage and the script.[108]

And, crucially, we each bring to this 'liberating process' our own 'zone of imagination', a 'busy, occupied, teeming place' in which the text's new material intermingles with our personal fears, hurts and vested interests, all in part influenced by the communities that shape our lives. It is here, once more, that we see the force of Paul Ricoeur's dictum that not only does the reader interpret the text, the text interprets the reader.

A powerful example of this imaginative endeavour is given by Walter Wink in his *Transforming Bible Study*. In this practical guide he looks to the studies carried out by Roger Sperry in which patients, who had had the connecting fibres between the right and left hemispheres of the brain severed on medical grounds, demonstrated a range of distinctive functions depending on which side of the brain was being used.[109] From such work it is established that the left hemisphere controls our sense of sequential time (*chronos*) and cause-and-effect: it is the seat of logic, analysis and abstract reasoning and enables achievement in grammar, mathematics and trained musicality. In contrast, the right hemisphere is concerned with the immediacy of time (*kairos*) and spatial relations: it is the centre of intuition, synthesis and imaginative reasoning and fosters an appreciation of metaphor, symbol, poetry, art and music at non-intellectualising levels.

In other words, human cognition is a process of knowing that is much richer than the resolute commitment to an analytical propositionalism of much, modernity-influenced evangelical theologising. Wink takes these insights and applies them as a powerful corrective to this solely 'left-brain' hermeneutic, declaring: 'We exegetes and theologians and pastors and people haven't been using *enough* of our brains when we encounter the Bible.' He seeks, rather, a holistic approach that embraces thinking *and* feeling, the cognitive *and* affective, careful analysis of the text *and* exposure to whatever God has for us as whole persons.

One recent example of this fuller engagement with Scripture was shared with me by David Runcorn, director of pastoral studies at Trinity College, Bristol,[110] who had led a group of sixteen theological students in an encounter with the narrative of Acts 10:23–48. This is the account of Peter's arrival at Caeserea at the behest of Cornelius, a 'devout and God-fearing' centurion. Both men had been spoken to by God and the air was pregnant with expectancy. After a careful reading of the text, David set a scene comprising four groups: the circumcised Jewish believers; Peter and his friends; Cornelius and the new Gentile converts; and the narrator and other observers. The students divided into these groups, assembled at the four corners of the room and were instructed to role-play their group, getting under the skin of the thoughts, feelings, prejudices and beliefs of their particular section. The observational group could circulate freely throughout; also, after a while, individual members of the other three groups, still in role, were invited to go to any other group they chose, to ask questions and enter into debate. Much to David's surprise, the cluster of 'Gentile converts' was left completely unvisited, whereas all the focus centred on the two remaining groups – 'Peter and friends', and the 'Jewish Christians' – who were locked into heated interchange. At this stage, David went to the isolated 'Gentiles' and asked them how they felt and in what way they would like to respond. It was suggested that they go to the other two groups and tell them what the Lord had done for them. This they did with waving arms, enthusiastically trying to interrupt the earnest theological debaters!

In the reflection following, once the students had come out of their roles, they were all powerfully struck with the realisation that this is just what they do in real life! If any has a difficulty about someone who is a puzzle or threat, he or she is much more likely to seek out a third party for, perhaps, intense discussion rather than face the person directly.[111] Here, analysis and reflection (left-brain) combined with imagination and emotion (right-brain) to inculcate transformative insight at a depth that simple rationality alone could not have achieved.

It is such methods as Brueggemann, Wink and Runcorn apply that can nudge evangelicalism, and its biblical counsellors, toward 'doing' a theology that is rendered more wholesome by owning an appropriate spirituality – a spirituality, as we saw in the last chapter (see pp. 181–3), that is 'relational, trinitarian, christocentric and liberational' and, within this fourfold structure, embraces evangelicalism's distinctive emphasis of Word- and Cross-centredness.

Cross-centredness

The shape of evangelical faith has always been avowedly cruciform. Its commitment to the Word inevitably means that the cross is taken very seriously. As has often been pointed out, the passion of Christ takes up a large proportion of each gospel account: over a third in the case of the Fourth Gospel. Anticipations of messianic suffering in the Old Testament, Jesus's own predictive words in the Gospels, the centrality of cross and resurrection in the Acts of the Apostles, the theological deliberations on the death of Christ in the Epistles and the heavenly vision of the 'Lamb slain' in the Book of Revelation, are all written deep into the unfolding story of the

Church, especially in its Reformed and evangelical sensibilities. John Bright, the nineteenth-century Quaker statesman, is said to have commented on hearing one evangelical divine, 'The atonement, always the atonement! Have they nothing else to say?'[112]

This preoccupation with the cross is pivotal, for example, in Martin Luther's declaration, 'the cross alone is our theology'.[113] Here is a theology which allows God to be God, permits the Lord of all to reveal himself as he chooses – not with trumpet fanfares, shouts of acclamation and the tread of countless marching feet, but through stable, open road, upper room, garden, court room, soldiers' barracks and a criminal's death. Such a 'hidden revelation'[114] turns the world upside down. Human autonomy and knowingness, from the revolt in Eden to modernity's intellectualism and postmodernity's multiple 'wisdoms', is challenged to its very roots by a theology of the cross – a theology that sees a model for greatness in Isaiah's suffering servant, honours the weak, poor and marginalised, calls disciples to a daily dying and reminds humanity of its creatureliness, fallenness and glorious hope of redemption. In the face of the Jewish bid for proof of God's power and the Greek commitment to philosophise its way to a higher state, St Paul preaches 'Christ crucified', declaring:

> Brothers and sisters, think of what you were when you were called. Not many of you were wise by human standards; not many were influential; not many were of noble birth. But God chose the foolish things of the world to shame the wise; God chose the weak things of the world to shame the strong . . . It is because of him that you are in Christ Jesus, who has become for us wisdom from God – that is, our righteousness, holiness and redemption. Therefore, as it is written, 'Let those who boast boast in the Lord.' (1 Cor. 1:23, 26–31)

Further, the centrality of the cross is the key to much that is most transformative in evangelical devotion and spirituality. We can see this motif in the streams of consecutive Reformed, Puritan and evangelical works: in, for instance, Luther's *The Bondage of the Will* (1525); John Owen's *The Death of Death in the Death of Christ* (1647); John Bunyan's *Pilgrim's Progress* (1682); the hymns of William Cowper and Isaac Watts in the eighteenth century and Frances Havergal and Charlotte Elliott in the nineteenth; James Denney's *The Death of Christ* (1902); and Amy Carmichael's *If* (1938). Jürgen Moltmann, taking the title of his *The Crucified God* from the medieval mystics and, through them, from Luther,[115] points to the treasures implicit in a cruciform spirituality:

> In his dying for us the risen Christ looks on us and draws us into his life. In the one who became poor for our sake, God's riches are opened up for us. In the one who became a servant for our sake, we are grasped by God's freedom. In the one who became sin for us, sinners become the righteousness of God in the world.[116]

Even so, just as, in the context of evangelicalism and the endeavours of biblical counselling, law needs story and the propositional needs the imaginative, so, I suggest, *a theology and spirituality of the cross needs a recovery of a theology and spirituality of creation*. There is no doubt that evangelicalism, with its roots in the soil of the Reformed faith, Puritanism and German Pietism,[117] has let slip to a varying extent the essential scriptural unity between the creative and redemptive. While the strand represented by John Calvin, holding to special *and* general revelation, presents a view that 'the creation reflects its creator at every point',[118] the Anabaptist emphasis within the Reformation pulled up the drawbridge of its faith commitment against a world seen to be sullied by fallenness and seductiveness. It is probably fair to say that evangelicalism has always struggled to maintain a more holistic stance which, through embracing a creation *as well as* redemption theology, explores and delights in the created order, celebrates the gift of humanness and takes God-given responsibility within the community. Tragically, that struggle has, from time to time, given way before the temptation to ghettoisation that is evangelicalism's particular susceptibility: the dispensationalist theology of John Nelson Darby (1800–82), for example, with its commitment to a view of Christ's return which seemed to warrant an attitude that was 'evangelistically active but socially passive';[119] and the controversy around 'fundamentalism'[120] in the United States in the 1920s which succeeded in splitting evangelicals into two factions – one aiming to meet human need through evangelism, the other through the 'social gospel'.[121]

As we have already seen, 'excluding' biblical counselling is especially prone to a selectivity toward Scripture which tends to focus on the didactic, the propositional and, through its sole commitment to special revelation, the redemptive. These are excellent and life-changing emphases as far as they go, but the neglect of general revelation and, consequently, a theology of creation can lead to an impoverished hermeneutic that excludes much of value in terms of a God who is abroad in his world, speaking through the wonders of the natural order and through the complex networks of human existence. Generally, biblical counsellors who engage with the integration of psychology and theology, and, more particularly, theorists like Guy, Farnsworth and Ingram who address the postmodern agenda, are at least on an exploratory journey which, at its best, incorporates law and story, the propositional and the imaginative and, hopefully, the redemptive and the creational. And, as we have already implied, these wider remits are simply outworkings of a commitment to both special and general revelation, to the God who orders all things in the cosmos in and through his Son and by his Spirit.

Further, since this is *the* grand narrative, we will not be surprised to find that the themes of creation and redemption interweave through the theology and spirituality of each of the pathways to wholeness. Including both the creational and redemptive threads within this seamless cloth, we can argue that in biblical counselling, as we have seen, there is the need for a recovery of story and imagination; in the healing ministries, the need for both the balance of a theology of suffering and of a fuller picture of creation's therapeutic gifts; in pastoral counselling, an emphasis on the covenantal and relational aspects of creation and redemption; in spiritual direction, a celebration of the wonder of the created and a call to worship its creator; and in social change, a continuing commitment to live out this twinned theology and spirituality in communal and ecological contexts.

To close this section, let me briefly share a small but significant part of my own story in terms of the intermingling of the creational and the redemptive. In the autumn of 1979 Joy and I were able to take a brief holiday on the Isle of Colonsay in the Inner Hebrides. After a year of travail in which I had experienced eight months of blindness, a major operation on my right eye, with a consequent gradual recovery of one-eyed sight, and the 'last straw' of developing a mysterious, debilitating malaise which had proved to be brucellosis, we were more than ready for a break. This last condition, also known as undulant fever, had dug itself well in by the time we took the overnight motor-rail to Scotland. We both slept fitfully that night as I tossed and turned, racked with fever, aching joints and a tiringly persistent cough. Arriving on the island by car-ferry the following evening, we looked forward to a restorative few days in Colonsay's only hotel as we rested and relaxed and sought strength for the unknown future.

I woke early on the third day to the realisation that I was blind once more! Initially, I had closed my eyes again, hoping and praying that the swirl of darkness that had greeted me was part of an unsettling dream, but there was no mistaking the all-too-familiar signs of a heavy vitreous bleed. It took a long time to declare the grim reality to a still-dozing Joy, whose patience through the darkness of my first period of blindness, and, more recently, with the unsociabality of a husband with brucellosis, had been sore stretched.

After breakfast, all we could do was to walk arm-in-arm across the nearby moorland, speechless and choked with tears. What was God up to? Had we not endured enough? Had not the 'lessons' learned through blindness, the prospect of long-term undulant fever, my loss of job as a student health doctor and resulting loss of income been adequately character-forming? The inner questions buzzed angrily.

Later, we drove to a lonely part of the island's west coast, where the close-cropped *machair* fringes a sweep of sand and rock. As we sat in the car, we were able to begin, falteringly, to express something of our supercharged feelings. In time, a silence descended upon us – not the earlier silence of our barely suppressed rage but a silence that was a stillness, in which our weariness had no more tears to shed. The peace of the place crept upon us. The stillness and the silence were of course both broken and reinforced by the sounds of nature: the restless, rhythmic sighing of Atlantic breakers, the shrill piping of bickering oyster-catchers. It was within this reassuring sense of connectedness with the order of things that we became aware of another voice, not audible, yet strangely real. It seemed as if the Lord of creation, the dayspring from on high, the one who, according to the Book of Proverbs, was the 'masterworker' at God's creative side, 'rejoicing in his whole world and delighting in the human race',[122] stood at our side, joyful yet sorrowful, glorious yet suffering, and saying, in effect, 'I know what you have been through, what you now struggle with and what lies ahead for you. I, too, have suffered and my suffering is exceeding great, so great that it encompasses all you endure and gives you strength for tomorrow.' I wrote of this encounter soon after, in *As Trees Walking*: 'We did not fully understand our plight and yet his compassion surrounded us and invaded our innermost selves.'[123]

Brueggemann sums up the mystery of God's largesse through creation and, by implication, a cross that assails our egocentricity:

> Creation faith, as an assertion that all that exists is wrought by the extravagant generosity of God, is reluctant to give reasons for God's intentions. It is enough to acknowledge, be awed, and delighted. This incredible past, to which we have only lyrical access, pushes one's *raison d'être* out beyond one's self, thus quickly refusing every notion of self-sufficiency and suiting us for an Other with whom we have by definition to do.[124]

Summary

This has been a chapter to explore both the strengths and weaknesses of biblical counselling in the contexts of late modernity and postmodernity. Of all the pathways to wholeness, this pathway is the one that lays the greatest claim to Scripture and is thus, paradoxically, most vulnerable to its misreading and mishandling. And yet, as I hope we have seen, it is in taking the Bible seriously that we most lay ourselves open to the dangerous but fulfilling business of transformation. The enterprise of biblical counselling, in both its excluding and integrational forms, has a particular commitment to a didactic mode that seeks a transformed mind and, thus, transformed behaviour. Without belittling the centrality of this emphasis in much of the biblical text, I hope we have shown that biblical counselling's project can be profoundly enhanced and made more effective by attending to both the full impact of Scripture's 'big story' and the subversive challenge of its sometimes idiosyncratic 'little stories'. This particular pathway is best travelled, amid the enticements of modernity's logical certitudes and postmodernity's bewildering options, with an ever-handy Bible, frequently thumbed as a sort of Rough Guide to the Universe. Here is a resource book, finely honed to 'make encyclopedias', to use Lovelace's phrase, with which we can engage with God's world, whether on the shop-floor or in the street, in a crowd or alone, on the shore or in a wood, in the study or in the counselling room. Thus provided for, we need to attend to that other voice within Scripture – to general as well as special revelation, to story as well as law, to imagination as well as proposition, to creation as well as redemption, to an everyday spirituality as well as to text-book theology. In Laurie Green's words, what is required is 'an earthy and communal spirituality of obedience and celebration' that is 'so at home in its own milieu that it knows how to see God in the secular world around it, and drink up spiritual resources through the pavements of the city or the fields of the countryside'.[125]

8

HEALING MINISTRIES:
THE FORWARD GAIN

*'The wound is healed,' he said, 'I am whole, I am free.' Then he bent over
and hid his face in his arms, weeping like a boy.*

Ursula Le Guin[1]

The year was 1979, the place was Christ Church Vicarage, Clifton,
Bristol, the situation was one of a month or two into my second
period of blindness with, it seemed at that stage, no prospect of
medical or surgical cure.[2] At the recommendation of a friend, Joy
and I were meeting with a visiting healer from the Midlands, a
woman in her early thirties, or thereabouts, who was a leading
member of a house church and was said to have been instrumental
in many dramatic experiences of healing. We felt mixed about the
large claims of her street-credibility and yet, after a first bout of
eight months' blindness, a few one-eyed, sighted months and
now, following the holiday on Colonsay, a return to physical
darkness, we also reckoned there was nothing to lose in continuing to look to God for reprieve through his servants' ministries.

The experience was not a happy one. There were five of us
present: Gloria, the healer, two younger women (our mutual
friend and one who worked with Gloria), Joy and myself. We
sat in a semi-circle about the hearth of an upstairs room and
discussed my condition – the diabetes, the consequent blindness
and the undulating symptoms of brucellosis. All seemed hopeful
until Gloria asked whether I had been 'baptised in the Spirit'. My
understanding of Scripture was such that I believed that a trinitarian God cannot be divided up, and, thus, having opened my life
to Jesus the Spirit-Baptiser, I replied in the affirmative. However,
this response did not fit with Gloria's 'second blessing' theology
and her view that healing is closely linked to 'receiving the Spirit'.
A further setback in this supposedly therapeutic encounter came a

little later when, in reply to another leading question, I had to declare that I could not be *sure* that God would heal me miraculously, either immediately or gradually, this side of heaven. Gloria was clearly unhappy with this apparent lack of faith and, in reply to my references to the stories of Job and St Paul's 'thorn in the flesh', she took the little remaining wind out of my expectant sails by saying, 'You can only claim Job's experience if you are as good as he was; you can only identify with Paul's situation if you have had the sort of visions of God that he had.'

What more could be said? We had reached a theological and pastoral impasse. And yet, wisely, we set the theorising aside, while Gloria laid her hands on my bowed head and prayed vehemently for my healing. Echoing her prayers in our hearts, Joy and I made our way out into the winter streets of Clifton. Two months later I had a second major operation on my recalcitrant right eye and the clearing of sight began once more. That unilateral vision, with the exception of the need for cataract surgery in 1990, has held well since; the brucellosis continued to debilitate over the following eighteen years or so, although its grip has lessened markedly during the last couple of years.

Clebsch and Jaekle, in evaluating the history of pastoral care, have written that the function of healing, compared with guiding, sustaining and reconciling, is, in the context of the last forty years of the twentieth century, both the 'most problematical' and the 'most open to new and fresh expression'.[3] In many ways our encounter with Gloria highlights both what is 'problematical' and what makes for hopeful change in Christian healing, raising innumerable questions – pastorally, experientially and theologically. Were we wise to engage with her in the first place? What exactly did we expect of her? of our friend? of God? Did our clash of biblical hermeneutics matter in terms of expectant faith and prayer? Was Gloria, after all, instrumental in some way in my improvement of sight, or was its restoration entirely due to the God who can heal through a surgeon's hands? And what of the brucellosis? Is a delay of eighteen years for answered prayer stretching the limits of credulity? What is healing anyway? Is peace of mind and heart through the trials of surgical intervention and chronically recurring illness not worth as much, or more, than a physical restoration that may work against life's learning curve?

It is questions like these, arising from the praxis of the so-called 'healing ministries,' that we need to consider in this chapter as we examine our second pathway to wholeness.[4] The subject is a big one and is fraught with a range of theoretical and practical issues that weave in and out of what may be called a theology of healing and a theology of suffering or, alternatively, a theology of power and a theology of weakness. To start with, we will consider something of the story of the Church's call to heal, in order to set the contemporary preoccupation with such methodologies as 'inner healing' and 'deliverance' in context. Finally, as with the previous chapter, we will explore a possible way ahead, seeking in this case to clarify some of the prevailing concerns in and around the healing ministries, both psychologically and theologically.

The Church and Healing

One might say that from the 1960s onward sections of the Christian Church, especially those influenced by the successive waves of the so-called 'charismatic movement', John Wimber's 'power healing' and the 'Toronto blessing', have developed an almost unhealthy preoccupation with health. And yet, behind this surge of interest, lies a long history of pastoral care in which the Church's call to heal in the name of Christ has waxed and waned through intermittent periods of scepticism and expectancy. Perhaps the most important thing for Christian healing ministries in today's culture is to steer a trusting (but not naïve) and hope-giving route between the rigorous scientism of modernity, where even the possibility of divine intervention is derisible, and the easy-believism of postmodern plurality, with its often tenuously held boundaries between meaning and magic.

Health and Healing

Before giving a brief overview of some of the salient features of the healing function throughout the history of pastoral care, it is worth clarifying something of what is meant by health and healing.

The word 'health' comes from the same Old English stock that gave us 'hale' (as in 'hale and hearty') in the northern dialect and 'whole' in the Midlands and southern parts of England. Although the word is commonly used today as a synonym of 'fitness', in the sense of 'soundness of body', its original meaning was much more closely linked with the concept of well-being in every aspect of human life. This comprehensiveness accords well with the Judaeo-Christian tradition, as is brought out by Morris Maddocks when he writes, 'Health can never be equated with human wellness and an absence of disease. Health is to do with the totality of creation, with the Creator himself.'[5]

With respect to 'healing', Clebsch and Jaekle declare, in a similar vein to Maddocks, that 'healing is more than mere restoration, for it includes *a forward gain* over the condition prevailing before illness'.[6] Here, we can contrast health and healing in their fuller senses with the notion of a medical or surgical cure, in which the normal expectation is, at the most, to return to one's previous state, as when recovering from pneumonia or coming through post-operative debility. We see the essentially biblical nature of these perspectives in, for example, the account of Jesus and the woman 'who had been subject to bleeding for twelve years'. He turns to her and says quite simply, 'Take heart, daughter, your faith has healed you' (Matt. 9:20–2). Here the Greek verb *sozo* expresses a healing of the whole person, giving the unnamed woman a 'forward gain' over her pre-haemorrhagic condition.[7]

That God is a God who heals is clear throughout Scripture. We see, for example, Yahweh's self-declaration at the waters of Marah: 'I am the LORD, who heals you' (Exod. 15:26); the psalmist's exultant, 'Praise the LORD, O my soul' and listing of Yahweh's 'benefits' to include, 'who . . . heals all your diseases' (Ps. 103:2–3); and, in the life of Jesus Christ, a powerful, God-centred ministry that heals 'every disease and sickness among the people' (Matt. 4:23). That the picture is less straightforward and more mysterious and disturbing than this becomes evident once we allow the texts' fuller impact, since we see, for instance, that Yahweh not only declares his ability to heal but also to inflict the 'diseases of Egypt' on his people if they should be disobedient (Exod. 15:26) and, with similar emphasis, Job says of the Almighty, 'He wounds, but he also binds up; he injures, but his hands also heal' (Job 5:18). And, although the impact of Christ's healings was profound in the *immediacy*, *completeness* and *permanence* of the changes he wrought, his was not a triumphalist crusade to make first-century Palestine the healthiest place on earth so much as an open portrayal of his divine authority and an affirming pronouncement of an 'inaugurated eschatology',[8] whereby the promise of the kingdom is initiated though, as yet, not consummated. Further, just as the Old Testament points to a 'dark mystery' with respect to healing and affliction, so the foretelling and realisation of Jesus's narrative is a blend of victory and apparent defeat, of conquering kingship and suffering servanthood, of, by inference, a theology of power and a theology of weakness.

Healing and Sustaining in the Church

This interweaving of a glorious, light-filled hope with the chequered landscape of present reality is written into the story of Christian pastoral care. In other words, the pastoral function of *healing* threads its way through church history entwined with, to use Clebsch and Jaekle's term, the function of *sustaining*, a ministry that helps people 'to endure and to transcend' affliction.[9] We thus see, in the earliest days of the Church, accounts of, on the one hand, God-given apostolic power to heal the sick (Acts 5:16) and perform 'miraculous signs and wonders' (Acts 14:3) and, on the other hand, divine sustenance given in the face of imprisonment (Acts 5:18–19), beatings (Acts 16:22), riot (Acts 19:29–41), and St Paul's unremitting 'thorn in the flesh' – the last offering up, it seems, through its very anonymity, the *general principle* that God's 'sufficient grace' is available in all situations of prolonged adversity (2 Cor. 12:7–10).

And so, throughout the unfolding story of pastoral care, we observe the continuing enmeshment of the 'forward gain' of healing and the 'holding the line' of sustaining.[10] We see the former in, for instance, the miracles witnessed by Irenaeus (c.130–c.200); the founding of hospitals by Basil the Great (329–79) and Hildegaard of Bingen (1098–1179); the miraculous healings recorded by John Wesley (1703–91); and the fresh outpouring of the Holy Spirit experienced among the people of the Black Forest in 1842 under the pastorship of Johann Christoph Blumhardt. The pastoral function of sustaining is exemplified in the exhortatory letters of Cyprian (c.200–58), Bishop of Carthage, written to the faithful during the Decian persecution; John Chrysostom's (c.347–407) consoling *Letter to a Young Widow*; Luther's *Fourteen Comforts for the Weary and Heavy Laden* (c.1519); and Jeremy Taylor's *The Rule and Exercise of Holy Dying* (1651).

It is when we come to the twentieth century that we meet, within a series of Spirit-impelled tidal waves that wash new life into a seemingly dessicated Church, a fresh healing impetus which, amid its claims of 'signs and wonders', is in recurring danger of glossing over the need for a complementary ministry of Christian sustenance: Pentecostalism, rising on a spring-tide of revival in 1906 and fed by the twin currents of Wesleyan Methodism and African spirituality;[11] charismatic renewal, eschewing Pentecostal denominationalism and penetrating the mainstream churches from the early 1960s;[12] John Wimber's so-called 'third wave' of 'power evangelism' and 'power healing', springing from his new openness to Pentecostalism in 1978;[13] and the possible 'first spray of a fourth wave' in the Toronto blessing of January 1994 and the subsequent spread of its dramatic, much-debated ecstatic phenomena.[14]

Although the debate on the lasting significance of all four 'waves' continues, there is no doubt that God has richly blessed his Church through these movements, not least through their burgeoning healing ministries. Over the same period, there has been a continuation of the more sacramental traditions of Christian healing, featuring laying-on of hands, anointing with oil and the centrality of the Eucharist.[15] Further, one of the hallmarks of twentieth-century pastoral care has been the steps taken to heal the ancient breach between the Church and medical practice.[16] Perhaps the most faithful mirroring of biblical models of healing is seen where these three traditions, charismatic, sacramental and medical, have joined forces.[17]

Bearing in mind Scripture's corrective that we need to engage a theology of suffering and weakness as well as a theology of healing and power, let us begin to grapple with some of the thornier pastoral and methodological issues raised by our very human desire for the 'forward gain' of healing and wholeness.

Healing Ministries Re-examined

As many are increasingly realising, the effectiveness of the healing ministries is particularly difficult to evaluate. In a sense there is a methodological challenge in all of our five pathways in terms of assessing the validity of claimed outcomes. However, it is more straightforward to measure improvement in, say, behavioural change as a response to biblical counselling, or environmental conditions resulting from social transformation, than in the inner world that is the target of spiritual direction or 'healing of the memories'. Moreover, and perhaps most surprisingly, the clarification of causative factors in a supposed 'forward gain' in something as explicit as *physical* healing can still prove to be fraught with evaluative difficulty. The dilemma of proof, as with the Pharisaical interrogators of the healed 'man blind from birth' in John 9, often lies more in the mind of the 'objective' investigator than in that of the one who can declare, with a mixture of exasperation and exultation, 'One thing I do know. I was blind but now I see!' (John 9:25).

Let us examine some of the knotty questions that surround the healing ministries and seek some resolution in relation to *healing and the burden of proof; inner healing and recovered memory;* and the methodological question, *healed or delivered?*

Healing and the Burden of Proof

If we take the biblical declaration that God is a God who heals, and at the same time accept the reality that that healing is, first, not inevitable[18] and, second, when it comes it may come through *natural, medical* or *miraculous* means, then the issue of proof is put into perspective. The reality is that no one needs convincing when a person 'gets over' a dose of flu or has clearly recovered after having an appendix removed or is fully active again after having a broken ankle set and remobilised. It is only where there are claims for the miraculous that the matter becomes an issue for the rational, scientifically attuned mind. For, as many have said, a miracle is, by definition, an exception: it is the intervention into the normally accepted order of things of a 'forward gain' that is way beyond what is anticipated or deemed possible. And if we take the miraculous healings of Jesus as our touchstone, we face transformative results which, more often than not, are *immediate, complete* and, presumably, *lasting*.[19]

Herein lies the dilemma for the contemporary mind. Many, following in the footsteps of such as D. F. Strauss,[20] will automatically exclude miracle – whether in first-century Palestine or in the globalised world of the new millennium – as lying outside the bounds of possibility in a universe which invariably obeys the laws of nature and is subject to nothing else but human knowingness and achievement. For others, the outright dismissal of the miraculous is not so straightforward. Many Christians, for example, especially those of evangelical persuasion, hold strongly to a belief in the veracity of the Bible's recorded miracles but, contrary

to many of their charismatic brothers and sisters, struggle with
what may be seen to be extravagant and unauthenticated claims of
dramatic healings today. Sometimes this incredulity relates, perhaps unwittingly, to an inherited diffidence not only to the
perceived excesses of Pentecostalism and, more recently, charismatic renewal but to a historic Reformed antipathy to Catholic
sacramentalist approaches to illness. The sound of B. B. Warfield's
indictments of 'counterfeit miracles'[21] still echoes in the Bible
study groups and prayer meetings of a large slice of fundamentalist and evangelical Christianity.

However, are we asking the wrong questions of today's healing
ministries?[22] A word of warning is given by M. A. H. Melinsky
who writes that 'to see a miracle is more akin to seeing a joke than
to seeing a red bus, and the more you analyse a joke, the less of a
joke does it become'.[23] Even so, does Christianity stand or fall on
the simple recounting (miracle as 'joke') of stories of discarded
wheelchairs, crutches thrown away, asymmetrically short limbs
lengthening, gold fillings appearing in carious teeth and cancerous
tissue rendered healthy again, all simply in response to the prayer
of faith? Or is the Christian story more honoured by a rigorous
and, at times, declamatory examination of such claims (miracle as
'red bus'), knocking down each questionably substantiated account like ten pins in a bowling alley?

It seems to me that the best approach lies neither in the potential
naivety of the first position or the ready scepticism of the second.
In this middle-ground stance we can concur that God *is* healer and
he can bring a 'forward gain' in people's lives through natural
recovery (for that is how he has made us), by medical and surgical
means (for that is how he has skilled and gifted us) and in direct
intervention, where God, in C. S. Lewis's words, 'short circuits' the
processes of nature.[24] And this third route of God's healing, that
we refer to as 'miracle', need not be seen, as modernity would
have it, as part of a natural/supernatural dichotomy, since all
healing is the province of the same creator and redeemer in a
world 'charged with the grandeur of God'.[25]

David Middlemiss tackles the methodological dilemma head-on
when he asks 'How can one assess the claim that a person has
encountered God in charismatic experience?'[26] With respect to
healing, he acknowledges that 'the elusiveness of hard evidence'
necessitates that the response to such questions as 'Did it happen?'
and 'How did it happen?' 'depends in which paradigm one is

situated'.[27] And so the judgments given on, say, an account from the 1985 Wimber conference in Brighton, in which, a year after prayer for healing, a middle-aged nurse described continuing freedom from her discomforts relating to a longstanding, severely painful arthritic condition of her neck spine,[28] will be many and various. In the case of a committed 'third wave' charismatic, there may be sheer delight in God's miraculous power; an evangelical, of the type who is persuaded that gifts of healing are tied inexorably to the 'dispensations' of the biblical record, will handle the story and its context with considerable caution; and a Western-trained doctor with no religious affiliation is likely to respond with downright disbelief, knowing the vagaries of cervical spondylosis and its attendant symptoms.

Pointing out that the traditional epistemological methods of deduction and induction are insufficient when confronted by 'charismatic experience',[29] Middlemiss puts forward Basil Mitchell's idea of a 'cumulative case argument'.[30] In this approach, 'The process of argument is not a chain of demonstrative reasoning. It is a presenting and representing of those features of a case which severally co-operate in favour of the conclusion.'[31]

If we were to take the story mentioned above, we are not left with a bald choice between seeing the episode as pure miracle or as palpable self-delusion. Human reality is usually much more complex. We may comment, first, that, as Christians, we can see that the encounter may well have been one of a genuine prayer of faith, which accords well with such scriptural declarations as, 'Ask and it will be given to you' (Matt. 7:7) and 'if we ask anything according to his will, he hears us' (1 John 5:14). Second, it may be that the woman had been under a great deal of stress, which in turn had tightened her neck and shoulder muscles and thus increased her symptoms, and that the care and support of those offering healing had played their part in relaxing her and giving a new sense of well-being. Third, it is likely that there would have been a close occupational connection between the frequent manoeuvring of heavy patients and her neck pain and that her year or so of improvement was, perhaps, also influenced by fresh care in her lifting technique. Other possible factors could be introduced into the narrative but these three – spiritual, psychological and physical – indicate the value of the 'cumulative case argument'. Taken together, they are likely to give a truer picture of interpreting charismatic experience than the more polarised stances frequently adhered to.[32]

Inner Healing and Recovered Memory

A major spill-over from the psychoanalytic tradition into the Christian healing ministries is the notion of 'inner healing', the central motif in a wide range of techniques which seek to bring God's wholeness not only to a person's inner life but to the past, pursuing 'the journey back' through such methodologies as prayer counselling, healing of the memories, primal integration, requiem healing and healing of the family tree.[33] In contrast to our first pathway of biblical counselling, with its objectifying emphasis on cognition and behaviour, the pathway of inner healing, in following the analyst's interest in the hidden past,[34] inevitably steps into the more subjective world of memory, imagination, fantasy and perceived human experience. We will examine this world under three headings: *inner healing*; *the place of hypnosis*; and *recovered memory: true or false?*

Inner Healing

The Spirit-charged soil of Pentecostalism and the charismatic movement proved fertile ground for the development of inner healing, decribed by Ruth Carter Stapleton as 'a process of emotional reconstruction experienced under the guidance of the Holy Spirit'.[35] The priority given to physical healing, especially in the earlier years of the first, second and third waves of renewal, increasingly acknowledged the claims of a bigger picture for healing in which a person's inner, emotional life was seen as an equally appropriate target for a God-given 'forward gain'. Here, there is a certain logic, not least from the point of view of a Judaeo-Christian anthropology, in extending the ambit of desired health to include interiority as well as physicality. Moreover, from the Second World War years onward, the progressively psychologised cultural climate, especially in its more analytic forms, inevitably created an atmosphere conducive to Christian stirrings in the direction of the buried past.

One of the earliest protagonists for inner healing, Agnes Sanford (1897–1976), an American Episcopalian whose fame spread through the publication of *The Healing Light* in 1947, openly acknowledges, albeit in unsophisticated form, the influence of analytic psychological concepts on her understanding of human need. Starting her healing ministry following an experience of the removal of her own 'mental depression' through a priest's prayer, and owning the centrality to her work of the 'baptism' and gifts of the Spirit, she writes of her self-understanding in terms of 'this unseen part of me, whether submerged beneath the depths of my conscious self or rising above it ... this also is myself'.[36] A distinctly Jungian flavour is shown when she argues that God 'incarnated Himself and became man, thus entering into the collective unconscious of the race, into the deep mind of every person' and is thus available 'for healing and for help' through a range of channels,[37] including friendship, counselling, prayer, interpreting dreams, and her own particular brand of inner healing.

Sanford's method, known as 'healing of the memories', has been a powerful influence on later proponents of inner healing, such as Ruth Carter Stapleton,[38] Francis MacNutt[39] and Leanne Payne.[40] In this approach, Sanford especially stresses the importance of the Holy Spirit's 'gift of knowledge', initially as a source for self-illumination during 'times of an inner dullness' which may indicate 'some old unpleasant memory is knocking on the doors of the consciousness'.[41] If a period of listening and self-examination fails to unlock the offending past, she acknowledges that the 'wounds' may be 'so deep that only the mediation of someone else can heal us',[42] through the confessional, the sacrament of penance or through listening and prayer. It is in the last of these that the healer, after exploring any accessible recall of the needy person's childhood, prays for forgiveness and healing, stage by stage back through the memories and beyond – 'back to the time of birth and even before birth', praying for 'the restoration of the soul ... of the real, original person'.[43]

In this retro-journey, the presence of the living Christ is seen as an essential companion for healing. Sanford describes her own experience of inner healing, prompted by a 'very discerning young woman' who had said to her that, while praying, she became aware of a fear in Sanford that was linked to the eighth year of her life.[44] After a difficult period of trying to pinpoint the past, Sanford began to recall that she had been 'sick with terror' that her father would die at that time. She writes:

> I went back to the memories and found that little child and, playing a game in the imagination, I told her that she was loved and comforted and that she would also be healed. Opening thus a door into the past, I

took Jesus with me and led Him to her that He might heal her with His love. And being of a sacramental church, I went to Communion service the next Sunday taking her with me.[45]

For Sanford, these were the first stages of a process of inner healing, in which a 'certain fear' had been identified and the possibility of its removal through Christ believed in.

Critiques of Inner Healing

Inner healing, and its attendant 'healing of the memories', has been criticised on a number of fronts, particularly from propositional, objectifying and deductive viewpoints within our Bible-based first pathway. Dave Hunt and T. A. McMahon,[46] for example, have attacked it with all guns blazing. Alarmed at the perceived poverty of biblical reference among inner healers, they accuse the methodology not only of merely offering 'psychological salvation' but also of conjuring up images of Jesus which may be more akin to dalliance with the 'spirit-guides' of shamanism than an authentic encounter with the living Lord.[47] The heart of their concern seems to lie with the very act of an imaginative return journey to the obscured past, with a 'visualization' which offers up a 'mental picture' that 'seems to be real'[48] but, in fact, may be a seductive delusion at best or, at worst, an opening up 'to demonic influence'.[49]

Although it is perfectly reasonable for Hunt and McMahon to challenge the slim biblical allusion of many in the inner healing ministry and to warn of the psychological and spiritual dangers of unguarded 'make-believe' excursions into a hidden childhood, their polemic against inner healing does not seem to allow for the Spirit-filled integrity of many of its practitioners nor for the legitimate use of the God-given gift of the imagination. Being 'Spirit-filled', of course, is no guarantee of Christian orthodoxy or orthopraxy but one cannot thus legitimately brush aside, I believe, the Christ-centred commitment to compassionate listening and healing of an Agnes Sanford or Leanne Payne. Further, recalling Nicholas Berdyaev's statement, 'God created the world by imagination', Payne sums up the counterbalance to Hunt and McMahon's anxiety-provoking critique:

[God] 'thought' the world, imagined it, then spoke it into being . . . We as makers do not create in this way, out of nothing . . . But we, in His image, 'make' according to the creative principle . . . An idea or a thought 'comes' to us: then we see with our mind's eye (i.e., we imagine) the painting, the building, the book, the project – whether the work of a conference, the creative work of parenting, or prayer for healing, etc. . . . If we are Christians, there is an added dimension, for we know that we are collaborating with the Spirit of our Creator God to bring to light this work of art.[50]

Two evangelicals from the Graduate School of Psychology at Fuller Theological Seminary, Jim M. Alsdurf and H. Newton Malony, provide a more particularising and systematic critique of inner healing by reviewing Ruth Carter Stapleton's ministry.[51] Their criticism overlaps that of Hunt and McMahon's in its concern for the perceived lack of biblical fibre in Stapleton's approach, but it also tackles the wider methodological issues linked with her personal background, theological framework and level of psychological insight.

It is perhaps no surprise that in such a ministry as inner healing, with its highly autobiographical mandate, that its proponents' personal narratives will tend to mould its assumptions, expectations and methods.[52] We have already seen this tendency in Sanford, albeit continually checked by her cautious self-awareness and humility. Further, in fairness to such as Sanford and Stapleton, we can say that it is not unique for the innovators of a 'new' methodology, particularly one whose story has been caught up with the heady days of charismatic renewal, to lag behind their successors in terms of attempts at theological and psychological systematisation.

One more recent approach to 'healing emotional wounds', which presents a more fully-fledged position, is that of David G. Benner.[53] Holding a theology of suffering in balance with a theology of healing, he puts forward a more holistic model than many of his predecessors. He acknowledges how very hard it is to get in touch with a past in which a person has been on the receiving end of, say, parental rejection and ill-treatment and how impossible it can then be to forgive the perpetrators. Benner sees many inner healing methodologies as inadequate in their effect since they often only address the need to heal *emotional* pain. He proposes, rather, a scheme that involves three tasks, each primarily involving a particular aspect of human personality: *re-experiencing the pain* (the emotions); *reinterpreting the hurt* (the intellect); and *releasing the anger* (the will).[54] The eventual goal of this programme is forgiveness – the 'hard work miracle' that can never be achieved easily or cheaply, since 'releasing the anger means giving it up . . . letting go of my right to revenge [and] forgiving other people for what they did to me'.[55]

Hypnosis and Inner Healing

A method which fills certain Christians with even more alarm than inner healing is that of hypnosis,[56] and yet, in responsible hands, this technique can be viewed as being as valid a contribution to the healing ministries as any. Hypnosis as an acceptable therapeutic method has had a chequered career: first systematised in the controversial, and later discredited, work of the Austrian physician Anton Mesmer (1734–1815),[57] applied to medical practice in Scotland by James Braid (1795–1860), used in psychiatric contexts by Jean-Martin Charcot (1835–93) in Paris and initially welcomed and then rejected by Freud.[58] Condemned from its earliest days in the guise of 'mesmerism' by the Church, and that view reinforced later by its assimilation into the practices of Mary Baker Eddy's Christian Science and its use and misuse as entertainment in stage settings, today's hypnosis has inherited the legacy of a suspicious Christian mindset. That mindset has been further reinforced during the recent decades of charismatic renewal by repeated attacks on hypnotic practice which have, for example, deemed it 'demonic at its worst and potentially damaging at its best'.[59] Concurrently, and in many ways paradoxically, hypnosis has become increasingly acceptable to the scientific community for its use in childbirth, surgery and dentistry, for its contribution to cognitive-behavioural cures for such well-defined conditions as phobic states and addiction to smoking, and for its value as an alternative therapeutic resource in the worlds of psychoanalysis and psychotherapy.

To understand the place of hypnosis, and its potential links with inner healing, it is important to emphasise that the hypnotic state is simply an example of a wide range of 'altered states of consciousness' (ASCs) to which the human frame is susceptible, such as sleep, anaesthesia, meditation, daydreaming, sexual ecstasy and inebriation. ASCs have a range of shared features and, as John H. Court, an Australian Christian psychologist and established hynotherapist, points out, these can be listed in order to clarify the nature of hypnosis itself.[60] Thus, hypnosis can be said to be characterised by *focused attention*, in which there is withdrawal from background distraction into a 'trance state'; *repetition*, such as the task of counting backwards; *disruption of critical thought processes*, accompanied by a shift to the visual imagery and non-rational thought of the right hemisphere of the brain; consequent *use of imagery; passivity*, which may be better described as 'receptivity', in which there is still the activity of choice; *trusting relationship*, the touchstone of many of the most effective therapies; *heightened suggestibility*, which Court describes as 'envisioning possibilities'[61] that may not normally be perceived; *physiological changes* comparable to those found in relaxation; and *demand characteristics*, referring to both the client's and therapist's expectations of the hypnotic state. All this may be summed up in the following simple definition by Z. Rubin and E. B. McNeil: '[Hypnosis is] an altered state of consciousness, in which the hypnotized subject can be influenced to behave and to experience things differently than she would in the ordinary waking state.'[62]

Although it is obvious from such a definition, and the preceding description, that hypnosis can be abused in unscrupulous hands, it is fair to say that so can *every* therapeutic approach to human need, including all the forms of Christian healing ministry discussed in this chapter. Even so, much Christian concern has been expressed around the basic presupposition that hypnosis inevitably entails a relinquishment of control from the client to the hypnotherapist, a bid for a trust that is seen as unwarranted in the life committed to God in Christ. Court takes this criticism seriously, but sees it as dependent on a misunderstanding about the nature of hypnosis in the hands of today's qualified practitioners. He writes:

In my view it is unethical to engage in a practice which removes freedom of choice from another person. My role is actually to enhance this freedom and to act in support of the principle that the Christian is to be characterized by self-control as an expression of the fruit of the Spirit (Gal. 5:23). Most Christians will acknowledge that they have less control than they wish over some areas of their lives – habits, addictions, fears, sins – and are seeking to enhance control . . . Effective management of this anxiety results in a return of control so that what was once impossible becomes possible again. The person has learned how to exercise self-control over an area of previous chaos. Hypnosis can be a tool to help those who are seriously motivated to change.[63]

Given the unarguable value of hypnosis in well-encapsulated conditions such as the phobic states, what of the relevance of this approach to the more clouded waters of the hidden past, the realm engaged upon by many inner healers? Here, Court sees both similarities and differences, where the two methods, 'although based on different assumptions, nonetheless converge on the human problems involving emotions and past trauma and the search for healing from negative experiences'.[64] We have already noted the shift from 'critical thought processes' to the non-rational thought and visual imagery of the brain's right hemisphere as a characteristic of the altered state of consciousness in hypnosis, and we have encountered a comparable movement in the visualisation techniques of the 'healing of memories'. Thus, with the newer, less directive style in contemporary hypnotherapy, there is a great deal of common ground between the two methodologies in terms of their 'journey back' approach – both using stepwise 'age regression' and guided imagery and both seeking engagement with obscured memory and repressed emotion.[65] Where hypnosis is in the hands of a qualified Christian therapist and inner healing is offered by a trusted and trustworthy Christian of experience and accountability, then there is likely to be a comparable openness to the leading of the Holy Spirit.

Court illustrates the complementarity between the two approaches in the case of Brenda, a 44-year-old single woman who had been helped previously in a 'prayer-healing context' but presented for the possibility of hypnotherapy in a state of incapacitating depression and low self-esteem. After eight counselling sessions, including seven occasions of induced hypnosis, in which a number of anxiety-provoking childhood experiences and a major episode of attempted rape in adult life (which had not surfaced in the inner-healing context) were accessed, Brenda's depression had lifted to the extent that she resolved to get back to work. The close parallels with inner healing are seen in Session 5, of which Court writes:

As she re-experienced her terror [at molestation by her friend's father when she was aged eight], feeling threatened and alone, I suggested that she might become aware of the presence of Jesus, recognizing that he had been there, unnoticed, all the time. She easily accepted the awareness of his presence as a source of comfort. Anxiety was progressively replaced by peace and reflectiveness.[66]

Recovered Memory: True or False?

Perhaps the most pressing question behind the 'journey back' methodologies, including inner healing and hypnosis, is: Are the recovered memories true or false? Or, a little more elegantly: Can we tell whether they are true or false?

I have an early memory that has stayed with me from childhood. I am barely a toddler and I am standing up in my cot holding on for grim life to the cotside. The small room I am in feels to be an upper room, the window opposite the cot is partly open, it is night-time and windy, for the curtains are billowing and blowing about. There is some light from somewhere, either from a small lamp in the room or from street lights outside. I can see a cupboard or a wardrobe against the right wall of the room, its mirror reflecting the restless shapes of light and dark that chase across walls and ceiling. And I am afraid . . .

Where did this memory come from? Does it relate to an actual situation seen through the inexperienced eyes of a small child? In other words, is it a 'true' flashback? Or, is it from a childish fancy, fantasy or dream? And, whether nightmare or reality, what was I afraid of? Does it matter whether the memory is true or false, given that somehow it is part of my remembered world? Checking my description through the years with my mother, her response has been that the details could relate to a particular address at which we lived for a short time and, if so, I could not have been older than eighteen months.

It is the 'truthfulness' of such recall that has been the centre of the debate since the early 1990s concerning childhood sexual abuse.[67] As is well known, two camps have taken up entrenched, either–or positions: one group often sees itself as made up of 'survivors' and insists on the accuracy of its memories; the other broadly sees itself as comprising 'the accused' and talks readily of the 'false memory syndrome'.[68] Between these two positions the psychotherapeutic profession is 'fighting for its life',[69] caught in the cross-fire from, on the one side, clients whose stories need to be heard and believed and, on the other, family members who plead their innocence.

Understandably, professional bodies are taking this debate very seriously. For example, the British Psychological Society (BPS) set up a working party in 1993 to examine the issues surrounding 'recovered memory'. One of its members, Phil Mollon, a psycho-

analytic psychotherapist, speaking in Bristol in 1997,[70] two years
after the BPS report, relates something of the 'pain, rage and fear'
generated among its recipients, not least with regard to the lack of
resolution in its findings. Declaring that 'false memory' and
'corroborated recovered memory' were both recorded in the
inquiry, Mollon explains the consequent angst among his colleagues in terms of the professional dislike for 'ambiguity'. He
urges that clinical psychologists, cognitive-behavioural therapists,
psychoanalysts, client-centred counsellors and hypnotherapists
combine their experience and perception to bring mutual understanding into this vexed field of childhood sexual abuse.

As Philip Roth the novelist puts it, 'Memories of the past are not
memories of the facts but memories of your imaginings of the
facts.'[71] This view of the 'trickiness of memory', to use Charles
Elliott's phrase,[72] was held by Freud who, in his earlier years,
wrote of the 'active nature of memory' in which 'remembering is
reconstruction'. Even so, his later emphasis postulated an 'archi-
val' view of memory,[73] in which prolonged psychoanalysis could
enter the depths of the stack room of the psyche's stored library
and thus retrieve its secrets. However, this view, although still
highly influential, has been largely dispelled by more recent
empirical evidence, which points to a great deal of memory
distortion through fantasy, defensiveness and the seduction of
being a 'centre-stage' storyteller.[74]

Peter Fonagy and Mary Target point out that contemporary
thinking on memory, from a psychodynamic perspective, describes two forms: 'autobiographical' and 'implicit' memory.
Although the act of remembering, particularly for life's earliest
events, is subject to distortion, there is a weight of research that
says that *autobiographical memory*, even for the third to fifth years of
life, is 'likely to be broadly accurate'.[75] Even so, experience with
post-traumatic stress disorder and work on the links between
brain function and repeated maltreatment indicate that childhood
trauma may 'disrupt the normal functioning of the memory
system', so that the autobiographical component of remembering
becomes unreliable.[76]

As well as the more self-evident autobiographical nature of
memory, there is thought to be an 'involuntary' or *implicit memory*
system, within which past experience is held intact, although
unreachable by conscious mental processes. It is believed by a
number of researchers that the emotional content of traumatic

memories may be stored permanently in implicit memory.[77] And, although the detailed story may not be recoverable in terms of time, place and situational context, it seems that the encoded experience may be accessible at the level of the senses and emotions; and, further, that accessibility may be revealed through present stimuli which resonate with these features in the original incident. Thus a particular smell, sound or sight can trigger the sensations associated with the buried trauma, releasing accompanying flashbacks or nightmares, reinforced by powerful emotions such as anxiety, rage or terror.[78] And so we can say that, for example, my own 'remembered' scene described above, with its disturbing visual imagery and intense fear, is more likely to arise from implicit memory than from the more factual and contextual storehouse of autobiographical memory.

But what of the now well-rehearsed dilemma concerning the nature of recovered memory and its relationship to *childhood trauma*, real or imagined? Even with an understanding of the complexity of memory with respect to its autobiographical and implicit elements, how is it that its retrieval can still prove so elusive? There is a web of theoretical consideration that surrounds the issue, but one of its strongest explanatory strands lies in the notion of 'dissociation'. Previously, in terms of the psyche's defence mechanisms, the Freudian idea of *repression* held sway as a 'motivated inability to retrieve relevant information' that is buried in the past.[79] Today, the concept of *dissociation* has taken root as a separating out of memories from their original context, where, although isolated and unreachable, they remain intact, 'influencing both behaviour and emotional disposition'.[80] With repression, 'memories unacceptable to consciousness' were thought to be ' "horizontally" split from awareness', like a collection of magazines whose earliest edition is inaccessibly buried at the bottom of the pile. With dissociation, such memories are held to be ' "vertically" split from the remainder of the patient's . . . functioning', like a group of upright box files whose respective contents are self-contained and 'split off' from their fellows. Although dissociation is a capacity that we all share to varying degrees, there is a close correlation between dissociative disorders[81] and the reporting of childhood abuse and related traumata. Such dissociated memories may be viewed, as it were, as blurred figures in a fog – vaguely familiar, yet their full identity shrouded. They are, to quote Christopher Bollas, 'not unknown thought but the unthought known'.[82]

What bearing does all this 'trickiness of memory' have on the claims of the healing ministries, especially on such 'journey back' methodologies as inner healing or, for that matter, hypnotherapy in Christian hands? It seems to me that such practitioners must take note of contemporary research with respect to the ambiguities of recovered memory. It is one thing to seek the Holy Spirit's guidance and discernment in the healing of memories, for example; it is quite another to insist that the recall of perceived childhood trauma, however vividly and compellingly presented, is, without doubt, the retrieval of historical event, correct in every detail. Such 'knowing' conclusiveness is in danger of not only spiritual arrogance before a God 'whose thoughts are above our thoughts', but of engulfment by the pastoral nightmare of uncertainty added to uncertainty, of false accusation compounded by vehement denial.

Amelia's story is typical of the uncertainties with which the inner healer or Christian counsellor must live. Seeing me in her mid-thirties over two years or so, she still mourned the death of her father from a road accident when she was only seven. An only child, she grew very close emotionally to her mother and was very upset when her mother remarried at the time of Amelia's tenth birthday. She seemed to be holding a great deal of anger toward her father for leaving her, toward her stepfather for his 'irritating' habits, toward older men generally and, as a Christian, toward all notions of God as 'a loving, heavenly Father'. Further, Amelia shared a range of brief snatches of 'stories' from the period between her father's death and her early teens, fragments of memory relating to various male friends of her mother's who visited the family home from time to time. These 'episodes' related to the way certain of these men 'looked at' her, were recounted, although very sketchily, with evident disgust and were clearly felt to be sexually abusive. How much of this recall was 'autobiographical' and historically accurate; how much 'implicit' and therefore only hinted at through strong present-day emotion and fragmentary 'flashback'; how much 'dissociative' and split-off from the 'real' Amelia? Or were there elements of fancy and fantasy contributing to the story, perhaps relating to a child's anxieties over maternal sexual activity? Over all, were the recovered memories true or false?

Most of these questions remained unresolved in Amelia's case. All I know is that, by the time the period of counselling had to be discontinued, she was less angry and more trusting toward the older men in her life (including her counsellor!) and had experienced a measure of healing in relation to the fatherly, motherly God whom, she had grown to accept, loved her and would not betray her.

Healed or Delivered?

When Joy and I rendezvoused with Gloria and friends at Christ Church Vicarage in 1979, we were open to the possibility of God's healing for my blindness. What surprised us at the time (although I had come across Gloria's approach elsewhere) was that she did not pray for healing so much as for *deliverance*. I wrote in *As Trees Walking*:

> After some minutes of collective prayer, Gloria rose and came to stand behind me, laying her warm hands on my head. She had seemed rather tense and, perhaps, unnerved by her encounter, but now she prayed with single-minded vehemence. She cried to God for my healing, commanding diabetes, blindness and brucellosis to depart. While she agonised her fingers kneaded into my scalp. We each echoed our prayers in our hearts, reaching out to God in our trust.[83]

Here an alternative paradigm of healing seemed to be operating, one that treats disease as an entity to be 'cast out', to be commanded, in the manner of Jesus encountering evil spirits: 'Depart!' Whether the imperative form of Gloria's prayer was appropriate in the context of illness or not, what place, if any, does the so-called ministry of deliverance have amid Christian healing ministries? Does it simply provide another choice among the 'charismatic' techniques of prayer for physical healing, of inner healing or the 'journey back' through hypnosis? Or, is there a quite different mindset behind the concept of deliverance, with its implications of the 'battle in the heavenlies' and a sometimes highly elaborated demonology?

The Bible demonstrates a clear belief that evil is abroad in God's world and that the impetus of that evil is ultimately laid at the door of the devil, or Satan, a personalised being dubbed as God's arch-adversary and hell-bent on leading humankind and its enculturation to destruction.[84] Although reference to this baleful influence is sparse in the Old Testament, the Gospel accounts,

particularly the Synoptics, are charged with a number of significant references to the Enemy and his allies, the evil spirits or
demons.[85] The coming of the incarnate Son of God, in announcing
the dawn of the kingdom of God, forces the hand of the powers of
darkness to a series of pitched battles, each of which is lost to the
tempted, resisting and victorious Jesus of Nazareth.[86] The Epistles,
although largely shifting their language from talk of demons to the
pervasiveness of sin and the dead hand of a law devoid of grace,[87]
declare the eternal outcome of the greatest battle of all, fought in
Gethsemane and on Golgotha:

> He forgave us all our sins, having cancelled the written code, with its
> regulations, that was against us and that stood opposed to us; he took it
> away, nailing it to the cross. And having disarmed the powers and
> authorities, he made a public spectacle of them, triumphing over them
> by the cross. (Col. 2:13–15)

Although many have sought to demythologise the supernatural
element in those forces that opposed Jesus and his followers, as
presented in the New Testament, it is worth asking how satisfactory alternative interpretations are. Perhaps the commonest produced by the modernist mindset is that Jesus was simply a man of
his time and that, just as he would have been unaware of the
geological timescale of the landscape he walked or the quantum
physics that operated in the air he breathed, so he naturally had
inherited the demonological views of his contemporaries, little
realising that, in 'casting out evil spirits', he was, in fact, dealing
with schizophrenia and grand-mal epilepsy. If only he had had
our psychiatric and neurological understanding!

I am not sure that this alternative explanation works, once the text
is taken seriously. At a general level, there is often a distinction
drawn between illnesses that Jesus heals and conditions which he
confronts by exorcism: 'The whole town gathered at the door, and
Jesus healed many who had various diseases. He also drove out
many demons . . .' (Mark 1:33–4). More specifically, encounters with
the possessed were often marked by certain features that distinguish
them from healings. These characteristics are typified in the engagement with the 'demon-possessed man' in the Gerasenes (Luke 8:26–
39): an uncanny knowingness toward Jesus's identity ('What do you
want with me, Jesus, Son of the Most High God?'); a superhuman
strength that could break his shackles and flee his guard (8:29); a

dialogue between Jesus and the many-voiced 'Legion', the collective name of the man's demons (8:30–1); and the evident 'need' of evil spirits for corporeality ('When the demons came out of the man, they went into the pigs'). Even though some might point out that certain psychotic states can possess an extraordinary degree of physical strength, and that pigs will always panic at crazed human behaviour(!), modern reductionism cannot quite explain away the full impact of such texts. We will examine a notable analysis of how we are to understand the powers of evil within contemporary society later in the chapter.

The deliverance ministry of Jesus and the early Church seemed to be part and parcel of their wider healing ministries. The practice of *exorcism*, 'the driving away of malevolent spirits by means of sacred words and holy rites',[88] thus became integral to the Christian tradition, in both its sacramental and charismatic forms.[89] Whereas, for example, the Western, Roman Church, set up the office of 'exorcist' as one of four minor orders of clergy, the Orthodox churches of the Eastern Church have always seen the deliverance ministry as a calling for 'charismatic' lay people, who may, in turn, be ordained as deacons or sub-deacons. In the light of the gross superstition and obsessive elaboration of medieval demonology, the Reformation and its aftermath treated exorcism with great caution, many following Luther's example that prayer alone was sufficient to counter Satan's devices.

Today, we see elements of the continuing division of viewpoint around this most controversial of ministries,[90] a division highlighted by the notorious 'Barnsley' Case of March 1975, 'in which a husband murdered his wife after an all-night exorcism during which a group of charismatic Christians claimed to have exorcized many demons from him, but failed to remove the demon of murder'.[91] This tragic episode highlighted the dangers of a so-called 'healing ministry' that was cut loose from the moorings of accountability through a wayward tendency to diagnose 'demons' as the direct cause of every perceived ill and idiosyncrasy. The minds of church hierarchies were concentrated wonderfully, and within the following year or so the Methodist Conference and the General Assembly of the Church of Scotland had issued reports on the vexed question of exorcism, the latter concluding tersely, 'There is no place in the Reformed Scottish tradition for such a rite to be devised . . . Any person encountering a case of alleged "possession" should refer it to a physician.'[92]

As early as 1965, when the second wave of the charismatic renewal was lapping at the doors of most local churches, the Bishop of Exeter convened a commission, comprising Roman Catholics as well as Anglicans, to investigate the phenomenon of deliverance. Although a report was published in 1972, recommending that 'every diocesan bishop should appoint a priest as diocesan exorcist' and that 'centres of training' should be established in each province, it took the tragedy at Barnsley, and a ruling from the subsequent General Synod in July 1975, to put forward guidelines that had staying power.[93] The Christian Exorcism Study Group, which arose out of the original 'Exeter' commission, has done much to encourage and effect a network of training, education and the establishment of diocesan advisers and teams for the 'ministry of deliverance'. Such teams 'should be seen as supplementing, strengthening and upbuilding the pastoral and priestly work of the parish clergy, and not as supplanting it'.[94]

In summary, we can say that the question, 'Healed or delivered?' although legitimate, is one that most pastoral carers and counsellors will not need to ask within much of their healing ministry.[95] The Christian Exorcism Study Group has been wise to stress the consultative nature of potential exorcism, the need for an ecclesial chain of responsibility and for the availability of psychiatric, medical, psychological and social work opinion. The pitfalls are numerous, both in terms of awareness of such disorders as the 'possession' syndrome,[96] psychotic conditions and dissociative states and in terms of spiritual discernment with respect to the exact nature of human need and how that is best met – sacramentally, through the laying-on of hands, anointing with oil, the use of holy water or a prayer of blessing, or, charismatically, through inner healing or a prayer for deliverance. Michael Perry, warning that 'major exorcism' is a procedure 'fraught with dangers both spiritual and physical for the unwary and ill-prepared', puts the Christian ministry of deliverance into perspective. He writes:

Let no one be deceived to think otherwise than that this [ministry] is a minor sphere of the activity of Satan. His great work is to be seen in such obscenities as the nuclear arms race, in the embattled and trustless negotiations between power blocs either internationally or between sections of societies, in apartheid and racial hatreds, in the million and one ways in which humankind behaves as though there were no God in heaven and no heaven for him to be in.[97]

The Way Ahead

Throughout our discussion of contemporary healing ministries the reader may have been struck by the recurring contrasts between this pathway and the first pathway we considered – that of biblical counselling, with its underlying evangelical and fundamentalist theologies and spiritualities. The latter pathway, as we saw in the last chapter, is propositional in its doctrines, didactic in its method, handles Scripture to cognitive and behavioural ends and embraces a theology that centres in the Word and the cross. For all its strengths, we suggested that for biblical counselling to be more *fully* biblical it needs story (*agada*) as well as law (*halacha*); spirituality as well as theology; imagination as well as proposition; and an emphasis on creation as well as redemption.

The strengths and weaknesses of the healing ministries, on the whole, pull in the opposite direction. As we have seen thoughout this chapter, healing and deliverance methodologies are brimful with 'stories' and this emphasis accords well with the spontaneity and hopefulness of the Jewish concept of *agada*. And yet, of course, this preoccupation with narrative can readily degenerate into unsubstantiated anecdote, where the cool-headed appraisals of *halacha* are neglected. In this tendency, we see something of George Lindbeck's 'experiential-expressivism' (see pp. 176–8),[98] in which the believer is in danger of a preoccupation with the expression of 'the experiences of the inner self', to the neglect of the objectifying givenness of the faith. By the same token, the corpus of the biblical canon can be handled in a highly selective way, in which, for example, favoured prophetic and eschatological passages are milked vigorously for their current applicability. Here we have a 'this-is-that' hermeneutic[99] in which the interpreter is at great pains to clinch that a contemporary phenomenon, such as the 'Toronto blessing', is just what a particular Scripture has predicted. Mark Stibbe, for instance, adopts a 'this-is-that' exegesis of the vision in Ezekiel 47:1–12, in which the four increasing depths of the river that flowed from the temple are identified as the four successive 'waves' of the Holy Spirit's work in the twentieth century and beyond.[100] At a much more modest level, Gloria, the charismatic healer we met at the beginning of the chapter, seemed to adopt a 'this-is-that' expectation in her approach to healing, except that, concluding that my situation did not match either Job's or Paul's, she adopted a 'this-is-*not*-that' interpretation in my case!

In all this, Pentecostal and charismatic spirituality, with their huge commitment to God-given transformative experience, are in ever-present need of a courageous theology that will face the hard questions raised by ecstatic, enspirited Christianity. Further, the 'right-brain' field of the imaginative, intuitive and inductive, not least in the 'journey back' methodologies, still needs the temperate, though more familiar, 'left-brain' voice of the propositional, systematic and deductive. And, third, the welcome rediscovery by the charismatic movement of the Holy Spirit's work can readily lead to unitarianism and a consequent neglect of the concept and relevance of the full Trinity.

We can seek a corrective to these trends under three headings: *releasing the affections; unmasking the powers;* and *integrating Word and Spirit.*

Releasing the Affections

One of the striking elements of the first decade of Pentecostalism was the palpable breaking down of barriers of race and sex, though not of class. The movement spread rapidly in the Afro-American community and among poor whites, while many women emerged as preachers, evangelists and healers. Although this early promise tragically gave way to renewed racism and sexism within the more middle- and upper-class echelons of the Pentecostal movement from the 1910s onward, the subsequent waves of charismatic renewal in the second half of the twentieth century have, at their best, seen the fresh breaking down of divisive barriers. It would be a mistake to exaggerate this liberative trend but there is no doubt that women, in particular, have been highly influential within the healing ministries. Many of the best-known names among Christian healers are those of women, including, for example, Agnes Sanford, Ruth Carter Stapleton, Kathryn Kuhlmann, Catherine Marshall, Anne White, Basilea Schlink and Leanne Payne. This observation stands in sharp contrast to that pertaining to biblical counselling, where, especially at the more 'excluding' end of the spectrum, there appears to be a singular lack of female leaders.

All in all, it is likely that we are seeing, within early Pentecostalism and the charismatic movement, the emergence of Schleiermacher's 'divinatory', 'psychological' or 'feminine' route of perception, as distinct from the 'comparative', 'technical' or 'masculine' principle so manifest in biblical counselling. Or, to put it another way, God's Spirit has been freshly reminding his people that they are not only 'all one in Christ Jesus' but that they are called to a fuller response to his humanising love, to a response that includes heart as well as head. Whereas modernity has long elevated reason over the emotions (and, as we saw in the last chapter, evangelicalism has often followed suit) and postmodernity tends to celebrate the irrational at the expense of the carefully reasoned (and Pentecostalism can slide in the same direction), charismatic renewal, if it will but grasp the nettle, could show the way to an integration of the cognitive and affective.

In Chapter 6, while considering effective pastoral theology, we discussed the prime importance of both right belief (orthodoxy) and right action (orthopraxy). Steven J. Land, in a perceptive critique of Pentecostal spirituality, puts forward the need for a third category – that of right affections (orthopathy)[101] – as integral to wholesome Christian living. Following John Wesley and Jonathan Edwards, he sees the concept of 'Christian affections' as abiding at a deeper level than 'feelings' or 'emotions', since they are 'objective, relational and dispositional': their object (and source) is God; they express 'a relationship with God, the church and the world'; and they 'dispose the person toward God and the neighbor'.[102] Further, Land takes three such affections – gratitude, compassion and courage – and, though acknowledging they are characteristic of all Christians, seeks to point out their 'distinctive Pentecostal ethos'.[103] We can take his cautionary note, I believe, for all who offer pastoral care within the healing ministries, especially those of a charismatic persuasion:

These three affections can . . . be seen as safeguards against certain dangers. A grateful, thankful walking in the light guards against presumption or mere mechanical duty . . . Compassionate, wholehearted love in and through Christ guards the soul against sentimentality, apathy and hardness of heart. The believer at peace through the cross is a peacemaker through compassion. The courage that is given to the grateful, compassionate seekers after righteousness is a hedge against despair . . . However, to go forth without the Spirit's leading is to go without his power . . . Power, like holiness and love and grace, is the believer's possession only in a derivative and relational sense.[104]

Thus, those involved with the healing ministries need to be acutely aware of their creatureliness and dependence on the redeeming, forgiving, empowering Lord for not only right belief and right action, but for the experience and expression of right Christian affection. There is a world of difference between the electronic detachment of a televangelist healer or the 'up-front' remonstrations with the Almighty from the leaders in a healing crusade and the thankful, compassionate and courageous dispositions of faithful women and men who humbly seek healing for others and themselves within pastoral or communal relationship. Here, there can be tangible movement toward the 'integration of beliefs, affections, and actions [of knowing, being and doing]'.[105]

Unmasking the Powers

More than any other pathway to be considered in this book, the healing ministries remind us, sometimes too sensationally and obsessively, of the grim reality of evil. Whereas biblical counselling may emphasise 'sin', pastoral counselling 'psychological blocks', spiritual direction 'the shadow' and social transformation 'injustice', the Pentecostal and charismatic spiritualities that undergird many approaches to healing often envision their calling in terms of a battle with the forces of darkness – with Satan, the archetypal evil one, and his lickspittle servants, the demons or evil spirits. It is here that, on the one hand, those influenced by modernist antipathy to the supernatural and, on the other, those caught up in charismatic renewal or, for that matter, the darker reaches of New Ageism, should take heed of C. S. Lewis's oft-quoted words from the Preface to his *Screwtape Letters*:

> There are two equal and opposite errors into which our race can fall about the devils. One is to disbelieve in their existence. The other is to believe, and to feel an excessive and unhealthy interest in them. They themselves are equally pleased by both errors and hail a materialist or a magician with the same delight.[106]

How can the dark forces, which many in the healing ministries seek to engage with in the name of Christ and in the power of the Holy Spirit, best be viewed as we seek to avoid the polar opposites of dismissive cynicism and obsessive preoccupation? Walter Wink puts the contemporary dilemma well when he writes: 'It is a virtue to disbelieve what does not exist. It is dangerous to disbelieve

what exists outside our current limited categories.'[107] Writing out
of his own personal despair at the suffering he met in Latin
America during the early 1980s, he sought to redefine those
categories through a fresh examination of the New Testament's
insistence 'that Christ is somehow, even in the midst of evil,
sovereign over the Powers'.[108]

In his critique, Wink demonstrates that the language of power is
not only pervasive throughout the New Testament but is presented as 'imprecise, liquid, interchangeable, and unsystematic'.
At the same time, the Powers themselves are 'both heavenly and
earthly, divine and human, spiritual and political, invisible and
structural', as well as 'both good and evil'.[109] It is from this
panoramic view that Wink is able to sit loose to the vexed question
as to whether the ancient perspectives on the *personified* nature of
good and evil, in the form of angels and demons, have a validity
for the contemporary mind. In fact, he argues, such beings,
although clear in the biblical record, are simply one aspect of
the whole. He writes that, in the New Testament,

> the theme of the Powers encompasses every concentration of power in
> any authorized agent or actor. If a worldview includes spiritual beings,
> then they naturally will be covered by the vocabulary of power. But
> they do not exhaust it or even have first call on it. The vast preponder-
> ance of uses of the terms for power is for its human bearers or the social
> structures that manifest it.[110]

In the first century, Wink argues, 'spirits' or 'angels' or 'demons', although 'actual entities', were not so much 'hovering in
the air' as 'incarnate in cellulose, or cement, or skin and bones, or
an empire, or its mercenary armies'.[111] Further, in translating
Scripture's language and concepts into those of today's culture,
he postulates that 'the "principalities and powers" are the inner
and outer aspects of any given manifestation of power', whether it
be government or armed forces, the health service or system of
education, the Women's Institute or local church. Although the
'outer form' of such structures is self-evident, they also have an
'inner essence' which can be seen as 'the spirituality of institutions,
the "within" of corporate . . . systems'.[112]

Such an 'unmasking of the Powers' can provide a sore needed
corrective to many in the healing ministries. Some may have
unconsciously sided with modernity and dispelled all notion of

evil as an affront to circumspect pastoral practice; others may be hugely preoccupied by an elaborated demonology where evil spirits lurk in every physical illness and psychological set-back. Wink, I believe, offers a way forward. On the one hand, his focus on the Powers exposes 'the soft underbelly' of contemporary philosophy's dismissal of 'all spirits from the earth'[113] and, on the other, his picture of the pervasiveness of institutional and structural 'spirituality' can help free the demon-obsessed healer from spiritual myopia. In this way, the power and influence of Satan, whether seen as a personal being or as a 'profound *experience* of numinous, uncanny power in the psyche and historic lives of real people',[114] is lifted from the merely parochial and narrowly localised and revealed in terms of its global enormity. Wink's analysis exposes the lie put about by this 'father of lies':

When television evangelists could try to terrorize us with Satan and then speak favorably of South African apartheid, we should have sensed something wrong. When the large evil went undetected, when the symbol no longer attracted to the fact, when evil ran roughshod through corporate boardrooms and even churches, unnoticed and unnamed, while 'Satan' was relegated to superego reinforcement and moralistic scare tactics, then we should have caught the stench – not of brimstone, but of putrefaction. Not that we had progressed beyond evil. On the contrary, *the evil of our time had become so gigantic that it had virtually outstripped the symbol and become autonomous, unrepresentable, beyond comprehension.*[115]

Integrating Word and Spirit

Whereas evangelicals and fundamentalists, in their commitment to Jesus Christ and the supremacy of the biblical text, have typically emphasised Word, Pentecostals and charismatics, fired with their experience of the Holy Spirit and his gifts to the Church, have manifestly stressed Spirit. Although some have sought to correct the imbalance of their tradition, there are still palpable differences of emphasis between many Word-oriented biblical counsellors and their Spirit-focused counterparts in the healing ministries. Behind a potential Word/Spirit split lie all the dangers of 'Jesus only' or 'Spirit only' unitarianism, as well as a fall into the trap of dividing a 'theology of the cross' from a 'theology of glory' or, to use Tom Smail's expressive language, of sliding from 'the power of love' toward 'the love of power'.[116]

Smail, a Calvinist Presbyterian influenced by charismatic renewal, in seeking to heal the breach between Word and Spirit, cross and glory, love and power, points out two models of renewal: the Pentecostal and the Paschal. In the former there is a tendency for a split between the 'biblical' and the 'experiential', between a first-stage encounter with the cross, 'located in the pardon department', and a second-stage point of arrival at Pentecost, 'in the power department'.[117] In contrast to this compartmentalised view, which always runs the danger of elevating the 'second stage' to 'top-floor' status, the Paschal model is unitive:

> There are no two circles, one with the cross at its centre and another with the Spirit at its centre, but only one circle with the crucified and risen Lord at its centre. It is to him that the Father has given the Spirit, and it is by him that the Spirit is given to his people, as the Spirit of his passion and only so as the Spirit of his power.[118]

Another integrational approach to the historic Word/Spirit split via a charismatic theology is offered by the Dutch theologian Jean-Jacques Suurmond. Where Smail concludes that Word and Spirit are held together at the cross, Suurmond points to their unity in creation. He follows Johan Huizinga's thesis on the primeval nature of play,[119] both among animals and human beings, and links this intrinsic creational dimension of life to the sabbath, the 'the crown of creation':[120] 'Word and Spirit are present at every level of creation, and work towards the eternal sabbath which has already become visible in a unique way in a man from Nazareth.'[121] Thus Jesus, who 'came eating and drinking' (Luke 7:34), 'emerges in the Gospels as God's troubadour *par excellence*': 'He is the perfect "charismatic" who in miraculous healings and preaching with authority manifests both the non-rational and the rational aspects of the Word and Spirit. His life displays the creativity, the passionate dedication and the surprising twist of a game.'[122]

If we take the combined insights of Smail and Suurmond we see a potential way forward for the theology and spirituality that underlies the healing ministries. Smail's integration of Word and Spirit at the cross and Suurmond's in creation do not need to be seen as oppositional, for, taken together, they provide a further corrective to the Church's historic tendency to sunder creation, redemption and glorification, the interrelating work of God the Father, Son and Holy Spirit.

Summary

Throughout this chapter on the 'forward gain' of healing we have been continually reminded of the two-dimensional nature of related pastoral care, that the Church is called both to heal and sustain, and that, where either is favoured at the expense of the other, distortions of Christian praxis occur. Where healing is vehemently demanded of God as a presumptuous birthright and resolutely claimed 'in faith', regardless of evidence to the contrary, then healer and suppliant may be caught in a web of arrogance, unreality and crushing disappointment. Where the possibility of healing is spurned and a 'no win' situation of 'grin and bear it' is invariably fostered, then the person in need may lose touch with all the potential for hope and consolation found in the Christian gospel. Both dimensions are needed for a pastoral care that is prepared to face the improvements and deteriorations, the encouragements and disappointments, the ups and downs of real, 'flesh and blood' people in a wondrous and hazardous world.

That pastoral sensitivity, as we have also seen, needs special grace and wisdom in the face of the healing ministries' many uncertainties: claims and counter-claims around miraculous healing; the relentless retro-quest for healed memories, birthings, 'in utero' experiences and family histories; accusations of childhood sexual abuse opposed by the indictment of 'false memory'; anxiety about hypnosis and compulsions to seek deliverance. Clebsch and Jaekle were right to see these callings as 'the most problematical' of the major pastoral functions!

We have not highlighted 'metaphor' with respect to the healing ministries, largely since the biblical parallels of healer and deliverer are self-evident on this pathway. However, as we conclude the chapter we can also see that our melding of Luther's *theologia gloriae* and *theologia crucis* necessitates a stepping away from any notion of triumphalism within the pastoral work of physical healing, inner healing or deliverance. If the orthodoxy of Word and Spirit, the orthopraxy of unmasking the Powers and the orthopathy of released affections are to be true to the trinitarian God – who is waiting Father, as well as Creator of all; Suffering Servant, as well as risen Lord; and groaning Go-Between, as well as Spirit of power – then we need a metaphor that addresses both the dark and light sides of life. The Jewish story of the 'wounded healer' provides such a metaphor with its depiction of the Messiah who has already come and is to be found sitting among the poor at the gates of the city. All have many wounds in this picture; but, whereas the others unbind their wounds all at once and then rebind them, the Messiah unbinds and rebinds his wounds one at a time, so that he is always ready to meet the needs of others. Henri Nouwen sees here a symbol of the pastoral carer, who is both a wounded minister and a healing minister, one who needs must attend to his own 'wounds' of loneliness and isolation and yet, at the same time, is available to bring healing through hospitality and community.[123]

Mary Grey, writing in the context of the abuse and oppression of women, sounds the right note for all would-be healers:

> But in our woundedness we are called to be healers. We are called to minister in mutuality to each other's brokenness. In our recovery of attending and tending to the lost rhythms and connectedness we are healers of each other. We re-discover 'care' through this recovery of connection. We are heard out of the depth into speech . . . by a listening of the heart, not by the speech of the expert. We minister to each other . . . through a kind of mutual messianism, where we participate in the relational, redeeming energy which was manifest in the life, death and resurrection of Jesus of Nazareth.[124]

It is these themes of relationality, heart-listening and communality that will provide the focus for our three remaining pathways: pastoral counselling, spiritual direction and social transformation.

9

PASTORAL COUNSELLING: THE MATURING PERSON

Only in the continuous encounter with other persons does the person become and remain a person. The place of this encounter is the community.

Paul Tillich[1]

Like millions of others, I could not quite believe the news on the morning of 1 September 1997. Diana, Princess of Wales dead? Killed in a car crash? That very same Diana who, earlier that year, had been seen in *Diary of a Princess* on BBC 1 – vital, beautiful, seemingly committed to rid the world of landmines, brushing aside an intrusive cameraman as she sat holding the hand of Sandra, a teenage Angolan who had waited three years to have an artificial limb fitted? Despite the ups and downs of her marriage and divorce, her self-evident psychological needs and her running battles with the insatiable press, she had emerged with a new confidence on to the world stage of human need. And here she was *dead*, with the rapidly mounting rumour that the ever-present paparazzi might have fatally overstepped their mark.

The subsequent story has been told, retold and interpreted countlessly. Joy and I were as mesmerised as anyone by the spectacle of national grief during her lying-in-state, the funeral procession and service in Westminster Abbey and the following journey to her resting place at Althorp Park. Of the innumerable images of those few days – the mute solemnity of the two young princes, the word 'Mummy' on the card of Prince Harry's wreath of white roses, Prince Charles's hand laid on his younger son's shoulder in the shadow of the exit from Horse Guards' Parade, the stricken faces of the onlookers and the ever-expanding tide of floral tributes at the palace gates – it was the dying moments of Lord Spencer's tribute, broadcast to the great crowd outside the Abbey, that seemed especially symbolic of the people's mood.

Spontaneous applause, picked up by worshippers just inside the West door, swept into the silent building to include the whole congregation. Here, surely, was a symbol of the Church needing to listen to the common people, needing to acknowledge a common-grace theology where God is abroad amid the communal and personal aspirations of humankind.

The hermeneutics of Diana's memory has fixated the minds of public analyst and private mourner alike. Interpretations of mass hysteria and media manipulation have vied with understandings of genuine national bereavement and the commonality of the religious instinct. Radio 4's *The Moral Maze*, broadcast soon after the funeral, typified the spread of public opinion. For Anne Lesley, the *Daily Mail* correspondent, there had been a conversion shift of viewpoint – from seeing the Princess as 'only good for shopping and suffering' to a realisation of 'the importance of the Diana myth' in the light of 'the self-policing, humble crowd'. Douglas Churnside, another witness in the programme, had slept on the pavement in The Mall the night before and declared that he was 'of a similar age to her, part of the Band-Aid generation' and that she 'epitomises that culture . . . glamorous . . . compassionate . . . able to confess its flaws'. He added: 'Diana worked one-on-one and we're told that's what we've got to do.'

This tragic death and its aftermath, in pointing to a widespread hunger for a spirituality that values human caring and acknowledges human vulnerability, is both challenge and inspiration for a Church whose pastoral care has often been insular and inward-looking.[2] In many ways, it is not the excluding tendencies of many within biblical counselling or the ecstatic highs of a number within charismatic renewal that provides the patient listening and empathetic understanding required. It is in our third pathway of *pastoral counselling* that, rightly perceived, there is the special capacity for coming alongside the broken, disillusioned and anxious and making some sense of life's disorder and dis-ease.

Pastoral Counselling

In Chapter 6 we were reminded that contemporary pastoral care inherits a long history of the Church's 'cure of souls', in which 'helping acts', carried out by 'representative Christian persons', are 'directed toward the healing, sustaining, guiding, and reconciling of troubled persons'.[3] We saw, too, that today's pastoral care seeks to be egalitarian in its calling (lay and ordained, women and men), communal in context and pluralistic in its frame of reference. In turn, we established an underlying pastoral theology that is transcendental, cautiously foundational, correlational and liberational. In the last two chapters, we have observed how our first two pathways are linked with certain elements within traditional pastoral praxis: theologically, both pathways have been seen to be transcendental and foundational; and, functionally, biblical counselling presents as a deductive form of guiding and the healing ministries as, at their best, an interplay of healing and sustaining. We need now to see how our third pathway, pastoral counselling, meshes with the traditions of pastoral care and the insights of present-day theology and psychology.

Definitions

In many ways, pastoral counselling is not easy to pin down. The adjective 'pastoral' evokes biblical imagery of God as shepherd of his people and a long history, through the Latin for shepherd, *pastorem*, of Christian pastoral ministry. The noun 'counselling' immediately brings the notion into the twentieth century and the pervasiveness of 'secular' psychology and therapy in contemporary society. Even so, the term 'pastoral counselling' often implies both more and less than the sum-total of these two words. We can identify at least five uses:

- counselling by the ordained carried out exclusively in the community of faith;
- counselling by the ordained that is available both for the community of faith and the wider community;
- counselling by believers, either lay or ordained, within the community of faith;
- counselling by believers, either lay or ordained, that is available for the community of faith and the wider community;
- counselling by people, regardless of their beliefs, in a range of communal and institutional contexts.

Thus expressed, these uses are descriptive of *any* form of pastoral counselling, whichever faith-system is involved.[4] If we take *Christian* pastoral counselling, the prime focus of this chapter, we can

see the practice of our first two mini-definitions in traditions that
strongly emphasise ministerial authority; and the next two in
churches that countenance the 'priesthood of all believers'. The
fifth usage is increasingly common in a pluralistic society where
the caring and personal tones of the word 'pastoral' have been
reclaimed in a number of organisational settings, including
schools, universities, hospitals and 'secular' counselling centres.

As we have previously noted, there is a close tie in the United
States between the pastoral calling and ordination. The founding
of the American Association of Pastoral Counselors (AAPC) in
1963, for example, has taken the route of a clericalised specialisa-
tion toward pastoral counselling, a commitment to those clergy
'who, having acquired specialized training and experience, have
chosen to identify themselves as specialists'.[5] Whereas the vocation of Christian pastoral counselling in North America, whether
parochially, in hospital settings or as a specific professional calling, is primarily a call to ordination, it is probably fair to say that,
in the United Kingdom, pastoral counsellors are as likely to be lay
as ordained, whether the context is the local church, a Christian
counselling centre or the wider community. Americans further
recognise *pastoral psychotherapy* as a comparable but more specia-
lised calling than pastoral counselling that, to quote Don Browning, 'addresses more completely ... the psychological and
developmental obstacles within a person's life which may be
impediments to free and confident thinking, decision making,
and action'.[6]

With this understanding of the variety of uses of the term,[7] I
would like to define *pastoral counselling* on a comprehensive base,
as follows:

> Pastoral counselling is that activity carried out by representative
> Christian persons, lay or ordained, which aims to help others toward
> constructive change in any or every aspect of life through a caring
> relationship, which has agreed boundaries and is accountable to a
> recognised community of faith or other authorising institution.

Such a definition emphasises *authorisation* ('representative Christian persons'); *comprehensiveness* among counsellors ('lay or ordained'), those helped ('others' implying individuals, couples,
families and other groupings) and counselling focus ('any or every
aspect of life'); the *relational* and *contractual* nature of the counsel-

ling ('agreed boundaries' pointing to some understood arrangement between the parties in terms of time, place, duration and frequency of contact); and the *accountability* of the counsellor within the wider context of pastoral care (the local church, Christian counselling centre, hospital setting, etc.).

Psychological Roots

It is as we explore the psychological roots and theological climate of pastoral counselling that we see its historic distinctiveness from the two pathways to wholeness so far examined. Whereas, with respect to theology's view of psychology, we have noted a more 'excluding' stance among biblical counsellors and, by implication, by many within the healing ministries of charismatic renewal, pastoral counselling, characteristically, has adopted a more 'assimilative' position (see pp. 190–4). As we have observed in biblical counselling and among the healing methodologies, and will discuss in the case of pastoral counselling, all three of these pathways – and, indeed, the whole five that this book considers – can move to a more truly 'integrational' theological and psychological viewpoint.

Thomas C. Oden has been one of the foremost commentators on the failure of nerve within the tradition of Christian pastoral care in the face of the rise of the secular psychologies and the consequent rapidly growing 'counselling movement' from the 1930s onward.[8] He has charted the slippage from a pastoral theology at the turn of the nineteenth and twentieth centuries, which was healthily cognisant of its rich biblical and pastoral heritage, to a posture adopted by mid century, under the newly erected banner of 'pastoral counselling', which had brushed aside the historic traditions for an eager celebration of a new-found faith – a Freudianism that replaced sin with neurosis and a Rogerianism that discarded God-dependence for a heady bid for human autonomy.

As we saw in Chapter 5, Anton Boisen's warning to the Clinical Pastoral Education (CPE) movement of the pending dangers of an uncritical assimilation of the psychoanalytic mindset was largely unheeded and, throughout the 1940s, Boisen's heirs encouraged clergy to cultivate the insights of Freud and his successors. This trend toward the psychologising of pastoral care and counselling was reinforced by the publication of Carl Rogers's *Counseling and*

Psychotherapy in 1942, a work that quickly became a standard textbook in many theological seminaries. At this time the influence of Seward Hiltner (1909–84) and his *Pastoral Counseling*, published in 1949, came to the fore. Once a student of Boisen's, Hiltner, although pioneering an *eductive* style of counselling ('drawing out' the client's needs and experiences as the central focus) that was comparable to the Rogerian approach, nonetheless increasingly held fast to the essentially church-based and pastoral aspects of pastoral counselling. In the 1960s, Hiltner was in the vanguard of the opposition to the specialist groundbase of the AAPC, arguing that private pastoral practice, cut off from the community of faith, was a contradiction in terms.

Inevitably, assimilative tendencies toward secular psychology travelled across the Atlantic to British shores through the return journeys of such London-based Christian pastors as Leslie Weatherhead (1893–1976) and William Kyle (1925–80), in the 1950s and 1960s respectively.[9] Even so, as with Hiltner, these two practitioners sought a measure of integration of psychological and theological insight and aimed to hold the linkage between pastoral counselling and the wider work of the Church. In 1969 Kyle founded the Westminster Pastoral Foundation (WPF), a body committed to church-based pastoral counselling during its first six or seven years. However, by the 1980s, WPF's increasing psychotherapeutic sophistication led to a crisis of identity between its Christian pastoral roots and the overt secularisation of its highly esteemed training programmes. As David Black, writing in 1991, records of WPF's decision to move its focus from the pastoral to the clinical:

> A new argument has prevailed: that, indeed, what is done and taught at WPF is not pastoral counselling. WPF, which now trains few clergy, is teaching and practising a secular activity to which the word pastoral has no application. Consonant with this, the word has been dropped from our official description of the work we do, which is now called psychotherapy or psychodynamic counselling, and is retained in our organisational title only to maintain continuity with our roots.[10]

The founding of WPF, along with other influential pastoral counselling bodies in the 1960s and early 1970s, such as Frank Lake's Clinical Theology Association (1962) and Louis Marteau's Dympna Centre (1971), led to widespread pressure for a British national pastoral organisation that would provide a platform for communication and debate and, perhaps at a later stage, a vehicle for standardisation and accreditation, with some parallels to the established American Association of Pastoral Counselors. Just as Hiltner had resisted the slide toward professionalisation of the pastoral calling in the United States, so a prophetic voice was raised against a comparable trend in the United Kingdom. Robert Lambourne (1917–72), general practitioner, psychiatrist and theologian, wrote in 1970 that he deplored 'the total lack of theological thrust in the so-called dialogue with psychoanalysis', which he had witnessed during a recent visit to the United States.[11] A year later he declared his opposition to the standardising, specialising American model and its incursion on to British soil:

> It is not enough to change our concepts of pastoral counselling to bring them up to date with those of the U.S.A. pastoral counselling organisations which though sophisticated and enlightened are trapped in their history of having been formed, and having flourished, under the pressure of clinical psychotherapy in a highly individualistic society. A model of healthy interpersonal life, of communal life as requiring mutual confrontation and mutual confirmation around the matter of values is essential for pastoral care.[12]

Lambourne went on to urge his British colleagues toward a 'concept and practice of pastoral care which is lay, communal, variegated, adventurous and diffuse'.[13] Here is a bid, against the tide of a psychologised, professionalised and clericalised pastoral ministry, for a recovery of the 'priesthood of all believers', in all its rich variety, interconnectedness and risk-taking commitment to others. Lambourne expressed the strong desire that pastoral counselling rediscover its rootedness in Christian pastoral care, breaking free from a 'hang up' theology[14] that leans heavily on the problem-solving clinical models of medicine and the psychoanalytic tradition.[15]

In spite of Lambourne's warning, a British pastoral organisation was set up in 1972: the Association for Pastoral Care and Counselling (APCC) which, later, became contributory to the formation of the British Association for Counselling (BAC). Even so, according to the Scottish pastoral theologian, David Lyall, 'it can be argued that Lambourne's critique did have an influence upon the issues that became important in APCC'.[16] We shall return later to the continuing debate between the psychological and pastoral root-edness of pastoral counselling.

Theological Climate

Just as biblical counselling has been cultivated in the theological climate of evangelicalism and fundamentalism, and the healing ministries in that of charismatic renewal and sacramentalism, pastoral counselling owes its nurture primarily to liberalism and, latterly, postliberalism. This is not to deny that many evangelicals, charismatics and sacramentalists engage with the pathway of pastoral counselling. It appears that those who do so are among the more 'open' and 'radical' sections of these stances, essentially because, it seems to me, such are freed up from a 'conservatism' that is tied exclusively to biblical proposition, ecstatic encounter or liturgical means respectively. Put another way, it is those members of the first two pathways that are more open to the rich variety of divine leading who may, in turn, combine their methods with a more *relational* emphasis which overlaps with pastoral counselling. Whereas the strength of biblical counselling lies in its theology of Word-centred redemption and that of the healing ministries in Spirit-centred sanctification, pastoral counselling, where it is most theologically aware,[17] is undergirded by the richly humanising perspectives of an *incarnational* theology.

First, let me make a brief comment on the use of the term 'liberal' in Christian contexts. It appears to me that just as the word 'conservative' is often used pejoratively of *other* Christians, from whom one wishes to distance oneself, so it is with the use of the word 'liberal'. Such adjectives are frequently handled dismissively and with very little appreciation of the range and variety of positions held under the stereotyping term. And so, for example, the word 'fundamentalist' is often used sweepingly, and inaccurately, of evangelicalism, with little thought of discernment between, say, conservative, liberal, open or radical evangelicals, let alone postevangelicals. Similarly, many in the more conservative end of evangelicalism will use the word 'liberal', with little or no differentiation between a whole spectrum of stances, from classical German Protestant liberalism of the fifty years up to the First World War, through the more existential styles of neo-orthodox theologians of the mid twentieth century, to the 'radicalised' liberalism of Don Cupitt and 'Sea of Faith' theology.[18] It is one of my aims in this book to seek to dispel something of this compartmentalising smokescreen by taking seriously the self-declarations of some of each pathway's advocates.

Let us consider certain of the key elements in the theological climate of pastoral counselling under two main headings: the *liberal tendency*; and *postliberal trends*.

The Liberal Tendency

We have already seen the pivotal influence of Schleiermacher's 'hermeneutics of understanding' in fostering a new emphasis on intuition and relationality in terms of the human comprehension of fellow-beings and of God himself. This psychologising legacy has been a cardinal ingredient in the leavening of European and American liberalism, an essentially anthropocentric theology that has disturbed the digestive processes of Christian orthodoxy by its questioning of supernaturalism, divine revelation, the veracity of the biblical record and the truths put forward by the faith 'once delivered'. At its most optimistic, liberal theology is heady with the notion of humanity's upward, self-achieving progress, purporting a 'gospel' in which, according to Richard Niebuhr, '[a] God without wrath brought men without sin into a Kingdom without judgement through the ministration of Christ without a cross'.[19]

Although we saw elements of George Lindbeck's 'experiential-expressive' approach to doctrine in Pentecostal and charismatic spirituality, in their case this stance is often tempered by the cognitive and propositional stances of evangelicalism. However, the liberal theologies which have the greatest influence in the history of pastoral counselling show a strongly *experiential-expressive* style, unfettered, by and large, by credal propositionalism. In experiential-expressivism, Lindbeck notes a Schleiermachean commitment to locating religion's ultimate verities 'in the prereflective experiential depths of the self', combined with a demonstration of that religion in terms of 'expressive and evocative objectificiations . . . of internal experience'.[20] In other words, there is a twinned emphasis on the *experience* of the 'inner life' and its *expression* through 'symbol'. Here we find a shift from life's 'givens' and conventions toward a world that can be shaped by human desire and whose realities can be moulded by metaphor.

We have seen examples of this modern and postmodern trend in Anthony Giddens's notion of 'the pure relationship' (see pp. 85–7) and in Richard Rorty's concept of the 'liberal ironist' (p. 149). Lindbeck summarises this universalising and self-actualising stance as follows:

> As we move into a culturally . . . post-Christian period . . . increasing numbers of people regard all religions as possible sources of symbols to be used eclectically in articulating, clarifying, and organizing the experiences of the inner self. Religions are seen as multiple suppliers of different forms of a single commodity needed for transcendent self-expression and self-realization.[21]

Among the 'experiential-expressive symbolists', to use Lindbeck's term, the contribution of certain 'neo-orthodox' theologians to the genesis and development of pastoral theology, and, thereby, pastoral counselling, is outstanding. For example, Don Browning, in fashioning his 'fundamental practical theology', looks to the influence of Reinhold Niebuhr (1892–1971) as the 'most powerful theological ethicist of the mid-twentieth century'.[22] Even so, among theologies broadly associated with neo-orthodoxy, it is probably Paul Tillich's (1886–1965) systematic theology that has most penetrated the world of pastoral care and counselling – through its dialogical commitment to psychology and psychoanalysis.

In Chapter 6 we noted pastoral theology's indebtedness to Tillich's *correlational method*, which 'makes an analysis of the human situation out of which the existential questions arise' and then 'demonstrates that the symbols used in the Christian message are the answers to these questions'.[23] It is this method that Tillich uses to great effect in *The Courage To Be*, in which he analyses the human predicament of anxiety, in both its existential and pathological forms, and offers a way forward through an exploration of Christian transcendence.[24] *Existential anxiety*, the main focus of the book, is seen as 'the anxiety of a finite being about the threat of non-being',[25] an anxiety which takes three forms, each threatening an aspect of human 'self-affirmation': the *anxiety of death*, an ontological threat; the *anxiety of meaninglessness*, a spiritual threat; and the *anxiety of condemnation*, a moral threat. Such anxieties are viewed as 'existential' in the sense that they belong 'to existence as such and not to an abnormal state of mind as in neurotic (or psychotic) anxiety'.[26] It is here that Tillich acknowledges the need for co-operation between psychothera-pists and theologians in order that a more integrated and discern-ing approach to human anxiety might be adopted.[27]

The way forward for the existentially anxious is, broadly speak-ing, twofold: 'the courage to be as a part', in which the need for *participation* in the world around is acknowledged; and 'the courage to be as oneself', in which the requirement for *individua-lisation* – 'ontological self-affirmation as an indivisible, unex-changeable self'[28] – is engaged with. Tillich sees the former as an 'interdependence' in which a person's relation to 'being-itself' (one of his symbolic phrases for the notion of God) has 'a mystical character', wherein the respondent 'plunges directly into the ground of being and meaning'.[29] In contrast, the latter 'expresses itself in the religious experience as a personal encounter with God' through a 'courage of confidence', exemplified in Luther's defiant stance shown forth in the German word *trotz*, 'in spite of': 'In spite of all the negativities he had experienced . . . he derived the power of self-affirmation from his unshakable confidence in God.'[30]

It is here that Tillich declares the touchstone of both Lutheran theology and existential psychology, of both Christian and secular personalism. Both the Pauline teaching on 'justification by faith' and psychotherapy's bid for the idea of 'acceptance' are closely interlinked: either way, for the guilt-ridden sinner, 'accepting acceptance though being unacceptable is the basis for the courage of confidence'.[31]

And yet, Tillich argues, there is a third and higher way for 'the courage to be' and this is where his *experiential-expressive* approach is at its most 'symbolist'. He declares that human beingness, although needing the mystical path of participation and the per-sonal encounter of individualisation, finds its ultimate fulfilment through facing the darkest of existential anxieties, that of a mean-inglessness that can lead to despair. It is here that Tillich, char-acteristically, resorts to symbolism in his effort to speak of God, since, he argues, the symbolic nature of the language he uses 'does not diminish its truth; on the contrary, it is a condition of its truth'; in short, he adds, '[To] speak unsymbolically about being-itself is untrue'.[32] He writes of the need to transcend theism and speaks of the 'God above God', who is the 'ultimate source of the courage to be' and is 'present, although hidden, in every divine–human encounter' – not least as the abyss of despair is faced. For Tillich, a church which raises itself in its message and its devotion to the God above the God of theism without sacrificing its concrete symbols can mediate a courage which takes doubt and meaninglessness into itself. It is the Church under the Cross which alone can do this, the Church which preaches the Crucified who cried to God who remained his God after the God of confidence had left him in the darkness of doubt and meaninglessness. To be as a part in such a church is to receive a courage to be in which one cannot lose one's self and in which one receives one's world.[33]

Tillich's voice is a rich and, at times, mystifying one and, inevitably, has its defendants and opponents. The breadth of its range, including correlations between theology and psychoanalysis, Lutheranism and socialism, Christian belief and existentialism, the self and the world, being and non-being, has been a great influence on pastoral care and counselling and its undergirding pastoral theology. His use of *symbol* is particularly open to misunderstanding. On the one hand, to quote David Kelsey, 'Paul Tillich has said that the "direct object of theology is not God; the direct object of theology is . . . religious symbols" and theology is to explicate the meaning of those symbols.'[34] On the other hand, it is important to realise that Tillich is especially influenced by Jung's notion that a symbol 'is the best possible description or formulation of a relatively unknown fact, *which is nonetheless known to exist or is postulated as existing*'.[35] For Elaine Graham, it is Tillich's assumption that theology and psychology converge into one central truth that is the sticking-point; this view runs the risk, she argues, 'of refusing any distinction between Christian truth-claims and the faith community, and secular culture'.[36] Perhaps it is Alister McGrath, writing in the context of postliberalism's critique of liberalism, who catches the fundamental dilemmas in Tillich's imprint on pastoral theology:

This [liberal] impulse, which is fundamentally apologetic in intent, is to find a common base for Christian theology and public discourse by a prior analysis of human knowledge, culture or experience. The merit of this critique is probably most evident in the case of Paul Tillich, whose apologetic theology is widely regarded as dictated by extrabiblical and non-Christian concerns, and inadequately grounded in the particularities of the Christian tradition.[37]

Postliberal Trends

Where Tillich's 'neo-orthodox' form of liberalism can still be seen as in thrall to the universalising agendas of modernity, postliberalism has, since its inception in the late 1970s and early 1980s, followed a quintessentially postmodern path. We have already met some of the key postliberal figures in Hans Frei (see pp. 102–3), David Kelsey (pp. 178–9) and George Lindbeck (pp. 176–8), linked with the movement's American roots at Yale Divinity School,[38] as well as in Stanley Hauerwas (pp. 53–6) and David Tracy (pp. 161–1). In such commentators we see a shift from liberalism's stress on the individual and the commonality of human experience to emphases on community and the differentness and otherness of human story. More comprehensively, Alister McGrath, in his critique of post-liberalism,[39] follows Willian C. Placher in identifying three cardinal features of the movement: the primacy of *narrative* 'as an inter-pretative category for the Bible'; the primacy of the *hermeneutics* 'of the world created by the biblical narratives' over the interpretation of 'the world of human experience'; and the primacy of *language* 'over experience'.[40] McGrath notes that among postliberal theolo-gians there is a particular appreciation of Alasdair MacIntyre's (see pp. 89–90) philosophical stance on 'the relation between narrative, community and the moral life' and thus concludes that 'postliber-alism reintroduces a strong emphasis on the *particularity* of the Christian faith, in reaction against the strongly homogenizing tendencies of liberalism'.[41]

This recovery of Christianity's particularity, coupled with a threefold commitment to Placher's three distinguishing features of postliberalism – narrative, hermeneutics and language – is self-evident in Lindbeck's *cultural-linguistic* approach to doctrine and religions (see pp. 177–8). Thus, for example, in handling Scripture, Lindbeck's interpretive style is *intratextual*, a style which takes the particularising story-line seriously, is committed to a close her-meneutic of the Bible's world and engages with 'the literary structure of the text itself'. In this way, postliberalism side-steps the extrapolating theologising of a great deal of christological reflection. It makes a bid, rather, for a simpler, more textually bound declaration, in which the 'believer' is 'to be conformed to the Jesus Christ depicted in the narrative'.[42]

What does cultural-linguistic postliberalism have to offer the everyday world of pastoral care and counselling – both through the interpretation of the biblical text and of the narrative of 'living human documents'? In many ways we have been seeking answers to such a question in a number of our earlier chapters: in our exploration of the particularising nature of process and goal, journey and story, as well as in the unpicking of postmodernity's antifoundationalism, deconstructionism and pluralism and their reassembling in a hermeneutical pastoral praxis which is committed to differentness and otherness.

Throughout this appraisal we have returned again and again to considerations of *culture* and *language* and their relevance to the pastoral encounter. It is easy, thus, for cultural-linguistic considerations to be held as a truism until it is realised that in Lindbeck's understanding it is their post-liberal *intratextuality* that is of the essence, in that it 'provides warrants for imaginatively and conceptually incorporating postbiblical worlds into the world of the Bible'.[43] Perhaps the cultural-linguistic emphasis is best illustrated in a clear cross-cultural example.

Emmanuel Lartey examines the cultural and linguistic characteristics of two Ghanaian tribes, the Ga and Akan peoples, and brings their world-views to the scrutiny of the biblical world of the Judaeo-Christian tradition. He unravels the meanings, for example, of the Ga name for God, the 'Supreme Being': *Ataa Naa Nyanma*, where *Ataa* signifies 'father', 'grandfather' or, perhaps, 'person who cares for'; *Naa* 'mother' or 'grandmother'; and *Nyanma* 'nocturnal being' or 'sky'. This 'personified creative life force' is thus seen as 'bisexual, nurturing, eternal and nocturnal (hidden or invisible) and associated with what is above (the sky)'.[44] Such notions of God are caught up with holistic views of life among both the Ga and Akan peoples, views that, for Ghanaian Christians, accord well with the biblical text. Following an examination of the concept of 'wholeness' in the Old and New Testaments, Lartey writes:

Such a conception of humanity is close to the essence of Akan and Ga humanity. The step from an individual related by spiritual bonds to father, father's lineage and God the Creator and by physical bonds to mother and mother's clan; to an individual related by spiritual bonds to God and community through faith in the self-giving love and offering of life in Jesus Christ, is a short one. The relationship between them is also plain. Each view enriches the other.[45]

Lartey goes on to show how an acute awareness of the cultural and linguistic contexts of the Ga and Akan peoples needs to infiltrate any pastoral practice among them. He gives the example of the Musama Disco Christo Church (MDCC) of West Africa, with branches in London and the United States, as a body, founded and led by Ghanaians, which offers a pastoral counselling that takes very seriously the ancient traditions of its people, without gainsaying its more recent Christian heritage. For instance, whereas Western missionary zeal attacks polygamy in African society, the MDCC declares that, as long as it is allowed by 'the laws of the state', their stance is a permitting one: 'The premise is not to encourage it, but we say that polygamy does not make a person a lesser Christian.'[46] As Lartey points out, Karl Barth's words resonate well with this view: 'We can hardly point with certainty to a single text [in the New Testament] in which polygamy is expressly forbidden and monogamy universally accepted.' And, where situations arise, 'It would be sheer brutality for the Christian Church to confront men with the choice between baptism and institutional polygamy.'[47] All in all, the MDCC demonstrates a quality of pastoral counselling that is sensitive to issues of culture and language, while seeking not to compromise the essentials of Christian particularity.

Even so, although Christian particularity is a welcome change from modernist liberalism's bland generalisations, Lindbeck admits that one problem with his cultural-linguistic postliberalism is that 'languages and cultures do not make truth claims, are relative to particular times and places, and are difficult to think of as having transcendent rather than this-worldly origins'.[48] This sums up postliberalism's dilemma: for all its commitment to the narratives and grammar of an intratextual hermeneutic, it cannot quite say whether, behind the story-line and the literary style, there lies the reality of a creator and redeemer God who engages compassionately with humanity in the multiple contexts of its culture and language. McGrath, while valuing postliberalism's emphases on Christianity's distinctiveness, the centrality of Jesus Christ and the pivotal nature of the biblical text, criticises Lindbeck's apparent suggestion that 'language *functions* within a cultural and linguistic world; it does not necessarily . . . *refer* to anything'.[49] Writing from an evangelical perspective, McGrath sums up postliberalism's tendency to give a greater loyalty to 'intrasystemic cohesion' than to external 'truth':

Postliberalism reduces the concept of 'truth' to 'internal consistency' . . .
[Although there is] no doubt that intrasystemic consistency is a quality
which is to be admired . . . it is perfectly possible to have an entirely
coherent system which has no meaningful relation to the real world.
Christianity is not simply about interpreting the narrated identity of
Jesus, or giving a coherent acount of the grammar of faith. It is about
recognizing the truth of Jesus Christ as Saviour and Lord.[50]

Even so, McGrath, writing in 1996, concedes that postliberalism
is 'perhaps best seen at present as a research programme, rather
than a definite set of doctrines'.[51] Just as post-evangelicalism can
be viewed as a reaction to evangelicalism's commitment to cognition and proposition and a move to a more experiential-expressive
form of spirituality, so postliberalism can be regarded as a reaction
to the blurred edges of liberalism's experiential-expressivism and
a step toward the more particularising and christocentric nature of
a cultural-linguistic approach. It is worth seeing something of the
circularity of this movement between the pathways to wholeness
in order to set, for example, the continuing debate between
McGrath's evangelicalism and Lindbeck's postliberalism in context.

The Maturing Person

As we consider pastoral counselling's focus on the maturing
person we can briefly recall a number of points in the book so
far which address both the concept of maturation and its contemporary cultural context: in Chapter 1, in examining the notion
of wholeness as 'process and goal', we encountered modern
methodologies which foster the ideas of self-actualisation, Gestalt
and psychosynthesis; in Chapter 3, in exploring selfhood in high
modernity, we met Anthony Giddens's descriptions of the quest
for 'the pure relationship' and for 'privatised passion'; and in
Chapter 5, in our survey of the hermeneutics of the life, we
observed something of the vulnerable, decentred state of the
postmodern self, typified among Richard Rorty's 'liberal ironists'
who bend language to their own ends within a self-serving
'therapeutic' society.
It is important at this stage that we remind ourselves of the
modernist and postmodernist enculturation within which pastoral

practice seeks to live out its Christian distinctiveness, whether within liberal, postliberal, evangelical or sacramentalist mode. The 'therapeutic' stance of Rorty's postmodern liberal ironist was foreseen in Philip Rieff's 'psychological man', who has 'nothing at stake beyond a manipulable sense of well-being' and is a potential 'hedger against his own bets, a user of any faith that lends itself to therapeutic use'.[52] Alasdair MacIntyre offers a comparable diagnosis of modernist individualism in his concept of 'emotivism', wherein 'all moral judgments are nothing but expressions of preference, expressions of attitude or feeling': so, for example, where someone might approve of a course of action and say 'This is good', what is meant is not an ethical evaluation so much as a declaration that means, 'I approve of this; do so as well'.[53]

Although the 'liberal ironist', 'psychological man' and the 'emotive' individual resonate strongly with some of the less theologically and spiritually anchored elements of 'experiential-expressive' forms of liberalism, Rieff's analysis gives us hope for pastoral care and counselling within a more postliberal, post-modern clime. He argues that, in general, 'all cultures have a therapeutic function', whether their unifying systems are 'called religious, philosophical, idealogical, or by any other name'.[54] Further, Rieff contrasts the 'commitment therapies' of classical history, in which 'positive communities' guarantee 'some kind of salvation of self' through transforming 'all personal relations by subordinating them to agreed communal purposes', with the 'analytic therapy' of modern, individualistic culture, wherein 'negative communities' are 'enabled to survive almost automatically by a self-sustaining technology', are devoid of offers of 'collective salvation' and are 'informative' rather than 'transformative'.[55]

As modernist experiential-expressivism gives way to post-modernist cultural-linguistic approaches, and the latter's dialogue with more orthodox and revelational forms of Christianity, we can take fresh hope, I believe, in a transition from a culture of individualistic 'analytic therapy' to a new form of 'commitment therapy' which, following the postmodern agenda we have dis-cussed in previous chapters, affirms 'otherness' and 'difference', set within a rediscovery of the transformative qualities of narrative and community. There is nothing automatic or inevitable in this transition since the postmodern self left to its own devices, as we have seen in Chapter 3 (see pp. 82–8), can slide from its celebration of human distinctiveness and value toward paranoia, cynicism and nihilism.

Once more, as we consider pastoral counselling's commitment to the 'maturing person', we can ask with Anthony Thiselton, 'whether either the self of modernity or the postmodern self need be the only possible selfhood'.[56] Let us consider such potential selfhood by using the methodology put forward by Robert Kegan; we will examine his notion of 'the evolving self' under two main headings: *personhood* and *maturation*.

Personhood

As we have seen, the theory and practice of pastoral counselling has grown from the psychological roots of a number of the secular psychologies, including those of the psychanalytical tradition and Rogerian humanism, and been cultivated in the theological climate of liberalism and postliberalism. This blend of influence, typified, for example, in Tillich's existential neo-orthodoxy, has led to a strong emphasis among pastoral counselling methodologies on concepts of 'selfhood' and 'personhood'. This is not the place to elaborate the welter of meanings of the 'self' and the 'person' used in counselling and psychotherapeutic contexts, since each of the innumerable strands in developmental psychology offers its own definitions. Although the terms are often used synonymously to refer, for instance, to 'the individual as a conscious being',[57] there has been a broad tendency in the unfolding of psychological theory to move from the more individualised notions of the 'self' toward the more relational understanding of the 'person'.[58] For example, in the field of object relations theory,[59] especially in its British school,[60] there has been a progressive movement from traditional Freudianism's preoccupation with the self as 'the subject as he experiences himself'[61] through a range of views that point more to the *inter*personal in child development, yet still holding to Freud's instinctual emphasis, to the 'self psychology' of Heinz Kohut, in which 'the relationship between the self and its selfobjects [is] central for self development'.[62]

The blend of a common humanity, with its potential for relatedness, and individual uniqueness in personhood has been well expressed by Clyde Kluckhohn and Henry A. Murray: 'Every person is in some respect like all others, like some others, like no other.'[63] In this statement we have, on the one hand, the viewpoint said to have been expressed by the Austrian innovative composer, Arnold Schoenberg, 'Someone had to be me!', and, on the other hand, the implied interconnectedness demonstrated in an African perspective in John Mbiti's, 'I am, because we are; and since we are, therefore I am.'[64]

Among the many theories of developmental psychology, it is the 'metapsychology' of Robert Kegan that provides a particularly rich and dynamic framework which pays due heed to both the autonomous and interdependent dimensions of personhood. He perceives that a fundamental reality of our humanness is to organise meaning: 'It is not that a person makes meaning, as much as that the activity of being a person is the activity of meaning-making.'[65] In assessing psychology's attempts to comprehend human 'meaning-making', Kegan is aware of the limitations of, on the one side, the 'rigorous but reductionistic' approaches of developmental psychologists like Jean Piaget (1896–1980) and Laurence Kohlberg[66] and, on the other, the 'vague but richer conception of psychological activity' in, for example, the existential psychologies.[67] Seeking to move beyond the purely psychological (hence a *meta*psychology) by adding biological and philosophical considerations, Kegan adopts a holistic approach to personality which explores 'the need for a sophisticated understanding of the relationship between the psychological and social, between the past and the present, and between emotion and thought'.[68] His balanced understanding of the place of separateness and connectedness in human personhood is summed up well by Joann Wolski Conn's views on Kegan's viewpoint:

> There is never an individual because the word refers only to that side of the person that is individuated or differentiated. There is always, as well, the side that is attached, is embedded. 'Person' refers to the fundamental motion of evolution itself: it is as much about the side of the self that is embedded in a context (family, school, church) as that which is individuated from it.[69]

Maturation

Sadly, as C. K. Barrett has put it, 'Mere lapse of time does not bring Christian maturity'[70] or, we might add, 'any other form of human maturity'; if it did, then all counsellors, pastoral and otherwise, would be out of work. The whole area of human maturation, both what it is and how it might be achieved, is fraught with a multiplicity of theoretical and practical considerations. Broadly speaking, the debate ranges from the more deterministic views that say we are at the mercy of Richard Dawkins's 'selfish gene'[71] to the more activist understandings that declare we can learn from and choose to progress through life's exigencies – as Aldous Huxley has it: 'Experience is not what happens to you, it's what you *do* with what happens to you.'[72]

As pastoral carers and counsellors, we will be acutely aware that, at a more sophisticated level, the problems of maturation which we encounter are often concerned with *an imbalance within the polarity of autonomy and dependency*. As I cast my mind back over a range of counsellees I have seen in recent years I can recall, for example, Benjamin, a resolutely independent businessman in his mid-forties, whose impulse in his teen years, having been out of favour with both his family and his school, was to shout out 'I'll show 'em!' and whose adult life was being lived out with the strongest of autonomous spirits. In contrast to this relentless show of a self-sufficiency which kept potentially intimate relationships at arm's length, Harriet's dilemma lay in her longing for physical and emotional closeness to other people. In her mid-twenties and struggling over 'comfort' bingeing, she was caught in a cycle of overeager desire for company that forced those around her to side-step her perceived demands, and so add to her misery. Kegan confirms this pull between 'differentiation' and 'embeddedness' in his own experience of clients as a therapist:

> One of these might be called the yearning to be included, to be part of, close to, joined with, to be held, admitted, accompanied. The other might be called the yearning to be independent or autonomous, to experience one's distinctness, the self-chosenness of one's directions, one's individual integrity.[73]

Keeping this polarity between connectedness and separateness in mind, Kegan sets out his plan of maturation in the form of a helix or ascending spiral of five progressive stages, each of which is an 'evolutionary truce' – 'a temporary solution to the lifelong tension between the yearnings for inclusion and distinctness'.[74] Taking on board the conclusions of his Harvard colleague, Carol Gilligan, that models of *differentiation* are 'stereotypically male' and models of *growth and development* are 'stereotypically female',[75] Kegan seeks to put forward a schema that is 'intrinsically about differentiation *and* integration' and is thus hopefully free of gender-based prejudice. Put simply, he gives 'equal dignity to each yearning' at whichever stage the maturing person has reached.[76]

Each of Kegan's five stages has its own 'particular culture of embeddedness', in which three functions operate: *confirmation*, a 'holding on to the person, to the me-I-am-becoming, to the experience of meaning-making'; *contradiction*, a 'letting go of the me-I-have-been, letting go of the made-meaning as new meaning evolves'; and *remaining in place*, 'staying put in the period of transformation so that what was me and gradually becomes not-me [can be] successfully reintegrated as the object of my new balance'.[77] The stages can be summarised as:

0. *incorporative* – the 'mothering culture' of infancy;
1. *impulsive* – the 'parenting culture' of childhood;
2. *imperial* – the 'role recognising culture' of school and family;
3. *interpersonal* – the 'culture of mutuality' of late adolescence and young adult life;
4. *institutional* – the 'culture of identity' in love or work;
5. *interindividual* – the 'culture of intimacy' of genuine adult love relationships.

Kegan handles this developmental sequence in the light of what he calls 'natural therapy' and it is here that we can see a hopeful link with Rieff's notion of the 'therapeutic culture' (see pp. 266–7), since Kegan's approach is closer to historic 'commitment therapy' than modernity's individualistic 'analytic therapy'. In *natural therapy*, the 'therapeutic process' which occurs naturally in 'those relations and human contexts which spontaneously support people through the sometimes difficult process of growth and change' is allowed to have full sway.[78] Thus, where counselling is needed, the counsellor seeks to join with 'the person in her meaning-making', rather than 'solve the problems which are reflective of that process'.[79]

Let us take just one transition from one culture of embeddedness to another that is commonly encountered in counselling: the move from the 'interpersonal' of Stage 3's 'culture of mutuality' to the 'institutional' of Stage 4's 'culture of identity'. In Penny's case this transition was proving highly problematic in her attempts to make meaning of life. Although living in a flat with two other young women and working as a secretary at a local estate agency, she was finding great difficulty in disengaging from the embedd-edness of primary relationships, particularly those with an aloof and dismissive father, a mother who was supportive but intensely loyal to her husband, and a married older sister, with whom Penny had always been compared adversely. Her father had repeatedly told her 'You'll never make the grade', and she had often feigned stupidity to annoy him further. She was torn between longing to be at home with her parents and wanting to stay away from them until they showed they valued her. Over the months, a unique row with her mother over her churlish attitude to her father, and a decision to write to him to apologise for her recent cold-shouldering, seemed to contribute toward a less cynical, more understanding attitude toward her parents. Gradually, though with many setbacks, she seemed to nudge toward a greater feeling of personal freedom and an increasing sense of autonomy, encouraged by some new potential friends at the church she was beginning to attend. Penny was making the transition, however tentatively, from the declaration, 'I *am* my relationships' to 'I *have* relationships'.[80]

It is at Kegan's fifth stage of 'interindividuality' that we can see something of the flowering of the 'culture of intimacy', the devel-opment of a 'psychospiritual' maturity, to use David Benner's term,[81] that is committed to responsible relationality. In Conn's words:

> Maturity is, basically, the deep personal openness which comes from having an independent identity, yet recognizing the personal limita-tions of independence and autonomy as the goal of development. Valuing, instead, the intimacy of mutual interdependence, the mature person is one who can freely surrender herself or himself, who can risk a genuinely mutual relationship with others and with God.[82]

The Way Ahead

In Chapter 6 we introduced Abraham Heschel's comments on the polarity within Hebrew law of *halacha* and *agada*, of proposition and relationship, of system and story. In Chapter 7 we observed biblical counselling's tendency to emphasise the propositional and systematic at the expense of the relational and narrational, thus buying into, to some extent, the agendas of modernity. Conversely, in Chapter 8, we noted the healing ministries' bias toward the experiential world of *agada* with their consequent neglect of the corrective ground rules of *halacha*. In this chapter, in considering the pathway of pastoral counselling, we have already seen something of the complexity of its psychological roots and its theological climate giving a range of modernist, liberal, experiential-expressive and postmodernist, postliberal, cultural-linguistic emphases. And, although within this matrix of disparate approaches we can discern elements of both *halacha* and *agada*, it seems to me that the strength and distinctiveness of pastoral counselling lies in its rich contribution to an understanding of *agada*, especially to the constituent concepts of relationality and narrative. Where that emphasis is wisely grounded in the *halacha* givenness of the Judaeo-Christian tradition, then the way ahead for an integrated style of pastoral counselling is promising.

Keeping in mind these considerations, particularly those of the twin perspectives of *relationality* and *narrative*, let us focus on two main dimensions of pastoral counselling that hold together its principal, life-affirming characteristics: a *formative hermeneutic* and a *covenantal theology*.

A Formative Hermeneutic

We set the scene of this chapter with the story of the tragic death of Diana, Princess of Wales and pointed out the crying need for the Church to hear the voice of the people, not least in its pastoral care and counselling. Commenting on this issue, the theologian John Drane draws a parallel with St Paul's encounter with the Athenians in Acts 17, a situation in which the apostle 'did not rubbish the spirituality he saw' but, rather, he 'pointed to the altar of the unknown God, to what they knew, and declared to them Jesus'. Drane goes on to suggest that the carpets of flowers laid in our cities at the time of Diana's funeral 'were placed on that altar' and that the Church does not need to 'reinvent' itself, but 'to return to our roots in the incarnation'.[83] It is this Pauline model – of listening to the people before speaking; of respecting their altar to the unknown God before voicing the Christian kerygma; and of being among others incarnationally before declaring the incarnation –

which, I believe, can provide the essence of pastoral counselling's hermeneutics, of both life and text.

Thomas Oden, in his *Kerygma and Counseling*, explores the notion that 'there is an implicit assumption hidden in all effective psychotherapy which is made explicit in the Christian proclamation'.[84] I believe this thesis resonates well with Paul's correlational approach to the citizens of Athens. Oden holds that the 'implicit assumption' that is covert in the effective therapeutic encounter is that the counsellee is not only accepted by the counsellor but is 'acceptable as a human being by the ground of being itself . . . the final reality [of] *Deus pro nobis*'.[85] This Tillichian language points to an *ontological* insight that, Oden argues, is borne out by the incarnation. He writes:

> The final power in life is for us, and . . . we are forgiven and acceptable. The Christ event clarifies this assumption. In our prodigality, alienation, estrangement, frustration, guilt, and hostility we find we are still loved by the Father and received into sonship. This divine love is not a reality we discover but a reality that discovers us. We do not win God, he wins us.[86]

And it is here that the *pastoral* counsellor, whether working in the context of the local church, a Christian counselling service, a hospital or in the wider community, is especially well placed, because, in Oden's terms, both the implicit nature of human acceptability (in the sense of being potentially recipient of God's forgiving largesse) *and* the explicit nature of the Christian proclamation may be consciously held in mind. For those pastoral counsellors, either ordained or lay, who are not only integrated within the community of faith, but also exercise more kerygmatic and didactic roles in the Church's life, this integration of insight is also given open expression. For many other Christians who counsel, whether they use the term *pastoral* counselling or not, the context of their work and their understanding of the counselling process may mean that the explicitly verbal side of the equation will not be a part of their general remit. Even so, Oden's 'implicit assumption' still operates in accordance with his argument that 'liberating divine acceptance can be mediated concretely through interpersonal relationships without overt witness to its ground and source'.[87]

This is a perspective that all Christian counsellors need to appreciate, not only on the perfectly reasonable grounds that counselling, with its rightful commitment to active listening and empathetic understanding toward the counsellee's story, is not to be *identified with* evangelism or teaching, but because there are certain biblical precedents for a less propositional and more relational approach. We have already seen the relevance of St Paul's approach at Athens as deeply respectful of the other's world-view and context. We can discern, too, in the life of Jesus Christ an approach to people in need that was exquisitely tailored to their specific needs and situations. In making a comparison with biblical counselling, it is worth noting that, although Jesus referred at times to the Old Testament Scriptures, most notably when facing the devil or religious leaders(!), his recorded encounters with the common people are seen to be essentially relational: a look, a question, a touch, a request, a rebuke, a story, rather than a quoted text. And so, Christians who counsel, especially in secular institutional contexts or within the wider community, need not feel guilty or second-rate in that their primary remit is to seek to build up a relationship of trust that is fashioned to the other's narrative. Biblical perspectives can still mould every aspect of the encounter: the counsellor's world-view, maturity and accountability; the counselling process, aims, methods; and, hopefully, the counsellee's responsiveness and commitment to constructive change.

Donald Capps, in his *Biblical Approaches to Pastoral Counseling*, gives a methodology that is particularly relevant to our discussion. In order to clarify the role the Bible plays in pastoral counselling, he looks to 'form criticism', a method of biblical criticism that 'tries to discern the original religious and social needs' which were served by the text's 'form or literary genre, such as saga, folk tale, legend, or prophetic saying'.[88] In Chapter 5, we saw how Capps, in his 'translation model' of pastoral hermeneutics, looks to Paul Ricoeur's 'analogy between texts and human actions'[89] and the consequent attention to the 'world-disclosive' power of 'genre' or 'form' within both the biblical record and the pastoral encounter (see pp. 137–48). Here we can view a more particularising example in Capps's creative use of the parallels between the form of the lament in the book of Psalms and the form of the grieving process.

Most Christian pastoral carers will be acutely aware of the value of the Psalms in bringing solace, encouragement and challenge to

those who struggle with life's demands. The Psalter has a gravitational pull for the careworn. During the long months that
followed my quadruple bypass in 1993 – months that encom-
passed the early stages of kidney failure, a pleural effusion, an
abscess in the chest wall and a protracted stretch of relentless
coughing from brucellosis – my limited attention span and dis-
couraged spirit made reading next to impossible. The only texts
that I could encounter – and that in very brief snatches – were
those of Psalms 34 and 116 and it was only a small handful of their
verses that seemed to have any staying power. There is no subtlety
in the fact that the two that hung most persuasively in my
conciousness were: 'This poor man called, and the LORD heard
him; he saved him out of all his troubles' (Ps. 34:6); and 'Be at rest
once more, O my soul, for the LORD has been good to you' (Ps.
116:7).

Given that every human emotion, from joy to sadness, from
praise to the desire for revenge, is represented in the Psalms, it is
no surprise that they are of profound relevance to the grieving
person – whatever the nature of the loss experienced. Capps points
out that over a third of the Psalms can be considered to be in the
form of the personal lament,[90] and that that form has a great deal
to say about how the people faced and overcame their suffering.
Walter Brueggemann, in his paper 'The Formfulness of Grief',[91]
shows how, in ancient Israel, the experience of life shaped what
was expressed to God and the pattern, or form, of that expression,
in turn, shaped experience. In the form of the lament, for example,
those who had experienced affliction – through sickness, betrayal
or defeat at the hand of enemies –were helped toward rehabilita-
tion and restoration within the community by the 'formfulness' of
the relevant psalm. The function of the form is a forward movement that both gives shape to the aggrieving experience and
defines a response. As Brueggemann puts it: 'The form not only
describes what is, but articulates what is expected and insisted
upon.'[92]

Capps takes Brueggemann's insights on the lament's formfulness, together with perspectives from the writings of Claus Westermann[93] and Bernhard W. Anderson,[94] and asks how the form of
the lament might 'shape the grief counseling process – its methods,
its objectives, its counselor-counselee relationship'.[95] Following
Brueggemann, and including Anderson's sixfold analysis of the
lament,[96] he makes a comparison between the form of lament in

the Psalms and the form of the grieving process as depicted by
Elisabeth Kübler-Ross:[97]

Psalms of Lament	Kübler-Ross
address to God	denial and isolation
complaint	anger
confession of trust	bargaining
petition	depression
words of assurance	acceptance
vow to praise	

Figure 2: Parallels between Psalmic Lament and the Grieving Process

There are similarities and dissimilarities within the parallelism of
these two formative processes. Among the similarities, the link
between the psalmist's 'complaint' and the grieving person's
anger is the most self-evident: in Brueggemann's words, Israel
'articulates rage against all comers as does Kübler-Ross's form'.[98]
Even so, however close the parallels might seem, Brueggemann
points to a fundamental difference between the formfulness of the
people of God's lament and the formfulness of the individual's
grief in the context of 'a death-denying production/consumption
society'.[99] Israel sees death 'as a conquered enemy'[100] and, more
fundamentally, has at the centre of its 'life-world . . . the abiding,
transforming presence of Yahweh'.[101]

From such considerations, Capps demonstrates *a formative hermeneutic* for pastoral counselling as he unravels the essentially
implicit moulding of the grieving process by the form of the
lament, which guides the process 'from complaint through petition to assurance and praise'.[102] We can briefly highlight these
four stages from within grief's formfulness.

1. *Complaint*: the counsellee is encouraged to express her feelings, however unpalatable they might be deemed. In the
   psalms of lament, there may be cries for vengeance or
   protestations of innocence, and the counsellee needs permis-

sion to declare, for example, in the instance of sexual abuse: 'I hate him! I could kill him! How could he have done that to me?' or, following a dependant's long illness and death: 'Nobody can accuse *me* of neglect! I did all I could!'

2. *Petition*: the counsellee needs to declare what she most wants. This *may* take the form of Kübler-Ross's 'bargaining', but Capps is right to stress that such attempts to do a deal with God ("If you'll make me better, I'll attend the Eucharist *every* Sunday") are really cries for help.[103] The pastoral counsellor will support the counsellee in her prayers, encouraging her to clarify her desires, motives and intentions for change.

3. *Assurance*: here there is a shift from the counsellee's sense of isolation to the realisation that she is not alone in her grief. This awareness will hopefully come through the support of family, friends and neighbours, but the counsellor's empathetic identification with her suffering may form the first pillar in the bridge toward a recovered sense of belonging. Even so, as Capps says, 'verbal assurance . . . cannot take the place of the *experience* of God's intervention', an experience that, especially in the early phases of adjustment, may be *mediated* by the counsellor's 'support of the counselee's petition'.[104]

4. *Praise*: in which the counsellee comes through to a more hope-giving perspective in which God may be thanked for his specific help. Sometimes circumstances make the notion of praise more accessible, as when a loved one dies and is thus spared further suffering after a long and harrowing illness, but for many the 'vow to praise' may seem elusive. It is essential that the pastoral counsellor allows the time needed for a change of attitude, a change which, given the bleakness of some people's situations, may finally evade the sufferer. It is the presence of Psalm 88 in the Psalter that acknowledges such human reality, a psalm that concludes with a continuing complaint: 'You have taken my companions and loved ones from me; the darkness is my closest friend' (v. 18). It is here that solace may be found in that God also mourns. In such a context, Capps writes, 'God seems to say to the bereaved, "If I were in your shoes, and you in mine, I would have difficulty praising you." '[105]

Thus Capps puts forward a handling of Scripture that can be distinguished from biblical counselling's more explicit and propositional approach and charismatic renewal's equally explicit 'this-is-that' style of interpretation. Here is an essentially implicit, formative hermeneutic that moulds the counselling process and, at the same time, provides a formfulness that can guide stage-by-stage objectives. The model is relational and is, at root, covenantal. Brueggemann summarises the heartland of this perspective: 'Israel affirmed covenant as the enduring context for grief and loss.'[106]

A Relational Theology

Pastoral counselling is not only characterised by, and needs, a confident 'formative hermeneutic', it is also an essentially 'relational' form of counselling[107] that requires a *relational theology*. And to establish such a theology, I suggest, we should take heed of two cardinal dimensions that give the *raison d'être* of our humanness and, thereby our potential for and calling to relatedness: a *trinitarian dimension* and a *covenantal dimension*.

A Trinitarian Dimension

Henri Nouwen, in his *Behold the Beauty of the Lord*, writes about praying with Russian Orthodox icons and devotes his first meditation to the icon of the Holy Trinity, painted by Andrei Rublev in 1425. The scene is inspired by the story of Abraham and Sarah's three heavenly visitors, described in Genesis 18, in which, following a generous meal with their hosts, they announced the unexpected birth of Isaac. The painting depicts the three figures, now translated to represent the Father, Son and Holy Spirit, sitting at table in 'intimate conversation' beneath the oak of Mamre and around the sacrificial lamb, set in their midst. The distinctiveness and relatedness of the three persons are symbolised in the interconnecting gestures of their hands and the gentle inclination of their heads toward one another. As Nouwen says, 'The movement from the Father toward the Son and the movement of both Son and Spirit toward the Father become a movement in which the one who prays is lifted up and held secure.'[108]

These beautiful symbols of divine relationality resonate with our own humanness and desire for connectedness. As we saw in Chapter 6, when considering a transcendental method in pastoral theology (see pp. 165–6), we noted the need for a perspective that looks to the concept of the Trinity[109] – where, in Moltmann's words, 'personhood is always being-in-relationship'[110] – as the inspiration for our call to 'otherness' and 'relatedness' as human beings, not least in the pastoral encounter. This linkage, of course, is not merely 'inspirational' since the very phrase 'being-in-relationship' reminds us that both divine and human relating concern *beingness* as well as *relationality*. As Martin Buber puts it, 'The primary word *I-Thou* can be spoken only with the whole being. . . as I become *I*, I say *Thou*.'[111] It is only as we have a sense of human *being* that we can respond genuinely to the 'other'. In Buber's words: 'The primary word *I-Thou* establishes the world of relation.'[112]

Colin Gunton explores these thought-provoking parallels and connections with regard to the ancient notion of *perichoresis*,[113] signifying 'the ontological interdependence and reciprocity of the three persons of the Trinity'.[114] Here is a term (from the Greek *peri*, about or around, and *choros*, dance) which signifies something of a divine choreography, an interweaving of figures that betokens both unity and diversity, enabling theology 'to preserve both the one and the many in dynamic interrelations'.[115] Furthermore, Gunton takes this evocative dance motif, with its profound ontological implications, and asks 'whether reality is on all its levels "perichoretic", a dynamism of relatedness'.[116] He concludes that it is; and, in contrast to the 'homogenising' project of modernity, that would see 'a Coca Cola advertisement in every village in the world',[117] he sees a universal perichoresis which, although it 'envisages close relatedness', it 'never does so to the detriment of particularity'.[118] For the modern mind, there is an individualism that holds back from the 'other' and yet strives for global similitude; for the perichoretic perspective, there is a *relationality* that moves toward the 'other' and, at the same time, is committed to *particularity*, a valuing of distinctiveness for its own sake. Gunton summarises his perichoretic world-view with these words:

> An account of relationality that gives due weight to both one and many, to both particular and universal, to both otherness and relation, is to be derived from the one place where they can satisfactorily be based, a conception of God who is both one and three, whose being consists in a relationality that derives from the otherness-in-relation of Father, Son and Spirit.[119]

We can close this section on 'the trinitarian dimension' of a relational theology by asking whether pastoral counselling, with its ostensible commitment to the counselling relationship,[120] can extend its theory and practice beyond its historic assimilation of secular personalism and allow the renewal of its praxis through a more fully perichoretic understanding of human createdness and contextualised relatedness. That context is a panoramic one that is also tied into a 'covenantal dimension'; as Jean-Jacques Suurmond has it: 'The Trinity [is] the perfected covenant' and 'that perfect covenant is like a mutual dance of Father, Son and holy community of creation'.[121]

A Covenantal Dimension

The links between vows of commitment and the need to relate to others can, at times, feel like a chain that shackles. Frances Dominica recalls her introduction to the Society of All Saints Sister of the Poor, when she first joined the order. The Mother Superior said to her, 'You haven't chosen your Sisters and, given the chance, you wouldn't do so either.'[122] And there is a sense in which this perceptive and realistic comment echoes the sentiments that the Israelites felt under the old covenant and that many Christians feel under the new.

And yet, although the word 'covenant' may be felt to be containing and restrictive, a right understanding can remind us that our perichoretic call to relatedness and particularity, although springing from the creative, trinitarian 'dance', also needs the containment of 'a service that is perfect freedom'. This covenantal calling, unlike many human contracts, is an agreement between unequals, between a generous and compassionate Yahweh and a people whose ragged psyches make them duck and weave beneath a largesse which, at times, seems too good to be true. The Mosaic covenant of Sinai is paradigmatic of such covenantal love. In J. D. Levenson's words:

> The special status of Israel rests not upon her merits, her strength or numbers or intelligence or honesty, but upon something irrational, a passion, an affair of the heart, not the mind, in short a love . . . Israel is singled out by and for the love of God . . . at the core of the covenant relationship lies a twofold love, the mysterious love of YHWH for Israel and the less baffling love of Israel for YHWH, her benefactor. Covenant-love is mutual; it distinguishes a relationship of reciprocity.[123]

In some small measure we can see that such a 'relationship of reciprocity' can be mirrored within the pastoral encounter. A number of theologians have explored the analogy for various approaches to pastoral care and counselling, including Oden, Brueggemann and David Atkinson.[124] For Oden the ontological aspect of covenant has been addressed in the juxtaposition of 'a therapy of human self-disclosure' in Carl Rogers and 'a theology in divine self-disclosure' in Karl Barth.[125] Atkinson draws a number of parallels between God's covenant with his people and the counselling relationship: for example, the contractual element of 'goals, terms and limits'; the modelling of grace whereby the counsellor says 'I am for you; I am with you; I am on your side'; and the recognition of 'moral boundaries within which human flourishing can be aided'.[126] It is in Brueggemann, though, that we see the fullest contribution on the relevance for covenant to pastoral care and counselling.

In his 'Covenanting as Human Vocation', Brueggemann uses the metaphor of covenant to undergird the ontological understanding 'that human persons are grounded in Another who initiates personhood and who stays bound to persons in loyal ways for their well-being'.[127] He pits this God-groundedness against modernity's commitment to 'self-groundedness' and argues, as we have done, that the latter perspective has penetrated 'much of the psychology used in pastoral care'.[128] Through exploring the main characteristics of the faithful 'covenant-making' God, Brueggemann distils three 'primary elements' in 'mature, covenantal personhood': *hoping, listening* and *answering*. He thus carries the analogy over to pastoral care, where the central issue is one of 'how persons who are hopeless, persistent speakers, and faithless listeners can be brought to faithful covenanting'.[129] An essential part of that maturing process, he further argues, is found in Israel's propensity to 'take God seriously'[130] in their expression of *rage, grief* and *praise* – aspects of human response to the divine that we have already met in the formative use of the psalms of lament. And, finally, we can take from Brueggemann the vital need for the communal aspect of a covenanting, trinitarian, 'being-in-relationship' God and a covenant-keeping, perichoretic, 'being-in-relationship' people to place pastoral counselling firmly in the context of the Church's covenant-based pastoral care:

Pastoral care . . . consists in the formation of a community holding to and practicing this radical, subversive metaphor [of covenant]. Pastoral care surely is not confined to psychology, but the metaphor has important implications for sociology, ethics, and ecclesiology. And in the life of the church, the issues of covenant are as urgent in preaching, liturgy, education, and administration as in counseling. All these are elements of pastoral care in which the vocation of covenanting is at issue.[131]

Summary

Throughout this chapter, we have been committed to an evaluation of the pathway of pastoral counselling as a route toward wholeness whose quintessence lies in the centrality of the notion of *relationship* – a commitment, at its best, to mutuality, reciprocity, otherness and particularity. Appropriately, it is the adjective 'pastoral' which reminds us of the biblical metaphor – that of the *shepherd* – which, rightly understood, resonates most faithfully with the relational emphasis of pastoral counselling. Although, especially in the years after the Second World War, the traditional usage of the metaphor in the 'cure of souls' has been challenged as too controlling and authoritative,[132] we can still, I suggest, learn a great deal from Hiltner's 'shepherding perspective'[133] and the pastoral overtones of Oden's 'pivotal analogy'.[134] The most fruitful paradigm lies in the biblical picture of Yahweh as Shepherd, of whom it is said:

> He tends his flock like a shepherd:
> He gathers the lambs in his arms
> and carries them close to his heart;
> he gently leads those that have young.
> (Isa. 40:11)

This tender portrait is carried over into the New Testament, where Jesus Christ, as the *good* shepherd, who 'lays down his life for the sheep' (John 10:11), presents a pastoral model that is gentle, considerate, nurturing, guiding, intimate and intent on a particularising relationality, in which he can say 'I know my sheep and my sheep know me' (10:14).

And so, where pastoral counselling, viewed, as we have seen in Lambourne and Brueggemann, in the communal context of pastoral care, can recover something of the more relationally based

aspects of the shepherdly metaphor and, at the same time, incorporate a biblical hermeneutic that is essentially implicit and
formative and a relational theology that is trinitarian and covenantal, then, I believe, it can play its integrative part more fully
within the field of pathways to wholeness. In this way, its liberal
experiential-expressivism and postliberal cultural-linguistic approaches can increasingly dialogue with the alternative theologies
and spiritualities of its neighbouring pathways. David Lyall
declares pastoral counselling's distinctive contribution to the
debate:

> I would simply affirm my belief that the truths of the Christian faith are
> not essentially propositional, but rather are relational: that 'the Word
> became flesh and dwelt among us, full of grace and truth' (St. John, 1:
> 14. RSV). In my pastoral relationships I can only be who I am; similarly
> those to whom I have the privilege to minister, and those with whom I
> work, can only be who they are. Yet the miracle of grace is that in the
> complexity and the simplicity of the pastoral relationship, when we
> have offered the best of our understanding and our skills, the God of all
> grace is at work deep within the human spirit with a power that
> transcends and encompasses all our knowing and all our skill.[135]

If the objective of pastoral counselling, as a pathway to wholeness, is to help the maturing person with the unblocking of that
pathway, in co-operation with 'the God of all grace', then spiritual
direction takes up the baton beyond the blockage. We now turn
our attention to the next limb of the journey.

10

SPIRITUAL DIRECTION:
THE UNCOMPLICATED HEART

But I understood at last that God breaketh not all men's hearts alike . . .
Richard Baxter[1]

I have just finished reading Helen Waddell's *Peter Abelard* and, although I have been aware of the essence of the tragic story of Abelard and Heloise for a long time, I was quite overwhelmed by the thwarted longings of these ill-starred lovers – longings for each other and for their elusive God. Even so, for both of them there was one individual – Gilles de Vannes, Canon of Notre Dame – who provided something of a still centre amid the exuberance and anguish of their passion. Gilles, as supportive confidant, was an unlikely figure – corpulent and pig-eyed, describing himself as a 'sensualist' in mind as well as body – and yet Abelard could say to him, 'I find it again, the truth of myself, with you.'[2] There was something about the canon, immured in his great chair and half in love with Heloise himself, that provided the sharp rebuke, the patient listening and the practical good sense that Abelard needed in his turbulent Christian journeying. We can see in Gilles, in spite of all his faults, something of the 'spiritual guide' or 'spiritual director' of an ancient tradition – a tradition that is, in essence, one of a 'mystical' spirituality.

By way of introduction to our fourth pathway to wholeness, let us focus on some of the salient points concerning its heritage of *mystical spirituality* and the pastoral calling of *spiritual direction*. We will then examine practical issues concerning *spiritual and psychological maturity*, a highly topical matter for pastoral counselling and spiritual direction, before making proposals for contemporary spirituality and spiritual direction as *the way ahead*.

Mystical Spirituality

Behind the notion of mystical spirituality lies the elusive concept of *mysticism*, the meaning of which has shifted its ground repeatedly within the Christian story. The situation ethicist Joseph Fletcher gives up on any attempt at definition, declaring that 'mysticism is something that begins in mist and ends in schism'![3] Evelyn Underhill (1875–1941), in her classic analysis of the subject, points to the *universality* of mysticism across the religious divides, referrng to Martin of Tours when she writes, 'All mystics . . . speak the same language and come from the same country.'[4] In contrast, within church history, we can see the origins of the mystical in the *mysterion* of the New Testament: ' . . . the mystery that has been kept hidden for ages and generations, but is now disclosed to the saints' (Col. 1:26). Here is the revealing of life's secret, an opening up of what was formerly closed, a sharing with all God's people of the *mysterion*, 'which is Christ in you, the hope of glory' (Col. 1:27). These Pauline statements exemplify the *particularising* voice of a christocentric revealed theology that is the heartland of a fully Christian mysticism.

Even so, Christian mystical spirituality not only has a voice that emphasises the specifics of belief, since there is also a tradition that stresses the incomprehensibility of the things of God. Although these two strands interweave throughout church history, they can be distinguished by two major orientations: 'kataphatic' and 'apophatic'. Following Gerald G. May, we can describe *kataphatic* spirituality as 'content-oriented', where there is a commitment to the contents of spiritual experience and an emphasis on the need for 'images of the divine' as essential 'for personal spiritual growth'. In contrast, *apophatic* spirituality is 'consciousness-oriented' and regards both content and image as potential impediments to the illumination of 'the divine Reality that is the source of human consciousness'.[5] Where kataphatic spirituality 'speaks according to' (from *kata*, according to, and *phanai*, to say) content, image and experience, apophatic 'speaks away from' (from *apo*, away from) these distracting entities.

Throughout the book so far, we have observed a duality of emphasis in paths toward wholeness: between 'reason' and 'intuition' in world religions in Chapter 1; between the 'comparative' and 'divinatory' in Schleiermacher in Chapter 4; and between *halacha* and *agada* in rabbinic Judaism in Chapters 6 onward. We find a comparable polarity in the realm of kataphatic and apophatic spirituality, for either of these can also demonstrate a *metaphysical* or *speculative* style, which is primarily cognitive and propositional, or an *affective* style, which is essentially emotional and experiential.[6]

The *kataphatic* orientation is a strong one in the history of Christian spirituality, its commitment to 'content' being *creational* and *incarnational*. Examples abound: in the anti-Gnostic writings of Irenaeus of Lyons (*c.*130–*c.*200), expressing a spirituality in which 'God's glory is the human person fully alive'; Francis of Assisi (1182–1226), celebrating the presence of the divine in the sun, moon, stars, birds and beasts; Martin Luther (1483–1546), focusing on the centrality of *theologia crucis*; Ignatius Loyola (1491–1556), declaring a content-filled and systematic spirituality that is trinitarian and christocentric; and Seraphim of Sarov (1759–1833), representative of an Orthodox spirituality that celebrates the interdependence of the created order.

The *apophatic* emphasis, that God is in some sense 'unknowable', also weaves in and out of the mystical tradition. Plotinus (205–70), a Greek philosopher from Egypt, emphasised the possibility for the soul to lose its distinctiveness by merging with the One; Gregory of Nyssa (*c.*330–95), one of the three Cappadocian Fathers,[7] declared that 'we can have no knowledge of the divine nature, which lies beyond the reach of the human mind';[8] the writings of Denys the Areopagite, attributed to the end of the fifth century, declare a 'theology of negation' in which 'the soul passes beyond anything it can perceive or know into the darknesss where God is';[9] *The Cloud of Unknowing* of fourteenth-century England pursued Denys's *via negativa*, wherein 'the most goodly knowing of God is that, the which is known by unknowing';[10] and the Spanish mystics, Teresa of Avila (1515–82) and John of the Cross (1542–91), declared a spirituality in which the soul needs to traverse the darkness of God's inaccessibility before experiencing union with the divine love.[11]

We will keep in mind this rich inheritance of mystical spirituality as we examine the tradition of its salient pastoral ministry – spiritual direction.

Spiritual Direction

Most, if not all, religions have within their framework a place, sometimes centrally, sometimes peripherally, for a 'spiritual guide', a man or woman who is seen to be a repository of a special wisdom that is in touch with the divine: the Hindu 'guru'; the Buddhist 'master'; the 'shaman' of northern Asian and native American traditional religion; and the 'rebbe' of Hasidic Judaism. It is the precursors of the last of these in the Old Testament priests, prophets and wise men and women that have the closest parallels with the genesis of Christian spiritual direction.[12] Guidance is no longer found through magic, the stars or casting lots; it is offered and received, rather, through the mediatoral voices of Yahweh's faithful servants – figures such as Moses, with whom the Lord would speak 'face to face, as one speaks to a friend' (Exod. 33:11), and Elijah, whose commitment to the younger Elisha was such that, even at his final departure, he could say, 'Tell me, what can I do for you before I am taken from you?' (2 Kgs 2:9). Such 'go-between' listening to God and nurturing of others is clear in Jesus's handling of his disciples: 'I have called you friends, for everything that I learned from my Father I have made known to you' (John 15:15) and in Paul's gentle but firm direction-giving to the young Timothy: 'What you heard from me, keep as the pattern of sound teaching, with faith and love in Christ Jesus' (2 Tim. 1:13).

We can discern three main metaphors for the spiritual director in the Christian tradition: he or she is *desert-dweller*, *soul-friend* and *midwife*. Behind these roles stands the biblical ministry of the *priest*, a ministry to Israel which, according to Walter Brueggemann, 'dealt with the problem of sin and guilt and the felt need for forgiveness and reconciliation'.[13] In each of these three priestly metaphors, the spirituality is a *spirituality of presence*.[14]

Desert-dweller

One major biblical theme that has proved relevant throughout the history of spiritual direction is that of the *desert* – tracts of wilderness in which the individual or group is tested to the limits and, through God's grace and power, emerges chastened, refined and obedient. This tradition is seen, for example, in the Sinai wanderings of the Israelites; in Elijah's flight from Jezebel (1 Kgs 19); in

Yahweh's allurement of Israel 'into the desert [to] speak tenderly to her' (Hos. 2:14); in John the Baptist's abstemious life as Christ's forerunner; in Jesus's forty-day encounter with the devil; and in Paul's post-Damascus Road sojourn in Arabia (Gal. 1:17).

We find that much of the sensibility of this scriptural perspective is carried over into the spirituality of the Desert Fathers. Responding, perhaps, to the blunting of Christianity's edge, once it became the state religion in AD 312 under Constantine (c.280–337), an increasing number of believers took to the Syrian, Palestinian and Egyptian deserts throughout the fourth century to embrace a life of solitude and abstenance.[15] One of the first precursors of this influx, Antony of Egypt (c.251–356), stands out for his resolve, as a young man, to sell all he had to give to the poor and for the longevity and profundity of his 'desert experience'.[16] Supportive of Athanasius in his fight against the Arian heresy[17] and sought out by many troubled Christians for counsel during the 'great persecution' (297–305) under Diocletian,[18] Antony was both a chief instigator of the monastic movement[19] and one of the principal prototypes for the long tradition of spiritual direction. Under his influence, 'spiritual fathers' and 'spiritual mothers' became available to guide their fellow-pilgrims on their journey with God, using the gift of 'discerning the spirits'[20] to illumine the way amid the warring factions of good and evil. This 'desert' ethos of the solitary 'abba' as director has been handed down through the centuries in both the Western[21] and Eastern Church. In the latter, for example, the role of the *staretz*, or elder, of Russian Orthodoxy was renewed in the late eighteenth and early nineteenth centuries as a calling to solitude in the 'desert' of the forest, a vocation whose offer of spiritual guidance enriched 'an entire people from the most humble levels to the most exacting intellectuals'.[22]

Soul-friend

Another ancient tradition that impinges on contemporary spiritual direction is that of the *soul-friend*. We have already picked up something of the biblical stress on the divine friendship extended to Christ's followers in John 15:14–17, a friendship that engenders love ('This is my command: Love each other'), obedience ('You are my friends if you do what I command') and the transformative effects of shared insight: ('Everything that I learned from my

Father I have made known to you'). In early Irish Christianity this offer of God's friendship, reinforced by brotherly and sisterly love, was made visible in the *anmchara*, the 'soul-friend', sometimes a priest, but often a lay man or lay woman, who 'was essentially a counsellor and guide'.[23] Here is the notion of fellow-pilgrim, one whose discerning and supportive wisdom was so valued that the Celtic saying – 'Anyone without a soul-friend is a body without a head'[24] – became proverbial.

Soul-friendship provides an egalitarian model for today's spiritual direction. One young ordinand who anticipated seeing me on a regular basis through her years of theological training jibbed at the authoritarian tone of the term 'spiritual director'. We discussed the question of 'labels' and decided to dispense with them, although we agreed that the idea of 'soul-friend' was the least threatening 'role' and the most indicative of the mutuality of Christian journeying.

Midwife

In the earlier part of my medical career, working in obstetrics on a hospital ward and, later, helping to deliver babies in patients' homes and at the local GP hospital, I was aware that, as doctor, I was most often called into the situation when the natural process of giving birth was in some way or other going wrong. On the whole, this interventionist role contrasted with that of the midwife, whose prime commitment was that of *being with* the woman in labour, to give support and encouragement, monitor progress and play a crucial, active part in the delivery itself.

Where the medical role is more akin to the problem-oriented nature of counselling, the role of the *midwife* is more comparable to spiritual direction. Margaret Guenther draws out the analogy in some detail: between the questioning uncertainties of early pregnancy and the tentative nature of beginnings in spiritual direction; between the long months of waiting and the need for patience amid the slow germination of God's new life in the believer; between the non-interventionist first stage of labour and the need for the spiritual director to resist premature action; between the active pushing of labour's second stage and the director's encouragement of the directee's 'hard and focused work'; and, finally, between the joy of a safe delivery and a healthy child and the celebration of 'spiritual friends' at the moment of God's richest blessing.[25]

Tilden Edwards takes the same notion, declaring that, although 'being a spiritual friend is being the physician of a wounded soul', the idea of 'midwife' is more accurately descriptive of the process of spiritual direction:

> The physician of souls explicitly is a midwife, providing an environ-ment for the birthing and nourishing of a whole soul. Always in the forefront of consciousness there is clarity that a three-way process is going on: between the midwife, the person struggling/allowing new life to come and take hold and the Royal One whose loving/healing/driving Spirit we would serve, reflect, and enflesh.[26]

A Spirituality of Presence

In the metaphors of desert-dweller, soul-friend and midwife, we are reminded that spiritual direction is a ministry of 'presence'. The director as *desert-dweller* is one who has experienced the refining process of solitude – not necessarily as a solitary, in isolation from others, but in what Henri Nouwen calls a 'solitude of the heart', wherein 'a man or woman . . . is able to perceive and understand this world from a quiet inner centre'.[27] The director as *soul-friend* is one who freely acknowledges the reality of a fellow-pilgrimage, a calling that is companionate and open to mutuality, in which both parties are aware of their vulnerabilities and needs and are willing to learn from the other. The director as *midwife* is one who both knows how to hold back, knows how to allow the process of generating and welcoming new life to unfold stage by stage, and how to step forward, not to dampen or gainsay the directee's efforts, but, rather, to encourage him or her in the painful business of bearing fruit in Christian discipleship. All three are undergirded by a *spirituality of presence*, a fellowship of solidarity which, in turn, depends on the ever-present Spirit of Christ. As David W. Augs-burger puts it, 'When one is truly there for another, a depth of communication occurs that is beyond words or style, or technique, or theory, or theology. It is presence gifted by Presence.'[28]

Spiritual and Psychological Maturity

Some years ago, while working in a student health service, I was gently, but firmly, reprimanded by a colleague in the department of mental health for raising spiritual matters with Trudy, a young student I was counselling. Her father happened to be a renowned American psychiatrist and, as I understood the episode, Trudy had declared this aspect of the counselling process to him and he, in turn, had been sufficiently incensed by the matter to ring the relevant head of department at the local university where I was employed. The criticism, on the face of it, seemed to be a valid one, although my exploratory questions had been tentative and, as I had seen it, simply part of a comprehensive approach to her story. Without denying the need for therapeutic sensitivity in many areas of people's lives – not least with respect to spirituality and personal belief, and acknowledging that my enquiry may have exceeded the mark in Trudy's case, this episode is, in some ways, a simple example of the deep split between modernist, secularised psychotherapeutic and psychiatric practice and the world of religious pastoral practice, between a psychological and a spiritual approach to people in need. And, although postmodernity's stirrings toward spirituality has helped blur the edges between these distinctive, excluding axes, modernity's cautious empiricism toward what is knowable and measurable in the human psyche still turns its back on the numinous and mysterious.

In many ways, the subtext of this book is to address this very split and to argue that, not least in a consideration of Christian pathways to wholeness, a truer and fuller view of our humanity, made in God's image, is to see the *fundamental inextricability* of psychology and spirituality – and, for that matter, physicality – in all our lives. This is not to gainsay, of course, that pastoral care may have a stronger focus in one direction or the other: where, for instance, pastoral counselling and pastoral psychotherapy may concentrate more on the psychological; the healing ministries, at times, more on the physical; and biblical counselling and spiritual direction more on the spiritual. But, I suggest, where human life is split and compartmentalised three ways by such methodologies, then the truncated approaches to people in need may greatly limit their advance toward Christian maturity.

Let us examine the call to a more integrated style under three main headings: *psychospiritual maturity; spiritual direction and pastoral counselling;* and *the uncomplicated heart.*

Psychospiritual Maturity

Martin came to see me, struggling over the childhood death of his older brother, Philip, and the powerful impress of his mother's control on his subsequent, 'only-child' upbringing. He had spent a lifetime trying to please his mother and fight off various fears around the awful possibility that if Philip could die aged seven, surrounded by family love, then he, Martin, single at forty-seven, could equally well succumb to some unknown disease or sudden accident. In the course of counselling, his comparable drive to please God and his fellow-Christians, and his attempts to ward off fear through prayer and faith, became a powerful theme that paralleled his life story. Were the issues here primarily psychological or were they essentially spiritual? Or were the psychological and spiritual indivisibly bound together? I am sure that David G. Benner is right when he declares:

> Our relationships with God are mediated by the same psychological processes and mechanisms as those that mediate relationships with other people. The spiritual quest is, at one level, a psychological quest, and every psychological quest in some way reflects the basic spiritual quest. Furthermore, psychological and spiritual aspects of human functioning are inextricably connected, and any segregation of spirituality and psychology is, therefore, both artificial and destructive.[29]

Benner holds to his concept of *psychospirituality* on the basis of the holism of the Judaeo-Christian understanding of human nature.[30] He takes the Dooyeweerdian perspective on our humanity,[31] put forward by A. Wolters, as comprising both specific *structure* and specific *direction*. The structural aspect refers to our createdness in God's image and points to the *psychological* mechanisms and processes that make up everyday human living; the directional aspect alludes to a person's *spiritual* orientation in life – ultimately, either toward God or away from him. And, although the structural and psychological and the directional and spiritual 'are not equivalent', they are closely interwoven and the one can only be talked about sensibly 'in the context of the other'.[32]

We can take the analogy of our created, fallen human nature as a 'glorious ruin',[33] like one of the beautiful monastic shells of Yorkshire or the Scottish borders. Such a building, although fragmented and a shadow of its original splendour, is nonetheless glorious in its ruined state: an incomplete colonnade here, a fractured arch there, still give some indication of the initial edifice's purpose – to provide an aesthetically arresting focus for the communal worship of God. Just as the building's structure *can* be studied while denying its directional purpose, so a person's psychological make-up *can* be attended to while his or her spiritual orientation in life is discounted. Either way, *raison d'être* is sacrificed.

Allowing, then, Wolters's and Benner's holistic perspectives, what can be said of the *maturing process* in terms of its psychological and spiritual aspects? We saw in the last chapter (see pp. 268–71) the importance of 'meaning-making' and 'embeddedness' in Robert Kegan's 'evolutionary' model of human maturation, and, also, that progress as a person is essentially *relational*, a bid for balance between the desires for separateness and connectedness. Benner carries over a similar emphasis, unpacking the broad brush strokes of human development in terms of the psychological and spiritual. Following Maslow's well-known 'hierarchy of needs',[34] in which requirements such as food, drink and shelter must be met at the basic level before people can aspire to 'higher' things, such as aesthetic appreciation and altruistic endeavour, Benner argues that 'until one *has* a self it is difficult to *transcend* self'.[35] Here, he points out, and this view accords well with Kegan's progressive stages, that it is only when we have resolved 'the unfinished business of the self' that 'we can better become aware of deeper needs and strivings'.[36]

It is here that Thomas Merton's (1915–68) notion of the 'false self' and the 'true self' offers another, complementary angle on the shaping of our psychospirituality.[37] For Merton, the *false self* is that aspect of who we are which is ensnared by the illusion that separateness from God and others is in our own best interest. The *true self* finds authenticity and freedom in self-surrender – a 'letting go' that is a paradoxical discovery of the true self, which, in turn, is also the discovery of 'the true God on whom we depend'.[38] This movement from the false, self-deceiving self to the true, self-sacrificing self is seen in human responsiveness to the divine 'missions', in which the Father 'communicates' to us 'His Word and His Spirit'. In Merton's words:

Our inner self awakens, with a momentary flash, in the instant of recognition when we say 'Yes!' to the indwelling Divine Persons. We are only really ourselves when we completely consent to 'receive' the glory of God into ourselves. Our true self is, then, the self that receives freely and gladly the missions that are God's supreme gift to His sons. Any other 'self' is only an illusion.[39]

This is the nub of all ideas of psychospiritual maturation. In terms of Benner's analysis, we can, of course, focus purely on the psychological as we seek to help others. In excluding human spirituality from the equation, though, we run the risk of encouraging a person's false self on its illusory path: in effect, we may appear to say, 'Of course, concentrate on *self*-fulfilment; forget others, forget God; be who *you* want to be, regardless.' In contrast, we can make the opposite mistake of discounting the psychological as we pursue a spiritual 'high' with, say, a directee. We may thus forget the close link between the 'givenness' of people's individuality (in terms of disposition, temperament, experience and story) and the direction of their spirituality, seeming to declare, 'Forget your hang-ups, conflicts, achievements and hopes; just let go, and let God . . .' Either way, we can collude with others that the false selves of pure 'self-actualisation' or unadulterated 'spiritualisation' are, in effect, forms of the true self. Henri Nouwen seems to hold the psychospiritual balance well when he writes: 'Put simply, life is a God-given opportunity to become who we are, to affirm our own true spiritual nature, claim our truth, appropriate and integrate the reality of our being, but, most of all, to say "Yes" to the One who calls us the Beloved.'[40]

Spiritual Direction and Pastoral Counselling

Let us briefly consider two cameo case histories: in the first Donna comes for spiritual direction; and in the second Gerry seeks pastoral counselling.

Donna is struggling in her Christian life as a mother of three children under the age of six. Her husband Ken has a demanding job that takes him away from home for at least three nights a week, but does what he can to help with the children at weekends. Donna feels trapped by tiredness, but also wants to make an effort to 'tune in' to God as best she can. She is a strongly intuitive person and likes to try new methods of prayer from time to time. She hopes that spiritual direction will give her a little space to explore God's will for her during a particularly demanding stretch of her life.

Gerry, single and in his late thirties, is also struggling, but for him the difficulties centre around a series of close friendships with women which he feels he has to step away from when they threaten to become 'too serious'. This leaves him dissatisfied, since he longs for intimacy and would like to marry, but is fearful of making 'a mistake'. He has had a good relationship with Christine, a member of the same local church, for the last eighteen months and he now feels she is becoming 'too fond' of him. He is worried by this, since she has been very depressed by a broken engagement in the past. He is increasingly irritated by her assumption that they will marry and yet still finds her attractive. He is in a turmoil over her and hopes that pastoral counselling will help him resolve the situation.

Following our discussion on psychospirituality, are we to see these two ministries on offer to Donna and Gerry as essentially the same, differing only in their degree of emphasis on spirituality and psychology respectively? Or, given the very different histories of spiritual direction and pastoral counselling – the former within an ancient pastoral tradition, the latter with its twinned roots in pastoral care and the secular counselling movement – are we to see these as two quite distinct pathways with little or nothing in common? As so often with such polarising questions, the answers seem to lie in a 'both/and' response. Let us seek to clarify the relationship between these two approaches by examining their *common ground*, before exploring their *distinctiveness*.[41]

Common Ground

We can, I suggest, see three main areas in which spiritual direction and pastoral counselling are similar: they are *contractual*, *relational* and *directional*.

The openly *contractual* nature of these two pathways is well established. Although both operate in the wider context of pastoral care and the Christian community, engagement with them requires a specific defining of boundaries and ground rules that is essentially contractual, or, as we saw in the last chapter (see pp. 280–2), *covenantal*. And so both spiritual direction and pastoral counselling are explicit in their agreed commitment to confidentiality, the accountability of supervision, the direction of the helping process and the framework of time and place within which that process can take place.

On the details of the last of these there will be characteristic differences. For Donna, a contract is negotiated for one-and-a-half-hour monthly sessions with her spiritual director initially, with the option to move to six-weekly once a helpful 'working pattern' is established. Here the contract is open-ended, although it can be concluded at any time by mutual agreement. For Gerry, embarking on pastoral counselling, the contract is a weekly one, with six sessions of fifty minutes each agreed on to start with. It will be understood that the arrangement is not open-ended and a concluding appointment will be made at some negotiated stage.

Both these pathways to wholeness are essentially *relational*. Although either can take place in group settings, they are typically one-to-one relationships, set within the agreed contractual boundaries just outlined. This relationality, as we saw in the last chapter, is a particular feature of pastoral counselling and is allowed to influence the therapeutic process through, for example, the use of transference.[42] Nonetheless, spiritual direction is also relational in the sense of offering a companionate soul-friendship as a fellow-traveller who is on the same journey.

For Donna, this enterprise would be a co-pilgrimage of seeking to discern God's will amid the domestic demands of her life. For Gerry, the counselling relationship itself will, at times, be the focus of therapy as counsellor and counsellee explore the relevance of other significant people in his life, both past and present, and their impingement on his relating difficulties with certain women friends.

Spiritual direction and pastoral counselling also share a certain *directional* emphasis. Both are committed to the path toward psychospiritual maturity, albeit, as we shall see, with different expectations of the route taken. Joann Wolski Conn notes that both counsellors and directors (or 'spiritual guides') are involved in 'a working alliance' which militates against 'another person's well-defended personality'. She concedes that both 'pastoral counselors and spiritual guides would agree with their secular colleagues' that the mainspring in the working alliance is 'the human drive toward life and growth', but, rightly, she argues that these Christian ministries seek to go further – extending 'the interpretation to include its ultimate source: the indwelling Spirit of the living God'.[43]

For Donna, the Godward aspect of her life is the ostensible focus of her seeking spiritual direction in the first place. For Gerry, it is likely that, in time, the relational struggles that brought him to counselling will be explored in the wider context of the church community and his own continuing Christian journey.

Distinctiveness

Given the common ground between spiritual direction and pastoral counselling as contractual, relational and directional ministries, let us now outline their cardinal differences. We can also summarise these under three headings: the *focus* of attention; the *orientation* of the pathway; and the *resources* used.

It is in their *focus* of attention that we find perhaps the most fundamental difference between these two complementary pathways. In terms of Christian journeying, we can say that spiritual direction focuses on *the continuing journey* toward God in Christ and through the power of the Holy Spirit. Pastoral counselling, although committed to the same pilgrimage, is more immediately concerned with *unblocking the route* when the way forward is hindered, disrupted or countered by life's existential and relational problems.

With these different foci in mind, we can see how requests for these distinctive forms of help can be misplaced. As Conn puts it, in both ministries the 'presenting objective' may need clarification. For example, someone may seek spiritual direction simply because, in her Christian circles, 'everyone who is anyone' has a 'soul-friend': just as it was fashionable in the 1960s and 1970s to have a counsellor, so in the 1980s, 1990s and beyond it can be deemed stylish to have a spiritual director. Another may seek spiritual direction because he would rather put a 'spiritual' label on his difficulties than face his psychological problems for what they are. Conversely, yet another may, mistakenly, pursue pastoral counselling in the belief that the Christian counsellor will be adept with advice on her prayer life or on placing her for a much-needed retreat. Spiritual directors and pastoral counsellors worth their salt will be used to such mismatching and will either be able to contain the person's needs within their own remit or refer him or her accordingly.

On the receiving side of the equation, directees may need to move on to counselling for a period within the course of their spiritual direction and counsellees may be advised to find a director once their period of counselling is concluded. For Donna, the continuing exploration of her Christian journey in spiritual direction may be disrupted, for a time, by a relational crisis with her husband Ken and expert marital counselling may be needed. For Gerry, once his anguish over his women friends has been faced, understood and, in substantial measure, resolved, regular spiritual direction may become a necessary support as he picks up with his continuing walk as a Christian disciple.

Where the focus of spiritual direction is on the unfolding Christian journey, and that of pastoral counselling is on those problems which impede that journey, the primary *orientation* of these two ministries is toward God and the goal of human maturity respectively. In the past, the remits of these pathways have often interpreted their stance somewhat narrowly. Spiritual direction has been 'concerned with religion, and intrinsically with nothing else',[44] frequently adopting an authoritarian clericalism. Comparably, pastoral counselling has been accused of harbouring a 'hang-up' theology[45] and being merely an expression of an 'ambulance syndrome', in which the pastor is simply 'there to pick up the pieces'.[46] However, as we have indicated with Benner's notion of psychospirituality, there is a more holistic emphasis abroad in both these ministries, an emphasis which, nonetheless, does not betray their distinctiveness. Conn puts her finger on the essence of that difference when she writes that, whereas those engaging in pastoral counselling 'seldom pay explicit and consistent attention to the theological dimension of their alliance', those seeking spiritual direction 'always pay explicit and consistent attention to God's presence'.[47]

For Donna, God, and his ways with her busy, exhausting motherhood, are the initial orientation of her spiritual direction; whatever the detail of her working alliance with her director, that orientation toward God will always be primary. For Gerry, struggling between his desire for independence from his women friends and his longing for connectedness, the orientation of pastoral counselling will be toward the greater maturity of interdependence, both with his fellow human beings and with his God.

One of the hallmarks of both spiritual direction and pastoral counselling is that of a sharing of inner states, a process that is facilitated by a range of *resources* in both ministries, including dream diaries, journal-keeping, letter writing, painting, sculpting, role-play, music, silence and meditation.

This range of methods is, ideally, undergirded and shot through with a primary resource, that of *prayer*. But it is here, once more, that we see a distinction of emphasis between spiritual direction and pastoral counselling. Both may be committed to the pervasiveness of prayer, but, characteristically, this dimension is handled differently in the two pathways. Conn points out that 'sharing one's deepest feelings and thoughts as they occur in prayer is often the focus of conversation in spiritual direction'; although all other aspects of life may be included in the working alliance, prayer is of special pertinence 'insofar as it mirrors or affects one's relationship with God'.[48]

In contrast, pastoral counselling will rarely be centred on the prayer life of the counsellee with that degree of intensity, although its relevance to the counsellee's psychological and relational struggles will not be denied. Even so, many pastoral counsellors will keep an open mind on whether to pray with the counsellee or not at the various stages of the counselling process. Here, the temptation to 'magic away' complex issues or to soften the impact of newly acquired insight by a formulaic approach to prayer must be resisted. And yet there may be times when a shared moment of prayer will help a counsellee find solace or encouragement in his or her continuing engagement with the maturing process. Spiritual direction is woven around a core of prayer: pastoral counselling is sensitive to prayer as an invaluable adjunct.

Donna, within spiritual direction, discovers the need to set aside her previously treasured times of daily quiet and prayerful solitude for an exploration of 'practising the presence of God', amid the distractions of the delights and demands of her children; she is encouraged, too, to explore the possibility of a silent weekend retreat, while Ken engages with the less-than-silent children. Gerry, although he would have 'run a mile' if his counsellor had offered to pray with him during the early weeks of counselling, is more than happy to request prayer for courage later in the process, once he has decided that he will share his clarified feelings and thoughts with Christine.

The Uncomplicated Heart

Sister Margaret Magdalen, Sister Provincial of the Community of St Mary the Virgin (Wantage), in South Africa, was one of the main speakers at the Swanwick Conference for Pastoral Care and Counselling (see p. xii) in 1994. The conference was in early

January, ten months after my quadruple bypass, and my mind was still vividly recalling that time of a near-death experience in the intensive care unit. During the conference I had received spiritual direction from the Rev. Anne Long and she had shared her thoughts with me on the simile of my heart operation and the metaphor of God as 'heart surgeon'. Knowing of my struggles over single-heartedness as a Christian, she had left me with the psalmist's prayer, 'Unite my heart to fear you, O God.' It was hearing Sister Margaret Magdalen's address during the conference's closing Holy Communion Service that brought together Anne's spiritual counsel and my own reflections, for her sermon's theme was 'The uncomplicated heart'.

It is this notion of the uncomplicated heart, I believe, that is the essential goal of psychospiritual journeying. The concept is as old as God's bid for human love and resonates in Yahweh's challenge to Israel, 'Love the LORD your God with all your heart and with all your soul and with all your strength' (Deut. 6:5), and Jesus's exhortation to his followers, 'store up for yourselves treasures in heaven . . . For where your treasure is, there your heart will be also" (Matt. 6:20–1).

Annice Callahan and others trace such 'spiritualities of the heart' through the unfolding story of the Church:[49] in the Christian discipleship of, for example, Augustine of Hippo (354–430), whose 'long conversion' was gradually translated 'into a single-hearted desire for God'; in Catherine of Siena (c.1347–80), in whom the heart of the crucified Christ drew out the responsive love of her own heart; in Martin Luther's prayer for a 'clean heart', created by God (Ps. 51); and in the Salesian spirituality of Francis de Sales (1567–1622) and Jeanne de Chantal (1572–1641) with its emphasis on relational love among human beings and toward God, mediated through the loving heart of Jesus.

Here the 'heart' is the personality's 'centre of gravity', the very core of a person's being, and, much Catholic spirituality argues, it is in *contemplation* that the uncomplicated heart moves toward psychospiritual maturity. Although this contemplation may be 'active', wherein, through the use of reason, imagination, the arts, prayer and liturgy, a person enters into joyful, attentive encounter with God, it is in 'passive' contemplation that Christian mystics such as Merton see the quintessence of the divine engagement: 'a vivid awareness of infinite Being at the roots of our own limited being.'[50] Christopher Bryant captures the awesome simplicity of this perspective when he tells the story of an old peasant, a parishioner of the Curé d'Ars. The priest was intrigued by the old man's nightly visit to the church, where he knelt and gazed in wrapt attention at the altar for an hour. When asked what he said in his vigil, he replied, 'I don't say anything. I look at him and he looks at me.' Bryant sums up this essentially 'imageless' contemplation as 'looking and loving'.[51]

Bringing together the threads of Benner's psychospiritual route to human maturity, Merton's call to a selfhood which can only be 'true' as it surrenders to God and a contemplative commitment to 'an uncomplicated heart', we can look to Annice Callahan for an essentially christological perspective on the mystical pathway to wholeness:

A spirituality of the heart is necessarily incarnational and holistic. It views the heart as a uniquely human reality that is both corporeal and spiritual. It represents the total mystery of the human person. It reflects on what it means to be human in the light of what it means to become divine. A spirituality of the heart is also redemptive and unitive. It describes a particular way of living the paschal mystery in our daily lives, that is, accepting the sufferings and joys that we and others experience. It is concerned with what can unify our fragmented selves, with what can heal our brokenness. It points to communion at a deep level, heart-to-heart.[52]

The Way Ahead

What might we consider on 'the way ahead' for this pathway to wholeness? Of all the pathways under consideration it is the one with the richest inheritance, because it rests most fully on the multiple strands of longstanding Christian spirituality, be they Augustinian, Benedictine, Cistercian, Carmelite, Franciscan, Dominican, Julian, Ignatian or Salesian. Without denying the profound value of these individual paths, it is worth considering, I suggest, the particular vulnerability in a postmodern age of mystical spirituality as a whole.

Since the pathway of spiritual direction has such an ancient lineage and since its mainspring is the mystical tradition, it is especially susceptible to an often unwitting osmosis of philosophies and theologies that are contrary to the Judaeo-Christian faith. In contemporary culture, there are two especially powerful voices that lay claim to much that is believed and practised within the spiritualities which nurture this pathway to wholeness: that of Carl Jung and his analytical psychology and that of the New Age movement. These voices are many-tongued and we cannot do justice to the breadth and depth of their multiple messages – both postive and negative –in this section. In many ways their potential influence on Christian spiritual direction can be summed up under two headings: *Jung and neo-Gnosticism*; and *New Age and pantheism*. In turn, we will explore an outline of that comparatively rare phenomenon in this pathway to wholeness: a theology that takes seriously a mystical spirituality and thus addresses the pastoral issues that arise from Jung and New Age. This gives us our third heading: *Rahner and christology*.

Jung and Neo-Gnosticism

Very few Christians in the pastoral ministries are neutral about Jung: he is either vilified as a charlatan and occultist or adulated as a spiritual guru and wise old man. On the whole, many in the evangelical and charismatic traditions of biblical counselling and the healing ministries are in the first camp and many in the liberal and Catholic traditions of pastoral counselling and spiritual direction are in the second.[53] It is the measure of the complexity, and frequent inconsistency, of Jung's prolific writings that Christian pastoral carers can take up such polarised stances on Freud's 'Apostle to the Gentiles'.[54]

Let us try to pinpoint certain elements in Jung's life and works that contribute to the confusion just mentioned and, hopefully, make a critical appraisal that will clarify both the value and danger of Jungian psychology for Christian pastoral care. Protagonists of Jung's methodology often point out that he never claimed more than an essentially *psychological* approach toward humanity and God, and thus, it is commonly argued, he cannot be criticised on philosophical and theological grounds. And yet, although he insisted on his purely psychological viewpoint, Jung clearly committed himself to reasoning that bore all the hallmarks of philosophy and theology. Thus, Swanee Hunt, in evaluating Jung's anthropology, writes that 'his disclaimers, while endearing, do not exempt his thought from careful analysis'.[55] With this proviso in mind, let us assess those dimensions of Jungianism

which have led to accusations of *neo-Gnosticism* under two headings – *the Gnostic heresy*; and *Jung: the Gnostic tendency* – and, then,
in the light of this discussion, re-examine *Jung and pastoral care*.

The Gnostic Heresy

In examining the contemporary view of Jung as a 'neo-Gnostic' it is
worth a brief appraisal of the 'Gnostic heresy', to use the language
of the early Church Fathers.[56] Here is a perspective on divine and
human nature that sees salvation, not in terms of faith or good
works, but as the prerogative of a chosen few to whom is revealed
special knowledge and understanding (*gnosis*). The origins of
Gnosticism are much disputed, believed, variously, to lie in ancient
Jewish mysticism, in the theological debates of New Testament
times or in essentially heretical aberrations of second- and third-
century Christianity. Kurt Rudolph, for example, sees some evidence of the seeds of a Gnostic view in the Pauline injuction to
Timothy to 'turn away from . . . the opposing ideas of what is
falsely called knowledge (*gnoseos*)' (1 Tim. 6:20). In the second
century, Irenaeus' treatise *Against Heresies* sought to counter such
'false knowledge' with the 'true gnosis' of the Church.[57]

Rudolph points out that, strictly speaking, Gnosticism 'has no
tradition of its own', borrowing from Greek, Jewish, Persian and
Christian sources and appropriating material 'to match its own
basic conception'.[58] Even though that 'basic conception', diluted as
it is by alien mythologies, proves so elusive, certain salient characteristics can be discerned. These arise from a profound *dualism*[59]
that infiltrates every belief about the deity, the cosmos and
humanity.[60] They include:[61]

1. *a doctrine of the 'unknown God'*, who is 'beyond all that is
   visible and sensible' and who is contrasted with a subordinate being – the creator of the world, or Demiurge, and his
   'auxiliary troops, the planets and the signs of the zodiac';[62]
2. *an 'anti-cosmic' world-view*, in which the divine pole of 'light'
   is seen to be over against the 'darkness' of the material and
   bodily;[63]
3. *a split understanding of humanity*, wherein the physical and
   psychological is deemed inferior to the spiritual – that part of
   a person, known as the divine 'spark', which can only be
   reawakened through redemptive 'knowledge' (*gnosis*);[64]

4. *A divided Christ-figure*, split into two quite separate entities – 'the earthly and transitory Jesus of Nazareth and the heavenly and eternal Christ'.[65]

Such elements from the Gnosticism of late antiquity can be seen to recur throughout the history of human thought and, by the eighteenth century, the general term 'Gnosticism' was used disparagingly for a spirituality that was the carefully guarded domain of an exclusive coterie of 'knowing ones'.[66] It can be argued that the esoteric nature of certain aspects of Jung's analytical psychology, and its attendant theologising, indicates a form of 'neo-Gnosticism'.

Jung: The Gnostic Tendency

It would be misleading to see Carl Gustav Jung (1875–1961) as a purely 'Gnostic' thinker, since the influences on his world-view were manifold,[67] including those of the Greek mystery cults, Platonism, Mithraism,[68] Christianity, medieval alchemy,[69] German Romanticism, Eastern mysticism and Western scientific endeavour. Even so, as we have seen, it is a Gnostic tendency to search and adapt the texts of a wide range of mythologies and understandings in order to establish its spirituality of 'knowingness', and Jung's single-minded search for meaning can be viewed in such a light. As the Jungian analyst Anthony Stevens puts it, Jung was 'a lifelong *gnostic* – one dedicated to knowing and experiencing the reality of the spirit'.[70]

As Jung freely acknowledged in his autobiographical *Memories, Dreams, Reflections*,[71] there was much in his family background and upbringing that shaped his quest for 'the reality of the spirit'. Brought up in Calvinist Switzerland, he was acutely aware of the scientific inheritance exemplified in his paternal grandfather, Carl Gustav Jung the Elder (1794–1864), a German physician and Rector of Basel University; the undermining of any potential trust in institutionalised Christianity through the negative influence of the doubt-racked faith of his clerical father, Paul Achilles Jung (1842–96); and the spiritualistic legacy from his mother, Emilie Preiswerk (1848–1923), and her family. The polarity of these strands, between, on the one side, the 'rational' and 'scientific' and, on the other, the 'irrational' and 'spiritual', was mirrored in the dual personality of Jung's mother: a kindly, reasonable 'daytime' personality and an 'uncanny' and prescient 'nighttime' one.[72] Jung had clearly inherited the seemingly incompatible traits of what he called, respectively, a 'No. 1' and a 'No. 2' personality and, later, as a medical student, in a revelatory flash, he saw that a career in psychiatry could unite these disparate facets of his life:

> Here alone the two currents of my interest could flow together and in a united stream dig their own bed. Here was the empirical field common to biological and spiritual facts, which I had everywhere sought and nowhere found. Here at last was the place where the collision of nature and spirit became a reality.[73]

Although Jung's earlier clinical years had their fair share of the scientific empirical method (the realm of his 'No. 1' personality),[74] his imaginative and intuitive style took his interests increasingly into the world of mythology, mysticism and the occult (the terrain of his 'No. 2' personality). The latter proclivity is shown throughout his career: in, for example, his avid reading of Goethe, Schopenhauer and Nietzsche in his late teens and early twenties;[75] in his doctorate on the mediumistic activities of his teenage cousin, Hélène Preiswerk;[76] in his withdrawal to Küsnacht in 1914, following his break with Freud, to 'confront the unconscious';[77] and in his pursuit of the mysteries of medieval alchemy in his later life, unlocking for him an 'uninterrupted intellectual chain back to Gnosticism' that 'gave substance' to his analytical psychology.[78] Jung's discovery of Gnosticism and his quintessentially Gnostic search for esoteric knowledge permeates both his psychology and his excursions into theology. Henri Ellenberger sees Jung's analytical psychology, like Freud's psychoanalysis, as a form of *hermeneutics*,[79] an interpretive enterprise which seeks to plumb the mysterious depths of the human psyche. In this endeavour, Jung moves beyond the narrow, deductive limits of science, as we have seen, and enters a place of unlimited horizons, the quest for Gnosis through the inductive process of experience, observation, active imagination and dream interpretation. And in this neo-Gnostic enquiry, we see both a Ricoeurian *hermeneutics of suspicion* toward orthodox Christianity, where Jung can ask, 'What then is so special about Christ? . . . Why not another model – Paul, or Buddha or Confucius or Zoroaster?',[80] and a *hermeneutics of affirmation*, in which he can declare that, in deeply psychological terms, 'Christ himself is the typical dying and self-transforming God.'[81] Peter

Homans sums up the paradoxes of Jung's analytical journey as demonstrating both a Christian and a post-Christian stance:[82]

> In order to emphasize the presence of a double movement in Jung's psychology, in which both rejection and affirmation were present, I call his approach a re-interpretation rather than simply one more interpretation. In all this Jung gave expression to an important facet of his personal identity – which existed alongside that of originative psychologist and social critic – that of prophet or re-interpreter of traditional Christianity.[83]

Jung and Pastoral Care

There is no dispute over Jung's rightly valued reinterpretive influence on Christian pastoral care, especially on the pathways of pastoral counselling and spiritual direction.[84] The close interplay between his concept of selfhood and divinity, his sharp awareness of the supernatural, his perception of life's polarities, his commitment to the imaginative and symbolic, and, not least, the influence of his theory of personality on the popular Myers-Briggs Type Indicator (MBTI),[85] have all contributed richly to the theory and practice of the pastoral ministries. Even so, as we have suggested, there is a darker side to the genesis and development of Jung's analytical psychology and, thus, an uncritical assimilation or a downright rejection of 'all things Jungian' miss out – the former by absorbing Gnostic and occultic perspectives unwittingly and the latter by discarding valid insights into the mystery of the human psyche. In the light of the discussion so far, let us briefly consider two areas that often lead to confusion among Christian pastoral carers: *the shadow and evil*; and *the self and God*.

The Shadow and Evil

In my own training as a spiritual director and as a qualified user of the MBTI, I have frequently come across the ready use of the term 'shadow' as something of a repository for knowing comments about somewhat puzzling features in another's behaviour: 'Aha! That sort of negative reaction is clearly from his "shadow"' or 'I'm sorry! She's definitely got to come to terms with her "shadow" before we can let her join the team.' Quite often such views, apart from their judgmental tone, are close to the mark in Jungian terms, since Jung declared that the shadow is 'the thing' a person 'has no wish to be'.[86] At the same time, such ready use of the word 'shadow' often seems to be a blanket term to preclude any notion of sin or evil, either at the personal, communal, national or international level. Thus, in its most universally psychologised form, the 'shadow' is blamed not only for an individual's transgressions and peccadilloes but for the worst excesses of a Hitler, Idi Amin or Pol Pot.

Interestingly, one of the tenets of the Gnosticism of late antiquity was a belief that the downward spiral of the cosmos was held at a 'darkened level of being', a 'degraded element of divinity', which seemed to see the sum-total of 'evil' as simply an 'ignorance' that could only be redeemed through 'knowledge' (*gnosis*).[87] Once more, we can see in Jung a tendency for a similar perspective, where his idea of the 'shadow' evokes the darker and hidden side of human nature, a side whose subversive influence can only be overcome through the light of knowledge:

> Everyone carries a shadow, and the less it is embodied in the individual's conscious life, the blacker and denser it is. If an inferiority is conscious, one always has a chance to correct it . . . But if it is repressed and isolated from consciousness, it never gets corrected, and is liable to burst forth suddenly in a moment of unawareness. At all events, it forms an unconscious snag, thwarting our most well-meant intentions.[88]

Here the notion of shadow as that aspect of our humanity that is, as it were, cast by the 'sun' of reality on the individual ego is clearly a useful one. Just as my physical shadow is uniquely shaped and goes wherever I go (as long as the sun is shining!), so the ego and Jungian 'shadow' are held in thrall. These concepts are of value in the pastoral calling, as long as the 'shadow' is not allowed to usurp and sanitise the dimension of human sinfulness, a dimension that, according to a biblical perspective, permeates every aspect of selfhood – conscious and unconscious, ego and shadow – and is highly resistant to dislodgment: 'The heart is deceitful above all things and beyond cure. Who can understand it?' (Jer. 17:9).

The Self and God
It is in the realm of selfhood and the Godhead that there can be special confusion for Christians seeking to understand Jung's

contribution to pastoral care, for in his analytical psychology we seem to meet both a divinised self and a psychologised God. Addressing this issue, Murray Stein demonstrates an 'intimate connection' between Jung as psychologist and Jung as theologian and shows how, in Jung's methodology, all 'words' and speculations, including those of all the '-ologies', 'are *also* words about the psyche, because they are words *of* the psyche'. Thus theology is as bound as any other discipline by this subjective stance, wherein 'words about God are also words about the psyche'.[89] For example, Jung defines the 'self' psychologically 'as the psychic totality of the individual'[90] and that totality is seen as 'indescribable and indistinguishable from a God-image'.[91] It is this Kantian inability to comprehend,[92] in which the psyche cannot reach beyond its own limitations, that characterises both Jung's psychology and his theology.[93] As Stein puts it:

> Jung's movement from psychology (words about the psyche) to theology (words about God) is . . . not based on establishing a privileged territory of image, experience, and discourse that lies beyond the reach of the psyche. Nor does he appeal to divine revelation. There is no gap. Theology for Jung is, rather, a transformation from psychology, a shift of language and understanding within the same territory and still within the realm of the psyche.[94]

Once more, we see in Jung a Gnostic tendency, for, in equating the inaccessible mystery of selfhood and the Godhead, he lays God as open to the penetration of darkness and evil[95] as the anti-cosmic perspectives of early Gnosticism did. For example, his studies of Gnostic and alchemical beliefs[96] and his commitment to a universal dialectic between opposite poles force him toward a notion of divinity as quarternarian rather than trinitarian, where the fourth aspect 'represents the devil'[97] and 'a common life unites not only the Father and the "light" son, but the Father and his *dark* emanation'.[98] Swanee Hunt sums up this confusion of self and God, good and evil and the subsequent circularity of the argument:

> [Jung] asserts that God must include evil. The strength of his claim rests on the concept of the shadow-side within each person. And the argument is that if one does not affirm evil as part of God, it is because one is afraid of God's shadow as one is of one's own shadow. To deny is to affirm. That is, to disclaim this premise is to have evidence of how true it is, else why would we need to repress it so thoroughly?[99]

Our assessment of Jung and his neo-Gnosticism is not a bid to discard the value of many of his insights into selfhood and the concept of God, and their usefulness in the pastoral ministries, so much as a plea for a careful *dialogue* between Christian theology and Jungian psychology. Within the pathway of spiritual direction, in particular, there is ready talk of the 'God within' and this immanentist God seems, at times, to be confused with a person's unique individuality. It is where these perceptions collapse God's transcendent otherness into, to use David Benner's phrase, 'the subterranean God who inhabits the collective unconscious'[100] that Jungianism is in danger of overreaching itself. Nonetheless, dialogue can help clarify a confused merging of ego and shadow, good and evil, God and self, without losing sight of the rich Judaeo-Christian understanding of human beings as made in God's image and likeness. Consequently, and without denying the mystery of the Johannine 'being in God' and 'Christ in us',[101] we need to hold to an awareness of human and divine *distinctiveness* if our journey toward wholeness is to be one of the heart's responsiveness to the divine Other – wherein, at the homecoming of journey's end, we can declare a true *gnosis*: 'Now we see but a poor reflection as in a miror; then we shall see face to face. Now, I know in part; then I shall know fully, even as I am fully known' (1 Cor. 13:12).

New Age and Pantheism

New Age is a polyglot movement, incorporating a widespread revival of interest in a range of 'wisdom' traditions, ancient mystery cults and complementary healing practices. Its 'newness', in following the astrological concept of the Zodiacal ages,[102] keenly awaits the imminent shift from the Age of Pisces (the Fish), an era of 'creative selfishness' which roughly coincides with the Judaeo-Christian period, to the Age of Aquarius (the Water-carrier), an era of global peace and harmony, reinforced by a 'decline of Christian influence' and anticipated to have dawned by the year 2062.[103] Under this banner of Aquarian hopefulness parades a great concourse of people who, with varying degrees of commitment, may engage, on the one hand, with crystal-gazing, astrology, shamanism, neo-paganism, astral projection, yoga or any one of a vast network of esoteric and mystical religious or occultic practices, or, on the other hand, with a host of ecological and 'green' issues based on a veneration for the Earth as a single, interactive system, the so-called Gaia hypothesis.[104]

Given what we have said earlier, it should be no surprise to find the bespectacled, benign figure of Carl Jung stepping out in imaginary company with today's New Agers. One survey[105] shows him to be one of the most important influences on the world-views of the New Age movement in America. We have already noted Jung's fascination with Gnosticism and alchemy, two mystical traditions that intrigue many New Agers, but it is worth pointing out that, not least with respect to the spiritualism that engaged his maternal family, he was very much a person of his time in terms of an incipient New Ageism.

Growing into young adulthood in the years either side of the *fin de siècle*, the end of the nineteenth century, Jung's life was powerfully shaped by the period's disillusionment with the religious conventions of Judaism and Christianity, the political polemics of Karl Marx and the emerging psychological secularism of Sigmund Freud.[106] Innumerable *'fin-de-siècle'* men and women turned, rather, to occultism and mysticism, drawn, in Richard Noll's words, by a 'sense of belonging to a community with shared goals and shared iconographies of the transcendent'.[107] Jung,[108] looking back to this period as containing 'the origin of all my ideas',[109] developed a great interest in Ascona, Switzerland, a centre that became a mecca for neo-paganism in the early decades of the twentieth century and can be seen as a precursor to those sacred sites, such as Glastonbury and Findhorn,[110] especially celebrated by the counterculture of the 1960s and 1970s, and the New Age movement from the 1980s onward.[111]

It is in the quintessentially Jungian notion of the *collective unconscious*, and the attendant archetypes, that we meet, I suggest, his most pervasive influence on the New Age movement, and this in turn can be seen to link with the perennial debate between *pantheism* and *panentheism*.

The Collective Unconscious

Jung declares that his idea of the collective unconscious began with a dream. He was in a multi-storied house ('It was "my house"') and found himself descending, storey-by-storey, into the bowels of the earth, where he reached 'a low cave cut in the rock' and containing 'scattered bones and broken pottery, like remains of a primitive culture'. On reflection, he came to the conclusion that he had reached 'the world of the primitive man within myself – a world which can scarcely be reached or illuminated by consciousness'.[112] Over the next few years he fashioned his understanding of the collective unconscious and its constituent archetypes, beginning the systematic use of these terms in 1916 and 1919 respectively.

Unlike Freud, Jung did not see the unconscious as simply 'the repository of repressed, infantile, personal experience' (Jung's notion of the *personal* unconscious'), but concluded, rather, that this aspect of the unconscious rested on a pervasive, deeper layer common to the whole of humankind: the *collective unconscious*. This layer can be viewed as without limit, like the lower reaches of a great, bottomless ocean which comprises, as part of its intrinsic structure, certain patterns that may, mysteriously, coalesce into the shapes and forms of innumerable sea-creatures – barely known, fantastical denizens of the deep that may, on occasions, rise into partial view to engage, inform or disturb. The 'patterns' are the *archetypes* and the 'sea-creatures' are the *archetypal images*, representations that may surface from the collective unconscious. Demaris S. Wehr summarises well the gradual evolution of Jung's views on the mysterious depths of the human psyche:

> The archetype . . . is the assumption of a patterning process in the human brain, instinctual and alike everywhere, expressing itself in universal human behavior patterns, motifs, themes, images, and symbols. Jung sometimes likens the archetype itself to a vortex of energy, drawing to itself certain themes and images. Archetypal images, he noted, are accompanied by much emotion. They are those typically human experiences and accompanying images that touch us the most deeply.[113]

And so, especially at momentous life-stages, such as adolescence, marriage, childbirth, mid-life, times of serious illness and death, archetypal images may arise from humanity's long story of engaging with such transitional events: figures of, for example, the boy-hero, the great earth mother, the trickster, the messiah figure or the sage. If psychological health is sought through the process of individuation, then such images, Jung argued, may need to be engaged with through the technique of *active imagination*. Described as 'The art of letting things happen',[114] this method entails an imaginative journey, such as descending into a cave, in which one is prepared to encounter and dialogue with any 'fantasy figures' that may present. Such an engagement may then be written out, painted, sculpted, danced or acted, in order that fresh insights needed may be ingrained into the maturing psyche.[115]

Clearly, such an enterprise, which for Jung himself proved hazardous, may be mishandled.[116] A headstrong and prayerless experimentation in this realm may unleash ill-understood psychological forces or, worse, unknown spiritual powers.[117] It is here, at the centre of Jungian methodology, that many New Agers and neo-pagans are enticed. Jung held strongly to the idea of a mythical 'pure religious instinct' that lies in the deepest layers of the collective unconscious and needs uncovering from the detritus of the Judaeo-Christian tradition. When such depths are plumbed, he argues, it is more likely that neo-Gnosticism will answer human need:

> An interior spiritual world whose existence we never suspected opens out and displays contents which seem to stand in sharpest contrast to all our former ideas. These images are so intense that it is quite understandable why millions of cultivated persons should be taken in by . . . modern gnostic systems [which] meet the need for expressing and formulating the wordless occurrences going on within ourselves *better* than any of the existing forms of Christianity.[118]

Pantheism and Panentheism

It is in the subterranean world of the unconscious that Jung saw the greatest hope for humankind. As Noll puts it, 'Reaching this hidden pagan layer of the collective unconscious within not only redeems the individual, but can lead to the birth of a new world.'[119] Among Jungians, such a vision forms 'their image of the great chain of being that unites them in a metaphysical belief system'.[120] And it is this heady and optimistic perspective of the spirituality of a new consciousness that is also the driving force of much New Ageism. Here is a world-view that hovers between pantheism and panentheism.

Charles Hartshorne says, quite simply, '*Pantheism* means that all is God; *panentheism*, that all is in God.'[121] The former can lead to 'a form of theological determinism',[122] since, if God is everything, then all he is and does is what everything is and does: he is the volcano that erupts, the river that floods, the forest that burns, the herd that stampedes, the people that love, hate, make peace and make war. The latter is, as John Macquarrie puts it, 'really a variety of theism, one which takes care to stress God's immanence equally with his transcendence'.[123] In pantheism, God is so immanent that he cannot be distinguished from the cosmos: in panentheism, his immanence (closeness) and transcendence (otherness) are such that he is both *in* his world, creatively and sustainingly, and *other than* his world – intimately involved, yet distinctive.

And just as we see in Jung a blurring of the edges between what is panentheistic and pantheistic, so in the New Age movement we find a see-sawing between a view that sees God, or the gods, as active in a created order and a perspective that God and the cosmos are 'one and the same'. It is inevitable, in the latter stance, that the earth and its inhabitants are *divinised* and, although that prospect may appear honouring to the natural world, it leads to a singular loss of autonomous value. Even as the wonder and mystery of, say, a Van Gogh painting or a Barbara Hepworth sculpture is obscured if their createdness cannot be distinguished from the artist, so the unique beauty and captivating characteristics of the created order can be devalued if they are simply seen as part of the Godhead. Richard Bauckham makes the point tellingly:

What we need to reverence and respect is the strange and particular way in which each kind of creature is itself, in all the extraordinary diversity of God's creation. It is not at all clear that this is what happens when nature is divinized. What people tend to treat as divine is the numinously impressive, the beautiful and the terrifying. They worship trees, not potatoes; pythons, not fleas.[124]

And yet, as we have seen with the place of Jung in the pastoral ministries, there is a great need for dialogue with the New Age movement.[125] Just as Christian counsellors and spiritual directors can learn from a Jungian understanding of human psychology, so they can profit from the challenges of New Age spirituality. Let us heed the plea of Michael Northcott as he examines the postmodern 'resurgence of the sacred':

Pastoral theology and ministry needs to recover a more holistic approach, a vision of community, and a direction for spiritual awareness which reflect and incarnate . . . New Age concerns. The church, far from rejecting New Age in paranoia, should rather embrace its agenda . . . [finding] a divine response in the story of the source of Being, the Incarnate Logos, Christ crucified and risen.[126]

Rahner and Christology

Philip Sheldrake has said that spirituality is 'theology on two feet'[127] and the sort of healthily bipedal theology that the spiritualities of this pathway to wholeness needs is expressed, I suggest, in the christology of Karl Rahner.

Karl Rahner (1904–1984), the German philosophical theologian, is an example of that comparatively rare phenomenon among academics, an intellectual rooted in the everyday needs of 'the common people'. William V. Dych describes how he had accompanied Rahner on more than one occasion on a visit to the supermarket, where the learned doctor would stock up with supplies and take these on to some poor family that he had kept in touch with through the years.[128]

There is a God-given continuity between Rahner's spirituality, his theology 'on two feet' and his pastoral commitment to others. This theology of praxis is an example of what George Lindbeck calls a 'two-dimensional outlook', combining 'the cognitively propositional and the expressively symbolic' approaches to doctrine.[129] Although Lindbeck prefers the 'cultural-linguistic' approach of postliberalism,[130] it seems to me that this melding of the cognitive and the experiential can, in the right hands, lead to an integrated theology and spirituality of both 'head' and 'heart', of *halacha* and *agada*.

Let us explore how Rahner's approach can encourage contemporary spiritual direction by addressing, on the one hand, the Gnostic tendency in Jung's influential psychology and, on the other, the pantheistic flavour of New Age spirituality. The possible antidote to these subversive trends can be considered under two headings: *knowing God through Christ: an ascending christology*; and *finding God in all things: an Ignatian spirituality*.

Knowing God through Christ: An Ascending Christology

In sharp contrast to the quest for 'knowingness' in Gnosticism, the Christian path to wholeness, according to Rahner,[131] is one in which personal knowledge is cut down to size in the face of divine mystery: 'In the depths of his being man knows nothing more surely than that his knowledge . . . is only a small island in a vast sea that has not been traveled.' Such a voyager needs to ask: 'Which does he love more, the small island of his so-called knowledge or the sea of infinite mystery?'[132] Here, Rahner seeks to avoid the route of both the Gnostic and the agnostic, since both try to grasp the centrality of knowledge – the first by owning it, the second by denying it.[133] It is, rather, that 'true theology' forces a person 'into the mystery of God', where he or she 'no longer grasps but rather is grasped'.[134]

Even so, Rahner does not leave his spirituality in an apophatic haze of 'unknowing'. While freely acknowledging 'God as mystery', he moves on to a more content- and experience-laden kataphatic stance by proclaiming 'the mystery made known' in Christ (Eph. 3:3). As Dych writes of Rahner's approach: 'The starting point for theology's talk, both about God and ourselves, is Jesus of Nazareth.'[135]

It is here that Rahner, although including the traditional and complementary 'descending Christology' of God 'made flesh in Christ', puts forward his notion of an 'ascending Christology', centred on 'an encounter with the historical Jesus'.[136] Instead of starting with a creedal faith *about* Jesus Christ, Rahner advocates a focus on the faith *of* Jesus Christ: rather than impose a system of what to believe from the 'givens' of the Faith, he proposes a *personal relationship*. Put differently, Rahner argues that 'faith precedes theology', in the sense that 'grace and free decision' generally come before major 'theoretical reflection'.[137] Jesus, as 'absolute saviour',[138] is 'the offer for us, and we ourselves are . . . the recipients of God's offer to us'.[139]

Jung's idea of *individuation* is quite often referred to in spiritual direction and it is instructive to compare this process and goal of personal wholeness with concepts of maturation implicit in Rahner's approach. Although Jung sometimes used theological language of individuation – as, for example, 'at-one-ment with oneself and . . . with humanity',[140] his notion is essentially a psychological one, in which there is a movement toward 'an integration of conscious and unconscious parts of the personality'.[141] Obviously these perspectives can be helpfully incorporated into Christian journeying, as we have seen, in principle, with David Benner's concept of psychospirituality (see pp. 292–4), and it is such viewpoints as Rahner's that can lift our eyes beyond the necessitous, but limited, horizon of personal maturation. He proposes a route to wholeness that embraces not only psychological growth but the progressive healing through God in Christ of every aspect of our humanity and, indeed, of the entire world order. Journey's end of completeness is universally achieved, in and through the redemption of humankind: 'In Rahner's cosmic vision the being of the whole created universe moves toward its fulfilment in human being, and human being moves toward its fulfilment in Jesus Christ. His cosmology, anthropology and Christology are intrinsically related moments within this single vision.'[142]

Finding God in All Things: An Ignatian Spirituality

Rahner became a Jesuit at eighteen and, looking back over his life in his later years, he declared that 'the spirituality of Ignatius himself . . . learned through the practice of prayer and religious formation' was more significant for him 'than all learned philosophy and theology inside and outside the Order'.[143] By the same token, he quotes with approval his fellow-Jesuit, Hans Urs von Balthasar, who said that part of theology must be done 'on one's knees'.[144] Besides the centrality of his relationship with Jesus – a truly Jesuitical hallmark[145] – Rahner's christology is also profoundly influenced by Ignatius' notion of 'finding God in all things',[146] a perspective that resonates constructively with much New Age spirituality.

For Ignatius, and thus for Rahner, the stance of 'finding God in all things' needs to grow out of an attitude of 'indifference' (*indiferençia*). This is not the disregarding mindset that shrugs its shoulders and looks the other way when faced with moral dilemmas or human need. It is, rather, in Rahner's words, 'a calm readiness for every command of God',[147] a willingness to sit loose to all activities, thoughts and preoccupations, however legitimate, in order to hear and obey God's 'still, small voice'. Here is a tiptoe eagerness to discern God's pathways to wholeness amid the clamouring voices of alternative routes, each claiming itself to be the *only* valid route. For Rahner the commitment is unremitting:

> Out of such an attitude of *indiferençia* there springs of itself the perpetual readiness to hear a new call from God to tasks other than those previously engaged in, continually to decamp from those fields where one wanted to find God and to serve him . . . [and] the courage to regard no way to him as being *the* way, but rather to seek him on all ways.[148]

It is such 'indifference' that opens the door to seeking God 'in *all* things'.[149] The vision here is one of pantheism's best face. 'The earth is the LORD'S, and everything in it' (Ps. 24:1). There is no confusion in the Ignatian perspective between the creator and Lord of all and the created cosmos, no slide into a Jungian divinisation of self or a New Age pantheism in which all is God and God is all.

Further, there is in Ignatian spirituality an integration of the two strands of piety we have stumbled across so many times in our pursuit of pathways to wholeness: between the cognitive and intuitive, between *halacha* and *agada*, between left brain and right brain, between the kataphatic and apophatic. For Rahner, as for Ignatius, 'indifference' and 'finding God in all things' lead to a deep 'joy in the world', fostered by the interweaving 'desert' way of the cross and the 'city' engagement of obedient living:

> Ignatian affirmation of the world is not a naïve optimism, not an installing ourselves in the world as though we had in it the centre of our lives. Ignatian joy in the world springs from the mysticism of conformity with him whom we have joined in the flight from the world contained in the foolishness of the Cross. But once we have found the God of the life beyond, then such an attitude will break out of deep seclusion in God into the world, and work as long as day lasts, immerse itself in the work of the time in the world and yet await with deep longing the Coming of the Lord.[150]

Summary

This chapter has sought to portray the fourth of our pathways to wholeness – a pathway characterised by an ancient tradition of mystical spirituality, the imaginative and symbolic use of Scripture, a 'two-dimensional' approach to doctrine that is cognitive and experiential-expressive, and pastoral metaphors of 'desert-dweller', 'soul-friend' and 'midwife'. The pathway's rich heritage of Celtic, Catholic and Eastern Orthodox spirituality has been outlined in the light of kataphatic and apophatic orientations, and its central pastoral ministry – spiritual direction – has been reviewed in its relationship to pastoral counselling and the notion of psychospiritual maturity. Given this pathway's special contemporary relationship with Jungian and New Age influence, the christology of Rahner and the spirituality of Ignatius have been put forward as a combined corrective to Gnostic and pantheistic trends.

It is probably true to say that the pathway of spiritual direction has witnessed the greatest number of new pilgrims of all the pathways we are considering. Within the Christian Church, biblical counsellors of evangelical persuasion, healers whose paths have been lit up by charismatic experience, and liberal and post-liberal pastoral counsellors, have all sought out a spirituality to widen the horizons of the upward journey. Bible-lovers, who formerly seemed to engage with just the propositional elements of their beloved text, have found their conceptual windows opened to a strange and new country which, on closer examination, proves to be just as biblical in its use of metaphor, symbol and human imagination as their more familiar cognitive terrain. Charismatics, who have lived with the celebration of the Holy Spirit's works of renewal for some time, have learned to face the darkness as well as the light, the cross as well as the glory, and have found new depths and heights of wonder in the mystical tradition. Liberals and postliberals, used to asking disturbing questions of their more happy-go-lucky or complacent brothers and sisters, have enlarged their vision of the symbolic and cultural, and hopefully of the numinous, in an engagement with the traditions of Christian spirituality.

It is thus that the pathway to wholeness that calls us to 'the uncomplicated heart' appeals to the whole of humankind. It is in this path of the 'mystic way', as we have seen, that a dialogue which takes seriously Jungian psychology and New Age spirituality, for example, is most likely to find sympathetic ears and voices. And yet it is in the universality of its appeal that the mystical journey has its particular dangers. Its very inclusiveness rightly welcomes all comers, but, where its spiritualities degenerate into a mishmash of isolated paths made in the image of each individual, the shadows of Gnostic elitism and pantheistic animism are never far away. This, once more, is where theology and spirituality need each other,[151] where, for example, Rahnerian christology and Ignatian spirituality go hand in hand, holding both the incomprehensibility of God and a Christ-centredness which, nonetheless, unlocks tthe door into the kingdom. And, if that kingdom is to be realised, then pathways to wholeness must include social change, and it is to that dimension that we now turn.

11

SOCIAL CHANGE:
THE REFORMED COMMUNITY

Thus says the LORD of hosts: Render true judgements, show kindness
and mercy to one another; do not oppress the widow, the orphan, the
alien, or the poor; and do not devise evil in your hearts against one
another. But they refused to listen . . .

Zechariah 7:9–11 (NRSV)

Luke, our grandson, now a sturdy nine-year-old, was in his
element. A keen supporter of Sheffield United, he had added
Glasgow Celtic to his short list of top football clubs since the
family's move to Scotland two-and-a-half years earlier. At the
beginning of a week's stay in the Lake District to celebrate his
Granny's sixtieth birthday with the wider family, he had his
much-loved Uncle Graham, another committed Sheffield United
supporter, all to himself. It was spring, the lakeland scenery hung
mistily around them, and, as they stepped out together, the talk
was serious. As a brief, ground-breaking manoeuvre amid an
interchange peppered with goals, brilliant saves and penalty
shoot-outs, Luke changed into conversational mode: 'There are
a lot of tourists in the Lake District, aren't there?' Graham had to
agree that there were. Some minutes later, once more interrupting
thoughts of league tables and the premier division, Luke asked,
'Graham, what *are* tourists?'

Luke had clearly heard the word before, probably each July and
August in the Highland community where he lived. Were they
cars, or motor-bikes, or walkers, or climbers, or, even, the hordes
of summer midges that swarmed above the local moorland?
Whatever they were, he had also picked up that weekends in
the Lakes were a good time for spotting them.

Interestingly, tourists are always other people. You and I, at our
most relaxed, are holiday-makers or just visitors; at our most

intrepid, we are travellers or explorers. We may be, as we shift the focus back to our postmodern journeying, pilgrims or nomads, venturing on our pathways to wholeness with single-minded purpose or with a responsiveness to the need of the moment. It is within this analogy, though, that we can, as pastoral carers, slip into a tourist mentality, and this danger is at its most pressing in this our fifth pathway, that of a communal care which seeks social and political change. Peter Selby warns of the trap in these words:

> If I seek any kind of encounter with God and suppose that I can set my mind free from the pressing issues which distress the world and distort the face of humanity, I make the spiritual journey into an exercise in tourism . . . To presume to care for other human beings without taking into account the social and political causes of whatever distress they may be experiencing is to confirm them in their distress while pretending to offer healing.[1]

It is this split between the private world of the individual and the public world of society at large that fosters a tourist mentality. For Selby it is as if life's journey 'becomes a luxury cruise in which the life of the crew is of no account'.[2] Conditions below deck are of no consequence to the fun-seeking, sun-soaking tourist and the first sign of any intrusion of the societal into the easy-going existence of the individual may be in a ship's mutiny at sea or the inconvenience of being stuck in port while the disaffected crew negotiate with captain or owner.

What is needed on all five of our pathways to wholeness is an awareness which engages both the communal and the individual, the societal and the personal, the public and the private, the context of the communal 'living human web'[3] as well as the text of the individual 'living human document'. Pastoral tourism must give way to fellow-pilgrimage, where we as pastoral carers live out our interconnectedness within community, lest, in Selby's words, we 'confirm [others] in their distress while pretending to offer healing'.

Let us explore the Christian call to social change, first, under the heading of *communal care*, by looking at two stories – one from the perspective of the care-giver and one from the perspective of the care-receiver. Second, let us examine the fundamental dimension of all true communally based pastoral care, that of *crossing the boundaries*, under whose title we will outline the contributions of radical theology to issues of poverty, gender, culture and ecology. Finally, we will enquire of *the way ahead* by a consideration of two ancient metaphors for communal care: the prophet and the wise one.

Communal Care

'Care in the community' has become a byword for a government policy that has been long on principle, but short on effective practice. Behind the phrase lies an ancient pastoral tradition wherein, in the words of the quote that heads this chapter, 'the widow, the orphan, the alien, [and] the poor' are provided for and incorporated within the nation's, the tribe's and the family's supportive generational structures. Such communal care, although urged by Yahweh on the Israelites again and again, was oft-times resisted, as it is today – the people 'refusing to listen', the easy-going 'tourism' of their lives turning a deaf ear to the cries of those bereft of a breadwinner, of their country of origin or of life's bare necessities. And yet, although many pastoral carers seem to be held captive in an individualised approach to counsel-ling and spiritual direction that dismisses the contextual and precludes the socio-political, there are still those whose sense of community – a 'sense that they are more alike than unlike'[4] their fellow-travellers – makes them step out into the public domain to listen to the distressed, cajole their oppressors and bring circum-stantial and structural change to lessen their plight and increase their hope. Let us consider the story of Vimla, a young Christian woman of Indian background with a deep commitment to social change, and the interconnected story of Sunita.

Vimla's Story

It all began with Claire. Vimla had read of Claire's need as a single mother with a small baby, living in 'bed and breakfast' accom-modation at a hostel for the homeless set in an affluent part of the city, and, after a great deal of heart-searching that she might be misunderstood as a 'Lady Bountiful', resolved to visit her. It was just before Christmas and Vimla was particularly moved by Claire's struggle to save up to buy presents amid a suburban environment that seemed engulfed by festive plenty. The hostel was a veritable rabbit warren of a place, temporarily housing fifty or so units, including single parents, men on remand, drug addicts and families with small children – all sharing two small 'galley' kitchens. One family, comprising two adults and four children, typifies the cramped lifestyle of many. They had been in the hostel for over a year, living out their lives in one room, the size of an average 'living room'. Mealtimes highlighted their plight. An extended journey up and down stairways, to and from one of the tiny kitchens, entailed the difficult choice as to whether to leave the children unattended in a sometimes hostile environment or to risk their presence amid the dangers of communal cooking. Further hazards lay in the return to their room, negotiating the crowded corridors and stairs with hot saucepans of food, all to vie for the one place to eat – sitting on their bed. As Vimla said to me, 'Here, there was nowhere to have an argument, to have sex, to watch TV.'

Although Vimla had worked previously in psychiatric settings and with the homeless, she was freshly struck by the level of unmet human need. Her own children were aged two and four at the time and she asked herself repeatedly, 'How would all this be for me?' Her initial desire to help was met in her encounter with Claire, since Vimla was able to give her the family travel-cot and assist in her move from the hostel into more adequate accommodation. However, Vimla had seen a great deal more than just Claire's plight. She had identified a particular dilemma among 'bed-and-breakfast' families: the need for somewhere for the children to play, so that both parents and their offspring could find some respite. She told Linda, a close friend at the church she attended, 'I need to do something' and Linda duly linked Vimla with Sophie, a new church member who had considerable experience in child-care provision.

And so these two women pooled their compassion and their expertise and, as Christians will, prayed, trusted and acted. They spread out a map of the city and charted all its bed-and-breakfast hostels. But where could they find a suitable centre where children and parents would have sufficient space to relax and enjoy a welcome break from their claustrophobic lives? It was Lucinda who provided the answer. Vimla had read in a local paper that this woman had recently bought a redundant church with the object of setting up a community centre. The map was consulted and the church was found to lie at the pivotal point of the clustering of hostels. Lucinda's response when phoned was simple and encouraging: 'Someone said to me only this morning, "You ought to run something for children from "B & Bs".' Seeing the site, Vimla and Sophie declared it to be 'perfect'. Looking back at these happy 'coincidences' nine years later, Vimla said, 'God was preparing the way. Our responsibility was just to walk that way.'

The church that Vimla and Sophie attended housed a large, affluent congregation – one to which Vimla, with her radical, 'hands-on', streetwise background, felt ill-fitted. Yet suddenly this body of professional and business people seemed the perfect resource for the money, skills and equipment that the play centre needed. Vimla admitted, 'It was our fault for not using all this.' She duly stood up in church, announced the potential centre's needs and was overwhelmed by the response – not only with all the furnishings and play things needed and with the ready covenanting of money, but with the volunteering of a small army of women – social workers, nursery nurses and young mums with small children of their own. The project was up and running.

But, it was asked, would the people come? Vimla had seen enough of how 'B-&-B' parents felt – depressed, lacking confidence, unable to negotiate with the world outside the hostel – to know that it would take great courage to venture out to an unknown place, and to unknown people. Health visitors were mobilised to spread news of the centre and the city council agreed to put details of its impending opening on the weekly housing benefit cheques they sent out. The day arrived, Vimla, Sophie and a handful of supporters paced up and down in their eagerness to welcome parents and children – and practically nobody came. And so a new phase had to be entered. Three or four women, all with children of their own, agreed to start the long haul of regular visiting. Each picked a hostel or two and, all alone, bravely went from door to door. As Vimla put it, it was less threatening for often suspicious and fearful 'bed-and-breakfasters' to be visited by a woman, especially one who knew first-hand what it is to have small toddlers around your feet all day and to experience frightened or ill babies in the middle of the night. The team of visiting women were able to say, 'We'll go with you to the centre', 'We'll take the children to give you a breather', or, confidently, yet perhaps unsure of the solution to a query, 'Sure, I could deal with that!' These personal contacts became the most important element in this venture of communal care. In fact, not least among those families who never ventured to the play centre, the regular visits by Vimla, Sophie and the team – simply 'fellow-women' – were the highlight of the week, since so many 'bed-and-break-fasters', once homeless, were completely shunned by their families and former friends.

Sunita's Story

Sunita, a married Gujerati Indian with three children, had been on the receiving end of visits by Sophie, who, in time, became one of these trusted 'fellow-women'. Sunita and her husband Justin had both been made redundant at the same time. Justin, like many men who lose work in their prime, felt as if he had been 'kicked in the teeth' and was determined to make ends meet by setting up his own business. However, the couple's loss of regular income and the large outlay needed for a new enterprise meant that they gradually fell behind with their mortgage payments. When Sunita was due to have her second child at Christmas, the building society began to claim back their property. They appealed against the decision and made every effort to find the needed money for a 'significant reduction in the arrears'. Now with two children, they were unable to put off the evil day beyond the following autumn. Sunita was ticked off by the man at the local housing advice shop for not approaching him before, as they could have been on the council housing list a year sooner. But no one had told them this. 'Where do we go?' she asked, and was told that arrangements could not be made until the family was out on the street. Telling me her story, she added, 'When you're homeless, you're treated like a criminal.'

On the day of their removal from their much loved home, their seven-year-old son asked, 'Mummy, where are we going to sleep tonight?' As she replied, 'I don't know', she felt the first pang of a betrayal of his trust in her. She had always been there for him, always as honest as she could be with him, and now she did not have the answer to the most basic of a child's questions. That night's destination, so it proved, was to be the hostel where Vimla had first met Claire. The family were allocated two rooms: one for Justin, Sunita and the baby, and one for their son – distressingly not adjacent to the parents' room, but about six rooms away on the opposite side of the corridor. Sunita and Justin's room was jam-packed with just a bed, a cot and a wardrobe, a far cry from one health visitor's notion of adequate living, expressed to Vimla: 'You can't be a family unless you can sit round a table and eat.' And so began the long haul of cramped living, sharing a remote kitchen and a bathroom with fifty or so other families, running the gauntlet of neighbours who included men on police bail, a wife-beater and drug addicts, and trying to prevent their son from premature contamination from a violent and foul-mouthed environment. Small wonder that he declared, 'I don't like it here', and applied himself to help his mum count the days to the thirteen weeks that they had been given as a deadline for their stay.

It was during their time at the hostel – which eventually proved to be of six months' duration – that Sunita picked up a note pushed under her door. It was from one of Vimla's friends and gave details of the newly opened play centre. Understandably, given their raw experience of other people, Sunita declined the invitation when Sophie appeared at the door soon after. At this time, Sunita remembers feeling so depressed that she would sit, motionless, on the bed all day, nursing her baby daughter. Sophie faithfully kept up her twice-weekly visits until, one day, Sunita decided to break from her reverie and give the play centre a try. After months of an imprisoning and dehumanising existence, which lacked the simple necessity of a chair to sit on and the luxury of coffee with milk (since they had no way of keeping milk fresh), Sunita broke down and wept at the gentle, genuine, normalising welcome she received. Here, she was treated 'as if normal, by normal, non-patronising people'; she was surrounded by room to walk in and turn round in; there was generous space and lots of toys for the children; and, best of all, she had a seat to herself and a cup of coffee *with* milk.

Returning from the play centre, Sunita cried for much of the rest of the day, for she had many tears to shed. Since her childhood in Gujerat, when she had reached out to the 'untouchables' in the village, she had 'always been of help'. And now, in her 'B-&-B' prison, she 'felt no purpose'. Somehow, though, Sophie, Vimla and their friends had rekindled Sunita's generous spirit. Unaware of their Christian commitment, but deeply impressed by the warm humanity of the women at the play centre, she began to talk with the people along the corridor, instead of brushing past them. She felt there must be something she could do for them and, in time, helped interpret the bureaucratic jargonese of their council letters, wrote replies for them, and offered to look after one of their children when she could.

Once she, Justin and the children had moved to their council house, her renewed vision for others' needs led to her continuing involvement with the play centre. Her harrowing experience of homelessness had opened a rich vein of practical compassion for her fellow-women in similar plight. Her articulate and lucid style led to many speaking engagements throughout the city, wherever churches and other bodies were willing to bend an ear toward the homeless and deprived. These commitments culminated in a meeting at the city centre when Sunita recounted her story to a packed, and visibly moved, assembly of members of parliament, councillors and business people. Now a mother of three, the latest project of this former village girl from India, who happens to be fearful of heights, is a parachute jump for the play centre!

Crossing the Boundaries

If a community is to be reformed it needs the Vimlas and Sophies of this world to cross the boundaries of status, wealth, health, gender, age, culture and environment. The boundaries of differentness so easily become the barriers of divisiveness. Vimla, Sophie and some of their fellow-workers, for example, found they needed to be acutely aware not to impose their middle-class cultural norms on those women who came to the play centre from different backgrounds. They learned, in time, to set aside their dietary scruples that favour brown bread and fruit over sweets for children and began to 'bracket out' their premise that parents need to play *with* their children as they concluded that the likes of Claire and Sunita were desperate for some space *from* their children. As Vimla said to me, in her concern for Justin and Sunita's plight of homelessness, 'We have money, power, influence and control, and thus have no clue what it feels like.'

If true theology is, as we have noted repeatedly, praxis – and Vimla and Sophie are among the first to acknowledge the centrality of Christian theology in their radical devotion to communal care – then we need to outline the part of such practical theology in crossing the boundaries of human need. It is here that we will consider the so-called 'liberation' theologies and, in doing so, I would join with Sallie McFague in seeing these theologies as central to contemporary society. She rightly does not regard them as 'marginal, strange, or even particularly novel enterprises' but, rather, views them within 'the classical traditions of fundamental reformulations of Christian faith', on a par with 'the theologies of Augustine, Luther, and Schleiermacher', men who were disturbers of the paradigms of their day. Aware that 'feminist, black, and Third World theologies' need to be 'qualified by an adjective', whereas 'white, male, Western theologies' are simply dubbed 'theology',[5] she adds:

> These other theologies are also just theology. As with all theology, they emerge out of a concrete, social context; they identify what they believe the central vision of Christianity to be; they offer particular insights, insights that emerge in part because of special perspectives – insights that ought to be seen as illuminating to all people . . . The crucial difference between these new theologies and classical theology is that for the first time they are coming from women, from people of color, and from the poor.[6]

Let us seek an overview of some of the cardinal aspects of these 'new', boundary-crossing theologies under four headings: *poverty and liberation theology; gender and feminist theology; culture and third-eye theology;* and *ecology and ecological theology.*

Poverty and Liberation Theology

The liberation theology of Latin America that, during the 1960s and 1970s, challenged the ivory towers of Western academic theology and the apolitical complacencies of conservative Christianity, in both its Catholic and evangelical forms, is here to stay – or at least until Jesus's words 'the poor you will always have with you' (Matt. 26:11) no longer apply. As Penny Lernoux puts it, forecasting conditions in Latin America by the year 2000, '210 million people [will be] living in tin and cardboard shacks with no running water, no electricity, no schools, no jobs – with nothing to hope for and nothing to lose.'[7] It is for such that the likes of the Peruvian Gustavo Gutiérrez, the Uruguayan Juan Luis Segundo and the Brazilian brothers Leonardo and Clodovis Boff have been carving out a theology of the poor – holding to orthopraxis rather than orthodoxy, an inductive reading of people's lives rather than a deductive extrapolation from Christian dogma, and a deep commitment to socio-political change rather than the individualism of an over-emphasis on personal transformation.[8]

Although a liberative struggle by certain evangelists and missionaries (on behalf of the oppressed native people of Central and South America in the face of European colonialisation) can be traced back to the sixteenth century,[9] the main impetus of what became known as 'liberation theology'[10] is seen in the social and political upheavals from the 1950s onward.[11] The Boff brothers outline a cycle of socio-economic expansion, deprivation, revolution and reaction: nationalistic governments, notably in Argentina, Brazil and Mexico, brought prosperity to the ruling and middle-classes but 'threw huge sectors of the peasantry into deeper rural marginalization or sprawling urban shantytowns'; this resulting inequality and injustice led, in turn, to the rise of powerful popular movements, which sought to redress the socio-economic imbalance; and, further, these stirrings of the people caused an increase in 'national security' and, in many cases, the vicious repression of all perceived opponents.[12] Within this social and political ferment there emerged a new, reflective consciousness (or 'conscientisation'), a closely bonded amalgam between a Marxist ideology that addressed society's inequities,[13] a 'grass-roots' liberative theology that gave voice to the poor and the proliferation of 'base communities' – church units, smaller than parishes, often led by lay people and committed to a socially active reinterpretation of the Scriptures in the light of material deprivation, governmental oppression and the earthed hopefulness of the Gospel. The climate for this newly emerging spirituality was further enhanced by the inclusive deliberations of the Second Vatican Council (1962–5), which opened new doors for clergy and laity alike toward an orthopraxis that got its hands dirty in its struggle for social change.

This blend of sociological, political and theological influences has shaped liberation theology not only in Latin America but worldwide: in the People's Church of South Korea, with its understanding of a theology of suffering;[14] in the prophetic voice of black and white in South Africa in the struggle against apartheid;[15] and in 'a new, questioning, critical and prophetic theology'[16] that fights to be heard in the mainstream churches of Europe and North America.[17] We saw an example of the last of these in Laurie Green's work with the people of Erdington, Birmingham (see pp. 171–4), and his liberational style of 'doing theology' echoes the schema put forward by the Boff brothers for liberation theology's method as three 'mediations', or 'means or instruments of the theological process': socio-analytical mediation; hermeneutical mediation; and practical mediation.

Socio-analytical Mediation

The first stage of the encounter with the needy, the Boffs argue, is one of careful appraisal of the social, economic and political contexts of deprivation. The question is asked: 'Why is there oppression and what are its causes?'[18] This question is not posed superficially because, behind all oppression, there is a history of attitude, prejudice, vested interests, market forces and imposition of control. In the stories of Vimla and Sunita questions need to be asked about the economics of high-interest loans and incurred debts, government housing policy, the perceived status of redundancy and unemployment, the empowerment of the bureaucratic and the disempowerment of those who 'break the rules'. Although the Boffs acknowledge the wide spectrum of human oppression – including that toward 'blacks, indigenous peoples, women', they regard its 'infrastructural' expression toward 'the socio-economically poor' as central to an understanding of inequity. Whereas the former group at least has a chance of dialogue with their oppressors, the latter, so the Boffs argue, are caught up in a struggle where 'basic interests are irreconcilable'.[19] And it is this institutionalised inflexibility that gives a sense of powerlessness, whether in the *relative* poverty of many in the affluent West[20] or in poverty's more extreme forms in parts of Africa, Asia or Latin America. Such deprivation, especially where to be poor is to be at best discounted and at worst criminalised, can sap all notion of human worth. As the Boffs put it:

> 'Poor' for the people means dependence, debt, exposure, anonymity, contempt, and humiliation. The poor do not usually refer to themselves as 'poor,' which would offend their sense of honor and dignity. It is the non-poor who call them poor. So a poor woman from Tacaimbó in the interior of Pernambuco, hearing someone call her poor, retorted: 'Poor, no! Poor is the end. We are the dispossessed, but fighting!'[21]

Hermeneutical Mediation

Once the socio-economic situation of the needy is understood at personal and structural levels, the liberation theologian turns to Scripture, asking 'What has the word of God to say about this?'[22] Here, the Bible is read, as it were, through the eyes of the oppressed: the text is approached 'bearing the whole weight of the problems, sorrows, and hopes of the poor'.[23] Once more we meet a variant of the *hermeneutical circle*. We have already noted (see pp. 129–30) the use of this term in exegetical and pastoral contexts and seen that, whichever the setting, the 'circularity' involves an interchange between the interpreter's pre-understandings and what is examined. In the task of a liberative interpretation of Scripture, the interchange occurs between the 'real life' pre-understandings of the socially disadvantaged and the conventional perceptions of the text. Inevitably, this process entails Ricoeur's *hermeneutics of suspicion* (see pp. 145–8), in which 'anything and everything involving ideas, including theology' is, according to Segundo, suspected of being 'intimately bound up with the existing social situation'.[24] Thus, the Bible is approached through the acknowledged filter of socio-political awareness, in which 'each new reality obliges us to interpret the word of God afresh, to change reality accordingly, and then to go back and reinterpret the word of God again, and so on'.[25] And so, a 'hermeneutic of liberation', in the light of Sunita and Justin's removal from their home, might reflect on the oppressive aspects of the nativity story, which, in turn, might illuminate God's solidarity with their plight. Any encouragement that might thus be found to endure the privations of the hostel and an insensitive bureaucracy may be given a further boost through the loving and practical support of Sophie, Vimla and the other women. The account of the early Church's commitment to social change in the book of Acts may then be freshly interpreted in relation to Sunita's return to the hostel to reach out to her neighbours up and down the corridor. In such an interpretive endeavour, to quote the Boffs, the Bible is read 'as a book of life, not as a book of strange stories'.[26]

Practical Mediation

The third stage of liberational method flows inexorably from the first two: a sequence that begins in socio-analytical action passes to an active engagement with Scripture and so leads to further liberative action. We have already met something of this action-reflection-action cycle in our discussion of Christian *praxis* in Chapter 6 (see pp. 171–4) and noted the transformative interplay between theory and practice. Stephen Pattison sums up liberation theology's methodology well when he writes, 'Its purpose is to fortify, inspire and inform Christian action within the overarching liberation struggle of the poor', and adds, 'It is thus severely *practical* theology.'[27] And Vimla, once more, can be seen to illustrate the frontline, pragmatic nature of this 'severely practical theology'. Concerning her work to date with the homeless, she said to me, 'We can only make a difference in bite-sized chunks, but even that can bring hope'. This realistic nibbling away at a problem is what the Boffs refer to as 'micro-actions'. However, Vimla's commitment is an expanding one – a commitment that aims not only to help the homeless find a home, but to help them find a sense of community too. By following up and supporting formerly homeless families in their newly acquired homes, it is hoped that 'not just individual families, but children too, and women fleeing domestic violence, given confidence to break out, will all be helped in integrating into the community'. Here is the attempt, in the Boffs' words, to co-ordinate *'micro-actions* with the *macro-system'*,[28] to knit together the personal and the interpersonal, the individual and the communal, the functional and the structural.

Gender and Feminist Theology

Although classical Latin American liberation theology, as we have seen, centres its focus on poverty as the essentially 'infrastructural' form of oppression, a range of other, complementary radical theologies rightly question the particularity of this emphasis. These include theologies that address the struggles of women and men, gays, lesbians and straights – all those who seek liberation from the mindset of a stereotyping and sexist society.[29] Looking, albeit briefly, at feminist theology as representative of these liberational struggles, we can quote Elisabeth Schüssler Fiorenza who challenges liberation theologians to acknowledge that 'their preferential "option" for the poor and oppressed' needs to be seen 'as the option of poor and Third World women because the majority of the poor and exploited today are women and children dependent on women for survival'.[30] Vimla and Sophie would agree with this appraisal in their encounters with homeless families: without denying the depth of struggle of many of the men – feeling disempowered and depressed at the apparent unfairness of their lot – they would see that, typically, the women were the ones who were left in their cramped 'bed-and-breakfast' quarters all day, caring for small children, running the gauntlet of addicts and men on remand in the corridors, and sallying forth from time to time to encounter the long waits, the puzzling paperwork and the bland replies and refusals of officialdom.

There are, of course, many strands in contemporary feminist theology, not least with respect to the relationship between feminism and postmodernity. Some feminists seem to be held by modernity in that, in their critique of its male-dominated, rational and objective metanarrative, they seem to offer an alternative metanarrative – female-centred, irrational and subjective.[31] Once more, we meet a tendency to polarise an understanding of human nature by opposing, in effect, *halacha* with *agada* (see p. 163). Other feminists, without betraying their critique of patriarchy, seek a closer affiliation with postmodern perspectives that celebrate differentness and otherness. Susan Hekman, for example, argues that postmodernity and feminism need each other, in that whereas 'the postmoderns see the error of Enlightenment dualism . . . the feminists complete this critique by defining these dualisms as gendered'.[32] A third position is taken up by Elaine Graham, whose feminist and liberational pastoral practice (see pp. 163–4) adopts a *post*-postmodern approach, in which she holds to postmodernity's rejection of the grand narrative and its celebration of human diversity. At the same time, she resists postmodernity's deconstructive tendencies, offering, rather, a *reconstructive* enterprise that establishes 'conversations between members of localized communities as the benchmark of sustainable norms of truth, value and morality'.[33]

It is in such interchange of life-stories between 'members of localized communities', as we have seen with Vimla and Sunita, that feminist theology faces the hermeneutical challenge. How are 'sustainable norms of truth, value and morality' to be verified in this narrative approach to pastoral and communal care? It is here that Mary Grey points to Schüssler Fiorenza's fourfold pattern of feminist interpretation.[34] First, as with Latin American liberation theology, a *hermeneutic of suspicion* is engaged in – in this case toward the biblical text, which is suspected of a strongly patriarchal mindset. Second, a *hermeneutic of proclamation* serves two purposes: to clarify those passages which threaten to hold women in continuing subjection (as when a battered wife encounters Jesus's call to take up her cross); and to highlight those texts which transcend the Bible's androcentrism (as in Christ's first resurrection appearance to Mary Magdalene). Third, a *hermeneutic of remembrance* in which 'new models of interpretation' enable the reader to perceive women at the centre of 'the biblical community' without forgetting their attendant 'suffering and struggles'. Finally, a *hermeneutic of creative actualisation* aims to take the biblical stories and retell them in the light of a feminist critique.

Such an interpretive approach to Scripture can focus, for example, on the story of Hagar in Genesis 16 and 21. It is here that we have a method that is, in essence, comparable to David Clines's notion of 'reading against the grain' (see p. 119), for most exegetes of these passages will concentrate on the 'with-the-grain' stories of Abraham and Sarah. Hagar, like so many women throughout history, is pushed from pillar to post. Socially, she is marginalised, since she is of servant 'class' and is Egyptian rather than a privileged Hebrew. Sexually, she is disempowered and has to submit to the plans of her owners. Physically, she is abused, flees for her safety and is eventually rendered homeless. And yet, as Mary Grey points out, 'she was one of the first mothers of a promised child, who received a revelation from God':[35] encountering the angel of the Lord, she declared, 'I have now seen the One who sees me' (Gen. 16:13).

It is the interplay between the stories of such as Hagar, Vimla, Claire and Sunita which is the quintessence of feminist theology's ability to cross the boundaries of gender, class and race.[36] Reflecting on her time in Manchester, Heather Walton writes:

> I walk through the streets of Moss Side and a thousand-and-one women's stories leap to heart and mind and soul. Some are easily linked by my scriptural imagination to the precious stories of tradition. Others are not, but still demand their place within a developing Christian pastoral narrative. They are stories relevant to us, owned by us, and useful to us, and they must be told . . . women's voices must be heard.[37]

Culture and Third-Eye Theology

We are all creatures of culture. None of us can escape the pain and privilege of 'enculturation'. This is well illustrated in David Guterson's *Snow Falling On Cedars*. Set on the island of San Piedro off Oregon's Pacific coast it is a story of two communities – one the descendants of European settlers, the other of immigrant Japanese stock. At the unprovoked bombing of Pearl Harbour by Japan in

1941 the island's Japanese men, strawberry farmers and fisher-
men, were rounded up and transported to a work camp in
Montana. One couple, the Imadas, had only been on San Piedro
since the 1920s and were still acutely aware of their Japanese
culture. At the arrest of her husband, Mrs Imada gathered her five
daughters around her to instruct them on the ways of the *hakujin*,
the island's white settlers. She warns the girls of 'the darkness in
the hearts' of the Americans and urges them to remember that
they, the Imadas, are Japanese through and through. Hatsue,
eighteen years of age and the eldest of the daughters, is half in
love with Ishmael Chambers, one of the white islanders. She
responds to their mother's homily by saying that not all the
Americans hate them and resists Mrs Imada's belief that the
hakujin are 'very much different' from the Japanese. Her mother
sums up that perceived difference as follows:

> The whites, you see, are tempted by their egos and have no means to
> resist. We Japanese, on the other hand, *know* our egos are nothing. We
> bend our egos, all of the time, and that is where we differ. That is the
> fundamental difference, Hatsue. We bend our heads, we bow and are
> silent, because we understand that by ourselves, alone, we are nothing
> at all, dust in a strong wind, while the *hakujin* believes his aloneness is
> everything, his separateness is the foundation of his existence. He seeks
> and grasps, seeks and grasps for his separateness, while we see that
> these are distinct paths we are traveling, Hatsue, the *hakujin* and we
> Japanese.

And like the Imadas, caught at the crossroads of two very
different cultures, Christian pastoral and communal carers need
to face the 'distinct paths we are traveling' – whether white
American or Japanese, Afro-Caribbean or Catholic Irish, Xhosa
or Zulu, Aboriginal Australian or British descendant, Malay
Muslim or Chinese Buddhist. Taking Roger Lundin's definition
of 'culture' once more (see p. 66), as that which 'designates that
complex, interlocking network of symbols, practices, and beliefs at
the heart of a society's life',[38] we need to ask how is it that, without
betraying the distincitive pathways to wholeness of the Judaeo-
Christian tradition, cultural boundaries can be crossed in response
to Christ's call to 'make disciples of all nations' (Matt. 28:19).

It is in answer to this question that some theologians, especially
since the Second Vatical Council of the 1960s, have put forward

the notion of *enculturation* (or *inculturation*). Although the term may be used simply as a synomym of 'socialisation', the Jesuit writer Marcello Azevedo defines it in this special sense as 'the dynamic relation between the Christian message and culture or cultures; and an ongoing process of reciprocal and critical inter-action and assimilation between them'.[39] Traditionally, Christian mission has often driven into 'alien' cultures within a one-way system, seeking to impose a Westernised form of Christianity on other peoples with little or no invitation to 'reciprocal and critical interaction'. Vincent J. Donovan, exercised over his call to the Masai of Tanzania, faces the inadequacy of the Western Church's missiology as he realises that these people have 'no word in their language for person or creation or grace or freedom or spirit or immortality'.[40] He finds the way forward through enculturation:

> The way people might celebrate the central truths of Christianity; the way they would distribute the goods of the earth and live out their daily lives; their spiritual, ascetical expression of Christianity if they should accept it; their way of working out the Christian responsibility of the social implications of the gospel – all these things, that is: liturgy, morality, dogmatic theology, spirituality, and social action would be a cultural response to a central, unchanging, supracultural, uninterpreted gospel.[41]

For Choan-Seng Song, writing in the context of Asian spiri-tuality, such crossing of cultural boundaries can be described as offering a 'third-eye' theology, incorporating 'a power of percep-tion and insight that enables [theologians] to grasp the meaning under the surface of things and phenomena'.[42] The term 'third eye' is derived from Buddhism and denotes, according to the Japanese Zen master Daisetz Suzuki, an opening up of inner vision, in which 'we see for the first time into the nature of our own being'.[43] Song contrasts such theological insight with 'a first- or a second-eye theology', whose 'two-dimensionality . . . canvasses a long stretch of terrain, which is the two thousand years of church history colored strongly by Western thought forms and life-styles'.[44] He sums up his bid to free Asian Christians from a Europeanised, second-hand form of Christianity in these words:

> The faith of the Reformation is the faith seen through German eyes. However definitive, influential, and far-reaching the Reformation faith

may have been, there is no reason why Chistians who are not heirs to the German spirit must see and interpret Christian faith through German eyes. Those who are not endowed with German eyes should not be prevented from seeing Christ differently. They must train themselves to see Christ through Chinese eyes, Japanese eyes, Asian eyes, African eyes, Latin American eyes.[45]

Thus third-eye theology, as with all radical theologies, offers a *hermeneutic of suspicion* toward the conventions of traditional Western theology. Seeking a way for Asian Christians 'to sing [their] own theological tune' by listening afresh to the stories – 'old and new' – of the indigenous people, Song views Westernised propositionalism as a theology that 'ironically, has become "disincarnated" ', wherein, rather than ' "the Word become flesh," theology becomes "the flesh become words" '.[46]

In his rediscovery of the language and culture of the people, seeking to discern something of God's 'eternal power and divine nature' (Rom. 1:20) within a common-grace theology, Song gives a number of 'enfleshed' examples of learning to 'see Christ' through Asian eyes. For instance, he points out how, in the Chinese language, one is obliged to declare 'the two words *love* and *pain* almost in the same breath' in the expression 'pain-love' (*thun-ai*).[47] The power of this term is seen, for example, in the intensity of a mother's love for her child, a love whose very expression at times of anguish may hold its object too closely, inflicting unwitting pain, a love that also feels pain deeply in its vehemence.[48] Pain-love is a self-sacrificing love and its zenith is seen in the cross – 'God's excruciating pain-love . . . rooted in the love of the God who bears pain for the world.'[49] And yet, for Song, without denying the uniqueness of Jesus Christ's sacrificial death, echoes of God's pain-love can be heard reverberating in, for instance, the compassion found in the bhakti religion of India and the Shin Buddhism of Japan, which bear 'some *substantial* resemblance to the Christian experience of God's love and grace'.[50]

Ecology and Ecological Theology

We have seen something of the call for pastoral carers to cross boundaries in order to pursue social change with respect to the interweaving concerns of poverty, gender and culture, but we need to see that considerations of the socio-political and socio-economic cannot be divorced from the socio-ecological if a truly reformed community is to be sought. We have referred to the need for a comprehensive creation theology and spirituality a number of times within our exploration of pathways to wholeness and there is no doubt that a fully biblical perspective on Christian journeying will hold the things of creation and community as indivisible. The tragedy is that we have allowed the severance of the material, creaturely and bodily from the realms of the spiritual and psychological for far too long. It seems that, in the contemporary world, it is only within the transition from modernity to postmodernity that humankind can wake up to its arrogant despoliation of the planet. The gross misreading of God's generous mandate to 'fill the earth and subdue it' (Gen. 1:28) as 'ravage the earth and exploit it' has been on an exponential curve within modernity's headstrong rush to acquire, control and consume. It is only within a postmodern, and belated Christian, celebration of difference and otherness that fresh stirrings of ecological concern seem to be gaining momentum – and that often where there seems to be no alternative. As Anthony J. Gittins points out, this recent 'acknowledgment of the madness of such excesses' has related as much to the 'Western discovery of its own "nest fouling"' as to 'the acquisition of wisdom from other traditions and cultures, or a rediscovery of social responsibilities'.[51] Even so, wise birds tidy up fouled nests, even when their environmental hedgerows are fast vanishing.

Gittins also reminds us of a Judaeo-Christian legacy that is faithful to the creator's mandate. Martin Luther, for example, when asked what he would do if he knew that the world would end the next day, replied, 'I would plant a tree in my garden.'[52] Something of the same sense of ecological urgency is seen today in a number of Christian theologies and spiritualities which are seeking the recovery of a holistic view of creational wholeness in the face of a continuing degradation of the earth's resources.[53] And such perspectives cut us down to size, reminding us, on the one hand, of a collective culpability that would rather plunder cosmic space than bring healing to the troubled land at our doorstep and, on the other hand, of a limited pastoral concern that would rather individualise human need than widen its horizons to encompass community and ecology.

Among ecological theologians, Sallie McFague brings a liberational and christological focus that unites our quest to cross the boundaries of humanly contrived dualisms in society and culture. She puts forward a perspective that just as humankind has oppressed the 'old poor' of the underclass, of women and of the culturally different, so humanity, in its greed, rapacity and neglect has oppressed the 'new poor' of the natural order. The breadth of her vision echoes the Pauline hope 'that the creation itself will be liberated from its bondage to decay' (Rom. 8:21):

> The liberating, healing, and inclusive ministry of Jesus that overturns hierarchical dualisms, heals sick bodies, and invites the outcasts to the table should in our time be extended to a new poor – nature. In addition to including oppressed, ailing, and rejected human beings, the Christic paradigm should now be extended to oppressed nature. We human beings in our misuse and exploitation of the natural world have caused nature to be the new poor. Our christology will extend the shape of Jesus' ministry to the scope of the entire planet, taking seriously the ancient belief that the redeemer is the savior of the *entire* creation.[54]

The Way Ahead

In this the most potentially inclusive of our five pathways to wholeness we have a cluster of radical theologies and spiritualities whose wide remit embraces and seeks to liberate the wealth of human communal existence. Without denying the vital roles played by evangelical propositionalism, charismatic and liberal experiential-expressivism and Catholic 'two-dimensional' approaches (see pp. 176–8) in pursuing social change, it seems to me that this fifth pathway looks especially to a cultural-linguistic perspective in Lindbeck's list of categories.[55] Its emphasis on cultural context and linguistic sensibilities is inevitable in its godly calling to cross social and creational boundaries, but, nonetheless, in looking for a way ahead that is faithful to the Judaeo-Christian heritage, it is vital that the desire for communal reformation does not slip into an interpretive praxis devoid of its theological and spiritual roots. Anthony Thiselton warns that such a *socio-pragmatic* hermeneutic, untethered as it is from consistent concepts of justice and mercy, is easy prey for any vested interests within a postmodern world:

> The problem . . . is that pragmatic hermeneutics is *diametrically opposed in practice* to the deepest theoretical concerns which lie behind liberation hermeneutics: those whose readings of texts win the day can only

be the power groups: the most militant, the most aggressive, the most manipulative.[56]

Let us continue, rather, with a *socio-critical* approach, to use Thiselton's alternative term, in which we do not aim to use texts 'instrumentally' to serve pre-determined agendas but 'transcendentally' in order to take seriously contexts of poverty, gender, culture and ecology that would help us 'define and evaluate in what justice would consist'.[57] Let us consider two biblical vocations whose metaphors will help us clarify something of the way forward for Christian social care and transformation: *the prophetic calling* and *the call of wisdom*.

The Prophetic Calling

The enemies of Jeremiah the prophet make plans against him, declaring that 'the teaching of the law by the priest will not be lost, nor will counsel from the wise, nor the word from the prophets' (Jer. 18:18). For Waldemar Janzen, the implication here is that, although 'Jeremiah has accused each of the three professional groups of failure in its own specific and proper calling', he does not deny their value when they are faithful to that calling.[58] As we have considered biblical metaphors of pastoral care, we have already attended to that of *teacher* in biblical counselling, *healer* and *deliverer* in the healing ministries, *shepherd* in pastoral counselling, and those of *desert-dweller*, *soul-friend* and *midwife* in spiritual direction – a mediatorial triad that can be subsumed under the call of the *priest*. Shortly we will examine the role of the *wise one*, but it is that of the *prophet* that can be regarded as of the essence in God's call for social reformation and transformation. Janzen sums up the distinctiveness of the prophetic call as a contrast to the 'subsidiary paradigms' of the priest, the wise one and the king – roles that could exemplify holiness, wisdom and justice respectively:

> It is different in the case of the prophets . . . a prophet could in no way ask others to emulate his or her 'prophetic life.' It was peculiar to the prophetic calling that it was uniquely addressed to certain persons by God. One could not aspire to it as a way of life or imitate those thus called.[59]

This 'peculiar' calling is one that comprises an *exodus spirituality* and a *suffering servanthood*.

All liberative theology which takes seriously the traditions of God's people looks to the great formative story of Israel's exodus from Egypt. Yahweh's stirrings on behalf of his beleaguered nation – 'the cry of the Israelites has reached me, and I have seen the way the Egyptians are oppressing them' (Exod. 3:9) – have given hope to countless abused, neglected and victimised individuals and communities. Padraic Leonard, for example, cites the basic ecclesial communities of the Brazilian poor as focal points of 'an exodus spirituality', wherein God 'invites the masses to become a people – his people' and in which the people respond, 'passing through the purifying desert of suffering and sacrifice'.[60]

Within the Old Testament the Exodus story acts as a template for a nation's ethical stance toward the poor, the widow, the orphan and the ethnic minority, and this stance is deeply embedded in the very nature of Yahweh:

> For the LORD your God is God of gods and Lord of lords, the great God, mighty and awesome, who shows no partiality and accepts no bribes. He defends the cause of the fatherless and the widow, and loves the alien, giving them food and clothing. And you are to love those who are aliens, for you yourselves were aliens in Egypt. Fear the LORD your God and serve him. Hold fast to him and take your oaths in his name. He is your praise. (Deut. 10:17–21)

Thus a covenant people, called out by the God of the oppressed, were to remember their own alienation in a foreign country as a source of compassion for others, whilst they journeyed toward the promised land. Their initial calling and the sustaining of that call was mediated through God's servant Moses, whose ministry, as Brueggemann puts it, 'represents a radical break with the social reality of Pharaoh's Egypt'.[61] That prophetic voice – whose task was 'to nurture, nourish, and evoke a consciousness and perception alternative to the consciousness and perception of the dominant culture'[62] – held out until the reign of Solomon in the tenth century, by which time there had been a profound shift from exodus radicalism to an autocratic mindset whose sole ambition was 'the self-securing of king and dynasty'.[63] By the eighth century the twinned remit of an exodus spirituality – the *covenant* and the *land* – was being denied as rulers and leaders betrayed

Yahweh's pact with Israel and usurped the inheritance of the common people.[64] Amos, Isaiah and Micah railed against the power-brokers, against those who 'covet fields and seize them, and houses, and take them' (Mic. 2:2). Since God's generous gift of grace – 'the Israelite family's claim to its inheritance/land' – was being violated, then that very gift would be withdrawn: exile loomed for those who were 'complacent in Zion' (Amos 6:1).[65]

And yet an exodus theology and spirituality survived – even as Israel was returned, as it were, to its ancient bondage. There was to be no new ethic: once more the prophetic voice sounded: 'Seek the peace and prosperity of the city to which I have carried you into exile. Pray to the Lord for it' (Jer. 29:7). As Janzen puts it, 'Even captivity has room for others, not only the other, but also the foreigner; in this case, the enemy.'[66] And so, as God's people follow a liberative agenda in seeking the 'shalom' (see pp. 27–30) and welfare of their oppressors, a 'new exodus' is inaugurated. Second Isaiah, that great prophet of the exile, declares, 'Comfort, comfort my people, says your God' (Isa. 40:1). In Brueggemann's words, there is to be an 'emergence of amazement' as a new hope is offered: the abused and abusing people have been judged; there is a new responsiveness to the needs of another race and culture; the oppressive might of Babylon is to be overthrown and God's people returned to their homeland.

It is such an exodus spirituality that resonates with the liberational work of Latin American base communities, Asian 'third-eye' theology, and feminist and womanist[67] groups throughout the world. In such endeavours a prophetic voice that is true to the God of Israel will not only seek the restoration of land and inheritance to the dispossessed but be mindful too of the oppressors' need for shalom. And it is here that the exodus perspective draws us toward the new beginnings promised by Second Isaiah, to the prophetic calling of a *suffering servanthood* – expressed initially as 'a personification of the people of Israel' and, in its eventual and greatest fulfilment, in 'the Suffering Servant of the New Covenant, Jesus Christ'. Thus the 'new exodus' leads, through suffering, toward a reformed and liberated community, one in which all barriers of race, class and gender are crossed, where there is 'neither Jew nor Greek, slave nor free, male nor female, for you are all one in Christ Jesus' (Gal. 3:28).

The Call of Wisdom

Vimla, I would suggest, is a true prophet. Her feisty campaigning spirit is not afraid to beard the bureaucratic lion in its den, to take up a strongly argued minority position where the underprivileged are being leaned on and, in her determination to find practical solutions for needy people, to adopt what Brueggemann calls 'the prophetic imagination',[68] daringly promising, for example, a homeless traveller that her newly acquired, empty council house would be filled with furniture by nightfall – through frantic phone-calls, a borrowed van and the generosity of a local church, it was!

And yet, in discussion with Vimla some time later, she pointed out to me that few of her fellow-workers retain their 'campaigning edge', often losing their initial prophetic voice and feeling 'corrupted and compromised' by an unyielding socio-political system. Caught between prophetic idealism and a necessitous pragmatism, is there an alternative and complementary metaphor for the likes of Vimla, Sophie and their 'fellow-women'? It is in the biblical notion of the *wise one* that we began to see the answer.

The development of 'wisdom' among God's people has its origins in comparable traditions among many of ancient Israel's neighbours. At a grass-roots level, there existed a folk wisdom held by the common people – the 'village circle', to use Ludwig Köhler's term.[69] Among such, Abigail, the wife of the well-to-do Nabal, can be considered a 'wise woman'. Hearing of her husband's surly and mean treatment of David's followers, who had been diligently protecting Nabal's livestock and herdsmen, she assembles enough food for an army and rides to meet Israel's future king with her peace-offering. David, having resolved to reek vengeance on Nabal's household, praises her for her 'good judgment' (1 Sam. 25:33) in saving him from bloodshed and a heavy conscience, accepting her generous provisions. In the meantime, Nabal is eating and drinking himself under the table and, the next morning, hearing Abigail's account of her meeting with David, has a heart attack, finally succumbing some ten days later, when 'the Lord struck Nabal and he died' (1 Sam. 25:38).

Here is a living parable of the nature of wisdom and folly, two opposing ways through life, wherein 'The way of fools seems right to them, but the wise listen to advice' (Prov. 12:15). Behind the choice of pathway lies the essence of what a person is really like:

Abigail is known as 'a woman of good understanding' (12:3, AV) and Nabal had presumably earned his nickname 'Fool' (12: 25). As Janzen points out, 'Wisdom and foolishness are seen as dimensions of *character* more than labels of individual actions.'[70]

Although Abigail is representative of the common people's wisdom, there was clearly also a calling for 'certain well-defined ranks among those wise who stood in the king's service'.[71] It is likely, according to Janzen, that specially trained scribes in both the royal court and the Temple were responsible for the literary production of such works as the book of Proverbs (from chapter 10 onward) and also for infusing the legacy of wisdom with 'insights from their own courtly tradition with its strong international flavor'.[72] That boundary-crossing perspective, with its 'expertise in politics and law'[73] became necessitous in the exilic and post-exilic periods, as Ronald E. Clements reflects:

> It is when we pause to think in terms of a situation in which Israel was no longer a nation [with its Temple destroyed and kingship and land lost] that we realize how important it was that concepts of morality and social order should have foundations that stretched beyond the boundaries of nationhood. This is why wisdom became such an important aspect of Israel's intellectual and cultural heritage in the post-exilic age.[74]

Thus God's people learned the universality of God-given social, political and moral instructions whose roots lay in the very creation of the cosmos.[75] It is this sense of the way things are in the world at large – often imponderable, seemingly perverse at times, yet responding to the mandate, 'The fear of the Lord is the beginning of wisdom' (Prov. 9:10) – that is the mainstay of the canonical wisdom literature, Job, Proverbs and Ecclesiastes. Brueggemann takes this universalising perspective within which to explore 'an alternative model for ministry'[76] in today's culture. In contrast to the confrontative, visionary role of the prophet with its quest for justice, and the liturgical, mediatorial role of the priest with its search for holiness, Brueggemann puts forward the role of the 'wise one' as an advisory and supportive ministry that seeks out wisdom. The call of the wise is as a 'second-string' operative who is self-effacing in his or her support of the power base, be it personal, organisational or institutional. It is a ' "ministry at the margin" of the faith community', not given to sermonising or

PATHWAYS TO WHOLENESS

proclamation, but, rather, tackling 'questions of value and reality [that] are wide open and unsettled'.[77] Above all:

> Because it is a ministry of insight which emerges *from below* rather than from above it makes no claim to transcendent authority. It has no commission, speaks for no other, has at its disposal no special power to achieve anything. What it has going for it comes from below, not from above. It relies only on the power to penetrate, the capacity to discern, the shrewdness to see clearly and deeply when others do not. Thus it has no authority than a functional one; no appeal beyond the authenticity of its insight.[78]

And this brings us full circle to my conversation with Vimla. We could see the value of the prophetic spirit and bemoaned the loss of its fire when campaigning zeal gives way to the routine decisions of organisational life. But this is where there is hope, I believe, for the way ahead in the Christian liberative struggle. It is in the dovetailing of the prophetic call with the call of the wise that boundaries of class, wealth, health, gender, age and race can be most effectively crossed. It is here, as the prophet's 'ministry of insight' which is 'from above' can enmesh with that of the wise 'from below', that both God's word and the people's voice can come together. It is where the idealism of the prophet can give way to the pragmatism of wise women and men that the Claires, Sunitas and Justins of this world can experience constructive social change and the wider communities they represent can begin to realise profound socio-political reformation.

Summary

We began the exploration of our fifth and final pathway to wholeness, that of social change which can lead toward a reformed community, in an awareness that this particular route stands out in its offer of an alternative. We can either adopt a 'tourist mentality' toward crying collective human need, bunkered safely, or so we may feel, in the privatised world of individual counselling or spiritual direction; or we can take courage to engage with the disturbing, unquantifiable public world of radical, socio-political praxis. This is not to dismiss the value of personal pastoral care, but to plead, rather, for a more acute and comprehensive contextual awareness on the part of the Christian carer. Thus, whether the care-giver's calling is essentially at the individual level or at a more communal or institutional level, the focus of care at least includes the societal, economic and environmental conditions and settings of the person's or group's life.

Having spelt out this directional challenge we engaged with two representational narratives within communal care: Vimla's story, from the point of view of the carer; and Sunita's story, from someone on the receiving end of such care. We found in the account of Vimla, Sophie and their 'fellow-women', and in the experiences of Sunita, Justin and their children, more than adequate material to demonstrate the desperate need for a Christian liberative practice that is prepared to stand alongside those who feel powerless, engage with the authorities on their behalf and seek constructive change in their social conditions.

Having clarified at least some of the issues that may arise in pastoral endeavours which pursue social change, we then looked at the picture worldwide in a consideration of crossing boundaries of class, gender, culture and ecology. In examining these four areas, which are representative of the human ability to divide, stereotype and reject in any aspect of life, we looked in outline at four overlapping, radical theological perspectives: those of liberation, feminist, third-eye and ecological theology respectively. Once more, we kept in mind our four parameters of each pathway's methodology – doctrinal stance, use of Scripture, metaphor of ministry, and spirituality. Having established a tendency for these radical theologies to be characterised by a cultural-linguistic approach to doctrine and a use of Scripture that engaged a powerful 'hermeneutic of suspicion', we then put forward the appropriateness for this pathway of not only the metaphor of the prophet, and its attendant exodus spirituality, but that of the wise one, and its accompanying spirituality of wisdom and godly pragmatism.

Once more, Peter Selby reminds us that we have a choice. We can either stir ourselves from life's deckchairs and sun-loungers and engage with the struggles of those we take for granted, whether they are the decision-makers and power-brokers of our collective journey, or the rank and file that sweats in the engine rooms below deck. Or we can continue as pastoral tourists, en-route yes, but quite content to exchange pleasantries and lend an occasional hand to the individuals of 'our set', as the situation may demand. As Selby puts it:

> We either do our own acting, thinking, feeling – or we get somebody else to do it for us; they either think or decide or act for us, if they are those to whom we have handed over our power of historic decision, or else they become sad, or sick, or imprisoned for us if they are those to whom we have handed over the work of suffering.[79]

May we, as Christian pastoral carers, act, think and feel liberationally, prophetically and with godly wisdom.

CONCLUSION

The ineffable is as much an integral part of the human mode of being-in-the-world as is the linguistic net in which one tries . . . to catch it.

Zygmunt Bauman[1]

Throughout this book we have been reminded that, in Korzybski's words, 'a map is not the territory'. As we have surveyed the 'territory' of contemporary life in Part I – in terms of process and goal, journey and story, cultural setting and the hermeneutics of both text and life – we have engaged with the rich, and sometimes daunting, complexity of society's transitions from modernity to postmodernity. Delineating the 'map' of pathways to wholeness in Part II in terms of Christian pastoral care, undergirded by pastoral theology and psychology, has been a more particularising affair as we have journeyed with five distinct yet overlapping clusters of methodology: biblical counselling, the healing and deliverance ministries, pastoral counselling, spiritual direction and the quest for social change. Yet the map is *not* the territory and we need now, in our concluding section, to return ourselves to the untidy, frustrating and yet infinitely rewarding enterprise of everyday living in a postmodern world that continues to entice and bewilder in turns.

What are we to say, by way of summary, concerning Christian pastoral care within the strictures and opportunities of postmodernity? Broadly, we have noted two polarising tendencies among pathways to wholeness: an inclination to step back from the postmodern agenda into a systematising propositionalism which seeks to reclaim 'the faith once delivered' but, at the same time, gets caught in the web of modernity's elevation of rationality and foundationalism; and an assimilative approach which uncritically welcomes postmodernity's deconstructionism, antifoundationalism and pluralism without, it seems, spotting the inevitable slide toward relativism and nihilism. Is there a third way that will enable us, through dialogue and a 'third-eye' perceptiveness, to hold on to the timeless truths of the Judaeo-Christian grand narrative and, at the same time, discern in the postmodern bid for 'otherness' and 'difference' perspectives that can enrich our pathways to wholeness? J. Richard Middleton and Brian J. Walsh put forward a constructive directional thrust when they write:

> Just as Israel after exile could not simply go back to its prior life in the land, to the status quo of temple, monarchy and guaranteed security, so we are not looking for a naive return to some modern or premodern Christian ideal. Neither a Dionysian embrace of chaos nor a fearful imposition of a prior orientation will do. We need to come through our disorientation to a reorientation, a return to our biblical roots, that propels us forward to grapple with life in a postmodern culture. Rejecting both postmodern abandonment and a myopic conservative retrenchment, we desire . . . a renewed encounter with the historic Christian faith that takes seriously where we have come historically. It is only this sort of reorientation that will be able to provide us with a genuine hope and critical guidance as we move into the twenty-first century.[2]

We have sought in this book such a way ahead, a route that seeks a 'reorientation' that is both true to pastoral care's 'biblical roots' and its vital part in the story of 'the historic Christian faith'. Even so, does our consideration of pathways to wholeness presuppose a major concession to postmodernity's thirst for an endless succession of alternatives in life's journeying? As Paul Goodliff, writing in the context of pastoral care and postmodern culture, says, 'Jesus Christ did not say, "I am a Way, a truth for those who choose to see things that way" but "I am the Way, the Truth, and the Life." It is this scandal of particularity that contradicts postmodern relativism.'[3]

In answer to Goodliff's rightly made point, I would state that, in our critique of the five pathways, we have aimed throughout to counter the claim that can be made by any one of them: the totalising claim that this particular methodology – be it one of counselling, healing, spiritual direction or social change – is *the* pathway to wholeness. The very plurality of pathways is a reflection of human differentness in temperament, experience, emphasis, style, understanding and objective and, more fundamentally, of the richly varied and mysterious ways in which the

God of surprises draws out human responsiveness in its theologies and spiritualities.

In all this we have returned again and again to the trinitarian nature of the Godhead, a nature whose perichoretic interrelatedness invites us to journey toward wholeness in relationality and community. It is as we have explored the kaleidoscopic range of metaphor, doctrinal approach, use of Scripture and spirituality among the five pathways that we have seen some reflection of the multifaceted face of God. Those facets come into sharpest focus incarnationally, in the face of Christ Jesus, 'the radiance of God's glory and the exact representation of his being, sustaining all things by his powerful word' (Heb. 1:3). It is on this christological note that I would like to conclude this book as we summarise the composite picture of pathways to wholeness in the pastoral calling of the One who declared his own pathway as authoritative.

It is Waldemar Janzen who, I believe, gives us a key to understand something of the exemplary nature of Jesus Christ's life, character, words and actions in such a way that is helpful in our attempt to draw a map of pastoral care within postmodernity's bewilderingly configured territory. In his comprehensive guide to the Old Testament's 'ethical message' for today's Christians[4] Janzen utilises the notion of the *paradigm*: 'For our purposes . . . paradigm will be used as a personally and holistically conceived image of a model (e.g., a wise person, good king) that imprints itself immediately and nonconceptually on the characters and actions of those who hold it.'[5]

Such influential paradigmatic images are part of everyday life, where we may internalise such concepts as the 'good neighbour', 'loyal friend', 'honest broker', 'wise pastor' or 'careful driver'. Before the Israelites' 'inner eye', Janzen argues, 'stood a vivid, lifelike yet ideal family member, worshiper, wise person, king, or prophet'. Such figures, culled from Israel's ancient stories, shape the personal and communal lives of God's people, reaching their paradigmatic acme in the person of Jesus Christ, who both fulfilled the messianic promise of 'one greater than' his godly forerunners[6] and, at the same time, brought the perspective of suffering servanthood to his singular callings:

[The] prophetic paradigm . . . became foundational for the suffering yet vindicated Servant Jesus Christ and the suffering yet redeemed community founded by him. Though Jesus Christ also embraced paradigmatically the offices of king, priest, and sage, these were qualitatively transformed by the attributes of suffering and redeemed servant. He was the lowly king; the self-sacrificing priest; the bringer of a wisdom not of this world. Above all, he was the Son of God, as Israel had been God's son. In that role he was the embodiment of Israel.[7]

And so, finally, as members of 'the suffering yet redeemed community founded by [Christ]', in continuity with that Israel which 'had been God's son', let us exercise our didactic, healing, shepherdly, priestly, prophetic and sapiential callings ever mindful of 'the suffering yet vindicated Servant Jesus Christ'. Whether our pastoral calling is that of counsellor, healer, spiritual director or as an agent of social, political or ecological change, let us, in the company of those we seek to help and those whose faithful lives are a resource and inspiration to us, trudge, stride or run ever onwards on our pathways to wholeness,

looking to Jesus the pioneer and perfecter of our faith, who for the sake of the joy that was set before him endured the cross, disregarding its shame, and has taken his seat at the right hand of the throne of God. (Heb. 12:2, NRSV)

NOTES

Preface

1 Michael Balint (1896–1970) was of the Hungarian school of psycho-analysis. He and his third wife Enid did a great deal to encourage a psychotherapeutic sensibility within general practice.
2 The momentum behind the Swanwick conferences has been influen-tial, both directly and indirectly, on a number of published works, including Francis Bridger and David Atkinson, *Counselling in Context: Developing a Theological Framework* (London: HarperCollins, 1994); Margaret Gill, *Free to Love: Sexuality and Pastoral Care* (London: HarperCollins, 1994); Paul Goodliff, *Care in a Confused Climate: Pastoral Care and Postmodern Culture* (London: Darton, Longman & Todd, 1998); Roger F. Hurding, *Roots and Shoots: A Guide to Counsel-ling and Psychotherapy* (London: Hodder & Stoughton, 1985); Roger F. Hurding, *The Bible and Counselling* (London: Hodder & Stoughton, 1992); Anne Long, *Listening* (London: Darton, Longman & Todd, 1990); Alistair Ross, *An Evaluation of Clinical Theology and its Con-tribution to Pastoral Theology and Training 1958–1969* (Oxford: Clinical Theology Association, 1994); and Alistair Ross, *Evangelicals in Exile: Wrestling with Theology and the Unconscious* (London: Darton, Long-man & Todd, 1997). Of these, Goodliff's masterly overview of pastoral care and postmodern culture is the one that resonates most with the subject matter of *Pathways to Wholeness*.
3 See Chapter 5 for an appraisal of Boisen's contribution to pastoral care and counselling.

Introduction

1 Alfred Korzybski, *Science and Sanity: An Introduction to Non-Aristo-telian Systems and General Semantics* (4th ed.; Lakeville, CT: The International Non-Aristotelian Library Publishing Company, 1958), pp. 58, 750.
2 Korzybski points to the parallels between maps and language in *Science and Sanity*, p. 58, as follows:

> A map is *not* the territory it represents, but, if correct, it has a *similar structure* to the territory, which accounts for its usefulness. If the map could be ideally correct, it would include, in a reduced scale, the map of the map; the map of the map, of the map; and so on, endlessly . . .
>
> If we reflect upon our languages, we find that at best they must be considered *only as maps*. A word is *not* the object it represents; and languages exhibit also this peculiar self-reflexiveness, that we can analyse languages by linguistic means.

3 Another important analysis of the need to reappraise the concepts of map and territory is given in Geoff King, *Mapping Reality: An Exploration of Cultural Cartographies* (London: Macmillan Press, 1996), where the author argues that the distinctions between them have always been arbitrary and, as J. Z. Smith also reasons, subject to Western imperialism. King makes the point that postmodernity blurs these distinctions further so that, to quote Jean Baudrillard, 'Henceforth, it is the map that precedes the territory . . .'; see King, p. 1.

4 Fritjof Capra, *The Tao of Physics: An Exploration of the Parallels Between Modern Physics and Eastern Mysticism* (3rd ed.; London: HarperCollins, 1992), p. 35.

5 ibid., p. 36.

6 ibid., p. 35.

7 J. Z. Smith, *Map Is Not Territory: Studies in the History of Religions* (Leiden: E. J. Brill, 1978), p. 292. Chapter 13 of Smith's book, titled 'Map is Not Territory', is his inaugural lecture on receiving a chair as Willon Benton Professor of Religion and the Human Sciences at The College, University of Chicago, in May 1974.

8 ibid. p. 294.

9 James George Frazer, *Totemism and Exogamy* (London, 1910), vol. 4, p. 61, quoted in Smith, *Map*, p. 296.

10 Smith, *Map*, pp. 296–7.

11 ibid., p. 309.

12 Sallie McFague, *Models of God: Theology for an Ecological, Nuclear Age* (London: SCM Press, 1987), p. 27.

Chapter 1 Pathways to Wholeness: Process and Goal

1 Padmasani J. Gallup, 'Pastoral Counselling in the Hindu Cultural Context' in Otto Stange (ed.), *Pastoral Care and Context* (Amsterdam: VU University Press, 1992), p. 78.

2 Ninian Smart, *The Religious Experience of Mankind* (London: Collins, 1971), p. 215.

3 ibid., p. 212.

4 Fritjof Capra, *The Tao of Physics: An Exploration of the Parallels between*

Modern Physics and Eastern Mysticism (3rd ed.; London: HarperCollins, 1992), pp. 41–2.

5 Gai Eaton, *Islam and the Destiny of Man* (London: George Allen & Unwin, 1985), p. 190. Eaton, a convert to Islam, writes powerfully of the 'human paradox' in relation to Islamic teaching and practice. He strongly emphasises a close link between disbelief, the ephemerality of non-believers' 'works' and a loss of reality: such a personality 'is cut off from its own centre, has a shadowy quality and the works of shadows can have no substance'. The chief sins in the Islamic lexicon, he writes, are *kufr*, meaning both 'unbelief' and 'ingratitude', the two inexorably linked, and *shirk*, associating other 'gods' with Allah (p. 191).

6 For a sympathetic handling of the Muslim-Christian dialogue, see Michael Nazir Ali, *Frontiers in Muslim-Christian Encounter* (Oxford: Regnum Books, 1987). He sees the Qur'an as a 'bridge' to this dialogue and writes:

> Surely we can accept the 'religious interrogative' of the *Qur'an* as a heart-cry and as genuine? We can accept that the *Qur'an* contains profound reflection on God's revelation of himself in nature and in conscience; we can accept that the *Qur'an* contains an accurate record of some biblical events; but we cannot accept it as the norm or standard by which all revelation is to be judged. (p. 128)

7 Eaton, *Islam*, p. 186, quoting Qur'an 33.6.

8 ibid., p. 189, quoting Qur'an 59.19.

9 ibid., p. 199.

10 I am indebted here to Smart, *Religious Experience*, pp. 508–20 and Fazlur Rahman, *Islam* (London: Weidenfeld and Nicolson, 1966), pp. 130–7.

11 Smart, *Religious Experience*, p. 520.

12 The profound influence of Platonic and Aristotelian philosophy on Western thought is well recognised. For example, Mary Stewart Van Leeuwen, in *The Person in Psychology: A Contemporary Christian Appraisal* (Leicester: Inter-Varsity Press, 1985), acknowledges the influence of Plato's 'innate ideas' – such as 'space, time, number, and causality' – on modern psychology (p. 33) and Aristotle's four-step method of 'observation, classification, intuitive abstraction, and deduction' in shaping contemporary scientific inquiry (p. 37).

13 Colin Brown, in *Christianity and Western Thought: A History of Philosophers, Ideas and Movements*, vol. 1 (Leicester: Inter-Varsity Press, 1990), p. 173, points out that, whereas 'rationalism' in its everyday sense tends to edit out the supernatural, rationalism as a 'technical, philosophical' term does not necessarily do so. He writes:

> The rationalists of the seventeenth and eighteenth centuries differed widely among themselves in the way they worked out their

different systems. But common to all was a belief in the rationality of the universe and the power of reason to grasp it. Behind all the complex machinery of nature there was a rational mind, and this could be known by the right use of reason.

14 From the preface of Isaac Newton, *Philosophiae Naturalis Principia Mathematica* (1687), cited in Brown, *Christianity*, p. 218.

15 Quoted in Brown, *Christianity*, pp. 285–6.

16 For a full examination of the four systems of psychology, see Roger F. Hurding, *Roots and Shoots: A Guide to Counselling and Psychotherapy* (London: Hodder & Stoughton, 1985). For other comprehensive surveys of psychology, psychotherapy and counselling from Christian perspectives, see Van Leeuwan, *The Person*; Stanton L. Jones and Richard E. Butman, *Modern Psychotherapies: A Comprehensive Christian Appraisal* (Downers Grove, IL: Inter-Varsity Press, 1991); and Paul D. Meier, Frank B. Minirth, Frank B. Wichern, and Donald E. Ratcliff, *Introduction to Psychology and Counseling: Christian Perspectives and Applications* (2nd ed.; Tunbridge Wells: Monarch, 1991).

17 On the cardinal methodologies of behaviourism and neo-behaviourism, see, for example, Richard Nelson-Jones, *The Theory and Practice of Counselling Psychology* (London: Holt, Rinehart & Winston, 1982), pp. 107–63.

18 For a more detailed appraisal of these methodologies, see Hurding, *Roots and Shoots*, pp. 75–105.

19 C. G. Jung, *Two Essays on Analytical Psychology*, vol. 7, tr. R. F. C. Hull, *The Collected Works of C. G. Jung*, ed. H. Read, M. Fordham and G. Adler (London: Routledge & Kegan Paul, 1953), para. 227.

20 See H. P. Rickman, *Wilhelm Dilthey: Pioneer of the Human Studies* (London: Paul Elek, 1979), pp. 163–79, where the influence of Dilthey's thought on the philosophers Edmund Husserl and Martin Heidegger, the sociologist Max Weber, and the hermeneutician Hans-Georg Gadamer and, through him, the theologian Jürgen Habermas, is clearly argued.

21 Kurt Goldstein, 'Organismic Approach to the Problem of Motivation', *Transactions of New York Academic Sciences*, vol. 9, 1947, p. 228, quoted in Robert S. Woodworth, *Contemporary Schools of Psychology* (8th ed.; London: Methuen & Co., 1951), p. 237.

22 See Abraham H. Maslow, *Motivation and Personality* (2nd ed.; New York: Harper & Row, 1970), pp. 164–9.

23 ibid., pp. 35–57.

24 Abraham H. Maslow, *Toward a Psychology of Being* (2nd ed.; New York: Van Nostrand Reinhold, 1968), p. 25.

25 Maslow, *Motivation*, p. xxii.

26 Maslow, *Psychology of Being*, pp. iii–iv.

27 For a fuller account of the early debate in the history of Gestalt psychology, see Woodworth, *Contemporary Schools*, pp. 120–51.

28 Frederick S. Perls, Ralph F. Hefferline, and Paul Goodman, *Gestalt Therapy: Excitement and Growth in the Human Personality* (3rd ed.; New York: Souvenir Press, 1972), pp. 25–6.

29 Vernon Van De Riet, Margaret P. Korb and John Jeffrey Gorrell, *Gestalt Therapy: An Introduction* (New York: Pergamon Press, 1980), p. xii.

30 For more detailed overviews of Gestalt therapy, see Petrushka Clarkson, *Gestalt Counselling in Action* (London: Sage Publications, 1989); Hurding, *Roots and Shoots*, pp. 199–207, and 'Gestalt Therapy' in *NDCEPT*, pp. 407–8; Malcolm Parlett and Faye Page, 'Gestalt Therapy' in Windy Dryden (ed.), *Individual Therapy: A Handbook* (Psychotherapy Handbooks; Milton Keynes: Open University Press, 1990), pp. 175–98; and Vernon Van De Reit in 'Gestalt Psychology and Psychotherapy' in *DPCC*, pp. 458–60.

31 Edgar Rubin, professor at the University of Copenhagen and writing in 1915, was perhaps the first to bring the concepts of *figure* and *ground* to the attention of the early Gestalt psychologists.

32 See, for example, Ian Davidson, *Here and Now: An Approach to Christian Healing through Gestalt* (London: Darton, Longman & Todd, 1991).

33 Clarkson, *Gestalt Counselling*, p. 17.

34 For more detailed overviews of Assagioli and his methodology, see Hurding, *Roots and Shoots*, pp. 155–64 and Douglas Mathers, 'Psychosynthesis' in David Jones (ed.), *Innovative Therapy: A Handbook* (Psychotherapy Handbooks; Buckingham: Open University Press, 1994), pp. 69–83.

35 Mathers in Jones, *Innovative Therapy*, p. 75.

36 Roberto Assagioli, *Psychosynthesis: A Manual of Principles and Techniques* (London: Turnstone Books, 1975), p. 21.

37 Mathers, 'Psychosynthesis', p. 75.

38 Assagioli, *Psychosynthesis*, p. 206, where he writes, 'The first three books of *The Imitation of Christ* . . . appear clearly to be a dialogue between the aspiring personality and the Self as the Inner Christ.'

39 ibid., p. 249.

40 ibid., p. 30.

41 Revelation 21:1.

42 Hartmut Beck and Colin Brown, 'Peace' in *NIDNTT*, vol. 2, p. 777.

43 ibid., p. 779.

44 See, also, Matthew 5:43–8; and Luke 6:27–36.

45 For examples of transcultural and cosmic levels of peace, brought through Christ's redeeming work, see Ephesians 2:11–22 for the former and Colossians 1:15–20 for the latter.

46 See, for example, the almost invariable formula, 'Grace and peace to you from God our Father and from the Lord Jesus Christ' in the opening verses of Paul's epistles, as well as 'Grace and peace be yours

in abundance' in 1 Peter 1:2 and 2 Peter 1:2 and 'Mercy, peace and love be yours in abundance' in Jude 2.

47 See Joann Wolski Conn, *Spirituality and Personal Maturity* (Mahwah, NJ: Paulist Press, 1989), pp. 136–43. Conn's case histories, although fictitious, are inspired by her pastoral ministry. Janice's handling of Annemarie's crisis is backed by her understanding of the writings of John of the Cross on 'spiritual darkness' and of Robert Kegan's notion of human maturation in Robert Kegan, *The Evolving Self: Problem and Process in Human Development* (Cambridge, MA: Harvard University Press, 1982).

48 Conn, *Spirituality*, p. 140.

49 Reinier Schippers in *NIDNTT*, vol. 2, p. 59.

50 ibid., p. 60. For a more detailed exposition of Plato's and Aristotle's stance on ethics, see Brown, *Christianity*, pp. 31–7 and pp. 48–9 respectively.

51 See *NIDNTT*, vol. 2, pp. 59, 64.

52 On the conjectured link between 'God Almighty' and 'God the Mountain One', see Derek Kidner, *Genesis: An Introduction and Commentary* (London: The Tyndale Press 1967), pp. 128–9, where he writes, 'More recently Shaddai has been equated with "mountain" . . . but there is no universal agreeement. A better guide is the study of its use, and this confirms the familiar emphasis on might, particularly over against the frailty of man.'

53 Frederick W. Bush, 'Images of Israel: The People of God in the Torah' in *Studies in Old Testament Theology*, ed. R. L. Hubbard Jr, R. K. Johnston and R. P. Meye (Dallas: Word, 1992), p. 102.

54 ibid., p. 101.

55 Wiord Popkes, 'New Testament Principles of Wholeness', *Evangelical Quarterly*, vol. 64, 1992, p. 323.

56 See *NIDNTT*, vol. 2, pp. 64–5, where Schippers argues that the 'eschatological and anthropological' aspects of this word-grouping 'are bound up with the general areas of meaning associated with *telos* on the one hand and *teleios* on the other'.

57 See Hans-Georg Link in *NIDNTT*, vol. 2, pp. 57–8.

58 ibid., p. 65.

59 See also 1 Corinthians 2:6, 14:20; Philippians 3:15; Colossians 1:28, 4:12; James 1:4, where *teleios* is rendered mature, complete, blameless, implying growth and progress toward 'adulthood'.

60 *NIDNTT*, vol. 2, p. 65.

61 Popkes, 'Wholeness', p. 322.

62 Jim Crumley, *Among Mountains* (Edinburgh: Mainstream Publishing, 1993), p. 12.

63 Walter Brueggemann, *The Bible and Postmodern Imagination: Texts under Negotiation* (London: SCM Press, 1993), pp. 21–5.

64 ibid., pp. 24–5.

65 ibid., p. 25.

Chapter 2 Pathways to Wholeness: Journey and Story

1 Carlos Castaneda, *The Teachings of Don Juan*, quoted in Fritjof Capra, *The Tao of Physics* (3rd ed., London: HarperCollins, 1992), p. 21.
2 John S. Dunne, *The Reasons of the Heart: A Journey into Solitude and Back Again into the Human Circle* (London: SCM Press, 1978), p. ix.
3 George Seaver, *Edward Wilson of the Antarctic: Naturalist and Friend* (London: John Murray, 1937), p. 1.
4 ibid., pp. 245–50.
5 Apsley Cherry-Garrard, *The Worst Journey in the World* (Harmondsworth: Penguin, 1948), p. 297.
6 John 15:5.
7 Cormac McCarthy, *The Crossing* (London: Macmillan, 1995), pp. 184–6.
8 ibid., p. 186.
9 See Günter Ebel in *NIDNTT*, vol. 3, pp. 935–42, where he points out the frequent usage in classical Greek literature of *hodos* to denote the two ways of 'virtue' and 'badness', a theme echoed and extended, shifting from an emphasis on 'the ethical problem of conduct' to 'the question of life and death, salvation or destruction', in Jesus's teaching on the 'two ways' and 'two gates' in the Sermon on the Mount (pp. 936, 940).
10 Stephen C. Barton, *The Spirituality of the Gospels* (London: SPCK, 1992), pp. 58–9.
11 ibid., p. 59.
12 See Acts 22:4 and 24:14.
13 Walter Brueggemann, *The Bible and Postmodern Imagination: Texts under Negotiation* (London: SCM Press, 1993), pp. 53–4.
14 ibid., p. 53.
15 ibid., p. 64.
16 Dunne, *Reasons*, p. 151.
17 ibid., p. 147.
18 ibid., p. 148.
19 Jon Nilson, 'Doing Theology by Heart: John S. Dunne's Theological Method', *Theological Studies*, vol. 48, 1987, pp. 65–86.
20 ibid., pp. 68–9, quoting 'Spiritual Adventure: The Emergence of a New Theology', John Dunne, interviewed by Kenneth L. Woodward, *Psychology Today*, vol. 11, no. 8, 1978, pp. 90 and 50 respectively.
21 See John S. Dunne, *A Search for God in Time and Memory* (London: Sheldon Press, 1975), pp. 33–4, where he sees the 'quest for the way, the truth, and the life' taking different forms in different periods of history 'according to the different prevailing forms of thought and life'. He examines three examples: the New Testament period as a 'story of deeds' in which Paul's quest carries him from Pharisaism to Christianity; a 'later period' as a 'story of experience' in which

Augustine moves from Manichaeism; and the modern period in which Kierkegaard's journey takes him from Hegelianism.

22 Dunne, *Reasons*, p. 149.

23 ibid., p. 150.

24 ibid., p. 149.

25 ibid., p. 151.

26 John S. Dunne, *The Church of the Poor Devil* (New York: Macmillan, 1982).

27 John S. Dunne, *The House of Wisdom* (San Francisco: Harper & Row, 1985).

28 Nilson, 'Doing Theology', pp. 79–80.

29 Dunne, *House of Wisdom*, p. xi.

30 Nilson, 'Doing Theology', p. 86.

31 John S. Dunne, *A Search for God in Time and Memory* (London: Sheldon Press, 1975), pp. 7–8.

32 For a useful discussion on 'metanarratives', 'narratives on a grand scale' (p. 130), with respect to biblical hermeneutics, see Mark Hargreaves, 'Telling Stories: Narrative and Biblical Authority', *Anvil*, vol. 13, no. 2, 1996, pp. 127–39. We will pick up with this debate more fully in Chapters 3 and 5.

33 Narrative theology, with its main rise to prominence occurring from the early 1970s onwards, is seen to have a precursor in H. Richard Niebuhr's *The Meaning of Revelation*, first published in 1941, where he introduces the notion of 'the story of our life'. There have been a number of analyses of the development of the discipline of narrative theology including those in Stanley Hauerwas and L. Gregory Jones, *Why Narrative? Readings in Narrative Theology* (Grand Rapids, MI: Eerdmans, 1989); and George W. Stroup, *The Promise of Narrative Theology* (London: SCM Press, 1981). Stroup (pp. 71–84) describes three 'broad camps': those writers, mainly in the United States and Germany and including James B. Wiggins and Johann Baptist Metz, who use 'narrative' as an introduction to religion, seeking to reinterpret traditional doctrines through the 'category of narrative'; those, including James William McClendon Jr, Stanley Hauerwas, John Dunne and Stephen Crites, who emphasise the importance of 'life-story and lived convictions'; and those who work primarily on 'biblical narrative', including Hans Frei, Brevard Childs and Sallie McFague. Of this third focus, Stroup points out the historic influence of the first two chapters of Eric Auerbach, *Mimesis: The Representation of Reality in Western Literature*, tr. Willard R. Trask (Princeton University Press, 1968), originally published in 1946, where the author argues that we are to fit our lives into the world of the biblical text, rather than the reverse. We will address narrative theology in this third category more fully in Chapter 4.

34 *OCEL*, p. 680.

35 Stanley Hauerwas, *A Community of Character: Toward a Constructive Christian Social Ethic* (Notre Dame, IN: University of Notre Dame Press, 1981), p. 94.

36 ibid., p. 96.

37 Hauerwas and Jones, *Why Narrative?* p. 5. In the introduction of this book, Hauerwas and Jones challenge the loose and oversimplified usage of 'narrative' and 'story' (pp. 1–5) without denying that narrative is 'central to theological and ethical reflection' (p. 1).

38 Hargreaves, 'Telling Stories', p. 128.

39 Hauerwas, *Community*, p. 10.

40 ibid., pp. 12–35.

41 ibid., p. 50.

42 ibid., p. 12.

43 ibid., pp. 13–14.

44 Richard Adams, *Watership Down* (Harmondsworth: Penguin, 1974), p. 102.

45 ibid., pp. 37–40.

46 Hauerwas, *Community*, pp. 34–5.

47 ibid., p. 37.

48 Two works by these authors of particular relevance to our discussion are Charles V Gerkin, *Living Human Documents: Re-Visioning Pastoral Counseling in a Hermeneutical Mode* (Nashville: Abingdon Press, 1984) and Donald Capps, *Pastoral Care and Hermeneutics* (Philadelphia: Fortress Press, 1984).

49 Gerkin, *Documents*, p. 112.

50 Erik H. Erikson, *Identity: Youth and Crisis* (London: Faber & Faber, 1968), p. 92.

51 Gerkin, *Documents*, p. 114.

52 Hauerwas, *Community*, p. 148.

53 Stroup, *Promise*, pp. 112–13.

54 ibid., p. 115.

55 ibid., pp. 115–16.

56 ibid., p. 116.

57 ibid., p. 171.

58 Ganzevoort here refers to Paul Ricoeur, 'L'identité Narrative' in P. Bühler and J. F. Habermacher (eds.), *La Narration* (Genève: Labor et Fides, 1988). We will consider Ricoeur's profound influence on narrative theology and biblical hermeneutics in Chapter 5.

59 R. Ruard Ganzevoort, 'Investigating Life-Stories: Personal Narratives in Pastoral Psychology', *Journal of Psychology and Theology*, vol. 21, no. 4, 1993, p. 277.

60 See ibid., p. 281.

61 Carolyn J. Bohler, 'The Use of Storytelling in the Practice of Pastoral Counseling', *Journal of Pastoral Care*, vol. 41, no. 1, 1987, pp. 63–71.

62 ibid., p. 67.

63 Here Bohler is referring to Henry Close, 'Metaphor in Pastoral Care', *Journal of Pastoral Care*, vol. 38, no. 4, 1984, p. 298. She also mentions (pp. 68–9) three other ways 'to engender twists of meaning': reframing the situation, where the counsellor draws a different picture of a narrative identity than the conventionally accepted one; asking the counsellee to retell the story from an alternative point of view (in our case, Louise to try to recount the story from, say, Mark's viewpoint); and, similarly, encouraging the counsellee to imagine herself in another perspective as she prays.

64 Bohlen, 'Use of Storytelling', p. 70.

65 W. A. H. Kox, *From Crisis to Christ* (Utrecht: Dissertation State University) in Ganzevoort, 'Life-Stories', p. 278.

66 Ganzevoort, 'Life-Stories', p. 278.

67 ibid., p. 283.

68 ibid.

69 Hauerwas, *Community*, p. 91.

Chapter 3 Pathways Today: Taking our Bearings

1 Karl Marx, *The Communist Manifesto*, quoted in Marshall Berman, *All That Is Solid Melts Into Air: The Experience of Modernity* (New York: Simon & Schuster, 1982), p. 89. See note 25.

2 *CED*, p. 387. More commonly, of course, the word 'cult' has the more perjorative sense of a 'sect' or, more specifically, 'a quasi-religious organisation using devious psychological techniques to gain and control adherents'.

3 Genesis 2:15.

4 Roger Lundin, *The Culture of Interpretation: Christian Faith and the Postmodern World* (Grand Rapids, MI: Eerdmans, 1993), p. 3, following Raymond Williams, *Keywords: A Vocabulary of Culture and Society* (New York: Oxford University Press, 1976), pp. 76–7, 80–1.

5 David W. Augsburger, *Pastoral Counseling Across Cultures* (Philadelphia: Westminster Press, 1986), p. 82.

6 H. Richard Niebuhr, *Christ and Culture* (New York: Harper & Brothers, 1951). See Roger F. Hurding, *Roots and Shoots: A Guide to Counselling and Psychotherapy* (London: Hodder & Stoughton, 1985), pp. 263–73, for a fuller discussion on the potential of Niebuhr's insights in the integration of psychology and theology.

7 Charles H. Kraft, *Christianity in Culture: A Study in Dynamic Biblical Theologizing in Cross-Cultural Perspective* (Maryknoll, NY: Orbis Books, 1979), pp. 104, 113.

8 ibid., pp. 104–15.

9 Niebuhr and Kraft are both critical of the 'Christ/God-against-culture' stance and both refer to the Johannine writings: Niebuhr,

quoting C. H. Dodd, sees 1 John as essentially 'Christ-against-culture', though not in the position's 'most radical form' (pp. 46-9); Kraft argues that the position adopts the 'serious error' of misreading John by interpreting *kosmos* negatively (p. 105).

10 Kraft, *Christianity in Culture*, p. 108.

11 Niebuhr, *Christ and Culture*, p. 145.

12 ibid., p. 154.

13 ibid., p. 191.

14 ibid., p. 194.

15 Kraft, *Christianity in Culture*, pp. 113–15.

16 Brian J. Walsh and J. Richard Middleton, *The Transforming Vision: Shaping a Christian World View* (Downers Grove, IL: InterVarsity Press, 1984), pp. 55–6. Although many see the cultural mandate to 'subdue the earth' as licensing human domination and despoliation of the planet, I join Walsh and Middleton in gainsaying that interpretation. They point out that the 'two fold task given to Adam was to develop and to *take care of*, or *preserve*, the garden. The intent of the biblical mandate is quite distinct from the modern Western vision of human conquest and exploitation of nature' (p. 58). We will return to this perspective later in the book.

17 David Harvey, *The Condition of Post-Modernity: An Enquiry into the Origins of Cultural Change* (Oxford: Blackwell, 1990), p. 99.

18 Anthony Giddens, *Modernity and Self-Identity: Self and Society in the Late Modern Age* (Cambridge: Polity Press, 1991), p. 146. Obviously, taking the example of the 'labouring poor' leaves out great slices of premodern Britain. However, Mary Abbott, researching English families from the sixteenth century to the end of the Great War, charts the rise in poverty through the Stuart and Georgian periods so that, in 1837 'the average Englishman was a farm labourer' and 'the average Englishwoman worked as a domestic servant until she married'. See Mary Abbott, *Family Ties: English Families 1540-1920* (London: Routledge, 1993), pp. 21, 132–3.

19 See Giddens, *Modernity*, as an example of this perspective.

20 Harvey, *Condition of Post-Modernity*, p. 48.

21 David Lyon, *Postmodernity* (Buckingham: Open University Press, 1994), p. 85.

22 René Descartes, *Discourse on Method and The Meditations*, tr. F. E. Sutcliffe (Harmondsworth: Penguin Books, 1968), pp. 53-4, quoted in Lundin, *Culture of Interpretation*, pp. 42-3.

23 Anthony C. Thiselton, *Interpreting God and the Postmodern Self: On Meaning, Manipulation and Promise* (Edinburgh: T & T Clark, 1996), p. 49. Schleiermacher's hermeneutical approach will be considered in Chapter 4.

24 J. M. Roberts, *The Pelican History of the World* (Harmondsworth: Penguin, 1980), p. 706.

25 From Samuel Moore's classic translation of *The Communist Manifesto* (London, 1888), authorised and edited by Friedrich Engels and universally reprinted, quoted in Berman, *All That Is Solid*, p. 89.

26 Berman, *All That is Solid*, p. 15, quoted in Harvey, *Condition*, p. 10.

27 Keith Tester, *The Life and Times of Post-Modernity* (London: Routledge, 1993), p. 151.

28 Lyon, *Postmodernity*, p. 4.

29 Alasdair MacIntyre, *After Virtue: A Study in Moral Theory* (London: Duckworth, 1981), p. 107.

30 MacIntyre, ibid., quoting Friedrich Nietzsche, *The Gay Science*, tr. by Walter Kaufmann (New York: Random House, 1974), p. 266.

31 Cardinal films that are dubbed 'postmodern' include David Lynch's *Blue Velvet* (USA, 1986) and television series *Twin Peaks* and Quentin Tarantino's *Pulp Fiction* (USA, 1994). *Blade Runner* has been especially focused on by writers on postmodernity; see Giuliano Bruno, 'Ramble City: Postmodernism and *Blade Runner*', *October*, vol. 41, 1987, pp. 61–74; Harvey, *Condition*, pp. 308–14; and Lyon, *Postmodernity*, pp. 1–3. The film is based on the novel by Philip K. Dick: *Do Androids Dream of Electric Sheep?*

32 The unedited edition of *Blade Runner* (1982) partly resolves the deep ambiguity at the end of the editor's cut edition by adding a scene in which Deckard and Rachel are seen flying in a spacecraft over a rolling landscape of snow-capped mountains and plunging valleys. Deckard had been told that Rachel has 'no termination date' and yet adds in a voice-over, 'I don't know how long we have together. Who does?' We can say that here is the promise of a partial return to modern romanticism, offset by the nagging uncertainties of a postmodernity that will not relinquish its grip.

33 Nicholas Wolterstorff, *Reason within the Bounds of Religion* (2nd ed.; Grand Rapids, MI: Eerdmans, 1984), p. 56.

34 See Nietzsche, *Gay Science*, where, in section 108, Nietzsche first declares his formulation 'God is dead'. This notion is elaborated in section 125, where he puts the words, 'God is dead. God remains dead' into the mouth of a madman as a prophetic declaration of a 'tremendous event' which 'is still on its way'.

35 Jean-François Lyotard, *The Postmodern Condition: A Report on Knowledge* (Manchester: Manchester University Press, 1984), p. xxiv. This book was originally published in French as *La Condition Postmoderne: Rapport sur le Savoir* in 1979.

36 ibid., p. 15. Lyotard follows Ludwig Wittgenstein in an emphasis on language games. For a critique of Wittgenstein in relation to the problem of hermeneutics, see Anthony C. Thiselton, *The Two Horizons: New Testament Hermeneutics and Philosophical Description with Special Reference to Heidegger, Bultmann, Gadamer and Wittgenstein* (Exeter: The Paternoster Press, 1980). Wittgenstein's complex think-

ing on linguistics seems less reductionist than Lyotard's. He writes, 'Only in the stream of thought and life do words have meaning'; quoted in Thiselton, p. 38.

37 Lyotard, *The Postmodern Condition*, p. 40.

38 Jean Baudrillard, *Simulations* (New York: 1983), p. 2, quoted in Geoff King, *Mapping Reality: An Exploration of Cultural Cartographies* (London: Macmillan Press, 1996), p. 1.

39 King, *Mapping Reality*, p. 5.

40 Baudrillard, 'The Reality Gulf', *Guardian* (1 January 1991), quoted in King, *Mapping Reality*, p. 7.

41 See Lyon, *Postmodernity*, pp. 11–17.

42 Jonathan Culler, *On Deconstruction: Theory and Criticism After Structuralism* (Ithaca, NY: Cornell University Press, 1982), p. 149, quoted in Susan Hekman, *Gender and Knowledge: Elements of a Postmodern Feminism* (Cambridge: Polity Press, 1990), p. 4. Here, Culler acknowledges the influence of William Warner on the shaping of this sentence and on making the link between 'sawing off the branch on which one is sitting' and Nietzsche's injunction in *The Gay Science* to 'live dangerously!'

43 See Thiselton, *Two Horizons*, p. 148, as part of his detailed discussion of Heidegger's classic work *Being and Time* (Oxford: Blackwell, 1962).

44 David Tracy, 'Theology and the Many Faces of Postmodernity', *Theology Today*, vol. 51, no. 1, 1994, p. 108.

45 Sean Hand (ed.), *The Levinas Reader: Emmanuel Levinas* (Oxford: Blackwell, 1989), p. 48.

46 Lyon, *Postmodernity.*, p. 76.

47 Harvey, *Condition*, pp. 113, 117.

48 In this section on 'the contemporary self' I am especially indebted to Anthony Giddens's analysis in *Modernity and Self-Identity*.

49 Giddens points to two possible sources of the term 'lifestyle': the writings of Alfred Adler, and thence taken up by radicals and advertisers in the 1960s; and Max Weber's 'style of life', eventually becoming 'lifestyle' in 'everyday language; see *Self-Identity*, footnote, p. 81.

50 Giddens, *Self-Identity*, p. 81.

51 ibid., p. 86.

52 Zygmunt Bauman, *Intimations of Postmodernity* (London: Routledge, 1992), p. 155.

53 Giddens, *Self-Identity*, p. 172.

54 ibid.

55 Classical psychoanalytic theory distinguishes between primary narcissism, 'the love of self which precedes loving others', and secondary narcissism, 'love of self which results from introjecting and identifying with an object'; see Charles Rycroft, *A Critical Dictionary of Psychanalysis* (Harmondsworth: Penguin Books, 1972), p. 94. In this

latter mechanism, the stance is a defensive one in which the narcissistic person has not faced the loss of the 'object', such as when an
adult man is caught up in a self-love that replaces the tentative love
(an incipient 'basic trust') he once had for a mother who has been
emotionally distanced since his childhood. For recent psychoanalytic
thinking on narcissism, see Andrew Samuels, Bani Shorter and Fred
Plaut, *A Critical Dictionary of Jungian Analysis* (London: Routledge,
1986), pp. 96–8.

56 Richard Sennett, *The Fall of Public Man* (Cambridge: Cambridge
University Press, 1977) and Christopher Lasch, *The Culture of Narcissism* (London: Abacus, 1980), evaluated in Giddens, *Self-Identity*, pp.
170–9.

57 ibid., p. 178.

58 *SOED* (1967) gives the first recognised usage of the word 'relationship' in 1744.

59 Nena O'Neill and George O'Neill, *Open Marriage* (London: Abacus,
1975), p. 211.

60 I take this phrase from A. C. Robin Skynner, *One Flesh: Separate
Persons: Principles of Family and Marital Psychotherapy* (London: Con-
stable, 1976).

61 Giddens, *Self-Identity*, pp. 89–90. For Giddens's detailed analysis of
the 'pure relationship', see pp. 88–98.

62 ibid., p. 186.

63 ibid., p. 187.

64 ibid., pp. 162–4.

65 *SOED* (1967).

66 Giddens, *Self-Identity*, pp. 162–3.

67 ibid., p. 164.

68 ibid., p. 65.

69 ibid., pp. 65–6. Erik Erikson saw shame and doubt as the linked
obverse side of autonomy in the two-year-old toddler, where the 'will
to be oneself' in early childhood is undermined by excessive shaming
or accusations of being 'dirty' or 'bad' by the adult world. See Erik H.
Erikson, *Identity: Youth and Crisis* (London: Faber & Faber, 1968), pp.
107–14. Giddens, *Self-Identity*, p. 65, refers to Helen B. Lewis, *Shame
and Guilt in Neurosis* (New York: International Universities Press,
1971), where Lewis describes two general states of shame: 'overt,
undifferentiated' shame, as when a child is 'in some way humiliated
by another person'; and 'bypassed' shame, which 'comes from
unconsciously experienced anxieties about inadequacies of self'.

70 Reported in Shere Hite, *Women and Love* (London, Viking, 1988), a
study of American women's 'extensive comments on their experiences and feelings in relation to men', quoted in Giddens, *Self-
Identity*, p.88, as an example of a striving for the 'pure relationship'.

71 In the context of post-1960s missiology, the word enculturation, or

inculturation, has been defined as 'the dynamic relation between the Christian message and culture or cultures; and an ongoing process of reciprocal and critical interaction and assimilation between them': see Marcello Azevedo, *Inculturation and the Challenges of Modernity* (Rome: Centre of Cultures and Religion, Pontifical Gregorian University, 1982), pp. 7-8, quoted in Judette A. Gallares, 'Toward a Multicultural Approach to Spiritual Direction' in *Common Journey: Different Paths: Spiritual Direction in Cross-Cultural Perspective*, ed. S. Rakoczy (Maryknoll, NY: Orbis Books, 1992), p. 159.

72 William A. Clebsch and Charles R. Jaekle, *Pastoral Care in Historical Perspective* (New York: Jason Aronson, 1975), p. 69.

73 For a major treatment on the Christian appraisal of contemporary psychologies see Roger F. Hurding, *Roots and Shoots: A Guide to Counselling and Psychotherapy* (London: Hodder & Stoughton, 1985).

74 My main sources for this brief section are Jürgen Habermas, *The Philosophical Discourse of Modernity: Twelve Lectures* (Cambridge: Polity Press, 1987); and Alasdair MacIntyre, *After Virtue: A Study in Moral Theory* (London: Duckworth, 1981).

75 Habermas gave his paper 'Modernity – An Unfinished Project' in September 1980 upon accepting the Adorno Prize; it was later published as Jürgen Habermas, 'Modernity: An Incomplete Project' in *The Anti-Aesthetic: Essays on Postmodern Culture*, ed. H. Foster (Port Townsend, WA: 1983).

76 Habermas, *Philosophical Discourse*, p. 43.

77 ibid., p. 337.

78 See ibid., pp. 23–44 for Habermas's analysis of Hegel's concept of modernity.

79 See, in particular, MacIntyre, *After Virtue*, pp. 114–53. Later in the book, following the notion of the medieval 'quest', he defines the 'virtues' as 'those dispositions which will . . . sustain us in the relevant kind of quest for the good' (p. 204).

80 ibid., p. 116.

81 ibid., pp. 244-5.

82 Thiselton, *Interpreting God*, p. 11.

83 Walter Brueggemann, *The Bible and Postmodern Imagination: Texts under Negotiation* (London: SCM Press, 1993), p. 49.

84 Tester, *Life and Times*, p. 124.

85 ibid., pp. 79-80.

86 ibid., p. 84.

87 Moltmann has compared theologies of hope with those of faith and love. He writes, 'Theologies of the Middle Ages were all theologies of love' while 'theologies of the Reformers . . . were decidedly theologies of faith.' Thiselton continues: 'But the fundamental issue of modern times "is the question of the future" which invites theology of hope. For Moltmann this entails a critique of the present which

brings about its transformation.' See Thiselton, *Interpeting God*, p. 121, quoting Jürgen Moltmann, *Theology Today* (London: SCM Press, 1988), p. 23.

88 Jürgen Moltmann, *Theology of Hope* (London: SCM Press, 1967), pp. 22–3.

89 ibid., pp. 24–5.

90 ibid., p. 16.

91 ibid., pp. 20–1.

92 Thiselton, *Interpreting God*, p. 117.

93 ibid., p. 134.

94 Ernst Hoffmann, 'Hope, Expectation' in *NIDNTT*, vol. 2, p. 238.

95 Moltmann, *Theology of Hope*, pp. 35–6.

96 ibid., pp. 33–4.

Chapter 4 Pathways Interpreted: Hermeneutics of the Text

1 Friedrich D. E. Schleiermacher, *Hermeneutics: The Handwritten Manuscripts* (Atlanta, GA: Scholars Press, 1977), p. 52; this edition is edited by Heinz Kimmerle and translated from the German by James Duke and Jack Forstman.

2 See Roger Lundin, *The Culture of Interpretation: Christian Faith and the Postmodern World* (Grand Rapids, MI: Eerdmans, 1993), p. 42, where Lundin argues that in the crisis at the end of the eighteenth century, in which the Enlightenment's rationalism and empiricism gave way to 'the pressure of skepticism' and 'the genesis of the romantic movement', 'epistemology was dethroned by hermeneutics, and the "culture of interpretation" was born'.

3 Julian Barnes, *A History of the World in 10½ Chapters* (London: Picador, 1990).

4 B. McHale, *Postmodern Fiction* (London, 1987), quoted in David Harvey, *The Condition of Post-Modernity: An Enquiry into the Origins of Cultural Change* (Oxford: Blackwell, 1990), p. 41. More fully, according to Harvey, McHale argues that the postmodern novel is 'characterized by a shift from an "epistemological" to an "ontological" dominant'. We can see this shift from the knowingness of the modern novel to the postmodern uncertainties of juxtaposed 'radically different realities' in, for example, Gabriel García Márquez, *One Hundred Years of Solitude* (1970) and Umberto Eco, *The Name of the Rose* (1983).

5 Barnes, *A History*, pp. 62–71.

6 ibid., pp. 4–5

7 ibid., pp. 12–14.

8 ibid., pp. 29–30.

9 M. Gertner, quoted in Anthony C. Thiselton's word-study 'Explain' in *NIDNTT*, vol. 1, p. 580.

10 Ulrich Luz, *Das Geschichtsverständnis des Paulus* (Munich: Kaiser, 1968), p. 134 (Thiselton's italics) in Anthony C. Thiselton, *New Horizons in Hermeneutics: The Theory and Practice of Transforming Biblical Reading* (London: HarperCollins, 1992), p. 149.

11 Thiselton, *New Horizons*, p. 149.

12 Lundin, *Culture*, p. 39.

13 John Goldingay, *Models for Interpretation of Scripture* (Carlisle: The Paternoster Press, 1995), p. 251.

14 Gillian R. Evans, *The Language and Logic of the Bible: The Earlier Middle Ages* (Cambridge: Cambridge University Press, 1984), pp. 14–15, quoted in Thiselton, *New Horizons*, pp. 144–5.

15 Thiselton, *New Horizons*, p. 145.

16 ibid., p. 183.

17 ibid., p. 168.

18 Edgar V. McKnight, *Post-modern Use of the Bible: The Emergence of Reader-Oriented Criticism* (Nashville: Abingdon Press, 1988), p. 32.

19 For a full discussion, see Thiselton, *New Horizons*, pp. 163–73. Here, Thiselton explores the beginnings of Christian allegorical interpretation in the early Church, citing the particular influence of Origen, who in turn legitimised his approach from what he saw as the Pauline precedent in Galatians 4:21–4; see pp. 169–70.

20 ibid., p. 163.

21 ibid., pp. 163–4; here, Thiselton discusses the pros and cons as to whether Paul is usisng allegory or typology. He concludes: 'Whether we use the word allegory, typology, or correspondence, it is clear that Paul has in view God's deeds in history, and the situational character of the analogy which he wishes to draw.'

22 McKnight, *Post-Modern Use*, pp. 29–30.

23 Augustine, *On Christian Doctrine* in vol. 2 of A Select Library of the Nicene and Post-Nicene Fathers of the Christian Church series, ed. Philip Schaff (Grand Rapids, MI: Eerdmans, 1956), 3.15.23.

24 Hans W. Frei, *The Eclipse of Biblical Narrative* (New Haven, CT: Yale University Press, 1974), p. 1.

25 Martin Luther, *On the Bondage of the Will* (Edinburgh: Clarke, 1957), pp. 128-9, quoted in Thiselton, *New Horizons*, p. 181.

26 Thiselton, *New Horizons*, p. 181.

27 Martin Luther, *Luther's Works*, vol. 54 (Philadelphia: Muhlinberg Press, 1960), p. 47, quoted in Thiselton, *New Horizons*, p. 181.

28 Luther, ibid., p. 406, quoted in Thiselton, *New Horizons* p. 181.

29 Thiselton, *New Horizons*, following Gerhard Ebeling.

30 Luther, *On the Bondage of the Will*, p. 71, quoted in Thiselton, ibid., p. 184.

31 Frei, *Eclipse*, p. 20.

32 Gerhard Ebeling, *Introduction to a Theological Theory of Language* (London: Collins, 1973), p. 17 in Anthony C. Thiselton, *The Two*

Horizons: New Testament Hermeneutics and Philosophical Description with Special Reference to Heidegger, Bultmann, Gadamer and Wittgenstein (Exeter: The Paternoster Press, 1980), p. xx.

33 Frei, *Eclipse*, pp. 21–2.

34 Frei, for example, cites the *Clavis Scripturae Sacrae* (1567) of Matthias Flacius Illyricus as 'the first writing on hermeneutics'; ibid., p. 37. Thiselton points out that it is generally understood, though, that the first use of the term 'hermeneutics' in the title of a study is in J. C. Dannhauer's *Hermeneutica Sacra* (1654); *New Horizons*, p. 194.

35 Frei, *Eclipse*, p. 43, quoting *The Chief Works of Benedict de Spinoza*, translated and introduced by R. H. M. Elwes (New York: Dover, 1951), p. 91.

36 Thiselton, *Two Horizons*, p. 11.

37 Francke was a 'spiritual son' of Phillip Jacob Spener (1635–1705), commonly thought to be the father of pietism, and founded many philanthropic and educational enterprises linked with the newly established University of Halle, which in turn became an international centre for the dissemination of pietism. One of Halle's best-known graduates was Count Ludwig von Zinzendorf (1700–60) who founded the missionary community of *Herrnhut* ('the Lord's watch') in 1724.

38 See Frei, *Eclipse*, p. 38, where Frei adds that 'emphasis' becomes 'a technical term' which 'stands for a doctrine or a way of seeing a meaning of scriptural words quite beyond what they appear to have in ordinary usage or in their immediate context'.

39 ibid., p. 51.

40 See Colin Brown, *Philosophy and the Christian Faith* (London: Tyndale Press, 1969), pp. 23, 33, 74.

41 Frei, *Eclipse*, pp. 52–3.

42 ibid., p. 111.

43 ibid., p. 109; see also Thiselton, *New Horizons*, pp. 195–6.

44 Frei, *Eclipse*, p. 56.

45 H. Richard Neibuhr, quoted by David L. Edwards in The *Church Times* (29 December 1989), p. 11.

46 For a well-known survey of this pursuit, see Albert Schweitzer, *The Quest of the Historical Jesus* (1906).

47 D. F. Strauss, *Life of Jesus* (1835), quoted in Frei, *Eclipse*, p. 272.

48 Strauss, *Life of Jesus*, in Frei, ibid., p. 234.

49 Karl Barth, *Protestant Theology in the Nineteenth Century* (London: SCM Press, 1972), p. 425, quoted in Thiselton, *New Horizons*, p. 209.

50 In this section on Schleiermacher, I am particularly indebted to Brown, *Philosophy*, pp. 108–16; Frei, *Eclipse*, pp. 284–322; Thiselton, *New Horizons*, pp. 204–36; and Anthony C. Thiselton, *Interpreting God and the Postmodern Self: On Meaning, Manipulation and Promise* (Edinburgh: T & T Clark, 1996), pp. 41–2, 48–60.

51 See Kant's *Critique of Pure Reason* (1781). Thiselton points out that Scheiermacher followed Kant in setting aside prior 'givens' in examining the process of understanding but, unlike Kant, he argues that the infinite is revealed 'in the finite particularities of individual or corporate human life' rather than in 'an idea' or 'an imperative'; see *New Horizons*, p. 213.

52 Friedrich D. E. Schleiermacher, *Hermeneutics*, p. 52.

53 Thiselton, *New Horizons*, p. 205.

54 Schleiermacher, *Hermeneutics*, pp. 150–1.

55 Thiselton, *Interpreting God*, p. 49.

56 Frei, *Eclipse*, p. 284.

57 Schleiermacher, *The Christian Faith* (Edinburgh: Clarke, 1948), p. 12, quoted in Brown, *Philosophy*, p. 111.

58 H. R. Mackintosh, *Types of Modern Theology: Scheiermacher to Barth* (London: Nisbet, 1937), p. 94, quoted in Thiselton, *New Horizons*, p. 229.

59 See Frei, *Eclipse*, pp. 293–4, 318–19; and Thiselton, *New Horizons*, pp. 228–33.

60 Thiselton, *New Horizons*, p. 208.

61 The term 'biblical theology' has been used in a variety of contexts. Frei points to its early post-Reformation use as a figural reading of the Scriptures 'which sought to establish the unity of religious meaning across the gap of historical and cultural differences'; see Frei, *Eclipse*, p. 8. The term was picked up again in the 1950s and 1960s in the so-called 'biblical theology movement' of which, in the context of 'New Testament theology', N. T. Wright writes, 'The text is . . . revelatory, and hence authoritative, insofar as it bears witness to the "real thing", that is, to the event(s) [especially concerning Jesus]'; see N. T. Wright, *The New Testament and the People of God*, vol. 1., Christian Origins and the Question of God (London: SPCK, 1992), p. 21.

62 See McKnight, *Post-modern Use.*, pp. 49–53, for a discussion of these major movements in historical criticism of the Bible. He refers to 'source criticism' in terms of its focus on primary sources to sort out the 'different historical traditions'; to 'form criticism' in relation to its study of the formation of stories within the oral tradition and its emphasis on 'individual units, studied in the light of their functions'; and to 'redaction criticism' with regard to its exploration of the 'editorial activity' within the Scriptures, revealing the 'situation and theology of writers and their communities'.

63 For an appraisal of Bultmann's hermeneutics, see Thiselton, *Two Horizons*, pp. 205–92.

64 H. A. Hodges, *Wilhelm Dilthey: An Introduction* (London: Kegan Paul, Trench & Trubner, 1944), p. 114, quoted in Thiselton, *Two Horizons*, pp. 235–6.

65 For an overview of Dilthey's notion of 'human understanding' as

370   PATHWAYS TO WHOLENESS

arising from comprehensions of history and a common humanity, see
Thiselton, *Two Horizons*, pp. 234–6.

66 See Hans-Georg Gadamer, *Truth and Method* (London: Sheed &
Ward, 1975), pp. 204–14 for Gadamer's criticism of Dilthey: for
example, 'He was always attempting to justify the knowledge of
what was historically conditioned as the achievement of objective
science, despite the fact of the knower's being conditioned himself'
(p. 204), and 'he expects the overcoming of the uncertainty and
unsureness of life to come not so much from the stability that the
experience of life provides but from science' (p. 211).

67 In *New Horizons*, pp. 314–15, Thiselton discusses three contributors to
the understandings of Gadamer's postmodern tendencies.

68 Thiselton, *The Two Horizons*, p. xix.

69 Gadamer, *Truth and Method*, p. 271, quoted in Thiselton, *Two Hoizons*,
p. 307.

70 Thiselton, *Two Horizons*, p. 307.

71 ibid., p. 326.

72 ibid., p. 320.

73 Susan Hekman, *Gender and Knowledge: Elements of a Postmodern
Feminism* (Cambridge: Polity Press, 1990), p. 14.

74 ibid., p. 107.

75 *CED*, p. 1407.

76 Desmond Morris, *Manwatching* (London: Panther, 1978).

77 For a sympathetic handling of de Saussure's work, see Thiselton, *New
Horizons*, pp. 83–8.

78 Lundin, *Culture*, p. 188.

79 See Thiselton, *New Horizons*, pp. 84–5.

80 Jean M. Aitchison in *OCEL*, p. 991, defines 'structuralism' as an
approach to linguistics 'which treats language as an interwoven
structure, in which every item acquires identity and validity only
in relation to the other items in the system'.

81 Terry Eagleton, *Literary Theory: An Introduction* (Minneapolis: University of Minnesota Press, 1983), p. 142, quoted in Lundin, *Culture*,
p. 194.

82 Jonathan Culler, *On Deconstruction: Theory and Criticism After Structuralism* (Ithaca, NY: Cornell University Press, 1982), p. 149, quoted in
Hekman, *Gender*, p. 4.

83 For detailed examination of Derrida's theories of textuality, and the
comparable work of Roland Barthes (1915–1980), see Thiselton, *New
Horizons*, pp. 80–132.

84 Thiselton, *New Horizons*, pp. 83–4.

85 Lundin, *Culture*, p. 192.

86 Jacques Derrida, *Of Grammatology* (Baltimore London: Johns Hopkins
University Press, 1976), p. 9, quoted in Thiselton, *New Horizons*, p.
104.

87 Nietzsche, 'On Truth and Lie in an Extra-Moral Sense' in *The Portable Nietzsche*, tr. and ed. Walter Kaufmann (New York: Penguin Books, 1976), p. 47, quoted in Lundin, *Culture*, pp. 187–8.

88 Derrida, 'Structure, Sign, and Play in the Discourse of the Human Sciences' (Johns Hopkins University, 1966), p. 292, quoted in Lundin, *Culture*, p. 194.

89 Lundin, *Culture*, p. 194.

90 See, for example, McKnight, *Post-modern Use*, pp. 75–93.

91 ibid., pp. 116, 131.

92 ibid., p. 15.

93 Stanley Fish, *Is There a Text in this Class? The Authority of Interpretive Communities* (Cambridge, MA: Harvard University Press, 1980), p. 10, quoted in Thiselton, *New Horizons*, p. 474.

94 Raymond Chapman in *OCEL*, p. 620.

95 McKnight, *Post-modern Use*, p. 254.

96 Quoted in Tony Castle (ed.), *The Hodder Book of Christian Quotations* (London: Hodder & Stoughton, 1982), p. 21.

97 McKnight, *Post-modern Use*, pp. 170–1.

98 ibid., p. 174.

99 See Thiselton, *New Horizons*, pp. 515–23, where Thiselton contrasts the reader-response approaches of Wolfgang Iser, which draws on 'a theory of perception to establish the role of readers in *filling in or completing* a textual meaning' that 'would otherwise remain only potential rather than actual' and Stanley Fish, which he sees as the 'most polemical and radical statement of a socio-pragmatic context-relative reader-response theory' (p. 515).

100 McKnight, *Post-modern Use*, p. 223.

101 ibid., p. 168, where McKnight quotes Jurij Lotman, *The Structure of the Artistic Text* (Ann Arbor: University of Michigan Press, 1977), pp. 23–4.

102 McKnight, *Post-modern Use*, p. 107.

103 ibid., p. 167.

104 ibid., p. 176.

105 ibid., p. 262.

106 Walter Brueggemann, *The Bible and Postmodern Imagination: Texts under Negotiation* (London: SCM Press, 1993), pp. 61–2, with reference to Stuart Hampshire, *Innocence and Experience* (Cambridge, MA: Harvard University Press, 1989).

107 David Clines, 'Images of Yahweh: God in the Pentateuch' in *Studies in Old Testament Theology*, ed. R. L. Hubbard Jr, R. K. Johnston and R. P. Meye (Dallas: Word, 1992), p. 82.

108 Brueggemann in, for example, Walter Brueggemann, *The Prophetic Imagination* (2nd ed.; Philadelphia, PA: Fortress Press, 1978); Walter Brueggemann, *Hopeful Imagination: Prophetic Voices in Exile* (2nd ed.; Philadelphia: Fortress Press, 1986); and Brueggemann, *Postmodern*

Imagination strongly stresses the need to reclaim the imaginative dimension in biblical hermeneutics. He writes, 'The great shift in interpretive practice I want to consider is that in this post-Cartesian situation, knowing consists not in settled certitude but in the actual work of imagination' (*Postmodern Imagination*, pp. 12–13).

109 Bernhard W. Anderson, 'Creation and Ecology' in Bernhard W. Anderson (ed.), *Creation in the Old Testament* (Philadelphia: Fortress Press, 1984), p. 154.

Chapter 5 Pathways Interpreted: Hermeneutics of the Life

1 Paul Ricoeur in Preface to Don Ihde, *Hermeneutic Phenomenology: The Philosophy of Paul Ricoeur* (Evanston, IL: Northwestern University Press, 1971), p. xv, quoted in Lewis S. Mudge (ed.), *Paul Ricoeur: Essays on Biblical Interpretation* (London: SPCK, 1981), p. 9.

2 Anthony C. Thiselton, *Interpreting God and the Postmodern Self: On Meaning, Manipulation and Promise* (Edinburgh: T. & T. Clark, 1996), p. 49.

3 For a useful overview of Ricoeur's complex and boundary-crossing hermeneutical theory, see Anthony C. Thiselton, *New Horizons in Hermeneutics: The Theory and Practice of Transforming Biblical Reading* (London: HarperCollins, 1992), pp. 344–78.

4 Paul Ricoeur, *Oneself as Another* (tr. by Kathleen Blamey; Chicago: University of Chicago Press, 1992), pp. 4–15. This book developed out of Ricoeur's Gifford Lectures, delivered in Edinburgh in 1986.

5 ibid., p. 15.

6 ibid., pp. 16, 18.

7 Anton T. Boisen, *Out of the Depths: An Autobiographical Study of Mental Disorder and Religious Experience* (New York: Harper & Bros., 1960), p. 51.

8 Boisen had a clear commitment to altering 'the basic structure of theological education', aiming to challenge the contemporary split between science and theology by 'seeking to make empirical studies of living human documents, particularly those in which men were breaking or had broken under the stress of moral crisis'; see ibid., p. 187.

9 Glenn H. Asquith, 'The Case Study Method of Anton T. Boisen', *Journal of Pastoral Care*, vol. 34, no. 2, 1980, p. 84.

10 Boisen, *Depths*, p. 197.

11 Clinical Pastoral Education, founded in the mid-1920s, is defined by Edward E. Thornton in *DPCC*, pp. 177–8 as:
professional education for ministry which brings theological students, ordained clergy, members of religious orders, and qualified laypersons into supervised encounter with living human docu-

ments in order to develop their pastoral identity, interpersonal competence, and spirituality; the skills of pastoral assessment, interprofessional collaboration, group leadership, pastoral care and counselling; and pastoral theological reflection.

12 See, for example, Boisen, *Depths*, p. 186, where he looks back over the first twenty years of CPE and expresses concern over 'a tendency to accept Freudian doctrine on authority without scrutinising it closely' and adds that he was 'especially troubled by a tendency to accept the easy solutions of some of the perennial problems of sin and salvation' by 'getting rid of the conflict by lowering the conscience threshold'. See also Roger F. Hurding, *Roots and Shoots: A Guide to Counselling and Psychotherapy* (London: Hodder & Stoughton, 1985), p. 215.

13 See Asquith, 'Boisen', pp. 86–9.

14 Anton Boisen, *The Exploration of the Inner World* (New York: Harper, 1952), p. 185.

15 ibid., p. 251.

16 Asquith, 'Boisen', p. 87, referring to Boisen's training manual (1946) for an introductory course on 'Types of Mental Illness'.

17 The 'verbatim', as an alternative approach in case study method to Boisen's careful history-taking from 'living human documents', was introduced in the 1930s by Russell L. Dicks for hospital ministry. Here, conversations with patients are recorded as recalled by the minister or theological student and the resulting material is highly educative in terms of the listener's misrememberings and gaps in memory recall. Boisen was unhappy with the trend within CPE of replacing the case history with verbatims, asking whether this might not mean 'a lessening of interest in the basic understanding of the experiences involved?'; see Boisen, *Depths*, p. 185.

18 Asquith, 'Boisen', p. 94.

19 See, in particular, John Patton, 'Clinical Hermeneutics: Soft Focus in Pastoral Counseling and Theology', *Journal of Pastoral Care*, vol. 35, 1981, pp. 157–68, where Patton traces his own use of the term 'soft focus' to Phillip Wheelwright, *The Burning Fountain: A Study in the Language of Symbolism* (Bloomington, IN: Indiana University Press, 1954) and Norman Perrin, *Jesus and the Language of the Kingdom* (Philadelphia, PA: Fortress Press, 1976). See also Charles V. Gerkin, *Living Human Documents: Re-Visioning Pastoral Counseling in a Hermeneutical Mode* (Nashville: Abingdon Press, 1984); and Charles V. Gerkin, 'Faith and Praxis: Pastoral Counseling's Hermeneutical Problem', *Pastoral Psychology*, vol. 35, no. 1, 1986, pp. 3–15. In the latter, for example, Gerkin seeks to integrate theological and psychological language, faith and praxis, in the hermeneutical task of pastoral counselling. He declares that this enterprise 'is more like a softly focused and continuing process of reflection and behavioural action than it is obedience to propositions' (p. 11).

20 Sister Wendy Beckett, *The Gaze of Love: Meditations On Art* (London: HarperCollins, 1993), p. 82.
21 Patton, 'Clinical Hermeneutics', p. 160.
22 Gerkin, *Documents*, p. 19.
23 ibid., p. 21.
24 ibid., p. 33.
25 ibid., p. 20.
26 ibid., pp. 122–3.
27 Thiselton disputes the popular view that Schleiermacher was the 'first major thinker to formulate the principle of the hermeneutical circle', although he concedes the probability that he was the first to 'address seriously' its implications for hermeneutics. See Thiselton, *New Hermeneutics*, p. 204.
28 Anthony C. Thiselton, *The Two Horizons: New Testament Hermeneutics and Philosophical Description with Special Reference to Heidegger, Bultmann, Gadamer and Wittgenstein* (Exeter: The Paternoster Press, 1980), p. 104. For a fuller discussion of the various nuances of the term 'hermeneutical circle' see pp. 103–10.
29 Thiselton, *Interpreting God*, p. 57.
30 Zygmunt Bauman, *Hermeneutics and Social Science* (New York: Columbian University Press, 1978), p. 17, quoted in Gerkin, *Documents*, p. 138.
31 Gerkin, *Documents*, pp. 138–9.
32 Cited in the context of Gadamer's handling of the hermeneutical circle in Susan Hekman, *Gender and Knowledge: Elements of a Postmodern Feminism* (Cambridge: Polity Press, 1990), p. 14.
33 Object relations theory arose within the field of psychoanalysis and put forward the concept that the infant progressively internalises influences from the outer world – initially 'part objects', such as the mother's breast, and, in time, 'whole objects', including, for example, the mother, father and older siblings. These 'object relations' in turn affect the relationships of adult life. For a comprehensive assessment of object relations theorists, see Howard A. Bacal and Kenneth M. Newman, *Theories of Object Relations: Bridges to Self Psychology* (New York: Columbia University Press, 1990).
34 Gerkin, *Documents*, p. 145. In assessing a range of methodological resources to effect change in pastoral counselling (pp. 143–60), Gerkin looks for approaches that are compatible with seeing 'the life of the soul' as involving 'the self-interpretive process within a framework of meaning that relates all aspects of life and relationships to a structure of ultimate meaning grounded in God' (p. 144). On balance, he favours the object relations theorists with their emphasis on 'integration and wholeness', although he greatly enlarges their 'integrative concern' to include the ultimate and Godward aspect of life.
35 The tradition of 'self', or personalistic, psychology lies primarily

within the orbit of humanism (as with Carl Rogers, Abraham Maslow and Erich Fromm) and gives emphasis to the self's inherent goodness, power to change and legitimate quest for autonomy. For Christian critiques of these psychologies, see Hurding, *Roots and Shoots*, pp. 106–23; Stanton L. Jones and Richard E. Butman, *Modern Psychotherapies: A Comprehensive Christian Appraisal* (Downers Grove, IL: Inter-Varsity Press, 1991), pp. 255–75; and Paul C. Vitz, *Psychology As Religion: The Cult of Self Worship* (Tring: Lion, 1981). Christian writers such as Hiltner and Gerkin seek to widen the remit of self psychology to include the person's 'life in God'. For an assessment of the self psychology of Heinz Kohut, in the psychoanalytic tradition, see Bacal and Newman, *Object Relations*, pp. 225–73.

36 Gerkin, *Documents*, pp. 146–7.
37 ibid., p. 155.
38 ibid., p. 159.
39 ibid., p. 156.
40 ibid., pp. 159–60.
41 ibid., p. 161.
42 See John Dominic Crossan, *The Dark Interval: Towards a Theology of Story* (Niles, IL: Argus Communications, 1975), p. 59, for Crossan's summary of his 'basic fivefold typology': 'Myth establishes world. Apologue defends world. Action investigates world. Satire attacks world. Parable subverts world.'
43 See, for example, F. F. Bruce in *NIDNTT*, vol. 2, p. 643, where the distinction between *mythos* as 'fiction' and *logos* as 'factual narrative' is traced back to as early as Pindar's writings in the fifth century BC.
44 Gerkin, *Documents*, pp. 161–2.
45 Crossan, *Dark Interval*, p. 60.
46 ibid., p. 57.
47 There are, of course, many analyses of Jesus's parables, including Crossan's, where he sees the parables as proclaiming 'the kingdom's temporality and the three simultaneous modes of its presence'. These are 'its *advent* as gift of God, its *reversal* of the recipient's world, and its empowering of life and *action*.' See Crossan, *In Parables: The Challenge of the Historical Jesus* (New York: Harper & Row, 1973), p. 35, quoted in Gerkin, *Documents*, p. 174. Sallie McFague, like Crossan, sees the parable as metaphor. She contrasts her approach with the traditional 'one-point' interpretation with its tendency 'to reduce the parables to their ideational possibilities' and argues for a metaphorical understanding that is 'generative of *new* meanings in the plural'; see Sallie McFague, *Speaking in Parables: A Study in Metaphor and Theology* (London: SCM Press, 1975), p. 72. See also Sallie McFague, *Models of God: Theology for an Ecological, Nuclear Age* (London: SCM Press, 1987), pp. 49–53.
48 McFague, *Speaking in Parables*, p. 79.

49 Gerkin, *Documents*, p. 171.

50 Richard Foster, *Prayer: Finding the Heart's True Home* (London: Hodder & Stoughton, 1992), p. 177. It was a photocopy of this page of Foster's book that gave me the quote from Bernard of Clairvaux.

51 Crossan, *Dark Interval*, p. 124. McFague traces this notion of Jesus as 'the Parable of God' to the writings of Robert W. Funk and Leander Keck, writing in the late 1960s and early 1970s; see McFague, *Speaking in Parables*, pp. 80–3.

52 Crossan, *Dark Interval*, p. 125.

53 Gerkin, *Documents*, pp. 176.

54 Donald Capps, *Pastoral Care and Hermeneutics* (Philadelphia: Fortress Press, 1984), p. 11.

55 Mudge (ed.), *Paul Ricoeur*, p. 1.

56 Paul Ricoeur, 'The Model of the Text: Meaningful Action Considered as a Text', *Social Research*, vol. 38, 1971, p. 558.

57 ibid., p. 547. In the 'Model of the Text', Ricoeur looks, *inter alia*, to the semiologists Ferdinand de Saussure and Claude Lévi-Strauss and argues that structural analysis is more than 'a sterile game, a divisive algebra': it can be seen 'as a stage – and a necessary one – between a naive interpretation and a critical interpretation', raising the possibility of locating explanation and understanding at two different stages of a unique hermeneutical arc' (p. 557).

58 ibid., p. 550.

59 ibid., pp. 561–2.

60 ibid., pp. 557, 561. Ricoeur summarises this 'world-disclosing' phenomenon: 'In the same way that a text is detached from its author, an action is detached from its agent and develops consequences of its own' (p. 541).

61 Capps, *Hermeneutics*, p. 43.

62 Ricoeur, 'Model', p. 534.

63 Capps, *Hermeneutics*, p. 43.

64 ibid.

65 See Ricoeur, 'Model', p. 534, where he writes, ' . . . every exegesis unfolds its procedures within the circumference of a meaning that has broken its moorings to the psychology of its author'.

66 Capps, *Hermeneutics*, p. 45.

67 Gerkin, *Documents*, p. 171.

68 Paul Ricoeur, 'Toward a Hermeneutic of the Idea of Revelation', in Mudge (ed.), *Paul Ricoeur*, p. 75.

69 ibid., p. 77.

70 ibid., p. 81.

71 ibid., p. 85.

72 ibid., p. 86.

73 ibid., p. 89.

74 ibid., p. 92. Ricoeur's schema for pastoral care has certain parallels in

the 'map' I put forward in Part II of this book, although I have only become aware of Ricoeur's analysis some years after clarifying my own.

75 Capps, *Hermeneutics*, p. 23.
76 ibid., p. 45.
77 Donald Capps, *Biblical Approaches to Pastoral Counseling* (Philadelphia: Westminster Press, 1981), p. 13.
78 Barbara Kingsolver, *Animal Dreams* (New York: HarperCollins, 1990).
79 ibid., p. 3.
80 Capps, *Hermeneutics*, p. 47.
81 ibid., p. 48.
82 ibid., p. 50.
83 See, for example, Paul Ricoeur, *Freud and Philosophy: An Essay in Interpretation* (New Haven, Yale University Press, 1970), p. 33.
84 See Roger Lundin, *The Culture of Interpretation: Christian Faith and the Postmodern World* (Grand Rapids, MI: Eerdmans, 1993), pp. 250–1, where Lundin sees Marx, Nietzsche and Freud as, 'ironically enough', taking up 'the Cartesian stance of doubt' and yet carrying it, to quote Ricoeur, 'to the very heart of the Cartesian stronghold'.
85 Capps, *Hermeneutics*, p. 31.
86 Thiselton, *Interpreting God*, p. 69.
87 Thiselton points out that, for Ricoeur, a symbol is 'a double-meaning linguistic expression which requires an interpretation'; here there is 'an intermixture or overlapping of multi-signification which exhibits the "richness" or "plurivocal" nature of language'. See Thiselton, *New Horizons*, p. 347.
88 Mudge (ed.), *Ricoeur*, p. 6, where Mudge cites Ricoeur's early attempt to help us reach a 'second naïveté' in the final chapter of his *The Symbolism of Evil* (Boston: Beacon Press, 1969).
89 Capps, *Hermeneutics*, p. 58.
90 Richard Rorty, *Contingency, Irony, and Solidarity* (Cambridge: Cambridge University Press, 1989), p. 27.
91 ibid., p. 5.
92 ibid., pp. 73–4.
93 ibid., p. 45.
94 ibid., p. 53.
95 ibid., p. 192.
96 ibid., p. 93.
97 Lundin, *Culture*, p. 35, where he refers to Richard Rorty, *Philosophy and the Mirror of Nature* (Princeton: Princeton University Press, 1979); see also Lundin, pp. 195, 199.
98 Lundin, *Culture*, p. 37.
99 ibid., p. 246.
100 ibid. 204–5.
101 Rorty, *Contingency*, p. 9.

102 Dietrich Bonhoeffer, *Letters and Papers from Prison*, ed. Eberhard Bethge (New York: Collier Books, 1971), p. 369, quoted in Lundin, *Culture*, p. 243.
103 Thiselton, *New Horizons*, p. 612.

Chapter 6 Pathways Charted: Map-making for the Journey

1 David W. Augsburger, *Pastoral Counseling Across Cultures* (Philadelphia: Westminster Press, 1986), p. 22.
2 ibid.
3 I am grateful to Philip Jenson of Trinity College, Bristol for this analogy.
4 Matthew 5:43–8.
5 On Samaritans, see Luke 10:25–37; 17:16–19; John 4:7–9; on women, Matthew 27:55–6; Mark 5:25–34; Luke 7:36–50, 8:1–3; John 4:1–42; on children, Matthew 11:25–6, 18:2–4, 19:13–5; Mark 9:36–7; on Sabbath-breaking, Matthew 12:1–14; Luke 13:10–17; John 5:2–18. For a detailed appraisal of Jesus's boundary-crossing, see Donald B. Kraybill, *The Upside-Down Kingdom* (Basingstoke: Marshall Morgan & Scott, 1985), pp. 167–72, 229–50.
6 Matthew 25:31–46.
7 Leanne Payne, *The Healing Presence* (Eastbourne: Kingsway, 1990), p. 132.
8 Jacob Firet, *Dynamics of Pastoring* (Grand Rapids, MI: Eerdmans, 1986), p. 68.
9 ibid., p. 82.
10 The roots of our continuing use of the term 'pastoral' care lie, of course, in the 'pivotal analogy', to use Thomas Oden's words, of the biblical connotation of the shepherd. See Thomas C. Oden, *Pastoral Theology: Essentials of Ministry* (Harper & Row, 1983), pp. 49–63.
11 See, for example, Stephen Pattison, *A Critique of Pastoral Care* (2nd ed.; London: SCM Press, 1993), pp. 11–13, where Pattison offers useful criticisms of Clebsch and Jaekle's definition and puts forward his own tentative version: '*Pastoral care is that activity, undertaken especially by representative Christian persons, directed towards the elimination and relief of sin and sorrow and the presentation of all people perfect in Christ to God.*'
12 William A. Clebsch and Charles R. Jaekle, *Pastoral Care in Historical Perspective* (New York: Jason Aronson, 1975), p. 4.
13 Pattison, *Critique*, pp. 11–13.
14 Seward Hiltner, *Preface to Pastoral Theology* (Abingdon Press, 1958), pp. 89–172, gives healing, sustaining and guiding as 'the three aspects of the shepherding perspective' (p. 146). Clebsch and Jaekle acknowledge their debt to this source, while declaring they have developed

their 'own meanings for these terms'; see Clebsch and Jaekle, *Pastoral Care*, p. 4.

15 Clebsch and Jaekle, *Pastoral Care*, p. 4.

16 *DPCC*, p. xii. Pattison first drew my attention to Hunter's definition in the Afterword of the second edition of his *Critique of Pastoral Care* (1993); see pp. 195–6.

17 Since the 1950s and 1960s there seems to have been a gradual evolution toward a more inclusive view as to who may be authorised to offer pastoral care. Whereas Hiltner expressed similar understandings to Clebsch and Jaekle (see Hiltner, *Preface*, pp. 37–9), more recent writers have moved to a more evenhanded attitude toward clergy and laity in this respect. For example, John Patton argues for a 'communal contextual paradigm' where the clergyperson is 'teacher of ministry and representative of the "whole" ministry of the community of faith, whereas the laity are more often than not "specialists" in a particular ministry, such as pastoral care'; see John Patton, *Pastoral Care in Context: An Introduction to Pastoral Care* (Louisville, KY: Westminster/John Knox, 1993), pp. 88–9.

18 Walter Brueggemann, *Genesis* (Atlanta, GA: John Knox Press, 1982), p. 48.

19 David Tracy, 'The Foundations of Practical Theology', in *Practical Theology: The Emerging Field in Theology, Church, and World*, ed. D. S. Browning (San Francisco: Harper & Row, 1983), p. 61.

20 David Tracy, *Blessed Rage for Order: The New Pluralism in Theology* (New York: The Seabury Press, 1975), p. 243.

21 Martin Luther, quoted in Hans W. Frei, *The Eclipse of Biblical Narrative* (New Haven, CT: Yale University Press, 1974), p. 176.

22 G. Ernest Wright, *God Who Acts: Biblical Theology as Recital* (London: SCM Press, 1952), p. 108.

23 David Tracy, 'The Foundations of Practical Theology' in Browning (ed.), *Practical Theology*, p. 62.

24 See, for example, Edward Farley, 'Theology and Practice Outside the Clerical Paradigm' in Browning (ed.), *Practical Theology*, p. 32. David Tracy also uses these three main subdivisions; see Tracy, 'Foundations', p. 62. Other categorisations of theology include, for example, biblical studies, church history, systematic theology, theological ethics and practical theology; see Stephen W. Sykes in *NDCT*, p. 566.

25 Hiltner refers to C. T. Seidel's *Pastoral-Theologie* (1749) as the earliest of innumerable German works that first used the term 'pastoral theology'; see Hiltner, *Preface*, p. 224.

26 The term 'dynamic psychology' covers those psychological approaches, such as psychoanalysis, which emphasise the 'cause-and-effect' nature of a person's or group's drives and motives.

27 The psychology of religion as an academic discipline was strongly influenced in its earlier years by William James's (1843–1910) func-

tionalism and pragmatism. See, for example, Roger F. Hurding, *Roots and Shoots: A Guide to Counselling and Psychotherapy* (London: Hodder & Stoughton, 1985), pp. 18–9, 42, 211–13.

28 Farley argues that practical theology needs rescuing from its 'clerical paradigm' and makes a plea for a praxis which is 'redemptively pervasive of any and all social, political, and cultural spaces', while retaining its distinctive Christian 'world-transforming' influence; 'Theology and Practice', p. 39.

29 ibid., p. 33.

30 Hiltner, *Preface*, p. 20.

31 See, for example, Paul H. Ballard (ed.), *The Foundations of Pastoral Studies and Practical Theology* (4 vols.; Cardiff: The Board of Studies for Pastoral Studies, University College, 1986); Paul H. Ballard, 'Pastoral Theology as Theology of Reconciliation', *Theology*, vol. 91, 1988, pp. 375–80; and Paul H. Ballard and John Pritchard, *Practical Theology in Action: Christian Thinking in the Service of Church and Society* (London: SPCK, 1996).

32 See Pattison, *Critique*, also Stephen Pattison and James Woodward, *A Vision of Pastoral Theology: In Search of Words that Resurrect the Dead* (Contact Pastoral Monograph, 1994); Stephen Pattison, *Pastoral Care and Liberation Theology* (Cambridge: Cambridge University Press, 1994); and Stephen Pattison, 'Should Pastoral Care have Aims and Objectives?', *Contact*, vol. 120, 1996, pp. 26–34. In the Afterword of the second edition of his *Critique* (1993), Pattison makes a plea for a pastoral care which pays 'less attention to verbalized theories, paradoxes and polarities on the abstract level' and 'more to the people and values' (pp. 208–9).

33 See Elaine L Graham and Margaret Halsey (eds.), *Life Cycles: Women and Pastoral Care* (London: SPCK, 1993); Elaine L. Graham, 'Towards a Theology of Desire', *Theology and Sexuality*, vol. 1 (1994); Elaine L. Graham, *Making the Difference: Gender, Personhood and Theology* (London: Mowbray, 1995); and Elaine L. Graham, *Transforming Practice: Pastoral Theology in an Age of Uncertainty* (London: Mowbray, 1996). We will look at Graham's contribution both in this chapter and Chapter 11.

34 In David Deeks, *Pastoral Theology: An Inquiry* (London: Epworth Press, 1987). Deeks equates the beginning of pastoral theology with the search 'for meaning in life', a theology that 'incorporates our conversations, and the narrative we tell of our lives' (p. 67).

35 In James N. Lapsley, 'Practical Theology and Pastoral Care: An Essay in Pastoral Theology' in Browning (ed.), *Practical Theology*, p. 167, Lapsley defines pastoral theology as 'the study of all aspects of the care of persons in the church in a context of theological inquiry, including implications for other branches of theology', a definition first published in 1969. Lapsley's is an important voice among pastoral theologians; his distinctive contribution lies in a blend of

psychoanalytic ego psychology and process theology, putting for-
ward a 'dynamic process model for relating salvation and health' in
James N. Lapsley, *Salvation and Health: The Interlocking Processes of Life*
(Philadelphia: Westminster, 1972), pp. 86ff.; for further material on
this 'interlocking' view, see James N. Lapsley, 'The Theology of
Salvation, Healing and Health' in *DPCC*, pp. 1107–10; also see
Rodney J. Hunter, 'The Lapsley Legacy', *The Princeton Seminary
Bulletin*, vol. 13, no. 2, 1992, pp. 176–86.

36 See, for example, Browning (ed.), *Practical Theology*; Don S. Browning,
Religious Ethics and Pastoral Care (Philadelphia: Fortress Press, 1983);
and Don S. Browning, *A Fundamental Practical Theology* (Minneapolis:
Fortress Press, 1991).

37 Ballard, 'Pastoral Theology, p. 375.

38 A. J. Heschel, *God in Search of Man* (New York: Farrar, Strauss &
Giroux, 1955), p. 336.

39 Browning offers a pastoral framework that addresses five levels of
human need: a *metaphorical* or *visional*, relating to the religious and
symbolic dimensions of life: an *obligational*, for the moral and ethical;
a *tendency-need* level, concerning human needs and values, a *con-
textual-predictive* or *environmental-social*, with respect to societal and
cultural contexts; and a *rule-role* level, regarding rules and roles for
everyday communication. See *Religious Ethics*, pp. 54–71 and *Fundamental Practical Theology*, pp. 105–9, 280–1.

40 Unlike Browning, who argues a foundational ethic as the mainspring
for congregational action, Graham puts forward a practical wisdom
that is the very 'medium by which truth-claims and value-commitments come into existence'. See *Transforming Practice*, p. 140.

41 Bernard Lonergan, *Method in Theology* (London: Darton, Longman &
Todd, 1972), pp. 4, 13–14.

42 William Shakespeare, *Hamlet*, II, ii, 211.

43 Lonergan, *Method*, p. xi. This 'collaborative creativity' is further
characterised by 'intentionality', where such 'operations' as imagin-
ing, understanding or formulating engage with, attend to and, thereby, 'intend' an object – such as a metaphor, insight or proposed
structure (pp. 6–7).

44 John S. Dunne, *The Reasons of the Heart: A Journey into Solitude and Back
Again into the Human Circle* (London: SCM Press, 1978), p. 151.

45 Colin E. Gunton, *The One, The Three and The Many: God, Creation and
Culture of Modernity* (Cambridge: Cambridge University Press, 1993),
p. 36.

46 ibid., p. 228.

47 Jürgen Moltmann, *The Spirit of Life: A Universal Affirmation* (London:
SCM Press, 1992), p. 11.

48 Nicholas Wolterstorff, *Reason within the Bounds of Religion* (2nd ed.;
Grand Rapids, MI: Eerdmans, 1984), pp. 24, 52.

49 Interestingly, although Graham sees Browning as still tied to some extent to the project of modernity, both she and he look to Jürgen Habermas as the way out of the impasse between modernity's foundationalism and postmodernity's deconstructionism. See Graham, *Transforming Practice*, pp. 88–90, 142–3, 151, and Browning, *Fundamental Practical Theology*, pp. 200–1.

50 In contrast to Stanley Hauerwas and Alastair McIntyre, whose ethics are 'entirely tradition-dependent', Browning argues that morality, although largely linked to tradition, does not entirely depend on it. Rather, as a *radical empiricist*, he writes that 'experience, as well as narrative, informs both our principles of obligation and our perception of human needs and tendencies'. He sums up the experiential and contextual emphases of his practical theology by declaring, 'We know the truth not by its roots (or foundations) but by its fruits (where it takes us).' See *Fundamental Practical Theology*, pp. 177–82.

51 Graham acknowledges, amid her declared 'antifoundationalism', pastoral theology's need to develop 'an adequate notion of *orthopraxis*' that can weather 'rapid social change, diversity of human need and cultural pluralism', without a collapse into 'an anti-theoretical or anti-epistemological account of pastoral care' (*Transforming Practice*, pp. 135–6). Thus, a commitment to a *right practice* that affirms 'some kind of (interim) truth and value' is made in Graham's theology – a theology that is earthed in community and cautiously defining in its transcendence (p. 209).

52 Gunton, *The One, The Three and The Many*, pp. 134–5.

53 Paul Tillich, *Systematic Theology*, vol. 1 (Welwyn: James Nisbet & Co, 1953), p. 70. Tillich sees religious symbols as 'a representation of that which is unconditionally beyond the conceptual sphere', thus 'opening up levels of reality which otherwise are hidden'; see Anthony C. Thiselton, *New Horizons in Hermeneutics: The Theory and Practice of Transforming Biblical Reading* (London: HarperCollins, 1992), p. 577.

54 Browning challenges Tracy's commitment to a transcendental 'fundamental theology' and seeks, rather, to extend Tracy's revisionist correlational approach into a fundamental *practical* theology that is 'the most inclusive and central theological enterprise'; see Browning, *Fundamental Practical Theology*, pp. 46–7.

55 Tracy, *Blessed Rage*, p. 32.

56 ibid., pp. 33–4. Elsewhere, Tracy writes that each subdiscipline of theology 'develops public criteria for its claims to meaning and truth'. These range from 'the necessary and abstract (transcendental and metaphysical) criteria of fundamental theology' through the 'hermeneutical criteria of truth as disclosure and concealment in systematic theologies' to the 'concrete praxis criteria of truth as personal, social, political, historical and natural transformations and ethical reflection in practical theology'. See Tracy, 'Foundations', pp. 62–3.

57 For example, in David Tracy, *The Analogical Imagination: Christian Theology and the Culture of Pluralism* (London: SCM Press, 1981), p. 24, he writes, 'On theological grounds, this [correlation] model can account for the full spectrum of possible relationships between "church" and "world" from identity through transformation to confrontation.'

58 Tracy, *Blessed Rage*, p. 46.

59 Tracy, 'Foundations', p. 62.

60 Tracy, *Blessed Rage*, pp. 249–50.

61 In Browning's schema we have, level-by-level, the religious, dutiful, needful, contextual and communicative aspects of human life. And so the practical theological task is to interpret the 'central witness of the Judeo-Christian tradition' at each of these five levels, then engage in a parallel enterprise with the relevant cultural setting, before entering 'a public conversation' that seeks to discern the 'relative adequacy' of the two viewpoints. See Browning, *Religious Ethics*, p. 56.

62 ibid., p. 48.

63 Jürgen Moltmann in Elisabeth Moltmann-Wendel and Jürgen Moltmann, *Humanity in God* (London: SCM Press, 1983), p. 59.

64 Graham, *Transforming Practice*, p. 140. Graham looks to the Aristotelian notion of practical wisdom (*phronesis*), where values are 'expressed not in abstract knowledge-claims but in the patterns and orderings of purposeful human activity' (p. 7).

65 ibid., p. 155.

66 ibid., p. 174.

67 ibid., p. 165, citing Nancy Fraser, 'What's Critical About Critical Theory?' in S. Benhabib and D. Cornell (eds.), *Feminism as Critique: Essays on the Politics of Gender in Late Capitalist Societies* (Cambridge: Polity Press, 1987), pp. 30–56.

68 Graham, *Transforming Practice*, pp. 164–5.

69 Laurie Green, *Let's Do Theology: A Pastoral Cycle Resource Book* (London: Mowbray, 1990), p. 22.

70 ibid., p. 25. For an overview of Green's 'Doing Theology Spiral', see pp. 24–32, where the spiral of care moves through a sequence of facing life's *experience* (acknowledging initial feelings and reactions), engaging with an *exploration* of the issues, followed by *reflection* to see how the Christian faith and tradition fit the situation and, finally, to *response*, in which those who are 'doing theology' use their new insights to assess a range of ways forward, from resolute action to a quiet acceptance of the freshly understood issues. Inevitably, in time, fresh experience leads to a *new situation* and a further opening up of the spiral of care.

71 Laurie Green, *Power to the Powerless: Theology Brought to Life* (Basingstoke: Marshall Pickering, 1987), pp. 16–17.

72 ibid, p. 10.

73 ibid., pp. 21–2.
74 ibid., p. 28.
75 ibid., pp. 30–1.
76 ibid., p. 32.
77 ibid., p. 34.
78 ibid., p. 39.
79 ibid., p. 43.
80 ibid., pp. 137–8.
81 George Lindbeck, *The Nature of Doctrine: Religion and Doctrine in a Postliberal Age* (London: SPCK, 1984), p. 74.
82 ibid., p. 79.
83 ibid., p. 16.
84 Lindbeck sees the roots of the experiential-expressive approach in the experiential tradition handed down from Kant and Schleiermacher; ibid., pp. 20–1.
85 Lindbeck argues the danger of confusing symbol with what it represents, of not differentiating adequately between 'form and content' in doctrine. See ibid., pp. 92–3.
86 Among these he makes mention of two 'ecumenically inclined Roman Catholics', Karl Rahner and Bernard Lonergan. Although Lindbeck concedes that this twofold outlook is preferable to either of its disparate components in accounting for both the 'variable and invariable aspects of religious traditions', he finds their efforts 'unpersuasive'. He does allow, though, for the possibility of a clearer integration of these two approaches. See ibid., pp. 16–17. See pp. 30–2 for a fuller appraisal of Lonergan's six theses, five of which, Lindbeck argues, are experiential-expressive, the sixth (in which biblical religions have 'another source in God's revelatory will') being propositional.
87 ibid., p. 17–18 (my italics). Lindbeck readily acknowledges the difficulty that the contemporary mind has when faced with the analogy of religion as language and its cultural context; see pp. 22–3. In spite of these major objections, he aims to show that the cultural-linguistic outlook 'is intellectually and empirically the most adequate' of the three approaches (p. 30).
88 ibid., p. 80.
89 ibid., p. 92.
90 David Kelsey, *The Uses of Scripture in Recent Theology* (London: SCM Press, 1975), p. 4. Kelsey insists that this book concerns 'a study of theologians' methods' and not an exercise in 'theological methodology'; see p. 7.
91 ibid., pp. 16–17.
92 ibid., p. 92.
93 *OCEL*, p. 653.
94 G. Lakoff and M. Johnson, *Metaphors We Live By* (1980), p. 19; reference from Philip Jenson.

95 Sallie McFague, *Models of God: Theology for an Ecological, Nuclear Age* (London: SCM Press, 1987), p. 33.

96 ibid., pp. 33–4.

97 ibid., p. 6.

98 ibid., p. xii.

99 McFague, for example, in exploring a 'theology for an ecological, nuclear age' puts forward metaphors for God as 'mother, lover, and friend of the world as God's body'. In doing this, she recognises the danger of such a monistic theology in tending 'toward identification of God and the world', but seeks to offset this difficulty through two riders to her argument. First, she concedes that 'as a metaphor, the relationship of divine agency and the world as God's body . . . both fits and does not fit': it both discloses 'the depths of divine love to imagine our world as God's body' and, at the same time, is nonsensical in terms of any close correspondence between God and the world and human beings and their bodies. Second, her metaphor is seen as a 'promising candidate to give imaginative reality to [the] sensibility' of 'the intricate, interdependent network of life, with God at its center as well as at every periphery'. See ibid., pp. 94–5.

100 ibid., p. 22.

101 ibid., p. 34.

102 Paul Ricoeur, 'Toward a Hermeneutic of the Idea of Revelation', in *Paul Ricoeur: Essays in Biblical Interpretation* ed. L. S. Mudge (London: SPCK, 1981), p. 92.

103 See Alastair V. Campbell, *Rediscovering Pastoral Care* (2nd ed.; London: Darton, Longman & Todd, 1986), pp. 24–5.

104 Donald Capps, *Pastoral Care and Hermeneutics* (Philadelphia: Fortress Press, 1984), pp. 76–7. Capps links each image with a distinctive model of 'theological diagnosis' that, taken together, can elucidate the pastoral encounter: the 'contextual' model (the shepherd), focusing on the causes of and resources for the problem; the 'experiential' model (the wounded healer), concentrating more on the emotional and interpersonal elements; and the 'revisionist' model (the wise fool), seeking new perspectives on the situation. See pp. 69–77.

105 Tom Lubbock, *Independent* (22 November 1988).

106 Two of the key figures of this movement were Jeanne-Marie Bouvier de la Motte Guyon (1648–1717) and François de Salignac de Lamothe Fénelon (*c*.1651–1715). Although initially critical, Fénelon became a proponent of 'la nouvelle spiritualité' of Madame Guyon, an approach which 'envisaged mystical union as a union of the human and divine wills such that the soul lost any capacity to distinguish between itself and God'; see Michael Richards in *DCS*, p. 184.

107 David G. Benner, *Psychotherapy and the Spiritual Quest* (Grand Rapids, MI: Baker Book House, 1988), pp. 104–6. In his analysis, Benner refers

to Gerald G. May, *Will and Spirit: A Contemplative Psychology* (San Francisco: Harper & Row, 1982), p. 33.

108 Paul Evdokimov, *L'Orthodoxie* (Neuchatel: Delachaux et Nestle, 1959), p. 113, quoted in Kenneth Leech, *Spirituality and Pastoral Care* (London: Sheldon Press, 1986), p. 5.

109 Joann Wolski Conn, *Spirituality and Personal Maturity* (Mahwah, NJ: Paulist Press, 1989), p. 30.

110 Leech, *Spirituality and Pastoral Care*, p. 74.

111 Wes Seelinger, *Western Theology* (Atlanta, GA: Forum House, 1973), quoted in Leech, *Spirituality and Pastoral Care*, p. 9.

112 Jonathan Culler, *On Deconstruction: Theory and Criticism after Structuralism* (Ithaca, NY, Cornell University Press, 1982), p. 149, quoted in Susan Hekman, *Gender and Knowledge: Elements of a Postmodern Feminism* (Cambridge: Polity Press, 1990), p. 4.

113 Kelsey, *Uses of Scripture*, p. 215.

Chapter 7 Biblical Counselling: The Transformed Mind

1 Richard F. Lovelace, *Dynamics of Spiritual Life: An Evangelical Theology of Renewal* (Exeter: The Paternoster Press, 1979), p. 219.

2 For a fuller account of the Christian responses to the secular psychologies in assimilation, reaction and dialogue, see Roger F. Hurding, *Roots and Shoots: A Guide to Counselling and Psychotherapy* (London: Hodder & Stoughton, 1985), pp. 211–42.

3 Although the term 'biblical counselling' is often seen as the prerogative of the more excluding brands of those Christian counselling approaches that hold to a high view of the Scriptures, I believe a case can be made (as I do in this chapter) for using the term to cover the whole spectrum of evangelical approaches that seek to be openly faithful to the Bible in their counselling methodologies.

4 I have followed the terms 'special' and 'general' revelation here as they are intrinsic to much of the debate between biblical counsellors of excluding and integational standings, with their often ready acknowledgment of the Reformed tradition. For a fuller discussion, see Hurding, *Roots and Shoots*, pp. 258–61.

5 ibid., pp. 277–90.

6 See Jay E. Adams, *Competent to Counsel* (Grand Rapids, MI: Baker Book House, 1970), pp. xiv–xviii, where he describes his reading of O. Hobart Mowrer, *The Crisis in Psychiatry and Religion* (Princeton: Van Nostrand Company, 1961) as 'an earth-shaking experience' (p. xvi).

7 Cornelius Van Til, *The Defense of the Faith* (Presbyterian and Reformed, 1955), pp. 286–99, 306.

8 For example: 'Biblically, there is no warrant for acknowledging the existence of a separate and distinct discipline called psychiatry. There

are, in the Scriptures, only three specified sources of personal problems in living: demonic activity . . . personal sin, and organic illness';
there is 'no room for a fourth: non-organic mental illness'. See Jay E.
Adams, *The Christian Counselor's Manual* (Presbyterian and Reformed, 1973), p. 9.

9 The terms are comparatively rare in the Greek texts: a handful of
references in the Septuagint's Wisdom literature and, in the New
Testament, *nouthesia* three times and *noutheteo* eight times. These are
quintessentially Pauline words; see, for example, Romans 15:14; 1
Corinthians 4:14; 10:11; Colossians 1:28; 3:16; and 1 Thessalonians
5:12, 14.

10 Van Til, *Defense of the Faith*, p. 286.

11 Jay E. Adams, *More Than Redemption: A Theology of Christian Counseling* (Grand Rapids, MI: Baker Book House, 1979), p. 326.

12 It is salutary to observe that *noutheteo* and *nouthesia* are derived from
nous (mind) and *tithemi* (put) and 'describe the exertion of influence
upon the *nous*, implying that there is resistance'. It is through
admonition, advice and warning that 'a person can be redirected
from wrong ways and his behaviour corrected'. See Georg Braumann
in *NIDNTT*, vol. 1, p. 568.

13 Jay E Adams, 'Nouthetic Counseling' in *Helping People Grow: Practical
Approaches to Christian Counseling*, ed. G. R. Collins (Santa Ana, CA:
Vision House, 1980), p. 158.

14 Interestingly, such prescriptive handling of Scripture in counselling
can be traced further back than Adams. See, for example, Clyde
Narramore, *The Psychology of Counseling* (Grand Rapids, MI: Zondervan, 1960), pp. 237–73.

15 For example, there are at least forty-five references to the Book of
Proverbs and just two from Isaiah in Adams, *Competent to Counsel*.

16 ibid., p. 51.

17 See, for example, Donald Capps, *Biblical Approaches to Pastoral Counseling* (Philadelphia: Westminster Press, 1981), pp. 32–6, 99–102, 114–
17; John D. Carter, 'Adams' Theory of Nouthetic Counseling', *Journal
of Psychology and Theology*, vol. 3, no. 3, 1975, pp. 143–55; Hurding,
Roots and Shoots, pp. 284–90; Stanton L. Jones and Richard E. Butman,
Modern Psychotherapies: A Comprehensive Christian Appraisal (Downers
Grove, IL: Inter-Varsity Press, 1991), pp. 18–26; and Richard D.
Winter, 'Jay Adams – Is He Really Biblical Enough?', *Third Way*,
vol. 5, no. 4, 1982, pp. 9–12. For a perceptive piece that even-
handedly seeks to build bridges between biblical counselling of
Adams's ilk and 'Christian psychology', see Philip G. Monroe,
'Building Bridges with Biblical Counselors', *Journal of Psychology
and Theology*, vol. 25, no. 1, 1997, pp. 28–37.

18 In a personal meeting with Jay Adams and a small group of Christian
counsellors in Hildenborough Hall, Kent, in May 1982, Adams

388 PATHWAYS TO WHOLENESS

expressed his regret at committing himself so resolutely to the term 'nouthetic'.

19 In David Powlison, 'Contemporary Biblical Counseling: An Annotated Bibliography', *Journal of Biblical Counseling*, vol. 12, no. 2, 1994, pp. 43–61, for example, Powlison writes of 'the modern biblical counseling movement founded by Jay Adams in the late 1960s' (p. 43).

20 David Powlison, '25 Years of Biblical Counseling: An Interview with Jay Adams and Jon Bettler', *Journal of Biblical Counseling*, vol. 12, no. 1, 1993, pp. 9–11.

21 John F. Bettler, 'Counseling and the Problem of the Past', *Journal of Biblical Counseling*, vol. 12, no. 2, 1994, p. 7.

22 Although Powlison describes Narramore as integrational, I see the latter's tripartite view of human need as essentially 'compartmentalised' or 'perspectival'; see Hurding, *Roots and Shoots*, pp. 234, 269–71. See Clyde Narramore, *The Psychology of Counseling* (Grand Rapids, MI: Zondervan, 1960); and *Encyclopedia of Psychological Problems: A Counseling Manual* (Grand Rapids, MI: Zondervan, 1966). In the latter (p. 14), Narramore puts foward a perspectivalist view in which the physical, emotional and spiritual components of human behaviour, although 'somewhat discrete', 'continually affect one another'. David Powlison, 'Integration or Inundation?' in *Power Religion: The Selling Out of the Evangelical Church?* ed. M. S. Horton (Chicago: Moody Press, 1992), pp. 191–218, describes Clyde Narramore as 'the first evangelical Christian well-known as a psychologist' and points to this 'trichotomist view' (body, spirit and soul) as attended to by the medical doctor, the pastor and the psychologist respectively. The 'new profession' of psychology thus 'first claimed legitimacy in evangelical circles' (see pp. 193–4).

23 For a succinct overview and critique, from an 'excluding' position, of the story of evangelical integration in psychology and theology, see Powlison, 'Integration or Inundation?', pp. 192–207. For an integrationist's assessment, see S. Bruce Narramore, 'Psychology and Theology: Twenty-Five Years of Theoretical Integration', *Journal of Psychology and Theology*, vol. 25, no. 1, 1997, pp. 6–10.

24 Among *integrational* contributions on the handling of Scripture in counselling, see Eric L. Johnson, 'A Place for the Bible Within Psychological Science', *Journal of Psychology and Theology*, vol. 20, no. 4, 1992, pp. 346–55; Eric L. Johnson, 'Christ, the Lord of Psychology', *Journal of Psychology and Theology*, vol. 25, no. 1, 1997, pp. 11–97; and H. Newton Malony, 'The Use of the Jewish/Christian Scriptures in Counseling', *Journal of Pastoral Counseling*, vol. 20, no. 2, 1985, pp. 116–24.

25 For appraisals of Frank Lake's (1914–82) distinctive approach in seeking an understanding between psychiatry and Christian theol-

ogy, see Carol Christian (ed.), *In the Spirit of Truth: A Reader in the Work of Frank Lake* (London: Darton, Longman & Todd, 1991); Hurding, *Roots and Shoots*, pp. 367–79, 383–6; John Peters, *Frank Lake: The Man and His Work* (London: Darton, Longman & Todd, 1989); and Alistair Ross, *An Evaluation of Clinical Theology and Its Contribution to Pastoral Theology and Training 1958–1969* (Oxford: Clinical Theology Association, 1994).

26 See Hurding, *Roots and Shoots*, pp. 299–301; Hughes acknowledges his debt to the influences of Clyde and Bruce Narramore and Lawrence Crabb, and in many ways holds a cautiously integrational approach, comparable to Crabb's.

27 During the three or four years leading up to the foundation of Network in 1986 there was a clear division among the steering committee between an excluding and an integrational approach to Christian counselling – the former influenced by Scope Ministries, Oklahoma City, which had links with Bristol through a previous Billy Graham mission. The integrational stance won the day and Network was established as something of a flagship in the United Kingdom in terms of both its commitment to integrate theology and psychology and to foster a training programme that is open to a wide spread of Christian emphases.

28 The original impetus for the formation of ABC is closely linked with seminars conducted by Jay Adams in 1981 and 1982, and by his colleagues John Bettler and Wayne Mack in the following years, at Hildenborough Hall, Kent.

29 Arthur F. Holmes, *All Truth Is God's Truth* (Grand Rapids, MI: Eerdmans, 1977), p. 8.

30 For an especially perceptive paper that tackles the vexed question of epistemology in modern psychology in the face of God's revealed truth, see Johnson, 'Christ, the Lord of Psychology'.

31 See John D. Carter and Bruce Narramore, *The Integration of Psychology and Theology: An Introduction* (Grand Rapids, MI: Zondervan, 1979). S. Bruce Narramore, 'Perspectives on the Integration of Psychology and Theology', *Journal of Psychology and Theology*, vol. 1, 1973, pp. 3–19, and John D. Carter and R. J. Mohline, 'The Nature and Scope of Integration: A Proposal', *Journal of Psychology and Theology*, vol. 4, 1976, pp. 3–14 are precursors of the Carter and Narramore book. Another seminal work published in the early days of integration is Gary R. Collins, *The Rebuilding of Psychology: An Integration of Psychology and Christianity* (Wheaton, IL: Tyndale House, 1977); for an appraisal of Collins's vital contribution to the debate, see Hurding, *Roots and Shoots*, pp. 235–7.

32 Carter and Narramore, *Integration*, p. 22.

33 ibid., p. 15.

34 ibid., p. 20.

35 ibid., p. 104; also see pp. 103–15.
36 For example, Crabb writes that in 'our view of general revelation we find warrant for scientific research as a valid means of looking for certain kinds of truth, but those of us who accept inerrancy hold to a view of special revelation which regards biblical data as uniformly true in all that it affirms'; Larry J. Crabb Jr, 'Biblical Authority and Christian Psychology', *Journal of Psychology and Theology*, vol. 9, no. 4, 1981, p. 306. In turn, he attacks the 'Two-Book View' and 'epistemological humility' of many integrationists, in which, respectively, general and special revelation are treated even-handedly as vehicles of God's truth and a certain diffidence is expressed before their revelatory power.
37 J. Guy Jr, 'Affirming Diversity in the Task of Integration: A Response to "Biblical Authority and Christian Psychology" ', *Journal of Psychology and Theology*, vol. 10, no. 1, 1982, p. 38.
38 Kirk E. Farnsworth, 'The Conduct of Integration', *Journal of Psychology and Theology*, vol. 10, no. 4, 1982, pp. 308–19. For critiques of Farnsworth, see Francis Bridger and David Atkinson, *Counselling in Context: Developing a Theological Framework* (London: HarperCollins, 1994), pp. 47–9; Stephen M. Clinton, 'A Critique of Integration Models', *Journal of Psychology and Theology*, vol. 18, no. 1, 1990, pp. 13–20; Michael J. De Vries, 'The Conduct of Integration: A Response to Farnworth', *Journal of Psychology and Theology*, vol. 10, no. 4, 1982, pp. 320–5; and H. Virkler, 'Response to "The Conduct of Integration" ', *Journal of Psychology and Theology*, vol. 10, no. 4, 1982, pp. 329–33.
39 Farnsworth, 'Conduct of Integration', p. 309.
40 ibid., p. 310.
41 ibid., p. 311.
42 ibid., p. 308.
43 Anthony C. Thiselton, *Interpreting God and the Postmodern Self: On Meaning, Manipulation and Promise* (Edinburgh: T. & T. Clark, 1996), p. 49.
44 Farnsworth, 'Conduct of Integration', p. 317.
45 Of particular note, see Clinton, 'Critique'; and 'The Foundational Integration Model', *Journal of Psychology and Theology*, vol. 18, no. 2, 1990, pp. 115–22.
46 Everett L. Worthington Jr, 'A Blueprint for Intradisciplinary Integration', *Journal of Psychology and Theology*, vol. 22, no. 2, 1994, pp. 79–86.
47 ibid., p. 79. See, too, Steve Bouma-Prediger, 'The Task of Integration: A Modest Proposal', *Journal of Psychology and Theology*, vol. 18, no. 1, 1990, pp. 21–31, where Bouma-Prediger 'proposes a framework, a typology of integration', comprising four basic kinds of integration: *interdisciplinary*, *intradisciplinary*, *faith-praxis* (between faith and 'way of life'), and *experiential* (within the self and/or between the self and

God).

48 Worthington, 'Blueprint', p. 79.
49 John A. Ingram, 'Contemporary Issues and Christian Models of Integration: Into the Modern/Postmodern Age', *Journal of Psychology and Theology*, vol. 23, no. 1, 1995, p. 3.
50 See Alister E. McGrath, *A Passion for Truth: The Intellectual Coherence of Evangelicalism* (Leicester: Inter-Varsity Press, 1996), pp. 167–70.
51 Colin Brown writes of Thomas Reid (1710–96), the founder of the Scottish 'common sense' philosophy, who strongly criticised Hume, a fellow-Scot, for his narrow view of human understanding in that nothing external to the mind can be known. Reid sought to refute this hypothesis as something which 'overturns all philosophy, all religion and virtue, and all common sense' (p. 260). See Colin Brown, *Christianity and Western Thought: A History of Philosophers, Ideas and Movements*, vol. 1 (Leicester: Inter-Varsity Press, 1990), pp. 259–83.
52 David Kelsey, for example, points to B. B. Warfield's commitment to the rational when he writes of Warfield's style of theology: 'traditional theological topics will be treated in the order of their logical dependence'; David Kelsey, *The Uses of Scripture in Recent Theology* (London: SCM Press, 1975), p. 162.
53 McGrath, *Passion*, p. 169.
54 ibid., p. 170, where McGrath quotes Carl F. H. Henry, *God, Revelation and Authority* (Waco, Tex: Word, 1976–83), vol. 1, p. 232 and vol. 3, p. 476. McGrath also refers to Donald G. Bloesch, *Essentials of Evangelical Theology* (2 vols.; San Francisco: Harper & Row, 1979), pp. 267–8 with regard to the influence of 'a strongly rationalist spirit' discernible in certain 'modern American evangelicals'.
55 McGrath, *Passion*, p. 170.
56 Powlison, 'Critiquing Modern Integrationists', pp. 30–1.
57 Powlison, 'Integration or Inundation?', p. 215.
58 Clinton, 'Critique'. See also Clinton, 'Foundational Integration Model', where part of his assumptive basis lies in a 'firm grounding in basic rationality, logic and perception' (p. 120).
59 Clinton, 'Critique', p. 17, with reference to Guy, 'Affirming Diversity' (in which, see p. 37).
60 Clinton, 'Critique', pp. 17–18.
61 Guy, 'Affirming Diversity', p. 36.
62 ibid., p. 37.
63 See Randie L. Timpe, 'Epistemological and Metaphysical Limits to Integration of Psychology and Theology', *Journal of Psychology and Theology*, vol. 2, no. 3, 1983, pp. 21–9. Timpe, in following Carter and Narramore's 'Parallels' model rather than their 'Integrates' model, does not openly acknowledge postmodern influences. Even so, his commitment to the 'divergent aims, goals, methods, and linguistic conventions' of traditional theology and psychology is consonant

with certain postmodern emphases.

64 Bouma-Prediger, 'Task of Integration', p. 26.

65 See J. F. Rychlak, 'A Suggested Principle of Complementarity for Psychology', *American Psychologist*, vol. 48, no. 9, 1993, pp. 933–42.

66 Ingram, 'Contemporary Issues', p. 4.

67 ibid., pp. 5–6.

68 ibid., p. 9.

69 ibid., pp. 6–7. Here, Ingram looks to R. W. Sperry's paper 'The Impact and Promise of the Cognitive Revolution', *American Psychologist*, vol. 48, no. 8, 1993, pp. 878–85, where Sperry offers a 'two way' model that 'integrates and blends aspects of prior opposed [objective and subjective] solutions into a novel unifying synthesis' (p. 879), quoted in Ingram, 'Contemporary Issues', p. 8.

70 In his theory of instincts, Freud postulated a *principle of constancy* which tends to restore inner equilibrium. Further, he put forward the notion of psychic *energy*, involved in achieving that constant state. The 'charges' of that energy he dubbed *cathexis*.

71 The three best known of the psychosociological school of the so-called neo-Freudians were Karen Horney (1885–1952), Harry Stack Sullivan (1892–1947) and Erich Fromm (1900–80); see Hurding, *Roots and Shoots*, pp. 92–5.

72 Viktor Frankl (1905) put forward his idea of *logotherapy* in 1926 as a form of psychotherapy that reaches beyond the psyche to 'the *logos*', or to the level of 'meaning'; see Hurding, *Roots and Shoots*, pp. 126–37, and Jones and Butman, *Modern Psychotherapies*, pp. 281–3.

73 We will assess Jung's contribution to pathways to wholeness in Chapter 10.

74 Ingram, 'Contemporary Issues', p. 7.

75 ibid., p. 9.

76 See ibid., pp. 11–12.

77 Adams refers to *pre*counselling, in which the counsellor's task is 'to confront unsaved men with the universal offer of the gospel', as essential in approaching the non-Christian. This is consistent with his commitment to biblical counselling as fundamentally 'nouthetic' and, thereby, placed in the context of Christian fellowship. See Adams, *Competent*, p. 70, and *Redemption*, p. 326. See also Hurding, *Roots and Shoots*, pp. 280, 282–3.

78 See above note. Powlison writes that the 'goal of biblically reinterpreting human experience . . . is the ministry of the Word that converts the soul'; 'Critiquing Modern Integrationists', p. 34.

79 Christopher Wright defines a paradigm as 'something used as a model or example for other cases where a basic principle remains unchanged, though details differ' and adds, 'a paradigm is not so much imitated as applied'; see Christopher J. H. Wright, *An Eye for an Eye: The Place of Old Testament Ethics Today* (Downers Grove, IL:

InterVarsity Press, 1983), p. 43. Waldemar Janzen finds this definition useful but says further that 'biblical Israelites did not carry with them a stock of maxims or principles, but mental images of model persons [such as Abraham] . . . In other words, before the Israelites' inner eye stood a vivid, lifelike yet ideal family member, worshiper, wise person, king, or prophet.' See Waldemar Janzen, *Old Testament Ethics: A Paradigmatic Approach* (Westminster/John Knox, 1994), pp. 26–7.

80 Powlison, '25 Years of Biblical Counseling', p. 10.

81 Lawrence J. Crabb Jr, *Understanding People: Deep Longings for Relationship* (Grand Rapids, MI: Zondervan, 1987), p. 26.

82 Gary R. Collins, *The Biblical Basis of Christian Counseling for People Helpers* (Colorado Springs, CL: NavPress, 1993), p. 57.

83 The commonest form of address for Jesus in the Gospels is 'teacher' or 'master' (Heb. *rabbî*; Gk. *didaskole*); see *NIDNTT*, vol. 3, pp. 115, 767.

84 See Matthew 5:17–20; compare Romans 3:31.

85 N. T. Wright, *The Climax of the Covenant: Christ and the Law in Pauline Theology* (Edinburgh: T. & T. Clark, 1991), p. 242.

86 On the instructional nature of Torah, see Hans-Helmut Esse in *NIDNTT*, vol. 2, p. 440.

87 I am grateful to Philip Jenson, Old Testament scholar at Trinity College, Bristol, for this analogy.

88 A. J. Heschel, *God in Search of Man* (New York: Farrar, Strauss & Giroux, 1955), p. 338.

89 Janzen, *Old Testament Ethics*, p. 59.

90 Walter C. Kaiser Jr, 'Images for Today: The Torah Speaks Today' in J. Robert L. Hubbard, R. K. Johnston and R. P. Meye (eds.), *Studies in Old Testament Theology* (Dallas: Word Publishing, 1992), p. 118.

91 For papers that make links between spirituality and the behavioural, and therefore have possible resonance for evangelicalism and biblical counselling, see Allen E. Bergin, 'Three Contributions of a Spiritual Perspective in Counseling, Psychotherapy, and Behavior Change', *Counseling and Values*, vol. 33, no. 1, 1988, pp. 21–33; E. P. Bolin and G. M. Goldberg, 'Behavioral Psychology and the Bible', *Journal of Psychology and Theology*, vol. 7, no. 3, 1979, pp. 167–75; and Howard P. Brown Jr, John H. Peterson Jr and Orville Cunningham, 'Rationale and Theoretical Basis for a Behavioral/Cognitive Approach to Spirituality', *Alcoholism Treatment Quarterly*, vol. 5 no. 1/2, 1988, pp. 47–59.

92 See, for example, Gustavo Gutiérrez, *We Drink from Our Own Wells: The Spiritual Journey of a People* (London: SCM Press, 1984), pp. 35–7, where Gutiérrez argues that in the early centuries every theology was a 'spiritual theology' but that, toward the fourteenth century, a divide began to open up between theology and spirituality to the detriment of both. See also Laurie Green, *Let's Do Theology: A Pastoral Cycle Resource Book* (London: Mowbray, 1990), p. 129.

93 In particular, see David K. Gillett, *Trust and Obey: Explorations in Evangelical Spirituality* (London: Darton, Longman & Todd, 1993); James Houston, *The Heart's Desire: A Guide to Personal Fulfilment* (Oxford: Lion, 1992); Alister McGrath, *Roots That Refresh: A Celebration of Reformation Spirituality* (London: Hodder & Stoughton, 1992); Alister McGrath, *Evangelicalism and the Future of Christianity* (London: Hodder & Stoughton, 1994); McGrath, *Passion*; James I. Packer, 'An Introduction to Systematic Spirituality', *Crux*, vol. 26, no. 1, 1990, pp. 1–8; and David Parker, 'Evangelical Spirituality Reviewed', *Evangelical Quarterly*, vol. 6, no. 3, 1991, pp. 123–48.

94 Packer, 'Systematic Spirituality', p. 7.

95 Mark Noll Jr, Cornelius Plantinga and David Wells, 'Evangelical Theology Today', *Theology Today*, vol. 51, no. 4, 1995, p. 502.

96 McGrath, *Passion*, p. 98.

97 See David Parker, 'Evangelical Spirituality Reviewed', *Evangelical Quarterly*, vol. 6, no. 3, 1991, pp. 123–48, where he declares both the danger and value in evangelicalism's current interest in other Christian traditions of spirituality. He maintains that there is much in the evangelical tradition that parallels other spiritualities and these practices can be re-evaluated and recovered. His main sticking point in assessing non-evangelical spirituality is where it threatens to deny God's grace 'by subtly appealing to human achievement or introducing a stand of legalism' (p. 141).

98 See McGrath, *Future of Christianity*, pp. 123–45.

99 See Dave Tomlinson, *The Post-Evangelical* (London: SPCK, 1995), and Graham Cray, Maggi Dawn, Nick Mercer, Michael Saward, Pete Ward and Nigel Wright, *The Post-evangelical Debate* (London: SPCK, 1997).

100 Tomlinson, *Post-Evangelical*, p. 90. Graham Cray, for example, challenges Tomlinson's equation of evangelicalism and modernity, seeing evangelicalism as 'a rooted movement whose primary doctrinal convictions far pre-date modernity' (Cray, et al. *Debate*, p. 4).

101 Nigel Wright, *The Radical Evangelical: Seeking a Place to Stand* (London: SPCK, 1996).

102 Alistair Ross, *Evangelicals in Exile: Wrestling with Theology and the Unconscious* (London: Darton, Longman & Todd, 1997).

103 D. W. Bebbington, *Evangelicalism in Modern Britain: A History from the 1730s to the 1980s* (London: Unwin Hyman, 1989), pp. 2–17.

104 See, for example, George Lindbeck, *The Nature of Doctrine: Religion and Doctrine in a Postliberal Age* (London: SPCK, 1984), p. 79. See the critique of Lindbeck's views on propositionalism in McGrath, *Passion*, pp. 137–41.

105 McGrath, ibid., p. 137.

106 Walter Brueggemann, *The Bible and Postmodern Imagination: Texts under Negotiation* (London: SCM Press, 1993), pp. 12–13.

107 ibid., p. 58.

108 ibid., p. 71.

109 Walter Wink, *Transforming Bible Study* (London: SCM Press, 1980), pp. 21–34. See Roger Sperry, *Science and Moral Priority: Merging Mind, Brain, and Human Values* (Oxford: Basil Blackwell, 1983), pp. 37–8, 55–9, where the distinctive but complementary functions of the two cerebral hemispheres, and their implications for social change, are laid down.

110 This account is used with permission.

111 Runcorn also pointed out to the students that, in this instance, 'the Gentiles had actually evangelised the Jewish Church (outsiders evangelising insiders) and that 'evangelism . . . is more than a one way process', in which it is 'not always clear who needs converting and from what'.

112 Quoted in Bebbington, *Evangelicalism in Modern Britain*, p. 14.

113 McGrath, *Roots That Refresh*, pp. 69–70, tells how Luther's statement *Crux sola est nostra theologica* 'proved to be the rock' on which McGrath's former liberalism 'foundered'.

114 McGrath (ibid., pp. 70–3) points to the notion of 'hidden revelation' in Luther's theology of the cross, in which, for instance, Luther, referring to Moses' 'glimpse' of God from the cleft in the rock (Exod. 33:21–3), writes, 'Whoever sees the visible rearward parts of God, as seen in suffering and the cross . . . deserve[s] to be called a theologian' (p. 70).

115 See Jürgen Moltmann, *The Crucified God: The Cross of Christ as the Foundation and Criticism of Christian Theology* (London: SCM Press, 1974), p. 47.

116 ibid., pp. 186–7.

117 See McGrath, *Future of Christianity*, pp. 14–18.

118 McGrath, *Roots That Refresh*, p. 128; for McGrath's sympathetic assessment of Calvin's 'world-affirming spirituality', see pp. 117–32.

119 Lovelace, *Dynamics of Spiritual Life*, p. 377, where the Darbyite influence on such evangelicals as D. L. Moody and F. B. Meyer is discussed.

120 In some circles the term 'fundamentalism' is still incorrectly applied to evangelicals generally. The term originally grew out of the publication in 1910–15 of a series of twelve books entitled *The Fundamentals* and took particular root in the United States in the 1920s and 1930s to describe a movement that was essentially reactive toward modernity. McGrath writes that certain 'central doctrines', notably 'the absolute literal authority of Scripture and the premillenial return of Christ' were 'treated as barriers . . . to alienate secular culture' as much as to give the movement 'a sense of identity and purpose'; McGrath, *Future of Christianity*, p. 21.

121 See Lovelace, *Dynamics*, pp. 376–9.

122 Proverbs 8:30–1. Although wisdom is here personified as feminine, it is possible to equate God's co-worker, who 'was there when he set the heavens in place' (8: 27), with the Word who 'was with God in the beginning . . . became flesh and made his dwelling among us' (John 1:2, 14).

123 Roger F. Hurding, *As Trees Walking* (Exeter: The Paternoster Press, 1982), p. 199.

124 Brueggemann, *Bible and Postmodern Imagination*, p. 29.

125 Green, *Let's Do Theology*, p. 22.

Chapter 8 Healing Ministries: The Forward Gain

1 Ursula Le Guin, *Earthsea Trilogy* (Harmondsworth: Pelican, 1979), p. 165.

2 This account is given more fully in Roger F. Hurding, *As Trees Walking* (Exeter: The Paternoster Press, 1982), pp. 213–15.

3 William A. Clebsch and Charles R. Jaekle, *Pastoral Care in Historical Perspective* (New York: Jason Aronson, 1975), p. 42.

4 It is worth pointing out at this stage that healing, because it is a comprehensive concept, can be seen to feature in all of the five pathways. In this chapter we shall primarily consider healing in relation to 'charismatic' spirituality, although its sacramental perspectives will feature more in Chapter 10. Colin Urquhart's methodology, with its strong emphasis on faith in scriptural promises and its questioning of much in 'journey back' approaches, straddles our first two pathways; see, for example, Colin Urquhart, *The Truth that Sets You Free* (London: Hodder & Stoughton, 1993), pp. 104–26.

5 Morris Maddocks, *The Christian Healing Ministry* (London: SPCK, 1981), p. 7.

6 Clebsch and Jaekle, *Pastoral Care*, p. 33.

7 See, for example, *NIDNTT*, vol. 3, p. 212, where Colin Brown points out that the use of *sozo* and *soteria* in the Synoptic accounts always refers to healing 'of the whole man'.

8 See John A. T. Robinson, *Jesus and His Coming: The Emergence of a Doctrine* (London: SCM Press, 1957), p. 101, where Robinson coins the term: 'For relating that hour [of the Son of Man] to the future and to the final consummation of God's purpose, "inaugurated eschatology" would appear the most satisfactory term. For at that hour *all* is inaugurated, yet *only* inaugurated.'

9 Clebsch and Jaekle, *Pastoral Care*, p. 8. Books on 'healing' often fail to balance their approach with a consideration of 'sustaining'. Stephen Pattison, *Alive and Kicking: Towards a Practical Theology of Illness and Healing* (London: SCM Press, 1989) is a notable exception.

10 For perspectives on the church history of healing and sustaining, see

Clebsch and Jaekle, *Pastoral Care*; Evelyn Frost, *Christian Healing* (London: Mowbray, 1940); Morton T. Kelsey, *Healing and Christianity: In Ancient Thought and Modern Times* (London: SCM Press, 1973); Maddocks, *Christian Healing Ministry*; and W. J. Sheils (ed.), *The Church and Healing: Papers Read at Meetings of the Ecclesiastical History Society* (Oxford: Blackwell, 1982). See also Roger F. Hurding, 'Healing', in *Medicine and the Bible*, ed. B. Palmer (Exeter: The Paternoster Press, 1986), pp. 191–216; and Roger F. Hurding, 'Healing' and 'Suffering' in *NDCEPT*, pp. 431–4 and 823–5.

11 For the influence of Wesleyan Methodism, including John Wesley's teaching on 'entire sanctification', on Pentecostalism, see D. W. Bebbington, *Evangelicalism in Modern Britain: A History from the 1730s to the 1980s* (London: Unwin Hyman, 1989), pp. 195–7; and Richard F. Lovelace, *Dynamics of Spiritual Life: An Evangelical Theology of Renewal* (Exeter: Paternoster Press, 1979), pp. 115–16, 120–1. Jean-Jacques Suurmond makes a powerful case for Pentecostalism's early links with African spirituality, in which there is no division between the spirit-world of dreams and visions and earthly reality; see Jean-Jacques Suurmond, *Word and Spirit at Play: Towards a Charismatic Theology* (London: SCM Press, 1994), pp. 3–19. Also see Suurmond and John Gunstone, *Signs and Wonders: The Wimber Phenomenon* (London: Darton, Longman & Todd, 1989), pp. 22–7, for discussions on the origins of and splits between black and white Pentecostalism. For the early spread of Pentecostalism to Britain, see Bebbington, *Evangelicalism*, p. 197; Michael Harper, *As At the Beginning: The Twentieth Century Pentecostal Revival* (London: Hodder & Stoughton, 1965), p. 45; and Peter Hocken, *Streams of Renewal: The Origins and Early Development of the Charismatic Movement in Great Britain* (Exeter: The Paternoster Press, 1986), pp. 67, 198–9.

12 For a thorough and detailed account of the early years of the 'charismatic movement', see Hocken, *Streams*. Hocken sees the two internationally known Pentecostalists, David du Plessis and Donal Gee, as pivotal figures in trying to prise Pentecostalism away from denominationalism toward a revival of the mainstream churches; see pp. 18–21 and 61–5. Hocken's painstaking research also establishes that the popular notion that charismatic renewal began in the United States and was thus exported to Britain is incorrect. He shows non-Pentecosalist anticipatory elements in the United Kingdom throughout the 1950s, including, for example, the influence of George Skinner Ingram and the interdenominational Nights of Prayer for World-wide Revival; see Hocken, *Streams*, pp. 82–3.

13 For Wimber's presentation of his own work, see John Wimber and Kevin Springer, *Power Evangelism: Signs and Wonders Today* (London: Hodder & Stoughton, 1985); and *Power Healing* (London: Hodder & Stoughton, 1986). For broadly sympathetic assessments, see Gun-

stone, *Signs and Wonders*; David C. Lewis, *Healing: Fiction, Fantasy or Fact?* (London: Hodder & Stoughton, 1989); and John White, *When the Spirit Comes With Power: Signs & Wonders Among God's People* (London, Hodder & Stoughton, 1989). For stronger critiques of Wimber and the 'signs and wonders' movement generally, see Wallace Benn and Mark Burkill, 'A Theological and Pastoral Critique of the Teaching of John Wimber', *Churchman*, vol. 101, no. 2, 1987, pp. 101–13; Martyn Percy, *Words, Wonders and Power: Understanding Contemporary Christian Fundamentalism and Revivalism* (London: SPCK, 1996); and Nigel Wright, 'The Theology and Methodology of "Signs and Wonders"', in *Charismatic Renewal: The Search for a Theology*, ed. T. Smail, A. Walker and N. Wright (London: SPCK, 1995), pp. 71–85. For a fine evangelical appraisal of healing and sustaining in the context of Wimber's links with Fuller Theological Seminary, see Lewis B. Smedes (ed.), *Ministry and the Miraculous: A Case Study at Fuller Theological Seminary* (Pasadena: Fuller Theological Seminary, 1987).

14 See Mark Stibbe, *Times of Refreshing: A Practical Theology of Renewal for Today* (London: HarperCollins, 1995). Mark Stibbe is cautious about the significance of the Toronto blessing and yet sees it as the harbinger of revival: 'There is a fourth wave coming, and . . . the Toronto phenomenon is the first sign of it' (p. 10; see also pp. 170–2). For charismatic appraisals of Toronto, see Lloyd Pietersen (ed.), *The Mark of the Spirit? A Charismatic Critique of the Toronto Blessing* (Carlisle: Paternoster Publishing, 1998), a systematic critique of Stibbe's book; and Tom Smail, Andrew Walker and Nigel Wright, 'From "The Toronto Blessing" to Trinitarian Renewal: A Theological Conversation' in *Charismatic Renewal*, pp. 152–66.

15 For an overview of the influence of charismatic renewal on the liturgical and sacramental traditions, see Peter Hocken, *The Strategy of the Spirit?* (Eagle, 1996). For reflections on the Holy Spirit's work in the Church from a leading Roman Catholic theologian, see Karl Rahner, *The Spirit in the Church* (London: Burns & Oates, 1979).

16 For writing that traces the story of the interrelationship between medical practice and Christian healing, see Maddocks, *Christian Healing*, pp. 97–112, 163–77; see also Hurding, 'Healing' in *Medicine and the Bible*, pp. 204–7. An influential example of this realignment is found in the work and writings of Robert A. Lambourne (1917–72), general practitioner, theologian and psychiatrist, Lecturer in Pastoral Studies in the Department of Theology, University of Birmingham (1964–72); see Robert A. Lambourne, *Community, Church and Healing: A Study of Some of the Corporate Aspects of the Church's Ministry to the Sick* (London: Arthur James, 1987); and Michael Wilson (ed.), *Explorations in Health and Salvation: A Selection of Papers by Bob Lambourne* (Birmingham: University of Birmingham, 1983).

17 For example, in the United States, Agnes Sanford, as an Episcopalian,

brought together a sacramentalist and charismatic approach to healing. She and her husband founded the 'School of Pastoral Care' in 1955 for ministers, doctors and nurses, where the Sanfords spoke of 'the power of the Holy Spirit working in men and women to the healing of their physical, mental, social and spiritual ills'; Hocken, *Streams*, pp. 181–2. Other comparable endeavours include the centres of Burrswood and Crowhurst in southern England, and, of wide influence throughout the British Isles, the Acorn Christian Healing Trust, founded in 1983 and committed to the 'vision of a nation renewed in the service of Christ the healer' through close ecclesio-medical links; see Morris and Anne Maddocks, 'Initiatives for the Kingdom', *Healing and Wholeness* (January 1995), p. 23.

18 A notable and much publicised instance, given its high-profile 'third wave' context, is seen in John Wimber's and the Vineyard Church's prayers for David Watson's healing from cancer in 1983 and early 1984, followed by Watson's death from the condition on 18 February 1984. See David Watson, *Fear No Evil: A Personal Struggle with Cancer* (London: Hodder & Stoughton, 1984) and Wimber, *Power Healing*, pp. 13–19. For biblical examples, see the extended delay in Job's recovery from multiple familial, economic and medical disasters; the continuation of Paul's 'thorn in the flesh' which, whether a physical affliction or not, was permitted by God; the episode of Epaphroditus' illness (Phil. 2:25–30); Paul's medicinal approach to Timothy's 'frequent illnesses' (1 Tim. 5:23); and the fact that Trophimus was left 'sick in Miletus' (2 Tim. 4:20).

19 See, for example, Henry W. Frost, *Miraculous Healing* (London: Marshall, Morgan & Scott, 1961), p. 115. For more recent overviews of New Testament healings, see Harold Remus, *Jesus as Healer* (Cambridge: Cambridge University Press, 1997); and John Wilkinson, *Health and Healing: Studies in New Testament Principles and Practice* (Edinburgh: 1980).

20 The nineteenth-century German theologian who in his influential *The Life of Jesus* (1835) dismissed not only the possibility of the miraculous but the very historicity of Jesus Christ (see Chapter 4).

21 See B. B. Warfield, *Miracles: Yesterday and Today, True and False* (Grand Rapids, MI: Eerdmans, 1965), later published as *Counterfeit Miracles* (Banner of Truth Trust, 1986). Warfield (1851–1921) held a dispensational view of healing, arguing that God has dispensed his miraculous gifts on humankind over certain crucial periods of biblical history, the last being 'the Apostolic age' (pp. 5, 6, 191).

22 Works that are favourably disposed to certain accounts of miraculous healing include Rex Gardner, *Healing Miracles: A Doctor Investigates* (London: Darton, Longman & Todd, 1986); Lewis, *Healing*; and White, *When The Spirit Comes*. More critical analyses include Peter May in John Goldingay (ed.), *Signs, Wonders and Healing* (Leicester:

IVP, 1989); David Middlemiss, *Interpreting Charismatic Experience* (London: SCM Press, 1996); and Percy, *Words, Wonders and Power*. Roland Howard, *Charismania: When Christian Fundamentalism Goes Wrong* (London: Mowbray, 1997), provides a more popular critique of the more sensationalist elements in charismatic renewal, including the healing ministries.

23 M. A. H. Melinsky, *Healing Miracles* (London: Mowbray, 1968), p. 69.

24 C. S. Lewis, *Miracles: A Preliminary Study* (London: Collins, 1960), p. 140.

25 From the first line of Gerard Manley Hopkins' 'God's Grandeur' in *Poems and Prose of Gerard Manley Hopkins* (Harmondsworth: Penguin, 1953), p. 27.

26 Middlemiss, *Interpreting*, p. xiv. By definition, the assessment of charismatic experience and its outcome is a field fraught with methodological difficulty. For valuable work in this area, see the research of the pastoral theologian, Leslie J. Francis: for example, Leslie J. Francis and Susan H. Jones, 'Personality and Charismatic Experience Among Adult Christians', *Pastoral Psychology*, vol. 45, no. 6, 1997, using the Revised Eysenck Personality Questionnaire and the Myers Briggs Type Indicator (MBTI), concludes that 'charismatic' Christians demonstrate 'stable extraversion' (Eysenck's index of 'sociability') and a preference for 'thinking' (MBTI).

27 Middlemiss, *Interpreting*, p. 163.

28 This story is discussed in Lewis, *Healing*, pp. 47–9.

29 Middlemiss, *Interpreting*, p. 118.

30 See Basil Mitchell, *The Justification of Religious Belief* (Macmillan, 1973), explored by Middlemiss, *Interpreting*, pp. 110–26.

31 John Wisdom in Mitchell, *Justification*, p. 45, quoted in Middlemiss, *Interpreting*, p. 120.

32 Middlemiss shows how Jonathan Edwards (1703–58), the great New England theologian of revival, displayed a comparable circumspection when faced with apparent divine intervention, arguing that 'Great effects on the body are no sure evidences that affections are spiritual': Jonathan Edwards, *The Religious Affections* (Banner of Truth Trust, 1961), Part II, Section II, quoted in Middlemiss, *Interpreting*, p. 217.

33 For an overview of many of these methodologies, see Roger F. Hurding, *Roots and Shoots: A Guide to Counselling and Psychotherapy* (London: Hodder & Stoughton, 1985), pp. 361–86. For works on 'primal integration' and the important work of Frank Lake (1914–82), see Carol Christian (ed.), *In the Spirit of Truth: A Reader in the Work of Frank Lake* (London: Darton, Longman & Todd, 1991); John Peters, *Frank Lake: The Man and His Work* (London: Darton, Longman & Todd, 1989); and Alistair Ross, *An Evaluation of Clinical Theology and Its Contribution to Pastoral Theology and Training 1958-1969* (Oxford:

Clinical Theology Association, 1994). See also Kenneth McAll, *Healing the Family Tree* (Sheldon Press, 1982) and Michael Mitton and Russ Parker, *Requiem Healing: A Christian Understanding of the Dead* (London: Darton, Longman & Todd, 1991); the latter includes an important critique of McAll's approach on pp. 86–104.

34 The parallel between inner healing and the psychoanalytic tradition is, of course, primarily limited to the *focus* of their gaze, i.e., on the 'hidden past': whereas analysis is committed to a painstaking 'archaelogical dig' to unearth personal history, the Christian 'journey back' methodologies, although often conceding the limited value of the 'talking cure', are avowedly dependent on the Holy Spirit's knowledge and guidance for illuminating the past.

35 Ruth Carter Stapleton, *The Experience of Inner Healing* (London: Hodder & Stoughton, 1978), Introduction.

36 Agnes Sanford, *Healing Gifts of the Spirit* (Evesham: Arthur James, 1966), p. 10.

37 ibid., p. 94.

38 See Stapleton, *Experience*, and Ruth Carter Stapleton, *The Gift of Inner Healing* (London: Hodder & Stoughton, 1977).

39 On Sanford's influence, see Francis MacNutt, *Healing* (Notre Dame, IN: Ave Maria Press, 1974), pp. 6–7; see, too, Francis MacNutt, *The Power to Heal* (Notre Dame, IN: Ave Maria Press, 1977).

40 On Payne's admiration for Sanford, see, for example, Leanne Payne, *The Healing Presence* (Eastbourne: Kingsway, 1990), pp. 161–2.

41 Sanford, *Healing Gifts*, pp. 86–7.

42 ibid., p. 101.

43 ibid., p. 107; for the detail of Sanford's method in helping others, see pp. 105–7.

44 ibid., p. 94.

45 ibid., p. 95.

46 Dave Hunt and T. A. McMahon, *The Seduction of Christianity: Spiritual Discernment in the Last Days* (Eugene, Oregon: Harvest House, 1985). See also Dave Hunt, *Beyond Seduction: A Return to Biblical Christianity* (Eugene, Oregon: Harvest House, 1987).

47 Hunt and McMahon, *Seduction*, pp. 171–88.

48 ibid., p. 165.

49 ibid., p. 173. This particular use of imagination has become an issue of major importance among both the proponents and critics of inner healing. For example, John Sandford in John Sandford and Mark Sandford, *Delivered or Healed? A Guide to Christian Wholeness* (London: HarperCollins, 1993), who defines his practice of inner healing as simply 'prayer and counsel for sanctification and transformation' (p. 18), defends his and his wife Paula's ministry against the unfair indictment of 'visualization': '[we] have always warned against [this] false use of imagination' (p. 20).

50 Payne, *Healing Presence*, p. 66.
51 J. Alsdurf and H. Newton Malony, 'A Critique of Ruth Carter Stapleton's Ministry of "Inner Healing"', *Journal of Psychology and Theology*, vol. 8, no. 3, 1980, pp. 173–84.
52 For a spirited defence of Stapleton, see William E. Buell, 'Reaction to Jim M. Alsdurf and H. Newton Malony's Critique of Ruth Carter Stapleton's Ministry of Inner Healing', *Journal of Psychology and Theology*, vol. 8, no. 3, 1980, pp. 185–90, where a similar point is made.
53 David G. Benner, *Healing Emotional Wounds* (Grand Rapids, MI: Baker Book House, 1990).
54 ibid., pp. 63–128.
55 ibid., p. 108.
56 See, for example, Martin and Deidre Bobgan, *Hypnosis and the Christian* (Minneapolis, MN: Bethany House, 1984); Hunt and McMahon, *Seduction*, pp. 185–6; and John and Mark Sandford, *A Comprehensive Guide to Deliverance and Inner Healing* (Grand Rapids, MI: Chosen Books, 1992). For a theologically and psychologically well-argued refutation of much of this anti-hypnosis literature, see John H. Court, *Hypnosis, Healing and the Christian* (Carlisle: Paternoster Press, 1997), pp. 37, 125–49. I am grateful to this last book for the essence of this section on hypnosis.
57 Court points to the animosity stirred in both the Church and science by Mesmer's theory of 'animal magnetism'; nonetheless, some were prepared to acknowledge that seemingly therapeutic changes were attributable to 'the power of suggestion and the use of the patients' imagination'; *Hypnosis*, p. 106.
58 Freud, although impressed by Charcot, in time discarded hypnosis, with which he was not particularly effective, in favour of his psychoanalytic 'talking cure'; thus, such was Freud's influence that hypnosis declined in popularity within the emerging profession of psychotherapy. See Court, *Hypnosis*, pp. 107–8.
59 Bobgans, *Hypnosis and the Christian*, p. 53, quoted in Court, *Hypnosis*, p. 127.
60 Court, *Hypnosis* pp. 6–18.
61 ibid., p. 145.
62 Z. Rubin & E. B. McNeil, *The Psychology of Being Human* (New York: Harper and Row, 1983), quoted in Court, *Hypnosis*, p. 22.
63 Court, pp. 36–7.
64 ibid., p. 92.
65 ibid., p. 93.
66 ibid., p. 98.
67 I am particularly indebted to Peter Fonagy and Mary Target, 'Memories are Irrelevant to Psychotherapy: Discuss,' in *Dilemmas in Psychotherapy in Royal College of Psychiatrists, Psychotherapy Section, Annual Residential Conference, Bristol* (1997), for the insights of this section.

68 This issue is taken seriously enough for the formation of two major organisations: the False Memory Syndrome Foundation in the USA in 1992, and the British False Memory Society in 1993.

69 Fonagy and Target, 'Memories', p. 184.

70 Meeting of the Bristol Psychotherapy Association, 3 December 1997, at which Phil Mollon spoke on 'The Memory Debate: Living with Uncertainty, Ambiguity and Complexity'. Also see, Phil Mollon, 'The Memory Debate: A Consideration of Clinical Complexities and Some Suggested Guidelines for Psychoanalytic Therapists', *British Journal of Psychotherapy*, vol. 13, no. 2, 1996, pp. 193–203.

71 Philip Roth, *The Facts: A Novelist's Autobiography* (New York: Harper, 1988), p. 8, quoted in Charles Elliott, *Memory and Salvation* (London: Darton, Longman & Todd, 1996), p. 20.

72 Elliott, *Memory*, pp. 20–30.

73 Fonagy and Target, 'Memories', p. 185.

74 See ibid., pp. 185–6, where five clusters of research relating to memory distortion are listed.

75 ibid., p. 186, referring to J. A. Usher and U. Neisser, 'Childhood Amnesia and the Beginnings of Memory for Four Early Life Events, *Journal of Experimental Psychology, General*, vol. 122, 1993, pp. 155–65.

76 The hippocampus, that part of the brain thought to be concerned with 'the meaningful integration of experience in memory', is found to be damaged in association with 'repeated experiences of maltreatment'; see Fonagy and Target, 'Memories', pp. 186–7.

77 See, for example, Jon G. Allen, 'The Spectrum of Accuracy in Memories of Childhood Trauma', *Harvard Review of Psychiatry*, vol. 3, 1995, pp. 84–95 who distinguishes between the 'implicit' nature of 'conditioned-emotional' memory and the 'explicit' nature of 'narrative-autobiographical' memory.

78 Fonagy and Target, 'Memories', pp. 187–8.

79 ibid., p. 195. See pp. 195–7 for a discussion of Freud's 'inconsistent' use of the term 'repression' and for its current use in psychoanalytic circles.

80 ibid., p. 197; for this section on dissociation, see pp. 197–9.

81 'Multiple personality disorder' (MPD), characterised by 'the existence within the person of two or more distinct personality or personality states', where at least two of these 'recurrently take full control of the person's behaviour', has been redesignated as 'dissociative identity disorder' (DID) in the *Diagnostic and Statistical Manual of Mental Disorders* (4th ed.; Washington, DC: American Psychiatric Press, 1994). See Court, *Hypnosis*, pp. 54–5; and John Morton, 'Cognitive Perspectives on Recovered Memories' in Joseph Sandler and Peter Fonagy (ed.), *Recovered Memories of Abuse: True or False?* (London: Karnac Books, 1997), pp. 58–63. 'Over 90% of patients with DSM-IV dissociative identity disorders report histories of severe physical and sexual abuse'; Fonagy and Target, 'Memories' p. 198.

82 Quoted in Fonagy and Target, 'Memories', p. 198.

83 Hurding, *As Trees Walking*, p. 214.

84 The verb *diaballo* (from the noun *diabolos*, slanderer, the devil), from *dia*, through, and *ballo*, to throw, means 'to throw over or across, divide, set at variance, accuse, bring charges, slander, inform, reject, misrepresent, deceive'. There is a clear progression from, in the Old Testament, seeing Satan, the Adversary, as simply an opponent (e.g., the word is used of the angel who stood in Balaam's way; Numbers 22:22, 32) through a tendency, in late Judaism, to see the devil as 'identified with the "evil inclination" and with the "angel of death" ' to, in the New Testament, an open confrontation between Jesus Christ and the forces of darkness. See *NIDNTT*, vol. 3, pp. 468–73.

85 Although popular Greek thinking and rabbinic Judaism were rife with a belief in demons, evil spirits who brought misery and disaster on humankind, the 'general trend in the OT is to exclude belief in demons'. In the New Testament angels and demons (*daimonion*) appear 'as opposites', the latter being subordinate to Satan and, where they possess men and women, cast out by the victorious Jesus (e.g., Matt. 12:28). See *NIDNTT*, vol. 1, pp. 450–3.

86 See, for example, Matthew 4:1–11; Mark 3:20–30; Luke 4:1–13; and John. 8:42–7. 'When the devil had finished all this tempting, he left [Jesus] until an opportune time' (Luke 4:13) indicates the recurring nature of these 'pitched battles'.

87 Walter Wink argues that Paul, in the light of ancient demonology, has 'taken key steps' toward 'depersonalizing it by means of the categories of sin, law, the flesh, and death'. See Walter Wink, *Naming the Powers: The Language of Power in the New Testament* (Philadelphia: Fortress Press, 1984), p. 104.

88 Clebsch and Jaekle, *Pastoral Care*, p. 38. Michael Perry sees 'deliverance' as the more general word for 'freeing people from the bondage of Satan' and 'exorcism' as 'a specific act of binding and releasing' to free a person 'believed to be possessed by a non-human malevolent spirit' or to cleanse a place 'believed to be infested by the demonic'; see Michael Perry (ed.), *Deliverance: Psychic Disturbances and Occult Involvement* (London: SPCK, 1987), p. 2 (also pp. 90–7).

89 For useful overviews on the church history of exorcism, see Clebsch and Jaekle, *Pastoral Care*, pp. 38–41, 190–208; and Perry, *Deliverance*, pp. 110–14. I am primarily indebted to these sources for this brief section.

90 In charismatic circles see, for example, Sandford and Sandford, *Delivered or Healed?* where a 'both/and' approach to inner healing and deliverance is adopted in the face of a climate of mutual criticism among practitioners (pp. 20–2). In the light of perceived excesses they offer 'a sensible view of deliverance', albeit within an advanced 'charismatic' demonology (pp. 23–47). Many of the leading charis-

matics see the deliverance ministry as integral to their calling; see, for example, MacNutt, *Healing*, pp. 189–210; and Wimber, *Power Healing*, pp. 111–38. For an overview of inner healing and deliverance in today's Roman Catholic Church, see Jim McManus, *Healing in the Spirit: Inner Healing and Deliverance in Today's Church* (London: Darton, Longman & Todd, 1994).

91 Perry, *Deliverance*, p. 112; for reports on the case, see *The Times* for 26 and 27 March 1975.

92 Perry, *Deliverance*. p. 112.

93 ibid., p. 113.

94 ibid., p. 115.

95 Many have pointed to the comparative scarcity of demon possession in 'Christianised' countries compared with, for example, certain parts of the Far East. See, for example, Sandford and Sandford, *Delivered or Healed?*, p. 39.

96 See, for example, the description in Perry, *Deliverance*, in which 'through a process of projection (and often associated identification) . . . people may become controlled by others, and by the perceptions and beliefs of others' (p. 72).

97 ibid., p. 97.

98 George Lindbeck, *The Nature of Doctrine: Religion and Doctrine in a Postliberal Age* (London: SPCK, 1984), p. 22.

99 This term is culled from Peter's Pentecostal sermon in which, seeing the Spirit's manifestations in tongues and fire, he declares, 'this is what was spoken by the prophet Joel' (Acts 2:16).

100 See Stibbe, *Times of Refreshing*, pp. 3–29. For a detailed refutation of Stibbe's approach, see Mark Smith, ' "This-is-That" Hermeneutics' in *The Mark of the Spirit? A Charismatic Critique of the Toronto Blessing*, ed. L. Pietersen (Carlisle: Paternoster Publishing, 1998), pp. 33–62.

101 See Steven J. Land, *Pentecostal Spirituality: A Passion for the Kingdom* (Sheffield: Sheffield Academic Press, 1993), pp. 13, 41–2.

102 ibid., pp. 135–6.

103 ibid., p. 138.

104 ibid., pp. 156–7.

105 ibid., p. 41.

106 C. S. Lewis, *Screwtape Letters* (London: Collins, 1955), p. 9.

107 Wink, *Naming the Powers*, p. 4.

108 ibid., p. x.

109 ibid., pp. 7–12.

110 ibid., p. 12.

111 ibid., p. 5.

112 ibid.

113 Walter Wink, *Unmasking the Powers: The Invisible Forces That Determine Human Existence* (Philadelphia: Fortress Press, 1986), p. 7.

114 ibid., p. 25.

115 ibid., pp. 9–10.
116 Tom Smail, 'The Love of Power and the Power of Love', *Anvil*, vol. 6, no. 3, 1989, pp. 223–33.
117 Tom Smail, 'The Cross and the Spirit: Towards a Theology of Renewal', in *Charismatic Renewal*, ed. Smail, Walker and Wright, pp. 56–7.
118 ibid., p. 60.
119 Johan Huizinga, *Homo Ludens: A Study of the Play Element in Culture* (London: Paladin, 1970).
120 Jean-Jacques Suurmond, *Word and Spirit*, p. 34.
121 ibid., p. 41.
122 ibid., p. 48.
123 Henri J. M. Nouwen, *The Wounded Healer* (New York: Doubleday & Co, 1979), pp. 81–96. Nouwen traces his legend of the wounded Messiah to the 'tractate Sanhedrin' in the Talmud (see pp. 81–2).
124 Mary Grey, 'Devouring Mother or Wounded Healer? Liberating New Models of Caring in Feminist Theology' in *Pastoral Care and Context*, ed. O. Stange (Amsterdam: VU University Press, 1992), p. 95.

Chapter 9 Pastoral Counselling: The Maturing Person

1 Paul Tillich, *The Courage To Be* (London: Nisbet & Co, 1952), p. 85.
2 For a measured Christian response to the pastoral implications of Princess Diana's death, see 'The Legacy that Diana left to the Churches', *Church of England Newspaper*, 13 February 1998, reporting on the consultation sponsored by the English Lausanne Movement at City Temple in London. For a perceptive article on some of the psychological aspects of her life, death and posthumous influence, see Bryan Jobbins, 'Diana: A Postscript', *Counselling*, vol. 9, no. 1, February 1998, pp. 13–15.
3 William A. Clebsch and Charles R. Jaekle, *Pastoral Care in Historical Perspective* (New York: Jason Aronson, 1975), p. 4.
4 For a valuable outline of pastoral counselling in Judaism, Islam, Hinduism and Buddhism, see David Lyall, *Counselling in the Pastoral and Spiritual Context* (Buckingham: Open University Press, 1995), pp. 42–50. For important works on intercultural pastoral care and counselling, see David W. Augsburger, *Pastoral Counseling Across Cultures* (Philadelphia: Westminster Press, 1986); Emmanuel Yartekwei Lartey, *Pastoral Counselling in Inter-Cultural Perspective* (Frankfurt am Main: Verlag Peter Lang, 1987); and Emmanuel Yartekwei Lartey, *In Living Colour: An Intercultural Approach to Pastoral Care and Counselling* (London: Cassell, 1997).
5 From the preamble to the AAPC constitution, quoted in Alastair V. Campbell, *Paid To Care? The Limits of Professionalism in Pastoral Care* (London: SPCK, 1985), p. 37.

6 Don S. Browning, 'Introduction to Pastoral Counseling' in *Clinical Handbook of Pastoral Counseling*, ed. R. J. Wicks, R. D. Parsons and D. E. Capps (New York: Paulist Press, 1985), p. 6; for a discussion of the definitions of pastoral care, pastoral counselling and pastoral psychotherapy, see pp. 5–7.

7 For valuable discussions on the sometimes bewildering range of usages of the term 'pastoral counselling', see Lyall, *Counselling*, pp. 36–8; Alistair Ross, 'The Future of Pastoral Counselling', *The Whitefield Institute Briefing*, vol. 1, no. 2, 1996, pp. 1–4; and Peter J. Van de Kasteele, 'Pastoral Counselling', *Clinical Theology Association Newsletter*, no. 67, 1996, pp. 4–5.

8 See, especially, Thomas C. Oden, 'Recovering Lost Identity', *Journal of Pastoral Care*, vol. 34, no. 1, 1980, pp. 4–18; Thomas C. Oden, *Pastoral Theology: Essentials of Ministry* (Harper & Row, 1983); Thomas C. Oden, *Pastoral Counsel*, vol. 3 (New York: Crossroad Publishing, 1989); and Thomas C. Oden, 'The Historic Pastoral Care Tradition: A Resource for Christian Psychologists', *Journal of Psychology and Theology*, vol. 20, no. 2, 1992, pp. 137–46.

9 For a fuller account of Weatherhead's and Kyle's contributions to pastoral counselling in Britain, see Roger F. Hurding, *Roots and Shoots: A Guide to Counselling and Psychotherapy* (London: Hodder & Stoughton, 1985), pp. 216–21, 224–7.

10 David Black, *A Place for Exploration: The Story of the Westminster Pastoral Foundation 1969–1990* (London: Westminster Pastoral Foundation, 1991), pp. 64–5.

11 R. A. Lambourne, 'With Love to the USA', *Religion and Medicine* (London: SCM Press, 1970), p. 132, quoted in Lyall, *Counselling*, p. 27.

12 R A Lambourne, 'Objections to a National Pastoral Organisation', *Contact*, no. 35, 1971, pp. 27–8.

13 ibid.

14 ibid., p. 27.

15 For the continuing debate around Lambourne's thesis, see Campbell, *Paid to Care?* pp. 37–40; Howard J. Clinebell, 'Debate: A National Pastoral Organisation', *Contact*, no. 36, 1971, pp. 26–9; Lyall, *Counselling*, pp. 26–9, 109–10; and Michael Northcott, 'The New Age and Pastoral Theology: Towards the Resurgence of the Sacred', *Contact*, Contact Pastoral Monograph, 2 (1992), pp. 22–5.

16 Lyall, *Counselling*, p. 28.

17 Among recent papers that urge pastoral counselling toward a greater theological sophistication, see Gordon Lynch, 'Moral Reflection and the Christian Pastoral Counsellor', *Contact*, no. 117, 1995, pp. 3–8; and Gordon Lynch, 'Where is the Theology of British Pastoral Counselling?', *Contact*, no. 121, 1996, pp. 22–8. For recent works that take this injunction seriously, see Francis Bridger and David Atkinson, *Counselling in Context: Developing a Theological Framework* (London: Har-

perCollins, 1994); and Paul Goodliff, *Care in a Confused Climate: Pastoral Care and Postmodern Culture* (London: Darton, Longman & Todd, 1998).

18 For a careful critique of Don Cupitt, Anthony Freeman and the 'Sea of Faith Network', see Anthony C. Thiselton, *Interpreting God and the Postmodern Self: On Meaning, Manipulation and Promise* (Edinburgh: T. & T. Clark, 1996), pp. 81–118.

19 Quoted by David L. Edwards, *Church Times*, 29 December 1989, p. 11.

20 George Lindbeck, *The Nature of Doctrine: Religion and Doctrine in a Postliberal Age* (London: SPCK, 1984), pp. 20–1.

21 ibid., p. 22.

22 Don S. Browning, *A Fundamental Practical Theology* (Minneapolis: Fortress Press, 1991), p. 142; see pp. 142–99, for a detailed examination of Reinhold R. Niebuhr, *The Nature and Destiny of Man*, vol. 1 (New York: Charles Scribner's Sons, 1943) and a reconstruction of Niebuhr: for example, Browning counters Niebuhr's insistence that self-sacrifice is 'the goal and norm of the Christian life' with his own view that, even though self-sacrifice is intrinsic to Christian living in a fallen world, the 'goal is fellowship and enjoyment between God and humans, and mutuality, sisterhood, and brotherhood between humans themselves' (p. 160).

23 Paul Tillich, *Systematic Theology*, vol. 1 (Welwyn: James Nisbet & Co, 1953), p. 70.

24 For a comparable discussion, exploring the value of existentialism and depth psychology to theology, see Paul Tillich, 'Psychoanalysis, Existentialism, and Theology', *Pastoral Psychology*, 9 October 1958, pp. 9–17.

25 Paul Tillich, *The Courage To Be* (London: Nisbet & Co, 1952), p. 37.

26 ibid., pp. 38–9.

27 See ibid., pp. 66–70.

28 ibid., p. 82.

29 ibid., p. 176.

30 ibid., pp. 152–3.

31 ibid., p. 156.

32 ibid., p. 171.

33 ibid., p. 178.

34 David Kelsey, *The Uses of Scripture in Recent Theology* (London: SCM Press, 1975), p. 131, quoting Paul Tillich, 'Theology and Symbolism' in F. E. Johnson (ed.), *Religious Symbols* (New York: Harper 1955), p. 108.

35 Carl Jung, *Collected Works*, vol. 6, para. 814, quoted in Andrew Samuels, Bani Shorter and Fred Plaut, *A Critical Dictionary of Jungian Analysis* (London: Routledge, 1986), p. 144.

36 Elaine L. Graham, *Transforming Practice: Pastoral Theology in an Age of Uncertainty* (London: Mowbray, 1996), p. 70.

37 Alister E. McGrath, *A Passion for Truth: The Intellectual Coherence of Evangelicalism* (Leicester: Inter-Varsity Press, 1996), p. 133. McGrath, in acknowledging the demise of classical liberalism, nonetheless is committed to interact with approaches to Christian theology which show liberal 'family resemblances', that is, 'an appeal to the "universals" of culture, experience or religion and a retreat from the affirmation of the particularity of the Christian faith' (p. 119).

38 ibid., p. 120.

39 ibid., pp. 120–61, where McGrath presents a sympathetic evangelical critique of postliberalism, especially focusing on the work of Lindbeck, Hauerwas and Frei.

40 ibid., p. 121.

41 ibid. (my italics).

42 Lindbeck, *Nature of Doctrine*, p. 120.

43 ibid., p. 123.

44 Lartey, *Pastoral Counselling*, pp. 25–6.

45 ibid., p. 68.

46 ibid., p. 146.

47 ibid., pp. 146–7, quoting Karl Barth, *Church Dogmatics*, ed. G. W. Bromiley and T. F. Torrance (Edinburgh: T. & T. Clark, 1961), vol. 3, part 4, pp. 199, 203.

48 Lindbeck, *Nature of Doctrine*, p. 23.

49 McGrath, *Passion For Truth*, p. 150.

50 ibid., pp. 153–4.

51 ibid., p. 161.

52 Philip Rieff, *The Triumph of the Therapeutic: Uses of Faith after Freud* (London: Chatto & Windus, 1966), pp. 13, 27.

53 Alasdair MacIntyre, *After Virtue: A Study in Moral Theory* (London: Duckworth, 1981), pp. 11, 12.

54 Rieff, *Triumph*, p. 67.

55 ibid., p. 73.

56 Thiselton, *Interpreting* p. 161.

57 J. P. Chaplin, *Dictionary of Psychology* (New York: Dell Publishing, 1975), p. 476, where 'self' is defined.

58 For comprehensive assessments on psychological and psychotherapeutic models of personhood, see Alan C. Tjeltveit, 'The Ubiquity of Models of Human Beings in Psychotherapy: The Need for Rigorous Refection', *Psychotherapy*, vol. 26, no. 1, 1989, pp. 1–10; and Mary Stewart Van Leeuwen, *The Person in Psychology: A Contemporary Christian Appraisal* (Leicester: Inter-Varsity Press, 1985). For a trinitarian, theological thesis on personhood, see Alistair I. McFadyen, *The Call to Personhood: A Christian Theory of the Individual in Social Relationships* (Cambridge: Cambridge University Press, 1990). McFadyen's approach is essentially relational; he writes: 'We are what we are in ourselves only through relation to others' (p. 9).

59 'Psychoanalytic theory in which the subject's need to relate to objects occupies the central position', in which 'objects' refer to 'persons, parts of persons, or symbols of one or the other'; Charles Rycroft, *A Critical Dictionary of Psychanalysis* (Harmondsworth: Penguin Books, 1972), pp. 100–1.

60 This school, which clustered around the figure of Melanie Klein (1882–1960), was anticipated by the much neglected work of Ian D. Suttie (1889–1935). For a comprehensive appraisal of the object relations theorists in Britain and the United States, see Howard A. Bacal and Kenneth M. Newman, *Theories of Object Relations: Bridges to Self Psychology* (New York: Columbia University Press, 1990).

61 Rycroft, *Dictionary of Psychoanalysis*, p. 149.

62 Bacal and Newman, *Object Relations*, p. 228. Kohut defines 'self-objects' as objects (see note 58) 'which are either used in the service of the self . . . or which are themselves experienced as part of the self'; Kohut (1979), quoted in Michael J. Patton and Naomi M. Meara, 'Kohut and Counselling: Applications of Self Psychology', *Psychodynamic Counselling*, vol. 2, no. 3, 1996, p. 331. Bacal and Newman regard Heinz Kohut, *The Restoration of the Self* (New York: International Universities Press, 1977) as the work in which he 'definitively introduced self psychology' (p. 225). See Bacal and Newman, *Object Relations*, pp. 225–73 for an assessment of Kohut's place in its links with object relations theory, and Patton and Meara, 'Kohut and Counselling', pp. 328–55, for an appraisal of his relevance to psychodynamic counselling.

63 Clyde Kluckhohn and Henry A. Murray, *Personality in Nature, Society and Culture* (New York: Alfred A. Knopf, 1948), p. 53, in Susan Rakoczy, 'Unity, Diversity, and Uniqueness: Foundations of Cross-Cultural Spiritual Direction' in *Common Journey, Different Paths: Spiritual Direction in Cross-Cultural Perspective*, ed. S. Rakoczy (Maryknoll, NY: Orbis Books, 1992), p. 10.

64 John S. Mbiti, *African Religions and Philosophy* (London: Heinemann Educational Books, 1969), pp. 108–9, quoted in Rakoczy, 'Unity', p. 14.

65 Robert Kegan, *The Evolving Self: Problem and Process in Human Development* (Cambridge, Massachusetts: Harvard University Press, 1982), p. 11.

66 Kegan expresses his indebtedness to both Piaget and Kohlberg, and their developmental frameworks for physical-cognition and moral reasoning respectively; see Kegan, *Evolving Self*, pp. 43–71. Nonetheless, Kegan seeks to move beyond their more reductionist understandings of 'meaning-making' in his 'constructive-developmental' approach, which takes 'the evolution of the activity of meaning . . . as the fundamental motion in personality' (p. 15).

67 ibid., p. 12.

68 ibid., p. 15.
69 Joann Wolski Conn, *Spirituality and Personal Maturity* (Mahwah, NJ: Paulist Press, 1989), pp. 57–8.
70 C. K. Barrett, quoted in David Prior, *The Message of 1 Corinthians* (Leicester: Inter-Varsity Press, 1985), p. 56.
71 Richard Dawkins, *The Selfish Gene* (London: Oxford University Press, 1976), in which the sociobiologist Dawkins postulates that it is in the survival 'interests' of their genetic make-up that individuals compete successfully and reproduce effectively.
72 Aldous Huxley, 'Visionary Experience' in *The Highest State of Consciousness*, ed. John White (New York: Archer, 1972), quoted in Kegan, *Evolving Self*, p. 11.
73 Kegan, *Evolving Self*, p. 107.
74 ibid., p. 108.
75 ibid., pp. 108–9. See Carol Gilligan, *In a Different Voice* (Cambridge, MA: Harvard University Press, 1982). Also see Conn, *Spirituality*, pp. 37–48, where she gives a sympathetic critique of Gilligan's work, but then concedes a preference for Kegan's methodology as 'a model of human maturity that is more helpful for pastoral counseling and spiritual direction' in that it accounts 'more adequately for the full range of women's and men's experience' (p. 50).
76 Kegan, *Evolving Self*, pp. 108–9.
77 Conn, *Spirituality*, p. 58. Conn gives an excellent summary of Kegan's material and I am indebted to both these authors in this section.
78 Kegan, *Evolving Self*, p. 256.
79 ibid., p. 274.
80 Conn, *Spirituality*, p. 56.
81 David G. Benner, *Psychotherapy and the Spiritual Quest* (Grand Rapids, MI: Baker Book House, 1988), p. 133. Benner writes: 'Psychospiritual maturity is characterized by integration of personality, which occurs within a context of significant interpersonal relationships and surrender to God.' See pp. 104–33 for his full treatment of this perspective.
82 ibid., p. 57.
83 'The Legacy', *Church of England Newspaper*.
84 Thomas C. Oden, *Kerygma and Counseling: Toward a Covenant Ontology for Secular Psychology* (2nd ed.; San Francisco: Harper & Row, 1978), p. 9 (Oden's italics removed here and in subsequent quotations).
85 ibid., p. 21.
86 ibid., pp. 23–4.
87 ibid.
88 Donald Capps, *Biblical Approaches to Pastoral Counseling* (Philadelphia: Westminster Press, 1981), p. 12.
89 Donald Capps, *Pastoral Care and Hermeneutics* (Philadelphia: Fortress Press, 1984), p. 23.

90 ibid., p. 59. Here Capps follows the reckonings of Bernhard W. Anderson and Hermann Gunkel – the latter generally credited with introducing the form critical method to the Old Testament with his commentary on Genesis (1901).

91 Walter Brueggemann, 'The Formfulness of Grief', *Interpretation*, vol. 31, no. 3, 1977, pp. 263–75; in this paper, Brueggemann seeks to extend the discussion in his 'From Hurt to Joy, from Death to Life', *Interpretation*, vol. 28, 1974, pp. 3–19, and in 'The Role of the Lament in the Theology of the Old Testament', *Interpretation*, vol. 28, 1974, pp. 20–38.

92 Brueggemann, 'Formfulness', p. 267.

93 Capps cites Westermann, 'The Role of the Lament', and *The Psalms: Structure, Content and Message* (Augsburg Publishing, 1980). Also see Claus Westermann, *The Praise of God in the Psalms* (Richmond: John Knox Press, 1965), and the more recent Claus Westermann, *Praise and Lament in the Psalms* (Edinburgh: T. & T. Clark, 1981), published in the same year as Capps's book.

94 Bernhard W. Anderson, *Out of the Depths: The Psalms Speak for Us Today* (Westminster Press, 1974).

95 Capps, *Biblical Approaches*, p. 73.

96 ibid., pp. 60–3.

97 Capps refers entirely to the classical study, Elisabeth Kübler-Ross, *On Death and Dying* (London: Tavistock Publications, 1970).

98 Brueggemann, 'Formfulness', p. 269.

99 ibid., p. 273.

100 ibid.

101 ibid., p. 271.

102 Capps, *Approaches*, p. 90.

103 See Capps's discussion on 'bargaining': ibid., pp. 80–2.

104 ibid., p. 83. On pp. 68–73, Capps, following Westermann, explores two other forms of lament: the 'lament of the mediator', as shown in Moses, Elisha, Jeremiah and the Suffering Servant of Deutero-Isaiah; and the 'lament of God', as demonstrated in the books of Isaiah, Hosea and Jeremiah. Capps sees these variants on the form of the psalmic lament as also relevant to pastoral counselling, as in the reality of the counsellor's own lament on behalf of the sufferer and in the way that the 'counselee's lament gains its meaning, ultimately, from the fact that God shares this lament' (pp. 72–3).

105 ibid., p. 87.

106 Brueggemann, 'Formfulness', p. 273.

107 For writing that links the relational aspect of humanity to the historic 'helping relationship', see Oden, *Pastoral Counsel*, where he argues that an 'embryonic theory of psychotherapeutic effectiveness has been implicitly operative in the classical pastoral tradition from its early times' (p. 7).

108 Henri J. M. Nouwen, *Behold the Beauty of the Lord: Praying with Icons* (Notre Dame, IN: Ave Maria Press, 1987), pp. 20–1.

109 For a stimulating theological treatise on the links between the Trinity and personhood, see McFadyen, *Call to Personhood*, he writes: 'A theory of human nature analogously informed by the nature of God as Trinity will lead to a specific understanding of individuality as a sedimentation of interpersonal relations which is instrinsically open to others as to God' (p. 24).

110 Jürgen Moltmann, *The Spirit of Life: A Universal Affirmation* (London: SCM Press, 1992), p. 11.

111 Martin Buber, *I and Thou* (2nd ed., tr. by Ronald Gregor Smith; Edinburgh: T. & T. Clark, 1959), p. 11.

112 ibid., p. 6.

113 Gunton prefers the more dynamic Greek concept of *perichoresis* than the Latinate derivative *coinherence*, in that the latter suggests 'a more static conception'; Colin E. Gunton, *The One, The Three and The Many: God, Creation and Culture of Modernity* (Cambridge: Cambridge University Press, 1993), p. 163, n.10. It has been pointed out that the term perichoresis does not occur before the seventh century and then it is used for 'the reciprocal natures of Christ'; even so, the notion was expressed in similar words from the same root earlier, especially among the Cappadocian Fathers in the fourth century; see H. E. W. Turner in *NDCT*, p. 112.

114 Gunton, *The One*, p. 152.

115 ibid., pp. 163–4.

116 ibid., p. 165.

117 ibid., p. 180.

118 ibid., p. 169.

119 ibid., pp. 6–7.

120 Relationship is clearly central to the ethos of the whole counselling movement, especially in its humanistic and existential roots. The personalism of the Judaeo-Christian tradition, in turn, has rediscovered the essence of relationality in a biblical anthropology. Among recent writing on 'person-centredness' and 'relationship' in counselling and psychology, see Ivan Ellingham, 'On the Quest for a Person-Centred Paradigm', *Counselling*, vol. 8, no. 1, 1997, pp. 52–5; Peter Holmes, Stephen Paul and Geoff Pelham, 'A Relational Model of Counselling', *Counselling*, vol. 7, no. 3, 1996, pp. 229–31; Dave Mearns, 'Working at Relational Depth with Clients in Person-Centred Therapy', *Counselling*, vol. 7, no. 4, 1996, pp. 307–11; and Joseph Tloczysnski, 'The Relationship Among Spirituality, Religious Ideology, and Personality', *Journal of Psychology and Theology*, vol. 25, no. 2, 1997, pp. 208–13.

121 Jean-Jacques Suurmond, *Word and Spirit at Play: Towards a Charismatic Theology* (London: SCM Press, 1994), pp. 218, 219. In the notion of

'Trinity as perfected covenant', Suurmond acknowledges he is in agreement with Hendrikus Berkhof; see Hendrikus Berkhof, *Christian Faith: An Introduction to the Study of the Faith* (Edinburgh: T. & T. Clark, 1980), pp. 330–7.

122 Account given by Sister Frances Dominica, *Songs of Praise*, BBC 1, July 1988.

123 J. D. Levenson, *Sinai and Zion* (Minneapolis: Winston, 1985), pp. 76–7.

124 See David Atkinson, 'Covenant and Counselling: Some Counselling Implications of a Covenant Theology', *Anvil*, vol. 1, no. 2, 1984, pp. 121-38; and Francis Bridger and David Atkinson, *Counselling in Context: Developing a Theological Framework* (London: HarperCollins, 1994).

125 Oden, *Kerygma and Counseling*, p. 5.

126 Bridger and Atkinson, *Counselling in Context*, pp. 151–2.

127 Walter Brueggemann, 'Covenanting as Human Vocation', *Interpretation*, vol. 33, 1979, p. 116.

128 ibid., p. 117.

129 ibid., p. 122.

130 ibid., p. 123.

131 ibid., p. 129.

132 See, for instance, Carroll Wise, *The Meaning of Pastoral Care* (New York: Harper & Row, 1966), p. 2 and *Pastoral Psychotherapy* (1980), pp. 223–4. In such writing there was an understandable rejection of the shepherding analogy in favour of the non-directive and non-judgmental style of Carl Rogers and his contemporaries. In a very different context, we see a comparable reaction, from the late 1960s onward, to the heavy shepherding element in a number of the burgeoning house churches with their dependency-inviting practice of 'covering', in which every major decision has to be checked with the elders or pastor. Shepherding and covering have been ascribed to, among others, Watchman Nee (1903–72), leader of the Little Flock churches in China in the 1920s and 1930s.

133 See, for example, Seward Hiltner, *Preface to Pastoral Theology* (Abingdon Press, 1958), p. 16, where Hiltner argues that, in the shepherding perspective, the Christian minister is freed from a rigid sense of 'office' to a pastoral flexibility which can respond relationally to 'the need and readiness of the other person or persons'.

134 Thomas C. Oden, *Pastoral Theology*, pp. 49–63.

135 Lyall, *Counselling*, pp. 146–7.

Chapter 10 Spiritual Direction: The Uncomplicated Heart

1 Richard Baxter, 1696, in *The Autobiography*, ed. J. M. Ll. Thompson (Dent, 1931), p. 7, quoted in Roger Pooley and Philip Seddon (eds.),

The Lord of the Journey: A Reader in Christian Spirituality (London: Collins, 1986), p. 80.

2 Helen Waddell, *Peter Abelard* (2nd ed.; London: The Reprint Society, 1950), p. 34.

3 Cited in Morton T. Kelsey, *The Other Side of Silence: A Guide to Christian Meditation* (London: SPCK, 1977), pp. 127–8, dating the remark to Cincinnati in 1941.

4 Evelyn Underhill, *Mysticism: A Study in the Nature and Development of Man's Spiritual Consciousness* (11th ed.; London: Methuen, 1926), p. ix.

5 Gerald G. May, *Will and Spirit: A Contemplative Psychology* (San Francisco: Harper & Row, 1982), p. 108.

6 U. Holmes, in his *A History of Christian Spirituality* (New York: Seabury Press, 1980), puts forward two bipolar scales for human relating to God: a kataphatic/apophatic scale and a speculative/affective scale. See the discussion in David G. Benner, *Psychotherapy and the Spiritual Quest* (Grand Rapids, MI: Baker Book House, 1988), pp. 75–9, where Benner refers to Holmes' view 'that full-orbed spirituality ideally contains a balance of all four ways of knowing God' (see p. 78). Gerald May follows a comparable analysis; see May, *Will and Spirit*, p. 23. Also see Martin Thornton, *Spiritual Direction: A Practical Introduction* (London: SPCK, 1984), pp. 32–7.

7 The other two Cappadocian Fathers were Gregory of Nyssa's older brother, Basil of Caeserea (330–79), and their friend, Gregory of Nazianzus (329–89). All three were strongly influenced by the writings of Origen (c.185–254), who, in turn, looked to the philosophy of Plato with respect to the natural human desire for God, or, in Plato's case, for 'the idea of absolute beauty'; see the discussion in Anthony Meredith, *The Cappadocians* (London: Geoffrey Chapman, 1995), pp. 10–17.

8 ibid., p. 59.

9 Andrew Louth in *DCS*, p. 109.

10 *The Cloud of Unknowing* (6th ed.; London: John M. Watkins, 1956) ch. 70, p. 256.

11 Although Teresa of Avila, in the sixth of the seven mansions of her *Interior Castle*, introduces affliction in the soul's journey toward union with God, it is in the *Dark Night of the Soul* by John of the Cross that we see the fullest poetic expression of the travail that accompanies the perceived absence of God.

12 Gerald May refers to Zalman Schachter's view that 'the spiritual direction of the Pharisees' provided 'a model for some of the Christian Desert Fathers'. May adds: 'In more recent Hasidism, great emphasis is placed upon the *yehidut*, a tri-union of the hasid (student), the rebbe (director) and God.' See May, *Will and Spirit*, p. 290.

13 Walter Brueggemann, *In Man We Trust: The Neglected Side of Biblical Faith* (Atlanta, GA: John Knox Press, 1972), p. 105.

14 For Waldemar Janzen, 'To live life in constant and zealous attention to Yahweh's holy presence constitutes the first great ethical imperative within the priestly paradigm of the good life'; see Waldemar Janzen, *Old Testament Ethics: A Paradigmatic Approach* (Westminster/John Knox, 1994), pp. 106–7. The relevance of this 'priestly paradigm' for the continuing Church tradition of spiritual direction is, I suggest, clear.

15 Origen bears witness to the fact that some believers were already engaging with the desert in the third century; see his *Against Celsus*, 3.9, cited in Andrew Louth, *The Wilderness of God* (London: Darton, Longman & Todd, 1991), p. 45.

16 Our biographical knowledge of Antony is based on *The Life of St Antony* by Athanasius (*c*.296–373). For an excellent introduction to his story and influence, see Louth, *Wilderness*, pp. 45–59.

17 Arius (*c*.250–*c*.336) and his followers believed that Christ was created by God and could not be of one substance with the Father.

18 Antony was more than a recluse, since he publicly visited Athanasius in Alexandria during the Diocletian persecution to support the cause against Arius and to encourage Christians who faced martyrdom. Louth writes: 'Antony was denied literal martyrdom for the sake of Christ: in his cell, in the desert, he became "a daily martyr in his conscience" ' (*Wilderness*, p. 48).

19 Antony, as 'founding father of the monastic movement', predicted a time when the majority would be 'mad' and would accuse those who resist their views as 'mad'. Rowan Williams writes: 'The world and the Church are mad when they circumscribe human possibilities of serving God; it is left for the ironic sanity of the monk or nun to demonstrate – at some personal cost – that God's call is a far stranger thing than any human social definitions might allow'; Rowan Williams, *The Wound of Knowledge* (2nd ed.; London: Darton, Longman & Todd, 1990), p. 94.

20 This gift of *diakrisis pneumaton*, based on 1 Corinthians 12:10, enables the pilgrim to clarify the way forward, choosing reality rather than illusion, good rather than evil. See, for example, Kenneth Leech, *Spirituality and Pastoral Care* (London: Sheldon Press, 1986), pp. 70–1, and David Lonsdale SJ, *Dance to the Music of the Spirit: The Art of Discernment* (London: Darton, Longman & Todd, 1992).

21 Seen, for example, in the solitary calling and spiritual directorship of Julian of Norwich (c.1342–1420) and in the wise counsel given by Abbé Huvelin (1838–1910) to Charles de Foucauld (1858–1916), during Foucauld's time as a Trappist monk in France and Syria and then through the earlier years of his work in the Saharan Desert with the Tuareg people. On the latter, see Louth, *Wilderness*, pp. 6–25, and René Voillaume, *Seeds of the Desert: The Legacy of Charles de Foucauld*, Willard Hill (Wheathampstead: Anthony Clarke, 1972).

22 Louis Bouyer, *Orthodox Spirituality and Protestant and Anglican Spirituality*, tr. Barbara Wall (New York: Seabury Press, 1969), p. 47. For
insight into the *startsy* (plural of *staretz*), see Bouyer, ibid., pp. 44–53;
Kenneth Leech, *Soul Friend: A Study of Spirituality* (London: Sheldon
Press, 1977), pp. 47–9; and Louth, *Wilderness*, pp. 123–42.

23 Leech, *Soul Friend*, p. 50. As Leech points out, the notion of the 'soul
friend' seems to have been inherited by Celtic Christians from their
druidic predecessors (see pp. 49–51). Also see Ian Bradley, *The Celtic
Way* (London: Darton, Longman & Todd, 1993), p. 73, and Regis A.
Duffy, *A Roman Catholic Theology of Pastoral Care* (Philadelphia:
Fortress Press, 1983), p. 37.

24 Leech, *Soul Friend*, p. 50.

25 See Margaret Guenther, *Holy Listening: The Art of Spiritual Direction*
(London: Darton, Longman & Todd, 1992), pp. 89–106. Besides
exploring the analogy of midwifery, Guenther also examines the
notions of spiritual direction as 'hospitality' and the spiritual director
as 'teacher'.

26 Tilden Edwards, *Spiritual Friend: Reclaiming the Gift of Spiritual
Direction* (New York: Paulist Press, 1980), p. 125.

27 Henri J. M. Nouwen, *Reaching Out: The Three Movements of the
Spiritual Life* (Glasgow: Collins, 1976), p. 38.

28 David W. Augsburger, *Pastoral Counseling Across Cultures* (Philadelphia: Westminster Press, 1986), p. 37. Here Augsburger writes in the
context of the 'pastoral therapist', but his point carries, nonetheless,
for all pastoral ministries, including spiritual direction.

29 Benner, *Psychotherapy*, p. 108.

30 See his argument in ibid., pp. 108–111. See also Roger F. Hurding,
Roots and Shoots: A Guide to Counselling and Psychotherapy (London:
Hodder & Stoughton, 1985), pp. 244–55, where I seek to put forward
a biblical anthropology for evaluating counselling methodologies.
For a contrasting view to Benner's integrative *psychospirituality*, see
Gerald May's *Will and Spirit*, where May, a Roman Catholic psychiatrist, declaring that 'much of psychology is really misplaced
spirituality' (p. 111), offers a *contemplative psychology*, which seeks
'to inform psychology with a certain amount of apophatic vision' and
aims to elevate *intuition* as 'the purest form of knowing' (p. 26).

31 As Benner points out, Herman Dooyeweerd (1894–1977), the Dutch
Calvinist philosopher, 'saw philosophy as the study of the structure
of creation, and theology as the study of the direction of those same
things'; Benner, *Psychotherapy*, p. 114n.

32 Benner, *Psychotherapy*, pp. 114–15, where Benner follows the argument in A. Wolters, *Creation Regained: Biblical Basics for a Reformational
Worldview* (Grand Rapids, MI: Eerdmans, 1985).

33 I am indebted to the writings of Francis Schaeffer (1912–84) for this
phrase.

34 See Abraham H. Maslow, *Motivation and Personality* (2nd ed.; New York: Harper & Row, 1970), pp. 35–58.

35 Benner, *Psychotherapy*, p. 123.

36 ibid.

37 See Thomas Merton, *Seeds of Contemplation* (2nd ed.; Wheathampstead: Anthony Clarke, 1972). On Merton's notion of selfhood, also see William H. Shannon, *Thomas Merton's Dark Path: The Inner Experience of a Contemplative* (New York: Farrar, Straus & Giroux, 1981), pp. 34–50.

38 Joann Wolski Conn, *Spirituality and Personal Maturity* (Mahwah, NJ: Paulist Press, 1989), p. 33, where she follows Shannon, *Dark Path*, in seeing 'Merton's model of spiritual development [as] basically a pattern of discovery'.

39 Merton, *Seeds*, p. 33.

40 Henri J. M. Nouwen, *Life of the Beloved: Spiritual Living in a Secular World* (London: Hodder & Stoughton, 1993), p. 106.

41 I am particularly indebted to Conn's excellent analysis for much of the thinking in this section; see Conn, *Spirituality*, pp. 96–125. For other useful comparative studies on spiritual direction and pastoral counselling, see David Bick, *Counselling and Spiritual Direction* (Edinburgh: The Pentland Press, 1997), and Leech, *Spirituality and Pastoral Care*, pp. 55–65.

42 Although the phenomenon of transference is often seen as the prerogative of the psychoanalytic tradition, the transferring of the counsellee's emotions, ideas and attitudes from a significant figure of his or her past to the counsellor can be experienced in any therapeutic approach, including pastoral counselling. Where relationality is thus misplaced the counselling process will seek to help the counsellee toward a clarification of the situation, so that in future the true, original object of the counsellee's feelings is discerned constructively.

43 Conn, *Spirituality*, p. 96.

44 Thornton, *Spiritual Direction*, p. 13. Thornton adopts an 'objective, professional and in a sense even clinical' approach (p. 14), which looks to the Bible, the historic creeds, ascetical and moral theology, and contemporary sociology; see pp. 48–53, 111–24.

45 R A Lambourne, 'Objections to a National Pastoral Organisation', *Contact*, no. 35, 1971, p. 27. Here, Lambourne sees pastoral theology as 'overinfluenced by the puzzle-solving view of human progress', espoused by 'medical clinical professional identity'.

46 Thornton, *Spiritual Direction*, p. 9.

47 Conn, *Spirituality*, p. 97.

48 ibid., p. 107. Here Conn summarises four aspects of prayer in spiritual direction – 'noticing my feeling-response to life's situations; how I express this to God, Jesus, the Spirit; how I listen for God's response to my expression of feeling; how I express my response to

God's being this way toward me' – based on William A. Barry and William J. Connolly, *The Practice of Spiritual Direction* (New York: The Seabury Press, 1982), pp. 69–79.

49 See Annice Callahan (ed.), *Spiritualities of the Heart: Approaches to Personal Wholeness in Christian Tradition* (Mahwah, NJ: Paulist Press, 1990).

50 Merton, *Seeds*, p. 2.

51 Christopher Bryant, *The River Within: The Search for God in Depth* (London: Darton, Longman & Todd, 1973), pp. 108–9.

52 Annice Callahan, *Spiritualities*, p. 1.

53 Negative views from Christians on Jung can be seen, for instance, in Dave Hunt, *Beyond Seduction: A Return to Biblical Christianity* (Eugene, Oregon: Harvest House, 1987), p. 197; Leanne Payne, *The Healing Presence* (Eastbourne: Kingsway, 1990), p. 112; and Jeffrey Satinover, *The Empty Self: Gnostic and Jungian Foundations of Modern Identity*, Grove Pastoral Series, no. 61 (Nottingham: Grove Books, 1995), pp. 27–8. For examples of positive responses, see Christopher Bryant, *Jung and the Christian Way* (London: Darton, Longman & Todd, 1983), p. vii; Morton T. Kelsey, *Christo-Psychology* (London: Darton, Longman & Todd, 1983), p. 4; and Robert J. Loftus, 'Depth Psychology and Religious Vocations' in *Jung and Christianity in Dialogue: Faith, Feminism and Hermeneutics* (ed. R.L. Moore and D. J. Meckel (Mahwah, NJ: Paulist Press, 1990), p. 220.

54 See, for example, Paul Roazen, *Freud and His Followers* (London: Allen Lane, 1976), pp. 238–9.

55 Swanee Hunt, 'The Anthropology of Carl Jung: Implications for Pastoral Care' in Moore and Meckle (eds.), *Jung and Christianity*, p. 235.

56 Until the publication of Gnostic codices in the nineteenth century, scholarship depended almost entirely on the polemical works of the early Church fathers for an understanding of second- and third-century Gnosticism. However, the discovery of Coptic Gnostic texts from Nag Hammadi in Upper Egypt in 1946 has done a great deal to disentangle the heresy's roots. See Kurt Rudolph, *Gnosis: The Nature and History of an Ancient Religion*, tr. Robert McLachlan Wilson (Edinburgh: T. & T. Clark, 1983), pp. 10–25, 34–52.

57 ibid., p. 55.

58 ibid., pp. 54–5.

59 Dualism can be said to exist 'when there are two substances, or powers, or modes, neither of which is reducible to the other', P. Helm in *NDT*, p. 210.

60 Rudolph sees Gnostic dualism as 'interwoven with a monistic idea . . . which is the basis for the identification of man and deity'; Rudolph, *Gnosis*, p. 58.

61 I rely heavily on Rudolph, *Gnosis* pp. 53–160, for this brief summary of Gnostic belief.

62 ibid., p. 58.
63 Rudolph shows the influence of Iranian Zoroastrian and Platonic dualism on Gnostic thought. The 'essentially ethical' orientation of Zoroastrian dualism and the *procosmic* stance of the dualism of Plato are contrasted with the *anti*-cosmic perspective of Gnosticism, in which there is 'an unequivocally negative evaluation of the visible world, together with its creator; it ranks as a kingdom of evil and of darkness' (p. 60). See the discussion in Rudolph, *Gnosis*, pp. 59–61.
64 ibid., pp. 57–8, 66–7.
65 ibid., p. 151.
66 Rudolph sees the term 'gnosticism', with its perjorative caste, as initiating in the French language; *Gnosis*, p. 56.
67 For one of the best recent resources on the breadth of influences on Jung, see Richard Noll, *The Jung Cult: Origins of a Charismatic Movement* (Fontana, 1996).
68 Noll shows how Jung's perception of Mithraism, a survival of ancient Persian Zoroastrianism that resurfaced in the Roman world of late antiquity, was linked with the notion of 'the true Aryan god within' that predated Christianity (ibid., p. 128); see pp. 123–9.
69 Alchemy was one of the central preoccupations of Jung's later years, in which he viewed the medievalist's commitment to turn base metal into gold as symbolic of the process of psychological maturation Jung called *individuation*. Jung pointed to the ancient Greek, Gnostic, Christian and Jewish roots of alchemy, commenting on its attempts 'to synthesize a unitary vision of the world in which the physical and the mystical aspects played equal parts'; C. G. Jung, *Aion: Researches into the Phenomenology of the Self* (2nd ed.; vol. 9, part 2, tr. R. F. C. Hull, *The Collected Works of C. G. Jung*, ed. H. Read, M. Fordham and G. Adler, (London: Routledge & Kegan Paul, 1968), para. 267. For an overview of Jung's alchemical insights into psychotherapy and religion, see Anthony Stevens, *On Jung* (Harmondsworth: Penguin, 1991), pp. 229–47.
70 ibid., p. 141.
71 C. G. Jung, *Memories, Dreams, Reflections* (Glasgow: Collins, 1977). Noll points to the heavy editing of this work by Aniela Jaffé, the Jung family and the original publishers, sees the work as 'the myth of a divine hero, a holy man, a saint' and argues that, to get to 'the historical Jung one must find a way to reach the "pre-Jaffé" biographical material'; Noll, *Cult*, p. 15 (also p. 301).
72 Jung, *Memories*, pp. 65–8.
73 ibid., p. 130.
74 Of particular note are Jung's work on the word-association test under Eugen Bleuler (1857–1939), the renowned psychiatrist, and his study of scientific epistemology; see Stevens, *Jung*, p. 264.
75 Jung identified his 'No. 2' personality with both Goethe's Faust and

Nietzsche's Zarathustra; *Memories*, pp. 123–4. Arthur Schopenhauer's (1788–1860) pessimistic philosophy, with its excursions into Hindu and Buddhist thought, was a great influence on the teenage Jung; *Memories*, pp. 88–9. For a detailed appraisal of Jung and these German writers, see Noll, *Cult*, pp. 24–6, 259–69.

76 Jung's thesis was published in 1902 under the title, 'On the Psychology and Pathology of So-Called Occult Phenomena'.

77 See Jung, *Memories*, pp. 194–225. Noll writes that between 1913 and 1916 Jung 'was engaging in intensely dissociative and potentially dangerous psychological exercises', a period that saw both his withdrawal from academic life and the stormy unfolding of his relationships with his wife Emma and his mistresses Antonia Wolff (1888–1953) and Sabina Spielrein (1885–1941); Noll, *Cult*, p. 219.

78 *Memories*, p. 231.

79 Henri F. Ellenberger, *The Discovery of the Unconscious* (New York: Basic, 1970), cited in Stevens, *Jung*, p. 267. Noll sees Ellenberger as the provider of the 'most informative biographical material on Jung'; Noll, *Cult*, p. 19.

80 Jung, 'Thoughts on the Interpretation of Christianity, with Reference to the Theory of Albrecht Ritschl' (1899), *The Zofingia Lectures*, *Collected Works*, A (Princeton: Princeton University Press, 1983), para. 251, quoted in Noll, *Cult*, p. 36.

81 Jung, *Collected Works*, vol. 11, para. 146.

82 I am indebted to Peter Homans, 'C. G. Jung: Christian or Post-Christian Psychologist?' in Moore and Meckel (eds.), *Jung and Christianity* (Mahwah, NJ: Paulist Press, 1990), pp. 21–30, for this analysis of Jung's hermeneutical viewpoint.

83 ibid., p. 23.

84 See, for example, Christopher Bryant, *Jung and the Christian Way* (London: Darton, Longman & Todd, 1983); E. Wayne Hill and Paul M. Mullen, 'Jungian Psychology and Pastoral Care', *Journal of Religion and Health*, vol. 31, no. 4, 1992, pp. 287–95; Kelsey, *Other Side;* Moore and Meckel (eds.), *Jung and Christianity*; Christopher Perry, *Listen to the Voice Within: A Jungian Approach to Pastoral Care* (London: SPCK, 1991); John A. Sanford, *Dreams: God's Forgotten Language* (2nd ed.; San Francisco: Harper & Row, 1989); and John Welch, *Spiritual Pilgrims: Carl Jung and Teresa of Avila* (Ramsey, NJ: Paulist Press, 1982). For a pastorally sensitive feminist appraisal of Jung, see Demaris S. Wehr, *Jung and Feminism: Liberating Archetypes* (London: Routledge, 1988).

85 The MBTI is an especially useful tool that has permeated much Christian practice in counselling and spiritual direction. Useful introductions are Gordon Lawrence, *People Types and Tiger Stripes* (2nd ed.; Gainesville, FL: Center for Applications of Psychological Type, 1982); and Isabel Briggs Myers, *Gifts Differing* (Palo Alto, CA: Consulting Psychologists Press, 1989); a standard text is provided by

Isabel Briggs Myers and Mary H. McCaulley, *Manual: A Guide to the Development and Use of the Myers-Briggs Type Indicator* (Palo Alto, CA: Consulting Psychologists Press, 1985); helpful applications of the theory are give in Eleanor S. Corlett and Nancy B. Millner, *Navigating Midlife: Using Typology as a Guide* (Palo Alto, CA: Consulting Psychologists Press, 1993); and Naomi L. Quenk, *Beside Ourselves: Our Hidden Personality in Everyday Life* (Palo Alto, CA: Consulting Psychologists Press, 1993). Those offering insight in the contexts of the Church include Malcolm Goldsmith and Martin Wharton, *Knowing Me – Knowing You: Exploring Personality Type and Temperament* (London: SPCK, 1993); W. Harold Grant, Magdala Thompson and Thomas E. Clarke, *From Image to Likeness: A Jungian Path in the Gospel Journey* (Ramsey, NJ: Paulist Press, 1983); Charles J. Keating, *Who We Are Is How We Pray: Matching Personality and Spirituality* (Mystic, CT: Twenty-Third Publications, 1987); and Chester P. Michael and Marie C. Norrisey, *Prayer and Temperament: Different Prayer Forms for Different Personality Types* (Charlottesville, VI: The Open Door, 1984). For a critical evaluation of MBTI, see Rowan Bayne, *The Myers-Briggs Type Indicator: A Critical Review and Practical Guide* (London: Chapman & Hall, 1995).

86 C. G. Jung, *The Practice of Psychotherapy: Essays on the Psychology of the Transference and Other Subjects* (*Collected Works*, vol. 16), para. 470.

87 Rudolph, *Gnosis*, p. 66, quoting the German existentialist scholar Hans Jonas, a pupil of Bultmann and Heidegger; see also, pp. 33–4.

88 C. G. Jung, *Psychology and Religion: West and East* (*Collected Works*, vol. 11), para. 131.

89 Murray Stein, 'C. G. Jung, Psychologist and Theologian' in Moore and Meckel (eds.), *Jung and Christianity*, pp. 5–6.

90 Jung, *Collected Works*, vol. 11, para. 232.

91 ibid., para. 233.

92 Put simply, Kant argued that the human mind 'conditions everything that it encounters'. As Colin Brown goes on to say, 'If Kant was sceptical about the possibility of knowing material things as they are in themselves, he was doubly so about realities which allegedly transcend the material'; see Colin Brown, *Philosophy and the Christian Faith* (London: Tyndale Press, 1969), pp. 96–7.

93 Stein, 'Jung', p. 7.

94 ibid., p. 13.

95 See, for example, Jung, *Collected Works*, vol. 9, para. 423, where he states: 'We do not know what good and evil are in themselves . . . If we call everything that God does or allows "good," then evil is good too, and "good" becomes meaningless.'

96 Jung, *Collected Works*, vol. 11, paras. 62n., 281.

97 ibid., para. 105.

98 ibid., para. 258.

99 Hunt, 'Anthropology', p. 245.

100 Benner, *Psychotherapy*, p. 55. The 'collective unconscious', with its attendant 'archetypes', is a quintessentially Jungian concept that will be discussed in the section on the New Age movement.

101 See, for example, Jesus's words in his 'high-priestly prayer' for those who will believe in him (John 17:21–3).

102 The Zodiacal ages are marked by the 'precession of the equinoxes', in which the sun, in moving in a direction contrary to the constellations, appears at a fresh constellation roughly every 2,100 years; see Eileen Campbell and J. H. Brennan, *The Aquarian Guide to the New Age* (Wellingborough: The Aquarian Press, 1990), p. 326.

103 See Wesley Carr, *Manifold Wisdom: Christians in the New Age* (London: SPCK, 1991), pp. 29–30.

104 James Lovelock is the originator of the controversial hypothesis that the earth is a living entity (Gaia, after the Greek earth goddess) that is self-regulating. See his *The Ages of Gaia: A Biography of Our Living Earth* (New York: W. W. Norton and Co., 1988).

105 A survey of leading American New Agers lists the influence of Jung second only to Teilhard de Chardin (1881–1955), the French Jesuit and palaeontologist: reported in Marilyn Ferguson, *The Aquarian Conspiracy: Personal and Social Transformation in the 1980s* (London: Routledge & Kegan Paul, 1981), pp. 418–20; see Lawrence Osborn, *Angels of Light? The Challenge of the New Age* (London: Darton, Longman & Todd, 1992), pp. 30, 193. It is no real surprise to find Teilhard de Chardin heading the list, since his deeply held belief in a hope-giving evolutionary process of increasing consciousness and complexity that unites the cosmic, the human and the divine accords well with the optimistic vision of the Age of Aquarius.

106 See Noll, *Cult*, p. 58. I am particularly indebted to Noll's book for his powerful analysis of Jung as a cult-hero.

107 ibid.

108 Among the more persuasive influences on Jung, along with the spiritualist movement we have already noted, was the perceptual climate created by theosophy. The Theosophical Society was founded in 1875 in New York by Helena Petrovna Blavatsky (1831–91), an emigré from Russia who was a spiritualist medium and, according to Noll, perhaps 'the single most influential woman in occultist circles in the nineteenth centurry'; ibid., p. 63. For an appraisal of theosophy's influence on Jung, see ibid., pp. 64–9. Lawrence Osborn sees theosophy as 'one of the factors in the twentieth-century revival of Hinduism and a major force within the New Age movement'; Osborn, *Angels*, p. 42.

109 C. G. Jung, *Analytical Psychology: Notes of the Seminar Given in 1925* (Princeton: Princeton University Press, 1989), p. 6, quoted in Noll, *Cult*, p. 26.

110 For an appraisal of the significance of Findhorn and Glastonbury, see Osborn, *Angels*, pp. xiii–xvi.

111 Noll, *Cult*, pp. 67–8.

112 Jung, *Memories*, pp. 182–4.

113 Wehr, *Jung and Feminism*, p. 52.

114 Jung, *Commentary on the Secret of the Golden Flower* (London: Routledge & Kegan Paul, 1962), p. 93, quoted in Stevens, *Jung*, p. 202.

115 For a full description of the technique of 'active imagination', see Stevens, *Jung*, pp. 201–4.

116 Jung acknowledged the dangers of 'confronting the unconscious' and in *Memories* describes a series of harrowing encounters with the numinous, including those with his principal archetype, Philemon, 'a pagan' who 'brought with him an Egypto-Hellenic atmosphere with Gnostic colouration' (p. 207); see pp. 200–10. Noll examines in detail Jung's own disturbing amplification of the account of his engagement with Philemon in a lecture delivered on 8 June 1925, entailing 'the long suppressed story of Jung's self-deification experience' (Noll, *Cult*, p. 211); see *Cult*, pp. 209–15.

117 Jung's unprotected approach can be contrasted with the imaginative use of all five senses in Ignatian spirituality, wherein the directee engages in a prayerful, Spirit-attentive, journey back to, say, a gospel story, in order to encounter the living Christ.

118 Jung, *Collected Works*, vol. 7, para. 118.

119 Noll, *Cult*, p. 99.

120 ibid., p. 293.

121 Charles Hartshorne in Mircea Eliade (ed.), *The Encyclopedia of Religion* (New York: Macmillan, 1987), vol. 11, p. 165.

122 ibid., p. 166.

123 John Macquarrie, *Principles of Christian Theology* (London: SCM Press, 1977), p. 120.

124 Richard Bauckham, 'The New Age Theology of Matthew Fox: A Christian Theological Response', *Anvil*, vol. 13, no. 2, 1996, p. 126.

125 For works which offer sympathetic dialogue with New Age from Christian perspectives, see Carr, *Manifold Wisdom*; John Drane, *What is the New Age Saying to the Church?* (London: Marshall Pickering, 1991); Michael Northcott, 'The New Age and Pastoral Theology: Towards the Resurgence of the Sacred', *Contact*, Contact Pastoral Monograph, 2 (1992); and Osborn, *Angels*.

126 Northcott, 'Resurgence, p. 31.

127 Philip Sheldrake, *Images of Holiness* (London: Darton, Longman & Todd, 1987), p. 2, quoted in Margaret Gill, *Free to Love: Sexuality and Pastoral Care* (London: HarperCollins, 1994), p. 231.

128 William V. Dych, *Karl Rahner* (London: Geoffrey Chapman, 1992), p. 9.

129 George Lindbeck, *The Nature of Doctrine: Religion and Doctrine in a Postliberal Age* (London: SPCK, 1984), p. 16. It is worth saying here

that both Lindbeck's two examples of a 'two-dimensional' approach, Bernard Lonergan and Karl Rahner, provide a transcendental theology (see Chapter 6).

130 ibid., p. 17.
131 In this section I am particularly indebted to Dych, *Rahner*; Gerald A. McCool, ed., *A Rahner Reader* (London: Darton, Longman & Todd, 1975); and K. Rahner, *Foundations of the Christian Faith: An Introduction to the Idea of Christianity* (London: Darton, Longman & Todd, 1978). Other volumes examined include K. Rahner, *Theological Investigations*, tr. David Bourke (London: Darton, Longman & Todd, 1975), vols. 4, 6 and 13.
132 Rahner, *Foundations*, p. 22.
133 See Dych, *Rahner*, pp. 20–1.
134 Rahner, *Investigations*, vol. 13, p. 8.
135 ibid., p. 22.
136 Rahner, *Foundations*, p. 177.
137 ibid., p. 204.
138 See ibid., pp. 204–6. Rahner calls the relationship to Jesus Christ 'absolute because we are dealing with the definitive salvation of the whole person and of the human race' (p. 205).
139 ibid., p. 202.
140 Jung, *Collected Works*, vol. 16, para. 227. Other examples include: in the therapeutic context, 'The "soul" . . . is . . . the very essence of relationship' (ibid., para. 504); and 'The progressive development and differentiation of consciousness . . . involves nothing less than a crucifixion of the ego' (*Collected Works*, vol. 9ii, para. 79, quoted in Perry, *Voice Within*, p. 174).
141 Jung, *Collected Works*, vol. 6, para. 762, quoted in Andrew Samuels, *Jung and the Post-Jungians* (London: Routledge, 1990), p. 102.
142 Dych, *Rahner*, p. 70.
143 Karl Rahner in *Dialogue: Conversations and Interviews 1965–1982*, ed. Paul Imhof and Hubert Biallowons, tr. and ed. Harvey Egan (New York: Crossroad, 1986), p. 191, quoted in Dych, *Rahner*, p. 6.
144 Dych, *Rahner*, p. 29.
145 Ignatius, the founder of the Society of Jesus (1540), once wrote, 'The more taste a man finds for Jesus Christ, the more distaste he will find for all which is not Christ'; *Epistolae et Instructiones S. Ignatii* I (Madrid, 1903–11), vol. 1, p. 705, quoted in Hugo Rahner, *Ignatius the Theologian*, tr. Michael Barry; London (Geoffrey Chapman, 1990), p. 18.
146 Margaret Hebblethwaite points out that the oft-quoted phrase 'finding God in all things' refers 'in a special way to the peak' of Ignatius's *Spiritual Exercises – The Contemplatio ad Amorem*; Margaret Hebblethwaite, *Finding God In All Things: The Way of St Ignatius* (London: HarperCollins, 1987), p. 14; see also, pp. 229–30.

147 Rahner, 'Ignatian Mysticism of Joy in the World' in *Investigations*, vol. 3, quoted in McCool, *Reader*, p. 315.

148 ibid.

149 ibid., p. 316.

150 ibid., p. 317.

151 See, for example, the seminal paper: Sandra M. Schneiders, 'Theology and Spirituality: Strangers, Rivals, or Partners?' *Horizons*, vol. 13, no. 2, 1986, pp. 253–74. Here, Sandra Schneiders shows how, in the past, theology ruled supreme, how spirituality has needed to exert its independence, and how, in the contemporary scene, spirituality has 'grown up', even though 'it belongs to the household of theology in the broad sense of that term' (pp. 273–4).

Chapter 11 Social Change: The Reformed Community

1 Peter Selby, *Liberating God: Private Care and Public Struggle* (London: SPCK, 1983), p. 76.

2 ibid.

3 I am indebted to Larry Kent Graham, 'From Relational Humanness to Relational Justice: Reconceiving Pastoral Care and Counseling' in *Pastoral Care and Social Conflict: Essays in Honor of Charles V. Gerkin*, ed. P. D. Couture and R. J. Hunter (Nashville: Abingdon Press, 1995), p. 222, for this metaphor to complement Anton Boisen's 'living human documents' (see Chapter 5 of this book). Graham writes, 'To conceptualize care for persons is to recognize the network of connections in the "living human web" which influences persons for good and ill, and to help persons relate in more loving and just configurations' (p. 227).

4 See Stanley Hauerwas, *A Community of Character: Toward a Constructive Christian Social Ethic* (Notre Dame, IN: University of Notre Dame Press, 1981), p. 60, where Hauerwas stresses the hermeneutical nature of community:

> A community is a group of persons who share a history and whose common set of interpretations about that history provide the basis for common actions. These interpretations may be quite diverse and controversial even within the community, but are sufficient to provide the individual members with the sense that they are more alike than unlike.

5 Sallie McFague, *Models of God: Theology for an Ecological, Nuclear Age* (London: SCM Press, 1987), pp. 46–7.

6 ibid., p. 47.

7 Penny Lernoux, *Cry of the People* (Harmondsworth: Penguin, 1982), p. 365, quoted in Stephen Pattison, *Pastoral Care and Liberation Theology* (Cambridge: Cambridge University Press, 1994), p. 20.

8 See, for example, Leonardo Boff, *Jesus Christ Liberator: A Critical Christology for Our Time*, tr. Patrick Hughes (London: SPCK, 1980); Leonardo Boff and Clodovis Boff, *Introducing Liberation Theology*, tr. Paul Burns; (Tunbridge Wells: Burns & Oates, 1987); Gustavo Gutiérrez, *A Theology of Liberation* (London: SCM Press, 1974); Gustavo Gutiérrez, *We Drink from Our Own Wells: The Spiritual Journey of a People* (London: SCM Press, 1984); and Juan Luis Segundo, *The Liberation of Theology*, tr. John Drury (Maryknoll, NY: Orbis Books, 1976).

9 Perhaps the best known figure is that of Bartolomé de Las Casas who arrived in South America in 1502 and fought long and hard for the right of the native Indians to be treated as equals by their Spanish conquerors; see Duncan B. Forrester, *Theology and Politics* (Oxford: Basil Blackwell, 1988), pp. 71–2.

10 Stephen Pattison points out that liberation theology 'first proclaimed itself as such at the second general conference of Latin American bishops at Medallín, Colombia in 1968'; see Pattison, *Pastoral Care*, p. 27.

11 For a concise history of 'liberation' in Latin America, see Boff and Boff, *Introducing Liberation Theology*, pp. 66–77. For a more detailed picture, see Alfred T. Hennelly (ed.), *Liberation Theology: A Documentary History* (Maryknoll, NY: Orbis Books, 1990) and Pattison, *Pastoral Care*, pp. 19–30.

12 Boff and Boff, *Introducing Liberation Theology*, pp. 66–7.

13 The Boffs summarise the links between Christian and Marxist notions of Liberation well when they write: 'Liberation theology uses Marxism purely as an *instrument*. It does not venerate it as it venerates the gospel.' They add that here there is simply a borrowing of 'methodological pointers' that have proved of value 'in understanding the world of the oppressed'; ibid., p. 28.

14 Duncan B. Forrester writes of Korea's Minjung theology, in which the Minjung, 'the ordinary people', responding to the translation of the Bible into their language, Hangul, have, over the last century or so, identified their sufferings with the Exodus story and the sufferings of Jesus and hold to the belief that 'the Gospel concerned both the religious and the political dimensions of life'; see Forrester, *Theology and Politics*, p. 95.

15 As expressed, for example, in *The Kairos Document* (1986); ibid., pp. 154–169.

16 ibid., p. 144.

17 As Forrester points out, 'there are hardly any churches *of* the poor in the northern hemisphere' (excepting, as we have seen, in South Korea); churches of the North are held, rather, in 'bourgeois captivity'. Even so, there are grounds for hope where, for example, 'the Church is still visibly present in the urban slums and the peripheral

housing estates' (see ibid., pp. 141–3).

18 Boff and Boff, *Introducing Liberation Theology*, p. 25.

19 ibid., p. 29.

20 See Bob Holman, *Putting Families First: Prevention and Child Care* (Basingstoke: Macmillan Education, 1988), p. 62, where Bob Holman defines the relativity of poverty in the United Kingdom of the 1980s: 'To be poor is not just about lack of food but concerns the extent of social differences between various sections of society.'

21 Boff and Boff, *Introducing Liberation Theology*, p. 31.

22 ibid., p. 32.

23 ibid.

24 Segundo, *The Liberation of Theology*, p. 8.

25 ibid. For a comprehensive appraisal of the hermeneutical circle in the light of liberation theology, see ibid., pp. 7–38.

26 Boff and Boff, *Introducing Liberation Theology*, p. 34.

27 Pattison, *Pastoral Care*, p. 29 (my italics).

28 Boff and Boff, *Introducing Liberation Theology*, p. 40.

29 Although the focus of this section is on feminist theology, there has been an increasing 'liberational' literature which, in the wake of the women's movement, offers Christian reflection on the emotional, psychological and spiritual needs of men in a sexist world. See, for example, Roy McCloughry, *Men and Masculinity: From Power to Love* (London: Hodder & Stoughton, 1992); and James B. Nelson, *The Intimate Connection: Male Sexuality, Masculine Spirituality* (Philadelphia: Westminster Press, 1988; London: SPCK, 1992). Important titles in the growing body of literature on lesbian and gay theology include Elizabeth Stuart, *Just Good Friends: Towards a Lesbian and Gay Theology of Relationships* (London: Mowbray, 1995); and Alison Webster, *Found Wanting: Women, Christianity and Sexuality* (London: Cassell, 1995).

30 Elisabeth Schüssler Fiorenza, 'For Women in Men's Worlds: A Critical Feminist Theology of Liberation, *Concilium*, vol. 171, 1984, p. 35, quoted in Pattison, *Pastoral Care*, p. 240. Pattison points out that one clear disadvantage of Latin American liberation theology's use of a Marxist social analysis is the latter's tendency to screen out gender issues in giving priority to the class struggle, thus 'contributing . . . to the invisibility of women and to their oppression in patriarchal society' (see p. 74).

31 For example, Susan Hekman points out that many contemporary feminists, in claiming the need for 'a feminist epistemology to replace the masculinist one' of modernity, oppose this stance by exalting 'the virtues of "female nature," nurturing, relatedness and community' in contrast to the ' "male" values of domination, rationality, and abstraction'. This polarising viewpoint, she argues, 'reifies the Enlightenment epistemology that it seeks to overcome'. See Susan Hekman, *Gender and Knowledge: Elements of a Postmodern Feminism* (Cambridge:

Polity Press, 1990), pp. 5–6.

32 ibid., p. 8. Hekman sees the philosophies of Foucault and Derrida as providing an escape route from modernity's epistemological impasse. For example, she writes, 'Derrida's . . . displacement of epistemology can be useful . . . because it provides a way of reconceptualizing the feminine in non-dualistic terms' (p. 163).

33 See Elaine L. Graham, *Transforming Practice: Pastoral Theology in an Age of Uncertainty* (London: Mowbray, 1996), pp. 142–3. Graham looks to the writings of Habermas, showing how he stops short of the full poststructuralist agenda in his argument that language not only shapes human identity and a sense of selfhood but it also 'guarantees some kind of faith in the possibility of rational discourse and human community'. Her hope is that Habermasian perspectives can help 'dislodge androcentric models of truth, rationality and emancipation', thus creating 'less coercive and essentializing metaphors and narratives of gender'. See pp. 146, 151, with reference to Habermas, *The Theory of Communicative Action* (Boston: Beacon Press, 1981).

34 Mary Grey, 'Devouring Mother or Wounded Healer? Liberating New Models of Caring in Feminist Theology' in *Pastoral Care and Context*, ed. O. Stange (Amsterdam: VU University Press, 1992), pp. 84–5, referring to Elisabeth Schüssler Fiorenza, *Woman-Church: The Hermeneutical Center of Feminist Biblical Interpretation* (Edinburgh: T. & T. Clark, 1990). See also Frederick W. Schmidt, 'Beyond a Biblicist Feminism: Hermeneutics, Women and the Church', *Feminist Theology*, vol. 11, 1996, pp. 55–71, where Frederick Schmidt explores Carolyn Osiek's analysis of feminist hermeneutical positions with respect to Scripture: the *rejectionist* model (as in Mary Daly); the *revisionist* model (Phyllis Trible) and the *liberation* model (Elisabeth Schüssler Fiorenza). Schmidt seeks to avoid what he calls the 'biblicistic' nature of the last two models and suggests the combination of their respective strengths in an understanding of revelation 'as a process . . . that . . . embraces not only the Bible and church tradition, but contemporary scholarship and moral reflection as well' (p. 70).

35 Grey, 'Devouring Mother', p. 83.

36 For a comprehensive global overview of feminist theology, see Ursula King (ed.), *Feminist Theology from the Third World: A Reader* (London: SPCK, 1994).

37 Heather Walton, 'Breaking Open the Bible' in *Life Cycles: Women and Pastoral Care*, eds. E. Graham and M. Halsey (London: SPCK, 1993), p. 198.

38 Roger Lundin, *The Culture of Interpretation: Christian Faith and the Postmodern World* (Grand Rapids, MI: Eerdmans, 1993), p. 3, quoting Raymond Williams, *Keywords: A Vocabulary of Culture and Society* (New York: Oxford University Press, 1976), pp. 76-7, 80-1.

39 Marcello Azevedo, Inculturation and the Challenges of Modernity (Rome: Centre of Cultures and Religion, Pontifical Gregorian University, 1982), pp. 7–8, quoted in Judette A. Gallares, 'Toward a Multicultural Approach to Spiritual Direction' in *Common Journey: Different Paths: Spiritual Direction in Cross-Cultural Perspective*, ed. S. Rakoczy (Maryknoll, NY: Orbis Books, 1992), p. 159.

40 Vincent J. Donovan, *Christianity Rediscovered: An Epistle from the Masai* (2nd ed.; London: SCM Press, 1982), p. 25.

41 ibid., pp. 30–1.

42 Choan-Seng Song, *Third-Eye Theology* (2nd ed.; Maryknoll, NY: Orbis Books, 1991), p. xiii.

43 Quoted in Song, *Third-Eye*, p. 27.

44 ibid.

45 ibid., referring to Seeberg, the German historian, who noted that 'the Reformation represents "Christianity in the understanding of the German spirit" ', quoted in Kazo Kitamori, *Theology of the Pain of God* (Richmond, VA: John Knox Press, 1965), p. 30.

46 Song, *Third-Eye*, p. 11.

47 ibid., p. 83.

48 ibid., pp. 83–4.

49 ibid., p. 84.

50 ibid., p. 90. The bhakti (meaning 'devotion') tradition and Shin Buddhism, founded by Shinran (1173–1263), both emphasise salvation by grace rather than 'good works'; see ibid., pp. 88–91.

51 Anthony J. Gittins, 'Toward Integral Spirituality: Embodiment, Ecology, and Experience of God' in Rakoczy (ed.), *Common Journey*, p. 48.

52 ibid., p. 44.

53 See, for example, Gittins, ibid., pp. 44–54, where an 'ecological spirituality' is explored, comprising a personal 'microspirituality', which may be narrowly 'microcosmic' and produce a spirituality of 'control', and a communal 'macrospirituality', which is open to the macrocosm and features a 'nurturing of self, others, and the earth' (p. 47). For detailed and systematic treatments of an ecological theology, see McFague, *Models of God*; and *The Body of God: An Ecological Theology* (London: SCM Press, 1993). Here, McFague puts forward 'immanental models of God' and a view of 'God's transcendence in an immanental way' respectively. In the latter book, writing from the point of metaphorical theology, she considers the world *as* God's body, set within 'a Christic framework' that encompasses creation and redemption – 'the liberation, healing, and fulfillment of all bodies' (p. 135). More controversially, Matthew Fox puts forward a 'creation spirituality' in, for example, his *Original Blessing: A Primer in Creation Spirituality* (Santa Fé, NM: Bear & Co., 1983), and *The Coming of the Cosmic Christ: The Healing of Mother Earth and the Birth of a Global Renaissance* (New York: HarperCollins, 1988). In the latter (p.

145) he writes that the 'appropriate symbol of the Cosmic Christ who became incarnate in Jesus is that of Jesus as Mother Earth crucified yet rising daily'. Rightly, he bemoans the neglect, despoliation and rape of 'Mother Earth' but then seems to move in a pantheistic direction when he summarises: 'In short, earth loved us – and still does – even though we crucify her daily.' For critiques of Fox, see Richard Bauckham, 'The New Age Theology of Matthew Fox: A Christian Theological Response', *Anvil*, vol. 13, no. 2, 1996, pp. 115–26; and Margaret Brearley, 'Matthew Fox and the Cosmic Christ', *Anvil*, vol. 9, no. 1, 1992 pp. 39–54.

54 McFague, *Body of God*, p. xii.

55 Lindbeck sees his cultural-linguistic approach as favouring an inter-religious dialogue that does not gloss over religious difference in order to find commonality, but, rather, 'can admit the unsubstitutable uniqueness of the God-willed missions of non-Christian religions'; George Lindbeck, *The Nature of Doctrine: Religion and Doctrine in a Postliberal Age* (London: SPCK, 1984), p. 54; see his argument on pp. 53–7, where he also acknowledges an alternative approach that 'saving faith . . . must be in some measure explicit: it comes, as Paul puts it, *ex auditu*, from hearing (Rom. 10:17)' (p. 57).

56 Anthony C. Thiselton, *New Horizons in Hermeneutics: The Theory and Practice of Transforming Biblical Reading* (London: HarperCollins, 1992), p. 603.

57 ibid., p. 602.

58 Waldemar Janzen, *Old Testament Ethics: A Paradigmatic Approach* (Westminster/John Knox, 1994), p. 164. I am particularly indebted to Janzen's insights for these sections on the 'prophetic paradigm'.

59 ibid., p. 155.

60 Padraic Leonard, 'Spiritual Direction and Religious Experience in the Cultural Environment of Brazil', in Rakoczy (ed.), *Common Journey*, p. 108.

61 Walter Brueggemann, *The Prophetic Imagination* (2nd ed.; Philadelphia: Fortress Press, 1978), p. 15.

62 ibid., p. 13.

63 ibid., p. 30. Brueggemann acknowledges that this major socio-political shift in the fortunes of Israel 'had no doubt begun and been encouraged by David'; even so the evidence for this decline 'is much clearer and unambiguous with Solomon'.

64 See Janzen, *Old Testament Ethics*, pp. 156–8.

65 ibid., pp. 158–9.

66 ibid., p. 167.

67 Elaine Graham cites the emergent theology of Chung Hyun Kyung from Korea as a theology that is 'very Third World, very Asian, very women'. Although Chung specifically addresses the social plight of Asian women – as 'Han of han', or 'the poorest of the poor' – her

theology has global application. Central to her argument is the notion of 'womanity', defined by Graham as 'a full humanity that values [women's] "gender specificity", rather than subsuming it under a universal (but covertly androcentric) human anthropology'. See Graham, *Transforming Practice*, pp. 133–4, referring to Hyun-Kyung Chung, *Struggle to be the Sun Again: Introducing Asian Women's Theology* (Maryknoll, NY: Orbis Books, 1990).

68 See, for example, Brueggemann, *Prophetic Imagination*; and Walter Brueggemann, *Hopeful Imagination: Prophetic Voices in Exile* (2nd ed.; Philadelphia: Fortress Press, 1986). Following Cornelius von Rad, Brueggemann, in *Hopeful Imagination*, notes how 'the poetry in the tradition of Jeremiah, Ezekiel, and 2 Isaiah embodies a most peculiar and important disjunction in the traditions of the Old Testament' (p. 1). These three prophetic poets '*discerned* [and] *wrought* the new actions of God by the power of their imagination, their tongues, their words. New poetic imagination evoked new realities in the community' (p. 2).

69 See Janzen, *Old Testament Ethics*, p. 122. Primarily for this section on wisdom, I am indebted to Janzen's book, as well as to Walter Brueggemann, *In Man We Trust: The Neglected Side of Biblical Faith* (Atlanta, GA: John Knox Press, 1972); Ronald E. Clements, *Wisdom in a Changing World: Wisdom in Old Testament Theology* (Berkeley, CA: Bibal Press, 1990); and Robert K. Johnston, 'Images for Today: Learning from Old Testament Wisdom' in *Studies in Old Testament Theology*, ed. R. L. Hubbard Jr, R. K. Johnston and R. P. Meye (Dallas: Word Publishing, 1992).

70 Janzen, *Old Testament Ethics*, p. 121. For Janzen's assessment of the story of Abigail, Nabal and David, in relation to 'folk wisdom', see pp. 120–2.

71 ibid., p. 120.

72 ibid., p. 122.

73 ibid., p. 164.

74 Clements, *Wisdom*, p. 23.

75 As Walter Zimmerli puts it, 'Wisdom thinks resolutely within the framework of a theology of creation'; Walter Zimmerli, 'The Place and Limit of the Wisdom in the Framework of the Old Testament', *Scottish Journal of Theology*, vol. 17, 1964, p. 148. 'Woman Wisdom', depicted in Proverbs 4–9, is clearly and closely associated with the created order; see especially Proverbs 8:22–31. For discussions on the symbolism entailed, see Clements, *Wisdom*, pp. 19–20 and Johnston, 'Images for Today', pp. 232–3.

76 Brueggemann, *In Man We Trust*, p. 109. See also Eugene H. Peterson, *Five Smooth Stones for Pastoral Work* (2nd ed.; Grand Rapids, MI: Eerdmans, 1992), pp. 165–70, where, in an examination of the book of Ecclesiastes, Peterson explores the value of wisdom in pastoral care.

77 ibid., p. 112.
78 ibid., p. 111 (italics removed).
79 Selby, *Liberating God*, p. 81.

Conclusion

1 Zygmunt Bauman, *Postmodernity and Its Discontents* (Cambridge: Polity Press, 1997), p. 165.
2 J. Richard Middleton and Brian J. Walsh, *Truth is Stranger Than It Used to Be: Biblical Faith in a Postmodern Age* (London: SPCK, 1995), p. 173.
3 Paul Goodliff, *Care in a Confused Climate: Pastoral Care and Postmodern Culture* (London: Darton, Longman & Todd, 1998), p. 69. Goodliff provides a masterly analysis of pastoral care's place within contemporary society, arguing a trinitarian, perichoretic position that pays due emphasis on relationality and community; see, in particular, pp. 58–70.
4 Waldemar Janzen, *Old Testament Ethics: A Paradigmatic Approach* (Westminster/John Knox, 1994), p. 1.
5 ibid., pp. 27–8.
6 See, for example, Matthew 12:41–2; 16:13–16; Mark 9:2–8; and Luke 20:41–4, in which Jesus Christ is seen to be greater than Jonah, Solomon, Jeremiah, Moses, Elijah and David respectively.
7 Janzen, *Old Testament Ethics*. p. 176.

BIBLIOGRAPHY

Adams, Jay E., *Competent to Counsel* (Grand Rapids, MI: Baker Book House, 1970).

Adams, Jay E., *The Christian Counselor's Manual* (Presbyterian and Reformed, 1973).

Adams, Jay E., *More Than Redemption: A Theology of Christian Counseling* (Grand Rapids, MI: Baker Book House, 1979).

Adams, Jay E., 'Nouthetic Counseling', in *Helping People Grow: Practical Approaches to Christian Counseling*, ed. G. R. Collins (Santa Ana, CA: Vision House, 1980), pp. 151–64.

Allen, Jon G., 'The Spectrum of Accuracy in Memories of Childhood Trauma', *Harvard Review of Psychiatry*, vol. 3, 1995, pp. 84–95.

Alsdurf, J. and Newton Malony, H., 'A Critique of Ruth Carter Stapleton's Ministry of "Inner Healing" ', *Journal of Psychology and Theology*, vol. 8. no. 3, 1980, pp. 173–84.

Anderson, Bernhard W. (ed.), *Creation in the Old Testament* (Philadelphia: Fortress Press, 1984).

Asquith, Glenn H., 'The Case Study Method of Anton T. Boisen', *Journal of Pastoral Care*, vol. 34, no. 2, 1980, pp. 84–94.

Assagioli, Roberto, *Psychosynthesis: A Manual of Principles and Techniques* (London: Turnstone Books, 1975).

Atkinson, David, 'Covenant and Counselling: Some Counselling Implications of a Covenant Theology', *Anvil*, vol. 1, no. 2, 1984, pp. 121–38.

Augsburger, David W., *Pastoral Counseling Across Cultures* (Philadelphia: Westminster Press, 1986).

Bacal, Howard A. and Newman, Kenneth M., *Theories of Object Relations: Bridges to Self Psychology* (New York: Columbia University Press, 1990).

Ballard, Paul H. and Pritchard, John, *Practical Theology in Action: Christian Thinking in the Service of Church and Society* (London: SPCK, 1996).

Ballard, Paul H., ed., *The Foundations of Pastoral Studies and Practical Theology* (Cardiff: The Board of Studies for Pastoral Studies, University College, 1986).

Ballard, Paul H., 'Pastoral Theology as Theology of Reconciliation', *Theology*, vol. 91, 1988, pp. 375–80.

Barton, Stephen C., *The Spirituality of the Gospels* (London: SPCK, 1992).

Bauckham, Richard, 'The New Age Theology of Matthew Fox: A Christian Theological Response', *Anvil*, vol. 13, no. 2, 1996, pp. 115–26.

Bauman, Zygmunt, *Intimations of Postmodernity* (London: Routledge, 1992).

Bauman, Zygmunt, *Postmodernity and its Discontents* (Cambridge: Polity Press, 1997).

Bayne, Rowan, *The Myers-Briggs Type Indicator: A Critical Review and Practical Guide* (London: Chapman & Hall, 1995).

Bebbington, D. W., *Evangelicalism in Modern Britain: A History from the 1730s to the 1980s* (London: Unwin Hyman, 1989).

Benner, David G., *Psychotherapy and the Spiritual Quest* (Grand Rapids, MI: Baker Book House, 1988).

Benner, David G., *Healing Emotional Wounds* (Grand Rapids, MI: Baker Book House, 1990).

Bergin, Allen E., 'Three Contributions of a Spiritual Perspective in Counseling, Psychotherapy, and Behavior Change', *Counseling and Values*, vol. 33, 1988, pp. 21–33.

Berman, Marshall, *All That Is Solid Melts Into Air: The Experience of Modernity* (New York: Simon & Schuster, 1982).

Bettler, John F., 'Counseling and the Problem of the Past', *Journal of Biblical Counseling*, vol. 12, no. 2, 1994, pp. 5–23.

Bick, David, *Counselling and Spiritual Direction* (Edinburgh: The Pentland Press, 1997).

Boff, Leonardo and Boff, Clodovis, *Introducing Liberation Theology*, tr. Paul Burns (Tunbridge Wells: Burns & Oates, 1987).

Bohler, Carolyn J., 'The Use of Storytelling in the Practice of Pastoral Counseling', *Journal of Pastoral Care*, vol. 41, no. 1, 1987, pp. 63–71.

Boisen, Anton T., *The Exploration of the Inner World* (New York: Harper, 1952).

Boisen, Anton T., *Out of the Depths: An Autobiographical Study of Mental Disorder and Religious Experience* (New York: Harper & Bros., 1960).

Bouma-Prediger, Steve, 'The Task of Integration: A Modest Proposal', *Journal of Psychology and Theology*, vol. 18, no. 1, 1990, pp. 21–31.

Bouyer, Louis, *Orthodox Spirituality and Protestant and Anglican Spirituality* vol. 3, tr. Barbara Wall; A History of Christian Spirituality, ed. L. Bouyer (New York: Seabury Press, 1969).

Bradley, Ian, *The Celtic Way* (London: Darton, Longman & Todd, 1993).

Brearley, Margaret, 'Matthew Fox and the Cosmic Christ', *Anvil*, vol. 9, no. 1, 1992, pp. 39–54.

Bridger, Francis and Atkinson, David, *Counselling in Context: Developing a Theological Framework* (London: HarperCollins, 1994).

Brown, Colin, *Philosophy and the Christian Faith* (London: Tyndale Press, 1969).

Brown, Colin, *Christianity and Western Thought: A History of Philosophers, Ideas and Movements*, vol. 1 (Leicester: Inter-Varsity Press, 1990).

Brown, Howard P., Jr, Peterson, John H., Jr and Cunningham, Orville,

'Rationale and Theoretical Basis for a Behavioral/Cognitive Approach to Spirituality', *Alcoholism Treatment Quarterly*, vol. 5, no. 1/2, 1988, pp. 47–59.

Browning, Don S. (ed.), *Practical Theology: The Emerging Field in Theology, Church, and World* (San Francisco: Harper & Row, 1983).

Browning, Don S., *Religious Ethics and Pastoral Care* (Philadelphia: Fortress Press, 1983).

Browning, Don S., 'Introduction to Pastoral Counseling', in *Clinical Handbook of Pastoral Counseling*, ed. R. J. Wicks, R. D. Parsons and D. E. Capps (New York: Paulist Press, 1985).

Browning, Don S., *A Fundamental Practical Theology* (Minneapolis: Fortress Press, 1991).

Brueggemann, Walter, *In Man We Trust: The Neglected Side of Biblical Faith* (Atlanta, GA: John Knox Press, 1972).

Brueggemann, Walter, 'The Formfulness of Grief', *Interpretation*, vol. 13, no. 3, 1977, pp. 263–75.

Brueggemann, Walter, *The Prophetic Imagination* (2nd ed.; Philadelphia: Fortress Press, 1978).

Brueggemann, Walter, 'Covenanting as Human Vocation', *Interpretation*, vol. 33, 1979, pp. 115–29.

Brueggemann, Walter, *Genesis* (Atlanta: GA: John Knox Press, 1982).

Brueggemann, Walter, *Hopeful Imagination: Prophetic Voices in Exile* (2nd ed.; Philadelphia: Fortress Press, 1986).

Brueggemann, Walter, *The Bible and Postmodern Imagination: Texts under Negotiation* (London: SCM Press, 1993).

Buber, Martin, *I and Thou* (2nd ed.; tr. Ronald Gregor Smith; Edinburgh: T. & T. Clark, 1959).

Buell, William E., 'Reaction to Jim M. Alsdurf and H. Newton Malony's Critique of Ruth Carter Stapleton's Ministry of Inner Healing', *Journal of Psychology and Theology*, vol. 8, no. 3, 1980, pp. 185–90.

Bush, Frederick W., 'Images of Israel: The People of God in the Torah' in *Studies in Old Testament Theology*, ed. R. L. Hubbard Jr, R. K. Johnston and R. P. Meye (Dallas: Word, 1992), pp. 99–115.

Callahan, Annice, (ed.), *Spiritualities of the Heart: Approaches to Personal Wholeness in Christian Tradition* (Mahwah, NJ: Paulist Press, 1990).

Campbell, Alastair V., *Paid to Care? The Limits of Professionalism in Pastoral Care* (London: SPCK, 1985).

Campbell, Alastair V., *Rediscovering Pastoral Care* (2nd ed.; London: Darton, Longman & Todd, 1986).

Campbell, Eileen and Brennan, J. H., *The Aquarian Guide to the New Age* (Wellingborough: The Aquarian Press, 1990).

Capps, Donald, *Biblical Approaches to Pastoral Counseling* (Philadelphia: Westminster Press, 1981).

Capps, Donald, *Pastoral Care and Hermeneutics* (Philadelphia: Fortress Press, 1984).

Capra, Fritjof, *The Tao of Physics: An Exploration of the Parallels Between Modern Physics and Eastern Mysticism* (3rd ed.; London: HarperCollins, 1992).

Carr, Wesley, *Manifold Wisdom: Christians in the New Age* (London: SPCK, 1991).

Carter, John D., 'Adams' Theory of Nouthetic Counseling', *Journal of Psychology and Theology*, vol. 3, no. 3, 1975, pp. 143–55.

Carter, J. D. and Mohline, R. J., 'The Nature and Scope of Integration: A Proposal', *Journal of Psychology and Theology*, vol. 4, 1976, pp. 3–14.

Carter, John D. and Narramore, Bruce, *The Integration of Psychology and Theology: An Introduction* (Grand Rapids, MI: Zondervan, 1979).

Chaplin, J. P., *Dictionary of Psychology* (New York: Dell Publishing, 1975).

Clarkson, Petrushka, *Gestalt Counselling in Action* (London: Sage Publications, 1989).

Clebsch, William A. and Jaekle, Charles R., *Pastoral Care in Historical Perspective* (New York: Jason Aronson, 1975).

Clements, Ronald E., *Wisdom in a Changing World: Wisdom in Old Testament Theology* (Berkeley, CA: Bibal Press, 1990).

Clinebell, Howard J., 'Debate: A National Pastoral Organisation', *Contact*, no. 36, 1971, pp. 26–9.

Clines, David, 'Images of Yahweh: God in the Pentateuch' in *Studies in Old Testament Theology*, ed. R. L. Hubbard Jr, R. K. Johnston and R. P. Meye (Dallas: Word, 1992), pp. 79–98.

Clinton, Stephen M., 'A Critique of Integration Models', *Journal of Psychology and Theology*, vol. 18, no. 1, 1990, pp. 13–20.

Clinton, Stephen M., 'The Foundational Integration Model', *Journal of Psychology and Theology*, vol. 18, no. 2, 1990, pp. 115–22.

Collins, Gary R., *The Rebuilding of Psychology: An Integration of Psychology and Christianity* (Wheaton, IL: Tyndale House, 1977).

Collins, Gary R., *The Biblical Basis of Christian Counseling for People Helpers* (Colorado Springs, CL: NavPress, 1993).

Conn, Joann Wolski, *Spirituality and Personal Maturity* (Mahwah, NJ: Paulist Press, 1989).

Court, John H., *Hypnosis, Healing and the Christian* (Carlisle: The Paternoster Press, 1997).

Crabb, Lawrence J., Jr, 'Biblical Authority and Christian Psychology', *Journal of Psychology and Theology*, vol. 9, no. 4, 1981, pp. 305–11.

Crabb, Lawrence J., Jr, *Understanding People: Deep Longings for Relationship* (Grand Rapids, MI: Zondervan, 1987).

Cray, Graham, Dawn, Maggi, Mercer, Nick, Saward, Michael, Ward, Pete and Wright, Nigel, *The Post-evangelical Debate* (London: SPCK, 1997).

Crossan, John Dominic, *The Dark Interval: Towards a Theology of Story* (Niles, IL: Argus Communications, 1975).

Deeks, David, *Pastoral Theology: An Inquiry* (London: Epworth Press, 1987).

De Vries, Michael J., 'The Conduct of Integration: A Response to Farnworth', *Journal of Psychology and Theology*, vol. 10, no. 4, 1982, pp. 320–5.

Donovan, Vincent J., *Christianity Rediscovered: An Epistle from the Masai* (2nd ed.; London: SCM Press, 1982).

Drane, John, *What is the New Age Saying to the Church?* (London: Marshall Pickering, 1991).

Dryden, Windy (ed.), *Individual Therapy: A Handbook* (Psychotherapy Handbooks; Milton Keynes: Open University Press, 1990).

Dunne, John S., *A Search for God in Time and Memory* (London: Sheldon Press, 1975).

Dunne, John S., *The Reasons of the Heart: A Journey into Solitude and Back Again into the Human Circle* (London: SCM Press, 1978).

Dunne, John S., *The House of Wisdom* (San Francisco: Harper & Row, 1985).

Dych, William V., *Karl Rahner* (London: Geoffrey Chapman, 1992).

Eaton, Gai, *Islam and the Destiny of Man* (London: George Allen & Unwin, 1985).

Edwards, Tilden, *Spiritual Friend: Reclaiming the Gift of Spiritual Direction* (New York: Paulist Press, 1980).

Erikson, Erik H., *Identity: Youth and Crisis* (London: Faber & Faber, 1968).

Farley, Edward, 'Theology and Practice Outside the Clerical Paradigm', in *Practical Theology: The Emerging Field in Theology, Church, and World*, ed. D. S. Browning (San Francisco: Harper & Row, 1983).

Farnsworth, Kirk E., 'The Conduct of Integration', *Journal of Psychology and Theology*, vol. 10, no. 4, 1982, pp. 308–19.

Firet, Jacob, *Dynamics of Pastoring* (Grand Rapids, MI: Eerdmans, 1986).

Fonagy, Peter and Target, Mary, 'Memories are Irrelevant to Psychotherapy: Discuss' in *Dilemmas in Psychotherapy in Royal College of Psychiatrists, Psychotherapy Section, Annual Residential Conference, Bristol* (1997).

Forrester, Duncan B., *Theology and Politics* (Oxford: Basil Blackwell, 1988).

Francis, Leslie J., and Jones, Susan H., 'Personality and Charismatic Experience Among Adult Christians', *Pastoral Psychology*, vol. 45, no. 6, 1997, pp. 421–8.

Frei, Hans W., *The Eclipse of Biblical Narrative* (New Haven, CT: Yale University Press, 1974).

Frost, Evelyn, *Christian Healing* (London: Mowbray, 1940).

Frost, Henry W., *Miraculous Healing* (London: Marshall, Morgan & Scott, 1961).

Gadamer, Hans-Georg, *Truth and Method* (London: Sheed & Ward, 1975).

Gallares, Judette A., 'Toward a Multicultural Approach to Spiritual Direction', in *Common Journey: Different Paths: Spiritual Direction in Cross-Cultural Perspective*, ed. S. Rakoczy (Maryknoll, NY: Orbis Books, 1992), pp. 156–70.

Ganzevoort, R. Ruard, 'Investigating Life-Stories: Personal Narratives in Pastoral Psychology', *Journal of Psychology and Theology*, vol. 21, no. 4, 1993, pp. 277–87.

Gardner, Rex, *Healing Miracles: A Doctor Investigates* (London: Darton, Longman & Todd, 1986).

Gerkin, Charles V., *Living Human Documents: Re-Visioning Pastoral Counseling in a Hermeneutical Mode* (Nashville: Abingdon Press, 1984).

Gerkin, Charles V., 'Faith and Praxis: Pastoral Counseling's Hermeneutical Problem', *Pastoral Psychology*, vol. 35, no. 1, 1986, pp. 3–15.

Giddens, Anthony, *Modernity and Self-Identity: Self and Society in the Late Modern Age* (Cambridge: Polity Press, 1991).

Gill, Margaret, *Free to Love: Sexuality and Pastoral Care* (London: HarperCollins, 1994).

Gillett, David K., *Trust and Obey: Explorations in Evangelical Spirituality* (London: Darton, Longman & Todd, 1993).

Gittins, Anthony J., 'Toward Integral Spirituality: Embodiment, Ecology, and Experience of God' in *Common Journey: Different Paths: Spiritual Direction in Cross-Cultural Perspective*, ed. S. Rakoczy (Maryknoll, NY: Orbis Books, 1992), pp. 44–54.

Goldingay, John, *Models for Interpretation of Scripture* (Carlisle: The Paternoster Press, 1995).

Goodliff, Paul, *Care in a Confused Climate: Pastoral Care and Postmodern Culture* (London: Darton, Longman & Todd, 1998).

Graham, Elaine L., *Transforming Practice: Pastoral Theology in an Age of Uncertainty* (London: Mowbray, 1996).

Graham, Elaine L. and Halsey, Margaret (ed.), *Life Cycles: Women and Pastoral Care* (London: SPCK, 1993).

Graham, Larry Kent, 'From Relational Humanness to Relational Justice: Reconceiving Pastoral Care and Counseling' in *Pastoral Care and Social Conflict: Essays in Honor of Charles V. Gerkin*, ed. P. D. Couture and R. J. Hunter (Nashville: Abingdon Press, 1995), pp. 220–34.

Green, Laurie, *Power to the Powerless: Theology Brought to Life* (Basingstoke: Marshall Pickering, 1987).

Green, Laurie, *Let's Do Theology: A Pastoral Cycle Resource Book* (London: Mowbray, 1990).

Grey, Mary, 'Devouring Mother or Wounded Healer? Liberating New Models of Caring in Feminist Theology', in *Pastoral Care and Context*, ed. O. Stange (Amsterdam: VU University Press, 1992), pp. 81–96.

Guenther, Margaret, *Holy Listening: The Art of Spiritual Direction* (London: Darton, Longman & Todd, 1992).

Gunstone, John, *Signs and Wonders: The Wimber Phenomenon* (London: Darton, Longman & Todd, 1989).

Gunton, Colin E., *The One, The Three and The Many: God, Creation and Culture of Modernity* (Cambridge: Cambridge University Press, 1993).

Gutiérrez, Gustavo, *We Drink from Our Own Wells: The Spiritual Journey of a People* (London: SCM Press, 1984).

Guy, Jr, J., 'Affirming Diversity in the Task of Integration: A Response to

"Biblical Authority and Christian Psychology"', *Journal of Psychology and Theology*, vol. 10, no. 1, 1982, pp. 35-9.

Habermas, Jürgen, *The Philosophical Discourse of Modernity: Twelve Lectures* (Cambridge: Polity Press, 1987).

Hand, Sean (ed.), *The Levinas Reader: Emmanuel Levinas* (Oxford: Blackwell, 1989).

Hargreaves, Mark, 'Telling Stories: Narrative and Biblical Authority', *Anvil*, vol. 13, no. 2, 1996, pp. 127-39.

Harvey, David, *The Condition of Post-Modernity: An Enquiry into the Origins of Cultural Change* (Oxford: Basil Blackwell, 1990).

Hauerwas, Stanley, *A Community of Character: Toward a Constructive Christian Social Ethic* (Notre Dame, IN: University of Notre Dame Press, 1981).

Hauerwas, Stanley and Jones, L. Gregory, *Why Narrative? Readings in Narrative Theology* (Grand Rapids, MI: Eerdmans, 1989).

Hebblethwaite, Margaret, *Finding God in All Things: The Way of St Ignatius* (London: HarperCollins, 1987).

Hekman, Susan, *Gender and Knowledge: Elements of a Postmodern Feminism* (Cambridge: Polity Press, 1990).

Heschel, A. J., *God in Search of Man* (New York: Farrar, Strauss & Giroux, 1955).

Hiltner, Seward, *Preface to Pastoral Theology* (Abingdon Press, 1958).

Hocken, Peter, *Streams of Renewal: The Origins and Early Development of the Charismatic Movement in Great Britain* (Exeter: The Paternoster Press, 1986).

Hocken, Peter, *The Strategy of the Spirit?* (Eagle, 1996).

Holman, Bob, *Putting Families First: Prevention and Child Care* (Basingstoke: Macmillan Education, 1988).

Holmes, Arthur F., *All Truth Is God's Truth* (Grand Rapids, MI: Eerdmans, 1977).

Homans, Peter, 'C. G. Jung: Christian or Post-Christian Psychologist?' in *Jung and Christianity in Dialogue: Faith, Feminism and Hermeneutics*, ed. R. L. Moore and D. J. Meckel (Mahwah, NJ: Paulist Press, 1990), pp. 21-37.

Hunt, Dave, *Beyond Seduction: A Return to Biblical Christianity* (Eugene, OR: Harvest House, 1987).

Hunt, Dave and McMahon, T. A., *The Seduction of Christianity: Spiritual Discernment in the Last Days* (Eugene, OR: Harvest House, 1985).

Hunt, Swanee, 'The Anthropology of Carl Jung: Implications for Pastoral Care', in *Jung and Christianity in Dialogue: Faith, Feminism, and Hermeneutics*, ed. R. L. Moore and D. J. Meckel (Mahwah, NJ: Paulist Press, 1990), pp. 234-62.

Hunter, Rodney J., 'The Lapsley Legacy', *The Princeton Seminary Bulletin*, vol. 13, no. 2, 1992, pp. 176-86.

Hurding, Roger F., *As Trees Walking* (Exeter: The Paternoster Press, 1982).

Hurding, Roger F., *Roots and Shoots: A Guide to Counselling and Psychotherapy* (London: Hodder & Stoughton, 1985).

Hurding, Roger F., 'Healing', in *Medicine and the Bible*, ed. B. Palmer (Exeter: The Paternoster Press, 1986), pp. 191–216.

Hurding, Roger F., *The Bible and Counselling* (London: Hodder & Stoughton, 1992).

Ingram, John A., 'Contemporary Issues and Christian Models of Integration: Into the Modern/Postmodern Age', *Journal of Psychology and Theology*, vol. 23, no. 1, 1995, pp. 3–14.

Janzen, Waldemar, *Old Testament Ethics: A Paradigmatic Approach* (Westminster/John Knox, 1994).

Johnson, Eric L., 'A Place for the Bible Within Psychological Science', *Journal of Psychology and Theology*, vol. 20, no, 4, 1992, pp. 346–55.

Johnson, Eric L., 'Christ, the Lord of Psychology', *Journal of Psychology and Theology*, vol. 25, no. 1, 1997 pp. 11–27.

Johnston, Robert K., 'Images for Today: Learning from Old Testament Wisdom', in *Studies in Old Testament Theology*, ed. R. L. Hubbard Jr, R. K. Johnston, and R. P. Meye (Dallas: Word Publishing, 1992), pp. 223–39.

Jones, David (ed.), *Innovative Therapy: A Handbook* (Psychotherapy Handbooks; Buckingham: Open University Press, 1994).

Jones, L. Stanton and Butman, Richard E., *Modern Psychotherapies: A Comprehensive Christian Appraisal* (Downers Grove, IL: Inter-Varsity Press, 1991).

Jung, C. G., *Two Essays on Analytical Psychology*, vol. 7, tr. R. F. C. Hull, *The Collected Works of C. G. Jung*, ed. H. Read, M. Fordham and G. Adler (London: Routledge & Kegan Paul, 1953).

Jung, C. G., *The Practice of Psychotherapy: Essays on the Psychology of the Transference and Other Subjects*, vol. 16, *Collected Works*.

Jung, C. G., *Aion: Researches into the Phenomenology of the Self*, 2nd ed., vol. 9, part 2, *Collected Works*.

Jung, C. G., *Psychology and Religion: West and East*, 2nd ed., vol. 11. *Collected Works*.

Jung, C. G., *Memories, Dreams, Reflections* (Glasgow: Collins, 1977).

Kaiser Jr, Walter C., 'Images for Today: The Torah Speaks Today', in *Studies in Old Testament Theology*, ed. J. Robert L. Hubbard, R. K. Johnston and R. P. Meye (Dallas: Word Publishing, 1992), pp. 117–32.

Kegan, Robert, *The Evolving Self: Problem and Process in Human Development* (Cambridge, MA: Harvard University Press, 1982).

Kelsey, David, *The Uses of Scripture in Recent Theology* (London: SCM Press, 1975).

Kelsey, Morton T., *Healing and Christianity: In Ancient Thought and Modern Times* (London: SCM Press, 1973).

King, Geoff, *Mapping Reality: An Exploration of Cultural Cartographies* (London: Macmillan Press, 1996).

Korzybski, Alfred, *Science and Sanity: An Introduction to Non-Aristotelian Systems and General Semantics* (4th ed.; Lakeville, CT: The International

Non-Aristotelian Library Publishing Company, 1958).

Kraft, Charles H., *Christianity in Culture: A Study in Dynamic Biblical Theologizing in Cross-Cultural Perspective* (Maryknoll, NY: Orbis Books, 1979).

Kraybill, Donald B., *The Upside-Down Kingdom* (Basingstoke: Marshall Morgan & Scott, 1985).

Kübler-Ross, Elisabeth, *On Death and Dying* (London: Tavistock Publications, 1970).

Lambourne, Robert A., 'Objections to a National Pastoral Organisation', *Contact*, no. 35, 1971, pp. 24–31.

Lambourne, Robert A., *Community, Church and Healing: A Study of Some of the Corporate Aspects of the Church's Ministry to the Sick* (London: Arthur James, 1987).

Land, Steven J., *Pentecostal Spirituality: A Passion for the Kingdom* (Sheffield: Sheffield Academic Press, 1993).

Lapsley, James N., *Salvation and Health: The Interlocking Processes of Life* (Philadelphia: Westminster, 1972).

Lapsley, James N., 'Practical Theology and Pastoral Care: An Essay in Pastoral Theology' in *Practical Theology: The Emerging Field in Theology, Church, and World*, ed. D. S. Browning (San Francisco: Harper & Row, 1983).

Lapsley, James N., 'The Theology of Salvation, Healing, and Health', in *Dictionary of Pastoral Care and Counseling*, ed. R. J. Hunter (Nashville: Abingdon Press, 1990), pp. 1107–10.

Lartey, Emmanuel Yartekwei, *Pastoral Counselling in Inter-Cultural Perspective* (Frankfurt am Main: Verlag Peter Lang, 1987).

Lartey, Emmanuel Yartekwei, *In Living Colour: An Intercultural Approach to Pastoral Care and Counselling* (London: Cassell, 1997).

Leech, Kenneth, *Soul Friend: A Study of Spirituality* (London: Sheldon Press, 1977).

Leech, Kenneth, *Spirituality and Pastoral Care* (London: Sheldon Press, 1986).

Leonard, Padraic, 'Spiritual Direction and Religious Experience in the Cultural Environment of Brazil', in *Common Journey: Different Paths: Spiritual Direction in Cross-Cultural Perspective*, ed. S. Rakoczy (Maryknoll, NY: Orbis Books, 1992), pp. 105–11.

Levenson, J. D., *Sinai and Zion* (Minneapolis: Winston, 1985).

Lewis, C. S., *Miracles: A Preliminary Study* (London: Collins, 1960).

Lewis, David C., *Healing: Fiction, Fantasy or Fact?* (London: Hodder & Stoughton, 1989).

Lindbeck, George, *The Nature of Doctrine: Religion and Doctrine in a Postliberal Age* (London: SPCK, 1984).

Loftus, Robert J., 'Depth Psychology and Religious Vocations', in *Jung and Christianity in Dialogue: Faith, Feminism and Hermeneutics*, ed. R. L. Moore and D. J. Meckel (Mahwah, NJ: Paulist Press, 1990), pp. 208–21.

Lonergan, Bernard, *Method in Theology* (London: Darton, Longman & Todd, 1972).

Long, Anne, *Listening* (London: Darton, Longman & Todd, 1990).

Louth, Andrew, *The Wilderness of God* (London: Darton, Longman & Todd, 1991).

Lovelace, Richard F., *Dynamics of Spiritual Life: An Evangelical Theology of Renewal* (Exeter: The Paternoster Press, 1979).

Lundin, Roger, *The Culture of Interpretation: Christian Faith and the Postmodern World* (Grand Rapids, MI: Eerdmans, 1993).

Lyall, David, *Counselling in the Pastoral and Spiritual Context* (Buckingham: Open University Press, 1995).

Lynch, Gordon, 'Moral Reflection and the Christian Pastoral Counsellor', *Contact*, no. 117, 1995, pp. 3–8.

Lynch, Gordon, 'Where is the Theology of British Pastoral Counselling?', *Contact*, no. 121, 1996, pp. 22–8.

Lyon, David, *Postmodernity* (Buckingham: Open University Press, 1994).

Lyotard, Jean-François, *The Postmodern Condition: A Report on Knowledge* (Manchester: Manchester University Press, 1984).

MacIntyre, Alasdair, *After Virtue: A Study in Moral Theory* (London: Duckworth, 1981).

MacNutt, Francis, *Healing* (Notre Dame, IN: Ave Maria Press, 1974).

MacNutt, Francis, *The Power to Heal* (Notre Dame, IN: Ave Maria Press, 1977).

Maddocks, Morris, *The Christian Healing Ministry* (London: SPCK, 1981).

Malony, H. Newton, 'The Use of the Jewish/Christian Scriptures in Counseling', *Journal of Pastoral Counseling*, vol. 20, no. 2, 1985, pp. 116–24.

Maslow, Abraham H., *Toward a Psychology of Being* (2nd ed.; New York: Van Nostrand Reinhold, 1968).

Maslow, Abraham H., *Motivation and Personality* (2nd ed.; New York: Harper & Row, 1970).

May, Gerald G., *Will and Spirit: A Contemplative Psychology* (San Francisco: Harper & Row, 1982).

McCool, Gerald A. (ed.), *A Rahner Reader* (London: Darton, Longman & Todd, 1975).

McFadyen, Alistair I., *The Call to Personhood: A Christian Theory of the Individual in Social Relationships* (Cambridge: Cambridge University Press, 1990).

McFague, Sallie, *Speaking in Parables: A Study in Metaphor and Theology* (London: SCM Press, 1975).

McFague, Sallie, *Models of God: Theology for an Ecological, Nuclear Age* (London: SCM Press, 1987).

McFague, Sallie, *The Body of God: An Ecological Theology* (London: SCM Press, 1993).

McGrath, Alister E., *Roots that Refresh: A Celebration of Reformation Spirituality* (London: Hodder & Stoughton, 1992).

McGrath, Alister E., *Evangelicalism and the Future of Christianity* (London: Hodder & Stoughton, 1994).

McGrath, Alister E., *A Passion for Truth: The Intellectual Coherence of Evangelicalism* (Leicester: Inter-Varsity Press, 1996).

McKnight, Edgar V., *Post-Modern Use of the Bible: The Emergence of Reader-Oriented Criticism* (Nashville: Abingdon Press, 1988).

Meier, Paul D., Minirth, Frank B., Wichern, Frank B. and Ratcliff, Donald E., *Introduction to Psychology and Counseling: Christian Perspectives and Applications* (2nd ed.; Tunbridge Wells: Monarch, 1991).

Merton, Thomas, *Seeds of Contemplation* (2nd ed.; Wheathampstead: Anthony Clarke Books, 1972).

Middlemiss, David, *Interpreting Charismatic Experience* (London: SCM Press, 1996).

Middleton, J. Richard and Walsh, Brian J., *Truth is Stronger than it Used to Be: Biblical Faith in a Postmodern Age* (London: SPCK, 1995).

Mollon, Phil, 'The Memory Debate: A Consideration of Clinical Complexities and Some Suggested Guidelines for Psychoanalytic Therapists', *British Journal of Psychotherapy*, vol. 13, no. 2, 1996, pp. 193–203.

Moltmann, Jürgen, *Theology of Hope* (London: SCM Press, 1967).

Moltmann, Jürgen, *The Crucified God: The Cross of Christ as the Foundation and Criticism of Christian Theology* (London: SCM Press, 1974).

Moltmann, Jürgen, *The Spirit of Life: A Universal Affirmation* (London: SCM Press, 1992).

Moltmann-Wendel, Elisabeth and Moltmann, Jürgen, *Humanity in God* (London: SCM Press, 1983).

Monroe, Philip G., 'Building Bridges with Biblical Counselors', *Journal of Psychology and Theology*, vol. 25, no. 1, 1997, pp. 28–37.

Mudge, Lewis S., (ed.), *Paul Ricoeur: Essays on Biblical Interpretation* (London: SPCK, 1981).

Narramore, Clyde, *The Psychology of Counseling* (Grand Rapids, MI: Zondervan, 1960).

Narramore, S. Bruce, 'Perspectives on the Integration of Psychology and Theology', *Journal of Psychology and Theology*, vol. 1, no. 1, 1973, pp. 3–19.

Narramore, S. Bruce, 'Psychology and Theology: Twenty-Five Years of Theoretical Integration', *Journal of Psychology and Theology*, vol. 25, no. 1, 1997, pp. 6–10.

Nazir Ali, Michael, *Frontiers in Muslim-Christian Encounter* (Oxford: Regnum Books, 1987).

Nelson-Jones, Richard, *The Theory and Practice of Counselling Psychology* (London: Holt, Rinehart & Winston, 1982).

Niebuhr, H. Richard, *Christ and Culture* (New York: Harper & Brothers, 1951).

Nietzsche, Friedrich, *The Gay Science*, tr. Walter Kaufmann (New York: Random House, 1974).

Nilson, Jon, 'Doing Theology by Heart: John S. Dunne's Theological Method', *Theological Studies*, vol. 48, 1987, pp. 48–65.

Noll Jr, Mark, Plantinga, Cornelius, and Wells, David, 'Evangelical Theology Today', *Theology Today*, vol. 51, no. 4, 1995, pp. 495–507.

Noll, Richard, *The Jung Cult: Origins of a Charismatic Movement* (Fontana, 1996).

Northcott, Michael, 'The New Age and Pastoral Theology: Towards the Resurgence of the Sacred' (Contact Pastoral Monograph, 1992).

Nouwen, Henri J. M., *Reaching Out: The Three Movements of the Spiritual Life* (Glasgow: Collins, 1976).

Nouwen, Henri J. M., *The Wounded Healer* (New York: Doubleday & Co, 1979).

Nouwen, Henri J. M., *Behold the Beauty of the Lord: Praying with Icons* (Notre Dame, IN: Ave Maria Press, 1987).

Nouwen, Henri J. M., *Life of the Beloved: Spiritual Living in a Secular World* (London: Hodder & Stoughton, 1993).

Oden, Thomas C., *Kerygma and Counseling: Toward a Covenant Ontology for Secular Psychology* (2nd ed.; San Francisco: Harper & Row, 1978).

Oden, Thomas C., 'Recovering Lost Identity', *Journal of Pastoral Care*, vol. 34, no. 1, 1980, pp. 4–18.

Oden, Thomas C., *Pastoral Theology: Essentials of Ministry* (Harper & Row, 1983).

Oden, Thomas C., *Pastoral Counsel* (New York: Crossroad Publishing, 1989).

Oden, Thomas C., 'The Historic Pastoral Care Tradition: A Resource for Christian Psychologists', *Journal of Psychology and Theology*, vol. 20, no. 2, 1992, pp. 137–46.

Osborn, Lawrence, *Angels of Light? The Challenge of the New Age* (London: Darton, Longman & Todd, 1992).

Packer, James I., 'An Introduction to Systematic Spirituality', *Crux*, vol. 26, no. 1, 1990, pp. 1–8.

Parker, David, 'Evangelical Spirituality Reviewed', *Evangelical Quarterly*, vol. 63, 1991, pp. 123–48.

Pattison, Stephen, *Alive and Kicking: Towards a Practical Theology of Illness and Healing* (London: SCM Press, 1989).

Pattison, Stephen, *A Critique of Pastoral Care* (2nd ed.; London: SCM Press, 1993).

Pattison, Stephen, *Pastoral Care and Liberation Theology* (Cambridge: Cambridge University Press, 1994).

Pattison, Stephen, 'Should Pastoral Care have Aims and Objectives?', *Contact*, no. 120, 1996, pp. 26–34.

Pattison, Stephen and Woodward, James, *A Vision of Pastoral Theology: In Search of Words that Resurrect the Dead* (Contact Pastoral Monograph, 1994).

Patton, John, 'Clinical Hermeneutics: Soft Focus in Pastoral Counseling and Theology', *Journal of Pastoral Care*, vol. 35, 1981, pp. 157–68.

Patton, John, *Pastoral Care in Context: An Introduction to Pastoral Care* (Louisville, KY: Westminster/John Knox, 1993).

Patton, Michael J. and Meara, Naomi M., 'Kohut and Counselling: Applications of Self Psychology', *Psychodynamic Counselling*, vol. 2, no. 3, 1996, pp. 328–55.

Payne, Leanne, *The Healing Presence* (Eastbourne: Kingsway, 1990).

Perls, Frederick S., Hefferline, Ralph F. and Goodman, Paul, *Gestalt Therapy: Excitement and Growth in the Human Personality* (3rd ed.; New York: Souvenir Press, 1972).

Perry, Christopher, *Listen to the Voice Within: A Jungian Approach to Pastoral Care* (London: SPCK, 1991).

Perry, Michael, ed., *Deliverance: Psychic Disturbances and Occult Involvement* (London: SPCK, 1987).

Peterson, Eugene H., *Five Smooth Stones for Pastoral Work* (2nd ed.; Grand Rapids, MI: Eerdmans, 1992).

Pietersen, Lloyd (ed.), *The Mark of the Spirit? A Charismatic Critique of the Toronto Blessing* (Carlisle: Paternoster Publishing, 1998).

Popkes, Wiord, 'New Testament Principles of Wholeness', *Evangelical Quarterly*, vol. 64, 1992, pp. 319-32.

Powlison, David, 'Integration or Inundation?' in *Power Religion: The Selling Out of the Evangelical Church?* ed. M. S. Horton (Chicago: Moody Press, 1992), pp. 191–218.

David Powlison, '25 Years of Biblical Counseling: An Interview with Jay Adams and Jon Bettler', *Journal of Biblical Counseling*, vol. 12, no. 1, 1993, pp. 8–13.

Powlison, David, 'Contemporary Biblical Counseling: An Annotated Bibliography', *Journal of Biblical Counseling*, vol. 12, no. 2, 1994, pp. 43–61.

Rahner, Hugo, *Ignatius the Theologian*, tr. Michael Barry (London: Geoffrey Chapman, 1990).

Rahner, Karl, *Theological Investigations*, vol. 13, tr. David Bourke (London: Darton, Longman & Todd, 1975).

Rahner, Karl, *Foundations of the Christian Faith: An Introduction to the Idea of Christianity* (London: Darton, Longman & Todd, 1978).

Rakoczy, Susan, (ed.), *Common Journey, Different Paths: Spiritual Direction in Cross-Cultural Perspective* (Maryknoll, NY: Orbis Books, 1992).

Rickman, H. P., *Wilhelm Dilthey: Pioneer of the Human Studies* (London: Paul Elek, 1979).

Ricoeur, Paul, 'The Model of the Text: Meaningful Action Considered as a Text', *Social Research*, vol. 38, 1971, pp. 529–62.

Ricoeur, Paul, 'Toward a Hermeneutic of the Idea of Revelation', in *Paul Ricoeur: Essays in Biblical Interpretation*, ed. L. S. Mudge (London: SPCK, 1981).

Ricoeur, Paul, *Oneself as Another*, tr. Kathleen Blamey (Chicago: University of Chicago Press, 1992).

Rieff, Philip, *The Triumph of the Therapeutic: Uses of Faith After Freud* (London: Chatto & Windus, 1966).

Rorty, Richard, *Contingency, Irony, and Solidarity* (Cambridge: Cambridge University Press, 1989).

Ross, Alistair, 'The Future of Pastoral Counselling', *The Whitefield Institute Briefing*, vol. 1, no. 2, 1996, pp. 1–4.

Ross, Alistair, *Evangelicals in Exile: Wrestling with Theology and the Unconscious* (London: Darton, Longman & Todd, 1997).

Rudolph, Kurt, *Gnosis: The Nature and History of an Ancient Religion*, tr. Robert McLachlan Wilson (Edinburgh: T. & T. Clark, 1983).

Rycroft, Charles, *A Critical Dictionary of Psychanalysis* (Harmondsworth: Penguin Books, 1972).

Samuels, Andrew, *Jung and the Post-Jungians* (London: Routledge, 1990).

Samuels, Andrew, Shorter, Bani and Plaut, Fred, *A Critical Dictionary of Jungian Analysis* (London: Routledge, 1986).

Sandford, John and Sandford, Mark, *Delivered or Healed? A Guide to Christian Wholeness* (London: HarperCollins, 1993).

Sandler, Joseph and Fonagy, Peter (eds.), *Recovered Memories of Abuse: True or False?* (London: Karnac Books, 1997).

Sanford, Agnes, *Healing Gifts of the Spirit* (Evesham: Arthur James, 1966).

Satinover, Jeffrey, *The Empty Self: Gnostic and Jungian Foundations of Modern Identity*, Grove Pastoral Series, no. 61 (Nottingham: Grove Books, 1995).

Schleiermacher, Friedrich D. E., *Hermeneutics: The Handwritten Manuscripts* (Atlanta, GA: Scholars Press, 1977).

Schmidt, Frederick W., 'Beyond a Biblicist Feminism: Hermeneutics, Women and the Church', *Feminist Theology*, vol. 11, 1996, pp. 55–71.

Schneiders, Sandra M., 'Theology and Spirituality: Strangers, Rivals, or Partners?', *Horizons*, vol. 13, no. 2, 1986, pp. 253–74.

Segundo, Juan Luis, *The Liberation of Theology*, tr. John Drury (Maryknoll, NY: Orbis Books, 1976).

Selby, Peter, *Liberating God: Private Care and Public Struggle* (London: SPCK, 1983).

Shannon, William H., *Thomas Merton's Dark Path: The Inner Experience of a Contemplative* (New York: Farrar, Straus & Giroux, 1981).

Sheils, W. J., ed., *The Church and Healing: Papers Read at Meetings of the Ecclesiastical History Society* (Oxford: Basil Blackwell, 1982).

Smail, Tom, 'The Love of Power and the Power of Love', *Anvil*, vol. 6, no. 3, 1989, pp. 223–33.

Smail, Tom, 'The Cross and the Spirit: Towards a Theology of Renewal' in *Charismatic Renewal: The Search for a Theology*, ed. T. Smail, A. Walker and N. Wright (3rd ed.; London: SPCK, 1995).

Smail, Tom, Walker, Andrew and Wright, Nigel, 'From "The Toronto Blessing" to Trinitarian Renewal: A Theological Conversation' in *Char-*

ismatic Renewal: The Search for a Theology, ed. T. Smail, A. Walker and N. Wright (London: SPCK, 1995).

Smart, Ninian, *The Religious Experience of Mankind* (London: Collins, 1971).

Smedes, Lewis B., ed., *Ministry and the Miraculous: A Case Study at Fuller Theological Seminary* (Pasadena: Fuller Theological Seminary, 1987).

Smith, J. Z., *Map Is Not Territory: Studies in the History of Religions* (Leiden: E. J. Brill, 1978).

Smith, Mark, ' "This-is-That" Hermeneutics' in *The Mark of the Spirit? A Charismatic Critique of the Toronto Blessing,* ed. L. Pietersen (Carlisle: Paternoster Publishing, 1998), pp. 33–62.

Song, Choan-Seng, *Third-Eye Theology* (2nd ed.; Maryknoll, NY: Orbis Books, 1991).

Sperry, Roger, *Science and Moral Priority: Merging Mind, Brain, and Human Values* (Oxford: Basil Blackwell, 1983).

Stange, Otto, ed., *Pastoral Care and Context* (Amsterdam: VU University Press, 1992).

Stapleton, Ruth Carter, *The Gift of Inner Healing* (London: Hodder & Stoughton, 1977).

Stapleton, Ruth Carter, *The Experience of Inner Healing* (London: Hodder & Stoughton, 1978).

Stein, Murray, 'C. G. Jung, Psychologist and Theologian' in *Jung and Christianity in Dialogue: Faith, Feminism and Hermeneutics,* ed. R. L. Moore and D. J. Meckel (Mahwah, NJ: Paulist Press, 1990), pp. 3–20.

Stevens, Anthony, *On Jung* (Harmondsworth: Penguin, 1991).

Stibbe, Mark, *Times of Refreshing: A Practical Theology of Renewal for Today* (London: HarperCollins, 1995).

Stroup, George W., *The Promise of Narrative Theology* (London: SCM Press, 1981).

Suurmond, Jean-Jacques, *Word and Spirit at Play: Towards a Charismatic Theology* (London: SCM Press, 1994).

Tester, Keith, *The Life and Times of Post-Modernity* (London: Routledge, 1993).

Thiselton, Anthony C., *The Two Horizons: New Testament Hermeneutics and Philosophical Description with Special Reference to Heidegger, Bultmann, Gadamer and Wittgenstein* (Exeter: The Paternoster Press, 1980).

Thiselton, Anthony C., *New Horizons in Hermeneutics: The Theory and Practice of Transforming Biblical Reading* (London: HarperCollins, 1992).

Thiselton, Anthony C., *Interpreting God and the Postmodern Self: On Meaning, Manipulation and Promise* (Edinburgh: T. & T. Clark, 1996).

Thornton, Martin, *Spiritual Direction: A Practical Introduction* (London: SPCK, 1984).

Tillich, Paul, *The Courage To Be* (London: Nisbet & Co, 1952).

Tillich, Paul, *Systematic Theology,* vol. 1 (Welwyn: James Nisbet & Co, 1953).

Tillich, Paul, 'Psychoanalysis, Existentialism, and Theology', *Pastoral Psychology,* vol. 9, October 1958, pp. 9–17.

Timpe, Randie L., 'Epistemological and Metaphysical Limits to Integration of Psychology and Theology', *Journal of Psychology and Theology*, vol. 2, no. 3, 1983, pp. 2–19.

Tomlinson, Dave, *The Post-Evangelical* (London: SPCK, 1995).

Tracy, David, *Blessed Rage for Order: The New Pluralism in Theology* (New York: The Seabury Press, 1975).

Tracy, David, *The Analogical Imagination: Christian Theology and the Culture of Pluralism* (London: SCM Press, 1981).

Tracy, David, 'The Foundations of Practical Theology', in *Practical Theology: The Emerging Field in Theology, Church, and World*, ed. D. S. Browning (San Francisco: Harper & Row, 1983).

Tracy, David, 'Theology and the Many Faces of Postmodernity', *Theology Today*, vol. 51, no. 1, 1994, pp. 104–14.

Underhill, Evelyn, *Mysticism: A Study in the Nature and Development of Man's Spiritual Consciousness* (11th ed.; London: Methuen, 1926).

Van de Kasteele, Peter J., 'Pastoral Counselling', *Clinical Theology Association Newsletter*, no. 67, 1996, pp. 4–5.

Van de Riet, Vernon, Korb, Margaret P. and Gorrell, John Jeffrey, *Gestalt Therapy: An Introduction* (New York: Pergamon Press, 1980).

Van Leeuwen, Mary Stewart, *The Person in Psychology: A Contemporary Christian Appraisal* (Leicester: Inter-Varsity Press, 1985).

Virkler, H., 'Response to "The Conduct of Integration" ', *Journal of Psychology and Theology*, vol. 10, no. 4, 1982, pp. 329–33.

Vitz, Paul C., *Psychology as Religion: The Cult of Self Worship* (Tring: Lion, 1981).

Walsh, Brian J. and Middleton, J. Richard, *The Transforming Vision: Shaping a Christian World View* (Downers Grove, IL: Inter-Varsity Press, 1984).

Walton, Heather, 'Breaking Open the Bible' in *Life Cycles: Women and Pastoral Care*, ed. E. Graham and M. Halsey (London: SPCK, 1993), pp. 192–9.

Warfield, B. B., *Miracles: Yesterday and Today, True and False* (Grand Rapids, MI: Eerdmans, 1965).

Wehr, Demaris S., *Jung and Feminism: Liberating Archetypes* (London: Routledge, 1988).

White, John, *When the Spirit Comes with Power: Signs and Wonders among God's People* (London: Hodder & Stoughton, 1989).

Williams, Rowan, *The Wound of Knowledge* (2nd ed.; London: Darton, Longman & Todd, 1990).

Wilson, Michael (ed.), *Explorations in Health and Salvation: A Selection of Papers by Bob Lambourne* (Birmingham: University of Birmingham, 1983).

Wimber, John and Springer, Kevin, *Power Evangelism: Signs and Wonders Today* (London: Hodder & Stoughton, 1985).

Wimber, John and Springer, Kevin, *Power Healing* (London: Hodder & Stoughton, 1986).

Wink, Walter, *Transforming Bible Study* (London: SCM Press, 1980).

Wink, Walter, *Naming the Powers: The Language of Power in the New Testament* (Philadelphia: Fortress Press, 1984).

Wink, Walter, *Unmasking the Powers: The Invisible Forces that Determine Human Existence* (Philadelphia: Fortress Press, 1986).

Winter, Richard D., 'Jay Adams – Is He Really Biblical Enough?', *Third Way*, vol. 5, no. 4, 1982, pp. 9–12.

Nicholas Wolterstorff, *Reason within the Bounds of Religion* (2nd ed.; Grand Rapids, MI: Eerdmans, 1984).

Woodworth, Robert S., *Contemporary Schools of Psychology* (8th ed.; London: Methuen & Co., 1951).

Worthington Jr, Everett L., 'A Blueprint for Intradisciplinary Integration', *Journal of Psychology and Theology*, vol. 22, no. 2, 1994, pp. 79–86.

Wright, Nigel, 'The Theology and Methodology of "Signs and Wonders" ' in *Charismatic Renewal: The Search for a Theology*, ed. T. Smail, A. Walker and N. Wright. (London: SPCK, 1995).

Wright, Nigel, *The Radical Evangelical: Seeking a Place to Stand* (London: SPCK, 1996).

Wright, N. T., *The Climax of the Covenant: Christ and the Law in Pauline Theology* (Edinburgh: T. & T. Clark, 1991).

Wright, N. T., *The New Testament and the People of God*, vol. 1, *Christian Origins and the Question of God* (London: SPCK, 1992).

INDEX OF NAMES

INDEX OF SUBJECTS